완전절친 LC+RC

실전 토익

5 회

The One 더원

global21.co.kr 온라인 무료 제공

실전&
복습용
음성파일

어휘리스트
+
어휘테스트

상세하고
친절한
해설집

LC
받아쓰기
워크북

완전
절친 **실전 토익 5회**

초판 1쇄 발행 2019년 7월 1일

지은이 이의걸·윤기원·글로벌21 어학연구소
기획 및 편집 오혜순
표지디자인 박윤정
본문조판 이미경
영업마케팅 정병건

펴낸곳 ㈜글로벌21
출판등록 2019년 1월 3일
주소 서울시 구로구 시흥대로 577-11
전화 02)6365-5169   팩스 02)6365-5179
www.global21.co.kr

ISBN 979-11-965975-1-1 13740

CONTENTS

NEW TOEIC

토익은 영어가 모국어가 아닌 사람들을 대상으로, 언어 본래의 기능인 의사소통능력에 중점을 두고 일상생활 또는 국제업무에 필요한 실용영어능력을 평가하는 세계적인 언어능력시험이다. 2016년 5월부터 신(新) 토익이 시행되어, 각 파트별 문항 수에 변화가 생겼으며, 새로운 유형의 문제와 지문이 추가되었다. 하지만 총 문항 수와 시험 시간은 동일하며, 전체적인 난이도 또한 유지되고 있다.

시험 구성

구성	파트	출제 내용			문항 수		배점
듣기 LC 45분	1	**사진 묘사**(문제지에 사진 인쇄) 4개의 짧은 문장을 듣고, 사진을 가장 정확하게 묘사한 것 고르기			6	100	495
	2	**질의 응답**(유일하게 보기가 3개) 제시 문장을 듣고, 그에 가장 어울리는 응답 고르기			25		
	3	**짧은 대화**(문제지에 문제와 보기 인쇄) 대화문을 듣고, 이에 대한 3개의 문제 풀기 # 신토익 문제 유형 3인 대화 및 주고받는 대화 수가 5회 이상인 대화 추가. 대화 속 화자의 의도를 묻는 문제[1]와 문제지의 시각정보를 연계하여 해결하는 문제[2] 추가			39		
	4	**짧은 담화**(문제지에 문제와 보기 인쇄) 내레이션을 듣고, 이에 대한 3개의 문제 풀기 # 신토익 문제 유형 대화 속 화자의 의도를 묻는 문제[1]와 문제지의 시각정보를 연계하여 해결하는 문제[2] 추가			30		
읽기 RC 75분	5	**단문 빈칸 채우기**(문법 · 어휘) 4개의 보기 중에서 불완전한 문장을 완성시키기에 가장 적당한 것 고르기			30	100	495
	6	**지문 빈칸 채우기** 4개의 보기 중에서 지문 속의 불완전한 문장을 완성시키기에 가장 적당한 것 고르기 # 신토익 문제 유형 문맥상 빈칸에 알맞은 문장을 고르는 문제 추가[3]			16		
	7	**독해** 단일 지문 또는 서로 연계된 2~3개의 복수 지문을 읽고, 이에 대한 2~5개의 문제 풀기 # 신토익 문제 유형 문자 메시지와 온라인 채팅 지문 추가. 지문 속 화자의 의도를 묻는 문제[1]와 주어진 문장의 적절한 위치를 찾는 문제[4] 추가	단일 지문	29	54		
			이중 지문	10			
			# 신토익 문제 유형 삼중 지문	15			
합계		7개 파트			200문항		990

신토익 문제 유형

1. 맥락상 화자가 한 말의 의도나 의미, 이유를 파악하는 문제로, LC와 RC 모두에서 출제된다.

⋯➡ What does the man mean when he says, " ~ ?"

⋯➡ Why does the woman say, " ~?"

⋯➡ At 2:34 PM, what does Ms. Marna mean when she writes, " ~ ?"

2. 파트 3과 4에서 문제지에 제시된 도표, 그래픽 등의 시각정보를 보고 해결하는 문제이다. 파트별로 2~3문제가 출제된다.

⋯➡ Look at the graphic. Where will the parade start?

3. 파트 6의 지문 속 4개의 빈칸 중, 지문의 흐름상 알맞은 한 문장을 찾는 문제이다. 지문당 1개씩 출제된다.

4. 문제에 제시된 문장의 적절한 위치를 지문 속에서 찾는 문제

⋯▶ In which of the positions marked [1], [2], [3], and [4] does the following sentence best belong?

출제 분야

▶ 전문 비즈니스 | 계약, 협상, 마케팅, 세일즈, 비즈니스 계획, 회의

▶ 제조 | 공장관리, 조립라인, 품질관리

▶ 금융과 예산 | 은행, 투자, 세금, 회계, 청구

▶ 개발 | 연구, 제품개발

▶ 사무실 | 임원회의, 위원회의, 편지, 메모, 전화, 팩스, 이메일, 사무 장비 및 가구

▶ 인사 | 구인, 채용, 퇴직, 급여, 승진, 취업지원과 자기소개

▶ 주택 · 기업 부동산 | 건축, 설계서, 구입, 임대, 전기와 가스

▶ 여행 | 기차, 비행기, 택시, 버스, 배, 유람선, 티켓, 일정, 역과 공항 안내, 렌터카, 호텔, 예약, 연기와 취소

시험 접수

웹사이트 exam.ybmnet.co.kr에 접속하여 시험 일정 및 접수 기간 등 세부 내용을 확인할 수 있다. 정기시험과 추가시험 일정을 확인하고, 원하는 시험 날짜를 선택해 접수한다. 접수한 시험의 응시일과 고사장을 정확히 확인한다.

준비물

▶ 규정 신분증: 주민등록증, 운전면허증, 기간 만료 전의 여권, 장애인 복지카드, 공무원증 등 (미지참 시 시험 응시 불가)
  불인정 신분증: 학생증(대학,대학원), 사원증, 각종 자격증, 사진이 부착된 신용카드, 국제운전면허증, 유효기간이 지난 신분증 등

▶ 필기구: 연필, 지우개 (볼펜이나 사인펜은 사용 불가)

▶ 시계: 아날로그 손목시계 (전자식 시계는 사용 불가)

시간표

오전 시험(일요일)	시험 진행	오후 시험(토요일)
9:20	입실	14:20
9:30 ~ 9:45	답안지 작성 오리엔테이션	14:30 ~ 14:45
9:45 ~ 9:50	쉬는 시간(이후 입실 불가)	14:45 ~ 14:50
9:50 ~ 10:05	신분증 확인	14:50 ~ 15:05
10:05 ~ 10:10	문제지 배부 및 파본 확인	15:05 ~ 15:10
10:10 ~ 10:55	듣기 평가(LC)	15:10 ~ 15:55
10:55 ~ 12:10	독해 평가(RC)	15:55 ~ 17:10

성적 확인

시험일로부터 통상 12일 후 인터넷과 ARS(060-800-0515)로 성적을 확인할 수 있다. 성적표는 우편으로 수령(발표 후 약 7~10일 정도 소요)하거나 온라인으로 접수한 웹사이트에서 직접 출력할 수 있다. 토익 성적은 시험 시행일로부터 2년 간 유효하다.

SELF CHECK

매회 실전에 임하는 마음으로 응시하세요. 응시 후 채점결과를 기록하면, 목표가 생기고 더 집중할 수 있습니다.

		시험 날짜	소요 시간	맞힌 개수	총 개수	다음 목표
Actual Test 1	LC					다 풀어버리겠다!
	RC					
Actual Test 2	LC					꿈은 원대하게!
	RC					
Actual Test 3	LC					나는 잘하고 있어!
	RC					
Actual Test 4	LC					머지않았다구!
	RC					
Actual Test 5	LC					할 수 있어!
	RC					

Actual Test 1

휴대폰은 OFF!
LC MP3는 ON!
2시간만 집중!

Check ▸ 시작 시간 _____ : _____

▸ 종료 시간 _____ : _____

LC MP3 바로듣기

LISTENING TEST

In the Listening test, you will be asked to demonstrate how well you understand spoken English. The entire Listening test will last approximately 45 minutes. There are four parts, and directions are given for each part. You must mark your answers on the separate answer sheet. Do not write your answers in your test book.

PART 1

Directions: For each question in this part, you will hear four statements about a picture in your test book. When you hear the statements, you must select the one statement that best describes what you see in the picture. Then find the number of the question on your answer sheet and mark your answer. The statements will not be printed in your test book and will be spoken only one time.

Statement (C), "They're sitting at the table," is the best description of the picture, so you should select answer (C) and mark it on your answer sheet.

1.

2.

GO ON TO THE NEXT PAGE

3.

4.

5.

6.

GO ON TO THE NEXT PAGE

PART 2

Directions: You will hear a question or statement and three responses spoken in English. They will not be printed in your test book and will be spoken only one time. Select the best response to the question or statement and mark the letter (A), (B), or (C) on your answer sheet.

7. Mark your answer on your answer sheet.

8. Mark your answer on your answer sheet.

9. Mark your answer on your answer sheet.

10. Mark your answer on your answer sheet.

11. Mark your answer on your answer sheet.

12. Mark your answer on your answer sheet.

13. Mark your answer on your answer sheet.

14. Mark your answer on your answer sheet.

15. Mark your answer on your answer sheet.

16. Mark your answer on your answer sheet.

17. Mark your answer on your answer sheet.

18. Mark your answer on your answer sheet.

19. Mark your answer on your answer sheet.

20. Mark your answer on your answer sheet.

21. Mark your answer on your answer sheet.

22. Mark your answer on your answer sheet.

23. Mark your answer on your answer sheet.

24. Mark your answer on your answer sheet.

25. Mark your answer on your answer sheet.

26. Mark your answer on your answer sheet.

27. Mark your answer on your answer sheet.

28. Mark your answer on your answer sheet.

29. Mark your answer on your answer sheet.

30. Mark your answer on your answer sheet.

31. Mark your answer on your answer sheet.

PART 3

Directions: You will hear some conversations between two or more people. You will be asked to answer three questions about what the speakers say in each conversation. Select the best response to each question and mark the letter (A), (B), (C), or (D) on your answer sheet. The conversations will not be printed in your test book and will be spoken only one time.

32. Where is the man going?
(A) To a bus stop
(B) To a concert hall
(C) To a sports venue
(D) To a theater

33. What is mentioned about Satellite Avenue?
(A) It is a new street.
(B) It is being repaired.
(C) It is closed.
(D) It is near downtown.

34. What does the woman suggest the man do?
(A) Catch a taxi
(B) Go home
(C) Ride the Blue Line
(D) Wait for the next bus

35. Who most likely is the man?
(A) A branch manager
(B) A job candidate
(C) A job recruiter
(D) A reporter

36. How long has the man been working in his current job?
(A) 2 months
(B) 3 months
(C) Half a year
(D) A year

37. What is mentioned about the man's family?
(A) His wife is not happy with his job.
(B) His wife got a new position.
(C) They are from Oak City.
(D) They do not want to relocate.

38. Why does the woman apologize?
(A) Because she has to cancel the appointment.
(B) Because she is late for the meeting.
(C) Because she needs to reschedule the meeting.
(D) Because she refused the man's offer.

39. What does the man mean when he says, "Works for me"?
(A) He is agreeing with the place to meet.
(B) He is fine with a video chat.
(C) The suggested schedule is convenient for him.
(D) The woman works in his department.

40. What will the speakers discuss at their meeting?
(A) A collaboration plan
(B) A merger
(C) The man's budget ideas
(D) The woman's qualifications

41. What did the woman do on the weekend?
(A) She did home repair works.
(B) She did some gardening.
(C) She visited an amusement park.
(D) She visited her parents.

42. What did the man have trouble doing?
(A) Deciding where to go
(B) Finding his destination
(C) Getting a parking space
(D) Making a reservation

43. What will the woman probably do next?
(A) Call her children
(B) Look at some photos
(C) Take a break
(D) Talk about her holiday

GO ON TO THE NEXT PAGE

44. How many people will accompany the man to the restaurant?

(A) 3
(B) 4
(C) 5
(D) 6

45. What is mentioned about one of the man's party?

(A) She has a serious allergy.
(B) She is a vegetarian.
(C) She likes the table with a view.
(D) She will show up late.

46. Why does the man say, "That's a relief"?

(A) He is concerned his guests will not like the restaurant.
(B) He is glad the chef can do what he asks.
(C) He is happy to get a reservation at a busy time.
(D) He is worried that there will not be enough menu choices.

---

47. Where is the conversation taking place?

(A) In a community center
(B) In a hotel
(C) In a library
(D) In a retirement home

48. What problem does the woman mention?

(A) The building is old.
(B) The construction outside is noisy.
(C) The heater is not working properly.
(D) The rooms are too cold.

49. What will the man do next?

(A) Call the maintenance department
(B) Have his lunch
(C) Listen to a lecture
(D) Retrieve his tools

---

50. Why is the man congratulating the woman?

(A) She got married.
(B) She got promoted.
(C) She received an honor.
(D) She won a contract.

51. What does the woman say about her group?

(A) They have not worked with her before.
(B) They put in a lot of effort.
(C) They were not cooperative with her.
(D) They will get reassigned soon.

52. What kind of products does the woman's company sell?

(A) Clothes
(B) Digital devices
(C) Automobile
(D) Medicine

---

53. What is the man's problem?

(A) He cannot find a photographer for a project.
(B) He does not have enough pictures for a catalog.
(C) He does not have the right kind of pictures.
(D) His deadline is already past.

54. What will happen in two weeks?

(A) A photographer will be available.
(B) An update will be finished.
(C) The man will get a job.
(D) The woman will take over the project.

55. What does the woman offer to do for the man?

(A) Accompany him to a photo shoot
(B) Call a different photographer
(C) Find a new studio
(D) Review a previous catalog

---

56. What are the speakers mainly discussing?
    (A) A business trip
    (B) A new company policy
    (C) Their new branch
    (D) Their recent vacations

57. What does the man mention about Singapore?
    (A) It has a lot of good food.
    (B) It has many sightseeing spots.
    (C) It is a beautiful city.
    (D) It is easy to get around.

58. What does the speakers' boss want them to do?
    (A) Go over the inspection checklist
    (B) Save on costs
    (C) Stay in a specific hotel
    (D) Treat a facility manager to dinner

59. What is the woman's problem?
    (A) She cannot find her ID.
    (B) She forgot her purse.
    (C) She is lost.
    (D) She is missing some papers.

60. Who most likely is the man?
    (A) A building security officer
    (B) A taxi driver
    (C) A traffic reporter
    (D) Her colleague

61. What does the woman imply when she says, "I won't be long"?
    (A) She does not want to go to the meeting.
    (B) She does not want to turn right.
    (C) She prefers a short conversation.
    (D) She will come back soon.

62. What is the purpose of the meeting?
    (A) To conduct an employee evaluation
    (B) To discuss a new branch
    (C) To interview a job candidate
    (D) To offer a position

63. Who most likely is Mr. Evans?
    (A) The company president
    (B) The overseas branch head
    (C) The Personnel Department director
    (D) The woman's direct supervisor

64. What does the woman need to do by the end of the month?
    (A) Find a new job
    (B) Get a visa
    (C) Make a decision
    (D) Move to Shanghai

GO ON TO THE NEXT PAGE

Name	Monthly Fee	Songs available /month	Devices
Music Depot	$8.50	unlimited	phone
PlayNow	$5.00	2,000	phone
Smartsound	$3.99	1,000	phone, PC
X Hits	$9.50	unlimited	phone, PC

65. What does the woman say about the service?
    (A) It is convenient.
    (B) It is high-tech.
    (C) It is priced fairly.
    (D) It is very popular.

66. Where does the man like to listen to music in particular?
    (A) At home
    (B) At the gym
    (C) At work
    (D) On the train

67. Look at the graphic. Which service will the woman most likely choose?
    (A) Music Depot
    (B) PlayNow
    (C) Smartsound
    (D) X Hits

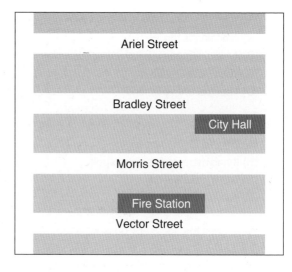

68. What can be said about the parade?
    (A) It was successful last year.
    (B) It will be canceled this year.
    (C) It will be held for the first time.
    (D) Its budget was increased.

69. Look at the graphic. Where will the parade start?
    (A) On Ariel Street
    (B) On Bradley Street
    (C) On Morris Street
    (D) On Vector Street

70. What does the woman say she will do?
    (A) Call City Hall
    (B) Fill out a job application
    (C) Help the man with the paperwork
    (D) Visit a government office

PART 4

Directions: You will hear some talks given by a single speaker. You will be asked to answer three questions about what the speaker says in each talk. Select the best response to each question and mark the letter (A), (B), (C), or (D) on your answer sheet. The talks will not be printed in your test book and will be spoken only one time.

71. What is implied about Orangeton?

(A) It is experiencing a lot of growth.

(B) It is getting a professional sports team.

(C) It is Mr. Jones' place of birth.

(D) It is the speaker's favorite place.

72. How long was Mr. Jones a professional athlete?

(A) For 5 years

(B) For 8 years

(C) For 10 years

(D) For 20 years

73. What did Mr. Jones recently do?

(A) Opened a store

(B) Left a hospital

(C) Played in a tournament

(D) Traveled around

74. Who is the caller?

(A) A business owner

(B) The listener's friend

(C) An engineer

(D) A weather forecaster

75. What can the listener provide?

(A) A catering service

(B) Locally-grown food

(C) A new window

(D) A quotation

76. What does Mr. Conklin ask the listener to do?

(A) Call back quickly

(B) Contact his assistant

(C) Reply by e-mail

(D) Stop by his office

77. What kind of business is being advertised?

(A) Childcare service

(B) Cleaning service

(C) Delivery service

(D) Elderly care service

78. What does the speaker mean when she says, "It will give you a big lift"?

(A) The service will make listeners save money.

(B) The service will be used to make listeners feel lighter.

(C) The service will make listeners happy.

(D) The service will take listeners where they need to go.

79. Who can get a discount?

(A) Those who give a discount code

(B) Those who have a certain size house

(C) Those who have not used the service before

(D) Those who live in a certain area

80. What will the new bridge go over?

(A) A lake

(B) A river

(C) A valley

(D) Some train tracks

81. Why was the project delayed?

(A) The citizens did not want to approve it.

(B) The city could not decide on a builder.

(C) The city did not have the money.

(D) The construction company had problems.

82. What is the construction company expected to do?

(A) Employ many people

(B) Give a press conference

(C) Start the bidding process

(D) Underbid its rivals

GO ON TO THE NEXT PAGE

83. Where is the announcement taking place?

(A) At a bookstore
(B) At a clothing store
(C) At a grocery store
(D) At a shoe store

84. What does the speaker imply when she says, "business really picked up between 5:00 and 7:00 PM"?

(A) A lot of customers came during the evening.
(B) The customers used a shuttle bus to come to the store.
(C) A special discount was offered in the evening.
(D) Those who work in the evening were paid double.

85. What will listeners receive if they work longer this weekend?

(A) A bonus
(B) Free merchandise
(C) Higher salary
(D) A paid day off

86. What is being advertised?

(A) A drink
(B) A health food
(C) A medication
(D) A supplement

87. Who can use the advertised product?

(A) Anyone
(B) Hospital patients only
(C) Students only
(D) Those over 15

88. Where can the product be purchased?

(A) At a health exhibition
(B) At all health food stores
(C) At any drugstore
(D) On the Web

89. What is the talk mainly about?

(A) An expansion of the office
(B) A new employee's first day
(C) Parking location changes
(D) Public transportation fees

90. What are listeners encouraged to do?

(A) Keep their desks clean
(B) Participate in a survey
(C) Ride to work together
(D) Welcome a new employee

91. According to the speaker, what might some listeners experience next week?

(A) A long walk
(B) Loud construction noise
(C) Low temperatures in the office
(D) A new desk assignment

Fern Grove Department Store	
♪♪ Thank you for shopping with us today. ♪♪	
Women's blouse	$55.00
Tax (10%)	$5.50
Total	$60.50

We appreciate our customer's feedback:
www.ferngrovedepart.com

92. What discount can a customer get on a child's jacket at most?

(A) 30 percent
(B) 40 percent
(C) 50 percent
(D) 60 percent

93. When does the sale end?

(A) This afternoon at 5:00
(B) Tonight at 8:00
(C) Tomorrow at 12:00
(D) Tomorrow night at 8:00

94. Look at the graphic. What can the customer receive?

(A) An extra discount
(B) A free gift
(C) Free parking
(D) A refund

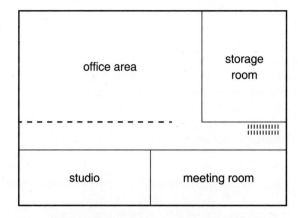

Platform	Time	Destination
1	15:30	Arendale
2	15:35	Hastings Cross
3	15:45	Gilmore Station
4	15:48	Green River

95. What industry does the speaker work in?

(A) Architecture

(B) Construction

(C) Medical

(D) Publishing

96. Look at the graphic. Which room will be smaller after the renovation?

(A) The meeting room

(B) The office area

(C) The storage room

(D) The studio

97. What most likely will the listeners do next?

(A) Discuss the office layout

(B) Have lunch together

(C) Plan a new product

(D) Speak with an architect

98. Who most likely is the speaker?

(A) A passenger

(B) A train conductor

(C) A train driver

(D) A train station staff

99. Look at the graphic. What time is the train to Gilmore Station going to leave?

(A) 15:35

(B) 15:45

(C) 15:48

(D) 15:55

100. Where should passengers with reserved tickets go?

(A) Car 1

(B) Car 2

(C) Car 4

(D) Car 8

This is the end of the Listening test. Turn to Part 5 in your test book.

GO ON TO THE NEXT PAGE

READING TEST

In the Reading test, you will read a variety of texts and answer several different types of reading comprehension questions. The entire Reading test will last 75 minutes. There are three parts, and directions are given for each part. You are encouraged to answer as many questions as possible within the time allowed.

You must mark your answers on the separate answer sheet. Do not write your answers in your test book.

PART 5

Directions: A word or phrase is missing in each of the sentences below. Four answer choices are given below each sentence. Select the best answer to complete the sentence. Then mark the letter (A), (B), (C), or (D) on your answer sheet.

101. If you would like to book one of our meeting rooms, please let us know if you need any ------- such as a projector or a video camera.
(A) equipment
(B) amenities
(C) instruments
(D) materials

102. AtoZ Industry offers plenty of ------- office furniture and supplies suitable for your needs.
(A) rent
(B) rental
(C) renter
(D) rents

103. If you have a problem installing our software on your computer, you can call ------- send an e-mail to our customer service staff.
(A) and
(B) nor
(C) or
(D) to

104. The city council ------- receives architectural proposals created by a group of graduate students.
(A) recently
(B) similarly
(C) highly
(D) regularly

105. As the keynote speech was cancelled at the last minute, the event organizer had to find a -------.
(A) replace
(B) replaceable
(C) replacing
(D) replacement

106. The leader talked at length about how practical his project plan was ------- all of his team members agreed to proceed.
(A) in case
(B) given that
(C) until
(D) whether

107. Sarah Luther had to hurry back to her office to attend a ------- seminar for the new intranet system.
(A) numerous
(B) mandatory
(C) versatile
(D) voluntary

108. Because of a heating problem, the sales team had to hold their meeting in an ------- cold room.
(A) exceed
(B) exceeded
(C) exceeding
(D) exceedingly

109. All employees are required to acknowledge that ------- have been informed of the new company policy and agree to it in all respects.

(A) theirs
(B) them
(C) themselves
(D) they

110. Melba Logistics is a licensed carrier ------- rapid and safe transportation services all over the world.

(A) forwarding
(B) equipping
(C) providing
(D) receiving

111. More than 300 people ------- 50 different countries took part in the 15th International Conference on Environmental Science.

(A) among
(B) from
(C) over
(D) through

112. With the board member's -------, Mr. Henderson will assume the post of chairperson next month.

(A) endorsable
(B) endorse
(C) endorsement
(D) endorser

113. If you have any problems with or questions about the network access -------, please ask our IT department.

(A) selection
(B) advance
(C) protocol
(D) sequence

114. According to the financial advisor, conducting ------- research beforehand is crucial for buying stocks.

(A) detail
(B) detailed
(C) detailing
(D) details

115. The personnel chief considers that asking an unexpected question can be useful to judge candidates ------- interviewing them.

(A) as well as
(B) unless
(C) still
(D) when

116. Rather than partially modifying it, the team manager thought they should reconsider the ------- design of the new product.

(A) center
(B) extra
(C) main
(D) whole

117. As the contract is coming to an end, the company will have to remove all possessions and ------- the rented property by the end of the week.

(A) vacancies
(B) vacancy
(C) vacant
(D) vacate

118. The consumer trends report found that people have recently spent ------- money on vacations and have saved it instead.

(A) fewer
(B) less
(C) many
(D) more

119. The new laptop, TGX 800, received many good reviews as it has been ------- improved from its old model and is a lot easier to use.

(A) mostly
(B) drastically
(C) scarcely
(D) temporarily

120. The CEO is extremely concerned that the company's stock price ------- steadily over the past few weeks.

(A) has dropped
(B) has been dropping
(D) is dropping
(D) will drop

GO ON TO THE NEXT PAGE

121. -------, the product launch went quite smoothly even though several urgent changes were made.
(A) Surprise
(B) Surprised
(C) Surprising
(D) Surprisingly

122. Mason Engineering has ------- some major changes over the year to become more customer-focused.
(A) underestimated
(B) undergone
(C) undermined
(D) understood

123. An e-mail was sent to notify all the participants that the event would take place at Hamilton Hall ------- Celia Hall.
(A) prior to
(B) instead of
(C) though
(D) thus

124. There were nearly 1,000 people ------- at the protest against the discontinuation of free bus passes for seniors.
(A) present
(B) presentation
(C) presented
(D) presenter

125. The collected personal information will not be disclosed to third parties without prior -------, except under court order.
(A) analysis
(B) consent
(C) discussion
(D) engagement

126. Compromise does not always resolve the issues ------- contain underlying interpersonal conflicts.
(A) what
(B) that
(C) where
(D) whose

127. Jade Private Hospital has established an excellent reputation in the community for its high ------- to patient satisfaction.
(A) commit
(B) commitment
(C) committal
(D) committed

128. As the restaurant has been -------, the owner is considering expanding his business in the region.
(A) productive
(B) prosperous
(C) strategic
(D) struggling

129. At the lecture, the renowned chef told the audience ------- such an easy recipe could result in such a delicious dish.
(A) as if
(B) despite
(C) how
(D) then

130. Even after spending long hours trying to fix it, the IT worker could not iron ------- the problem with the network.
(A) down
(B) off
(C) out
(D) over

PART 6

Directions: Read the texts that follow. A word, phrase, or sentence is missing in parts of each text. Four answer choices for each question are given below the text. Select the best answer to complete the text. Then mark the letter (A), (B), (C), or (D) on your answer sheet.

Questions 131-134 refer to the following e-mail.

To: Amanda Green
From: Exciting Travel Co.
Subject: Visit Costa Rica
Date: March 19

Exciting Travel's Top Three Reasons You Should Visit Costa Rica

1. ------- you crave adventure, Costa Rica is definitely the place for you. You can go white-water
    131.

rafting, kayaking, scuba diving, cliff diving, sky diving… the list is endless.

2. -------. Both public and private beaches are sure to please lovers of sun and sand like -------.
    132.   **133.**

3. Costa Rica has been called the happiest country on Earth, and for good reason. The people are

peaceful, friendly and go out of their way to make every visitor feel at home.

For details about our travel ------- to Costa Rica, please visit our Website: www.excitingtravel.net.
                              134.

131. (A) If
(B) Probably
(C) Where
(D) Whether

132. (A) Costa Rica has a world-famous rainforest and many environmental organizations give tours of it.
(B) If you have kids, you'll definitely want to take advantage of our resort's six swimming pools.
(C) We have several great travel deals to Costa Rica, but they expire soon so don't put it off —call today.
(D) With almost 1,000 miles of coastline, Costa Rica is home to some of the world's loveliest beaches.

133. (A) ourselves
(B) them
(C) themselves
(D) yourself

134. (A) agency
(B) insurance
(C) package
(D) tips

GO ON TO THE NEXT PAGE

Questions 135-138 refer to the following article.

Media Company to Relocate to Stamford

STAMFORD — Blasted, a live-streaming media company ------- **135.** in Westville, plans to move within the next few months to an office park in Stamford's south end. The firm is set to make the move during the second quarter of this year after ------- **136.** a long-term lease for 9,500 square feet at Brookbend Center.

"Brookbend Center has been home to many high technology companies ------- **137.** its founding, and we're pleased Blasted is making Brookbend its future home," property manager Jonathan Turner said in a statement. Situated next to the Norton River, Brookbend Center covers 40 acres. It features a conference room that can hold up to 200 people, an auditorium, and six meeting rooms. -------. **138.**

135. (A) base
(B) based
(C) is basing
(D) was based

136. (A) creating
(B) losing
(C) proposing
(D) signing

137. (A) by
(B) since
(C) until
(D) yet

138. (A) Mr. Turner is taking applications from other prospective tenants for an available office unit.
(B) The company will expand its domestic manufacturing capacity after the move, sources say.
(C) The office center also includes a cafeteria, 1,457 parking spaces, and several walking trails.
(D) Time will tell if the move by Blasted will result in higher earnings for their struggling products.

MEMORANDUM

To: All Employees
From: Oscar Mendelson
Date: May 25
Subject: Welcoming our new employee

I'm happy to announce that Ms. Joanne Remnick is joining Medifast, Inc. to fill the open position

in customer service. Joanne ------- for more than five years in customer service at BioServe. She
                            139.

earned several employee-of-the-month awards while there and she comes ------- recommended by
                                                                          140.

her superiors.

Joanne's direct supervisor will be Robert Vesper, so if you have questions, you can ------- with
                                                                                      141.

Robert before she starts.

We are delighted to have Joanne join the Medifast team. Joanne's first day will be Tuesday, June 13.

142.

---

139. (A) is working
    (B) will have worked
    (C) worked
    (D) works

140. (A) highly
    (B) mainly
    (C) mostly
    (D) fairly

141. (A) share
    (B) solve
    (C) talk
    (D) think

142. (A) As we will have safety inspectors here next week, please don't be late to work.
    (B) If you see Joanne around the building, be sure to welcome her to the company.
    (C) Joanne was one of our best employees in customer service and we will miss her.
    (D) Please make sure to submit your suggestion for employee of the month by then.

GO ON TO THE NEXT PAGE

Questions 143-146 refer to the following e-mail.

To: Atlas Property Management Agency
From: Rita Hanson, Buildmore Co.
Date: May 13
Subject: Necessary repairs

As a follow-up to our conversation on May 12, this is a ------- for repairs at our office located in
143.

the Bradford Building, Number 301. The office was in need of these repairs ------- we moved in,
144.

not through any fault, abuse, or negligence on our part. These are the items in need of repair: one

inner office door (latch broken) and the heating unit on south side of office (doesn't turn on and off

properly).

------- It regrettably interferes with our ability ------- business in this location. Please let me know
145. **146.**

when you will be making the repairs.

Sincerely,

Rita

143. (A) bill
(B) quote
(C) reply
(D) request

144. (A) although
(B) because
(C) when
(D) whether

145. (A) Our firm has recently earned several
awards for design and efficiency.
(B) This office has many great attributes like
spaciousness and natural light.
(C) We look forward to hearing back from you
about our collaboration proposal.
(D) We would like this matter to be taken care
of as soon as possible, of course.

146. (A) conducting
(B) conducted
(C) conducts
(D) to conduct

PART 7

Directions: In this part you will read a selection of texts, such as magazine and newspaper articles, e-mails, and instant messages. Each text or set of texts is followed by several questions. Select the best answer for each question and mark the letter (A), (B), (C), or (D) on your answer sheet.

Questions 147-148 refer to the following product instructions.

TopSpeed

Thank you for purchasing the Trine Blender TopSpeed. We pride ourselves on easy-to use high-quality kitchen appliances and utensils.

To start using your new blender, first you will need to remove the pieces from the container and begin setup. The blender base will be heavy, so please be aware it might fall if opened from the bottom of the package.

The contents of the box will include: one base, two blade attachments, one pitcher attachment, and four serving cups. Before using, make sure to thoroughly clean all parts of the machine. Choose the blades needed (one large and one small blade; other sizes sold separately) and screw the blade attachment to the base. Once secured, it will be ready to use. Next, plug it in, add your ingredients, and make sure the pitcher is on tight. You will be then ready to use the Trine Blender TopSpeed.

---

147. What should customers pay attention to when removing the product?

(A) The installation instructions
(B) The sharpness of the blades
(C) The type of knife to open the box with
(D) The way the box is opened

148. How many types of blades are included in the box?

(A) 1
(B) 2
(C) 3
(D) 4

GO ON TO THE NEXT PAGE

Questions 149-150 refer to the following text message chain.

Steve Bedrosian   9:34 AM
Hey Mark, sorry to bother you. I know it's almost time for your appointment with the new client, but I have a favor to ask.

Mark Fitz   9:37 AM
Sure, What's up?

Steve Bedrosian   9:39 AM
I'm stuck in meetings at the office all day, so I was wondering if you could swing by our westside office and grab the design documents for the Bunker Hill project on your way back here for the meeting this evening.

Mark Fitz   9:41 AM
No problem. I'm heading into my customers office now. It's not too far, so I can stop and get them after we finish here. Is the project back on the schedule?

Steve Bedrosian   9:43 AM
Thanks. I appreciate it. We are having discussions about using the designs either to restructure the original BH project or possibly using them to start the new Wilder project next spring.

Mark Fitz   9:48 AM
Wow, that's good to hear! I was hoping it would be picked up again for something. I really liked the way it was shaping up when it was pitched. I'll message you once I have then and am heading your way.

149. What is preventing Mr. Bedrosian from getting the meeting documents?

(A) He has to go to Bunker Hill.
(B) He has to stay at the company.
(C) His colleague took a day off.
(D) The documents are not ready yet.

150. At 9:48 AM, what does Mr. Fitz mean when he writes "I really liked the way it was shaping up"?

(A) He thought that the design of the project was good.
(B) He thought that the meeting was well-organized.
(C) He thought that the project was losing unnecessary things.
(D) He thought that the schedule would work.

Questions 151-152 refer to the following notice.

Rosa's Italian Homestead is proud to announce that we will be reopening our 52nd Street location on Saturday, April 16, and we would like to invite everyone to come see our new look and menu. For over 30 years, we have served the area the finest dishes possible, but wanted to modernize and update our design and the meals for you.

To show our gratitude for your time in the Mariemont area, we will be offering a few special items that will only be available this month! Come and enjoy traditional Sicilian Pasta alla Norma, Manicotti, and a fresh seafood plate of Pesce spada alla ghiotta. During the first week, we will be offering a special three-course meal for the price of a large pizza. Come in and experience the fresh new tastes at Rosa's!

151. When will the special discount end?

(A) In a few days
(B) At the end of the week
(C) At the end of the month
(D) At the end of next month

152. Which kind of plate is Rosa's NOT offering in the special reopening menu?

(A) A large pizza
(B) Manicotti plate
(C) Seafood plate
(D) Sicilian pasta

GO ON TO THE NEXT PAGE

Questions 153-154 refer to the following e-mail.

	e-mail
To:	James McCullen
From:	Sebastian Bludd
Subject:	The Winterholm Project
Date:	April 20

Dear Mr. McCullen,

The Winterholm Project has been given clearance to start, but I think I am going to need your help on a few things. This will be my first time as lead of a new construction site, but I know you've had a lot of experience in situations like this, so I would appreciate your input.

First, we only have 14 months to complete it, but we will have to start construction in November, so the winter air will make it more difficult for our construction team. Do you think we should start with the smaller construction crew and add more later? It will be a large structure, and we will need quite a bit of time for creating the best workspaces for all of our recruits. I understand that speed is as important as quality in this matter, but I want to do it right. Let me know what ideas you can come up with.

Sebastian Bludd

153. Why does Mr. Bludd ask Mr. McCullen for his advice?

(A) He does not want to be responsible for the project.

(B) He has no experience in construction.

(C) He thinks he needs approval to start it.

(D) He trusts his opinion about the project.

154. What problem does Mr. Bludd mention?

(A) The placement of the offices

(B) The price of the building

(C) The size of the land

(D) The weather during construction

ATTENTION: ALL EMPLOYEES

The Annual Summer Warehouse Sale will begin on June 5! All employees can participate in the sale, which will offer merchandise for 60-80 percent off and includes anything currently housed in our warehouse located near the main office. That means televisions, ovens, radios, and more.

We have updated the Employee Sale section of the company intranet so that you can start searching the catalog now! Please note, once the sale begins, the Web page data may be incorrect, as it will take some time to update sales that week. All items will be sold on a first come first served basis, so don't wait if you see something you are interested in.

Make sure to bring your company badge with you for entry into the warehouse. The sale will only last two weeks, so take advantage of this once-a-year savings opportunity!

155. What kind of products will be available at the sale?

(A) Electronics
(B) Kitchen utensils
(C) Office equipment
(D) Summer clothing

156. When does the sale end?

(A) June 5
(B) June 19
(C) June 30
(D) July 1

157. How can people find out about sale items before the sale begins?

(A) By accessing a Website
(B) By asking for a list
(C) By contacting someone in the main office
(D) By visiting the warehouse

GO ON TO THE NEXT PAGE

JD Turk Cleaners will come to your office, store, or warehouse and create a safe clean working environment for your team. We have been in business for six years and have been the recipient of numerous awards for our thoroughness and work attitude. You can put your faith in us to take care of your office, wherever it may be. We have members of our staff ready at any time required by you. Our team leader Glen Matthews, has over 20 years of experience in the field, and will be able to get the job done for you.

We don't want to interrupt your important work time, so we are available 24 hours a day and seven days a week, whenever you need us. To contact JD Turk, you can call our office number: 916-555-2342 or send us a message to jdturk@mailme.com or you can send forms to our address:

4023 Sacred Heart Boulevard,

San Difrangeles,

CA 94207

158. What is true about JD Turk Cleaners?

(A) They can finish the job quickly.

(B) They can work at any time.

(C) They only hire the top workers in the industry.

(D) They started their business 20 years ago.

159. What does Mr. Matthews do?

(A) He answers the phone at the office.

(B) He hires new employees for the company.

(C) He is the field manager for JD Turk.

(D) He responds to all e-mails directly.

160. How can a customer NOT contact JD Turk Cleaners?

(A) By mail

(B) By phone

(C) Via e-mail

(D) Via the Website

Questions 161-163 refer to the following article.

Garibaldi Security Services was celebrating today after receiving word that they had received the prized Londo Award for Internet protection and safeguarding of clients. GSS is responsible for over 235 customers, and had zero server failures of service during the timeframe of the award. In recent years, GSS has overcome past mistakes and become a leader in security technology, as well as new security measures to prevent loss of corporate and consumer information.

This is the first time that GSS has won the award, and a spokesperson said, "This award recognizes all of the efforts our company has made in the last year to ensure that our clients can trust us with their privacy." The spokesperson continued to say that the reorganization of the company five years ago helped create a stronger commitment to staying on top of new hacking techniques and espionage from outside sources. GSS is also looking to expand their services in the next year, in an effort to maximize profits and name recognition.

161. What is the article mainly about?
(A) A company recognized for outstanding service
(B) A failure of a newly established company
(C) A major change in personnel at an IT company
(D) A recent trend in the information technology industry

162. Why did the company restructure five years ago?
(A) To expand their business overseas
(B) To get better ideas to support clients
(C) To purchase updated technology
(D) To replace older workers

163. What is the company NOT looking to do in the near future?
(A) Improve brand awareness
(B) Make their profits
(C) Expand their business
(D) Pursue government contracts

GO ON TO THE NEXT PAGE

Questions 164-167 refer to the following advertisement.

Do you want to spend your summer working as a mentor to children? If so, come join us for an exciting six-week program at Camp Crystal. — [1] —. We will spend two weeks working and training together at camp, doing all the fun things you remember from your own childhood.

We have three areas at Camp Crystal where children can learn and have fun. — [2] —. Sharing the duties and helping with chores set the example of teamwork. Campers will help create the decorations and meals in the cabins.

— [3] —. Next, in the forest that surrounds the camp, everyone will see wildlife up-close and personally, as many kinds of interesting animals live around Camp Crystal. In past treks, we've seen everything from insects to foxes and bears! Trained outdoor leaders supervise all nature walks, so there won't be any danger of getting hurt or lost.

Finally, in our most popular area, we have a large lake, where counselors and campers alike will enjoy swimming, boat rides and if they are lucky, they might see Old Jason, a large tortoise that has lived near the lake for 100 years!

We also offer music, cooking, and painting lessons at an additional cost. If you have a class that you can teach, please let us know. Come to Camp Crystal and see what everyone is screaming about! — [4] —.

164. What is the main purpose of the advertisement?

(A) To draw tourists to Camp Crystal

(B) To hire new camp counselors for the summer

(C) To inform people of changes in Camp Crystal

(D) To introduce outdoor summer activities

165. How long will employees train before the camp begins?

(A) A few days

(B) A week

(C) Half a month

(D) A month

166. Which additional lessons does Camp Crystal NOT offer?

(A) Cooking

(B) Horseback riding

(C) Music

(D) Painting

167. In which of the positions marked [1], [2], [3], and [4] does the following sentence best belong?

"First, in the lodging area, we live, cook, clean, and have fun as a group."

(A) [1]

(B) [2]

(C) [3]

(D) [4]

Questions 168-171 refer to the following e-mail.

To	Sarah McGinly
From	Frank Tyson
Subject	Our products
Date	April 14

Dear Ms. McGinly,

We recently received an e-mail from you about our lineup of educational products that you recently used and we appreciate your wonderful words about your experience with them. —[1]—. We always love hearing from those who are satisfied with our products and would be excited to offer you a chance to help decide what kinds of future apps, games, and software we will release.

In our customer beta program, you would be sent versions of apps or computer software that we are currently working on. You would be able to download and use them for free and all we need for you to do is answer short questionnaires and give feedback via our preferred customer Website.

—[2]—. If interested, please fill out the form attached, which includes sections such as preferences of what kind of apps and software you would most enjoy beta testing and how often you would want to be included in the test. —[3]—. Once we receive these forms and after we find products you are most interested in, we will contact you to start your first test period. —[4]—.

Thanks and have a wonderful day.

Frank Tyson, Product Manager
Brain Games Entertainment

168. What type of product would Brain Games NOT send to Ms. McGinly?

(A) Apps
(B) Books
(C) Games
(D) Software

169. What would Ms. McGinly have to do as part of the program?

(A) Come to the office to work
(B) Fill out reports for the manager
(C) Respond to questions about the products
(D) Speak to reporters about the new products

170. What should Ms. McGinly do to participate in the program?

(A) Call Mr. Tyson directly
(B) Download an application form
(C) Send back the attachment
(D) Visit Brain Games Entertainment

171. In which of the positions marked [1], [2], [3], and [4] does the following sentence best belong?

"We would also need you to sign a secrecy agreement to be included in the preferred customer program."

(A) [1]
(B) [2]
(C) [3]
(D) [4]

GO ON TO THE NEXT PAGE

Questions 172-175 refer to the following online discussion.

Steve Banner 2:23 PM		Hi, Brand and Kate. Thanks for giving me a few minutes. I need to ask about the traffic on our Website. I have checked the data and it shows that customer traffic has been declining sharply for the last few days. Any ideas what's happening?
Brand Thompson 2:24 PM		There was a special report on the news a few days ago saying that one of our products caused an injury, which might have something to do with it.
Kate Marna 2:26 PM		What? I hadn't heard anything about this. What happened?
Steve Banner 2:27 PM		This is news to me as well. Can you fill us in, Brand?
Brand Thompson 2:30 PM		A local news channel interviewed a parent about learning to ride a bicycle with training wheels, the Cubby 200. The parent said that the wheels just popped off, which made the child fall and scrape up his legs and face a bit.
Steve Banner 2:32 PM		Why was this not brought to my attention? We need to contact this parent and extend our apologies, as well as we offer a replacement. Let's try to turn this around to show that we do care about our products and customers.
Kate Marna 2:34 PM		Brand, message me which news station it was, and I will get in touch with them so I can help straighten out the situation. Let's put out this fire before it's too late!
Brand Thompson 2:35 PM		OK. I'll have to find the information, but I will send it over today.
Steve Banner 2:37 PM		OK. Thanks for the update. Looks like concerned parents are hearing about this by word of mouth, causing the traffic drop, so you two need to work together to help get these customers back.

172. What caused a drop in Website traffic?

(A) A defective product

(B) A hike in prices

(C) A new company policy

(D) A piece of incorrect information

173. How will they try to solve the problem?

(A) By giving a new Cubby 200

(B) By sending an apology letter

(C) By using the media to promote their products

(D) By warning customers not to use a product

174. Who will contact certain news media?

(A) Mr. Banner

(B) Mr. Thompson

(C) Ms. Marna

(D) Their boss

175. At 2:34 PM, what does Ms. Marna mean when she writes, "Let's put out this fire before it's too late!"?

(A) They need to encourage other employees of the company to do better.

(B) They need to address the issue quickly before they lose more customers.

(C) They need to start offering more discounts to customers who are loyal to the company.

(D) They need to keep the customers updated.

GO ON TO THE NEXT PAGE

Questions 176-180 refer to the following information and application form.

Expanse Engineering has started an online board for employees who wish to rent, buy, sell, or trade housing, furniture, appliances, and more. There is a small fee for positing, but replying or trading in the employee lounge is always free. To post an ad, please fill out all of the required information on the application, pay the fee.

Price

Item listing (under 50 words)	$2.00
Item listing (50-99 words)	$3.00
Item listing (100 words or more)	$4.00
Pictures	$.10 per picture

---

www.expanseengineering.com/board

Employee name: Mary Logan

Section: Sales/Furniture

Date: March 23

Item Description:

I am preparing to move after this fiscal year and want to sell some of my furniture. I have three things for sale. First is a large wooden dresser with four drawers. I've had it for four years and it is in excellent condition. I also have a small, white computer desk that is big enough for working, but won't get in the way inside a room. Finally is a small refrigerator that can hold several containers and up to around six drink cans. I would like to sell them together, but will sell piece by piece if needed. Check out the pictures for each piece included and contact me to make an offer!

Words: 114

Photos attached: 3

How many days posted: 30 days

176. What kind of services does the company board offer?

(A) Exchanging goods
(B) Collecting unwanted items
(C) Delivering appliances
(D) Translating documents

177. How is the price of the service determined?

(A) By the category
(B) By the number of items
(C) By the number of words
(D) By the posting period

178. Why is Ms. Logan selling the items?

(A) She is going to buy new ones.
(B) She is leaving the company.
(C) She needs the money.
(D) She will relocate.

179. How can a person know about the condition of the items?

(A) By contacting a Web administrator
(B) By looking at photos online
(C) By sending Ms. Logan an e-mail
(D) By visiting Ms. Logan's place

180. How much did Ms. Logan probably spend for the advertisement?

(A) $2.10
(B) $3.30
(C) $4.30
(D) $9.30

GO ON TO THE NEXT PAGE

Questions 181-185 refer to the following schedule and e-mail.

New Hires – Orientation Schedule
April 3rd – 7th

Schedule	Times
Welcome Breakfast	8:00 AM – 10:00 AM
Introduction to Policies and Procedures	10:15 AM – 11:05 AM
System Training (Customer Service Reps Only) – Lana Carney	11:15 AM – 12:00 PM
System Training (Engineers) – Vince Turner	11:15 AM – 12:00 PM
Lunch	12:15 PM – 1:15 PM
System Training (Inside and Outside Sales) – Richard Bird	1:15 PM – 2:00 PM
System Training (Management Trainees) – Lori Stevens	1:15 PM – 2:00 PM
Breakout Session with Division Managers (Division Leads Only)	1:30 PM – 2:00 PM
Breakout Session into Department groups – Manager Introductions	2:15 PM – 3:00 PM
Team Breakout Session – All Groups	3:15 PM – 4:45 PM
End of Orientation Day	5:00 PM

---

	e-mail
To:	Richard Bird; Lori Stevens
From:	Vince Turner
Subject:	Orientation Schedule
Date:	March 31, 2:43 PM

Hello Rich and Lori

I know that orientation for new employees is coming up next week, but a Towson manager asked me if I had time to work with them directly next week to assist with building their new database. They would need me to be at their offices in the morning to start the process. If possible, I would need to switch training times with one of you.

Normally I wouldn't ask, but this is a Top 10 client, so I didn't want to say no. Since I was the captain of the ship for our databases, they said they needed me to come in and guide them through it. I feel it is important for me to show loyalty to our customers for the installation.

It would only be from Monday to Wednesday, but I think it would be easier for all involved if we could reschedule the entire week. Can either of you switch times with me so I can work with Towson in the mornings?

Thank you,
Vince Turner

181. How long will the session take for the team?

(A) For half an hour
(B) For 45 minutes
(C) For an hour
(D) For one and a half hours

182. What is the purpose of the e-mail?

(A) To ask what will be discussed at the orientation
(B) To determine which managers are attending
(C) To find out who is running the training programs
(D) To request a change in schedule

183. In the e-mail, the word "building" in paragraph 1, line 2, is closest in meaning to

(A) adding
(B) creating
(C) enlarging
(D) constructing

184. Why doesn't Mr. Turner want to turn down the customer's request?

(A) He promised to help them anytime.
(B) They are an important company.
(C) They cannot use the database without him.
(D) They paid for a tour.

185. When would Mr. Turner like to talk to new engineers?

(A) 11:15 AM
(B) 1:15 PM
(C) 1:30 PM
(D) 5:00 PM

GO ON TO THE NEXT PAGE

Damaged Baggage

If your checked baggage arrives damaged, you'll need to report the damage within seven days of receiving your bag. You can contact one of our ground staff at the airport or send a message to our Customer Service section. cs@forwardair.com

Forward Airlines responsibility for damaged baggage is limited. Please see full details of our Baggage Policy here. Forward Airlines Baggage Policy

As a general rule, we do not assume responsibility for normal wear and tear to baggage. This includes:

* Cuts, scratches, scuffs, dents and marks that may occur despite careful handling
* Damage to, or loss of, protruding parts of the baggage including: straps, pockets, pull handles, hanger hooks, wheels, external locks, security straps, or zippers
* Unsuitably-packed luggage (e.g. over-packed)

To	Forward Airlines Customer Services <cs@forwardair.com>
From	Beverly Rodriguez <brodriguez@pronto.net>
Subject	Damaged luggage
Date	May 22

To whom it may concern,

I recently returned to Los Angeles from Hong Kong on Forward Airlines. I was dismayed to see that my checked suitcase had been damaged. I took it to a luggage repair shop the same day and got it fixed. I have attached the bill to this message. I expect to be reimbursed for the full amount of the repair. This is my first bad experience with Forward Airlines and I hope to have this problem resolved quickly.

Beverly Rodriguez

THREE STAR LUGGAGE REPAIR

Date received	May 17	Invoice number	5V803
Customer name	Beverly Rodriguez	Staff member	Yannick
Bag type	Large rolling bag, black	Date finished	May 21
Bag maker	Stenson, Inc.		

Description of repair:
Replacement of retracting handle mechanism

Note: All repairs completed according to manufacturer's standard using parts from original manufacturer.	Subtotal	$35.50
	Tax	$5.00
	Total	$40.50

186. What is true about the information?

(A) Customers should report the damage within a week.

(B) Damaged luggage is covered by insurance.

(C) Customers should bring their luggage to the office.

(D) Worn baggage is dealt separately.

187. When did Ms. Rodriguez arrive in Los Angeles?

(A) May 15

(B) May 17

(C) May 21

(D) May 22

188. What does Ms. Rodriguez imply in her e-mail?

(A) She has flown on Forward Airlines before.

(B) She has recently moved overseas.

(C) She repaired the luggage by herself.

(D) She flew to Hong Kong.

189. Why might Forward Airlines deny Ms. Rodriguez's claim?

(A) She did not report it to the proper staff.

(B) She had a damaged handle.

(C) She had over-packed her bag.

(D) She didn't make the claim.

190. What is mentioned about the repair?

(A) It cost less than expected.

(B) It was finished earlier than requested.

(C) The item was sent to the manufacturer.

(D) The replacement parts were from Stenson, Inc.

GO ON TO THE NEXT PAGE

Castle Clothing Order Summary

Customer: Eric Pratchett
5400 Hanover Rd.   **Order Date:** May 14
Smith Village, Ca 94423   **Ship Date:** May 17

Item #	Item name	Color	Qty.	Unit Price	Total
SW99	Sweater	Blue	1	$50.00	$50.00
CR67	Men's pants	Gray/Black	2	$80.00	$160.00
BL02	Light blazer	Brown	1	$150.00	$150.00
SH14	Shirt	White	2	$40.00	$80.00
				Subtotal	$440.00
				Total Order	$440.00

* For residents of CA, tax is included in unit price.
** No shipping charges for orders over $300

---

	e-mail
To:	Eric Pratchett <ericpratchett@strongly.net>
From:	Castel Clothing Customer Care <cccc@castelclothing.com>
Subject:	Your order
Date:	May 29

Dear Mr. Pratchett,

Unfortunately, the following item that you ordered is now out of stock: #BL02. Although we try our best to maintain 100-percent accuracy with inventory, there are rare occasions where we experience an inventory error.

Attached is a description of an item that is similar to the one you purchased that we currently have in stock. This item is cheaper than the one you purchased, so the difference would be refunded. Please let us know if you would like this one as a replacement or if you would like to wait until your original item becomes available.

Sincerely,
Raleigh Mclntosh
Castel Clothing Customer Care

Graveline Sports Jacket

This jacket for men is light enough to wear on a warm spring day or with a sweater underneath on a chilly day. Made of 100-percent breathable cotton, the jacket has five front buttons, two roomy side pockets, and one inner breast pocket. The wind-blocking stand-up collar is stylish and practical. Available in a variety of colors for $140 (incl. Tax)

191. What can be inferred in the order form?
(A) It was shipped on the day of the purchase.
(B) Additional tax has been charged.
(C) The items were shipped at no charge.
(D) The items can be returned.

192. Which item Mr. Pratchett ordered is NOT immediately available?
(A) Black pants
(B) Gray pants
(C) The blue sweater
(D) The brown blazer

193. What information does Mr. McIntosh want?
(A) A credit card number
(B) A customer's decision
(C) The delivery address
(D) The item number

194. How much can Mr. Pratchett get a refund on a new jacket?
(A) $10
(B) $40
(C) $50
(D) $80

195. What material is BL02 most likely made of?
(A) Silk
(B) Nylon
(C) Cotton
(D) Wool

ITINERARY FOR SINGAPORE TRIP

May 10–13

Wednesday, May 10
- 4:00 PM   Arrive in Singapore
- 7:00 PM   Dinner with team (at your discretion)

Thursday, May 11
- 10:00 AM–4:00 PM   Tour of manufacturing facility, led by Mr. Chang
- 7:00 PM   Dinner cruise with Mr. Chang

Friday, May 12
- 10:00 AM   Sightseeing around Singapore
- 2:00 PM   Presentation by product development team
- 6:30 PM   Dinner reservations at Waverly Point

Saturday, May 13
- 10:00 AM   Check out of hotel
- 12:00 noon   Flight departs for San Francisco

Where to Eat in Singapore

Pavilion
Located in the Western Hotel, Pavilion offers travelers a taste of home when away from home. We will pair your meal with a great glass of wine.

Open 7 days/week

Fortini
Don't ask for the menu. We don't have one. Allow our award-winning chef to choose for you. We promise you won't regret it.

Open 7 days/week

Aubergine
French chef Paul Desautel left his comfortable Parisian life to start Aubergine five years ago. One of Singapore's most delightful restaurants.

Closed Wednesdays

Chantilly
Located in the heart of Marina Bay, Chantilly takes fusion very seriously. Combines the best culinary tastes from around the world.

Closed Mondays

To	Jocelyn Woods
From	Brandon Ainsley
Subject	Recommendation
Date	April 28

Hi Jocelyn,

I heard you're going to Singapore. That's fantastic! You absolutely cannot miss this great restaurant called Fortini. It sounds Italian and they do have delicious Italian dishes, but they serve so much more. I've been there three times and each time I come away thinking that was the best meal I've ever had. And you don't need to worry about Megan either, since the chef always has something terrific for vegetarians. I guarantee you all will love it!

Safe travels,
Brandon Ainsley

196. According to the schedule, when will the team visit some tourist places?

(A) Wednesday
(B) Thursday
(C) Friday
(D) Saturday

197. Which restaurant will the team be unable to visit on the first day?

(A) Pavilion
(B) Fortini
(C) Aubergine
(D) Chantilly

198. In the list, the word "pair" in line 3, is the closest in meaning to

(A) combine
(B) double
(C) keep
(D) treat

199. What is mentioned about the restaurant Mr. Ainsley recommends?

(A) It has no menu.
(B) It has outdoor seating.
(C) It serves fusion food.
(D) It serves only vegetarian food.

200. What is implied about a member of the group?

(A) She went to the diner before.
(B) She doesn't like Italian food.
(C) She has a dietary restriction.
(D) She is not going on the trip.

Stop! This is the end of the test. If you finish before time is called, you may go back to Parts 5, 6, and 7 and check your work.

Actual Test 2

휴대폰은 OFF!

LC MP3는 ON!

2시간만 집중!

Check ▸ 시작 시간 _____ : _____

▸ 종료 시간 _____ : _____

LC MP3 바로듣기

LISTENING TEST

In the Listening test, you will be asked to demonstrate how well you understand spoken English. The entire Listening test will last approximately 45 minutes. There are four parts, and directions are given for each part. You must mark your answers on the separate answer sheet. Do not write your answers in your test book.

PART 1

Directions: For each question in this part, you will hear four statements about a picture in your test book. When you hear the statements, you must select the one statement that best describes what you see in the picture. Then find the number of the question on your answer sheet and mark your answer. The statements will not be printed in your test book and will be spoken only one time.

Statement (C), "They're sitting at the table," is the best description of the picture, so you should select answer (C) and mark it on your answer sheet.

1.

2.

GO ON TO THE NEXT PAGE

3.

4.

5.

6.

GO ON TO THE NEXT PAGE

PART 2

Directions: You will hear a question or statement and three responses spoken in English. They will not be printed in your test book and will be spoken only one time. Select the best response to the question or statement and mark the letter (A), (B), or (C) on your answer sheet.

7. Mark your answer on your answer sheet.

8. Mark your answer on your answer sheet.

9. Mark your answer on your answer sheet.

10. Mark your answer on your answer sheet.

11. Mark your answer on your answer sheet.

12. Mark your answer on your answer sheet.

13. Mark your answer on your answer sheet.

14. Mark your answer on your answer sheet.

15. Mark your answer on your answer sheet.

16. Mark your answer on your answer sheet.

17. Mark your answer on your answer sheet.

18. Mark your answer on your answer sheet.

19. Mark your answer on your answer sheet.

20. Mark your answer on your answer sheet.

21. Mark your answer on your answer sheet.

22. Mark your answer on your answer sheet.

23. Mark your answer on your answer sheet.

24. Mark your answer on your answer sheet.

25. Mark your answer on your answer sheet.

26. Mark your answer on your answer sheet.

27. Mark your answer on your answer sheet.

28. Mark your answer on your answer sheet.

29. Mark your answer on your answer sheet.

30. Mark your answer on your answer sheet.

31. Mark your answer on your answer sheet.

PART 3

Directions: You will hear some conversations between two or more people. You will be asked to answer three questions about what the speakers say in each conversation. Select the best response to each question and mark the letter (A), (B), (C), or (D) on your answer sheet. The conversations will not be printed in your test book and will be spoken only one time.

32. What will the woman do in October?

(A) Attend a seminar
(B) Go on vacation
(C) Study abroad
(D) Take a business trip

33. What does the man say about the suspension of service?

(A) It cannot be done.
(B) It has to be longer than a month.
(C) The procedure needs to be done online.
(D) There will be a charge.

34. What information will the woman give next?

(A) Her account number
(B) Her e-mail address
(C) Her home address
(D) Her phone number

35. Who most likely is Ms. Jackson?

(A) A receptionist
(B) A school owner
(C) A student
(D) An instructor

36. Why is the woman calling?

(A) To book an appointment
(B) To cancel an appointment
(C) To confirm an appointment
(D) To reschedule an appointment

37. What did the woman decide to do?

(A) Call the man back later
(B) Choose a different person
(C) Make an appointment next week
(D) Talk to Ms. Jackson

38. What are the speakers discussing?

(A) A company symbol
(B) A new building design
(C) A painting
(D) A photograph

39. What does the woman mean when she says, "That's it"?

(A) She has said what she wants to say.
(B) She is amused by his opinion.
(C) She thinks the man made a good point.
(D) She wants to end the conversation.

40. What does the woman say she will do?

(A) Ask another co-worker for help
(B) Contact an artistic firm
(C) Hire a different firm
(D) Think of new slogans

41. What is the cause of the delay?

(A) A mechanical problem
(B) A staffing problem
(C) A traffic jam
(D) A car accident

42. Who most likely is the man?

(A) A mechanic
(B) A passenger
(C) A station worker
(D) A Website designer

43. What does the man give the woman?

(A) A line map
(B) A refund
(C) A URL of his company
(D) An update on the delay

GO ON TO THE NEXT PAGE ➡

44. What will the woman's family most likely do tomorrow?

(A) Go fishing
(B) Purchase mementos
(C) Return home
(D) See a friend

45. What does the man mention about the boat?

(A) It is fast.
(B) It is small.
(C) It needs some repairs.
(D) It runs only once a day.

46. How did the woman hear about the tour?

(A) From a brochure
(B) From a friend
(C) From a TV show
(D) From an online advertisement

47. What does the woman imply about the finances?

(A) The speakers are in debt to the bank.
(B) The speakers are making a lot of money.
(C) The speakers have enough money for advertising.
(D) The speakers do not have extra money.

48. Why does the woman say, "word of mouth doesn't cost us a thing"?

(A) She believes there is a cheaper way.
(B) She does not like what the man said.
(C) She is not sure how much advertising costs.
(D) She knows referrals are free.

49. What does the man say he will do?

(A) Give free drinks out
(B) Take a class in finance
(C) Talk to some friends
(D) Upload a photo online

50. Why is the man in a hurry?

(A) He has a job interview.
(B) He has an appointment.
(C) He needs to catch a train.
(D) He wants to get home quickly.

51. What is mentioned about the food at the restaurant?

(A) It is all from local suppliers.
(B) It is all organic.
(C) It is prepared ahead of time.
(D) It is prepared when ordered.

52. What will the woman bring the man first?

(A) A hamburger
(B) A salad
(C) An iced tea
(D) Potato soup

53. Where most likely are the speakers?

(A) At a university
(B) At an awards ceremony
(C) In a radio station
(D) In a TV studio

54. What is the man's research about?

(A) Environmental concerns
(B) Political issues
(C) Private sector growth
(D) World economy

55. What will the speakers do next?

(A) Continue with an interview
(B) Listen to audience questions
(C) Look at some data
(D) Watch a video

56. Who most likely is the man?

(A) A dentist

(B) A medical assistant

(C) A patient

(D) A receptionist

57. What is mentioned about Dr. McCloud?

(A) She is completely booked this week.

(B) She is leaving the office soon.

(C) She will go to a conference.

(D) She will take a break now.

58. When will Mr. Stuart's next appointment be?

(A) Next Thursday morning

(B) Next Thursday afternoon

(C) Next Friday morning

(D) Next Friday afternoon

---

59. What will the speakers do at the store tomorrow?

(A) Get ready for a sale

(B) Make a list of stock

(C) Pack items in boxes

(D) Put out new merchandise

60. Why is John unable to stay late tomorrow?

(A) He has a doctor's appointment.

(B) He has another job.

(C) He is going out of town.

(D) He is in school.

61. What can be said about the woman?

(A) She does not like to work overtime.

(B) She has some free time tomorrow.

(C) She is not sure of her schedule.

(D) She wants to get promoted.

```
┌─────────────────────────────────────┐
│        Lacy's October Sale          │
│           7th – 13th                 │
│                                      │
│  The earlier you shop, the more you SAVE! │
│                                      │
│  25% OFF!    Friday thru Sunday     │
│  20% OFF!    Monday and Tuesday     │
│  15% OFF!    Wednesday              │
│  10% OFF!    Thursday               │
└─────────────────────────────────────┘
```

62. What does the man want to buy?

(A) A bag

(B) A jacket

(C) A pair of shoes

(D) A shirt

63. What will the woman do this weekend?

(A) Attend an event

(B) Buy some clothes

(C) Relax at home

(D) Take a business trip

64. Look at the graphic. What discount will the speakers most likely get?

(A) 10 percent

(B) 15 percent

(C) 20 percent

(D) 25 percent

GO ON TO THE NEXT PAGE

Board Meeting Schedule
November 1

10:00	Ms. Erin Sinclair
10:30	Mr. Leo Anderson
11:30	Sales team
12:00	President Matt Moore

Products	Band Material	Band Color
Chater 400	Metal	Silver
Elling 2Z	Metal	Gold
Millseed CR	Leather	Brown
Vextron 7T	Leather	Black

65. What will the woman's boss do before 11:00 tomorrow?

(A) Attend the board meeting
(B) Interview candidates
(C) Prepare for the presentation
(D) See a client

66. Look at the graphic. What time will the sales team present their report?

(A) 10:00
(B) 10:30
(C) 11:30
(D) 12:00

67. What does the man say he will do?

(A) Edit a schedule
(B) Finish a report
(C) Send an invitation
(D) Talk to the sales team

68. What was wrong with the first watch the man tried?

(A) It was not the right color.
(B) It was too expensive.
(C) It was too heavy.
(D) It was uncomfortable.

69. Look at the graphic. Which watch will the man probably order?

(A) Charter 400
(B) Elling 2Z
(C) Millseed CR
(D) Vextron 7T

70. What does the woman offer the man for free?

(A) An extra band
(B) Delivery service
(C) Gift wrapping
(D) Parking

PART 4

Directions: You will hear some talks given by a single speaker. You will be asked to answer three questions about what the speaker says in each talk. Select the best response to each question and mark the letter (A), (B), (C), or (D) on your answer sheet. The talks will not be printed in your test book and will be spoken only one time.

71. Who most likely is the speaker?
    (A) An IT employee
    (B) A police officer
    (C) A postal worker
    (D) A store owner

72. According to the speaker, what is unique about her business?
    (A) It is the cheapest.
    (B) It is the fastest.
    (C) It is the largest.
    (D) It is the oldest.

73. What does the speaker say she will do soon?
    (A) Move to a different location
    (B) Open a new branch
    (C) Post an advertisement
    (D) Visit the listener's office

74. What is the broadcast mainly about?
    (A) A new sports facility
    (B) A new sports team
    (C) A retiring player
    (D) A sports tournament

75. What is mentioned about Stanleyville?
    (A) It has a new mayor.
    (B) It has an excellent ice rink.
    (C) It has hosted sporting events before.
    (D) It has more than one professional team.

76. What will listeners hear next?
    (A) A city leader's speech
    (B) A reporter's story
    (C) A weather report
    (D) Advertisements

77. What type of store is the announcement for?
    (A) A deli
    (B) A department store
    (C) A grocery store
    (D) A wine shop

78. When is the announcement most likely being made?
    (A) On Monday
    (B) On Wednesday
    (C) On Friday
    (D) On Sunday

79. What is mentioned about the online option?
    (A) It offers more selection than the store.
    (B) It has recently been redone.
    (C) It is cheaper than the store.
    (D) It is secure.

80. What is the speaker mainly discussing?
    (A) A new government policy
    (B) A new local facility
    (C) Personnel changes at his work
    (D) Recent economic news

81. Who most likely is Kevin Chang?
    (A) A biotechnology expert
    (B) A company owner
    (C) A government spokesperson
    (D) A news person

82. What will listeners hear next?
    (A) An advertisement
    (B) A biotechnology report
    (C) A press briefing
    (D) An interview

GO ON TO THE NEXT PAGE

83. Why is the woman calling?

(A) To change an appointment

(B) To express appreciation

(C) To make a reservation

(D) To recommend a restaurant

84. What does the woman say she needs to decide about her party?

(A) What to serve

(B) When to hold it

(C) Where to hold it

(D) Who to invite

85. What does the speaker imply when she says, "They are filling up quickly"?

(A) The customers have eaten enough.

(B) The customers want to go home early.

(C) The hall has few nights left to reserve.

(D) The staff will finish their work soon.

86. When can listeners ask questions?

(A) As they are leaving

(B) At anytime

(C) During lunch

(D) In the afternoon session

87. What does the speaker mean when he says, "We'll be covering all the basics of running a small business"?

(A) They will apply for small business insurance.

(B) They will instruct listeners on many aspects of starting a business.

(C) They will interview listeners for a job at a small business.

(D) They will review all the skills learned at a previous seminar.

88. What will the listeners do next?

(A) Fill out a form

(B) Get into small groups

(C) Have lunch

(D) Listen to talks

89. What department does Robert most likely work in?

(A) Accounting

(B) IT

(C) Office administration

(D) Sales

90. What will Jocelyn do in less than a week?

(A) Hire a moving company

(B) Clean the new office

(C) Organize supplies

(D) Pack boxes

91. Why does the speaker say, "on second thought"?

(A) She wants the listeners to think about something again.

(B) She wants to do something different than what she first said.

(C) She thinks that time is running out for the move.

(D) She thinks that the move should happen sooner.

92. Who most likely are the listeners?

(A) Bookstore workers

(B) Club members

(C) Professors

(D) Students

93. What will listeners hear next?

(A) A book excerpt

(B) A movie summary

(C) A university lecture

(D) Questions and answers

94. What does the speaker ask the listeners to do?

(A) Come up on stage

(B) Get into small groups

(C) Make a line at the microphone

(D) Stand up if they have a question

Mr. Black's Schedule

	10:00	1:00	3:00
Monday 14	Recording		
Tuesday 15	Sales call		Interview
Wednesday 16	Board meeting	Teleconference	Client outing
Thursday 17	Business trip --------	----------------	---------->
Friday 18	Seminar	Presentation	

95. What type of business is the speaker in?

(A) Audio recording

(B) Electronics sales

(C) Restaurant business

(D) Musical instruments sales

96. Look at the graphic. When can Mr. Black visit the speaker's business?

(A) At 10:00 on Monday

(B) At 1:00 on Tuesday

(C) At 1:00 on Thursday

(D) At 3:00 on Friday

97. What does the speaker offer Mr. Black?

(A) A discount

(B) A free gift

(C) Free parking

(D) Free upgrades

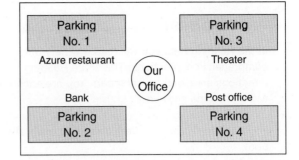

Parking No. 1		Parking No. 3
Azure restaurant	Our Office	Theater
Bank		Post office
Parking No. 2		Parking No. 4

98. What is mentioned about the current parking lot?

(A) It is being torn down.

(B) It is closing for repairs.

(C) It is giving employees security concerns.

(D) It is raising its prices.

99. Look at the graphic. Where does the speaker prefer the new parking to be located?

(A) Near Azure restaurant

(B) Near the bank

(C) Near the post office

(D) Near the theater

100. What is most important to the speaker when choosing a parking lot?

(A) Hours

(B) Location

(C) Price

(D) Safety

This is the end of the Listening test. Turn to Part 5 in your test book.

GO ON TO THE NEXT PAGE

READING TEST

In the Reading test, you will read a variety of texts and answer several different types of reading comprehension questions. The entire Reading test will last 75 minutes. There are three parts, and directions are given for each part. You are encouraged to answer as many questions as possible within the time allowed.

You must mark your answers on the separate answer sheet. Do not write your answers in your test book.

PART 5

Directions: A word or phrase is missing in each of the sentences below. Four answer choices are given below each sentence. Select the best answer to complete the sentence. Then mark the letter (A), (B), (C), or (D) on your answer sheet.

101. After reading the incident report, the factory director realized his workers had different ------- on safety issues.

(A) looks
(B) sights
(C) views
(D) watches

102. In the financial industry, Mark Hudson has been known as an ------- business leader for many years.

(A) accomplish
(B) accomplishable
(C) accomplished
(D) accomplishment

103. The security software giant VESCO ------- their latest product around the world sometime next spring.

(A) has been launching
(B) has launched
(C) is launching
(D) will be launched

104. When an ------- version of Catfox browser is available, it will be automatically downloaded.

(A) invited
(B) edited
(C) interested
(D) updated

105. The employee had spent only a year in the IT department before getting a ------- to supervisor.

(A) promote
(B) promotion
(C) promotional
(D) promoted

106. ------- the hotel's billing error, the Smiths were excessively overcharged for their two-night stay.

(A) Due to
(B) Except for
(C) In case
(D) So that

107. The data transfer rates, usually from 100 to 150 kilobytes per second, ------- depending on the type of device you have.

(A) emerge
(B) convert
(C) record
(D) vary

108. Although Kyle Boyd was inexperienced in sales, his ------- cheerful character was a great benefit in selling products.

(A) naturally
(B) naturalness
(C) nature
(D) natural

109. The fashion magazine chose Amy Kitano as Designer of the Year for ------- a new line for young women.

(A) create
(B) created
(C) creates
(D) creating

110. It was obvious that Jim Barrow was not ------- prepared for his presentation since he could barely answer the questions.

(A) fully
(B) generously
(C) securely
(D) widely

111. Despite its convenient location, the new restaurant was not busy at all even ------- weekends.

(A) around
(B) for
(C) in
(D) on

112. The mayor announced the new city hall would have a special ceiling that two architectural firms ------- on.

(A) collaborated
(B) collaboration
(C) collaborative
(D) collaboratively

113. As the last meeting did not go well, the leader hopes to reach a ------- on the upcoming project this time.

(A) consensus
(B) definition
(C) match
(D) satisfaction

114. Mr. Patterson is a well-known business consultant whose career goal is to help his clients achieve -------.

(A) theirs
(B) them
(C) themselves
(D) those

115. Because of the last-minute venue change, the organizers had to contact all the attendees ------- had registered for the event.

(A) that
(B) what
(C) which
(D) whom

116. The purpose of the following survey on behavior analysis is to research ------- reactions to shocking news.

(A) capable
(B) formal
(C) typical
(D) terminal

117. Lisa Foster realized that working ------- from home was more difficult than she thought as there were so many distractions.

(A) efficiencies
(B) efficiency
(C) efficient
(D) efficiently

118. The marketing chief was satisfied with the survey results as ------- respondents found the new product "useful" or "very useful."

(A) almost
(B) most
(C) mostly
(D) the most

119. The development team had a small party to celebrate the completion of a home-use robot that can be ------- controlled by mobile phone.

(A) hardly
(B) jointly
(C) manually
(D) remotely

120. Gene Electronics' new 100-inch flat-screen TV will be available ------- five different colors next spring.

(A) from
(B) in
(C) of
(D) with

GO ON TO THE NEXT PAGE

121. The mining firm believed the vast region to be an immense storehouse of natural resources and thought it was a wise -------.

(A) invest
(B) invested
(C) investment
(D) investor

122. Hoping to improve the company's performance, the automaker's president decided to ------- its management structure.

(A) overestimate
(B) overhaul
(C) overlook
(D) overtake

123. The increased ------- for a thorough investigation showed how upset people are with the company's alleged secret funds.

(A) call
(B) called
(C) calling
(D) calls

124. The new recruit's project plan was so ------- that everyone in the department, including the manager, was quite impressed.

(A) elaborate
(B) elaborating
(C) elaborately
(D) elaboration

125. The study suggests that the elementary and middle school years are the best times for the ------- of a second language.

(A) acquisition
(B) buyout
(C) possession
(D) takeover

126. The newly-opened hotel is close to downtown and has luxurious amenities; -------, it is reasonably priced.

(A) in addition
(B) instead
(C) on the other hand
(D) otherwise

127. The data that the supervisor uploaded to the intranet was missing, which according to the technician, happens only -------.

(A) occasion
(B) occasional
(C) occasionally
(D) occasions

128. As visitors can have a full view of the office from the reception area, the manager told everyone to keep their desks -------.

(A) closely
(B) fairly
(C) orderly
(D) properly

129. In the interview, the company head said he has been successful because he always values integrity ------- profits.

(A) across
(B) over
(C) than
(D) upon

130. ------- the outcome is, it was a great honor for Sarah Daly to be considered for manager of the new branch.

(A) Indeed
(B) Nevertheless
(C) Whatever
(D) While

PART 6

Directions: Read the texts that follow. A word, phrase, or sentence is missing in parts of each text. Four answer choices for each question are given below the text. Select the best answer to complete the text. Then mark the letter (A), (B), (C), or (D) on your answer sheet.

Questions 131-134 refer to the following notice.

Attention all Marshburg City residents:

The Marshburg City Office will be under ------- from October 10 through October 21. All offices will
                                          131.

be operating from the City Library for those two weeks, but will be closed from October 24 through

October 28 ------- we move back into the City Office. Telephone and fax numbers will remain the
            132.

same for the duration of the construction. ------- .
                                            133.

> **Our new office hours are as follows:**
> M – F 10:00 AM – 4:00 PM
> Closed Saturday and Sunday

-------, if any local residents wish to help with the move between October 24 and October 28, please
134.

sign up at the library. Lunch and drinks will be provided to anyone who volunteers.

---

131. (A) renovate
(B) renovated
(C) renovation
(D) renovator

132. (A) as
(B) if
(C) though
(D) whether

133. (A) Our mailing address can be found below.
(B) Our new phone numbers are listed on our Website.
(C) Our office hours, however, will be changing.
(D) Our office hours will remain the same.

134. (A) Additionally
(B) Second
(C) Therefore
(D) Yet

GO ON TO THE NEXT PAGE

To: Samantha Patel
From: Perry Fonda
Subject: Help on November 8
Date: November 2

Hi Samantha,

I've got a ------- to ask. I'm meeting with the people from the Tolliver Fund next Tuesday, November
                135.

8 at 4:00 and I could really use some backup. This is my first big chance to land an important client

and I don't want to -------. Since I'm fairly new, I'm not sure they will take me seriously -------
                    136.   137.

a senior partner like you in the room. Do you have time, even to just stop in and introduce yourself?

It would really help. -------. Just a few tips from when you started out here.
                        138.

Thank you in advance.

Perry

135. (A) favor
    (B) job
    (C) request
    (D) wish

136. (A) fail
    (B) mistake
    (C) stop
    (D) upset

137. (A) among
    (B) before
    (C) except
    (D) without

138. (A) After you look over the file, let me know
       what you think.
    (B) If you are busy at that time, maybe you
       could give me some pointers.
    (C) If you can't make it, I understand and I'll do
       my best.
    (D) Let me know your schedule, and I'll try to
       match it.

Questions 139-142 refer to the following article.

Junko Cosmetics announced Wednesday that it will ------- a new line of moisturizers just in time for
139.

the dry winter weather. -------. Junko CEO said of Skin Drink, "They're aimed at any person of any
140.

age who wants their skin to feel ------- and comfortable. We will offer a fragrance-free moisturizer
141.

and a type with sunscreen." The lotions ------- between £ 5.00 and £ 6.50 at any drugstore or
142.

cosmetics counter that sells the Junko brand.

139. (A) consider
(B) launch
(C) open
(D) test

140. (A) Like other Skin Drink products, the
moisturizers include all natural ingredients.
(B) The company is keeping the product name
under wraps until just before its release.
(C) The line, called Skin Drink, will feature four
lotions for different types of skin.
(D) With its sales forecast looking gloomy, the
future of the company is uncertain.

141. (A) smooth
(B) smoothen
(C) smoothly
(D) smoothness

142. (A) could price
(B) have been priced
(C) priced
(D) will be priced

GO ON TO THE NEXT PAGE

Questions 143-146 refer to the following information.

JOB FAIR

1:00-5:00 PM
Sunday, November 13
Canary Family Fun Park

A unique and exciting job fair is going to be held in Canary Family Fun Park this month. It is focused

entirely on ------- jobs all in Canary Family Fun Park! If you've always wanted to work at the
     143.

region's number-one entertainment venue for people of all ages, come see us on Sunday, November

13. -------. Some of the jobs will be extended beyond the end of the year too! With ------- one
  144.   **145.**

application, you will be considered for positions at all of the restaurants, hotels, and attractions at

Canary Family Fun Park.

Don't ------- this chance to get the job of your dreams!
    146.

---

143. (A) advertising
(B) engineering
(C) hospitality
(D) research

144. (A) Be sure to include three letters of reference in your application and send it by November 13.
(B) Please encourage your friends and family to attend our grand opening event this weekend.
(C) We are looking for experienced managers in all areas of marketing and advertising.
(D) You will have the opportunity to apply for any of 150 temporary jobs.

145. (A) another
(B) each
(C) either
(D) just

146. (A) win
(B) grab
(C) break
(D) miss

PART 7

Directions: In this part you will read a selection of texts, such as magazine and newspaper articles, e-mails, and instant messages. Each text or set of texts is followed by several questions. Select the best answer for each question and mark the letter (A), (B), (C), or (D) on your answer sheet.

Questions 147-148 refer to the following coupon.

NOW 30% OFF

at TOMAS BROWN
when you spend over $100 online.

OFFER ENDS November 1st

ENJOY SHOPPING

We will donate every $1 spent over $100 to Blue Triangle.

Terms
*Only valid online clothing purchases.
*Only valid in the U.S.
*Limit once per customer.
*Cannot be used in conjunction with any other offer.

147. What can this coupon be used for?

(A) A bag
(B) A shirt
(C) A watch
(D) Shoes

148. What limit is placed on the coupon?

(A) It can be used only by itself.
(B) It is only valid on certain brands.
(C) It is only valid on November 30.
(D) It is valid after spending $1.

GO ON TO THE NEXT PAGE →

ATTENTION: MEMBERS

Please be aware that there will be an annual maintenance check of the gymnasium and its facilities on November 9. This check ensures the safety of all equipment, studios, pool areas, changing rooms, and all other member locations.

The maintenance will last the entirety of November 9, starting from 6:00 AM. The gym will re-open to members at 6:00 AM on November 10. Due to this closure, the opening time on November 8 will be extended to 11:00 PM. Please note: this only includes the gymnasium. It does not include the studios or pool areas. Please contact the manager if you have any concerns.

We apologize for any inconvenience caused and thank you for your continued patronage.

149. When will the maintenance be completed?

(A) By noon on November 9
(B) By the beginning of November 10
(C) By lunchtime on November 10
(D) By the beginning of November 11

150. Which facilities can a member use later than usual on November 8?

(A) The dance studio
(B) The gymnasium
(C) The pool
(D) The sports shop

Questions 151-152 refer to the following text message chain.

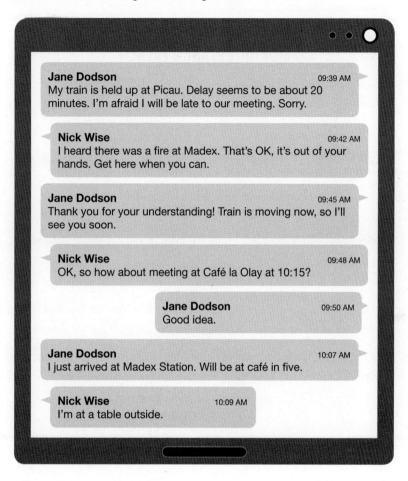

TEST 2

151. At 09:42 AM, what does Mr. Wise most likely mean when he writes, "it's out of your hands"?

(A) Another colleague will take over Ms. Dodson's project.

(B) Ms. Dodson isn't a specialist in that field.

(C) The delay started at Madex.

(D) The delay was not in Ms. Dodson's control.

152. Where was Ms. Dodson at 10:00?

(A) At Café la Olay

(B) At her office

(C) At Madex Station

(D) On a train

GO ON TO THE NEXT PAGE

MONIQUE BLANC'S FRENCH

You:
- Speak
- Have fun
- Learn

Me:
- Relaxed lessons
- Creative style
- Exam preparation

Come learn French with a native speaker!
All ages and abilities welcome.

Telephone: 080-5555-3245   **E-mail:** monique.blanc@bisco.com

Testimonials:

" Monique's class was so much fun! I was a beginner in French but now feel confident enough to travel to France and use what I learned. Thank you! " — Mary Newman

" It was hard for me to learn French, but I had to prepare for my exams. Mme. Blanc helped me achieve the highest possible grade, which I'm so grateful for. " — Gary Bush

153. What is mentioned about Mme. Blanc?

(A) Her academic achievements
(B) Her location
(C) Her native language
(D) Her work history

154. Why is Mr. Bush appreciative of Mme. Blanc?

(A) She advised him where to travel in France.
(B) She gave private lessons.
(C) She helped with his academic success.
(D) She gave a good grade.

SILVER FERN HOTEL GROUP
Customer Satisfaction Survey

Please complete the following survey based on the experience of your stay with us.
Mark a number from 0 to 4 in the corresponding box, in accordance to the scale below.

Extremely dissatisfied	Dissatisfied	No opinion	Satisfied	Extremely satisfied
0	1	2	3	4

- Customer Service (reception, waiting/bar staff, housekeepers) ·· __4__
- Room Service (timeliness, ease, choice) ·· __4__
- The Restaurant (ambience, food, tableware) ·· __4__
- The Bar (ambience, choice of drinks) ·· __1__
- Cleanliness (all areas) ··· __4__
- Noise levels (external and internal) ··· __3__
- Location (distance from points of interest) ·· __3__
- Cost (general) ··· __3__
- Amenities (choice, functionality, age) ··· __2__

Other comments

Overall, I was very pleased with my stay at Silver Fern. The staff were exceptional, particularly Mr. Smyth, who went the extra mile to make my stay comfortable. However, even though the bar had a large variety of drinks available, I could not find my favorite cocktail and the bar staff did not know of it. I hope it will be on the menu when I return next year! I didn't have time to make use of the amenities, although the free shuttle service into town was an added bonus. Thank you again. I look forward to next time!

155. How does the customer rate the hotel?

(A) Average
(B) Excellent
(C) Mostly satisfying
(D) Poor

156. Who is Mr. Smyth?

(A) A hotel employee
(B) A hotel guest
(C) A hotel manager
(D) A taxi driver

157. What was the customer NOT satisfied with?

(A) The choice of amenities
(B) The distance from the town
(C) The diversity of drinks
(D) The friendliness of the staff

GO ON TO THE NEXT PAGE

Questions 158-160 refer to the following article.

Mobile phones are now said to provide us with twice as much information as libraries or schools do. This raises the question: should we continue to teach children in the traditional way? Education ministers and teachers are firmly on the yes side of this issue, but tech companies and most young people are calling for a new approach to learning.

Companies such as Poko and Djiib are pioneering the technology to make home-schooling or "anywhere-schooling" more possible and likely for the future. "The depth and breadth of knowledge a child can receive from this type of technology is much vaster than what a teacher can offer in the classroom," said Jim Frank, the CEO of Poko. "We are holding our children back by not changing the methods of education, as society and our lives develop."

Talks have been held by government officials in an attempt to fully comprehend this new idea and establish how viable it could be. The officials would like to hold a public meeting on October 3 so they can hear from parents and other concerned citizens. "For everyone's sake, I urge the public attend this town hall meeting. We need the input from everybody on this important issue." Education minister Paul Simonson commented.

158. What is the article mainly about?

(A) A different way of schooling

(B) A new private school

(C) A special commemoration on October 3

(D) The future of mobile phones

159. What field does Jim Frank work in?

(A) Finance

(B) Government

(C) Publishing

(D) Technology

160. What does a government official encourage people to do?

(A) Start home-schooling their children

(B) Invest in tech companies

(C) Voice their opinions at a meeting

(D) Talk to some local teachers

Questions 161-163 refer to the following e-mail.

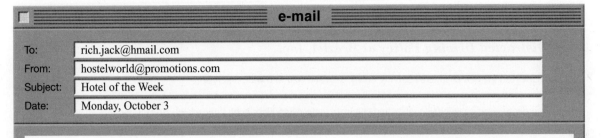

To:	rich.jack@hmail.com
From:	hostelworld@promotions.com
Subject:	Hotel of the Week
Date:	Monday, October 3

HOTELWORLD
The World is Your Oyster.

HOTEL OF THE WEEK
Golden Arms Inn: Bleat, The United Kingdom

Situated on a brilliant, lush green piece of land in the English countryside, this inn is the perfect weekend getaway for Londoners or those looking to explore Northern England. There is a vast area of lawn surrounding the house, where guests can enjoy evening strolls, bowls, or even a spot of croquet. The inn itself displays a remarkable piece of architecture: reminiscent of the 19th century gothic style. Sit on the porch, under the archway and enjoy your free breakfast.

All rooms offer guests an insight into the inn's history, through careful restoration preserving the former charm. Each also has suite facilities (including a separate bath), queen-size beds, and 24-hour room service. Other amenities include a large dining hall, a ballroom, a library, an 18-hole golf course, and horse stables all within the grounds of the inn.

We are offering the second night's stay at a 50-percent discount, if you book before the end of the month. Do it now to avoid disappointment!

161. What is true of the inn?

(A) It displays modern architecture.
(B) It is located in a rural area.
(C) It is mainly for businesspeople.
(D) It offers a free lunch.

162. How are the guest rooms described?

(A) As cozy
(B) As historical
(C) As luxurious
(D) As spacious

163. How long is the discount?

(A) A week
(B) Two weeks
(C) Nearly a month
(D) A month and a half

GO ON TO THE NEXT PAGE

Questions 164-167 refer to the following notice.

Distracted Driving Policy at Breztel, Inc.

Please read the new Distracted Driving Policy, sign and return to your supervisor.

In order to increase employee safety and eliminate unnecessary risks behind the wheel, Breztel, Inc. has enacted a Distracted Driving Policy, effective September 1. —[1]—. We are committed to ending the epidemic of distracted driving, and have created the following rules, which apply to any employee operating a company vehicle or using a company-issued cellphone while operating a personal vehicle:

* Employees may not use a handheld cellphone while operating a vehicle—whether the vehicle is in motion or stopped at a traffic light. This includes, but is not limited to: answering or making phone calls; engaging in phone conversations; and/or reading or responding to e-mails, instant messages, and/or text messages. —[2]—.
* If employees need to use their phones, they must pull over safely to the side of the road or another safe location.
* Additionally, employees should:
  (A) Turn cellphones off or put them on silent or vibrate mode before starting the car.
  (B) Consider changing their voice mail greetings to indicate that they are unavailable to answer calls or return messages while driving.
  (C) Inform clients, associates, and business partners of this policy as an explanation of why calls may not be returned immediately.

—[3]—. Any employee of Breztel, Inc. who is found to be out of compliance with the above regulations will first be given a written warning. —[4]—. A second infraction will result in a mandatory unpaid leave of absence of one week. The third infraction will result in the employee being terminated from Breztel, Inc.

---

164. What is the purpose of the new policy?

(A) To follow regional laws
(B) To prevent accidents
(C) To teach good driving techniques
(D) To remind drivers to stay awake

165. What is suggested regarding voice mail?

(A) It should be checked regularly.
(B) It should be turned off.
(C) It should state when the call will be returned.
(D) It should state why calls are not being answered.

166. What would an employee receive who violated the company policy twice?

(A) A position change
(B) A warning letter
(C) Termination from the company
(D) Suspension without pay

167. In which of the positions marked [1], [2], [3] and [4] does the following sentence best belong?

"This warning will be added to the employee's permanent personnel file."

(A) [1]
(B) [2]
(C) [3]
(D) [4]

Questions 168-171 refer to the following letter.

March 18

Dear Mr. Vaughn,

Thank you for taking the time to write of your unsatisfactory experience with our company and may I express my sincerest apologies about this matter. —[1]—. It is of utmost importance to meet our customers' expectations and in the instance that we fail, provide resolutions.

Therefore, we will accept your request and offer a replacement sofa of the same product number and color free of charge, which will be dispatched to you tomorrow morning. In light of the poor delivery service you received, we have conducted new training sessions for all drivers and I hope you recognize a difference tomorrow. —[2]—.

In addition, I would like to take this opportunity to offer you our personal services to show you we can do a much better job with our customer service. —[3]—. Please find enclosed a $50 voucher and my signed business card. If you decide to visit the store, please show the card to a staff member, who will personally assist you during your time there.

Thank you once again for bringing to our attention that there appears to be discrepancies within the company. —[4]—. We hope you will trust us again and continue to be a satisfied customer in the coming years.

Yours Sincerely,

Arun Devdas

Manager, Customer Services

---

168. Why did Mr. Devdas send the letter to Mr. Vaughn?

(A) To convey his regret
(B) To express his satisfaction
(C) To inform him about a company product
(D) To request new contact information

169. What did Mr. Devdas promise to Mr. Vaughn?

(A) To conduct training sessions soon
(B) To offer free delivery on his next order
(C) To provide a new sofa at no extra charge
(D) To respect Mr. Vaughn's decision

170. What will Mr. Vaughn receive by using the enclosed card?

(A) A free gift
(B) An extra discount
(C) An updated catalog
(D) Special assistance

171. In which of the positions marked [1], [2], [3], and [4] does the following sentence best belong?

"It is highly appreciated in ensuring growth and the future success of our business."

(A) [1]
(B) [2]
(C) [3]
(D) [4]

GO ON TO THE NEXT PAGE

Questions 172-175 refer to the following online discussion.

Ken Brown 13:02	Hello to both of you! Have you finished the orders yet?
Jack Taylor 13:12	Afternoon Ken. Not yet. It's taken longer than anticipated due to the unexpected fire drill.
Ken Brown 13:14	Yes, that was unusual. Where are you up to?
Jack Taylor 13:15	We were halfway through today's orders when the system shut down. Levi is back down in the stockroom, preparing boxes for the last half of orders.
Ken Brown 13:15	OK. Have you remembered the orders in the black book?
Jack Taylor 13:16	Oh, I totally blanked on those! I'll call down to Levi and get him to pick it up on his way back to the office.
Ken Brown 13:17	It's OK, I'm on my way back to the office from the shop floor. I'll grab it.
Levi O'Conner 13:25	Hi Ken, just checking in. The stockroom is a real mess. It'll take me a while to straighten things out.
Ken Brown 13:27	No worries Levi. Just do as best you can and get back to the office as soon as possible. We need to get the order finished by 15:00 today.
Levi O'Conner 13:28	Thanks Ken! If you have anyone to spare, I could use some help down here.
Jack Taylor 13:30	I've just asked Bruce to leave the shop floor. He's on his way to give you a hand.
Levi O'Conner 13:31	Good news. Thanks.

172. What are they mostly discussing?

(A) A fire drill

(B) A merchandise recall

(C) A new customer

(D) Order processing

173. At 13:16, what does Mr. Taylor mean when he writes, "I totally blanked on those!"?

(A) He cannot see well.

(B) He forgot all about something.

(C) He has a lot of free time.

(D) He is not ready to start working again.

174. Who will pick up the black book?

(A) Mr. Brown

(B) Mr. O'Conner

(C) Mr. Taylor

(D) Mr. Taylor's assistant

175. Where will Bruce go?

(A) To the entrance

(B) To the office

(C) To the shop

(D) To the stockroom

GO ON TO THE NEXT PAGE

E-Street Model X

There had been so many leaks about the new electric car from Matcha Motors, I was expecting to see no surprises at the unveiling this weekend. Was I ever wrong! Once I peeked inside the new model, I realized that this vehicle is a game-changer. Like the Model B, it has no instrument panels in front of either the driver or passenger. Instead, you control the car from a computer monitor mounted in the center. This makes sense for Matcha since it saves costly changes when shipping to either left-driving or right-driving countries. The technology is also a sight to see. From battery charge gauges to entertainment to climate control, the monitor in the Model X is simple and intuitive to use.

What's truly unbelievable about this model, though, is the price. Starting at just under $40,000, this is an e-car for the masses. Of course, to get the dual motor, you have to pay about $10,000 more, but it's worth it for those who like speed and longer distance driving on one charge.

Speaking of charge, Matcha Motors CEO promises 300 more charging stations across the country before the Model X ships. Yes, you'll have to wait two and a half more years for your Model X, but pre-orders are being taken on their Website, www.matchamotors.com. Just to reserve a car, you'll need to commit at least $4,000 depending on the extras you want. As for this reviewer, I'm hooked. I'm counting down the days until delivery...

—Shaun Hansen

To	Shaun Hansen <shaunh@wheels.com>
From	Olga Malayov <omalayov@matchamotors.com>
Subject	Review of the Model X

Dear Mr. Hansen,

Thank you for your glowing review of our latest model. We are sure you won't be disappointed once you are sitting behind the wheel of your new E-Street car. I had a few more pieces of information about the car I thought you might like to pass along to your readers.

Firstly, I'm sorry to say that there was a mistake in the press packet we handed out at the event you attended. The pricing for the second motor is about $2,000 less than you mentioned in your review. This makes the Model X even more attractive to consumers.

Secondly, we have upped our production targets and now expect drivers to take delivery of the Model X six months earlier than previously stated. By the end of next year, Matcha Motors will be manufacturing more vehicles than the country's top three automakers combined.

Lastly, we have had to start a waiting list for the Model X since the pre-orders exceeded even our high expectations. However, we do hope that because of our heightened production goals, we will be able to serve all consumers who want a Model X within the next three years.

Sincerely,
Olga Malayov

176. According to the review, on what feature does Matcha Motors save money?

(A) The batteries
(B) The control panels
(C) The motors
(D) The seats

177. Who most likely is Mr. Hansen?

(A) A Matcha Motors spokesperson
(B) A journalist
(C) A technology expert
(D) An advertising specialist

178. What does the extra motor on the Model X cost?

(A) $2,000
(B) $8,000
(C) $10,000
(D) $40,000

179. What does Ms. Malayov mention about production?

(A) It has been delayed.
(B) It has been sped up.
(C) It is being done overseas.
(D) It is being restructured.

180. In the review, the word "masses" in paragraph 2, line 2, is closest in meaning to

(A) public
(B) quantity
(C) variety
(D) wealth

GO ON TO THE NEXT PAGE

Questions 181-185 refer to the following e-mail and information.

```
┌──────────────────────────────────────────────────────────────┐
│                          e-mail                              │
├──────────┬───────────────────────────────────────────────────┤
│ To:      │ info@yoganation.com                               │
│ From:    │ Evel Hun <e-hun@foro.com>                         │
│ Subject: │ Package deals                                     │
│ Date:    │ Sunday, June 30                                   │
└──────────┴───────────────────────────────────────────────────┘
```

Dear Sir/Madam,

I came across a copy of a pamphlet describing your package deals at the local gym and wonder if you could answer some questions.

I would like to get back into yoga and am interested in joining your group as often as possible. I noticed the BAI package allows me to practice whenever there is a class available. Could you tell me if you offer mature students a discount?

I picked up this flyer today but seeing as it's a weekend, you will not see my e-mail until Monday — by which time it'll be July 1. Would I still be entitled to a reduction in sign-up costs?

My friend and I are not sure which day is better to attempt the trial lesson. Could you make any suggestions?

I look forward to hearing from you.

Kind regards,
Evel Hun

 **YogaNation**

Please check out our monthly deals below if you're interested in becoming a permanent member of YogaNation.

PACKAGES	DETAILS	FEES (extra classes)
BAI	Attend however much you like	$400/month
PUR	Attend up to twelve classes a month	$360/month ($30/class)
GAR	Attend up to six classes a month	$210/month ($35/class)
CHA	A 'pay-as-you-go' system	$40/class

A membership fee of $200 for the year is charged as a one-time fee when initially purchasing packages.

Receive a 20-percent discount on membership with this pamphlet.

Valid until June 30.

181. What is the main purpose of the e-mail?

(A) To check if a price cut would be offered

(B) To inform the instructor of her attendance to regular classes

(C) To make the instructor aware of her interest

(D) To suggest starting a mature students' class

182. What should YogaNation do for Ms. Hun?

(A) Explain the deals in a more detailed way

(B) Recommend a good gym

(C) Respond with information about dates

(D) Sign her and her friend up for a trial lesson

183. Which package offers cheaper extra classes?

(A) BAI

(B) PUR

(C) GAR

(D) CHA

184. Who would pay $40 for a class?

(A) BAI members

(B) PUR members

(C) GAR members

(D) CHA members

185. How much at most would Ms. Hun pay to become a member?

(A) $200

(B) $400

(C) $560

(D) $600

GO ON TO THE NEXT PAGE

Redlands Community Center announces NEW adult classes for the winter

* **Come join your friends and neighbors in interesting classes**

* **Learn a new skill or revive an old interest**

* **All classes are taught by local experts in their fields**

* **Choose from among the following classes:**

- Outdoor Photography for Any Season
- Growing Your Own Herbs
- Introduction to Pilates
- Computer Basics

- French Cooking
- Sketching and Drawing
- Creative Writing
- Investing for Beginners

These and many others are listed on our Website: www.redlandscommctr.com. You can also fill out our online registration form and pay via credit card on the site. For questions, contact Jolene at joleneb@redlandscommctr.com. We look forward to seeing you in class!

---

www.redlandscommctr.com/registration

REGISTRATION FORM

Redlands Community Center Adult Learning

Name: _Whitney Burke_ **Age:** _43_ **Address:** _46 Wilderest Lane, Redlands_

◊ Have you ever taken a Redlands Community Center class before? _NO_

◊ How did you hear about the classes? _My friend told me about them after taking a class._

Class ID	Class name	Teacher
RAD 105	Growing Your Own Herbs	Ralph Munez
RAD 148	Investing for Beginners	Jennifer Cho
RAD 197	Computer Basics	Neil Jackson
RAD 239	Advanced Photography	Suzanne Olsen

To	wburke@firemail.com
From	frankdodds@redlandscommctr.com
Date	October 28
Subject	Your registration for the Redlands classes

Dear Ms. Burke,

Thank you for registering for the Redlands Community Center classes. We were able to fit you into all classes except one. Unfortunately, Suzanne Olsen is unable to teach her class this winter. She has to relocate suddenly due to her husband's job. We are sorry for the inconvenience. We hope to offer this same class with a new instructor in the spring.

Also, since you mentioned in your application that you have a friend who has taken classes with us, I wanted to let you know about our referral discount. If you refer anybody to our classes, you both get 5 percent off the cost of all the classes for that term. Let us know your friend's name so we can offer him or her the discount.

Thanks again for registering. See you soon.

Frank Dodds

TEST 2

186. How can neighbors sign up for the classes?

(A) By visiting the center
(B) By completing a form
(C) By paying in advance
(D) By contacting staff

187. How did Ms. Burke find out about the courses?

(A) From a referral
(B) From a TV ad
(C) From the Internet
(D) From the notice

188. What can be said about Mr. Munez?

(A) He has taught the same course for many years.
(B) He is a local herb specialist.
(C) He is taking the same courses as Ms. Burke.
(D) He is moving out of the area.

189. Which class has an issue in the winter?

(A) RAD 105
(B) RAD 148
(C) RAD 197
(D) RAD 239

190. Why is one course unavailable?

(A) It is only offered in the spring.
(B) It was mistakenly added to the course list.
(C) The instructor is ill.
(D) The instructor is moving.

GO ON TO THE NEXT PAGE

Questions 191-195 refer to the following e-mails and coupon.

To	Customer Service <cs@steelworks.com>
From	Brian W <brianw@pershing.com>
Subject	My trusty iron
Date	November 29

To whom it may concern,

I have used my Press-on 400 iron for about six years and been quite satisfied with this reliable item. Recently, I had a problem that the temperature didn't rise. I checked the cord and there didn't seem to be any problem. I also cleaned off the surface, but it didn't change. I don't want to give up on this great iron, so I am wondering if it would be possible to have it repaired. Please let me know if there is a repair shop nearby in the Glendale Valley area. If not, I am willing to mail it outside of my immediate area if you'd let me know where to send it.

Thank you in advance for your help.

Brian Wilcox

---

e-mail

To:	Brian W <brianw@pershing.com>
From:	Customer Service <cs@steelworks.com>
Subject:	Re: My trusty iron
Date:	November 30

Dear Mr. Wilcox,

We are sorry to inform you that the Press-on 400 was discontinued about two years ago. We are unable to offer repair service on that model, but we value your loyalty and would like to retain you as a customer. To that end, I have enclosed a coupon for $30 off our newest model, the PressMagic 500, which has all the features of your iron, plus more. Our improved steaming features will reduce even difficult wrinkles. Additionally, the PressMagic can handle heavier fabrics than our previous models. We hope you will take advantage of our offer at any of the retail locations listed on the certificate.

We appreciate your business.

Jane Carver
Customer Relations
Steel Works

STEEL WORKS

Present this certificate at any of the following retail outlets for $30 off any Steel Works product.

B's Home Store	Appliances and More	Home Super Store	Johnson Goods
25081 Highway 53 Rosedale, UT	85 South Mall Drive Carsonville, NY	5903 E. Styx Way Glendale Valley, UT	898 Beverly St. Tatterville, NV

*This coupon is not valid in combination with any other promotion.

*This coupon may not be redeemed for cash.

*This coupon must be used on or before December 31.

191. What is wrong with Mr. Wilcox's product?

(A) The control button is broken.

(B) The cord is split.

(C) The heating element is broken.

(D) The steam function does not work.

192. Why can't Ms. Carver grant Mr. Wilcox's request?

(A) He does not have an extended warranty.

(B) He lives outside the store's range.

(C) His product has been recalled.

(D) His product is not being made anymore.

193. What is mentioned about the PressMagic 500?

(A) It has a better design.

(B) It has a higher heat range.

(C) It is more reliable.

(D) It works on thick clothes.

194. Where most likely would Mr. Wilcox use the coupon?

(A) At Appliances and More

(B) At B's Home Store

(C) At Home Super Store

(D) At Johnson Goods

195. How long can Mr. Wilcox use the coupon?

(A) For about one week

(B) For about two weeks

(C) For about one month

(D) For about one year

GO ON TO THE NEXT PAGE

Three Brothers Catering

No job too small or too large — we aim to please!

Three Brothers Catering has been in business for over a decade and has pleased hundreds of hungry customers over the years. We can provide lunch or dinner for your corporate events, community organization or private party. No matter how many you're expecting, we have something sure to please everyone. Until the end of the month, first-time customers get free delivery on office lunches! Take a look at our menu (full color pictures!) online at www.3broscatering.com. If you like what you see, give us a call at 555-8139.

Three Brothers Catering

Three Brothers Catering

8391 Castle View Drive
Los Animas, NM

Customer Name: Leslie Jones   Date: November 7   Venue: Jones and Co.

Order	Qty.	Unit Price	Total
Variety of sandwiches	12	3.95	47.40
Green side salad	5	3.50	17.50
Variety of bottled drinks	12	1.00	12.00
Appetizer tray	1	12.00	12.00

```
┌─────────────────────────────────────────────────────────────────────┐
│  ▣  ════════════════════════  e-mail  ════════════════════════      │
├─────────────────────────────────────────────────────────────────────┤
│  To:       │ rep@3broscatering.com                                  │
│  From:     │ ljones@jonesnco.com                                    │
│  Subject:  │ Changes to my order                                    │
│  Date:     │ November 5                                             │
└─────────────────────────────────────────────────────────────────────┘
```

Hi Joseph,

I hope it's not too late to make a few changes to my order for the day after tomorrow. I just got word that three people from our branch in Youngston will be joining us at our meeting. They won't be having lunch with us, but I will need beverages for them. So, that brings up the number to 15.

I also had a change in the salads. One person said he doesn't want a salad. Otherwise, everything else is fine. I understand that it's short notice for you, but it couldn't be helped. As this is our first order with your company, I hope we're still eligible for the special deal.

Thanks so much,
Leslie Jones

196. What is mentioned about Three Brothers Catering?

(A) It also offers cooking classes.

(B) It has won some awards.

(C) It is a new service.

(D) It opened more than ten years ago.

197. What event is Ms. Jones holding?

(A) A business lunch

(B) A grand opening

(C) A retirement party

(D) An open house

198. Why does Ms. Jones need to change her beverage order?

(A) More people are coming.

(B) More people would like coffee.

(C) Some people requested diet sodas.

(D) Some people will not be coming.

199. How many salads does Ms. Jones need?

(A) 3

(B) 4

(C) 5

(D) 12

200. What does Ms. Jones expect to receive?

(A) A 15-percent discount

(B) A free gift

(C) A loyalty program

(D) No delivery charge

**Stop! This is the end of the test. If you finish before time is called,
you may go back to Parts 5, 6, and 7 and check your work.**

Actual Test 3

Check ▸ 시작 시간 _____ : _____

▸ 종료 시간 _____ : _____

LC MP3 바로듣기

LISTENING TEST

In the Listening test, you will be asked to demonstrate how well you understand spoken English. The entire Listening test will last approximately 45 minutes. There are four parts, and directions are given for each part. You must mark your answers on the separate answer sheet. Do not write your answers in your test book.

PART 1

Directions: For each question in this part, you will hear four statements about a picture in your test book. When you hear the statements, you must select the one statement that best describes what you see in the picture. Then find the number of the question on your answer sheet and mark your answer. The statements will not be printed in your test book and will be spoken only one time.

Statement (C), "They're sitting at the table," is the best description of the picture, so you should select answer (C) and mark it on your answer sheet.

1.

2.

GO ON TO THE NEXT PAGE

3.

4.

5.

6.

GO ON TO THE NEXT PAGE

PART 2

Directions: You will hear a question or statement and three responses spoken in English. They will not be printed in your test book and will be spoken only one time. Select the best response to the question or statement and mark the letter (A), (B), or (C) on your answer sheet.

7. Mark your answer on your answer sheet.

8. Mark your answer on your answer sheet.

9. Mark your answer on your answer sheet.

10. Mark your answer on your answer sheet.

11. Mark your answer on your answer sheet.

12. Mark your answer on your answer sheet.

13. Mark your answer on your answer sheet.

14. Mark your answer on your answer sheet.

15. Mark your answer on your answer sheet.

16. Mark your answer on your answer sheet.

17. Mark your answer on your answer sheet.

18. Mark your answer on your answer sheet.

19. Mark your answer on your answer sheet.

20. Mark your answer on your answer sheet.

21. Mark your answer on your answer sheet.

22. Mark your answer on your answer sheet.

23. Mark your answer on your answer sheet.

24. Mark your answer on your answer sheet.

25. Mark your answer on your answer sheet.

26. Mark your answer on your answer sheet.

27. Mark your answer on your answer sheet.

28. Mark your answer on your answer sheet.

29. Mark your answer on your answer sheet.

30. Mark your answer on your answer sheet.

31. Mark your answer on your answer sheet.

PART 3

Directions: You will hear some conversations between two or more people. You will be asked to answer three questions about what the speakers say in each conversation. Select the best response to each question and mark the letter (A), (B), (C), or (D) on your answer sheet. The conversations will not be printed in your test book and will be spoken only one time.

32. Who most likely is the woman?

(A) A clothing designer

(B) A department store clerk

(C) A researcher

(D) The man's colleague

33. Why is the man in a hurry?

(A) He is late to work.

(B) He is not feeling well.

(C) He is on his way to see someone.

(D) He just got an urgent call.

34. What does the man say about his purchase?

(A) It is a new brand.

(B) It is not for himself.

(C) It was easy to find.

(D) It was on sale.

35. Why is the woman worried?

(A) She has to speak in public.

(B) She will forget the changes.

(C) She cannot be on time.

(D) She will make a mistake.

36. What does the woman want to do now?

(A) Go home

(B) Practice more

(C) Visit the doctor

(D) Write some notes

37. Where will the speakers go next?

(A) To a cafeteria

(B) To a meeting room

(C) To the break room

(D) To the president's office

38. Where is this conversation most likely taking place?

(A) At a bank

(B) At a kitchenware store

(C) At a restaurant

(D) At a supermarket

39. What does the man complain about?

(A) Fewer choices

(B) Noisy atmosphere

(C) Poor quality

(D) Rude people

40. Why does the man say, "I'm afraid you've just lost some loyal customers"?

(A) He is not happy with the price increase.

(B) He will not visit the place anymore.

(C) Some people left because of bad service.

(D) Some people think the manager is incompetent.

41. Who most likely is the man?

(A) A customer service representative

(B) A librarian

(C) A post office worker

(D) A delivery person

42. What caused the woman's problem?

(A) A computer error

(B) A mistake in delivery

(C) A stock shortage

(D) A user oversight

43. What will the woman receive within two weeks?

(A) A coupon

(B) A refund

(C) Additional items

(D) Promotions

GO ON TO THE NEXT PAGE

TEST 3

44. What are the speakers mainly discussing?
   (A) A manager's proposal
   (B) A new job candidate
   (C) A public service Website
   (D) A transportation delay

45. What will the woman do next?
   (A) Call a city information line
   (B) Check something on the Internet
   (C) Go to her manager's office
   (D) Visit a new client

46. Where does the man ask the woman to go?
   (A) To a client meeting
   (B) To a coffee shop
   (C) To a manager's office
   (D) To a train station

47. What did the woman do last week?
   (A) Attended a seminar
   (B) Had a job interview
   (C) Took a business trip
   (D) Went on vacation

48. What does the man say about the sales department?
   (A) It is moving to a new floor.
   (B) Its seminar was unsuccessful.
   (C) New employees started there recently.
   (D) The new head is unpopular.

49. What does the woman think the president should do?
   (A) Change the company policy
   (B) Communicate with all staff soon
   (C) Hire a new sales department manager
   (D) Instruct the manager to go easy

50. Why is the man calling the gym?
   (A) He forgot something there.
   (B) He wants to get some information.
   (C) He forgot to pick up an application form.
   (D) He wants to make sure they are open.

51. How does the man get to work?
   (A) By bicycle
   (B) By bus
   (C) By car
   (D) By train

52. Why might the man not join the gym?
   (A) It costs too much.
   (B) It is far from his house.
   (C) It does not have the equipment he likes.
   (D) It is not open at the times he needs.

53. What are the speakers mainly discussing?
   (A) A co-worker's promotion
   (B) The man's work experience
   (C) The woman's assignment
   (D) Their boss's retirement

54. What does the man mean when he says, "I'm the wrong person to ask"?
   (A) He cannot make an objective judgment.
   (B) He has no preference in the matter.
   (C) He is not familiar with marketing.
   (D) He needs time to think of an answer.

55. What does the woman say about Steve?
   (A) He has an idea for a new product line.
   (B) He has been at the company the longest.
   (C) He has more experience than Iris.
   (D) He has to make an announcement soon.

56. What is the man asked to do?

(A) Fill out a survey
(B) Negotiate a contract
(C) Pay money
(D) Sign his name

57. Where are the women most likely working?

(A) At a bank
(B) At a construction company
(C) At a law office
(D) At a real estate office

58. What does Carol promise to do?

(A) Contact the man later
(B) Prepare more paperwork
(C) Talk to a bank officer
(D) Visit the man's company

---

59. What is the woman shopping for?

(A) A birthday gift
(B) A good-bye gift
(C) A retirement gift
(D) A wedding gift

60. What does the woman ask the man to do?

(A) Check the stockroom
(B) Give her a discount
(C) Recommend a different item
(D) Send her the item

61. What will the woman be doing tomorrow at noon?

(A) Attending a gathering
(B) Paying for the delivery
(C) Making food for a party
(D) Taking a colleague to the airport

T-REX CINEMAS	
Screen 1	
All Star Players	▸ 5:30 – 7:40
	▸ 8:00 – 10:10
Screen 2	
Brave And Braver	▸ 5:40 – 7:30
	▸ 7:50 – 9:40

62. What does the man say he is doing later?

(A) Sharing his thoughts
(B) Cooking dinner
(C) Going back to his office
(D) Meeting a friend

63. Look at the graphic. What time will the man probably watch a movie?

(A) 5:30
(B) 5:40
(C) 7:50
(D) 8:00

64. What type of movie is *Brave And Braver* most likely?

(A) A comedy
(B) A documentary
(C) A drama
(D) A science fiction

GO ON TO THE NEXT PAGE ⟶

Customer Satisfaction Survey	
Business	**Comment**
Anderson&Associates	Poor quality cleaning
Blackmoor, Inc.	Schedule problems
Parker&Sons	Too expensive
Vesper Group	Always satisfactory

Serenity Spa Options
- Massage ·············· $50
- Facial ················· $35
- Manicure ············· $25
- Pedicure ············· $20

¶Or choose our Full Package for $100 when you show this online coupon.

65. Where do the speakers most likely work?

(A) At a cleaning business

(B) At a law firm

(C) At a rental agency

(D) At a training school

66. What explanation does the woman give for the poor quality comment?

(A) Lazy workers

(B) Low-quality supplies

(C) New management

(D) Untrained staff

67. Look at the graphic. Who will the woman most likely call soon?

(A) Anderson&Associates

(B) Blackmoor, Inc.

(C) Parker&Sons

(D) Vesper Group

68. Look at the graphic. How much will the woman pay?

(A) $25

(B) $35

(C) $50

(D) $100

69. When will the woman get a treatment?

(A) Today at 4:30

(B) Today at 5:00

(C) Tomorrow at 4:30

(D) Tomorrow at 5:00

70. Who will the woman bring with her?

(A) Her husband

(B) Her colleague

(C) Her daughter

(D) Her mother

PART 4

Directions: You will hear some talks given by a single speaker. You will be asked to answer three questions about what the speaker says in each talk. Select the best response to each question and mark the letter (A), (B), (C), or (D) on your answer sheet. The talks will not be printed in your test book and will be spoken only one time.

71. Where is the speaker?
    (A) At a community center
    (B) At a city office
    (C) At a computer repair shop
    (D) At a library

72. What does the speaker ask the listeners to do?
    (A) Learn about software
    (B) Deliver lunches
    (C) Recruit more volunteers
    (D) Use some devices

73. What is offered by local businesses?
    (A) Computer lessons
    (B) Discount coupons
    (C) Free software
    (D) Meals

74. What type of business is the message for?
    (A) An amusement park
    (B) A community center
    (C) A kids' theater
    (D) A school

75. How many days is the business closed in the summer?
    (A) One day
    (B) Two days
    (C) Three days
    (D) Never

76. What should a listener do for ticket pricing information?
    (A) Press "1"
    (B) Press "2"
    (C) Press "3"
    (D) Visit the Website

77. What is being advertised?
    (A) Air travel
    (B) A bus company
    (C) Train travel
    (D) A travel agency

78. What does the company offer customers?
    (A) Changeable tickets
    (B) Fast service
    (C) Low prices
    (D) Many destinations

79. According to the advertisement, what can be found on the Website?
    (A) Customer reviews
    (B) Scheduling information
    (C) Ticket prices
    (D) Tourist information

80. What is being reported?
    (A) A product design
    (B) A product display
    (C) A product recall
    (D) A product sales

81. What problem does the speaker mention?
    (A) The color
    (B) The functions
    (C) The price
    (D) The weight

82. What can customers get at the end of next month?
    (A) A discount
    (B) A feedback form
    (C) A free gift
    (D) A special invitation

GO ON TO THE NEXT PAGE

83. What is the audience asked to do?

(A) Be patient with the speaker
(B) Clap for the speaker at the end
(C) Refrain from taking pictures
(D) Wait until later to ask questions

84. Why does the speaker say, "I'm just going to bite the bullet and do this"?

(A) She is going to eat her lunch soon.
(B) She is going to speak even though she is afraid.
(C) She wants to hear what the audience thinks.
(D) She wants to stop violence in the town.

85. What will the speaker talk about next?

(A) How to involve people in voting
(B) How to solve the town's problems
(C) Ways to improve local schools
(D) Ways to recycle unwanted items

---

86. What has the listener asked the speaker to do?

(A) Design a piece of equipment
(B) Design a piece of luggage
(C) Make some handles
(D) Make some locks

87. What is mentioned about the speaker's business?

(A) It has won design awards.
(B) It is expanding overseas.
(C) It is having financial trouble.
(D) It is not a large firm.

88. What does the speaker imply when he says, "After all, that's only six weeks away"?

(A) The deadline is too soon.
(B) The order can be finished soon.
(C) The schedule is perfect.
(D) The summer is going quickly.

---

89. What does the speaker mean when she says, "What I'm about to say shouldn't be a surprise to anyone"?

(A) It is not the first time the company has tried to save money.
(B) It is unexpected that the speaker has to mention the topic again.
(C) The listeners have not understood the policy well before now.
(D) The listeners may have forgotten what the speaker said.

90. What unnecessary cost does the speaker want to reduce?

(A) Color toner
(B) Electricity
(C) Paper
(D) Computer server

91. What does the speaker ask the listeners to do to their computers?

(A) Change their settings
(B) Reset their passwords
(C) Save their files to the backup server
(D) Use a new printer

---

92. What is the seminar about?

(A) Building a new Website
(B) Helping local businesses
(C) Increasing visitors to Websites
(D) Updating Websites

93. What does the speaker mention about his experience?

(A) He designed his first Website 15 years ago.
(B) He has been helping businesses for a long time.
(C) He has received awards for his Web designs.
(D) He learned about new technology from attending seminars.

94. What are listeners encouraged to do during the presentations?

(A) Ask questions
(B) Make suggestions
(C) Take notes
(D) Use a recorder

SHOE SIZE CHART	
U.S.	Europe
6	36
7	38
8	40
9	42

FREE PUBLIC SEMINARS
sponsored by City Hospital

May 22	Exercise for Everyone, Young and Old
June 19	Healthy Diets for a Long Life
July 24	Healthy Eating Even on Vacation
August 21	Keeping Your Heart Happy

95. Why is the speaker calling?

(A) To ask for a refund

(B) To get return information

(C) To request a size chart

(D) To reschedule a trip

96. Look at the graphic. What size shoe does the speaker need?

(A) 36

(B) 38

(C) 40

(D) 42

97. Where is the speaker going soon?

(A) On a camping trip

(B) On a cruise

(C) On a walking tour

(D) On a work trip

98. Who most likely is the speaker?

(A) An administrator

(B) A doctor

(C) A city official

(D) A travel agent

99. What will the speaker do for the listener next week?

(A) Conduct a tour

(B) Host a party

(C) Perform an operation

(D) Speak at a seminar

100. Look at the graphic. When would Ms. Morris most likely attend a seminar?

(A) May 22

(B) June 19

(C) July 24

(D) August 21

This is the end of the Listening test. Turn to Part 5 in your test book.

GO ON TO THE NEXT PAGE

READING TEST

In the Reading test, you will read a variety of texts and answer several different types of reading comprehension questions. The entire Reading test will last 75 minutes. There are three parts, and directions are given for each part. You are encouraged to answer as many questions as possible within the time allowed.

You must mark your answers on the separate answer sheet. Do not write your answers in your test book.

PART 5

Directions: A word or phrase is missing in each of the sentences below. Four answer choices are given below each sentence. Select the best answer to complete the sentence. Then mark the letter (A), (B), (C), or (D) on your answer sheet.

101. Online reviewers of Hotel Lila complained that the rates were too expensive, but the Smiths thought they were -------.

(A) excessive
(B) fancy
(C) reasonable
(D) valuable

102. TGS Publishing is looking for an experienced ------- who can draw for our new series of children's books.

(A) illustrate
(B) illustrated
(C) illustration
(D) illustrator

103. Sophie Anderson started ------- own business, Real Wear Co., right after she graduated from high school.

(A) her
(B) hers
(C) herself
(D) she

104. If you wish to apply for the ------- of nighttime shift worker, please complete our online application form.

(A) employment
(B) obligation
(C) position
(D) responsibility

105. The survey results show that over 95 percent of participants have received information or promotions that are not ------- to them.

(A) relevance
(B) relevancy
(C) relevant
(D) relevantly

106. ------- the building expansion is close to completion, we will have to plan the opening ceremony.

(A) As long as
(B) Even though
(C) If only
(D) Now that

107. Suri Tech's products are not only high quality, but also ------- more economical than most brand-name items.

(A) ever
(B) highly
(C) much
(D) very

108. The shuttle runs between the shopping mall and Central Station ------- from 9:00 AM to 8:00 PM.

(A) continuation
(B) continuing
(C) continuous
(D) continuously

109. The administrative affairs division was having trouble deciding ------- they should cancel or postpone the company picnic.

(A) before
(B) even
(C) what
(D) whether

110. The sales representative was glad but nervous when she was told to ------- the CEO to a luncheon with a major client.

(A) accompany
(B) accomplish
(C) include
(D) involve

111. After he was transferred to the payroll department, Matt Bender needed some time to get ------- with the calculation software.

(A) acquaint
(B) acquainted
(C) acquainting
(D) acquaints

112. John Harris was promoted to manager three years after joining the company due to his ------- to the organization.

(A) contribute
(B) contributed
(C) contributing
(D) contribution

113. Incentive bonuses will be given twice a year, in June and December, depending on individual -------.

(A) background
(B) finance
(C) inspection
(D) performance

114. The exact date ------- the winners of the design competition will be announced has not been decided yet.

(A) when
(B) where
(C) which
(D) whose

115. When searching ------- the thousands of resources available online, it often takes some skills to get the results you want.

(A) beneath
(B) over
(C) through
(D) under

116. While the candidate has more than ------- experience for the job, the personnel chief thought he lacked a positive attitude.

(A) enormous
(B) enough
(C) expert
(D) extra

117. ------- speaking, the country's biofuel industry has improved greatly over the past few decades.

(A) Technological
(B) Technologically
(C) Technologies
(D) Technology

118. The marketing chief tried to fix his computer problem himself ------- than waiting for a technician to show up.

(A) better
(B) later
(C) rather
(D) other

119. The executive director thoroughly enjoyed his trip to a local branch as he was ------- treated by the employees there.

(A) effectively
(B) especially
(C) generally
(D) generously

120. If Elton Corp. could purchase the land at a fair price, they ------- to the new location by the end of the year.

(A) have been moved
(B) moved
(C) are moved
(D) will move

GO ON TO THE NEXT PAGE

TEST 3

121. As the wage-hike negotiations didn't reach a consensus, the union was left with no choice but to ------- a strike.

(A) initiate
(B) initiation
(C) initiative
(D) initiatively

122. After several years of struggle, there are some ------- of recovery in the logistics industry.

(A) implications
(B) impressions
(C) indications
(D) interventions

123. At Acro Hill Hotel, visitors are sure to experience a comfortable stay ------- magnificent views from the rooftop terrace.

(A) enjoy
(B) enjoyed
(C) enjoying
(D) enjoys

124. Two teams were sitting at ------- sides of the table at the meeting, trying to push each of their plans through.

(A) opposing
(B) oppose
(C) opposite
(D) opposition

125. The national supermarket chain sought to ------- its debt by selling 50 of its 90 stores to a competitor.

(A) charge
(B) input
(C) offset
(D) release

126. In order to keep up ------- the latest technology in the industry, the automaker's president regularly reads several specialized magazines.

(A) along
(B) for
(C) to
(D) with

127. According to the pharmaceutical maker's report, it is estimated that ------- one in three people have some kind of food allergy.

(A) rough
(B) rougher
(C) roughly
(D) roughness

128. The experienced salesperson ------- mentored the new recruit for six months, leading him to remarkable achievements.

(A) enthusiastically
(B) periodically
(C) relatively
(D) potentially

129. Mildred Hospital is ranked ------- the best in the country for patient outcomes and state-of-the-art facilities.

(A) among
(B) highly
(C) providing
(D) that

130. A skilled pilot -------, Jeff Long is also an instructor at a flight school and a columnist for an aviation magazine.

(A) he
(B) him
(C) himself
(D) his

PART 6

Directions: Read the texts that follow. A word, phrase, or sentence is missing in parts of each text. Four answer choices for each question are given below the text. Select the best answer to complete the text. Then mark the letter (A), (B), (C), or (D) on your answer sheet.

Questions 131-134 refer to the following notice.

Eat Healthy, Be Active Community Workshop Series

The Eat Healthy, Be Active community workshops were developed by nutritionists and fitness ------- **131.** based on *The Dietary Guidelines for Health and Fitness* from the government. ------- of the six **132.** workshops in the series includes a lesson plan, learning objectives, hands-on activities, videos, and handouts. The workshops were designed for community educators, health promoters, nutritionists, and others to teach adults in a wide variety of community settings. These workshops will be offered free of charge at the River City Community Center every weekend in June. -------. Please enroll **133.** ------- the center or online at www.rivercitycommcenter.org **134.**

---

131. (A) special
    (B) specialists
    (C) specialize
    (D) specializing

132. (A) Few
    (B) Each
    (C) Every
    (D) Total

133. (A) All participants will receive a continuing education certificate upon completion of the series.
    (B) Comments or suggestions to make the community center classes better are always welcome.
    (C) Since the renovations will take longer than expected, we've had to cancel some of the classes.
    (D) We're pleased to announce that the center now accepts all major credit cards, as well as cash.

134. (A) for
    (B) by
    (C) in
    (D) to

GO ON TO THE NEXT PAGE

Questions 135-138 refer to the following e-mail.

To: Gina Caruso
From: Yuki Madison
Date: July 5
Subject: Performance request

Dear Ms. Caruso,

I was in the audience at the Bluebird Café last Friday night and I was ------- impressed with your
                                                                        135.
acoustic guitar and piano pieces. I'm in charge of booking musicians for the annual music festival in

Starling City and one of our performers has just -------. I know this is last-minute, but ------- there's
                                                 136.   **137.**
any way you could step in for her, I would be eternally grateful. -------. Could you look it over and get
                                                                 138.
back to me at your earliest convenience?

Sincerely,

Yuki Madison
Organizer
Starling City Music Festival

135. (A) hardly
    (B) nearly
    (C) evenly
    (D) deeply

136. (A) cancelled
    (B) continued
    (C) played
    (D) attended

137. (A) even as
    (B) if
    (C) because
    (D) moreover

138. (A) I won't be in the office until Friday, but I will
       check my messages.
    (B) I've attached a document with the fee offer
       and other details.
    (C) The festival is to be held July 30 and 31 at
       Starling City Park.
    (D) There are three other singers I'm
       considering for the concert.

Weekend Delays in the Valley Ridge Tunnel

Due to ongoing restoration and repair work in the Valley Ridge Tunnel by Valley Ridge City

Engineers, ------- significant delays to weekend service on the 32, 89, 171 and 482 express buses
    139.

in both directions through the end of the summer. Tunnel ------- will temporarily cause the closure of
      140.

one tube, while two-way traffic is accommodated in the other tube. ------- The traffic on Friday nights
      141.

going out of the city is expected to be especially heavy, so please allow ------- travel time whether in
      142.

private vehicles or public transportation.

---

139. (A) expect
(B) expected
(C) expecting
(D) expects

140. (A) repairs
(B) services
(C) shutdown
(D) traffic

141. (A) As a result, there will only be one lane of traffic open in each direction.
(B) City buses can now accommodate baby strollers in a designated space.
(C) In fact, all roads in Valley Ridge have been inspected recently by city engineers.
(D) The engineers have said that the repair work could continue into next year.

142. (A) add
(B) addition
(C) additional
(D) additionally

Questions 143-146 refer to the following memo.

Dear Staff,

I have recently gotten a number of ------- regarding the state of the conference room on the fourth
143.

floor. Apparently, some of you have eaten your lunch in there and not ------- your trash with you
144.

when you leave. It makes it very unpleasant for people who have afternoon meetings in there. Please

don't put smelly food trash in the wastebaskets in that room. -------. If the problems persist, I may be
145.

forced to lock the room ------- lunch.
146.

Thank you very much.

Timothy Reynolds
Office Manager

---

143. (A) complaints
(B) compliments
(C) conflicts
(D) controversies

144. (A) take
(B) taken
(C) taking
(D) to take

145. (A) All of us can do better in submitting our time
sheets on time.
(B) For this type of trash, use the garbage can
in the break room.
(C) The president will address the importance
of the recycling policy.
(D) We will be catering the meeting, so get your
order in soon.

146. (A) during
(B) in
(C) when
(D) while

PART 7

Directions: In this part you will read a selection of texts, such as magazine and newspaper articles, e-mails, and instant messages. Each text or set of texts is followed by several questions. Select the best answer for each question and mark the letter (A), (B), (C), or (D) on your answer sheet.

Questions 147-148 refer to the following notice.

Attention: Residents of the Robinson Park District

This is notification of the temporary closing of Olonda Park for remodeling of the children's area and construction of the amphitheater for free concerts. It is expected to take 4–6 months for all of the work to be completed and we look forward to the big reopening festival next spring. It will be finished in time to celebrate the 100th anniversary of the founding of Meyer Springs, and we will hold a party in the park for the occasion. For the duration of Olonda Park's closure, we would like to encourage visitors to check out other nearby parks, such as Lindley Park and Jinat Park, which are conveniently located near schools in the area. If you have any questions, please send them to the office of the mayor (mayorsoffice@meyersprings.gov) or come to the next city council meeting on July 5.

147. Why is the park closing?

(A) To prepare for a big event next weekend
(B) To renovate and add a building
(C) To repair the park's roads and sidewalks
(D) To tear down old facilities

148. What are residents encouraged to do on July 5?

(A) Ask about construction in the park
(B) Express opposition to the city's plan
(C) Get a brochure regarding the new city parks
(D) Listen to the details of urban development

GO ON TO THE NEXT PAGE

Questions 149-150 refer to the following text message chain.

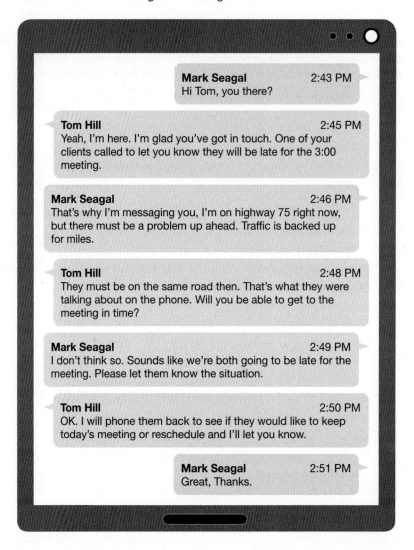

Mark Seagal   2:43 PM
Hi Tom, you there?

Tom Hill   2:45 PM
Yeah, I'm here. I'm glad you've got in touch. One of your clients called to let you know they will be late for the 3:00 meeting.

Mark Seagal   2:46 PM
That's why I'm messaging you, I'm on highway 75 right now, but there must be a problem up ahead. Traffic is backed up for miles.

Tom Hill   2:48 PM
They must be on the same road then. That's what they were talking about on the phone. Will you be able to get to the meeting in time?

Mark Seagal   2:49 PM
I don't think so. Sounds like we're both going to be late for the meeting. Please let them know the situation.

Tom Hill   2:50 PM
OK. I will phone them back to see if they would like to keep today's meeting or reschedule and I'll let you know.

Mark Seagal   2:51 PM
Great, Thanks.

149. What caused the meeting to be deferred?

(A) Because of a car breakdown
(B) Because of a traffic jam
(C) Because of a train delay
(D) Because of road construction

150. At 2:49 PM, what does Mr. Seagal mean when he says, "I don't think so"?

(A) He believes the data was incorrect.
(B) He cannot make it to the meeting on time.
(C) He disagrees with Mr. Hill's idea.
(D) He doubts the train will arrive on time.

Waypoint is proud to announce the new Armada series of media players, being released this fall. These state-of-the-art devices are packed with space and choice. We know being able to watch and share the hottest videos on the go is important to keep current at work or school, so HD video comes standard in every Armada. Taking the music you love with you has become a staple today, and Waypoint has found a way to increase storage without losing the fidelity of the music. At the highest quality settings, the Armada 1 can hold 3,000 songs. Each step up generates another 3,000 more songs for your collection! If you decide that you want as much music as you can get, the Armada 5 can hold 15,000 songs at the highest quality. We are taking pre-orders now, so don't let this amazing device slip through your fingers.

151. What is true about the Armada series?

(A) They are available in many colors.

(B) They can hold movies.

(C) They can record music.

(D) They weigh less than other devices.

152. How many songs can an Armada 2 hold?

(A) 3,000

(B) 6,000

(C) 9,000

(D) 15,000

GO ON TO THE NEXT PAGE

Questions 153-154 refer to the following e-mail.

To	Melissa Scroggins
From	Harold Lloyd
Date	August 4
Subject	Conducting a class

Dear Melissa,

Thank you for asking me to conduct a lecture at your university. Although it means a great deal to me to be considered, I am unfortunately unable to accept your request at this time. I am currently required to be on site for the project my team is working on. With any luck, we will wrap it up around the first of the year, but there are, of course, no guarantees. I would be happy to discuss possible dates for next year, if your offer still stands. It always gives me great pleasure to see, speak to, and develop young minds passionate about physics. Towards the end of this year, if you could send me some details about which points or topics you would like me to speak about, I will get something prepared for your students. I also look forward to finally putting a face to your name after many months of e-mails.

Sincerely,

Dr. Harold Lloyd
Astrophysics Head, Andromeda Industries

153. When is Dr. Lloyd's project supposed to be complete?
(A) By January
(B) By March
(C) By August
(D) By December

154. What does Mr. Lloyd ask Ms. Scroggins to do?
(A) Meet him in person to discuss details
(B) Prepare a lecture at the university
(C) Send him an e-mail about the project proposal
(D) Send him some details about a lecture

Questions 155-157 refer to the following information.

Welcome to Schmidt's, Copper City's newest center for all of your home electronics and DIY needs. Please take this opening celebration coupon booklet to the store and choose the coupon that best suits you. For example, if you are looking to purchase new appliances for your home, present the first coupon to not only save 15 percent off the price of the product, but also get free home delivery. Or, if there is a TV you have in mind, the next coupon will give you free installation plus three months of satellite TV service! Finally, if you consider yourself handy around the house, the third coupon in here will entitle you to a complimentary set of tools. Let us know what you need and we will be happy to assist. We look forward to seeing you at Schmidt's Grand Opening Celebration, starting July 1.

155. Why is Schmidt's offering the coupons to customers?

(A) To begin their holiday sales week

(B) To celebrate the store's anniversary

(C) To celebrate the store's first day of operation

(D) To show customers that they appreciate them

156. How many services are offered with the coupons?

(A) 1

(B) 2

(C) 3

(D) 4

157. What kinds of items would customers most likely NOT find at Schmidt's?

(A) Automobile goods

(B) Home entertainment

(C) Kitchen appliances

(D) Paint brushes

GO ON TO THE NEXT PAGE

Questions 158-160 refer to the following e-mail.

```
┌──────────────────────────────────────────────────────────────────────┐
│                              e-mail                                    │
├──────────────────────────────────────────────────────────────────────┤
│  To:      Rohm Ellington <rellington@vastmail.com>                     │
│  From:    Pathway Tours <csr@pathwaytours.com>                         │
│  Subject: Canada tour                                                  │
│  Date:    June 1                                                       │
└──────────────────────────────────────────────────────────────────────┘
```

Dear Mr. Ellington,

Thank you for choosing Pathway Tours. This e-mail is a confirmation of your trip to Canada. We are happy to answer any questions that you might have about your tour, so please let us know if we can assist in any way. It looks like there will be a total of 38 people on this tour, so everyone will be sharing a room with one other guest. If you are traveling with more than one person, we can set up a family room for you. As we will be traveling to many restaurants and markets, please let us know if you or anyone you are traveling with has any allergies or restrictions with food.

The tour's flight is scheduled to leave at 9:32 AM, so we are requesting that everyone meet at the airport at 7:30 AM on the 17th. If you experience any trouble, contact one of the tour guides as soon as possible. The flight won't be able to wait, but if needed, one of them will meet you in Canada after your flight arrives. After arrival, the tour will be led by two guides, Ms. Gina Lyons and Mr. John Hogan. Both are Canadian born, and have lived in the area for most of their lives. They will show you not just the most popular spots, but also those hidden treasures that only locals know about.

Pamela Strathmore
CSR, Pathway Tours

158. What is the main purpose of the e-mail?

(A) To ask for assistance with guiding the tour

(B) To confirm a trip with a customer

(C) To offer a trip to a customer

(D) To tell a customer not to be late for the flight

159. Who will wait at the airport if a customer should miss a flight?

(A) A local travel agent

(B) A taxi driver

(C) A tour guide

(D) Ms. Strathmore

160. Why does Ms. Strathmore believe that the two guides are the best choice for this tour?

(A) They are both experts in the history of the area.

(B) They are very patient and will wait for others.

(C) They can speak the local dialect and translate.

(D) They were both born and raised in the area.

Questions 161-163 refer to the following questionnaire.

We at *Fair Trade Magazine* are asking our readers for feedback on the magazine. We want to know what you like and dislike about what you read every month. At the end of this period, we will be offering a prize to three randomly chosen participants. Everyone who sends us a filled out form will be entered into the contest.

Q. What sections in the magazine are you favorites?

A. Since my company has branches in multiple countries, I have to attend meetings all around the world, so the business etiquette section is a must-read. My other favorite is the largest section, the monthly report. It gives me invaluable insight into the business mind from the perspective of industry leaders.

Q. Do you have the least favorite section?

A. I think the least useful section is the cover story. It is usually a fluff piece about some hot shots or company presidents that don't tell the readers much about how they achieved success. It usually just details what he or she does when vacationing or away from the office. It doesn't encourage anyone who isn't a CEO or in upper management to read that. What about replacing this with articles of the regular people who work hard every day? Represent those of us who make Fair Trade possible.

Q. Are there other ways that we can improve the magazine?

A. Since the Website runs in conjunction with the magazine, how about bonus features for those who have a subscription to the magazine? It could have access to a members' section of the Website, or special features that have weekly updates or news about sales strategies, etc.

161. What does the reader enjoy about the etiquette pages?

(A) How employees in other countries work
(B) How other companies work
(C) How to act in unfamiliar situations
(D) How to greet new customers

162. Why does the reader believe the main article is not useful?

(A) It does not offer enough information.
(B) It does not profile famous people.
(C) It is too specialized for the general reader.
(D) It only covers easy subjects.

163. What does the reader propose for the magazine?

(A) Allowing readers to ask questions to famous leaders
(B) Arranging meetings between readers and newsmakers
(C) Creating a special section of the Website for some readers
(D) Giving an extra discount to magazine subscribers

GO ON TO THE NEXT PAGE

Questions 164-167 refer to the following article.

At Odds with Business, the new book by Ellison Waters, is a wonderful account of how anyone can easily overcome the toughest work decisions, if you have a little help along the way. —[1]—.

Mr. Waters said that this book is "the culmination of twenty-two years of hard work and experience, documenting all I picked up during my younger days." Waters' book, which is a partial biography and partial how-to book, begins with his childhood and takes us through his university days. —[2]—. For example, future competitors like Sam Nash opened the door to the business world for Mr. Waters. He also includes choices he made early in his business life to show that failures can teach lessons and show us how not to do something. These failures can also be valuable to others so they won't make the same mistakes. —[3]—.

Understanding the techniques that Mr. Waters lists in his book won't make you the next industry giant, but it does give a bit of insight into how his mind works and how he uses his company to create new ideas. —[4]—. This book is recommended for anyone that is breaking into business or wants to learn new ways to create a product demand for your company.

164. What does the reviewer think of the book?

(A) It does not give enough business tips.

(B) It is a great way to learn business.

(C) It is hard to understand the writer's background.

(D) It spends too much time on failures.

165. What is stated in the first part of the book?

(A) Business books to read

(B) Business techniques

(C) Mr. Waters' business life

(D) Mr. Waters' school days

166. Who is Sam Nash?

(A) Mr. Waters' advisor

(B) Mr. Waters' partner

(C) Mr. Waters' relative

(D) Mr. Waters' rival

167. In which of the positions marked [1], [2], [3], or [4] does the following sentence best belong?

"After that, it moves on to introducing those who influenced him to become the business legend that he is today."

(A) [1]

(B) [2]

(C) [3]

(D) [4]

— [1] —. Many businessmen and women from around the globe will be coming to Los Angeles next week for the biggest trade show of the year. Leaders from electronics, computers, and gaming will be bringing out their best to show both consumers and competitors what is coming down the line.

As the week-long expo starts, we should expect to see many items, such as televisions, cameras, even new gaming consoles or mobile devices on display. — [2] —. More than 25,000 people are expected to be at the show for at least one of the five days, with many consumers attending all of the three public days of the show.

Non-industry individuals are considered vital to the show, as they will spend the most time with products, as well as give comments after use and receive free giveaways to show off back home. — [3] —. When asked, more than 40 percent of consumers polled said that seeing new products make them feel like kids in a candy store. Amazingly, 74 percent of confirmed attendees for this year said that they are coming to see the technical design of the products. — [4] —.

168. What is purpose of the event?

(A) To buy and sell new electronics

(B) To conduct marketing research

(C) To showcase future products

(D) To share technology advances

169. How many days is the event open to the general public?

(A) 1

(B) 3

(C) 5

(D) 7

170. According to the article, why do most people attend the event?

(A) To look at the product design

(B) To purchase the newest gadgets

(C) To talk with experts in the field

(D) To try new electronics before they're released

171. In which of the positions marked [1], [2], [3] or [4] does the following sentence best belong?

"Most of the surprises come during the first three days of the show, so we should know much more soon."

(A) [1]

(B) [2]

(C) [3]

(D) [4]

Questions 172-175 refer to the following online discussion.

Drew Manson
12:34 PM

Hello, everyone. Thanks for joining me. With only three weeks left before we are due to present our group project, I was thinking we should see where we are, and if need be, ask for some help.

Michael Ino
12:35 PM

My team and I could definitely use some backup. We've hit the wall creatively.

Elaine Gregg
12:35 PM

I'd be glad to help out. What can I do?

Michael Ino
12:37 PM

Well, any thoughts about how we can show management how the product works in the real world? It doesn't translate well in presentation form.

Drew Manson
12:38 PM

Maybe we could show them a short demonstration of how it works. What do you think?

Michael Ino
12:40 PM

That's a good idea, but how can we get a demo unit built in less than three weeks? I'm worried that if it's rushed, it may not work at all. That would be a disaster.

Elaine Gregg
12:42 PM

I could have my team focus on the unit this week, and then pass it off to your team after that. When the time comes for the demo, it would be a great help if both teams knew how to use it properly, right?

Michael Ino
12:43 PM

That's a great idea. I'll let my team know that they will be working in tandem with you all.

Drew Manson
12:44 PM

Excellent. I look forward to hearing a progress report about it next week.

172. Why does Mr. Ino need help with his part of the project?

(A) He got a tough request from management.
(B) He has had trouble correcting some data.
(C) He must find cheaper materials.
(D) He wants to present the product well.

173. Who will work on the unit first?

(A) Mr. Ino's team
(B) Mr. Manson's team
(C) Ms. Gregg's team
(D) All IT staff

174. What will happen in a week?

(A) They will have a meeting with their managers.
(B) They will show their client a trial.
(C) They will start the new project.
(D) They will update Mr. Manson on the project.

175. At 12:37 PM, what does Mr. Ino mean when he says, "It doesn't translate well"?

(A) It is difficult to talk about the product effectively.
(B) It will be difficult to demonstrate in other countries.
(C) The pictures do not make sense to anyone else.
(D) The words are hard for many people to understand.

GO ON TO THE NEXT PAGE

TEST 3

Jericho, Inc. is looking for NEW TEAM MEMBERS to join us this summer. If you have experience with customer service and sales, we want to speak to you about a position. Our talented sales staff is trained to use both traditional and modern techniques, such as in newspaper and magazines, search engines, and commercials, to speak to individuals and companies about marketing and advertising of their products domestically and internationally.

Two men with a vision started the company in 1983, wanting to take the industry by storm. After their first eight years of operations, Jericho, Inc. is considered to be one of the top five companies in advertising today. We are looking for people who can be determined when it comes to advertising, sales, marketing, and negotiation. Over 200 million people have seen our campaigns, and we want to expand our vision by double this year. Big ideas are always welcome and we want to hear how you could transform our business into a world leader. Recent college graduates are encouraged to apply as well.

If interested, please contact Lance Everson at the Irvine office at 864-555-7093 or e-mail us at: jobsjericho@walls.com.

e-mail	
To:	Lance Everson <jobsjericho@walls.com>
From:	Robert Gibson <robertgib11@smokeymt.edu>
Date:	May 20
Subject:	Job position

Dear Mr. Everson,

I am very interested in a position with Jericho, Inc. and would like to speak with you about a possible job opportunity at your earliest convenience. I am a senior at Smokey Mountain University and will be earning a degree in business economics at the end of this year. I am at the top of my class and am working part-time at Hunter&Michaels, a local advertising office in town. I share the passion of advertising and would like to use my experience in local advertising and marketing in a larger role. I am always thinking about new ways to introduce products into markets around the country, and would bring skills in Internet marketing and analytics to help ensure that our brands are seen by a larger percent of consumers. For these reasons, I feel that I would be a good fit for your company.

Thank you in advance for your consideration.

Robert Gibson

176. What kind of company is Jericho, Inc.?

(A) An advertising company
(B) An IT company
(C) A publisher
(D) A retailer

177. What is NOT mentioned in the advertisement?

(A) Staff training
(B) Sales figures
(C) Job qualifications
(D) Company history

178. What is the main purpose of the e-mail?

(A) To accept a job offer
(B) To apply for a job
(C) To ask about job details
(D) To follow up on an interview

179. What might prevent Mr. Gibson from getting the position?

(A) His current academic status
(B) His grades at school
(C) His major at the university
(D) Lack of recommendations

180. In the e-mail, the word "share" in line 4, is closest in meaning to

(A) divide
(B) give
(C) have
(D) match

GO ON TO THE NEXT PAGE

TEST 3

Questions 181-185 refer to the following schedule and memo.

Meeting Agenda July 17	Time
Amory Brothers Representatives arrive	9:00 AM
Introductions and first proposal	9:30 AM
Multimedia showcase *Make sure to use the audio files with this.	10:00 AM
Discussions about how our company can achieve growth *May also be some Q&A during this time.	11:00 AM
Lunch with Amory Brothers President	12:00 PM
Group discussions with management from both companies	1:00 PM
Final negotiations *We are hoping to reach this part earlier, but will stress it at this time.	2:00 PM
Preliminary contracts drawn up	2:30 PM
End of the day's meeting	4:00 PM

MEMO

To: Mark Reynolds, Amy Abbott
From: Jennifer Tyson
Date: July 15
Subject: Meeting Agenda July 17

Hello, Mark and Amy,

Here is some information regarding the meeting with Amory Brothers on July 17th. I wanted to make sure to inform you of everything that should happen that day, since it is a big meeting for us.

This contract could help our company regain its foothold in the audio industry, and I know that I can count on you to help us do just that. When the reps from Amory arrive, please take them to meeting room D, where we will have everything ready to go for you.

Amory Brothers is a blue-chip company in the audio industry and works with everyone from the top singers to the best movie companies in the world. Their specialty is creating small equipment to offer assistance to space programs and governments that need to use the smallest audio listening devices available. They expect fast-thinking project leaders to respond to their concerns, and I know the two of you will show how we can be a leading part of the future in audio. I have every confidence they will see that we are the best choice for their future projects!

Jennifer Tyson
President, Hitbox Sound

181. What is the purpose of the meeting?

(A) To explain a new audio device

(B) To show new programs to representatives

(C) To try to encourage a merger

(D) To win a contract for the company

182. What does Ms. Tyson remind Mark and Amy to do during the showcase?

(A) To answer the client's questions

(B) To finish as quickly as possible

(C) To explain as many details as they can

(D) To use the prepared files

183. What does the client have leading technology in?

(A) Audio equipment

(B) Computers

(C) Vehicles

(D) Video equipment

184. What does Ms. Tyson NOT think about Amory Brothers?

(A) They are a small company.

(B) They are one of the best companies.

(C) They need responsive companies to work with.

(D) They will consider the contract beneficial.

185. When will Mark and Amy meet the visitors?

(A) At 9:00 AM

(B) At 9:30 AM

(C) At 10:00 AM

(D) At 12:00 PM

GO ON TO THE NEXT PAGE

Peter Solvang — A Brief Summary of the Artist's Work

- **Early Period:** Solvang worked in multiple colors (acrylic), using the broad brush strokes he would become famous for later in life.

- **Mid-career:** Solvang branched out with a few modern portraits during this time, bringing to mind the influence of Carson and Eustace.

- **Final Works:** In the decade before his death, Solvang expressed emotions only in black. The bold, dark strokes reflected their own light, he said.

Public Access Channel July Programming Schedule

Monday, July 17   <u>Getting Started on Your Retirement Fund</u>   17:00-17:15
Investment guru, Ravita Singh, tells viewers it's never too early to start investing for your retirement. Tune in for tips and warnings about the best and safest investments.

Tuesday, July 18   <u>Taco Tuesday and Other Treats</u>   15:30-16:00
Mexican chef Juanita Valdez shares another terrific recipe with us. Using ingredients easily found in any supermarket, you'll be able to please your hungry crowd tonight.

Wednesday, July 19   <u>Peter Solvang Retrospective</u>   20:00-21:30
Solvang has been called France's greatest modern painter. The second in a series, tonight's program examines the works in the middle of his seven-decade career.

Thursday, July 20   <u>This Beautiful Old House</u>   20:30-21:30
Owners of older houses have a lot of work to do. We make it easier with our weekly show that teaches you the basics of home repair and maintenance. Save money and DIY!

```
┌─────────────────────────────────────────────────────────────────────────┐
│ □ ══════════════════════════ e-mail ══════════════════════════════════   │
├─────────────────────────────────────────────────────────────────────────┤
│ To:        │ Public Access Channel Information <pacinfo@pacabroadcasting.gov> │
│ From:      │ Riley Springer <rspringer@vastmail.com>                       │
│ Date:      │ July 20                                                       │
│ Subject:   │ Question about a program                                      │
└─────────────────────────────────────────────────────────────────────────┘
```

Hello,

I would like to know if you are re-broadcasting the program from last night, about the painter. I only caught the last ten minutes of it, so I don't know the name of it. I teach art history at the local college and I'd like to use some of it in my class. Could you tell me how to view it again or how to purchase a recording of it, if possible?

Riley Springer

186. When did Peter Solvang use black paint only?

(A) In his early days

(B) Before he met Eustace

(C) During the middle of his career

(D) In the latter part of his life

187. What does the art TV program focus on?

(A) A tutorial on brush strokes

(B) An artist's portrait period

(C) Bright colors in nature

(D) Using acrylic in paintings

188. When does a show about money air?

(A) Monday

(B) Tuesday

(C) Wednesday

(D) Thursday

189. What program does Ms. Springer ask about?

(A) Getting Started on Your Retirement Fund

(B) Peter Solvang Retrospective

(C) Taco Tuesday and Other Treats

(D) This Beautiful Old House

190. What is mentioned about Ms. Springer?

(A) She is an artist.

(B) She is an investment banker.

(C) She owns an older home.

(D) She works in education.

GO ON TO THE NEXT PAGE →

Auburn Motors Special Lease Offer

If you're not quite ready to make the commitment to buy a car for whatever reason, our lease option is perfect — and sometimes less costly in the long run than buying brand-new!

Lease any of our brand-new models* for just $200 per month for 36 months and pay only $2,500 at signing. That's a lower down payment than any of our competitors.

No security deposit. Walk-away anytime during lease agreement. For 36 months, take up the option to purchase a vehicle for value for money (cheaper than buying one). This offer will be made to qualified candidates. Thorough credit background check will be made by Verify, Inc.

*Wellspring 5000 sedan, Fox Trot XR sports car, Jasmine 33 hybrid, Emerald Bay mini van

Final Invoice for Car Lease

Make/Model: Hybrid

Mileage Upon return: 12,389

Name: Timothy Loins

Total time on lease: 12 months

Maintenance: New brake pads

Mileage charge	389 x 0.15	58.35
Local tax		49.50
Maintenance		245.25
Final month charge		200.00
Total		553.10

*Vehicle leases include 12,000 free miles per year. Above that, customers are charged $.15 per mile.

From	Timothy Lions <timothylions@bizplus.net>
To	Auburn Motors <info@auburnmotors.com>
Date	July 3
Subject	Car lease charges

I just received the final invoice from my car lease with Auburn Motors and I'm afraid there's been an error, probably just a clerical one. At the time I turned the car back in, I recorded the miles as 10,389. I even took a picture of the odometer, which I've attached to this message. Please refund me the extra mileage charge.

Thank you,
Timothy Lions

191. How much did Mr. Lions likely pay as a down payment?

(A) $200
(B) $553.10
(C) $1,200
(D) $2,500

192. What type of car did Mr. Lions lease?

(A) Emerald Bay
(B) Fox Trot XR
(C) Jasmine 33
(D) Wellspring 5000

193. When did Mr. Lions return the vehicle?

(A) A week after signing the lease
(B) A few months after signing the lease
(C) One year after signing the lease
(D) Three years after signing the lease

194. How much is Mr. Lions asking to be refunded?

(A) $49.50
(B) $58.35
(C) $200.00
(D) $245.25

195. What has Mr. Lions sent with his e-mail?

(A) A picture of the car's control panel
(B) A picture of the car's exterior
(C) His original contract
(D) The lease advertisement

GO ON TO THE NEXT PAGE

San Marcos 25th Annual Home Decor Exhibition

July 21–24   9:30 AM–5:30 PM   Javier Center   San Marcos, CA

Program for July 21

- Opening Presentation   10:00 AM – 10:30 AM   Main Stage
  Exhibition organizer Felicia Knowles of Westbrook Designs will give a welcome speech.

- Trends in Home Fashion   11:30 AM – 12:30 PM   East Room
  Staff from local business Bridget Homes will explain what is trending now.

- Forecast for Next Year   1:30 PM – 2:00 PM   West Pavilion
  Design icon Robert Waxman will share his insights on hot designs in the coming year.

- New Exhibitors' Gallery   All Day   Center Section
  Don't miss the newest businesses showing off their products.

---

e-mail

From:	Marc Ephraim <mephraim@ephraimdes.com>
To:	Janessa Blackwell <jblackwell@ephraimdes.com>
Date:	July 17
Subject:	Home Decor Exhibition

Hi Janessa,

I was hoping you could help me with the upcoming event at Javier Center. My team and I can cover the booth itself, but we need to rotate some people to the gallery throughout the first day. I was wondering what your availability would be from 1:00 to 5:00? I could actually use two more people, so if you have any recommendations, let me know. One more thing. Could you look over the attached product list and confirm the price on CSH-45? I know that particular one costs more because of the specialty fabric, but I don't know what price we finally settled on.

Thanks a lot,
Marc Ephraim
Ephraim Designs

Ephraim Designs Exhibition Product List

	Item Number	Dimensions	Price
Upholstery Fabrics			
Woven	UF-WV21	Varies (remnants)	Individually labeled
Modern	UF-MO11	"	"
Traditional	UF-TR95	"	"
Small Cupboards			
Mottled Green	CPB-MG3	H85/W76/D40	$125
French Grey	CPB-FG5	"	$125
Provence Blue	CPB-PB7	"	$135
Mediterranean Blue	CPB-MB9	"	$130
Cushion Covers			
Floral	CSH-55	40x40	$45
Animals	CSH-32	40x40	$45
Designer	CSH-45	55x55	$50
Traditional	CSH-64	55x55	$50

196. Where can participants hear about future trends?

(A) Center Section

(B) East Room

(C) Main Stage

(D) West Pavilion

197. When does Mr. Ephraim want Ms. Blackwell's help?

(A) On July 21

(B) On July 22

(C) On July 23

(D) On July 24

198. In the e-mail, the word "cover" in line 1, is the closest in meaning to

(A) decorate

(B) hide

(C) wrap

(D) include

199. What item does Mr. Ephraim ask Ms. Blackwell about?

(A) The designer cushion cover

(B) The floral cushion

(C) The modern upholstery fabric

(D) The woven table cloth

200. What is common to the cupboards in the list?

(A) The color

(B) The material

(C) The price

(D) The size

Stop! This is the end of the test. If you finish before time is called, you may go back to Parts 5, 6, and 7 and check your work.

Actual Test 4

Check ▸ 시작 시간 _____ : _____

▸ 종료 시간 _____ : _____

LC MP3 바로듣기

LISTENING TEST

In the Listening test, you will be asked to demonstrate how well you understand spoken English. The entire Listening test will last approximately 45 minutes. There are four parts, and directions are given for each part. You must mark your answers on the separate answer sheet. Do not write your answers in your test book.

PART 1

Directions: For each question in this part, you will hear four statements about a picture in your test book. When you hear the statements, you must select the one statement that best describes what you see in the picture. Then find the number of the question on your answer sheet and mark your answer. The statements will not be printed in your test book and will be spoken only one time.

Statement (C), "They're sitting at the table," is the best description of the picture, so you should select answer (C) and mark it on your answer sheet.

1.

2.

GO ON TO THE NEXT PAGE

3.

4.

5.

6.

GO ON TO THE NEXT PAGE ➡

PART 2

Directions: You will hear a question or statement and three responses spoken in English. They will not be printed in your test book and will be spoken only one time. Select the best response to the question or statement and mark the letter (A), (B), or (C) on your answer sheet.

7. Mark your answer on your answer sheet.

8. Mark your answer on your answer sheet.

9. Mark your answer on your answer sheet.

10. Mark your answer on your answer sheet.

11. Mark your answer on your answer sheet.

12. Mark your answer on your answer sheet.

13. Mark your answer on your answer sheet.

14. Mark your answer on your answer sheet.

15. Mark your answer on your answer sheet.

16. Mark your answer on your answer sheet.

17. Mark your answer on your answer sheet.

18. Mark your answer on your answer sheet.

19. Mark your answer on your answer sheet.

20. Mark your answer on your answer sheet.

21. Mark your answer on your answer sheet.

22. Mark your answer on your answer sheet.

23. Mark your answer on your answer sheet.

24. Mark your answer on your answer sheet.

25. Mark your answer on your answer sheet.

26. Mark your answer on your answer sheet.

27. Mark your answer on your answer sheet.

28. Mark your answer on your answer sheet.

29. Mark your answer on your answer sheet.

30. Mark your answer on your answer sheet.

31. Mark your answer on your answer sheet.

PART 3

Directions: You will hear some conversations between two or more people. You will be asked to answer three questions about what the speakers say in each conversation. Select the best response to each question and mark the letter (A), (B), (C), or (D) on your answer sheet. The conversations will not be printed in your test book and will be spoken only one time.

32. Where are the speakers going next week?

(A) On a business trip

(B) On a camping trip

(C) To a client's office

(D) To a holiday resort

33. How are the speakers going to get to their destination?

(A) By airplane

(B) By bus

(C) By car

(D) By train

34. What is mentioned about this Friday?

(A) No company vehicles are available.

(B) The man will spend time with his family.

(C) The woman will move to a new place.

(D) There is a company picnic.

35. What does the woman say she likes?

(A) Greek food

(B) Modern art

(C) New cafés

(D) Pop music

36. Where are the speakers planning to meet?

(A) At a gallery

(B) At a restaurant

(C) At an art supply store

(D) At the woman's apartment

37. What will the speakers do tomorrow at 7:30?

(A) Cook dinner

(B) Listen to an artist talk

(C) Participate in an art class

(D) Try a new restaurant

38. What does the man ask the woman about?

(A) A college application

(B) A promotional campaign

(C) His checking account

(D) His son's scholarship

39. Why does the woman say, "We've had a lot of calls about that today"?

(A) Many people have complained that the line is busy.

(B) She has talked with the same customer repeatedly.

(C) She is tired of all the calls.

(D) The new offer is popular.

40. What does the woman recommend to the man?

(A) To ask a friend for advice

(B) To come see her again

(C) To call back later

(D) To hurry up

41. Where are the speakers?

(A) At an airport

(B) At a luggage store

(C) At a train station

(D) At a travel agency

42. What is the problem?

(A) The man forgot to make a reservation.

(B) The man overcharged the woman.

(C) The woman's item did not arrive with her.

(D) The woman's name was spelled wrong.

43. Where will the woman probably go next?

(A) To a clinic

(B) To a hotel

(C) To Atlanta

(D) To her home

GO ON TO THE NEXT PAGE ➡

TEST 4

44. What are the speakers mainly discussing?

(A) A customer order

(B) A feedback form

(C) A new Website

(D) A trial product

45. What change does the woman suggest?

(A) Decreasing the font size

(B) Emphasizing the logo

(C) Making the type darker

(D) Modifying the whole design

46. What does the man mean when he says, "I think I can handle it"?

(A) The man can set up the system by himself.

(B) The man needs no feedback from the woman.

(C) The woman does not have to see the designers.

(D) The woman does not need to give the man a ride.

---

47. Who most likely is the man?

(A) A credit card company representative

(B) A customer service representative

(C) A new customer

(D) A store clerk

48. What is the woman's problem?

(A) Her computer is not working.

(B) Her order has not arrived yet.

(C) Her order is incorrect.

(D) Her payment method is not accepted.

49. What might the man do next?

(A) Call the credit card company

(B) Check the woman's purchase record

(C) Explain a procedure

(D) Transfer the woman's call

---

50. What are the speakers mainly discussing?

(A) A food delivery service

(B) A neighborhood event

(C) The man's schedule

(D) The woman's new job

51. What change would the woman like to see?

(A) A variety of services

(B) A different schedule

(C) Friendlier staff

(D) Lower prices

52. What does the woman say she will do?

(A) Move to a different area

(B) Change her jobs

(C) Sign up for a service

(D) Talk to her neighbors

---

53. What problem are the speakers discussing?

(A) A customer complaint

(B) A financial problem

(C) A product recall

(D) A supply problem

54. What does the woman imply when she says, "The summer will nearly be over by then"?

(A) She is happy that it will be less hot then.

(B) The company will close after summer.

(C) The product will not be needed then.

(D) The workers will be busier then.

55. What will happen at the end of the day?

(A) A manufacturer will call back.

(B) A clearance sale will begin.

(C) The speakers will do an inventory.

(D) The products will be put on the market.

---

56. What is mentioned about the speakers' company?

(A) It is doing well.
(B) It is hiring new employees.
(C) It is moving to an overseas location.
(D) It is spending more than it takes in.

57. What does the woman say she will do?

(A) Contact her friend
(B) Look at some contracts
(C) Make a reservation
(D) Visit a new branch office

58. What is the reason for the higher rent prices in the area?

(A) Better transportation
(B) Economic growth
(C) Improved safety
(D) New office building construction

59. What does Ellen dislike about her new place?

(A) The access to work
(B) The crowded station
(C) The color of the house
(D) The size of her room

60. What can be said about Seven Oaks Station?

(A) It is a new station.
(B) It is in the western part of the city.
(C) The women did not know about it.
(D) Two lines go through it.

61. What will Nina do next?

(A) Look for a new place
(B) Check the departure time
(C) Show Ellen an app
(D) Take a train

62. Who most likely is the man?

(A) A caterer
(B) A city official
(C) A grocery store manager
(D) A reporter

63. What is mentioned about the woman's business?

(A) It almost won the award last year.
(B) It relocated last year.
(C) It remodeled its office this year.
(D) It started this year.

64. What will happen next Monday?

(A) The contest results will be announced.
(B) The magazine issue will be released.
(C) The speakers will meet at the woman's office.
(D) The woman will have a job interview.

GO ON TO THE NEXT PAGE

HOTEL SINCLAIR

1. Room charge	....	$80
2. Mini bar	....	$17
3. Room service	....	$12
4. Service charge	....	$8
Total		$117

65. Look at the graphic. How much will be taken off of the bill?

(A) $8

(B) $12

(C) $17

(D) $80

66. What does the man say caused the problem?

(A) A cleaning staff mistake

(B) A computer error

(C) A name mix-up

(D) A reservation change

67. What will the man most likely do next?

(A) Call his supervisor

(B) Check something on the computer

(C) Give the woman a key

(D) Process a payment

ABC Furniture
Discount Coupon

Sofas, Couches	10% OFF!
Dining tables	20% OFF!
Beds	20% OFF!

9 791196 597504

(Expires July 31)

68. What does the man mention about the item?

(A) It is his favorite color.

(B) It is suitable for his home.

(C) It is big for his place.

(D) It is within his budget.

69. Look at the graphic. What discount will the man get on his purchase?

(A) 10%

(B) 15%

(C) 20%

(D) 25%

70. What will the man most likely do next?

(A) Arrange delivery

(B) Check the price online

(C) Look for a different item

(D) Measure the item

PART 4

Directions: You will hear some talks given by a single speaker. You will be asked to answer three questions about what the speaker says in each talk. Select the best response to each question and mark the letter (A), (B), (C), or (D) on your answer sheet. The talks will not be printed in your test book and will be spoken only one time.

71. What type of business is the message for?
    (A) A hotel
    (B) An airline
    (C) An electronics store
    (D) An online clothing store

72. What are callers asked to have ready?
    (A) Their membership number
    (B) Their mobile phone number
    (C) Their order number
    (D) Their passport number

73. When is a caller directed to call back for a shorter wait time?
    (A) At 10:00 AM
    (B) At 5:30 PM
    (C) At 7:00 PM
    (D) At 8:30 PM

74. Why is the speaker meeting with the listeners?
    (A) To explain how some software works
    (B) To find out what they need in a new system
    (C) To inform new employees of company policies
    (D) To introduce a piece of equipment

75. According to the speaker, what is a benefit of his product over the competitor's?
    (A) It is cheaper.
    (B) It is faster.
    (C) It is higher quality.
    (D) It is lighter.

76. What will the listeners do next?
    (A) Listen to a presentation
    (B) Log into a new system
    (C) Use some office equipment
    (D) Watch a video

77. What is mentioned about the Air Space K shoes?
    (A) They are made for new runners only.
    (B) They are only available online.
    (C) They are the cheapest on the market.
    (D) They use a new type of fabric.

78. What does the store's technology do?
    (A) Make custom shoes
    (B) Measure foot size
    (C) Teach customers how to run
    (D) Show customers where to run

79. What does a customer have to do to get a free gift?
    (A) Bring in a coupon
    (B) Buy two pairs of shoes
    (C) Fill out a questionnaire
    (D) Say they heard the advertisement

80. Where are the listeners?
    (A) At a concert venue
    (B) At a grocery store
    (C) At a movie theater
    (D) At a sports venue

81. What will happen in five minutes?
    (A) A game will begin.
    (B) A performer will appear.
    (C) Another announcement will be made.
    (D) Snacks will be available.

82. What will listeners who show a subway card receive?
    (A) A copy of a magazine
    (B) A food discount
    (C) A free gift
    (D) A special seat

GO ON TO THE NEXT PAGE

83. What does the speaker mean when she says, "we will stop taking breakfast orders in about ten minutes"?

(A) The listeners should be in a hurry to leave.
(B) The listeners should decide what they want soon.
(C) The speaker is nearly finished with her shift.
(D) The speaker is running out of breakfast items.

84. What does the speaker suggest the listeners do?

(A) Order drinks separately
(B) Pay for their meals individually
(C) Share a common beverage
(D) Try an appetizer

85. What will the speaker bring the listeners soon?

(A) Coffee
(B) Menus
(C) Silverware
(D) Water

86. Who most likely is giving the report?

(A) A fire official
(B) A product designer
(C) A Web designer
(D) An IT staff member

87. What was the problem?

(A) A fire in the office damaged some equipment.
(B) A product was found to be defective.
(C) A Website had been hacked.
(D) An employee used an unsafe Website.

88. When will the problem be fully resolved?

(A) By tomorrow
(B) By the middle of next week
(C) At the end of next week
(D) Next month

89. What type of item is the speaker reporting on?

(A) A gadget
(B) A laptop computer
(C) A music player
(D) A video camera

90. What does the speaker imply when she says, "the store opened at 9:00 and it's almost 2:00 now"?

(A) The line at the cashier's is getting shorter.
(B) The popular item may be gone by now.
(C) The store clerks are tired already.
(D) The store will be closing soon.

91. When can a customer receive their online order?

(A) In three weeks
(B) In six weeks
(C) In about two months
(D) In six months

Expense Report

Trip purpose: <u>Trade Show</u>   Department: <u>Sales</u>
Name: <u>Catherine Snow</u>   Manager: <u>Isabelle Perkins</u>

Date	Description	Air/Transp.	Hotel	Meals	Others
8/20, 23	RT flight to LA	$350			
8/20-22	3 nights stay		$800		
8/20-22	Meals			$300	
8/20-22	Rental car	$200			

92. Which department does the caller work in?

(A) Accounting
(B) Administration
(C) Personnel
(D) Sales

93. Look at the graphic. For what amount does Catherine have to produce receipts?

(A) $50
(B) $200
(C) $250
(D) $350

94. What is Catherine asked to do soon?

(A) Book the air tickets
(B) Bring a paper to the caller
(C) Change a reservation
(D) Fill out a form

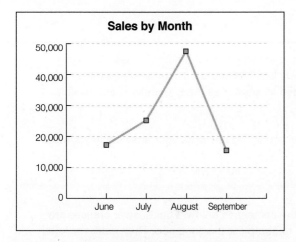

Sales by Month

www.walshassoc.com

B

MEDICAL RESEARCH

A   **FUN RUN**   C

Saturday, July 22
Bring the Whole Family.
Sponsored by Walsh&Assoc.

D

Tel. 555-6332

95. Where most likely does the speaker work?

(A) At a cable services firm
(B) At a home furnishings company
(C) At a telecommunications company
(D) At a travel agency

96. Look at the graphic. When was the sale held?

(A) June
(B) July
(C) August
(D) September

97. What will Rachel talk about?

(A) A branch grand opening
(B) A new sales staff member
(C) Some new sales strategies
(D) The disappointing sales numbers

98. Where most likely does the speaker work?

(A) At a print shop
(B) At a sports gym
(C) In a business office
(D) In a shopping mall

99. Look at the graphic. Where does the speaker want to put the Web address?

(A) A
(B) B
(C) C
(D) D

100. What will the listeners do next?

(A) Attend an event
(B) Get a flyer printed
(C) Give their opinions
(D) Help the speaker hand out flyers

This is the end of the Listening test. Turn to Part 5 in your test book.

TEST 4

GO ON TO THE NEXT PAGE

READING TEST

In the Reading test, you will read a variety of texts and answer several different types of reading comprehension questions. The entire Reading test will last 75 minutes. There are three parts, and directions are given for each part. You are encouraged to answer as many questions as possible within the time allowed.

You must mark your answers on the separate answer sheet. Do not write your answers in your test book.

PART 5

Directions: A word or phrase is missing in each of the sentences below. Four answer choices are given below each sentence. Select the best answer to complete the sentence. Then mark the letter (A), (B), (C), or (D) on your answer sheet.

101. The express train that the division head took to work was delayed an hour because of mechanical -------.
(A) harm
(B) mistake
(C) revision
(D) trouble

102. Long-term testing was required to refine the business risk management process to make it more ------- and consistent.
(A) predict
(B) predictability
(C) predictable
(D) prediction

103. Two poster samples were presented to the team leader, but ------- struck him and the team had to think of something else.
(A) both
(B) each
(C) either
(D) neither

104. The nonprofit organization was fortunate to receive ------- assistance in the amount of $30,000 from the local bank.
(A) educational
(B) informative
(C) monetary
(D) personnel

105. Sunshine Security offers free on-site estimates with no ------- to buy for your home or business.
(A) obligate
(B) obligation
(C) oblige
(D) obliged

106. ------- the scheduled staff meeting, the assistant had to print out all the handouts for everyone.
(A) As far as
(B) Except for
(C) Just about
(D) Prior to

107. Although he was offered the position of overseas branch manager last week, Ian Lee is ------- considering if he should take the opportunity.
(A) almost
(B) only
(C) still
(D) yet

108. Owing ------- to the cooler-than-usual summer, the sales of air conditioners have dropped nationwide.
(A) large
(B) largely
(C) largeness
(D) larger

109. A voucher ------- to this e-mail in pdf format; please show it to the hotel clerk when you check in.

(A) attached
(B) attaching
(C) is attached
(D) is attaching

110. The magazine article succeeded in ------- public attention to the rural agricultural issues.

(A) directing
(B) forcing
(C) promoting
(D) reaching

111. Naomi Boomer rushed to the Fairmont Hotel, ------- she was scheduled to see her client.

(A) when
(B) where
(C) which
(D) who

112. The administrative manager thought that Central Park would be perfectly ------- for the company's outdoor event.

(A) suit
(B) suitability
(C) suitable
(D) suitably

113. The most noticeable ------- of the new smartphone series, Xtreme, is a fingerprint sensor to authenticate the user.

(A) fascination
(B) feature
(C) trademark
(D) treasure

114. The tour bus will stop at a spot to enjoy a panoramic view of the city ------- at least 20 minutes.

(A) by
(B) for
(C) until
(D) with

115. The CEO was delighted to hear the news that his firm recorded the ------- sales last quarter.

(A) higher
(B) highest
(C) lower
(D) lowest

116. The marketing chief was truly impressed with the new recruit's ------- analysis of the survey results.

(A) considerate
(B) desperate
(C) respectful
(D) thorough

117. Thanks to the success of its new products, Catty, Inc. was able to reduce its accumulated ------- by 8.5 million dollars last year.

(A) lose
(B) losing
(C) losses
(D) lost

118. This Website allows anyone who is interested in our city cleaning project ------- its progress.

(A) follow
(B) followed
(C) following
(D) to follow

119. As he ------- talked about his colorful career, the lecturer did not realize he had already gone over his time.

(A) confidentially
(B) cooperatively
(C) enormously
(D) passionately

120. With technology advancing so fast every day, ------- is critical for professionals and job seekers to stay up-to-date in their fields.

(A) it
(B) one
(C) that
(D) there

GO ON TO THE NEXT PAGE

TEST 4

121. In order to fully ------- the vision of our clients, we make every effort to establish a close relationship with them.

(A) realizable
(B) realization
(C) realize
(D) realized

122. Working for more than 20 years at a charity organization, Tim Davidson gained ------- in fund-raising activities.

(A) commitment
(B) comprehension
(C) expertise
(D) access

123. Everyone seemed exhausted after the long discussion; ------- the supervisor wrapped up the meeting quickly.

(A) accordingly
(B) likewise
(C) meanwhile
(D) nonetheless

124. The local bakery is famous for its ------- display of assorted bread and pastries in the window.

(A) appetite
(B) appetizer
(C) appetizing
(D) appetizingly

125. Please forward us the amount -------, which is indicated on the invoice, by the end of the month.

(A) counted
(B) balanced
(C) owed
(D) refunded

126. The botanist says that River City Garden benefits ------- from the mild climate of the area.

(A) rich
(B) richer
(C) richly
(D) richness

127. The waterfront development project ------- done a week ago, but it is nowhere near completion yet.

(A) had been
(B) should have been
(C) was
(D) would be

128. The division head was really looking forward to reading Molly Shannon's report, but she had not ------- finished yet.

(A) barely
(B) far
(C) quite
(D) very

129. The Emerson Group is dedicated to ------- people with limited finances or other special needs.

(A) help
(B) helped
(C) helping
(D) helps

130. To enforce the security, Madison Corp. decided to ------- a security guard at each of its three entrances.

(A) layout
(B) moving
(C) premises
(D) station

PART 6

Directions: Read the texts that follow. A word, phrase, or sentence is missing in parts of each text. Four answer choices for each question are given below the text. Select the best answer to complete the text. Then mark the letter (A), (B), (C), or (D) on your answer sheet.

Questions 131-134 refer to the following notice.

Harvey Collins: A Special Cinema Screening

Saturday 15 July

From *West End Lovers* to *All the Beautiful Tomorrows*, Harvey Collins' acting career ------- over **131.** five decades. Now, for the first time, the Creststone Picture House Archives has ------- together **132.** highlights from Mr. Collins award-winning career. Some clips from the collection are never-before-seen outtakes and behind-the-scenes footage while filming in locations all over the world. Films will be introduced by Creststone Archives Officer Kathryn Villa. ------- . **133.**

Seats are limited at this free event, so book yours soon. Please follow the link below for ------- . **134.**

https://www.eventbook/harveycollins/creststonearchives.com

---

131. (A) had spanned
     (B) is spanned
     (C) spanned
     (D) spans

132. (A) gone
     (B) got
     (C) moved
     (D) put

133. (A) She is in charge of all public inquiries about the works.
     (B) She will also be taking audience questions after each film.
     (C) The Creststone Cinema is undergoing renovation at this time.
     (D) There is a $5 charge for each adult, while children are free.

134. (A) discounts
     (B) lists
     (C) purchases
     (D) reservations

GO ON TO THE NEXT PAGE

Questions 135-138 refer to the following e-mail.

To: cs@bbluggage.com
From: matildaikeda@greenmail.com
Subject: PakTek40
Date: August 10

To whom it may concern:

I bought your PakTek40 backpack about three weeks ago. I really like all the different pockets and pouches. Since I bike to work, I need a lot of ------- to carry my stuff. -------. I tried applying a bit of
135.   136.
oil on it, but it won't move at all. I'm not sure ------- I should send it back to you or take it back to the
137.
store where I bought it. Please let me know ------- to do to resolve this. Thank you.
138.

135. (A) compartments
     (B) efforts
     (C) parts
     (D) alternatives

136. (A) I discovered yesterday that the small pouch
         in front has a tear on the bottom.
     (B) Just after getting home from the store,
         I spilled paint on it.
     (C) The straps are too short for me to use it on
         my bicycle.
     (D) Unfortunately, the main zipper got stuck
         and I haven't been able to fix it.

137. (A) as
     (B) if
     (C) though
     (D) where

138. (A) how
     (B) what
     (C) when
     (D) whom

Citywide Ferry Service to Launch Soon

The Rockridge ------- 139. will be the first citywide ferry service to hit the water, with a launch coming in

October. The two other planned routes will begin early next year. -------. 140. The route includes a stop at

the City Center Terminal on the way from Rockridge to the ------ 141. stop, Pier 7 in Brantley. Rides will

cost $3.00, but fares won't be integrated with the rest of the city's transportation, meaning that riders

won't get a ------- 142. transfer from boat to subway.

---

139. (A) bridge
(B) direction
(C) map
(D) route

140. (A) City officials are hoping to attract tourists to the new park by offering free bus rides from the station.
(B) Rockridge is getting the first service since the area has among the longest commute times in the city.
(C) The city council is expected to vote on the new service's cost and stops at its next monthly meeting.
(D) The ferry was traveling at the usual speed when the accident occurred, according to safety inspectors.

141. (A) final
(B) finalized
(C) finalize
(D) finally

142. (A) fast
(B) free
(C) complete
(D) secure

GO ON TO THE NEXT PAGE

Questions 143-146 refer to the following notice.

The annual company picnic will be held at Doe Reservoir Beach on Saturday, July 3, starting at

11:00 AM. All employees and their families ------- . This year we again plan to ------- volleyball,
                                              143.   **144.**

softball, swimming, and water-skiing (with at least three boats in the water!). ------- . The company
                                                                                  145.

will provide basic barbecue fare (including vegetarian entrées) and sporting equipment, but all are

------- to bring along their own fun. And don't forget your dessert! Please let Luke Harris know by
146.

June 21 how many people you'll be bringing. Looking forward to a wonderful time!

---

143. (A) are invited
(B) invited
(C) inviting
(D) will be inviting

144. (A) promote
(B) feature
(C) operate
(D) sustain

145. (A) All of us were happy to welcome our newest
member, Josh, to the company last week.
(B) If you have any ideas about the ceremony,
please let Marie know before next Saturday.
(C) Of course, the dessert contest will likely be
the most popular part of the whole day.
(D) Those who have used goods to donate to
the charity, you can bring them up till July.

146. (A) encouraged
(B) encouragement
(C) encourager
(D) encourages

PART 7

Directions: In this part you will read a selection of texts, such as magazine and newspaper articles, e-mails, and instant messages. Each text or set of texts is followed by several questions. Select the best answer for each question and mark the letter (A), (B), (C), or (D) on your answer sheet.

Questions 147-148 refer to the following memo.

After 40 years of service with Parker&Sons, Mr. Howard Trumbo will retire at the end of this month. Mr. Trumbo is known in the industry for his humor and hard work, and has said that he wants to use his golden years to travel and see parts of the globe he has never experienced before. We wish him all the best.

Ms. Janet Newsome, who has been selected to fill the seat, is expected to lead the company to a successful future after being our group leader for the last five years. The transition will take a few weeks, as new team members get acquainted with new responsibilities and tasks.

147. What is the purpose of the notice?
   (A) To congratulate someone on winning a prize
   (B) To give information about merger transition
   (C) To inform staff about someone leaving the company
   (D) To welcome a new team member to the company

148. What is true about Ms. Newsome?
   (A) She retired a few weeks ago.
   (B) She will go on a business trip abroad.
   (C) She will transfer to a different office.
   (D) She has led a team over years.

GO ON TO THE NEXT PAGE

Questions 149-150 refer to the following text message chain.

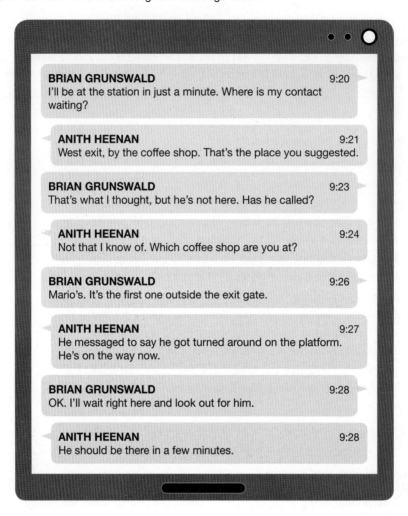

BRIAN GRUNSWALD   9:20
I'll be at the station in just a minute. Where is my contact waiting?

ANITH HEENAN   9:21
West exit, by the coffee shop. That's the place you suggested.

BRIAN GRUNSWALD   9:23
That's what I thought, but he's not here. Has he called?

ANITH HEENAN   9:24
Not that I know of. Which coffee shop are you at?

BRIAN GRUNSWALD   9:26
Mario's. It's the first one outside the exit gate.

ANITH HEENAN   9:27
He messaged to say he got turned around on the platform. He's on the way now.

BRIAN GRUNSWALD   9:28
OK. I'll wait right here and look out for him.

ANITH HEENAN   9:28
He should be there in a few minutes.

149. Where will Mr. Grunswald meet his contact?

(A) Beside the exit gate
(B) By a café
(C) Near the station
(D) On the platform

150. At 9:27, what does Ms. Heenan mean when she says, "he got turned around on the platform"?

(A) He got confused about the direction he needed to go.
(B) He started walking around the platform to look at things.
(C) He wanted to meet at a different place.
(D) He was walking in a large crowd.

The Conway Accounting Firm is proud to announce a getaway program for all employees! We want to show our appreciation for all the hard work you do during the year, and an office party isn't always the best answer, so starting the first week in September, we will be offering complimentary rotating day trips to various parts of the tri-state area.

These day trips will offer everyone a chance to relax, unwind him- or herself after the tough month of hard overtime. We want everyone to be able to enjoy these, so each trip will be within three hours of the office, and some of the choices include a day spa, first-class service at a lodge, or the virtual world at VirtuaPlex. There will be over 20 to choose from!

Everyone is eligible to use this program, but the dates are first come, first served; so don't wait too long. Sign up through the company intranet and look for the link marked "Employee Days" to select your day to getaway.

151. Why is the company offering day trips to the workers?

(A) As a reward for finishing a project
(B) As a thank-you for their effort
(C) As a thank-you for winning a prize
(D) As a year-end bonus for workers

152. What is NOT true about the programs?

(A) They are mainly outdoor activities.
(B) They are offered for free.
(C) They will not take long to travel to.
(D) They will start in early September.

TEST 4

GO ON TO THE NEXT PAGE

Questions 153-154 refer to the following article.

In potentially bad news for their rivals, it is being reported that TES Systems and Holiday Technologies are entering a new business partnership to work together to increase market share in the very competitive technology market. Combined, the two companies will create one of the largest computer software companies in the world.

If approved, TES Systems will begin making parts for Holiday in an effort to increase margin by using cost-effective technology. It is reported that TES Systems uses refurbished materials, greatly reducing costs for the manufacturer. Although both companies are reluctant to use the word "merger," it looks to be the case in this situation. TES spokesman Greg Harrison said, "This partnership will help both companies increase profits, while benefiting each company with lower production costs."

153. What is the article mainly about?

(A) Company's fiscal condition
(B) A potential merger
(C) Developing new technology
(D) Raising recycling awareness

154. How does TES Systems keep costs down?

(A) They have an efficient manufacturing process.
(B) They outsource their manufacturing overseas.
(C) They will cut the costs by half.
(D) They use cheaper materials for their parts.

Attention: All Dream Net Employees

After a few months of negotiation, we have made the decision to bring in some new equipment to our office, and we want everyone to get a chance to be introduced to it, as well as learn how to use it. Starting on Monday, you will notice a section of the second floor will be blocked off in preparation of its installation. What is this new equipment? We think you will be very excited to learn that we will now be able to do the highest level Medical 3D printing, right here in the building.

As many of our clients have stated, this new technique is something they are interested in bringing to their network of rehabilitation clinics, and we believe that we can be the number one provider of these services. A number of our clients have stated their preference to use this technology with those they are trying to assist, and with the Wish Foundation, we can help those dreams become a reality. Whether it be a 3D printed hand or leg, we can now do our very best to be a part of the team that supports everyone in need.

Once installed, there will be a few basic training days, and then some more intensive programs for teams working directly with the machines. Questions or any other comments should be sent to Jackie Stevens at extension 49 or e-mail her at: jstevens@dreamnet.com.

155. Where will the new equipment introduced?

(A) At a medical clinic
(B) At a new client's office
(C) At Dream Net's office
(D) At the Wish Foundation's office

156. What kind of work does the company most likely do?

(A) Aid people with disabilities
(B) Create images with high-tech scanners
(C) Sell office equipment
(D) Use technology to create servers

157. What will take place next week?

(A) The company will announce a partnership with the Wish Foundation.
(B) The company will discuss new product designs.
(C) The company will join a medical network.
(D) The company will offer training programs.

TEST 4

GO ON TO THE NEXT PAGE

Questions 158-160 refer to the following estimate.

Ken Brockton's Auto Repair

1928 Ball Road
Culver City, CA 90232
August 7

Damage	- Front left fender partially crushed - Front left headlight and casing - Bumper has cracks and paint scrapes
Repairs	- Repair and smooth front left fender - Replace headlight - Fix bumper cracks - Polish and wax bumper
Estimated Repair Time	4 days*
Estimated Cost	$850.00*
Insurance Details	- Automobile Insurance (pay for 60 percent) - Policy # 0323-268-9890
Auto Body Technician	Clark Flynn
Mechanic	Aaron Bernard
Customer	Nicholas Tunney 65 Arrow Lane Los Angeles, CA 90096 424-555-7404

Please note: Time and costs are subject to change. It is our policy to notify the customer of these changes before action is taken.

---

158. How many automobile parts will be fixed by the service?

(A) 1

(B) 2

(C) 3

(D) 4

159. When is the soonest the repairs could be finished?

(A) August 9

(B) August 11

(C) August 13

(D) August 15

160. What is indicated about the cost?

(A) An insurance company will partly cover it.

(B) It is due on August 30.

(C) It is the final amount.

(D) Mr. Tunney should pay $850.

Questions 161-163 refer to the following e-mail.

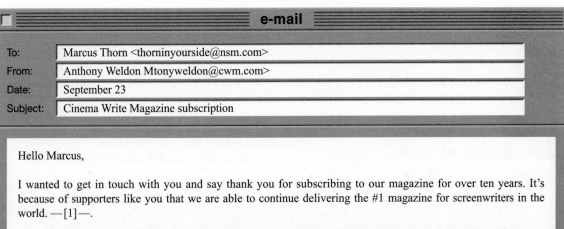

	e-mail
To:	Marcus Thorn <thorninyourside@nsm.com>
From:	Anthony Weldon Mtonyweldon@cwm.com>
Date:	September 23
Subject:	Cinema Write Magazine subscription

Hello Marcus,

I wanted to get in touch with you and say thank you for subscribing to our magazine for over ten years. It's because of supporters like you that we are able to continue delivering the #1 magazine for screenwriters in the world. —[1]—.

I noticed that your subscription is ending towards the end of next month, and thought I should see if you are ready to renew it today. Since you are in our top-rank subscribers, I am authorized to offer this "for your eyes only" special. —[2]—. With this special, you will receive a 60-percent discount on a two-year subscription, as well as receive commemorative copies of two original scripts used for the best picture winners from the last 50 years.

—[3]—. A chance to meet and interact with some of the hottest screenwriters in the business today! We will be having a Platinum Tier online course for everyone that wishes to attend. Here you can listen to experts, ask questions, and even get advice on how to best sell your script in today's market.

So what do you say, Marcus? Are you ready to continue with us and have the best to be delivered to your door every month? —[4]—.

Regards,
Anthony Weldon

161. When will Mr. Thorn's subscription expire?

(A) At the end of September
(B) At the beginning of October
(C) At the end of October
(D) At the beginning of November

162. Why is Mr. Thorn offered a special program?

(A) He has a top-level membership.
(B) He has donated a large amount of money.
(C) He has worked for the magazine for over ten years.
(D) He introduced the magazine to his friend.

163. In which of the positions marked [1], [2], [3], or [4] does the following sentence best belong?

"Act today and you will find something else coming to you as well."

(A) [1]
(B) [2]
(C) [3]
(D) [4]

GO ON TO THE NEXT PAGE

Mayor West and the City Council today announced a plan to resurrect the riverbank area of our fine city. —[1]—. The plan, called the "Banks of Riverdale," will remove many of the older warehouses and buildings and replace them with more family friendly attractions to help visitor experience of downtown Riverdale. There will also be at least two new parks built next to the river with playgrounds, swings, and more for everyone to enjoy. —[2]—.

More than half of citizens polled said that the downtown area needed to be beautified to enhance what many consider to be one of the best cities in the region already. —[3]—. Project leaders said that this complete renovation of the area was considered years ago, but could only be funded now, thanks to the successful projects involving the city's sports teams and the revenue they are generating.

According to Mayor West, initial parts of the project will begin this spring, with the areas closest to the sports stadiums being renovated or removed first. From there, leaders are hoping new restaurants and shopping areas will catch on with those new and familiar to the area. —[4]—.

164. How will the city improve the waterfront area?

(A) By building restaurants and tourist sites

(B) By creating an amusement park for kids

(C) By making the river water safer and cleaner

(D) By moving warehouses to another part of the city

165. What is mentioned about Riverdale?

(A) It is close to a lake.

(B) It is looking for professional sports teams.

(C) It is opening a new stadium soon.

(D) It is seen as one of the top cities in the area.

166. Why did the city government decide to proceed with the renovation plan?

(A) The voters in the area agreed it upon after many debates.

(B) Money was finally available for it.

(C) They wanted to upgrade the city before a big sporting event.

(D) They wanted to update the city's look after criticism from the media.

167. In which of the positions marked [1], [2], [3], or [4] does the following sentence best belong?

"We are excited to hear more about this project as the plans become finalized over the next few weeks."

(A) [1]

(B) [2]

(C) [3]

(D) [4]

Questions 168-171 refer to the following notice.

We at Streamline would like to inform all our customers and clients that we are moving to larger offices next month. We have had such an unbelievable growth in the last few years thanks to all of you, and we wanted to say thank you for the kind reviews and helping spread the word about us. We at Streamline believe that the customer is the reason that we are here, and we want to make sure that we are doing the best we can to serve you.

Starting on September 1, we will begin our move across town to our new offices located in the Geraldine district. Our offices will be on the corner of 97th and Taft Street, in the Houseman Building, on floors one through five. Parking for the Houseman offices is in the rear of the building offering almost one hundred spaces. The first floor will be where most of the day-to-day operations will take place, our second floor will be for meetings and interviews, but on floors three through five, we are going to have production studios, where we will have some stages and sets to help create the perfect ideas for your business.

As we begin our transition into our new headquarters, we will make sure to have representatives at both the old and new locations, just in case you have questions. You can contact us via our Website at www.streamline.com or by calling 555-2389.

168. What is the reason Streamline has decided to change offices?

(A) The business has had much success recently.
(B) The customers asked them to move closer to downtown.
(C) They needed to make room for their new products.
(D) They streamlined their business operations.

169. Where should people park when visiting the new office?

(A) Behind the building
(B) In front of the building
(C) Next to the building
(D) Underneath the building

170. Which floor will a client visit if they give a presentation?

(A) On the first floor
(B) On the second floor
(C) On the third floor
(D) On the fourth floor

171. Why will some employees stay at the old office?

(A) To answer customers' questions
(B) To clean up old equipment
(C) To complete ongoing projects
(D) To meet some important customers

GO ON TO THE NEXT PAGE

Questions 172-175 refer to the following online discussion.

⬤	**GREG HUNT**	Hello everyone. Any news about the exhibition next month?	11:30
⬤	**TONY PLAYER**	I received an e-mail about it yesterday. Didn't you get it?	11:31
⬤	**JIM JONSON**	I got it. Said we were all going to be sharing a room. Is that right?	11:33
⬤	**GREG HUNT**	What? How can we fit four of us in one room? We'll be stuffed in like sardines!	11:34
⬤	**TONY PLAYER**	How do they expect that to work? The rooms only have two beds.	11:36
⬤	**JIM JONSON**	That is a problem. I don't want to sleep on the floor for a week either.	11:37
⬤	**RON BURKE**	I'm here now. I asked management about the room. They said they would look into it.	11:39
⬤	**GREG HUNT**	Great. OK, let's think about how we will present the products this year.	11:39
⬤	**TONY PLAYER**	I was thinking that we should have some kind of interactive display.	11:40
⬤	**JIM JONSON**	I like that. Then people can try it out as we talk about it.	11:42
⬤	**RON BURKE**	Good plan. How about Tony and Jim handle the first presentation?	11:42
⬤	**TONY PLAYER**	OK. I'll work on it this afternoon.	11:44
⬤	**JIM JONSON**	What is the game plan for length of the demo? We don't want to go long.	11:47
⬤	**GREG HUNT**	No more than 10 to 15 minutes. We want as many people to see it as possible.	11:48
⬤	**TONY PLAYER**	We should prevent anyone from taking photos at the event as well.	11:49
⬤	**RON BURKE**	Of course. We wouldn't want competitors to "borrow" any ideas from us.	11:50
⬤	**GREG HUNT**	OK, let's get to work and meet again Friday with how we want to proceed.	11:51

172. What is the team preparing for?

    (A) A presentation for a client

    (B) An industry event

    (C) A competition

    (D) A sales meeting

173. Why did Mr. Burke contact management?

    (A) To ask about the project

    (B) To lower the cost

    (C) To request new equipment

    (D) To talk about the room size

174. Who will give the first speech?

    (A) Mr. Burke and Mr. Player

    (B) Mr. Hunt and Mr. Burke

    (C) Mr. Jonson and Mr. Hunt

    (D) Mr. Jonson and Mr. Player

175. At 11:47, what does Mr. Jonson mean when he says, "We don't want to go long"?

    (A) He does not like photo sessions.

    (B) He expects the event will end early.

    (C) He is reluctant to travel far.

    (D) He prefers the demo to be short.

GO ON TO THE NEXT PAGE

Questions 176-180 refer to the following e-mails.

To	Brian Sinclair
From	John Sheridan
Subject	New company policy
Date	July 17

Hi Brian,

Here's the draft for the new company summer shape-up program. I would appreciate some feedback from you on it.

Now that the summer is here, we would like to introduce an exciting new way for employees at Lang&Huston to begin the day. Starting at 8:00 AM, we will begin a 30-minute warm-up exercise class for everyone to attend. We are pushing everyone to be as healthy and active as possible this year! We will have a special guest to kick off our first week of morning sessions, but I don't want to spoil the surprise.

This will be a great way to stretch both our bodies and minds. After that, we will hold an office meeting to discuss what we can do to improve our daily missions. We want everyone to attend, so please make sure to be in Meeting Room A by 8:00 AM, starting Monday the 3rd.

John Sheridan
VP of Personnel
Lang&Huston, Inc.

To	John Sheridan
From	Brian Sinclair
Subject	RE: New company policy
Date	July 17

Hi John,

I am encouraged to read your e-mail about the morning shape-up program; however, I think we may have to make some changes to it. When I read it, I felt as though it was mandatory, and we cannot force anyone to join a workout class at work. How about we offer free classes to anyone that wants to have them? They would have to be offered at a few different times, since we can't exclude anyone from the opportunity. Also, we probably should also remove the special guest mystery. If you have someone special booked to make everyone excited to join, we should use that to encourage attendance. And why don't we schedule the sessions on the first and last day of the week, so we can begin and end the week with some team building?

Brian Sinclair
Sales Manager
Lang&Huston, Inc.

176. What does Mr. Sheridan want employees to do?

(A) Be industry leaders in health services

(B) Be more competitive with each other

(C) Have a better sales record than last year

(D) Have a workout with colleagues

177. In the first e-mail, the word "spoil" in paragraph 2, line 4, is closest in meaning to

(A) assist

(B) create

(C) repair

(D) ruin

178. When does Mr. Sinclair propose revealing a special guest?

(A) As late as possible

(B) At the first session

(C) Next Monday

(D) Sometime before August 3

179. What does Mr. Sinclair offer to do?

(A) Offer classes for recruits

(B) Open various times

(C) Register in advance

(D) Check personal preferences

180. Which days does Mr. Sinclair believe would be best for the classes?

(A) On Monday and Tuesday

(B) On Monday and Friday

(C) On Thursday and Friday

(D) On Saturday and Sunday

TEST 4

GO ON TO THE NEXT PAGE

Office Supply Wholesale Order Form

Name: Wolffe Marketing
Address: 66 Order Ave
Springfield, IL
62702
Date: June 24
Invoice #: C2032

Shipping Address: 2002 Republic Boulevard
Nashville, TN
37201

Item	Qty.	Unit Price	Total Price
Printer paper (case)	10	$40.00	$400.00
Office desk 30x48x23	10	$100.00	$1,000.00
Office chairs (black)	10	$60.00	$600.00
Total			$2,000.00
Member Discount*: 10%			$1,800.00 (#OSW23789)
Tax**: 10%			$180.00
Total Cost			$1,980.00

*Member discount requires membership #
**No sales tax for orders shipped to KY, TN, MS, or AL

---

e-mail

To:	Customer Service <csr@osw.com>
From:	Leila Saldana <leilasaldana@packmail.com>
Subject:	Order #OSW23789
Date:	July 1

Attn: Customer Service Department

Our office ordered some new furniture for our new staff (order #2032) from your online store. The order was placed last month.

Everything arrived fine at our receiving address today, but there are two errors that do need attention. The office chairs that we ordered were black, but all ten that we received were red. While these are very nice chairs, we would prefer something a little more suited for our office design. Another problem is about the sales tax on the items I have bought. Can I get a price adjustment for that?

We would like to exchange the chairs as soon as possible, as our new employees start at the office on the 12th. I would like an authorization label to switch the chairs, as well as reimbursement for the shipping cost for returning them to your warehouse.

Thank you very much for your attention to this issue.

Sincerely,
Leila Saldana
Floor Manager
Wolffe Marketing

181. What can be inferred in the invoice?

(A) The billing and shipping addresses are the same.

(B) A shipping charge has been added.

(C) Each item has the same quantity.

(D) Only office furniture has been ordered.

182. How long did Wolffe Marketing wait for the supplies?

(A) For a few days

(B) For about a week

(C) For a few weeks

(D) For about a month

183. How much will Ms. Saldana get back?

(A) $150

(B) $180

(C) $200

(D) $380

184. What is Ms. Saldana requesting from the supply company?

(A) A discount on their next purchase

(B) Approval to return the order

(C) An exchange permission form

(D) Reimbursement for the entire order

185. What was the problem with the order?

(A) The color of an item was wrong.

(B) The items were shipped to the wrong address.

(C) The number of items was wrong.

(D) The price of the chairs was incorrect.

GO ON TO THE NEXT PAGE

TEST 4

Questions 186-190 refer to the following advertisement, application, and Web review.

Just moved and need your cable TV and Internet service set up? Having trouble with your cable services? Call Jim the Cable Guy today.

- Low prices
- Convenient service times
- Locally owned and operated

The following packages are available to most customers within the region.

TV+Internet $50/month	Internet only $25/month
- Includes 200 channels and HD for free - Standard speed Internet	- Standard speed Internet - Free installation (online orders only)
TV only $40/month	**Deluxe $75/month**
- Includes 200 channels - Extra charge for HD	- Includes 250 channels and HD - High-speed Internet and free installation

Jim the Cable Guy
Service Application

Name: Candace Bauman
Best time of day*: 12:00-1:00 Monday, Wednesday, or
Thursday, before noon on weekends
Address: 3801 San Carlos Drive Esposito, California
Phone: 555-2839
Type of residence: Apartment

*We can't guarantee we'll make it at these times, but we strive to match your schedule.

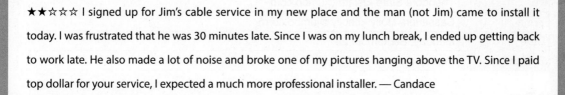

★★☆☆ I signed up for Jim's cable service in my new place and the man (not Jim) came to install it today. I was frustrated that he was 30 minutes late. Since I was on my lunch break, I ended up getting back to work late. He also made a lot of noise and broke one of my pictures hanging above the TV. Since I paid top dollar for your service, I expected a much more professional installer. — Candace

186. What is mentioned about the owner of Jim the Cable Guy?

(A) He has an engineering degree.
(B) He has owned the business for decades.
(C) He lives in the area.
(D) He recently moved to a new place.

187. In the application, the word "strive" in line 8 is closest in meaning to

(A) affect
(B) compete
(C) oppose
(D) try

188. When did an employee of Jim the Cable Guy most likely visit Ms. Bauman's home?

(A) On Monday morning
(B) On Wednesday noon
(C) On Friday noon
(D) On Saturday morning

189. Which package did Ms. Bauman get?

(A) Deluxe
(B) Internet only
(C) TV and Internet
(D) TV only

190. What did Ms. Bauman complain about?

(A) The behavior of the installer
(B) The cable service price
(C) The quality of her TV picture
(D) The speed of her Internet

TEST 4

GO ON TO THE NEXT PAGE

Questions 191-195 refer to the following e-mails and list.

To	Theodore Slate <tslate@jumbo.com>
From	Cassandra Holly <cholly@jumbo.com>
Date	Monday, September 26
Subject	Pop-up store

Hi Theo,

I was wondering if you could do some research for me? I want to put some of our top-selling products in a pop-up store somewhere in town for the week-long vacation starting on October 6. We've done well selling our products online, which is good. I'm just not sure how many residents around here know about our products. Could you look around and see if there are any empty storefronts or even outdoor venues where we could set up shop? Thanks.

Cassie

---

e-mail

To:	Cassandra Holly <cholly@jumbo.com>
From:	Customer Service <cs@steelworks.com>Theodore Slate <tslate@jumbo.com>
Date:	Monday, October 3
Subject:	Re: Pop-up store

Hi Cassandra,

I'm really excited about your idea to feature our homemade bags in a visible way in Oaktown. I found several places that might be of interest for the pop-up store. I've attached a list to this message. I'm thinking maybe the first or second would be the best, since they are the biggest and are available now. Although from a traffic standpoint, the last one could be perfect since it's on a busy corner downtown.

Let me know what you think. I can set up appointments with the owners of these places if you'd like to see any of them.

Theo

Type Property	Location	Size	Details
Storefront	391 Main Street	45 ㎡	Available now
Mall space	Oaktown – east wing	42 ㎡	Expensive
Kiosk near station	Greenbay Station exit	31 ㎡	Security concerns
Storefront	208 Redmond Blvd.	40 ㎡	Available mid Oct.

191. Why does Ms. Holly want to have a pop-up store?

(A) She has extra merchandise to sell.

(B) She has just started her business.

(C) She hopes to gain more local customers.

(D) She wants to introduce a new product line.

192. What type of product does Mr. Slate's company make?

(A) Clothing

(B) Cosmetics

(C) Jewelry

(D) Purses

193. Why would the location on the Redmond Boulevard likely not be chosen?

(A) It is not available at the right time.

(B) It is too expensive.

(C) It is too far away.

(D) It is too small.

194. What does Mr. Slate offer to do?

(A) Do more research

(B) Make a list of properties

(C) Make some appointments

(D) Show Ms. Holly some new products

195. What is mentioned about the kiosk?

(A) It is close to a mall.

(B) It is downtown.

(C) It is the largest location.

(D) It might not be safe.

TEST 4

GO ON TO THE NEXT PAGE

THE BROWN HOTEL
... in the heart of Center Grove

The Brown Hotel is one of Center Grove's most well-known landmarks, just off of King Square near the convention center. We feature an in-house coffee shop and a full-service dining room. Here are the specials for the month of September.

- Stay two weeknights for the price of one.*
- Groups booking 3 or more double rooms can receive a 20% off discount.**

   *Offer does not apply to Mondays if it is a national holiday.

   **Not to be combined with any other offer.

Itinerary for Exhibition in Center Grove
September 23 – 25

Saturday, September 23	
10:00 AM	Arrive in Center Grove
11:00 AM	Set up booth for exhibition
1:00 – 5:00 PM	Exhibition at Welch Convention Center
Sunday, September 24	
10:00 AM	Doors open at exhibition
10:00 AM – 4:00 PM	Exhibition
7:00 PM	Dinner with your team
Monday, September 25 (national holiday)	
9:00 AM	Breakfast meeting with Center Grove director
11:00 AM	Campaign planning with Center Grove team (working lunch)
3:30 PM	Flight back to Winchester

To	Kate Johnson <kjohnson@mytex.com>
From	Bradley Dexter <bdexter@mytex.com>
Date	Monday, September 11
Subject	Your upcoming trip

Hi Kate,

I understand you're going to the exhibition at Center Grove. I went last year and it was really fun. Our people at the branch office are very nice and they will show you a good time. Be sure to ask the director to take you to this great breakfast place right on the water called Stanley's. The omelets are fantastic.

Anyway, I found this advertisement about the Brown Hotel. That's where we stayed last year. It's really convenient to the exhibition venue and the views of the bay are great, so ask for a bayside room.

Hope you can get one of the two discounts they're offering this month.
Have a nice trip.

Bradley Dexter

196. What is mentioned about the Brown Hotel?

(A) It has just been renovated.

(B) It is a renowned place.

(C) It offers 24-hour room service.

(D) It serves mostly businesspeople.

197. What will Ms. Johnson and her team be doing around noon on Monday?

(A) Discussing a business strategy

(B) Eating out

(C) Taking down the booth

(D) Working at the exhibition

198. Why will the team not be eligible for the hotel's half price discount?

(A) They are not staying long enough.

(B) They are staying at the hotel on the weekend.

(C) They do not have a membership card for the hotel.

(D) They will not book enough rooms.

199. When could Ms. Johnson go to Stanley's with her colleagues?

(A) On Saturday lunchtime

(B) On Sunday morning

(C) On Sunday evening

(D) On Monday morning

200. What does Mr. Dexter recommend doing at the hotel?

(A) Asking for extra pillows

(B) Getting a room on a certain side

(C) Going to the music hall

(D) Visiting a gift shop

Stop! This is the end of the test. If you finish before time is called, you may go back to Parts 5, 6, and 7 and check your work.

Actual Test 5

휴대폰은 OFF!
LC MP3는 ON!
2시간만 집중!

Check ▸ 시작 시간 _____ : _____

▸ 종료 시간 _____ : _____

LC MP3 바로듣기

LISTENING TEST

In the Listening test, you will be asked to demonstrate how well you understand spoken English. The entire Listening test will last approximately 45 minutes. There are four parts, and directions are given for each part. You must mark your answers on the separate answer sheet. Do not write your answers in your test book.

PART 1

Directions: For each question in this part, you will hear four statements about a picture in your test book. When you hear the statements, you must select the one statement that best describes what you see in the picture. Then find the number of the question on your answer sheet and mark your answer. The statements will not be printed in your test book and will be spoken only one time.

Statement (C), "They're sitting at the table," is the best description of the picture, so you should select answer (C) and mark it on your answer sheet.

1.

2.

GO ON TO THE NEXT PAGE

TEST 5

3.

4.

5.

6.

GO ON TO THE NEXT PAGE

TEST 5

PART 2

Directions: You will hear a question or statement and three responses spoken in English. They will not be printed in your test book and will be spoken only one time. Select the best response to the question or statement and mark the letter (A), (B), or (C) on your answer sheet.

7. Mark your answer on your answer sheet.

8. Mark your answer on your answer sheet.

9. Mark your answer on your answer sheet.

10. Mark your answer on your answer sheet.

11. Mark your answer on your answer sheet.

12. Mark your answer on your answer sheet.

13. Mark your answer on your answer sheet.

14. Mark your answer on your answer sheet.

15. Mark your answer on your answer sheet.

16. Mark your answer on your answer sheet.

17. Mark your answer on your answer sheet.

18. Mark your answer on your answer sheet.

19. Mark your answer on your answer sheet.

20. Mark your answer on your answer sheet.

21. Mark your answer on your answer sheet.

22. Mark your answer on your answer sheet.

23. Mark your answer on your answer sheet.

24. Mark your answer on your answer sheet.

25. Mark your answer on your answer sheet.

26. Mark your answer on your answer sheet.

27. Mark your answer on your answer sheet.

28. Mark your answer on your answer sheet.

29. Mark your answer on your answer sheet.

30. Mark your answer on your answer sheet.

31. Mark your answer on your answer sheet.

PART 3

Directions: You will hear some conversations between two or more people. You will be asked to answer three questions about what the speakers say in each conversation. Select the best response to each question and mark the letter (A), (B), (C), or (D) on your answer sheet. The conversations will not be printed in your test book and will be spoken only one time.

32. What are the speakers discussing?

(A) A company celebration
(B) An annual salary
(C) A leadership change
(D) A new product's sales

33. What did the man do last year?

(A) He got promoted.
(B) He moved departments.
(C) He overspent on a project.
(D) He planned an event.

34. What did the company president tell the woman to do?

(A) Book a larger venue
(B) Make a payment
(C) Increase sales soon
(D) Use less money

35. What is the purpose of the call?

(A) To cancel an appointment
(B) To change an appointment
(C) To confirm an appointment
(D) To make an appointment

36. When will the man go to the woman's office?

(A) This morning
(B) This afternoon
(C) Tomorrow at 3:00
(D) Tomorrow at 6:00

37. What does the woman remind the man about?

(A) His annual checkup
(B) His appointment next week
(C) His insurance information
(D) His payment from last month

38. Why is the man selling his couch?

(A) He bought a new one.
(B) He is moving overseas.
(C) It is rather old.
(D) It is too big for his new apartment.

39. What can be said about the woman?

(A) She has been in the man's apartment before.
(B) She is an apartment owner.
(C) She is having a party soon.
(D) She just moved to a new town.

40. What does the man imply when he says, "I'm showing it to somebody this afternoon"?

(A) He does not want the woman to buy his apartment.
(B) He may have found a buyer for the couch.
(C) He thinks someone is interested in his apartment.
(D) He wants to sell the couch quickly.

41. What is the woman's difficulty in making a decision?

(A) She has no suitable candidates.
(B) She has pressure from her boss.
(C) She has time pressure.
(D) She has two good choices.

42. Where do the speakers work?

(A) At a factory
(B) At a clothing store
(C) At a fast food restaurant
(D) At a supermarket

43. What does the man suggest?

(A) Advertising the position online
(B) Going to different stores to get data
(C) Having a joint interview
(D) Reading an essay from the candidates

GO ON TO THE NEXT PAGE

44. What is the problem about the event?

(A) It is largely over budget.

(B) The speakers cannot find the venue.

(C) The weather may be bad.

(D) There are not enough participants.

45. What does the man say he will do?

(A) Call a staff meeting

(B) Inform the media about the event

(C) Post a notice on the staff bulletin board

(D) Put information on an internal network

46. When will the event probably be held?

(A) Today

(B) Thursday

(C) Friday

(D) Next Monday

---

47. Where does the man most likely work?

(A) At a conference center

(B) At a hotel

(C) At a travel agency

(D) At an airline

48. What is the purpose of the woman's trip?

(A) Wedding

(B) Business

(C) Vacation

(D) Family gathering

49. What will the woman give the man next?

(A) Her contact information

(B) Her credit card number

(C) Her flight information

(D) Her reservation number

---

50. What is mentioned about the man?

(A) He is new at the office.

(B) He wants to be president.

(C) He was assigned a new project.

(D) He would like to help the woman.

51. What does the woman mean when she says, "you have my vote"?

(A) She hopes the man will run in an election.

(B) She supports the man's idea.

(C) She wants to elect the man to a managerial position.

(D) She will give the man a good review.

52. Where will the man most likely go next?

(A) To the City Hall

(B) To the president's office

(C) To the voting place

(D) To the woman's office

---

53. What was changed over the weekend?

(A) The computer network

(B) The department spaces

(C) The employees' desks

(D) The office location

54. What does the woman say she needs to do?

(A) Finish her report

(B) Find her presentation notes

(C) Get onto her computer

(D) Give the man his assignment

55. What does the man offer to do for the woman?

(A) Call the IT department

(B) Change her password

(C) Listen to her speech

(D) Show her around the office

---

56. Why is the woman surprised?

(A) Her boss is leaving the company.
(B) Robert was late to the meeting.
(C) The applicants were not qualified.
(D) There are many job candidates.

57. What does Robert suggest?

(A) Advertising on more Websites
(B) Asking for some help
(C) Calling some universities
(D) Scheduling interviews soon

58. What will Tony probably do next?

(A) Fill out an application
(B) Enter data into a computer
(C) Interview a candidate
(D) Look through some applicants

---

59. Who most likely is the man?

(A) A board member
(B) A caterer
(C) A clerical assistant
(D) An organizer

60. What event is the woman calling about?

(A) A birthday party
(B) A retirement party
(C) An awards banquet
(D) An executive gathering

61. What will the man send the woman?

(A) A brochure
(B) A menu
(C) A price estimate
(D) A wine list

Rockford Natural History Museum Ticket Prices
•Regular Exhibits $18
−with audio tour $22
•Dinosaur Exhibit $10
−plus movie $14

62. Look at the graphic. How much did the man pay for his ticket?

(A) $10
(B) $14
(C) $18
(D) $22

63. What does the woman say about the movie?

(A) It explains the special exhibits.
(B) It has some special effects.
(C) It is very long.
(D) It runs every hour.

64. What does the man say he will do?

(A) Come back to the museum later
(B) Consider the woman's suggestion
(C) Join a museum club
(D) Watch the movie another day

GO ON TO THE NEXT PAGE

TEST 5

Mystery	Biography
Science Fiction	Horror
History	Fantasy

65. What does the woman say about the book?

(A) It has gotten mixed reviews.

(B) It is difficult to read.

(C) It is popular.

(D) It is set in Europe.

66. Why does the man want to read the book?

(A) He needs to read it for an assignment.

(B) He wants to see if it is worth recommending.

(C) He read a rare review of the book.

(D) The woman highly recommended it.

67. Look at the graphic. What type of book is the man looking for?

(A) Fantasy

(B) History

(C) Horror

(D) Mystery

— Inventory List —

Item No.	Fabric	Amount in Stock
C92	Cotton	18 meters
Ch19	Chiffon	1 meter
G05	Gauze	10 meters
W83	Wool	7 meters

68. Where is this conversation most likely taking place?

(A) At a restaurant

(B) At a clothing store

(C) At a fabric store

(D) At an art store

69. What does the woman say she is doing this weekend?

(A) Going to a gallery

(B) Completing a piece of art

(C) Checking inventory

(D) Working at her company

70. Look at the graphic. Which fabric will the woman buy?

(A) C92

(B) Ch19

(C) G05

(D) W83

PART 4

Directions: You will hear some talks given by a single speaker. You will be asked to answer three questions about what the speaker says in each talk. Select the best response to each question and mark the letter (A), (B), (C), or (D) on your answer sheet. The talks will not be printed in your test book and will be spoken only one time.

---

71. What event is the speaker attending next week?

(A) A building dedication
(B) A local festival
(C) A restaurant opening
(D) A winery tour

72. Why does the speaker ask the listener to contact her?

(A) To answer a question about the event
(B) To confirm an additional guest
(C) To cancel her attendance
(D) To give directions to the event

73. Who does the speaker mention is coming to visit?

(A) A business contact
(B) A business owner
(C) A friend
(D) A relative

---

74. Who most likely are the listeners?

(A) Book club members
(B) Bookstore employees
(C) Community leaders
(D) Cooking club members

75. According to the speaker, what will Mr. Pascal be doing soon?

(A) Demonstrating a skill
(B) Reading from his book
(C) Signing his book
(D) Taking questions from listeners

76. When did Mr. Pascal's interest in his chosen field start?

(A) After he wrote his first book
(B) In his childhood
(C) When he left France for the first time
(D) While he was in cooking school

77. Where is the announcement being made?

(A) On a boat
(B) On a tour bus
(C) On a train
(D) On an airplane

78. What is located near the snack bar?

(A) A tourist information counter
(B) Stairs to the exit
(C) The bathrooms
(D) The only available exit

79. Who speaks multiple languages?

(A) Restaurant servers
(B) Staff at a service center
(C) The snack bar employees
(D) The crew of the boat

---

80. What product is being advertised?

(A) A learning app
(B) A book series
(C) A language camp program
(D) A language private lesson

81. According to the advertisement, how does *Say Hello!* keep users motivated?

(A) By offering discounts regularly
(B) By offering level-up incentives
(C) By using interesting images
(D) By using popular music

82. What is mentioned about EduLang?

(A) It has received honors.
(B) It is a start-up in the software industry.
(C) It is the most popular company in the industry.
(D) It was started by technology experts.

GO ON TO THE NEXT PAGE

TEST 5

83. What department does the speaker work in?

(A) Marketing

(B) Payroll

(C) Personnel

(D) Sales

84. What does the speaker mean when she says, "I was hoping to finalize everything later today"?

(A) She wants Dominic to call her soon.

(B) She wants Dominic to hurry up.

(C) She wants help on her final report.

(D) She wants to leave early.

85. Who needs to visit the speaker's office today?

(A) Dominic

(B) George

(C) The marketing boss

(D) The payroll director

---

86. What type of radio program does the speaker host?

(A) Classical music

(B) Local news

(C) Rock and roll

(D) Talk show

87. According to the speaker, who is Marshall Young?

(A) A bank employee

(B) A local business leader

(C) An orchestra conductor

(D) A radio station worker

88. What does the speaker imply when he says, "Seating is limited"?

(A) Listeners are eligible to reserve special tickets.

(B) Listeners can get only front seats.

(C) Listeners can reserve tickets for Wednesday only.

(D) Listeners have to get tickets soon.

---

89. What is the main purpose of the call?

(A) To congratulate a colleague

(B) To inform a colleague of an award

(C) To invite a colleague out for dinner

(D) To request help from a colleague

90. What does the speaker mean when she says, "No one deserves this more than you"?

(A) Everyone hoped the listener would win.

(B) No other worker should get the award.

(C) There is no one else on the speaker's team.

(D) We all deserved a better result.

91. What is mentioned about the speaker's company this year?

(A) It expanded to other places.

(B) It hired many people.

(C) It moved to a new location.

(D) It won an award.

---

92. What kind of business is Stronghold, Inc.?

(A) Information security

(B) Investment

(C) Law firm

(D) Real estate

93. Why has this year been good for the company?

(A) They expanded overseas.

(B) They hired experienced employees.

(C) Their reputation increased.

(D) Their sales hit a record high.

94. What is the speaker offering the listeners?

(A) Management positions

(B) Extra security

(C) Larger offices

(D) Year-end bonuses

Store Sales by Week
(November)

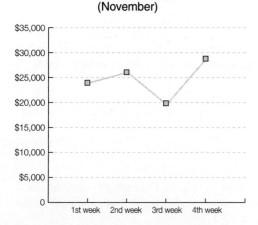

95. What type of business is the speaker in?

(A) Hospitality
(B) Manufacturing
(C) Retail sales
(D) Construction

96. Look at the graphic. When will the store likely relocate?

(A) The 1st week in November
(B) The 2nd week in November
(C) The 3rd week in November
(D) The 4th week in November

97. What does the speaker say about sales?

(A) They are about the same year to year.
(B) They go up during seasonal campaigns.
(C) They have been lower than usual this year.
(D) They vary greatly within a month.

DIAMOND DEPARTMENT STORE
FLOOR DIRECTORY

4th Floor	Women's Wear
3rd Floor	Shoes
2nd Floor	Men's Wear
1st Floor	Cosmetics

98. How often does the store have a sale?

(A) Every quarter
(B) Every six months
(C) Once a month
(D) Once a year

99. Look at the graphic. Where can a customer receive an extra discount today?

(A) On the 1st floor
(B) On the 2nd floor
(C) On the 3rd floor
(D) On the 4th floor

100. What would a customer do for a chance to win a prize?

(A) Fill out a survey
(B) Purchase a minimum amount of goods
(C) Show a coupon
(D) Use their loyalty card

This is the end of the Listening test. Turn to Part 5 in your test book.

GO ON TO THE NEXT PAGE

TEST 5

READING TEST

In the Reading test, you will read a variety of texts and answer several different types of reading comprehension questions. The entire Reading test will last 75 minutes. There are three parts, and directions are given for each part. You are encouraged to answer as many questions as possible within the time allowed.

You must mark your answers on the separate answer sheet. Do not write your answers in your test book.

PART 5

Directions: A word or phrase is missing in each of the sentences below. Four answer choices are given below each sentence. Select the best answer to complete the sentence. Then mark the letter (A), (B), (C), or (D) on your answer sheet.

101. Cosmos House is a leading firm in the industry with a staff of over 200 ------- architects and designers.

(A) advanced
(B) calculated
(C) interested
(D) talented

102. Immigration ------- do not permit foreigners to work in the country without the appropriate status.

(A) regulate
(B) regulation
(C) regulations
(D) regulatory

103. ------- on Mr. Gibson's team contributed to the success of the new shoe line.

(A) Everyone
(B) Whoever
(C) One another
(D) Each other

104. We welcome your ------- to help us continually provide you with first-class service.

(A) motivation
(B) feedback
(C) invitation
(D) operation

105. This week only, easybuy.com is offering special discounts on ------- items.

(A) selected
(B) selecting
(C) selection
(D) selections

106. ------- the software company is relatively unknown, its new product could help it become popular.

(A) Although
(B) Despite
(C) In addition
(D) Until

107. While the delivery fee was supposed to be $300, the supplier charged the retailer $100 ------- on the bill.

(A) above
(B) high
(C) more
(D) up

108. Our customer care line is available seven days a week, ------- that no question goes unanswered.

(A) convincing
(B) deciding
(C) ensuring
(D) featuring

109. ------- for the marketing team, the sales campaign went exceptionally well and received wide media coverage.

(A) Fortunate
(B) Fortunately
(C) Fortune
(D) Fortunes

110. Wayfair Company is committed to ------- the latest software at affordable prices.

(A) provide
(B) provided
(C) provision
(D) providing

111. According to the specialist, wind turbines generally work ------- better in open, rural areas than mounted on rooftops in cities.

(A) far
(B) further
(C) less
(D) more

112. If you are a ------- to the digital version of *Movie Times*, you have access to our online archives.

(A) subscribe
(B) subscriber
(C) subscribers
(D) subscription

113. The division head was having a hard time choosing white ------- light gray for the wallpaper of his new office.

(A) and
(B) but
(C) nor
(D) or

114. The CEO always says that conducting ------- research and analysis can minimize the risk of failure.

(A) complicated
(B) redundant
(C) tentative
(D) thorough

115. Mark Tyler worked at Zane Industries in the early years of the company, ------- there were only a few employees.

(A) when
(B) where
(C) which
(D) whose

116. Despite her colleagues' enthusiasm about the merger, the news was ------- little interest to Lisa Olsen.

(A) at
(B) in
(C) of
(D) with

117. Although the job offer was almost too ------- to pass up, Lee Boule was reluctant to commute to a different state.

(A) attracting
(B) attraction
(C) attractive
(D) attractively

118. Please note that the accounting department will only provide ------- for expenses when a receipt is included with the form.

(A) reassessment
(B) reference
(C) reimbursement
(D) replica

119. As Amy Lynn ------- the speech every day since last week, her colleagues believe she is ready to deliver it.

(A) could have practiced
(B) had practiced
(C) has practiced
(D) practices

120. ------- your inquiry about joining our association, we will be more than happy to discuss membership details.

(A) Because
(B) Likewise
(C) Regarding
(D) With

GO ON TO THE NEXT PAGE

TEST 5

121. Milan Properties acquired Colton Tech's former sites, which ------- nearly one million square feet.
(A) gross
(B) net
(C) sum
(D) total

122. If the administrative manager had ------- his client Ms. Ford on the street, he would have said hello to her.
(A) recognition
(B) recognize
(C) recognized
(D) recognizing

123. If you return the product without a receipt, you will be given a store credit, which can be applied ------- your next purchase.
(A) above
(B) over
(C) through
(D) toward

124. Sue Ellis became a section chief three years ago and was ------- promoted to the sales manager the next year.
(A) chronologically
(B) continually
(C) sincerely
(D) subsequently

125. The last chapter of ZDE Steel's corporate history features the company's ------- in the 1980s.
(A) expand
(B) expandable
(C) expander
(D) expansion

126. Under the company regulations, factory inspections have to be carried out ------- every two months.
(A) during
(B) once
(C) then
(D) within

127. With the most ------- carry-on luggage, travelers will avoid the inconveniences during the trip.
(A) rigorous
(B) comparable
(C) vigorous
(D) durable

128. The automobile company has announced a recall of over one million cars because their airbags were ------- manufactured.
(A) defect
(B) defective
(C) defectively
(D) defects

129. Some psychological treatments may have more ------- effects than other treatments.
(A) last
(B) lasting
(C) lasted
(D) lastly

130. To make an official purchase agreement, a director must hand in ------- from at least two potential vendors.
(A) applications
(B) estimates
(C) requirements
(D) comprises

PART 6

Directions: Read the texts that follow. A word, phrase, or sentence is missing in parts of each text. Four answer choices for each question are given below the text. Select the best answer to complete the text. Then mark the letter (A), (B), (C), or (D) on your answer sheet.

Questions 131-134 refer to the following notice.

Oak Grove Library Presents Business Lunch Hour

On Tuesday, November 7 from 11:30 AM to 12:30 PM, the Oak Grove Library will ------- a free
131.

Business Lunch Hour. Entrepreneurs and small business owners are invited to bring ------- own
132.

lunch and meet at the Oak Grove Library to learn digital skills to help their businesses grow. James

Olson, owner of Digital Age, will share ten ways you can boost your visibility online for free. This

event is presented in ------- with the Monroe Country Chamber of Commerce. -------.
133.   **134.**

---

131. (A) cater
(B) establish
(C) host
(D) plan

132. (A) theirs
(B) them
(C) their
(D) themselves

133. (A) collaborate
(B) collaboration
(C) collaborative
(D) collaboratively

134. (A) For more information, call James at 555-2591.
(B) Participants will be charged a small fee at the door.
(C) The event will be called off in case of rain.
(D) The library will be closed on Monday, November 6.

GO ON TO THE NEXT PAGE

Questions 135-138 refer to the following article.

San Marcos opening new store in Harriston

HARRISTON — Harriston is getting its first San Marcos. The coffee shop chain announced its ------- **135.**

for a store in Harriston on Tuesday. It says the store, due to open in February next year, is part of its

initiative, which ------- three years ago to invest in more rural communities across the nation. -------.
136. **137.**

San Marcos also plans to work with locally-owned businesses to supply products for the store.

Harriston officials have said they're excited about the store, believing it will help ------- more foot
138.

traffic to the downtown area.

---

135. (A) developments
(B) operations
(C) plans
(D) promises

136. (A) began
(B) had begun
(C) have begun
(D) will have begun

137. (A) Company officials say their goal is to create job opportunities for local youth.
(B) San Marcos grows its own beans in several Latin America and African countries.
(C) The investment is expected to be safe for retired couples and young people alike.
(D) Rural communities are usually the last to benefit from economic upturns.

138. (A) bring
(B) keep
(C) offer
(D) occur

Questions 139-142 refer to the following e-mail.

From: Henri Saveaux <hsaveaus@visitparis.fr>
To: Amalia Francis <amaliaf@bloggers.net>
Date: December 12
Subject: Permission to reprint

Dear Ms. Francis,

I work for a small publishing company in Paris. We put out an English tourist magazine about France every quarter. We noticed your blog post on toursaroundtheworld.com. It was very ------- written **139.** and has some good pictures and maps. -------. Of course, we would pay you the ------- rate for **140.** **141.** contributions to our magazine. Your writing is so captivating — we're wondering if you'd like to be a regular contributor. Please let us know if you agree to ------- or both offers. **142.**

Thank you,

Henri Saveaux

139. (A) entertain
(B) entertaining
(C) entertainingly
(D) entertainment

140. (A) Each of our issues is focused on a different city around the world, and next time it's Berlin.
(B) Your illustrations were beautiful and we'd like to hang them in our gallery in Paris.
(C) We think our readers would like it and are wondering if we can print it in our February issue.
(D) When you return to Paris, please visit our new office near the River Seine.

141. (A) beneficial
(B) less
(C) reduced
(D) usual

142. (A) all
(B) either
(C) many
(D) neither

GO ON TO THE NEXT PAGE

TEST 5

Museums Saver Ticket

Buy a museums saver ticket to the Fashion Museum, the Roman Museum, and Torrance Art Gallery and save big on entry prices! ------- . You can ------- a saver ticket online, at the front desks, or from
       143.   **144.**
the Tourist Information Center.

- Adults: £21.50
- Seniors (65 and over) / Students: £18.50
- Children (age 6–16): £11.75
- Groups of more than 20 people: £13.00 each

Season Ticket

------- value for entry for one full year to the Fashion Museum, the Roman Museum, and Torrance
 145.

Art Gallery, the season ticket is also available in the same ways as described above. The season

ticket is ------- if you live in the region or even if you just visit Torrance regularly.
        146.

- Adults: £30.00
- Seniors (65 and over) / Students: £25.00
- Children (age 6–16): £14.00

---

143. (A) All of the buildings are unfortunately closed for renovation at this time.
(B) You can buy three tickets to these three locations, all within ten minutes' walk of each other.
(C) There are more museums set to open in the Torrance area next year.
(D) When you visit Torrance by train, please get off at Torrance West Station.

144. (A) apply
(B) confirm
(C) purchase
(D) reserve

145. (A) Accessible
(B) Available
(C) Best
(D) Obvious

146. (A) perfect
(B) perfection
(C) perfectly
(D) perfectness

PART 7

Directions: In this part you will read a selection of texts, such as magazine and newspaper articles, e-mails, and instant messages. Each text or set of texts is followed by several questions. Select the best answer for each question and mark the letter (A), (B), (C), or (D) on your answer sheet.

Questions 147-148 refer to the following information.

In an effort to extend the life of your new Haven sweater, we would like to offer some advice and tips on how to take care of your new favorite top. First, since the material is very delicate, we do not recommend cleaning it in a conventional washer and dryer. The tossing and tumbling can cause the cloth to stretch, and after a few washes, it could possibly tear. Please take the sweater to a cleaning professional, such as a dry cleaner, to have it cleaned properly.

We also recommend keeping it in a dry, dark box when not wearing it, as it will help keep the colors bright and the materials fresh. Once taken out to wear, a soft felt brush should be used to clean lint or hair from the sweater. If you choose to use something else, it may work fine, but anything with coarse, plastic or metal bristles could cause damage to your top.

147. What could happen if the product is not taken to an experienced cleaner?

(A) It might get wrinkled.
(B) It might rip.
(C) It might shrink.
(D) The color might change.

148. According to the information, where should a user keep the product?

(A) In a bright room
(B) In a closet
(C) In a dry, covered container
(D) In a well-ventilated place

GO ON TO THE NEXT PAGE

TEST 5

Questions 149-150 refer to the following notice.

This is a notice to all employees of Yongwater, Inc. in regard to the new vacation policy that will be implemented on October 1. All employees will be required to inform management at least two weeks prior to their target vacation date. If a time-off request comes up unexpectedly, we will review the need at that time. The updated policy is made to make sure that the company can continue operations without interruption, even if some employees are not available at their regular time. This will also enable the company to fill temporary positions if necessary. Please include the dates and reason for taking time-off and it will be reviewed by the management. Thank you for your cooperation.

149. What will happen in October?

(A) A new computer system will be introduced.
(B) New rules regarding holiday time will begin.
(C) The company will have temporary workers.
(D) The management will change.

150. When should an employee submit a document?

(A) At the beginning of every month
(B) About half a month before a day off
(C) In two weeks
(D) The next day

At Martinez Goods, we are working hard to create the things that we believe you will not want to live without. Therefore, we are proud to announce the Jericho 5000 line of microwaves. Our designers put in many hours of testing, including safety tests, to make sure that these appliances have all the features you need.

As someone who has purchased Jericho models in the past, we would like to invite you to participate in helping us decide what is important for the newest model of our line. We want to make the best product we can for our loyal customers, and with your help, we think we can. The survey below should only take about 5–7 minutes to complete, and as a thank-you, we will send a 10-percent-off coupon for your next purchase on our Website.

151. Who does Martinez Goods ask to join the survey?

(A) Any visitors to their Website
(B) Parents of young children
(C) Previous customers
(D) Their designers

152. What is a responder offered after filling out the survey?

(A) A voucher
(B) A free gift
(C) A link to a special sale
(D) A thank-you e-mail

GO ON TO THE NEXT PAGE

TEST 5

Questions 153-154 refer to the following text message chain.

Brad Young   1:32 PM
What did you think of the new human resources proposal Ray
sent this morning? It seems like it will fit onto the company
vision for the coming year nicely.

Jessica Imono   1:36 PM
I haven't had much time to look it over yet, but from what I've
seen, it looks good.

Brad Young   1:37 PM
I wanted to get your input on something. Did you read the
extra section marked "bonus" in the e-mail?

Jessica Imono   1:40 PM
No, where was it? I didn't see any attachments on the e-mail.
Let me check again.

Brad Young   1:42 PM
It should either be attached or maybe a link on the bottom on
the e-mail. I could forward it to you now.

Jessica Imono   1:43 PM
That would be great. It's definitely not here.

Brad Young   1:44 PM
OK. Check again in a few minutes and then we can talk about
it.

153. What is the conversation topic?

(A) A company employee

(B) A company problem

(C) A personnel plan

(D) A missing item

154. At 1:43PM, what does Ms. Imono most likely
mean when she writes, "It's definitely not
here"?

(A) She cannot access a Web page.

(B) She cannot find the information.

(C) The e-mail must be missing.

(D) The information must be posted somewhere
else.

Questions 155-157 refer to the following e-mail.

e-mail

To:	Emerson Palmer <emersonp@nextmail.com>
From:	Reginald Teller <representative@dasexpress.com>
Date:	September 28
Subject:	Order #820-00812

Hello Mr. Palmer,

I am writing to you about your order with us for the digital antenna and speaker. Unfortunately, we had very strong storms near our warehouses this week, which caused some serious damage to our buildings. Therefore, we are unable to immediately ship the items you purchased. It will take 1-2 weeks for the buildings to be repaired and then another few days for order preparation before we anticipate orders resuming.

We have few options that you may choose for your order. First, approval of a delay will keep your order active, and we will ship it as soon as possible. Next, we can substitute a similar product and have it sent from another warehouse in the country to your location. Lastly, if you would prefer, we can cancel the order for you. Please let us know which is best for you in the next 48 hours. If we do not receive a response, we will keep the order active. We apologize for any inconvenience this may cause.

Thank you and have a nice day.

Reginald Teller
Service Representative

155. Why is the shipping delayed?

(A) Due to a delivery problem

(B) Due to inclement weather

(C) Due to mislabeling

(D) Due to a stock shortage

156. Which option is NOT given to the customer?

(A) An alternate item

(B) The order cancellation

(C) The later shipping of an item

(D) The refund for shipping costs

157. What will happen if Mr. Palmer does not respond in two days?

(A) The order will be canceled.

(B) The order will be charged.

(C) The order will be processed.

(D) The order will be delivered.

GO ON TO THE NEXT PAGE

TEST 5

Questions 158-160 refer to the following advertisement.

Fall is almost upon us and now is the best time to get in shape for next year! At Gregg's Gym, we offer the most up-to-date techniques in aerobics, cardio, yoga, martial arts, muscle building, and weight loss programs. If you want to shed some pounds before the holidays, or just get some exercise, we have a plan for you.

Our off-season Body Saver series offer a little something for everyone. You can choose to take only one type of class for the full season, choose a pair of classes for the price of one, or use the mix-and-match system, joining any classes you want during your visit. Drop in and take a test drive with any of our qualified instructors and see how you can improve your well-being, and have fun while doing it.

Gregg's is open 7 days a week, from 6:00 AM to 12:00 AM every day, so we can fit into your schedule at any time you need. We are conveniently located at the corner of 17th and Winslow Avenue, right in the heart of the city, and only a two-block walk from the subway.

158. What is NOT mentioned in the ad?

(A) A type of exercise

(B) Business hours

(C) A location

(D) Requirements

159. According to the advertisement, what features does Gregg's have?

(A) A lot of staff members

(B) Right next to a station

(C) Open 24 hours a day

(D) Special offers

160. How can a person try out a service?

(A) By accompanying a friend

(B) By applying online

(C) By becoming a member at the site

(D) By going directly to the site

To	Amelia Hunters <ahunters@sloanefoundation.com>
From	Rachel Benson <rbenson@nextmail.com>
Date	October 10
Subject	Sloane history exhibition

Hi Amelia,

I wanted to get in touch and see if you wanted to come with us to the Sloane history exhibition this weekend. —[1]—. It's supposed to be one of the best displays of the fall. —[2]—.

The arts director received permission to show everything in the museum's collection about our area's history and many things from our foundation will be included. There are so many items that I have wanted to see, but were always in the vault and unavailable to the public. —[3]— I know that you are a big fan of history and wouldn't want to miss a chance to see this.

If you can get back to me before 8:00 tomorrow night, I will be picking up tickets for everyone who wants to go at that time. —[4]—. There will be a group of us, maybe six or so, and we will be meeting at the office before heading over.

Rachel

161. What is the purpose of the e-mail?

(A) To ask Ms. Hunters to an event
(B) To get permission to leave work early
(C) To invite Ms. Hunters to lunch
(D) To respond to an e-mail

162. Where does Ms. Benson want to meet Ms. Hunters this weekend?

(A) At the box office
(B) At the city hall
(C) At the foundation office
(D) At the museum

163. In which of the positions marked [1], [2], [3], or [4] does the following sentence best belong?

"I heard that even the original designs for the city will be shown."

(A) [1]
(B) [2]
(C) [3]
(D) [4]

Questions 164-167 refer to the following e-mail.

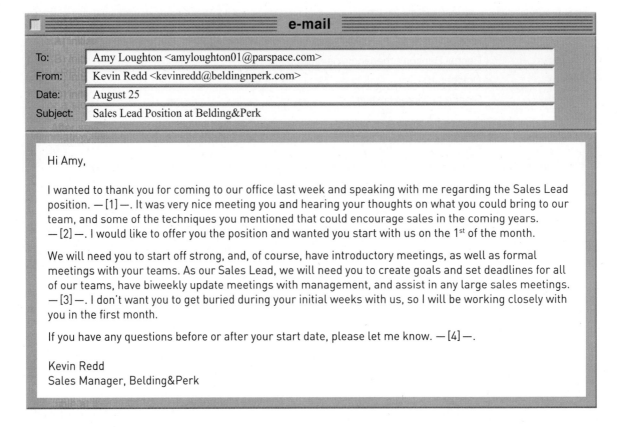

	e-mail
To:	Amy Loughton <amyloughton01@parspace.com>
From:	Kevin Redd <kevinredd@beldingnperk.com>
Date:	August 25
Subject:	Sales Lead Position at Belding&Perk

Hi Amy,

I wanted to thank you for coming to our office last week and speaking with me regarding the Sales Lead position. — [1] —. It was very nice meeting you and hearing your thoughts on what you could bring to our team, and some of the techniques you mentioned that could encourage sales in the coming years. — [2] —. I would like to offer you the position and wanted you start with us on the 1st of the month.

We will need you to start off strong, and, of course, have introductory meetings, as well as formal meetings with your teams. As our Sales Lead, we will need you to create goals and set deadlines for all of our teams, have biweekly update meetings with management, and assist in any large sales meetings. — [3] —. I don't want you to get buried during your initial weeks with us, so I will be working closely with you in the first month.

If you have any questions before or after your start date, please let me know. — [4] —.

Kevin Redd
Sales Manager, Belding&Perk

---

164. What does Mr. Redd like about the interview with Ms. Loughton?

(A) Her cheerful personality
(B) Her experience in sales
(C) Her management skills
(D) Her sales ideas

165. How will Ms. Loughton get ready for her first week at the company?

(A) She will attend training with other employees.
(B) She will complete assigned tasks.
(C) She will write a speech for her subordinates.
(D) She will have several meetings.

166. Who will help Ms. Loughton in September?

(A) Mr. Redd's assistant
(B) Sales team members
(C) The previous Sales Lead
(D) The Sales Manager

167. In which of the positions marked [1]. [2], [3], or [4] does the following sentence best belong?

"I know it sounds like quite a bit of work at first, but we believe that you can keep up."

(A) [1]
(B) [2]
(C) [3]
(D) [4]

To	Jackson Waters <jwaters@noratech.com>
From	Emily Brewer <eb001@goerslove.com>
Date	Wednesday, November 1
Subject	Meeting about our products

Hi Mr. Waters,

I hope you are doing well. I wanted to see if it would be okay to reschedule tomorrow's meeting for the next week. We want to be able to share with you all of the most up-to-date product information we can, but won't receive the report until this evening. We would like to read and thoroughly go over the report before presenting it to you. Overall, it should take two or three days to read and confirm the product information.

Should we receive the product report earlier, I will, of course, let you know. We will have a little extra time to process and work with this information over the weekend, so we will have a demonstration prepared for you during the meeting. The beginning of next week should be fine for us. Would that be okay for you as well?

I look forward to hearing back from you and thank you for working with us on such an important project for both of our companies.

Thank you,
Emily Brewer

---

168. What is the purpose of the e-mail?

(A) To ask for an item description

(B) To ask to delay a meeting time

(C) To extend the meeting time

(D) To give an update on the meeting

169. How much time will the team spend going through the information?

(A) A few hours

(B) A day

(C) A few days

(D) A week

170. What does Ms. Brewer offer Mr. Waters?

(A) A completed unit

(B) A demo

(C) Printed reports

(D) Support documents

171. What day would Ms. Brewer most likely to meet with Mr. Waters?

(A) On Monday

(B) On Thursday

(C) On Friday

(D) On Saturday

GO ON TO THE NEXT PAGE

Questions 172-175 refer to the following online discussion.

Randal Bunch 11:34 AM		Have anyone seen Francis today? I was supposed to speak with him.
Ingrid Colane 11:35 AM		He got a phone call this morning and said he needed to leave. I think he was heading to a client's office.
Randal Bunch 11:35 AM		I see. Does anyone have an update on Kilnesmith?
Brian Lagerwood 11:40 AM		I think I can assist with that. I was working with Francis on that account.

— Ingrid Colane has exited the chat. —

Randal Bunch 11:41 AM		Great, thanks Brian. I know that Francis has been working with them for quite some time. Do you think they will accept our offer?
Brian Lagerwood 11:41 AM		Francis and I have met with them multiple times over the last few months. It will come down to us or another company. They should decide by October 13.
Randal Bunch 11:44 AM		Hmm, OK. I was hoping to know by September. I need to know if there is anything we can do to encourage them to accept our offer. If they don't, it would set our finances back quite a bit for next fiscal year.
Brian Lagerwood 11:45 AM		Well, I heard that Bromley offered Klinesmith more money, but it was a short-time deal. Ours would be twice as long. Should we sweeten the pot?
Randal Bunch 11:46 AM		Maybe, but let's make sure that we can work with them on this. We can't afford to find another supplier in such a short amount of time.
Brian Lagerwood 11:47 AM		I will let you know as soon as I get an update.

172. What does Ms. Colane mention that Francis is doing?

(A) Going on a business trip

(B) Seeing with a client

(C) Trying to get a better deal

(D) Visiting a family member

173. How does Mr. Bunch describe a deal with Kilnesmith?

(A) Complex

(B) Demanding

(C) Essential

(D) Long-lasting

174. What has Mr. Lagerwood been involved with recently?

(A) Looking for a new location for a warehouse

(B) Meeting with a potential supplier

(C) Preparing for a business trip

(D) Working on financial details for next year

175. At 11:45 AM, what does Mr. Lagerwood most likely mean when he writes, "should we sweeten the pot?"

(A) He wants to know if he should explain why their contract is better.

(B) He wants to know if he should extend the time for them to decide.

(C) He wants to know if he should invite them for a meeting.

(D) He wonders if he should make a better offer.

GO ON TO THE NEXT PAGE

Shade: The Mark on Banker Hill

Written by Steven Bird
Directed by Lindy Allen

Richard Shade is a tough-talking, hard-boiled detective who knows the city like the back of his hand. He's had the respect of his peers since he was a fresh face on his first case. The city is dark and chilling and he feels that today is either his lucky day or maybe the worst day of his life. One of film's iconic crime detectives, Shade works outside the police and has many disputes with Maxwell Young, the one cop he trusts. Steven Bird has taken the original film and transformed it for today's audiences, using current technology to create the modern atmosphere that surrounds the story.

We also meet a mysterious woman, Gloria Grey, who believes someone is trying to steal her husband's inheritance, showing up at Shade's office and asking for his help. She lets herself in as Shade naps in his office, and proves to be a woman willing to do anything to get her hands on the money. The streets around Banker Hill are dangerous, but for someone like Richard Shade, it could be murder.

Running Time: 117 minutes

---

https://www.freshtomatoes.com/review

Shade: The Mark on Banker Hill is a remake of a classic movie, which tells us the story of a down-on-his-luck detective who is looking for a break. Originally, this was one of a series of films about Shade released in the 1950s and is now considered to be one of the classics of the genre.

This version of the Shade character has been given a softer side, and the private eye is now more of a fast-thinking joker. Stepping into the shoes of Richard Shade is Johnny Baxter, who has been cast historically as a more comedic and musical actor. But Baxter comes through with a performance that I believe the classic cast would be proud of. It's definitely a different take on the original, but Baxter handles the scenes like he was born for the role. Marianne Lewis is fantastic in the lead female role and will be seen as an up-and-coming star for sure. Since much of the story revolves around these two, it should be noted how well they work off of each other in the film, but there are memorable scenes with the rest of the small cast, too.

Shade is designed to be the first in a new film series for Grand Studios, and although this film isn't going to change the way we view crime movies, it is a good way to establish the characters in today's world.

176. Who is the person that Richard Shade has faith in?

(A) Gloria Grey

(B) Johnny Baxter

(C) Lindy Allen

(D) Maxwell Young

177. In the program, the word "fresh" in paragraph 1, line 2 is closest in meaning to

(A) additional

(B) energetic

(C) new

(D) raw

178. What is NOT true about the film?

(A) It's been reproduced.

(B) The director didn't change the original film.

(C) There are two main characters in the film.

(D) It has reflected the today's trend.

179. What change to the new version does the review focus on?

(A) The lead character

(B) The music

(C) The overall atmosphere

(D) The scenario

180. What kind of job is Mr. Baxter usually offered?

(A) Action

(B) Comedy

(C) Drama

(D) Horror

GO ON TO THE NEXT PAGE

Questions 181-185 refer to the following e-mails.

To	Elijah Graham <elijah2019@inoutbox.com>
From	Tower Hotel <frontdesk@towerhotelten.com>
Date	September 5
Subject	Confirmation of reservation

Dear Mr. Graham,

We have received your request to book a room for October 3–12 and can confirm that we have Room 711 ready for you then. We can also confirm the wake-up call from October 4–6, at 5:30 AM for the three days.

The hotel and the surrounding areas will be very busy during your stay, as the Richmond Harvest Festival will be taking place. The city is expecting around 100,000 people to visit on at least one of the days during the week-long celebration. We appreciate your business and if there is anything we can do to make your stay even better, please do not hesitate to ask.

Service included	Wake-up call Complimentary breakfast Room cleaning
Room 711 at $92/night (Oct. 3–12, 9 nights)	Total: $828

Thank you for choosing Tower Hotel.

Jason Richards
Hospitality Manager
Tower Hotel, Richmond, Tennessee

To	Tower Hotel <frontdesk@towerhotelten.com>
From	Elijah Graham <elijah2019@inoutbox.com>
Date	September 6
Subject	Reservation and correction

Dear Mr. Richards,

Thank you for confirming the booking so quickly, but I noticed that there was an error with it. I will be leaving on the 11th, so I will not need the room on the 12th. Can you re-book and confirm the new dates?

Also, I was unaware of the Richmond Harvest Festival, so that may present a problem. I will be in town working with a client and I've requested a wake-up call not to be late. I am now worried that traffic may be difficult during the week. Do you offer shuttle service or hotel buses for your guests? I don't want to be late for my meetings because I have to wait for a public taxi.

Thank you,
Elijah Graham

181. When will the festival take place?

(A) At the end of September

(B) At the beginning of October

(C) In mid-October

(D) At the end of October

182. What service will the hotel provide for Mr. Graham?

(A) Refreshments

(B) Laundry

(C) Room service

(D) A free meal

183. When is Mr. Graham expected to have a meeting?

(A) On October 3−5

(B) On October 4−6

(C) On October 3−11

(C) On October 11−12

184. How many nights is Mr. Graham planning to stay at the hotel?

(A) 6

(B) 7

(C) 8

(D) 9

185. What does Mr. Graham ask the hotel about?

(A) A parking space

(B) The festival dates

(C) The room size

(D) Transportation

GO ON TO THE NEXT PAGE

Questions 186-190 refer to the following e-mails and gift certificate.

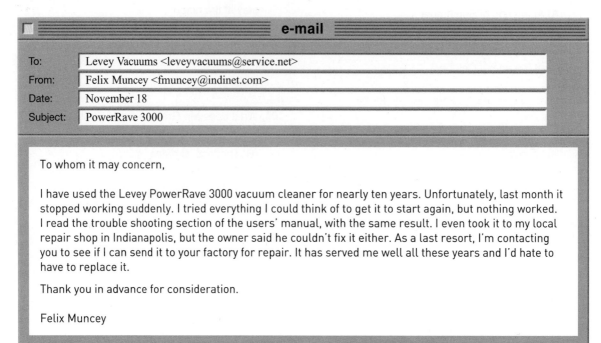

	e-mail
To:	Levey Vacuums <leveyvacuums@service.net>
From:	Felix Muncey <fmuncey@indinet.com>
Date:	November 18
Subject:	PowerRave 3000

To whom it may concern,

I have used the Levey PowerRave 3000 vacuum cleaner for nearly ten years. Unfortunately, last month it stopped working suddenly. I tried everything I could think of to get it to start again, but nothing worked. I read the trouble shooting section of the users' manual, with the same result. I even took it to my local repair shop in Indianapolis, but the owner said he couldn't fix it either. As a last resort, I'm contacting you to see if I can send it to your factory for repair. It has served me well all these years and I'd hate to have to replace it.

Thank you in advance for consideration.

Felix Muncey

	e-mail
To:	Felix Muncey <fmuncey@indinet.com>
From:	Levey Vacuums <leveyvacuums@service.net>
Date:	November 19
Subject:	RE: PowerRave 3000

Dear Mr. Muncey,

Thank you for your inquiry. We are sorry to hear that your PowerRave 3000 is no longer functioning. We regret to inform you that this model has been discontinued. However, since you liked the PowerRave so much, we're confident that you'll also like our new model, the Clean Machine XT (retail price: $250).

The Clean Machine XT is our newest model cleaner and has many attractive features. Its "one-of-a-kind material" means it is much lighter than any other comparable machine on the market, without sacrificing power. Also, the Clean Machine's revolutionary design allows for access into small corners and under furniture.

To honor your loyalty to the Levey vacuum brand, I'd like to offer you a discount on the purchase of the Clean Machine XT. I've attached the coupon to this message, so you can print it out and show it to one of our authorized outlets near you. We hope that we can retain you as a customer for many years to come.

Sincerely,
Marcia Lopez
Customer Care

Date of issue: November 19

Present this coupon (on a mobile device or in paper form) to any of the dealers below to receive 20% off the Clean Machine XT.

| **Al's Vacuums** | **Morristown Appliance** | **Flat Irons Appliance** | **S&B Vacuums** |
| Gary, IN | Morristown, IN | Evansville, IN | Indianapolis, IN |

*Offer not good on any other make or model.
*Not to be combined with any other discounts or deals.
*Coupon expires six months after date of issue.

---

186. What is the purpose to the fist e-mail?

(A) To ask about repair shops nearby

(B) To complain about a product

(C) To inquire about factory repair

(D) To request a refund

187. What makes the Clean Machine XT unique?

(A) Its power

(B) Its price

(C) Its size

(D) Its weight

188. How much is the vacuum with the coupon?

(A) $100

(B) $150

(C) $200

(D) $250

189. Which retailer is located in the same town as Mr. Muncey?

(A) Al's Vacuums

(B) Morristown Appliance

(C) Flat Irons Appliance

(D) S&B Vacuums

190. When will the coupon expire?

(A) On November 30

(B) On December 31

(C) On January 19

(D) On May 19

GO ON TO THE NEXT PAGE

TEST 5

Award-winning author Roland Evans has made us wait four long years, but finally, the follow-up to his best-selling smash *Surprise, Surprise!* is here. November 25 is the day to mark on your calendars: the release of *No Surprise Is a Good Surprise* in hardback. Mr. Evans was holed up in his mountain cabin for nearly six months last year finishing the book, according to his publicist. And it's worth the wait, say all reviewers lucky enough to get an advance copy.

Apparently, *No Surprise Is a Good Surprise* blends all the terrific characters and exciting actions readers loved in *Surprise, Surprise!* The question we're all asking now: is there a movie in the works, bringing these great books to the big screen? On that, Mr. Evans is being suspiciously quiet. We'll just have to see what surprise may await us.

Franklin Books Schedule of Events for December

Date	December 4 8:00 PM	December 7 3:00 PM	December 11 7:00 PM	December 14 1:00 PM	December 20 8:00 PM
Author	Lucia Tanak	Elise Pauley	Roland Evans	Emil Vargus	Erin Gutierrez
Type of book	Fantasy	Children's	Young Adult	History	Science Fiction

To	Johan Klein <jkdemon@fastline.com>
From	Franklin Books <customer@franklinbooks.com>
Date	December 21
Subject	Event calendar

Dear Mr. Klein,

Thank you for your message. We are sorry your experience at Mr. Evans's event was unsatisfactory. We do mention on our Website that seating is first come, first served as space is limited. If you arrived a bit late, as you indicated, it's not surprising you weren't able to get a seat. As for the long line for signatures, again, we cannot really help the popularity of our guest authors.

I will pass along your idea to have more than one event for each author. My supervisor takes customer feedback seriously. I hope you will join us again when another of your favorite authors comes to town.

Thank you.

Frannie Poleman
Franklin Books

191. What is mentioned about Mr. Evans?

(A) He has a shelter in the mountains.

(B) He is making a movie.

(C) He is taking a long vacation.

(D) He wants to quit writing.

192. What type of book is *No Surprise Is a Good Surprise*?

(A) Children's

(B) Fantasy

(C) Science Fiction

(D) Young adult

193. What can be said of Franklin Books?

(A) It closes at 8:00 PM.

(B) It did not hold morning events in December.

(C) It has a large event space.

(D) It holds an event once a week.

194. When did Mr. Klein likely attend an event at Franklin Books?

(A) On December 4

(B) On December 11

(C) On December 14

(D) On December 20

195. What does Ms. Poleman promise to do for Mr. Klein?

(A) Call him the next time an author comes

(B) Give his suggestion to her boss

(C) Save him a seat at an event

(D) Send him a discount coupon

GO ON TO THE NEXT PAGE

Questions 196-200 refer to the following e-mails and product information.

From	Jarvis Sloan <jsloan@allproav.net>
To	Stephanie Ross <sross@ultrawave.com>
Date	November 7
Subject	Presentation equipment

Dear Ms. Ross,

Thank you for your e-mail about our line of presentation equipment. I have attached a spec sheet to this e-mail. On the attachment, you will find a brief of features, plus the price ranges. For more details, including color pictures and a helpful video on each of these products, please see our Website at www.allproav.net. You can also set up an account and purchase any item directly from us via our Website.

Please don't hesitate to contact me if I can be of further assistance to you in meeting your company's audio-visual needs.

Sincerely,
Jarvis Sloan
All-Pro Audio-Visual, Inc.
555-2839

All-Pro Audio-Visual, Inc.

Projectors – portable and in-house
- Choose from 2.5 or 4 GB internal memory
- Wi-Fi connectivity
- USB capability
- Portable models are lightweight for easy travel
- LED lamp never needs replacing
- Price range $299-$495, depending on memory size

Screens
- Portable – easy set up and break down (includes travel case)
- Mounted (permanent) – electric or manual pull-down
- 92-120 inches
- Prices range from $99 to $159, depending on size

Smartboards
- Like a giant tablet in your conference room
- Interactive screen makes input from multiple people possible
- Multi-touch screen
- Dry-erase surface for drawing and writing
- Prices range from $559 to $999

The latest in presentation technology, these SMART boards are truly cutting-edge! Though a bit pricey, the collaboration they inspire makes it worth the cost.

To:	Jarvis Sloan <jsloan@allproav.net>
From:	Stephanie Ross <sross@ultrawave.com>
Date:	November 9
Subject:	RE: Presentation equipment

Dear Mr. Sloan,

Thank you for your quick reply, While I'm interested in having a smartboard, the budget for our new start-up does not allow for this type of purchase right now. Please keep me informed of any reduction in price as you introduce new lines in the future.

For the moment, I'm interested in the cheapest projector, plus the 92-inch screen. Please let me know how I can purchase these, as I didn't see that information on the spec sheet.

Thank you for your help.

Stephanie Ross
Ultra Wave

---

196. Why does Mr. Sloan send the e-mail to Ms. Ross?

(A) To respond to her complaint
(B) To respond to her inquiry
(C) To schedule a meeting time with her
(D) To thank her for her business

197. According to the information, what is an advantage of a smartboard?

(A) Groups can work together more easily on it.
(B) It can be used as a video screen.
(C) It can be easily carried in a case.
(D) It is cheaper than a projector.

198. How much will Ms. Ross most likely pay for a screen?

(A) $99
(B) $159
(C) $299
(D) $495

199. What does Ms. Ross mention about the smartboard?

(A) Her boss does not understand its functions.
(B) Her company cannot afford to buy it.
(C) Her company does not need it.
(D) Her co-workers have never used one before.

200. What is implied about Ms. Ross?

(A) She did not look at the Website.
(B) She is the head of an established company.
(C) She is new at Mr. Sloan's company.
(D) She will give a presentation to Mr. Sloan.

Stop! This is the end of the test. If you finish before time is called, you may go back to Parts 5, 6, and 7 and check your work.

TEST 5

215

Answer Sheet

TEST NO. _____

완전 정복 실전 토익 5회

응시일 | 년 | 월 | 일
성명 | 한글 |
| 영어 |

결과 | LC |
| RC |

맞은 개수

Listening Comprehension (Part I~IV)

NO.	ANSWER	NO.	ANSWER	NO.	ANSWER	NO.	ANSWER	NO.	ANSWER
1	a b c	21	a b c d	41	a b c d	61	a b c d	81	a b c d
2	a b c	22	a b c d	42	a b c d	62	a b c d	82	a b c d
3	a b c	23	a b c d	43	a b c d	63	a b c d	83	a b c d
4	a b c	24	a b c d	44	a b c d	64	a b c d	84	a b c d
5	a b c	25	a b c d	45	a b c d	65	a b c d	85	a b c d
6	a b c	26	a b c d	46	a b c d	66	a b c d	86	a b c d
7	a b c	27	a b c d	47	a b c d	67	a b c d	87	a b c d
8	a b c	28	a b c d	48	a b c d	68	a b c d	88	a b c d
9	a b c	29	a b c d	49	a b c d	69	a b c d	89	a b c d
10	a b c	30	a b c d	50	a b c d	70	a b c d	90	a b c d
11	a b c	31	a b c d	51	a b c d	71	a b c d	91	a b c d
12	a b c	32	a b c d	52	a b c d	72	a b c d	92	a b c d
13	a b c	33	a b c d	53	a b c d	73	a b c d	93	a b c d
14	a b c	34	a b c d	54	a b c d	74	a b c d	94	a b c d
15	a b c	35	a b c d	55	a b c d	75	a b c d	95	a b c d
16	a b c	36	a b c d	56	a b c d	76	a b c d	96	a b c d
17	a b c	37	a b c d	57	a b c d	77	a b c d	97	a b c d
18	a b c	38	a b c d	58	a b c d	78	a b c d	98	a b c d
19	a b c	39	a b c d	59	a b c d	79	a b c d	99	a b c d
20	a b c	40	a b c d	60	a b c d	80	a b c d	100	a b c d

Reading Comprehension (Part V~VII)

NO.	ANSWER	NO.	ANSWER	NO.	ANSWER	NO.	ANSWER	NO.	ANSWER
101	a b c d	121	a b c d	141	a b c d	161	a b c d	181	a b c d
102	a b c d	122	a b c d	142	a b c d	162	a b c d	182	a b c d
103	a b c d	123	a b c d	143	a b c d	163	a b c d	183	a b c d
104	a b c d	124	a b c d	144	a b c d	164	a b c d	184	a b c d
105	a b c d	125	a b c d	145	a b c d	165	a b c d	185	a b c d
106	a b c d	126	a b c d	146	a b c d	166	a b c d	186	a b c d
107	a b c d	127	a b c d	147	a b c d	167	a b c d	187	a b c d
108	a b c d	128	a b c d	148	a b c d	168	a b c d	188	a b c d
109	a b c d	129	a b c d	149	a b c d	169	a b c d	189	a b c d
110	a b c d	130	a b c d	150	a b c d	170	a b c d	190	a b c d
111	a b c d	131	a b c d	151	a b c d	171	a b c d	191	a b c d
112	a b c d	132	a b c d	152	a b c d	172	a b c d	192	a b c d
113	a b c d	133	a b c d	153	a b c d	173	a b c d	193	a b c d
114	a b c d	134	a b c d	154	a b c d	174	a b c d	194	a b c d
115	a b c d	135	a b c d	155	a b c d	175	a b c d	195	a b c d
116	a b c d	136	a b c d	156	a b c d	176	a b c d	196	a b c d
117	a b c d	137	a b c d	157	a b c d	177	a b c d	197	a b c d
118	a b c d	138	a b c d	158	a b c d	178	a b c d	198	a b c d
119	a b c d	139	a b c d	159	a b c d	179	a b c d	199	a b c d
120	a b c d	140	a b c d	160	a b c d	180	a b c d	200	a b c d

※ 사용 필기구 : 연필(연필 이외의 사인펜, 볼펜 등은 절대 사용 불가)

※ 1개의 정답만 골라 아래 <보기>의 올바른 표기대로 정확히 작성해야 합니다. 잘못된 필기구 사용과 잘못된 표기는 OMR기기가 판독한 결과에 따르며, 그 결과는 본인 책임입니다.

<보기> 올바른 표기 : ●   잘못된 표기 : ○ ⦿ ◖ ◑ ◐

Answer Sheet

TEST NO. ____

완전 절친 실전 토익 5회

LC MP3 바로듣기

응시일		년	월	일
성명	한글			
	영어			

결과	LC	
맞은 개수	RC	

Listening Comprehension (Part I~IV)

NO.	ANSWER	NO.	ANSWER	NO.	ANSWER	NO.	ANSWER	NO.	ANSWER
1	ⓐⓑⓒⓓ	21	ⓐⓑⓒⓓ	41	ⓐⓑⓒⓓ	61	ⓐⓑⓒⓓ	81	ⓐⓑⓒⓓ
2	ⓐⓑⓒⓓ	22	ⓐⓑⓒⓓ	42	ⓐⓑⓒⓓ	62	ⓐⓑⓒⓓ	82	ⓐⓑⓒⓓ
3	ⓐⓑⓒⓓ	23	ⓐⓑⓒⓓ	43	ⓐⓑⓒⓓ	63	ⓐⓑⓒⓓ	83	ⓐⓑⓒⓓ
4	ⓐⓑⓒⓓ	24	ⓐⓑⓒⓓ	44	ⓐⓑⓒⓓ	64	ⓐⓑⓒⓓ	84	ⓐⓑⓒⓓ
5	ⓐⓑⓒⓓ	25	ⓐⓑⓒⓓ	45	ⓐⓑⓒⓓ	65	ⓐⓑⓒⓓ	85	ⓐⓑⓒⓓ
6	ⓐⓑⓒⓓ	26	ⓐⓑⓒⓓ	46	ⓐⓑⓒⓓ	66	ⓐⓑⓒⓓ	86	ⓐⓑⓒⓓ
7	ⓐⓑⓒⓓ	27	ⓐⓑⓒ	47	ⓐⓑⓒⓓ	67	ⓐⓑⓒⓓ	87	ⓐⓑⓒⓓ
8	ⓐⓑⓒⓓ	28	ⓐⓑⓒ	48	ⓐⓑⓒⓓ	68	ⓐⓑⓒⓓ	88	ⓐⓑⓒⓓ
9	ⓐⓑⓒⓓ	29	ⓐⓑⓒ	49	ⓐⓑⓒⓓ	69	ⓐⓑⓒⓓ	89	ⓐⓑⓒⓓ
10	ⓐⓑⓒⓓ	30	ⓐⓑⓒ	50	ⓐⓑⓒⓓ	70	ⓐⓑⓒⓓ	90	ⓐⓑⓒⓓ
11	ⓐⓑⓒⓓ	31	ⓐⓑⓒ	51	ⓐⓑⓒⓓ	71	ⓐⓑⓒⓓ	91	ⓐⓑⓒⓓ
12	ⓐⓑⓒⓓ	32	ⓐⓑⓒ	52	ⓐⓑⓒⓓ	72	ⓐⓑⓒⓓ	92	ⓐⓑⓒⓓ
13	ⓐⓑⓒⓓ	33	ⓐⓑⓒ	53	ⓐⓑⓒⓓ	73	ⓐⓑⓒⓓ	93	ⓐⓑⓒⓓ
14	ⓐⓑⓒⓓ	34	ⓐⓑⓒ	54	ⓐⓑⓒⓓ	74	ⓐⓑⓒⓓ	94	ⓐⓑⓒⓓ
15	ⓐⓑⓒⓓ	35	ⓐⓑⓒ	55	ⓐⓑⓒⓓ	75	ⓐⓑⓒⓓ	95	ⓐⓑⓒⓓ
16	ⓐⓑⓒⓓ	36	ⓐⓑⓒ	56	ⓐⓑⓒⓓ	76	ⓐⓑⓒⓓ	96	ⓐⓑⓒⓓ
17	ⓐⓑⓒⓓ	37	ⓐⓑⓒ	57	ⓐⓑⓒⓓ	77	ⓐⓑⓒⓓ	97	ⓐⓑⓒⓓ
18	ⓐⓑⓒⓓ	38	ⓐⓑⓒ	58	ⓐⓑⓒⓓ	78	ⓐⓑⓒⓓ	98	ⓐⓑⓒⓓ
19	ⓐⓑⓒⓓ	39	ⓐⓑⓒ	59	ⓐⓑⓒⓓ	79	ⓐⓑⓒⓓ	99	ⓐⓑⓒⓓ
20	ⓐⓑⓒⓓ	40	ⓐⓑⓒ	60	ⓐⓑⓒⓓ	80	ⓐⓑⓒⓓ	100	ⓐⓑⓒⓓ

Reading Comprehension (Part V~VII)

NO.	ANSWER	NO.	ANSWER	NO.	ANSWER	NO.	ANSWER	NO.	ANSWER
101	ⓐⓑⓒⓓ	121	ⓐⓑⓒⓓ	141	ⓐⓑⓒⓓ	161	ⓐⓑⓒⓓ	181	ⓐⓑⓒⓓ
102	ⓐⓑⓒⓓ	122	ⓐⓑⓒⓓ	142	ⓐⓑⓒⓓ	162	ⓐⓑⓒⓓ	182	ⓐⓑⓒⓓ
103	ⓐⓑⓒⓓ	123	ⓐⓑⓒⓓ	143	ⓐⓑⓒⓓ	163	ⓐⓑⓒⓓ	183	ⓐⓑⓒⓓ
104	ⓐⓑⓒⓓ	124	ⓐⓑⓒⓓ	144	ⓐⓑⓒⓓ	164	ⓐⓑⓒⓓ	184	ⓐⓑⓒⓓ
105	ⓐⓑⓒⓓ	125	ⓐⓑⓒⓓ	145	ⓐⓑⓒⓓ	165	ⓐⓑⓒⓓ	185	ⓐⓑⓒⓓ
106	ⓐⓑⓒⓓ	126	ⓐⓑⓒⓓ	146	ⓐⓑⓒⓓ	166	ⓐⓑⓒⓓ	186	ⓐⓑⓒⓓ
107	ⓐⓑⓒⓓ	127	ⓐⓑⓒⓓ	147	ⓐⓑⓒⓓ	167	ⓐⓑⓒⓓ	187	ⓐⓑⓒⓓ
108	ⓐⓑⓒⓓ	128	ⓐⓑⓒⓓ	148	ⓐⓑⓒⓓ	168	ⓐⓑⓒⓓ	188	ⓐⓑⓒⓓ
109	ⓐⓑⓒⓓ	129	ⓐⓑⓒⓓ	149	ⓐⓑⓒⓓ	169	ⓐⓑⓒⓓ	189	ⓐⓑⓒⓓ
110	ⓐⓑⓒⓓ	130	ⓐⓑⓒⓓ	150	ⓐⓑⓒⓓ	170	ⓐⓑⓒⓓ	190	ⓐⓑⓒⓓ
111	ⓐⓑⓒⓓ	131	ⓐⓑⓒⓓ	151	ⓐⓑⓒⓓ	171	ⓐⓑⓒⓓ	191	ⓐⓑⓒⓓ
112	ⓐⓑⓒⓓ	132	ⓐⓑⓒⓓ	152	ⓐⓑⓒⓓ	172	ⓐⓑⓒⓓ	192	ⓐⓑⓒⓓ
113	ⓐⓑⓒⓓ	133	ⓐⓑⓒⓓ	153	ⓐⓑⓒⓓ	173	ⓐⓑⓒⓓ	193	ⓐⓑⓒⓓ
114	ⓐⓑⓒⓓ	134	ⓐⓑⓒⓓ	154	ⓐⓑⓒⓓ	174	ⓐⓑⓒⓓ	194	ⓐⓑⓒⓓ
115	ⓐⓑⓒⓓ	135	ⓐⓑⓒⓓ	155	ⓐⓑⓒⓓ	175	ⓐⓑⓒⓓ	195	ⓐⓑⓒⓓ
116	ⓐⓑⓒⓓ	136	ⓐⓑⓒⓓ	156	ⓐⓑⓒⓓ	176	ⓐⓑⓒⓓ	196	ⓐⓑⓒⓓ
117	ⓐⓑⓒⓓ	137	ⓐⓑⓒⓓ	157	ⓐⓑⓒⓓ	177	ⓐⓑⓒⓓ	197	ⓐⓑⓒⓓ
118	ⓐⓑⓒⓓ	138	ⓐⓑⓒⓓ	158	ⓐⓑⓒⓓ	178	ⓐⓑⓒⓓ	198	ⓐⓑⓒⓓ
119	ⓐⓑⓒⓓ	139	ⓐⓑⓒⓓ	159	ⓐⓑⓒⓓ	179	ⓐⓑⓒⓓ	199	ⓐⓑⓒⓓ
120	ⓐⓑⓒⓓ	140	ⓐⓑⓒⓓ	160	ⓐⓑⓒⓓ	180	ⓐⓑⓒⓓ	200	ⓐⓑⓒⓓ

※ 1개의 정답만 골라 아래 〈보기〉의 올바른 표기대로 정확히 작성해야 합니다. 잘못된 필기구 사용과 올바르지 못한 표기로 인한 불이익은 본인 책임입니다.
잘못된 표기는 OMR기기가 판독한 결과에 따르며, 그 결과는 본인 책임입니다.

〈보기〉 올바른 표기 : ●   잘못된 표기 : ⊙ ◐ ① ◑ ◯

※ 사용 필기구 : 연필(연필 이외의 사인펜, 볼펜 등은 절대 사용 불가)

Answer Sheet

TEST NO. ____

완전 철저 실전 독의 5회

응시일		년	월	일	맞은 개수	
성명	한글				결과	LC
	영어					RC

Listening Comprehension (Part I~IV)

NO.	ANSWER	NO.	ANSWER	NO.	ANSWER	NO.	ANSWER	NO.	ANSWER
1	ⓐⓑⓒ	21	ⓐⓑⓒ	41	ⓐⓑⓒⓓ	61	ⓐⓑⓒⓓ	81	ⓐⓑⓒⓓ
2	ⓐⓑⓒ	22	ⓐⓑⓒ	42	ⓐⓑⓒⓓ	62	ⓐⓑⓒⓓ	82	ⓐⓑⓒⓓ
3	ⓐⓑⓒ	23	ⓐⓑⓒ	43	ⓐⓑⓒⓓ	63	ⓐⓑⓒⓓ	83	ⓐⓑⓒⓓ
4	ⓐⓑⓒ	24	ⓐⓑⓒ	44	ⓐⓑⓒⓓ	64	ⓐⓑⓒⓓ	84	ⓐⓑⓒⓓ
5	ⓐⓑⓒ	25	ⓐⓑⓒ	45	ⓐⓑⓒⓓ	65	ⓐⓑⓒⓓ	85	ⓐⓑⓒⓓ
6	ⓐⓑⓒ	26	ⓐⓑⓒ	46	ⓐⓑⓒⓓ	66	ⓐⓑⓒⓓ	86	ⓐⓑⓒⓓ
7	ⓐⓑⓒ	27	ⓐⓑⓒ	47	ⓐⓑⓒⓓ	67	ⓐⓑⓒⓓ	87	ⓐⓑⓒⓓ
8	ⓐⓑⓒ	28	ⓐⓑⓒⓓ	48	ⓐⓑⓒⓓ	68	ⓐⓑⓒⓓ	88	ⓐⓑⓒⓓ
9	ⓐⓑⓒ	29	ⓐⓑⓒⓓ	49	ⓐⓑⓒⓓ	69	ⓐⓑⓒⓓ	89	ⓐⓑⓒⓓ
10	ⓐⓑⓒ	30	ⓐⓑⓒⓓ	50	ⓐⓑⓒⓓ	70	ⓐⓑⓒⓓ	90	ⓐⓑⓒⓓ
11	ⓐⓑⓒ	31	ⓐⓑⓒⓓ	51	ⓐⓑⓒⓓ	71	ⓐⓑⓒⓓ	91	ⓐⓑⓒⓓ
12	ⓐⓑⓒ	32	ⓐⓑⓒⓓ	52	ⓐⓑⓒⓓ	72	ⓐⓑⓒⓓ	92	ⓐⓑⓒⓓ
13	ⓐⓑⓒ	33	ⓐⓑⓒⓓ	53	ⓐⓑⓒⓓ	73	ⓐⓑⓒⓓ	93	ⓐⓑⓒⓓ
14	ⓐⓑⓒ	34	ⓐⓑⓒⓓ	54	ⓐⓑⓒⓓ	74	ⓐⓑⓒⓓ	94	ⓐⓑⓒⓓ
15	ⓐⓑⓒ	35	ⓐⓑⓒⓓ	55	ⓐⓑⓒⓓ	75	ⓐⓑⓒⓓ	95	ⓐⓑⓒⓓ
16	ⓐⓑⓒ	36	ⓐⓑⓒⓓ	56	ⓐⓑⓒⓓ	76	ⓐⓑⓒⓓ	96	ⓐⓑⓒⓓ
17	ⓐⓑⓒ	37	ⓐⓑⓒⓓ	57	ⓐⓑⓒⓓ	77	ⓐⓑⓒⓓ	97	ⓐⓑⓒⓓ
18	ⓐⓑⓒ	38	ⓐⓑⓒⓓ	58	ⓐⓑⓒⓓ	78	ⓐⓑⓒⓓ	98	ⓐⓑⓒⓓ
19	ⓐⓑⓒ	39	ⓐⓑⓒⓓ	59	ⓐⓑⓒⓓ	79	ⓐⓑⓒⓓ	99	ⓐⓑⓒⓓ
20	ⓐⓑⓒ	40	ⓐⓑⓒⓓ	60	ⓐⓑⓒⓓ	80	ⓐⓑⓒⓓ	100	ⓐⓑⓒⓓ

Reading Comprehension (Part V~VII)

NO.	ANSWER	NO.	ANSWER	NO.	ANSWER	NO.	ANSWER	NO.	ANSWER
101	ⓐⓑⓒⓓ	121	ⓐⓑⓒⓓ	141	ⓐⓑⓒⓓ	161	ⓐⓑⓒⓓ	181	ⓐⓑⓒⓓ
102	ⓐⓑⓒⓓ	122	ⓐⓑⓒⓓ	142	ⓐⓑⓒⓓ	162	ⓐⓑⓒⓓ	182	ⓐⓑⓒⓓ
103	ⓐⓑⓒⓓ	123	ⓐⓑⓒⓓ	143	ⓐⓑⓒⓓ	163	ⓐⓑⓒⓓ	183	ⓐⓑⓒⓓ
104	ⓐⓑⓒⓓ	124	ⓐⓑⓒⓓ	144	ⓐⓑⓒⓓ	164	ⓐⓑⓒⓓ	184	ⓐⓑⓒⓓ
105	ⓐⓑⓒⓓ	125	ⓐⓑⓒⓓ	145	ⓐⓑⓒⓓ	165	ⓐⓑⓒⓓ	185	ⓐⓑⓒⓓ
106	ⓐⓑⓒⓓ	126	ⓐⓑⓒⓓ	146	ⓐⓑⓒⓓ	166	ⓐⓑⓒⓓ	186	ⓐⓑⓒⓓ
107	ⓐⓑⓒⓓ	127	ⓐⓑⓒⓓ	147	ⓐⓑⓒⓓ	167	ⓐⓑⓒⓓ	187	ⓐⓑⓒⓓ
108	ⓐⓑⓒⓓ	128	ⓐⓑⓒⓓ	148	ⓐⓑⓒⓓ	168	ⓐⓑⓒⓓ	188	ⓐⓑⓒⓓ
109	ⓐⓑⓒⓓ	129	ⓐⓑⓒⓓ	149	ⓐⓑⓒⓓ	169	ⓐⓑⓒⓓ	189	ⓐⓑⓒⓓ
110	ⓐⓑⓒⓓ	130	ⓐⓑⓒⓓ	150	ⓐⓑⓒⓓ	170	ⓐⓑⓒⓓ	190	ⓐⓑⓒⓓ
111	ⓐⓑⓒⓓ	131	ⓐⓑⓒⓓ	151	ⓐⓑⓒⓓ	171	ⓐⓑⓒⓓ	191	ⓐⓑⓒⓓ
112	ⓐⓑⓒⓓ	132	ⓐⓑⓒⓓ	152	ⓐⓑⓒⓓ	172	ⓐⓑⓒⓓ	192	ⓐⓑⓒⓓ
113	ⓐⓑⓒⓓ	133	ⓐⓑⓒⓓ	153	ⓐⓑⓒⓓ	173	ⓐⓑⓒⓓ	193	ⓐⓑⓒⓓ
114	ⓐⓑⓒⓓ	134	ⓐⓑⓒⓓ	154	ⓐⓑⓒⓓ	174	ⓐⓑⓒⓓ	194	ⓐⓑⓒⓓ
115	ⓐⓑⓒⓓ	135	ⓐⓑⓒⓓ	155	ⓐⓑⓒⓓ	175	ⓐⓑⓒⓓ	195	ⓐⓑⓒⓓ
116	ⓐⓑⓒⓓ	136	ⓐⓑⓒⓓ	156	ⓐⓑⓒⓓ	176	ⓐⓑⓒⓓ	196	ⓐⓑⓒⓓ
117	ⓐⓑⓒⓓ	137	ⓐⓑⓒⓓ	157	ⓐⓑⓒⓓ	177	ⓐⓑⓒⓓ	197	ⓐⓑⓒⓓ
118	ⓐⓑⓒⓓ	138	ⓐⓑⓒⓓ	158	ⓐⓑⓒⓓ	178	ⓐⓑⓒⓓ	198	ⓐⓑⓒⓓ
119	ⓐⓑⓒⓓ	139	ⓐⓑⓒⓓ	159	ⓐⓑⓒⓓ	179	ⓐⓑⓒⓓ	199	ⓐⓑⓒⓓ
120	ⓐⓑⓒⓓ	140	ⓐⓑⓒⓓ	160	ⓐⓑⓒⓓ	180	ⓐⓑⓒⓓ	200	ⓐⓑⓒⓓ

Answer Sheet

TEST NO. ___

완전 철철 실전 토익 5회

응시일		년 월 일
성명	한글	
	영어	

결과	LC	
맞은 개수	RC	

Listening Comprehension (Part I~IV)

NO.	ANSWER	NO.	ANSWER	NO.	ANSWER	NO.	ANSWER	NO.	ANSWER
1	a b c	21	a b c d	41	a b c d	61	a b c d	81	a b c d
2	a b c	22	a b c d	42	a b c d	62	a b c d	82	a b c d
3	a b c	23	a b c d	43	a b c d	63	a b c d	83	a b c d
4	a b c	24	a b c d	44	a b c d	64	a b c d	84	a b c d
5	a b c	25	a b c d	45	a b c d	65	a b c d	85	a b c d
6	a b c	26	a b c d	46	a b c d	66	a b c d	86	a b c d
7	a b c	27	a b c	47	a b c d	67	a b c d	87	a b c d
8	a b c	28	a b c	48	a b c d	68	a b c d	88	a b c d
9	a b c	29	a b c	49	a b c d	69	a b c d	89	a b c d
10	a b c	30	a b c	50	a b c d	70	a b c d	90	a b c d
11	a b c	31	a b c	51	a b c d	71	a b c d	91	a b c d
12	a b c	32	a b c	52	a b c d	72	a b c d	92	a b c d
13	a b c	33	a b c	53	a b c d	73	a b c d	93	a b c d
14	a b c	34	a b c	54	a b c d	74	a b c d	94	a b c d
15	a b c	35	a b c	55	a b c d	75	a b c d	95	a b c d
16	a b c	36	a b c	56	a b c d	76	a b c d	96	a b c d
17	a b c	37	a b c	57	a b c d	77	a b c d	97	a b c d
18	a b c	38	a b c	58	a b c d	78	a b c d	98	a b c d
19	a b c	39	a b c	59	a b c d	79	a b c d	99	a b c d
20	a b c	40	a b c	60	a b c d	80	a b c d	100	a b c d

Reading Comprehension (Part V~VII)

NO.	ANSWER	NO.	ANSWER	NO.	ANSWER	NO.	ANSWER	NO.	ANSWER
101	a b c d	121	a b c d	141	a b c d	161	a b c d	181	a b c d
102	a b c d	122	a b c d	142	a b c d	162	a b c d	182	a b c d
103	a b c d	123	a b c d	143	a b c d	163	a b c d	183	a b c d
104	a b c d	124	a b c d	144	a b c d	164	a b c d	184	a b c d
105	a b c d	125	a b c d	145	a b c d	165	a b c d	185	a b c d
106	a b c d	126	a b c d	146	a b c d	166	a b c d	186	a b c d
107	a b c d	127	a b c d	147	a b c d	167	a b c d	187	a b c d
108	a b c d	128	a b c d	148	a b c d	168	a b c d	188	a b c d
109	a b c d	129	a b c d	149	a b c d	169	a b c d	189	a b c d
110	a b c d	130	a b c d	150	a b c d	170	a b c d	190	a b c d
111	a b c d	131	a b c d	151	a b c d	171	a b c d	191	a b c d
112	a b c d	132	a b c d	152	a b c d	172	a b c d	192	a b c d
113	a b c d	133	a b c d	153	a b c d	173	a b c d	193	a b c d
114	a b c d	134	a b c d	154	a b c d	174	a b c d	194	a b c d
115	a b c d	135	a b c d	155	a b c d	175	a b c d	195	a b c d
116	a b c d	136	a b c d	156	a b c d	176	a b c d	196	a b c d
117	a b c d	137	a b c d	157	a b c d	177	a b c d	197	a b c d
118	a b c d	138	a b c d	158	a b c d	178	a b c d	198	a b c d
119	a b c d	139	a b c d	159	a b c d	179	a b c d	199	a b c d
120	a b c d	140	a b c d	160	a b c d	180	a b c d	200	a b c d

Answer Sheet

TEST NO. ____

완전 철친 실전 토익 5회

LC MP3 바로듣기

응시일   년 월 일

맞은 개수

성명	한글	
	영어	
결과	LC	
	RC	

Listening Comprehension (Part I~IV)

NO.	ANSWER	NO.	ANSWER	NO.	ANSWER	NO.	ANSWER	NO.	ANSWER
1	ⓐⓑⓒⓓ	21	ⓐⓑⓒⓓ	41	ⓐⓑⓒⓓ	61	ⓐⓑⓒⓓ	81	ⓐⓑⓒⓓ
2	ⓐⓑⓒⓓ	22	ⓐⓑⓒⓓ	42	ⓐⓑⓒⓓ	62	ⓐⓑⓒⓓ	82	ⓐⓑⓒⓓ
3	ⓐⓑⓒⓓ	23	ⓐⓑⓒⓓ	43	ⓐⓑⓒⓓ	63	ⓐⓑⓒⓓ	83	ⓐⓑⓒⓓ
4	ⓐⓑⓒⓓ	24	ⓐⓑⓒⓓ	44	ⓐⓑⓒⓓ	64	ⓐⓑⓒⓓ	84	ⓐⓑⓒⓓ
5	ⓐⓑⓒⓓ	25	ⓐⓑⓒⓓ	45	ⓐⓑⓒⓓ	65	ⓐⓑⓒⓓ	85	ⓐⓑⓒⓓ
6	ⓐⓑⓒⓓ	26	ⓐⓑⓒⓓ	46	ⓐⓑⓒⓓ	66	ⓐⓑⓒⓓ	86	ⓐⓑⓒⓓ
7	ⓐⓑⓒ	27	ⓐⓑⓒⓓ	47	ⓐⓑⓒⓓ	67	ⓐⓑⓒⓓ	87	ⓐⓑⓒⓓ
8	ⓐⓑⓒ	28	ⓐⓑⓒⓓ	48	ⓐⓑⓒⓓ	68	ⓐⓑⓒⓓ	88	ⓐⓑⓒⓓ
9	ⓐⓑⓒ	29	ⓐⓑⓒⓓ	49	ⓐⓑⓒⓓ	69	ⓐⓑⓒⓓ	89	ⓐⓑⓒⓓ
10	ⓐⓑⓒ	30	ⓐⓑⓒⓓ	50	ⓐⓑⓒⓓ	70	ⓐⓑⓒⓓ	90	ⓐⓑⓒⓓ
11	ⓐⓑⓒ	31	ⓐⓑⓒⓓ	51	ⓐⓑⓒⓓ	71	ⓐⓑⓒⓓ	91	ⓐⓑⓒⓓ
12	ⓐⓑⓒ	32	ⓐⓑⓒⓓ	52	ⓐⓑⓒⓓ	72	ⓐⓑⓒⓓ	92	ⓐⓑⓒⓓ
13	ⓐⓑⓒ	33	ⓐⓑⓒⓓ	53	ⓐⓑⓒⓓ	73	ⓐⓑⓒⓓ	93	ⓐⓑⓒⓓ
14	ⓐⓑⓒ	34	ⓐⓑⓒⓓ	54	ⓐⓑⓒⓓ	74	ⓐⓑⓒⓓ	94	ⓐⓑⓒⓓ
15	ⓐⓑⓒ	35	ⓐⓑⓒⓓ	55	ⓐⓑⓒⓓ	75	ⓐⓑⓒⓓ	95	ⓐⓑⓒⓓ
16	ⓐⓑⓒ	36	ⓐⓑⓒⓓ	56	ⓐⓑⓒⓓ	76	ⓐⓑⓒⓓ	96	ⓐⓑⓒⓓ
17	ⓐⓑⓒ	37	ⓐⓑⓒⓓ	57	ⓐⓑⓒⓓ	77	ⓐⓑⓒⓓ	97	ⓐⓑⓒⓓ
18	ⓐⓑⓒ	38	ⓐⓑⓒⓓ	58	ⓐⓑⓒⓓ	78	ⓐⓑⓒⓓ	98	ⓐⓑⓒⓓ
19	ⓐⓑⓒ	39	ⓐⓑⓒⓓ	59	ⓐⓑⓒⓓ	79	ⓐⓑⓒⓓ	99	ⓐⓑⓒⓓ
20	ⓐⓑⓒ	40	ⓐⓑⓒⓓ	60	ⓐⓑⓒⓓ	80	ⓐⓑⓒⓓ	100	ⓐⓑⓒⓓ

※ 사용 필기구 : 연필(연필 이외의 사인펜, 볼펜 등은 절대 사용 불가)

Reading Comprehension (Part V~VII)

NO.	ANSWER	NO.	ANSWER	NO.	ANSWER	NO.	ANSWER	NO.	ANSWER
101	ⓐⓑⓒⓓ	121	ⓐⓑⓒⓓ	141	ⓐⓑⓒⓓ	161	ⓐⓑⓒⓓ	181	ⓐⓑⓒⓓ
102	ⓐⓑⓒⓓ	122	ⓐⓑⓒⓓ	142	ⓐⓑⓒⓓ	162	ⓐⓑⓒⓓ	182	ⓐⓑⓒⓓ
103	ⓐⓑⓒⓓ	123	ⓐⓑⓒⓓ	143	ⓐⓑⓒⓓ	163	ⓐⓑⓒⓓ	183	ⓐⓑⓒⓓ
104	ⓐⓑⓒⓓ	124	ⓐⓑⓒⓓ	144	ⓐⓑⓒⓓ	164	ⓐⓑⓒⓓ	184	ⓐⓑⓒⓓ
105	ⓐⓑⓒⓓ	125	ⓐⓑⓒⓓ	145	ⓐⓑⓒⓓ	165	ⓐⓑⓒⓓ	185	ⓐⓑⓒⓓ
106	ⓐⓑⓒⓓ	126	ⓐⓑⓒⓓ	146	ⓐⓑⓒⓓ	166	ⓐⓑⓒⓓ	186	ⓐⓑⓒⓓ
107	ⓐⓑⓒⓓ	127	ⓐⓑⓒⓓ	147	ⓐⓑⓒⓓ	167	ⓐⓑⓒⓓ	187	ⓐⓑⓒⓓ
108	ⓐⓑⓒⓓ	128	ⓐⓑⓒⓓ	148	ⓐⓑⓒⓓ	168	ⓐⓑⓒⓓ	188	ⓐⓑⓒⓓ
109	ⓐⓑⓒⓓ	129	ⓐⓑⓒⓓ	149	ⓐⓑⓒⓓ	169	ⓐⓑⓒⓓ	189	ⓐⓑⓒⓓ
110	ⓐⓑⓒⓓ	130	ⓐⓑⓒⓓ	150	ⓐⓑⓒⓓ	170	ⓐⓑⓒⓓ	190	ⓐⓑⓒⓓ
111	ⓐⓑⓒⓓ	131	ⓐⓑⓒⓓ	151	ⓐⓑⓒⓓ	171	ⓐⓑⓒⓓ	191	ⓐⓑⓒⓓ
112	ⓐⓑⓒⓓ	132	ⓐⓑⓒⓓ	152	ⓐⓑⓒⓓ	172	ⓐⓑⓒⓓ	192	ⓐⓑⓒⓓ
113	ⓐⓑⓒⓓ	133	ⓐⓑⓒⓓ	153	ⓐⓑⓒⓓ	173	ⓐⓑⓒⓓ	193	ⓐⓑⓒⓓ
114	ⓐⓑⓒⓓ	134	ⓐⓑⓒⓓ	154	ⓐⓑⓒⓓ	174	ⓐⓑⓒⓓ	194	ⓐⓑⓒⓓ
115	ⓐⓑⓒⓓ	135	ⓐⓑⓒⓓ	155	ⓐⓑⓒⓓ	175	ⓐⓑⓒⓓ	195	ⓐⓑⓒⓓ
116	ⓐⓑⓒⓓ	136	ⓐⓑⓒⓓ	156	ⓐⓑⓒⓓ	176	ⓐⓑⓒⓓ	196	ⓐⓑⓒⓓ
117	ⓐⓑⓒⓓ	137	ⓐⓑⓒⓓ	157	ⓐⓑⓒⓓ	177	ⓐⓑⓒⓓ	197	ⓐⓑⓒⓓ
118	ⓐⓑⓒⓓ	138	ⓐⓑⓒⓓ	158	ⓐⓑⓒⓓ	178	ⓐⓑⓒⓓ	198	ⓐⓑⓒⓓ
119	ⓐⓑⓒⓓ	139	ⓐⓑⓒⓓ	159	ⓐⓑⓒⓓ	179	ⓐⓑⓒⓓ	199	ⓐⓑⓒⓓ
120	ⓐⓑⓒⓓ	140	ⓐⓑⓒⓓ	160	ⓐⓑⓒⓓ	180	ⓐⓑⓒⓓ	200	ⓐⓑⓒⓓ

※ 1개의 정답만 골라 아래 <보기>의 올바른 표기대로 정확히 작성해야 합니다. 잘못된 필기구 사용과 잘못된 표기는 OMR기기가 판독하지 못한 결과에 따르며, 그 결과는 본인 책임입니다.

<보기> 올바른 표기 : ●   잘못된 표기 : ◐ ◑ ⊘ ○ ●

Answer Sheet

TEST NO. _____

응시일	년	월	일
성 명	한글		
	영어		

	년	월	일

맞은 개수	LC	
결과	RC	

완전 절친 실전 토익 5회

Listening Comprehension (Part I~IV)

NO.	ANSWER	NO.	ANSWER	NO.	ANSWER	NO.	ANSWER	NO.	ANSWER
1	a b c	21	a b c d	41	a b c d	61	a b c d	81	a b c d
2	a b c	22	a b c d	42	a b c d	62	a b c d	82	a b c d
3	a b c	23	a b c d	43	a b c d	63	a b c d	83	a b c d
4	a b c	24	a b c d	44	a b c d	64	a b c d	84	a b c d
5	a b c	25	a b c d	45	a b c d	65	a b c d	85	a b c d
6	a b c	26	a b c d	46	a b c d	66	a b c d	86	a b c d
7	a b c	27	a b c d	47	a b c d	67	a b c d	87	a b c d
8	a b c	28	a b c d	48	a b c d	68	a b c d	88	a b c d
9	a b c	29	a b c d	49	a b c d	69	a b c d	89	a b c d
10	a b c	30	a b c d	50	a b c d	70	a b c d	90	a b c d
11	a b c	31	a b c d	51	a b c d	71	a b c d	91	a b c d
12	a b c	32	a b c d	52	a b c d	72	a b c d	92	a b c d
13	a b c	33	a b c d	53	a b c d	73	a b c d	93	a b c d
14	a b c	34	a b c d	54	a b c d	74	a b c d	94	a b c d
15	a b c	35	a b c d	55	a b c d	75	a b c d	95	a b c d
16	a b c	36	a b c d	56	a b c d	76	a b c d	96	a b c d
17	a b c	37	a b c d	57	a b c d	77	a b c d	97	a b c d
18	a b c	38	a b c d	58	a b c d	78	a b c d	98	a b c d
19	a b c	39	a b c d	59	a b c d	79	a b c d	99	a b c d
20	a b c	40	a b c d	60	a b c d	80	a b c d	100	a b c d

Reading Comprehension (Part V~VII)

NO.	ANSWER	NO.	ANSWER	NO.	ANSWER	NO.	ANSWER	NO.	ANSWER
101	a b c d	121	a b c d	141	a b c d	161	a b c d	181	a b c d
102	a b c d	122	a b c d	142	a b c d	162	a b c d	182	a b c d
103	a b c d	123	a b c d	143	a b c d	163	a b c d	183	a b c d
104	a b c d	124	a b c d	144	a b c d	164	a b c d	184	a b c d
105	a b c d	125	a b c d	145	a b c d	165	a b c d	185	a b c d
106	a b c d	126	a b c d	146	a b c d	166	a b c d	186	a b c d
107	a b c d	127	a b c d	147	a b c d	167	a b c d	187	a b c d
108	a b c d	128	a b c d	148	a b c d	168	a b c d	188	a b c d
109	a b c d	129	a b c d	149	a b c d	169	a b c d	189	a b c d
110	a b c d	130	a b c d	150	a b c d	170	a b c d	190	a b c d
111	a b c d	131	a b c d	151	a b c d	171	a b c d	191	a b c d
112	a b c d	132	a b c d	152	a b c d	172	a b c d	192	a b c d
113	a b c d	133	a b c d	153	a b c d	173	a b c d	193	a b c d
114	a b c d	134	a b c d	154	a b c d	174	a b c d	194	a b c d
115	a b c d	135	a b c d	155	a b c d	175	a b c d	195	a b c d
116	a b c d	136	a b c d	156	a b c d	176	a b c d	196	a b c d
117	a b c d	137	a b c d	157	a b c d	177	a b c d	197	a b c d
118	a b c d	138	a b c d	158	a b c d	178	a b c d	198	a b c d
119	a b c d	139	a b c d	159	a b c d	179	a b c d	199	a b c d
120	a b c d	140	a b c d	160	a b c d	180	a b c d	200	a b c d

Answer Sheet

TEST NO. ____

완전절친 실전토익 5회

LC MP3 바로듣기

Listening Comprehension (Part I~IV)

NO.	ANSWER	NO.	ANSWER	NO.	ANSWER	NO.	ANSWER	NO.	ANSWER
1	ⓐⓑⓒⓓ	21	ⓐⓑⓒⓓ	41	ⓐⓑⓒⓓ	61	ⓐⓑⓒⓓ	81	ⓐⓑⓒⓓ
2	ⓐⓑⓒⓓ	22	ⓐⓑⓒⓓ	42	ⓐⓑⓒⓓ	62	ⓐⓑⓒⓓ	82	ⓐⓑⓒⓓ
3	ⓐⓑⓒⓓ	23	ⓐⓑⓒⓓ	43	ⓐⓑⓒⓓ	63	ⓐⓑⓒⓓ	83	ⓐⓑⓒⓓ
4	ⓐⓑⓒⓓ	24	ⓐⓑⓒⓓ	44	ⓐⓑⓒⓓ	64	ⓐⓑⓒⓓ	84	ⓐⓑⓒⓓ
5	ⓐⓑⓒⓓ	25	ⓐⓑⓒⓓ	45	ⓐⓑⓒⓓ	65	ⓐⓑⓒⓓ	85	ⓐⓑⓒⓓ
6	ⓐⓑⓒⓓ	26	ⓐⓑⓒⓓ	46	ⓐⓑⓒⓓ	66	ⓐⓑⓒⓓ	86	ⓐⓑⓒⓓ
7	ⓐⓑⓒ	27	ⓐⓑⓒ	47	ⓐⓑⓒⓓ	67	ⓐⓑⓒⓓ	87	ⓐⓑⓒⓓ
8	ⓐⓑⓒ	28	ⓐⓑⓒ	48	ⓐⓑⓒⓓ	68	ⓐⓑⓒⓓ	88	ⓐⓑⓒⓓ
9	ⓐⓑⓒ	29	ⓐⓑⓒ	49	ⓐⓑⓒⓓ	69	ⓐⓑⓒⓓ	89	ⓐⓑⓒⓓ
10	ⓐⓑⓒ	30	ⓐⓑⓒ	50	ⓐⓑⓒⓓ	70	ⓐⓑⓒⓓ	90	ⓐⓑⓒⓓ
11	ⓐⓑⓒ	31	ⓐⓑⓒ	51	ⓐⓑⓒⓓ	71	ⓐⓑⓒⓓ	91	ⓐⓑⓒⓓ
12	ⓐⓑⓒ	32	ⓐⓑⓒ	52	ⓐⓑⓒⓓ	72	ⓐⓑⓒⓓ	92	ⓐⓑⓒⓓ
13	ⓐⓑⓒ	33	ⓐⓑⓒ	53	ⓐⓑⓒⓓ	73	ⓐⓑⓒⓓ	93	ⓐⓑⓒⓓ
14	ⓐⓑⓒ	34	ⓐⓑⓒ	54	ⓐⓑⓒⓓ	74	ⓐⓑⓒⓓ	94	ⓐⓑⓒⓓ
15	ⓐⓑⓒ	35	ⓐⓑⓒ	55	ⓐⓑⓒⓓ	75	ⓐⓑⓒⓓ	95	ⓐⓑⓒⓓ
16	ⓐⓑⓒ	36	ⓐⓑⓒ	56	ⓐⓑⓒⓓ	76	ⓐⓑⓒⓓ	96	ⓐⓑⓒⓓ
17	ⓐⓑⓒ	37	ⓐⓑⓒ	57	ⓐⓑⓒⓓ	77	ⓐⓑⓒⓓ	97	ⓐⓑⓒⓓ
18	ⓐⓑⓒ	38	ⓐⓑⓒ	58	ⓐⓑⓒⓓ	78	ⓐⓑⓒⓓ	98	ⓐⓑⓒⓓ
19	ⓐⓑⓒ	39	ⓐⓑⓒ	59	ⓐⓑⓒⓓ	79	ⓐⓑⓒⓓ	99	ⓐⓑⓒⓓ
20	ⓐⓑⓒ	40	ⓐⓑⓒ	60	ⓐⓑⓒⓓ	80	ⓐⓑⓒⓓ	100	ⓐⓑⓒⓓ

응시일		년	월	일
성 명	한글			
	영어			

결과	LC	
	RC	

맞은 개수

Reading Comprehension (Part V~VII)

NO.	ANSWER	NO.	ANSWER	NO.	ANSWER	NO.	ANSWER
101	ⓐⓑⓒⓓ	121	ⓐⓑⓒⓓ	141	ⓐⓑⓒⓓ	161	ⓐⓑⓒⓓ	181	ⓐⓑⓒⓓ
102	ⓐⓑⓒⓓ	122	ⓐⓑⓒⓓ	142	ⓐⓑⓒⓓ	162	ⓐⓑⓒⓓ	182	ⓐⓑⓒⓓ
103	ⓐⓑⓒⓓ	123	ⓐⓑⓒⓓ	143	ⓐⓑⓒⓓ	163	ⓐⓑⓒⓓ	183	ⓐⓑⓒⓓ
104	ⓐⓑⓒⓓ	124	ⓐⓑⓒⓓ	144	ⓐⓑⓒⓓ	164	ⓐⓑⓒⓓ	184	ⓐⓑⓒⓓ
105	ⓐⓑⓒⓓ	125	ⓐⓑⓒⓓ	145	ⓐⓑⓒⓓ	165	ⓐⓑⓒⓓ	185	ⓐⓑⓒⓓ
106	ⓐⓑⓒⓓ	126	ⓐⓑⓒⓓ	146	ⓐⓑⓒⓓ	166	ⓐⓑⓒⓓ	186	ⓐⓑⓒⓓ
107	ⓐⓑⓒⓓ	127	ⓐⓑⓒⓓ	147	ⓐⓑⓒⓓ	167	ⓐⓑⓒⓓ	187	ⓐⓑⓒⓓ
108	ⓐⓑⓒⓓ	128	ⓐⓑⓒⓓ	148	ⓐⓑⓒⓓ	168	ⓐⓑⓒⓓ	188	ⓐⓑⓒⓓ
109	ⓐⓑⓒⓓ	129	ⓐⓑⓒⓓ	149	ⓐⓑⓒⓓ	169	ⓐⓑⓒⓓ	189	ⓐⓑⓒⓓ
110	ⓐⓑⓒⓓ	130	ⓐⓑⓒⓓ	150	ⓐⓑⓒⓓ	170	ⓐⓑⓒⓓ	190	ⓐⓑⓒⓓ
111	ⓐⓑⓒⓓ	131	ⓐⓑⓒⓓ	151	ⓐⓑⓒⓓ	171	ⓐⓑⓒⓓ	191	ⓐⓑⓒⓓ
112	ⓐⓑⓒⓓ	132	ⓐⓑⓒⓓ	152	ⓐⓑⓒⓓ	172	ⓐⓑⓒⓓ	192	ⓐⓑⓒⓓ
113	ⓐⓑⓒⓓ	133	ⓐⓑⓒⓓ	153	ⓐⓑⓒⓓ	173	ⓐⓑⓒⓓ	193	ⓐⓑⓒⓓ
114	ⓐⓑⓒⓓ	134	ⓐⓑⓒⓓ	154	ⓐⓑⓒⓓ	174	ⓐⓑⓒⓓ	194	ⓐⓑⓒⓓ
115	ⓐⓑⓒⓓ	135	ⓐⓑⓒⓓ	155	ⓐⓑⓒⓓ	175	ⓐⓑⓒⓓ	195	ⓐⓑⓒⓓ
116	ⓐⓑⓒⓓ	136	ⓐⓑⓒⓓ	156	ⓐⓑⓒⓓ	176	ⓐⓑⓒⓓ	196	ⓐⓑⓒⓓ
117	ⓐⓑⓒⓓ	137	ⓐⓑⓒⓓ	157	ⓐⓑⓒⓓ	177	ⓐⓑⓒⓓ	197	ⓐⓑⓒⓓ
118	ⓐⓑⓒⓓ	138	ⓐⓑⓒⓓ	158	ⓐⓑⓒⓓ	178	ⓐⓑⓒⓓ	198	ⓐⓑⓒⓓ
119	ⓐⓑⓒⓓ	139	ⓐⓑⓒⓓ	159	ⓐⓑⓒⓓ	179	ⓐⓑⓒⓓ	199	ⓐⓑⓒⓓ
120	ⓐⓑⓒⓓ	140	ⓐⓑⓒⓓ	160	ⓐⓑⓒⓓ	180	ⓐⓑⓒⓓ	200	ⓐⓑⓒ

global21.co.kr

여러분의 목표 달성을 응원합니다!

LC+RC

실전 토익

5 회

정답 및 스크립트

온라인 무료 제공 global21.co.kr ▶

완전절친 LC+RC

실전 토익

5 회

정답 및 스크립트

◁)) LC MP3 Actual Test 1

1 (B)	2 (D)	3 (A)	4 (D)	5 (B)	6 (D)	7 (A)	8 (A)	9 (B)	10 (A)
11 (B)	12 (C)	13 (B)	14 (B)	15 (B)	16 (A)	17 (B)	18 (A)	19 (C)	20 (C)
21 (B)	22 (A)	23 (A)	24 (C)	25 (C)	26 (A)	27 (A)	28 (B)	29 (B)	30 (A)
31 (C)	32 (C)	33 (B)	34 (C)	35 (B)	36 (C)	37 (B)	38 (C)	39 (C)	40 (A)
41 (B)	42 (C)	43 (B)	44 (C)	45 (A)	46 (B)	47 (A)	48 (C)	49 (D)	50 (C)
51 (B)	52 (B)	53 (C)	54 (B)	55 (A)	56 (A)	57 (D)	58 (B)	59 (D)	60 (B)
61 (D)	62 (D)	63 (C)	64 (C)	65 (C)	66 (D)	67 (D)	68 (A)	69 (B)	70 (D)
71 (C)	72 (B)	73 (D)	74 (A)	75 (D)	76 (A)	77 (B)	78 (C)	79 (C)	80 (B)
81 (B)	82 (A)	83 (B)	84 (A)	85 (C)	86 (D)	87 (D)	88 (D)	89 (C)	90 (C)
91 (A)	92 (D)	93 (D)	94 (C)	95 (D)	96 (A)	97 (A)	98 (D)	99 (D)	100 (D)
101 (A)	102 (B)	103 (C)	104 (D)	105 (D)	106 (C)	107 (B)	108 (D)	109 (D)	110 (C)
111 (B)	112 (C)	113 (C)	114 (B)	115 (D)	116 (D)	117 (D)	118 (B)	119 (B)	120 (B)
121 (D)	122 (B)	123 (B)	124 (A)	125 (B)	126 (B)	127 (B)	128 (B)	129 (C)	130 (C)
131 (A)	132 (D)	133 (D)	134 (C)	135 (B)	136 (D)	137 (B)	138 (C)	139 (C)	140 (A)
141 (C)	142 (B)	143 (D)	144 (C)	145 (D)	146 (D)	147 (D)	148 (B)	149 (B)	150 (A)
151 (B)	152 (A)	153 (D)	154 (D)	155 (A)	156 (B)	157 (A)	158 (B)	159 (C)	160 (D)
161 (A)	162 (B)	163 (D)	164 (B)	165 (C)	166 (B)	167 (B)	168 (B)	169 (C)	170 (C)
171 (C)	172 (A)	173 (A)	174 (C)	175 (B)	176 (A)	177 (C)	178 (D)	179 (B)	180 (C)
181 (D)	182 (D)	183 (B)	184 (B)	185 (B)	186 (A)	187 (B)	188 (A)	189 (B)	190 (D)
191 (C)	192 (D)	193 (B)	194 (A)	195 (C)	196 (C)	197 (C)	198 (A)	199 (A)	200 (C)

PART 1

1

◁)) 캐나다

(A) A person is holding a camera in his hand.

(B) A person is looking at a notebook.

(C) A person is putting something in a box.

(D) A person is taking a picture.

(A) 한 사람이 손에 카메라를 들고 있다.
(B) 한 사람이 수첩을 보고 있다.
(C) 한 사람이 상자 안에 무언가를 넣고 있다.
(D) 한 사람이 사진을 찍고 있다.

어휘 take a picture 사진을 찍다

2

◁)) 영국

(A) The bus is pulling into a parking lot.

(B) A car is picking up a passenger.

(C) Cars are lined up next to the bus.

(D) People are boarding the bus.

(A) 버스가 주차장으로 들어오고 있다.

(B) 차 한 대가 승객을 태우고 있다.

(C) 차들이 버스 옆에 나란히 있다.

(D) 사람들이 버스에 탑승하고 있다.

어휘 pull into (탈것이) ~에 들어오다 line up 줄을 서다 board (탈것에) 타다

3

◁)) 호주

(A) They are crossing a street.

(B) They are entering a driveway.

(C) They are turning a corner.

(D) They have their feet on the pedals.

(A) 사람들이 길을 건너고 있다.

(B) 사람들이 진입로에 진입하고 있다.

(C) 사람들이 코너를 돌고 있다.

(D) 사람들이 페달 위에 발을 올려놓고 있다.

어휘 cross (가로질러) 건너다 driveway 자동차 진입로

4

◁)) 미국

(A) They are leaving a building.

(B) They are putting their luggage on the counter.

(C) They are shopping for coats.

(D) They are waiting in line.

(A) 사람들이 건물에서 나오고 있다.

(B) 사람들이 짐을 카운터에 두고 있다.

(C) 사람들이 코트를 사고 있다.

(D) 사람들이 줄지어 기다리고 있다.

어휘 luggage 짐 wait in line 줄을 서서 기다리다

5

◁)) 호주

(A) Chairs are being folded up.

(B) Screens are hanging from the ceiling.

(C) Seats are filled with people.

(D) A speaker is standing on the stage.

(A) 의자가 접히고 있다.

(B) 스크린이 천장에 매달려 있다.

(C) 좌석이 사람들로 가득 차 있다.

(D) 발표자가 무대 위에 서 있다.

어휘 fold up 접다 hang from the ceiling 천장에 매달리다 be filled with ~로 가득 차다 stage 무대

6

◁)) 미국

(A) A ship is being painted.

(B) A ship is docking at a pier.

(C) People are getting on a ship.

(D) People are standing on the beach.

(A) 배에 페인트가 칠해지고 있다.

(B) 배가 항구에 정박하고 있다.

(C) 사람들이 배에 탑승하고 있다.

(D) 사람들이 해변에 서 있다.

어휘 dock 정박하다 pier 부두 get on ~에 탑승하다

PART 2

7 ◁)) 영국···미국

Does your university still offer night classes?

(A) Yes, on Tuesdays and Thursdays.

(B) It has a library on campus.

(C) Many students go to the school.

당신의 대학에서는 아직도 야간 수업을 하나요?

(A) 네, 화요일과 목요일이에요.

(B) 캠퍼스에 도서관이 있습니다.

(C) 많은 학생이 학교에 갑니다.

어휘 offer 제공하다

---

8 ◁)) 호주···캐나다

Whose mobile phone keeps ringing?

(A) It seems to be Jerry's.

(B) I think it's a good song.

(C) The caller is his sister.

누구 휴대폰이 계속 울리나요?

(A) Jerry의 휴대폰 같아요.

(B) 좋은 노래 같아요.

(C) 발신자가 그의 동생이에요.

어휘 ring 벨이 울리다 seem to ~인 것 같다

---

9 ◁)) 미국···호주

When did you go to the store?

(A) Across from the bank.

(B) I went this morning.

(C) The total was $24.92.

언제 그 가게에 갔습니까?

(A) 은행 건너편이에요.

(B) 오늘 아침에 갔습니다.

(C) 총 24.92달러입니다.

어휘 total 총(액)

---

10 ◁)) 캐나다···영국

The traffic is bad today.

(A) It's always like this on Fridays.

(B) The train was delayed due to the accident.

(C) I think that piece is fantastic.

오늘 교통체증이 심하군.

(A) 금요일마다 항상 이렇다고요.

(B) 사고 때문에 열차가 연착되었습니다.

(C) 제 생각에 그 작품은 환상적이에요.

어휘 due to ~ 때문에 accident (불의의) 사고, 재난 piece 작품, 물건

---

11 ◁)) 영국···캐나다

They haven't sold all of the new books by Mr. Martin, have they?

(A) Yes, if you want to see a movie.

(B) There are still a few left on the table over there.

(C) His latest book won an award.

그들은 Martin씨의 신간을 전부 팔지는 못했죠?

(A) 당신이 영화 보는 걸 원한다면, 그래요.

(B) 저쪽 탁자에 아직 몇 권이 남아 있습니다.

(C) 그의 최근 저서는 상을 받았습니다.

어휘 see a movie 영화를 보다 win an award 상을 타다

12 〔◁》 호주···미국〕

What was the last thing you read?

(A) It's a good way to spend a night.

(B) The event will last about 30 minutes.

(C) A great ghost story set in England.

어휘 last 계속되다 set in ~를 배경으로 하다

최근에 읽은 것이 무엇인가요?

(A) 밤을 보내는 좋은 방법이에요.

(B) 행사는 30분간 계속될 거예요.

(C) 영국을 배경으로 한 재미있는 유령 이야기예요.

---

13 〔◁》 영국···호주〕

Is Mr. Stark still the president of Wolf's Creek?

(A) The company is growing.

(B) He retired last year.

(C) I think they sell auto parts.

어휘 retire 은퇴하다 auto parts 자동차 부품

Stark씨는 아직 Wolf's Creek의 사장입니까?

(A) 그 회사는 성장하고 있습니다.

(B) 그는 작년에 은퇴했습니다.

(C) 그 회사는 자동차 부품을 판매하는 것 같습니다.

---

14 〔◁》 캐나다···미국〕

Why are the lights off in this room?

(A) There are four of them.

(B) No one was using it.

(C) The lunchroom is on the first floor.

어휘 lunchroom 구내식당

왜 이 방은 불이 꺼져 있나요?

(A) 넷이 있습니다.

(B) 아무도 사용하지 않아서요.

(C) 구내식당은 1층에 있어요.

---

15 〔◁》 미국···호주〕

Where should we meet next time?

(A) Probably in the morning.

(B) Let's go to a restaurant.

(C) Once a week is best.

다음에 어디서 만날까요?

(A) 아마도 아침에요.

(B) 식당에 갑시다.

(C) 일주일에 한 번이 제일 좋아요.

---

16 〔◁》 캐나다···영국〕

How often do you visit your hometown?

(A) Every two years or so.

(B) It's a few hours from here.

(C) My parents still live there.

어휘 or so ~ 정도

고향에 얼마나 자주 방문하나요?

(A) 대략 2년마다요.

(B) 여기서 몇 시간 걸립니다.

(C) 제 부모님은 여전히 그곳에서 사십니다.

17 ◁)) 미국···호주

Is she planning on flying to the conference?

(A) From Wednesday through Friday.

(B) She was, but all the flights were booked.

(C) These plans look great!

그녀는 회의에 비행기를 타고 갈 계획인가요?

(A) 수요일부터 금요일까지요.

(B) 그녀는 그럴 계획이었지만, 모든 항공편이 예약되어 있었어요.

(C) 이 계획들은 훌륭해 보여요!

어휘 plan on ~할 계획이다 book 예약하다

---

18 ◁)) 캐나다···미국

Where did the marketing team go?

(A) They're at a seminar.

(B) It's all in this folder.

(C) We need two additional members.

마케팅 팀은 어디 갔나요?

(A) 그들은 세미나에 참석 중입니다.

(B) 이 폴더 안에 다 들어 있습니다.

(C) 우리는 추가 인원이 두 명 필요합니다.

어휘 seminar 강연 additional 추가적인

---

19 ◁)) 영국···캐나다

He's taken on a lot of extra responsibility, hasn't he?

(A) No, he arrived five minutes ago.

(B) We'll take extra precautions, of course.

(C) Yes, and it's rather surprising.

그는 막중한 책임을 지고 있죠?

(A) 아뇨, 그는 5분 전에 도착했습니다.

(B) 물론 우리는 각별히 주의할 것입니다.

(C) 네, 놀라울 정도예요.

어휘 take on (책임을) 지다 precaution 예방책 rather 상당히

---

20 ◁)) 미국···호주

How did everything go at the convention?

(A) I'll try to be on time.

(B) In Los Angeles, I believe.

(C) Very well. I wish you had been there.

회의는 어땠나요?

(A) 제시간에 오도록 노력하겠습니다.

(B) 로스앤젤레스에서 하는 걸로 알고 있어요.

(C) 좋았어요. 당신도 있었더라면 좋았을 거예요.

어휘 convention 대규모 회의, 집회 on time 제시간에

---

21 ◁)) 영국···캐나다

I'm thinking about changing apartments.

(A) I pay nearly $2,000 a month.

(B) Oh, really? Why?

(C) We have only one more candidate.

아파트를 바꿀까 생각 중이에요.

(A) 저는 한 달에 거의 2,000달러를 지불해요.

(B) 정말이요? 왜죠?

(C) 후보자는 한 명 밖에 없습니다.

어휘 pay 지불하다 candidate 후보

22 〔◁» 호주···미국〕

Have all the attendees received a packet?

(A) Yes. I handed them out as they arrived.

(B) This package is addressed to someone else.

(C) No. We need to collect more data.

모든 참석자가 꾸러미를 받았나요?

(A) 네. 그들이 도착했을 때 나누어줬어요.

(B) 이 소포는 다른 사람 수신으로 되어 있네요.

(C) 아니요. 더 많은 자료를 수집해야 해요.

어휘 packet 소포, 꾸러미 hand out 나누어 주다 package 소포, 상자 address (우편물을) 보내다 collect 수집하다

---

23 〔◁» 호주···영국〕

When is a good time to reach Mr. Thompson?

(A) He's in the office by 8:00 every morning.

(B) I'm sorry, we've run out of time.

(C) It opened last week.

Thompson씨에게 언제 연락하는 게 좋을까요?

(A) 그는 매일 오전 8시에는 사무실에 있습니다.

(B) 죄송해요. 우리가 시간이 부족합니다.

(C) 그곳은 지난주에 문을 열었습니다.

어휘 run out of time 시간이 부족하다

---

24 〔◁» 캐나다···호주〕

Could you help me with next quarter's budget?

(A) Which floor are you going to?

(B) We went over by quite a bit.

(C) Yes, but I'm busy until noon.

다음 분기 예산안 좀 도와주시겠어요?

(A) 어느 층으로 가시나요?

(B) 우리 예산이 꽤 초과됐습니다.

(C) 네. 그런데 저는 정오까지는 바빠요.

어휘 quarter (4분의 1) 분기 go over 초과하다 quite a bit 꽤 많은

---

25 〔◁» 캐나다···미국〕

His sales numbers are slipping, unfortunately.

(A) All of our accessories are on sale today.

(B) I don't have time right now.

(C) What should we do about it?

안됐지만, 그의 영업 실적은 부진해요.

(A) 오늘 저희 액세서리 모두 판매 중입니다.

(B) 제가 지금은 시간이 없습니다.

(C) 그 일을 어떻게 해야 할까요?

어휘 sales number 판매 실적 slip (낮은 수준으로) 떨어지다 on sale 판매되는

---

26 〔◁» 미국···영국〕

Should we buy these supplies online or at the store?

(A) Whichever is cheaper.

(B) I'd rather take the train.

(C) We accept all types of credit cards.

이 공급품들을 온라인에서 사야 할까요, 상점에서 사야 할까요?

(A) 어느 쪽이든 저렴한 곳이요.

(B) 저는 차라리 기차를 타겠습니다.

(C) 저희는 모든 종류의 신용카드를 받고 있습니다.

어휘 supply 공급품 accept 받아들이다

27 🔊 호주…캐나다

The new clients have been entered in the system, right?

(A) I'm just finishing the last one.

(B) No. They're staying overnight.

(C) Yes. They just left.

시스템에 신규 고객이 입력되었죠?

(A) 이제 막 마지막 고객 등록을 마무리하고 있어요.

(B) 아뇨. 그들은 하룻밤 묵을 거예요.

(C) 네. 그들이 방금 떠났습니다.

어휘 stay overnight 하룻밤 묵다

---

28 🔊 미국…호주

Who is that waiting in the conference room?

(A) The client suddenly postponed the meeting.

(B) It must be my 10:00 appointment.

(C) The equipment is all ready.

회의실에서 기다리는 사람은 누구죠?

(A) 고객이 갑자기 회의를 연기했습니다.

(B) 10시에 저와 약속한 사람인가 봐요.

(C) 장비가 모두 준비되었습니다.

어휘 postpone 연기하다

---

29 🔊 캐나다…영국

Have you decided on a section leader yet?

(A) All seats in this section are reserved.

(B) It's between Logan and Maria.

(C) Not everyone is happy about it.

분단장을 아직 결정하지 못했나요?

(A) 이 구역의 모든 좌석이 예약되어 있습니다.

(B) Logan과 Maria 중 한 명입니다.

(C) 모두가 그에 만족하는 건 아닙니다.

어휘 section leader 반장 decide on ~로 결정하다 reserve 예약하다

---

30 🔊 캐나다…미국

You picked up the new brochures, didn't you?

(A) No, I'm just leaving to do that now.

(B) Whenever you decide to go is fine.

(C) Yes, they'll be ready tomorrow.

새로 나온 브로슈어를 가지고 왔죠?

(A) 아뇨. 지금 가져오려고 막 나가려던 참이에요.

(B) 당신이 언제 가기로 하든 괜찮아요.

(C) 네. 내일이면 준비될 거예요.

---

31 🔊 미국…영국

Will the company change its name after the merger?

(A) Everyone agrees on the amount.

(B) Yes, to Vancouver.

(C) We have no intention of doing so.

회사가 합병 후에 이름을 바꿀까요?

(A) 모든 사람이 액수에 동의해요.

(B) 네. 밴쿠버로요.

(C) 우리는 그럴 의향이 없어요.

어휘 merger (회사의) 합병 agree on ~에 동의하다 intention 의도

PART 3

Questions 32–34 refer to the following conversation. (◁)) 영국…호주

M Excuse me. ³²I'm going to City Stadium to watch the baseball game with my son. Is this the bus we should take?

W Yes, this bus goes to the stadium but I heard ³³there's long delay on Satellite Avenue because of road construction. If I were you, I'd take the subway.

M Oh, I didn't know I could get there on the subway.

W Yes, it's a new station. ³⁴Just get on the Blue Line and get off at 14th Street.

M Thank you very much.

남 실례합니다. 아들과 ³²야구 관람을 위해 City 스타디움으로 가려고 해요. 이 버스를 타면 되나요?

여 네. 이 버스가 경기장으로 가요. 그런데 ³³도로 공사 때문에 Satellite가에서 많이 지체된다고 들었어요. 저라면 지하철을 타겠어요.

남 지하철로 갈 수 있는지 몰랐어요.

여 네, 새로 생긴 역이에요. ³⁴파란 노선을 타고 14번가에서 내리면 돼요.

남 정말 감사합니다.

어휘 delay 지연, 지체 road construction 도로 공사 get off (탈것에서) 내리다

32 남자는 어디로 가는가?
(A) 버스정류장
(B) 콘서트홀
(C) 스포츠 경기장
(D) 극장

33 Satellite가에 대해 언급된 것은 무엇인가?
(A) 그 길은 새로 생긴 길이다.
(B) 그 길은 보수 중이다.
(C) 그 길은 폐쇄되었다.
(D) 그 길은 시내와 가깝다.

34 여자는 남자에게 무엇을 하라고 제안하는가?
(A) 택시 타기
(B) 집으로 돌아가기
(C) 파란 노선 타기
(D) 다음 버스 기다리기

어휘 venue 장소, 현장 theater 극장 repair 수리하다 downtown 시내 ride (탈것을) 타다

Questions 35–37 refer to the following conversation. (◁)) 캐나다…미국

W Well, Mr. French, from all I've heard today, ³⁵you are our strongest choice for the position. I just have a few more questions.

M Of course. And please call me Chris. Mr. French sounds like my father.

W Okay, Chris. ³⁵,³⁶Your resume shows you started the job you have now just six months ago. Why are you looking for a different job so soon?

M Actually, ³⁷my wife got promoted to branch manager here in Oak City, and we decided to relocate.

여 French씨, 제가 오늘 들어본 것을 종합해보면 ³⁵당신이 이 직책에 가장 유력하네요. 몇 가지 질문이 더 있습니다.

남 좋습니다. Chris라고 불러주세요. French씨는 제 아버지를 부르는 것처럼 들리거든요.

여 그래요, Chris. ³⁵,³⁶당신의 이력서를 보면 지금 일을 시작한 지 6개월 밖에 되지 않았어요. 왜 이렇게 빨리 다른 일을 찾고 있죠?

남 사실, ³⁷아내가 이곳 Oak시 지점장으로 승진했고, 우리 가족은 이사를 결심했거든요.

어휘 strongest choice 유력한 선택 position 자리, 직책 resume 이력서 branch 지점 relocate 이동하다

35 남자는 누구인가?
(A) 지점장
(B) 입사 지원자
(C) 모집자
(D) 기자

36 남자는 현재 직장에서 얼마나 일했는가?
(A) 2달
(B) 3달
(C) 반 년
(D) 1년

37 남자의 가족에 대해 언급된 것은 무엇인가?
(A) 아내가 그의 직업에 만족하지 않는다.
(B) 아내가 새로운 직위를 얻었다.
(C) 그들은 Oak시 출신이다.
(D) 그들은 옮기기를 원하지 않는다.

어휘 candidate 지원자 recruiter 모집자

Questions 38-40 refer to the following conversation. 〈📢 캐나다…영국〉

W Marcus, this is Sylvia from Three Rivers Inc. I'm sorry to do this to you at the last minute, but <u>³⁸I have to change our appointment tomorrow.</u> Something urgent came up and I have to leave the office early.

M That's no problem, Sylvia. Do you have time earlier in the day, like around noon?

W Actually, no. That's why I'm apologizing. I really have no time at all tomorrow. But the next day, <u>³⁹Thursday, I'm free in the morning.</u>

M <u>³⁹Works for me.</u> Why don't we say 10:00?

W Sounds good, Marcus. Thanks so much for your understanding. <u>⁴⁰I look forward to hearing your proposal for our joint project.</u>

여 Marcus, 저 Three Rivers사의 Sylvia예요. ³⁸임박해서 이런 말을 해서 미안하지만, 내일 약속 시간을 변경해야겠어요. 급한 일이 생겨서 빨리 퇴근을 해야 해요.

남 괜찮아요, Sylvia. 그날 좀 더 일찍 시간 괜찮아요? 정오쯤이라든가?

여 실은, 시간이 안 돼요. 그래서 사과드리는 거예요. 내일은 정말 시간이 없어요. 하지만 다음 날인 ³⁹목요일 아침에는 시간이 나요.

남 ³⁹전 좋아요. 10시 어때요?

여 좋아요, Marcus. 이해해줘서 정말 고마워요. ⁴⁰우리 공동 프로젝트 관련 제안 기대할게요.

어휘 at the last minute 임박해서 appointment 약속 urgent 긴급한 apologize 사과하다 Why don't we say ~? ~하는 것 어때요? joint project 공동 프로젝트

- - - - -

38 여자는 왜 사과하는가?
(A) 약속을 취소해야 해서
(B) 회의에 늦어서
(C) 회의 일정을 변경해야 해서
(D) 남자의 제안을 거절해서

39 〈신유형〉 남자가 Works for me라고 말한 의도는 무엇인가?
(A) 남자는 만나는 장소에 대해 동의하고 있다.
(B) 남자는 화상 대화가 괜찮다.
(C) 제시된 일정이 그에게 편하다.
(D) 여자가 그의 부서에서 일한다.

40 화자들은 회의에서 무엇을 논의할 것인가?
(A) 공동작업 계획
(B) 합병
(C) 남자의 예산안
(D) 여자의 자격요건

어휘 cancel 취소하다 reschedule 일정을 변경하다 refuse 거절하다 offer 제안 convenient 편한 department 부서 collaboration 공동작업 budget 예산 qualification 자격요건

- - - - -

Questions 41-43 refer to the following conversation. 〈📢 미국…호주〉

M Hi, Elizabeth. How are you? Did you do anything over the three-day weekend?

W Oh, hi Ben. Nothing special. <u>⁴¹Just worked in the garden.</u> You know, it was great weather to be outside. How about you?

M I took my family to the new amusement park on the west side of the city. It was absolutely packed with people. <u>⁴²We couldn't find a parking spot for about 30 minutes.</u>

W Sounds stressful. But I'm sure your kids loved it.

M Yes, once we finally got into the park, they had a great time. The roller coaster was their favorite. <u>⁴³I'll show you some pictures I took.</u>

남 안녕하세요, Elizabeth. 지난 3일 연휴 동안 뭐 좀 했어요?

여 안녕하세요, Ben. 별것 없었어요. ⁴¹그냥 정원에서 일했어요. 야외에 있기 정말 좋은 날씨였잖아요. 당신은요?

남 저는 가족들 데리고 시 서쪽에 생긴 놀이공원에 갔어요. 거긴 진짜 사람들로 꽉 찼었어요. ⁴²주차공간 찾는 데 30분이나 걸렸어요.

여 힘들었겠네요. 그래도 애들은 좋아했겠죠.

남 네, 일단 공원에 들어가니까 재미있게 놀더라고요. 아이들이 롤러코스터를 제일 좋아했어요. ⁴³제가 찍은 사진 몇 장 보여줄게요.

어휘 amusement park 놀이공원 packed with ~로 가득 찬 parking spot 주차장

41 여자는 주말에 무엇을 했는가?
(A) 집수리를 하였다.
(B) 정원에서 일하였다.
(C) 놀이공원을 방문했다.
(D) 그녀의 부모를 방문했다.

42 남자는 어떤 일에 어려움을 겪었는가?
(A) 어디로 갈지 결정하기
(B) 목적지를 찾아가기
(C) 주차공간을 확보하기
(D) 예약하기

43 여자는 다음에 무엇을 할 것인가?
(A) 자기 아이들에게 전화한다.
(B) 몇 장의 사진을 본다.
(C) 휴식을 취한다.
(D) 자기가 보낸 휴일을 이야기한다.

어휘 destination 목적지 make a reservation 예약하다 take a break 휴식하다

Questions 44-46 refer to the following conversation. 🔊 미국…캐나다

M Hello, ⁴⁴I'd like to make a reservation for six for next Monday night. I also have a question about your menu.

W Okay. We have a lovely table with a view that would seat six. What would you like to know about the menu?

M One woman in our party has a dietary restriction. ⁴⁵She's allergic to soy, so she can't have any soy based products or oil on any of her food.

W That won't be a problem. ⁴⁶Our chef is familiar with this type of restriction. He can prepare everything without soy for her.

M ⁴⁶That's a relief. It hasn't been easy finding a suitable restaurant for her.

남 여보세요? 다음 주 월요일 밤에 ⁴⁴여섯 명을 예약하려고 합니다. 그리고 그곳 메뉴에 관해 질문이 있습니다.

여 알겠습니다. 여섯 명이 앉아서 경치도 볼 수 있는 근사한 자리가 있습니다. 메뉴에 대해서는 무엇을 알고 싶으신가요?

남 우리 일행 중 여자 한 분이 식사 제한이 있습니다. ⁴⁵콩 알레르기가 있어서 콩으로 만든 제품이나 콩기름이 들어간 음식은 안 됩니다.

여 문제없습니다. ⁴⁶저희 주방장이 이런 종류의 식사 제한은 잘 알고 있어요. 그분 음식에는 콩이 들어가지 않게 준비해드릴 수 있습니다.

남 ⁴⁶그럼 안심이 되네요. 그분한테 맞는 식당을 찾는 게 쉬운 일이 아니었거든요.

어휘 with a view 전망이 좋은 party 일행 dietary 식이 요법의 restriction 제한 allergic to ~에 알레르기가 있는 prepare 준비하다 relief 안도 suitable 적합한

---

44 식당에 몇 명의 인원이 남자와 동행할 것인가?
(A) 3명
(B) 4명
(C) 5명
(D) 6명

45 남자의 일행 중 한 명에 대해 언급된 것은 무엇인가?
(A) 그녀는 심각한 알레르기가 있다.
(B) 그녀는 채식주의자다.
(C) 그녀는 경치가 좋은 자리를 좋아한다.
(D) 그녀는 늦게 참석할 것이다.

46 남자는 왜 That's a relief라고 하는가?
(신·유·형)
(A) 자기 손님들이 식당을 좋아하지 않을까 걱정하고 있다.
(B) 주방장이 그의 요청을 들어줄 수 있어서 기쁘다.
(C) 바쁜 시간에 예약할 수 있어서 만족한다.
(D) 메뉴 선택이 충분치 않을까 걱정하고 있다.

어휘 accompany 동반하다 serious 심각한 vegetarian 채식주의자 show up 나타나다 be concerned 걱정하다

Questions 47-49 refer to the following conversation. (호주…영국)

W Louis, ⁴⁸I've been getting complaints about the heater in Room C. I guess it's making a loud noise every time it turns on and off.

M Hmm, I just fixed that last week. I guess ⁴⁷this community center is just getting old. I'll look at it after lunch.

W It would be great if you could look at it now because there's a group coming at 1:00 to use the room. They're going to be listening to a lecture about the town's history.

M Okay. ⁴⁹Let me get my tools and I'll go over there.

여 Louis, ⁴⁸C호실의 난방기에 대한 민원이 들어오고 있어요. 전원을 키고 끌 때마다 소음이 나는 거 같아요.

남 흠, 지난주에 난방기를 고쳤는데요. 제 생각에는 ⁴⁷이 주민센터가 노후하고 있는 것 같아요. 점심 먹고 한번 확인해 볼게요.

여 지금 확인해준다면 좋을 것 같아요. 그 방을 사용하는 단체가 1시에 오거든요. 그분들은 마을 역사에 대한 강의를 들을 거예요.

남 알겠어요. ⁴⁹공구 챙겨서 거기로 갈게요.

어휘 complaint 불만 fix 고치다 tool 공구

---

47 대화가 이루어지고 있는 장소는 어디인가?
(A) 주민센터
(B) 호텔
(C) 도서관
(D) 양로원

48 여자가 언급한 문제는 무엇인가?
(A) 건물이 노후했다.
(B) 밖에서 하는 공사가 시끄럽다.
(C) 난방기가 제대로 작동하지 않는다.
(D) 방들이 너무 춥다.

49 남자는 다음에 무엇을 할 것인가?
(A) 관리부에 전화하기
(B) 점심 먹기
(C) 강의 듣기
(D) 공구 가져오기

어휘 retirement home 양로원 construction 공사 properly 적절하게 maintenance department 관리부, 유지보수 부서 retrieve 가져오다

Questions 50-52 refer to the following conversation. (영국…캐나다)

M Wendy, ⁵⁰congratulations on your Employee of the Year award. You deserve it after all your hard work on the new product line.

W Oh, thanks, Russell. It's a bit embarrassing since ⁵¹I was just part of a large group that worked really hard on the new line. It really was a team effort.

M But you were the leader of the team. Their cheerleader, so to speak. I know you put in extra-long hours over several months.

W Yes, it was a lot of work. But it paid off. ⁵²We have the number one tablet computer in the market now.

남 Wendy, ⁵⁰올해의 직원상을 받은 거 축하해요. 신제품 라인에 심혈을 기울여 일한 만큼, 당신은 그 상을 받을 자격이 있어요.

여 고마워요, Russell. ⁵¹저는 신제품 라인을 위해 열심히 일한 여러 사람들 중 한 명일 뿐이라서 좀 쑥스럽네요. 그건 정말 팀 전체의 노력이었어요.

남 하지만 당신이 팀의 리더였잖아요. 말하자면 치어리더인 셈이죠. 당신이 몇 달 동안 추가 근무를 한 거 알아요.

여 네, 일이 정말 많았어요. 하지만 성과를 거뒀죠. ⁵²이제 태블릿 컴퓨터 시장에서 우리가 1위예요.

어휘 deserve ~를 받을 만하다, ~할 가치[자격]이 있다 hard work 노고 embarrassing 난처한, 쑥스러운 so to speak 말하자면

---

50 남자는 왜 여자를 축하하는가?
(A) 여자가 결혼을 해서
(B) 여자가 승진해서
(C) 여자가 상을 받아서
(D) 여자가 계약을 따내서

51 여자는 자신의 팀에 대해서 뭐라고 말하는가?
(A) 그들은 전에 그녀와 같이 일한 적이 없다.
(B) 그들은 많은 노력을 기울였다.
(C) 그들은 그녀에게 협조적이지 않았다.
(D) 그들은 곧 전출될 것이다.

52 여자의 회사는 어떤 종류의 제품을 판매하는가?
(A) 옷
(B) 디지털 기기
(C) 자동차
(D) 의학품

Questions 53–55 refer to the following conversation. (◁)) 미국…호주 신 유 형

M Sarah, I'm having a lot of trouble with this catalog update. I was wondering if you could help me.

W Of course, Stephen. When I did the update a few years ago, I was surprised how much work it was. What seems to be the problem?

M ⁵³It's the photographer. He doesn't understand that the pictures of the new products should look similar to the older ones.

W That doesn't sound good. Are you using Cathryn Jacobs, the photographer I used?

M No, she wasn't available. I went with someone she recommended, but now I wish I had waited until Ms. Jacobs was free. And it's too late now since ⁵⁴the deadline is in two weeks.

W ⁵⁵Maybe if I went with you to the studio, I could try to explain what we want.

M That would be great. I'm sorry to take up your time like this.

W It's no problem. I'm happy to help.

남 Sarah, 제가 이 카탈로그를 업데이트하는 데 애를 먹고 있어요. 저 좀 도와줄 수 있나요?

여 물론이죠, Stephen. 몇 년 전에 제가 업데이트할 때, 작업 분량 때문에 놀랐죠. 무슨 문제예요?

남 ⁵³사진작가 때문이에요. 신제품 사진들이 구형 제품 사진들과 비슷해 보여야 한다는 것을 사진작가가 이해하지 못하고 있어요.

여 문제가 있네요. 제가 함께 일했던 사진작가 Cathryn Jacobs와 같이 하고 있어요?

남 아뇨, 그분은 같이 작업할 수 없었어요. 그녀가 추천한 사람하고 같이 했는데, 지금은 Jacobs 씨와 같이 일할 수 있을 때를 기다렸다면 좋겠다 싶어요. 그런데 지금은 ⁵⁴마감일이 2주 남아서 너무 늦었어요.

여 ⁵⁵제가 스튜디오에 같이 가면 우리가 원하는 것을 설명할 수 있을 것 같네요.

남 그러면 좋죠. 이렇게 시간을 뺏어서 죄송해요.

여 괜찮아요. 도울 수 있어서 기뻐요.

- - - - - -

53 남자의 문제는 무엇인가?
(A) 프로젝트를 위한 사진작가를 찾을 수 없다.
(B) 카탈로그에 넣을 사진이 충분하지 않다.
(C) 딱 맞는 종류의 사진이 없다.
(D) 마감일이 벌써 지났다.

54 2주 후에 어떤 일이 일어날 것인가?
(A) 사진작가가 일을 할 수 있을 것이다.
(B) 업데이트가 완료될 것이다.
(C) 남자는 직장을 구할 것이다.
(D) 여자는 프로젝트를 넘겨받을 것이다.

55 여자는 남자에게 무엇을 제안하는가?
(A) 남자와 함께 사진 촬영장에 가기
(B) 다른 사진작가 부르기
(C) 새로운 스튜디오 찾기
(D) 이전 카탈로그 검토하기

Questions 56-58 refer to the following conversation with three speakers. 🔊 캐나다…호주…미국 신유형

W1 It looks like ⁵⁶we're all ready for the facility inspection in Singapore. I've gotten our tickets and Jane, you booked the hotel, right?

W2 Yes, I found a place very close to the facility. It will be just a ten-minute taxi ride away.

W1 So we don't need to rent a car?

M I've been to Singapore before. ⁵⁷The public transit system is fantastic. Nobody needs to use a car in the city center, especially visitors.

W1 That's good news since ⁵⁸our boss wants us to keep expenses as low as possible. Well, be sure to bring your inspection checklists and passports. See you tomorrow.

여1 ⁵⁶싱가포르 공장 점검 준비가 다 된 것 같네요. 우리 항공권은 제가 가지고 있고, Jane은 호텔을 예약했죠?

여2 네, 공장과 아주 가까운 곳을 찾았어요. 택시를 타고 10분 거리에 있어요.

여1 그러면 차를 빌릴 필요가 없네요?

남 ⁵⁷전에 싱가포르에 갔던 적이 있어요. 대중교통 시스템이 아주 훌륭합니다. 시내 중심가에서 차를 사용할 필요가 없어요. 방문객들은 특히 그래요.

여1 좋은 소식이네요. 왜냐하면 ⁵⁸사장님이 가능한 한 적게 경비를 쓰라고 하셨거든요. 그럼, 점검 체크리스트와 여권을 반드시 지참해주세요. 내일 봐요.

어휘 facility 시설 inspection 점검 close to ~와 가까운 public transit 대중교통 expense 비용

---

56 화자들이 주로 논의하는 것은 무엇인가?
(A) 출장
(B) 회사의 새로운 정책
(C) 회사의 새로운 지점
(D) 그들의 최근 휴가

57 남자는 싱가포르에 대해 무엇을 언급하는가?
(A) 훌륭한 음식이 많다.
(B) 관광지가 많다.
(C) 아름다운 도시이다.
(D) 돌아다니기 편리하다.

58 화자들의 사장이 그들에게 원하는 것은 무엇인가?
(A) 점검 체크리스트 검토하기
(B) 비용 절감하기
(C) 특정 호텔에 머무르기
(D) 시설 관리자에게 저녁 대접하기

어휘 business trip 출장 policy 정책 recent 최근의 sightseeing spot 관광지 get around 돌아다니다 go over ~를 점검하다 cost 비용 specific 특정한 treat 대접하다

Questions 59-61 refer to the following conversation. 🔊 캐나다…미국

W Oh, no. I just realized ⁵⁹I forgot something at my office. Can you turn around and go back to where you picked me up?

M Uh, ⁶⁰I can't do a U-turn right here. So, I'll have to go around the block.

W That's fine. ⁵⁹I can't believe I left such an important file for my meeting there. I'm just glad I remembered if before we got too far.

M Okay, here we are. I'll wait here, but of course ⁶⁰the meter will be running.

W I understand. ⁶¹I won't be long.

여 오, 안 돼. 이제 알았는데, ⁵⁹사무실에 뭔가 놓고 온 것 같아요. 저 태운 곳으로 다시 되돌아갈 수 있으세요?

남 ⁶⁰여기서 유턴을 할 수는 없어요. 그래서 구역을 돌아서 가야 해요.

여 괜찮아요. ⁵⁹회의에 필요한 중요한 파일을 놓고 왔다니 믿을 수가 없네. 더 멀리 가기 전에 생각나서 다행이지.

남 자, 도착했습니다. 여기서 기다릴게요. 하지만 당연히 ⁶⁰미터기는 돌아가고 있을 겁니다.

여 알겠어요. ⁶¹오래 걸리지 않아요.

어휘 realize 깨닫다 do a U-turn 유턴하다 meter 계량기

59 여자의 문제는 무엇인가?
(A) 신분증을 찾을 수 없다.
(B) 지갑을 잃어버렸다.
(C) 길을 잃었다.
(D) 서류를 빠뜨렸다.

60 남자는 누구인가?
(A) 건물 경비원
(B) 택시기사
(C) 교통 기자
(D) 여자의 동료

61 🛈🛈🛈 여자의 말 I won't be long이 의미하는 것은 무엇인가?
(A) 그녀는 회의에 참석하고 싶지 않다.
(B) 그녀는 우회전하고 싶지 않다.
(C) 그녀는 짧은 대화를 선호한다.
(D) 그녀는 곧 돌아올 것이다.

어휘 lost 길을 잃은 security officer 경비원 make mad 화나게 하다

Questions 62-64 refer to the following conversation with three speakers. 🔊 미국…영국…호주 🛈🛈🛈

M1 Thank you for coming, Ellen. We have something we want to ask you.

M2 ⁶²How would you like to work at our overseas branch, you know, the one in Shanghai?

W Oh, I hadn't thought about it. I mean, ⁶³I thought this meeting was going to be an employee evaluation or something. I thought that's why you're here, Mr. Evans.

M2 Well, ⁶³as head of personnel I wanted to explain some of the details if you were to take us up on the offer.

M1 We've heard good things about you from your supervisor and we thought the time was right to give you some more responsibility.

W I'm really flattered, uh, honored. Since it's quite sudden, can I have some time to think it over?

M2 Of course. But there are a lot of things my department needs to sort out, like visas. So ⁶⁴we'll need an answer by the end of the month.

남1 와줘서 고마워요, Ellen. 당신에게 물어보고 싶은 것이 있어요.
남2 상하이에 있는 ⁶²우리 해외 지사에서 일해보는 것 어때요?
여 생각지도 못했어요. 제 말은, ⁶³이 회의가 직원평가 같은 것일 거라고 생각했어요. 그래서 Evans씨 당신이 여기에 온 거라 생각했어요.
남2 만약 Ellen씨가 이 제안을 받아들인다면 ⁶³인사과 부장으로서 제가 자세하게 설명하고 싶었습니다.
남1 Ellen씨의 상사에게서 당신에 대해 좋은 평가를 들어서, 지금이 당신에게 더 많은 직무를 주는 적기라고 생각했습니다.
여 정말 기쁘고 영광스러워요. 너무 갑작스러워서 그러는데, 생각할 시간을 좀 가져도 될까요?
남2 물론이죠. 하지만 비자나 그런 일로 저희 부서에서 처리해야 할 업무가 많아요. 그러니 ⁶⁴이번 달 말까지는 답변해주세요.

어휘 overseas branch 해외 지사 employee evaluation 직원평가 personnel 인사과 detail 세부 사항 supervisor 관리자 flattered 으쓱해지는 sudden 갑작스러운 sort out 정리하다

---

62 회의의 목적은 무엇인가?
(A) 직원평가를 실시하기 위해
(B) 새 지점에 대해 논의하기 위해
(C) 입사 지원자를 면접하기 위해
(D) 일자리를 제안하기 위해

63 Evans씨는 누구인가?
(A) 회사의 사장
(B) 해외 지사장
(C) 인사 부장
(D) 여자의 직속상관

64 여자는 이번 달 말까지 무엇을 해야 하는가?
(A) 새로운 직업 찾기
(B) 비자 받기
(C) 결정 내리기
(D) 상하이로 이사하기

어휘 conduct 실행하다 offer a position 일자리를 제안하다 director 부장 direct 직접적인

Questions 65-67 refer to the following conversation and list. (◁)) 호주…영국)

W Hey, Mark, ⁶⁵I found the list of music streaming services on the Internet. These services are pretty reasonable.

M Oh, thanks for this, Janice. ⁶⁶I want to be able to listen to music anywhere, especially when I'm on the train. I guess I can go for the cheap one since I just like hip hop.

W ⁶⁷I really like the idea of no limits since my musical taste is pretty varied. And I'd like to be able to listen to it on both my phone and PC.

여 Mark, ⁶⁵인터넷에서 음악 스트리밍 서비스 목록을 찾았어. 서비스 이용료가 아주 적당해.

남 고마워, Janice. ⁶⁶나는 어디에서든지 음악을 들을 수 있길 바라거든. 기차 안에서는 특히. 나는 힙합만 좋아하니까, 싼 걸로 고르면 될 것 같아.

여 ⁶⁷나는 무제한으로 들을 수 있다는 게 정말 좋아. 내 음악 취향은 굉장히 넓으니까. 그리고 음악을 전화와 컴퓨터 둘 다로 들을 수 있으면 좋겠어.

이름	요금(월)	이용 가능한 음악 개수(월)	기기
Music Depot	8.50달러	무제한	휴대폰
PlayNow	5달러	2,000	휴대폰
Smartsound	3.99달러	1,000	휴대폰, PC
⁶⁷X Hits	9.50달러	무제한	휴대폰, PC

어휘 reasonable 합리적인 taste 취향 varied 다양한

---

65 여자는 서비스에 대해 뭐라고 말하는가?
(A) 편리하다.
(B) 첨단기술이다.
(C) 요금이 적당하다.
(D) 아주 유명하다.

66 남자는 특히 어디에서 음악을 듣는 것을 좋아하는가?
(A) 집
(B) 체육관
(C) 일터
(D) 기차

67 목록에 의하면, 여자는 어떤 서비스를 선택할 것인가? (신유형)
(A) Music Depot
(B) PlayNow
(C) Smartsound
(D) X Hits

어휘 price 값을 매기다 fairly 적당한

Questions 68-70 refer to the following conversation and map. (◁)) 캐나다…영국)

W Mark, ⁶⁸the parade went really well last year. We got so many positive comments. And now we have to decide where we want the parade to start this year. Of course, it should be somewhere downtown.

M Well, we can't start it on Morris Street because it's too narrow. And Vector Street is out because of the fire station. That leaves two possible streets.

W ⁶⁹Why don't we start it at City Hall? There is a big plaza to gather in front.

M Sounds good. Now, all we need to do is get the permit.

W I've already filled out the permit application form. I just need to add the starting place information and the time. ⁷⁰Then I'll drop it at the city office on my way home this evening.

여 Mark, ⁶⁸작년 퍼레이드는 정말 순조로웠잖아요. 긍정적인 의견을 아주 많이 받았어요. 이제 올해 퍼레이드의 출발점은 어디로 할지 정해야 해요. 물론, 시내 어딘가가 되겠지요.

남 Morris가는 너무 비좁아서 거기부터 출발할 수는 없어요. 그리고 Vector가는 소방서가 있으니 제외하죠. 이렇게 되면 두 거리가 가능성이 있네요.

여 ⁶⁹시청에서 시작하는 것은 어때요? 앞에 모일 수 있는 큰 광장이 있잖아요.

남 좋은 생각이에요. 이제 우리가 해야 할 일은 허가를 받는 것뿐이네요.

여 허가신청서는 제가 이미 작성했어요. 출발지 정보와 시간만 추가하면 돼요. ⁷⁰제가 오늘 저녁 퇴근하는 길에 시청에 들러서 낼게요.

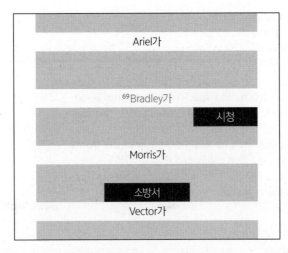

Ariel가

⁶⁹Bradley가

시청

Morris가

소방서

Vector가

어휘 go well 순조로이 진행되다 positive 긍정적인 narrow 좁은 gather 모이다 permit 허가 fill out (양식을) 채우다 application form 신청서

68 퍼레이드에 대해 뭐라고 말할 수 있는가?
(A) 작년에 성공적이었다.
(B) 올해는 취소될 것이다.
(C) 처음으로 개최될 것이다.
(D) 퍼레이드 예산이 증액되었다.

69 🆕🔰 지도에 의하면, 퍼레이드는 어디서 시작될 것인가?
(A) Ariel가
(B) Bradley가
(C) Morris가
(D) Vector가

70 여자는 무엇을 할 것이라고 말하는가?
(A) 시청에 전화하기
(B) 입사 지원서 작성하기
(C) 남자의 서류 작성을 돕기
(D) 관공서 방문하기

어휘 hold 열리다 increase 증가하다 paperwork 서류 작업

PART 4

Questions 71–73 refer to the following news report. 🔊 호주

Well, after more than ten years away, hometown hero and basketball star ⁷¹Harrison Jones is finally returning home. Mr. Jones has just announced his retirement and relocation back here to Orangeton. ⁷²After nearly eight years in the professional league, Mr. Jones suffered an injury in a game last season. Though doctors did everything they could, he eventually had to give up playing. Since then ⁷³he's been to 20 different cities talking about his book and now he's coming back here to open up a sports gym chain.

10여 년이 흘러, 마침내 고향의 영웅이자 농구 스타인 ⁷¹Harrison Jones가 고향에 돌아옵니다. Jones씨는 막 자신의 은퇴와 함께 이곳 Orangeton으로 거취를 옮길 것이라고 발표했습니다. ⁷²프로 리그에서 8년에 가까운 활약을 했던 Jones씨는 지난 시즌 경기 도중 부상을 입었습니다. 의사들이 할 수 있는 모든 것을 다 했지만, 결국 Jones씨는 운동을 포기해야 했습니다. 이후 ⁷³그는 20개의 도시를 돌며 자신의 책에 대해 이야기했으며, 이제 이곳으로 돌아와 스포츠 체육관 체인점을 열려고 합니다.

어휘 return 돌아오다 announce 발표하다 retirement 은퇴 relocation 이전, 이사 suffer 고통 받다 injury 부상 give up 포기하다 chain 체인점

---

71 Orangeton에 대해 암시하는 것은 무엇인가?
(A) 크게 성장하고 있다.
(B) 프로 스포츠 팀을 모으고 있다.
(C) Jones씨가 태어난 곳이다.
(D) 화자가 좋아하는 장소이다.

72 Jones씨는 몇 년간 프로선수로 활동했는가?
(A) 5년
(B) 8년
(C) 10년
(D) 20년

73 Jones씨는 최근에 무엇을 했는가?
(A) 가게를 열었다.
(B) 병원을 떠났다.
(C) 경기에 참여했다.
(D) 여러 곳을 다녔다.

어휘 imply 암시하다 experience 경험하다 growth 성장

Questions 74-76 refer to the following telephone message. 🔊 미국

Hello, this is Vince Conklin. **74I own the East End Diner on Main Street.** A friend recommended **75I call you to get an estimate on putting window coverings** on our south facing windows. The customers are complaining about the late afternoon sun in the front part of our restaurant. **76Could you give me a call at 555-2839 when you get this message?** I'd like to get started on this as soon as possible since the weather is warming up.

안녕하세요? 74저는 Vince Conklin입니다. Main 가에 있는 East End Diner의 주인입니다. 친구의 추천으로 전화드렸는데 75저희 가게의 남쪽 창문에 창문 덮개를 설치하는 건으로 견적을 받고 싶습니다. 늦은 오후에 식당 정면으로 들어오는 햇빛에 손님들이 불평하거든요. 76이 메시지를 확인하시면 555-2839로 전화주세요. 날씨가 따뜻해지고 있기 때문에 가급적 빨리 이 일을 시작하고 싶어요.

어휘 get an estimate 견적을 뽑다 customer 손님

---

74 전화를 건 사람은 누구인가?
(A) 사업주
(B) 수신자의 친구
(C) 엔지니어
(D) 기상 요원

75 수신자는 무엇을 제공해줄 수 있는가?
(A) 출장연회 서비스
(B) 현지 식품
(C) 새 창문
(D) 견적서

76 Conklin씨는 수신자에게 무엇을 부탁하는가?
(A) 빨리 회신하기
(B) 그의 조수에게 연락하기
(C) 이메일로 회신하기
(D) 그의 사무실에 들르기

어휘 forecaster 예측하는 사람 locally grown 현지에서 재배된 quotation 견적 contact 연락하다 assistant 조수 reply 대답하다 stop by ~에 들르다

Questions 77-79 refer to the following advertisement. 🔊 캐나다

Does your house of apartment need a thorough cleaning but you just don't have the time? If you're an older couple who just can't keep up with the tasks or a busy working mom who's just plain tired, let Merry Workers help you out. **77Our cheerful staff of cleaners** can come in and do what might take you several days in a few hours. **78It will give you a big lift** to walk into your fresh-smelling and orderly house after a long day. **79Call us today for a new customer discount of up to 25 percent,** depending on the size of your place. 555-3829.

아파트는 대청소가 필요한데, 당신은 시간이 부족한가요? 그런 일을 정기적으로 할 수 없는 노부부이거나, 그저 피곤하고 바쁜 워킹맘이라면 Merry Worker가 도와드리겠습니다. 77저희 쾌활한 청소 직원이 방문해서 여러분이 며칠이 걸릴 일을 단 몇 시간 내에 해드릴 수 있습니다. 긴 하루를 마치고 산뜻한 향기가 가득한 정돈된 집에 들어가는 것으로 78기분이 좋아질 것입니다. 오늘 전화주세요. 79신규 고객을 대상으로 최대 25%의 할인이 집 크기에 따라 적용됩니다. 전화번호는 555-3829입니다.

어휘 thorough cleaning 대청소 keep up with ~를 계속 해나가다 cheerful 쾌활한 give a big lift 기분을 좋아지게 하다 orderly 정돈된 discount 할인 depending on ~에 따라

77 어떤 업종을 광고하고 있는가?
(A) 보육 서비스
(B) 청소 서비스
(C) 배송 서비스
(D) 노인 요양 서비스

78 화자가 It will give you a big lift라고 말한 의도는 무엇인가?
(A) 서비스로 인해 광고를 듣는 사람들이 돈을 절약할 것이다.
(B) 서비스가 광고를 듣는 사람들이 가뿐해지는 데 이용될 것이다.
(C) 서비스로 인해 광고를 듣는 사람들이 행복해질 것이다.
(D) 서비스가 광고를 듣는 사람들이 가야 하는 곳으로 데려다줄 것이다.

79 할인받을 수 있는 사람은 누구인가?
(A) 할인 코드를 대는 사람
(B) 특정한 크기의 집을 가진 사람
(C) 전에 서비스를 이용하지 않은 사람
(D) 특정 지역에 거주하는 사람

어휘 childcare 보육 delivery 배송의 feel light 가뿐하다 certain 특정한 area 지역

Questions 80-82 refer to the following broadcast. 〈)) 영국

Good evening. I'm Rex Madison with your news update. Our top story tonight is ⁸⁰the approval of a new bridge over the Marble River. While the river is our city's most visible landmark, it makes it rather inconvenient to get from one side of town to the other. Now we'll have two bridges to choose from. Taxpayers approved the bridge last November, but ⁸¹it has taken six months for city officials to choose a construction company. They finally went with the lowest bidder, ⁸²Nine Point Construction, a local business that expects to hire more than 50 people for the five-year project.

좋은 저녁입니다. Rex Madison이 최신 뉴스를 전달합니다. 오늘 밤 헤드라인은 ⁸⁰Marble강에 새로 놓일 다리의 승인에 대한 뉴스입니다. 이 강은 우리 시에서 가장 눈에 띄는 명소지만, 마을 한쪽에서 다른 쪽으로 이동하는 데 오히려 불편이 되었습니다. 이제 선택할 수 있는 다리가 두 개 생깁니다. 납세자들은 다리 건설을 지난 11월에 찬성했지만 ⁸¹시 관계자들이 건설사를 선택하는 데 6개월이 걸렸습니다. 최종 최저액 입찰사인 ⁸²현지 업체 Nine Point 건설은 향후 5년의 사업기간 동안 50명이 넘는 일자리를 창출하리라 예상하고 있습니다.

어휘 approval 승인 visible (눈에) 보이는 inconvenient 불편한 taxpayer 납세자 construction company 건설사 bidder 입찰자

---

80 새로운 다리는 어디를 지나갈 것인가?
(A) 호수
(B) 강
(C) 계곡
(D) 일부 열차 선로

81 프로젝트는 왜 지연되었는가?
(A) 시민들이 승인하고 싶지 않았다.
(B) 시가 건설업자를 결정하지 못했다.
(C) 시에 돈이 없었다.
(D) 건설사에 문제가 있었다.

82 건설사가 할 것으로 예상되는 일은 무엇인가?
(A) 다수의 사람을 고용하는 것
(B) 기자 회견을 여는 것
(C) 입찰 절차를 시작하는 것
(D) 경쟁사보다 싼 가격에 입찰하는 것

어휘 builder 건축업자 employ 고용하다 press conference 기자 회견 bidding 입찰 process 절차 underbid 낮은 가격에 입찰하다

Questions 83-85 refer to the following talk. 〈)) 호주

Just a quick word before we open this morning. As you know, we're having our big annual sale this weekend. ⁸³Many customers wait to buy all their clothes at this sale, so it gets pretty busy. Based on last year's sales, ⁸⁴business really picked up between 5:00 and 7:00 PM, so I need more of you for that time. I've adjusted the schedule and posted it on the bulletin board in the break room. Please check it before you leave today. Of course, ⁸⁵anybody working a longer shift will be paid overtime, which is double your hourly wage.

오늘 아침 개장 전에 잠시 말씀드리겠습니다. 아시다시피, 이번 주말에 연례 세일 행사가 있습니다. ⁸³많은 고객들이 이 세일 행사 때 옷을 사려고 기다리기 때문에 정말 바쁠 겁니다. 작년 판매를 보면, ⁸⁴오후 5시에서 7시 사이가 가장 바빠서 그 시간에 더 많은 분이 필요합니다. 일정을 조정해서 휴게실 게시판에 붙여놨습니다. 오늘 퇴근 전에 확인해주세요. 물론, ⁸⁵연장 근무자는 초과 수당을 받을 겁니다. 초과 수당은 시급의 두 배입니다.

어휘 annual 매년의 based on ~에 근거하여 pick up 바쁘다 adjust 조정하다 bulletin board 게시판 shift 교대 근무 hourly wage 시급

83 안내는 어디에서 이루어지고 있는가?
- (A) 서점
- (B) 옷 가게
- (C) 식료품 가게
- (D) 신발 가게

84 business really picked up between 5:00 and 7:00 PM이라는 화자의 말이 암시하는 것은 무엇인가?
- (A) 많은 손님이 저녁 시간에 방문했다.
- (B) 고객들이 셔틀버스를 이용해 가게에 왔다.
- (C) 저녁에 특별 할인이 제공되었다.
- (D) 저녁에 일하는 사람은 두 배의 보수를 받았다.

85 안내를 듣는 사람들은 이번 주말에 연장 근무를 하면 무엇을 받을 것인가?
- (A) 보너스
- (B) 무료 상품
- (C) 더 높은 급여
- (D) 유급 휴가

어휘 grocery 식료품의 merchandise 물품 salary 급여 day off 휴가

Questions 86–88 refer to the following advertisement. (◁») 미국

Are you unreasonably tired at the end of the day? Do you have trouble staying awake after lunch? **86**Then you need our all-natural energy supplement, Pep Pills. **87**These supplements are nonaddictive and perfectly safe for people over 15. Made with ginseng and vitamin B₁₂, Pep Pills give you a big boost of energy quickly. Available in capsule or convenient gel form. Don't look for Pep Pills at the drug store. **88**They're only sold online at www.peppills.com. Visit our Website for a free sample sent right to your door. No obligation, no charge.

하루가 끝날 무렵이면 턱없이 피곤한가요? 점심식사 후에 깨어 있기 어려우신가요? **86**그렇다면 여러분은 천연 에너지 보충제 Pep Pills가 필요합니다. **87**이 보충제는 중독성이 없으며, 15세 이상에게도 완벽하게 안전합니다. 인삼과 비타민 B₁₂로 만들어진 Pep Pills는 여러분에게 대량의 에너지를 빠르게 공급해줍니다. 캡슐 또는 편리한 젤 형태로 구입하실 수 있습니다. 약국에서 Pep Pills를 찾지 마세요. **88**온라인 www.peppills.com에서만 구매하실 수 있습니다. 저희 웹사이트를 방문하시면 무료 샘플을 집에서 받아보실 수 있습니다. 의무사항이 아니며 지불하실 필요도 없습니다.

어휘 unreasonably 지나칠 정도로 supplement 보충제 nonaddictive (약이) 중독되지 않는 obligation 의무 charge 요금

86 무엇을 광고하는가?
- (A) 음료
- (B) 건강식품
- (C) 의약품
- (D) 보충제

87 광고 제품을 누가 사용할 수 있는가?
- (A) 누구나
- (B) 입원 환자 전용
- (C) 학생 전용
- (D) 15세 이상인 사람

88 제품은 어디서 구입이 가능한가?
- (A) 건강 박람회
- (B) 모든 건강식품 가게
- (C) 모든 약국
- (D) 인터넷

어휘 exhibition 박람회 drugstore 약국

Questions 89–91 refer to the following talk. (◁») 캐나다

Just wanted to let everybody know before they leave for the weekend that the parking lot to the north side will be closed next week, Monday through Friday, for resurfacing. **89**That means we will be restricted to the east end parking lot, which is smaller. **90**I encourage you to carpool or take public transportation because parking in that lot will be first come, first served. With only 25 spots, **91**some of you may have to find street parking, which is expensive and far from the office.

여러분이 주말을 맞이하기 전에 알립니다. 북쪽에 있는 주차장이 다음 주 월요일부터 금요일까지 재포장으로 인해 폐쇄됩니다. **89**따라서 동쪽 끝에 있는 더 작은 주차장만 사용하도록 제한됩니다. 선착순으로 주차를 하기 때문에 **90**카풀이나 대중교통을 이용하실 것을 권장합니다. 25대만 주차를 할 수 있으니 길거리 주차장을 찾아야 하는 분들도 있을 텐데, **91**요금은 비싸고 사무실에서 멀리 있습니다.

어휘 resurface 재포장하다 restrict 제한하다 encourage 권장하다 first come, first served 선착순 spot 자리

89 주로 무엇에 대해 이야기하는가?
(A) 사무실 확장
(B) 신입직원의 첫날
(C) 주차 장소 변경
(D) 대중교통 요금

90 직원들에게 무엇을 장려하는가?
(A) 책상의 청결 상태 유지하기
(B) 설문 조사 참여하기
(C) 차를 함께 타고 출근하기
(D) 신입직원 환영하기

91 화자에 의하면, 다음 주에 몇몇 직원들은 어떤 일을 겪게 될 것인가?
(A) 먼 거리 걷기
(B) 시끄러운 공사 소음
(C) 서늘한 사무실
(D) 새 책상 배정

어휘 expansion 확장 location 위치 fee 비용 survey 설문조사 participate in ~에 참여하다 temperature 온도 assignment 배정

Questions 92-94 refer to the following announcement and receipt. (◁) 영국

Attention customers. Thank you for shopping with us at Fern Grove Department Store today. As a reminder, our annual sale is ongoing on all floors. 92 Discounts between 40 and 60 percent can be found on all items in some sections, such as kids' clothing and women's shoes. 93 The sale ends tomorrow at closing, so don't delay. Remember to bring your receipt and parking ticket for validation to any of our customer service desks throughout the store. 94 Free parking is offered for those with purchases over 50 dollars. 93 We will be closing in 30 minutes, at 8:00, as usual.

고객께 안내 말씀드립니다. 오늘 Fern Grove 백화점을 찾아주셔서 감사합니다. 다시 한 번 알려드리면, 저희 연례 세일이 전 층에서 진행 중입니다. 92 아동 의류와 여성 제화 등 몇몇 구역에서 40~60퍼센트를 할인하는 상품을 보실 수 있습니다. 93 세일은 내일 영업 종료와 동시에 끝나니 미루지 마세요. 백화점 곳곳에 있는 고객서비스 데스크에서 영수증과 주차확인증을 잊지 말고 지참하세요. 94 50달러 이상 구매하신 분들께 무료 주차가 제공됩니다. 93 저희는 평소처럼 30분 후 8시에 영업을 종료할 예정입니다.

Fern Grove 백화점	
♪♪ 저희 백화점을 이용해주셔서 감사합니다. ♪♪	
여성 블라우스	55달러
부가세(10%)	5.50달러
94 총액	60.50달러
고객님의 소중한 의견 감사합니다.	
www.ferngrovedepart.com	

어휘 reminder 상기시키는 것 ongoing 계속 진행 중인 delay 미루다 validation 확인

---

92 고객은 아동 재킷을 최대 얼마까지 할인 받을 수 있는가?
(A) 30%
(B) 40%
(C) 50%
(D) 60%

93 세일은 언제 끝나는가?
(A) 오늘 오후 5시
(B) 오늘 밤 8시
(C) 내일 12시
(D) 내일 밤 8시

94 영수증에 의하면, 고객은 무엇을 받을 수 있는가?
신 유 형
(A) 추가 할인
(B) 공짜 선물
(C) 무료 주차
(D) 환불

어휘 refund 환불(금)

Questions 95-97 refer to the following excerpt of meeting and layout. (ⓘ 호주)

[95]Thanks everyone for your hard work on the next issue. Our subscribers are really going to like the beautiful photographs we're adding to the magazine. Now I'd like to mention a change to the office renovation plans. I've talked with the architect and she said that to get the most light in our studio, we should add one more set of windows. [96]That will mean the room next to the studio will be smaller. [97]I'd like to hear from anyone who has any objections or concerns about this now. What do you think?

[95]다음 호를 작업해주신 여러분의 노고에 감사드립니다. 구독자들은 우리가 잡지에 넣는 아름다운 사진들을 정말 좋아할 것입니다. 이제 사무실 개조 계획 관련 변경 사항에 대해 말씀드리겠습니다. 건축가와 이야기를 나누었는데 스튜디오를 더 밝게 하려면 창문을 한 세트 더 추가해야 한다고 합니다. [96]그로 인해 스튜디오 옆방이 더 작아집니다. [97]이 상황에 대해 이의가 있거나 우려하는 사람이 있으면 지금 의견을 듣고 싶습니다. 어떻게 생각하시나요?

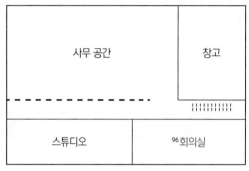

어휘 subscriber 구독자 renovation 개조 architect 건축가 objection 이의 concern 우려 storage 저장(소)

95 화자는 어떤 업종에 종사하는가?
(A) 건축
(B) 건설
(C) 의료
(D) 출판

96 (신유형) 설계도에 의하면, 개조 후 어느 방이 작아질 것인가?
(A) 회의실
(B) 사무 공간
(C) 창고
(D) 스튜디오

97 직원들이 다음에 할 일은 무엇인가?
(A) 사무실 배치에 대해 토론한다.
(B) 함께 점심을 먹는다.
(C) 신제품 계획을 짠다.
(D) 건축가와 이야기한다.

어휘 layout 배치

Questions 98-100 refer to the following announcement and timetable.

Attention passengers. [98]Please be aware that we've had a change of time for one of our trains leaving soon. [99]The express to Gilmore Station will leave ten minutes later than scheduled. We apologize for this delay. If you are taking the express to Gilmore Station, please go to Platform 3. The local to Green River is leaving from Platform 4. As a reminder, [100]cars 5 to 9 are for passengers with reserved tickets only. If you have an unreserved ticket, please enter at the front of the train, in cars 1 to 4.

승객 여러분께 안내드립니다. [98]곧 출발하는 기차의 출발 시간이 바뀌었다는 것을 알려드립니다. [99]Gilmore역 행 급행열차는 예정보다 10분 늦게 출발합니다. 지연에 대해 사과드립니다. Gilmore역 행 급행열차를 타신다면 3번 승강장으로 가시기 바랍니다. Green River행 완행열차는 4번 승강장에서 출발합니다. 안내드리면, [100]5번부터 9번 칸은 예약된 승차권을 소지한 승객들을 위한 차량입니다. 예약하지 않은 티켓을 소지하고 있으신 경우에는 열차의 앞쪽 1번부터 4번 칸에 탑승해주시기 바랍니다.

승강장	시간	목적지
1	15:30	Arendale
2	15:35	Hastings Cross
3	⁹⁹15:45	Gilmore역
4	15:48	Green River

어휘 passenger 승객 be aware 알다 express (탈것의) 급행 platform (역의) 승강장 reserved 예약된 unreserved 예약되어 있지 않은 enter 들어가다

---

98 화자는 누구인가?
(A) 승객
(B) 열차 차장
(C) 열차 기관사
(D) 기차역 직원

99 신유형 시간표에 의하면, Gilmore역으로 가는 기차는 몇 시에 출발할 것인가?
(A) 15:35
(B) 15:45
(C) 15:48
(D) 15:55

100 예약된 승차권을 가진 승객은 어디로 가야 하는가?
(A) 1번 차량
(B) 2번 차량
(C) 4번 차량
(D) 8번 차량

어휘 train conductor 열차 차장

PART 5

101

저희 회의실을 예약하고 싶다면 프로젝터나 비디오카메라 같은 장비가 필요한지 알려주세요.

(A) 장비   (B) 편의 시설
(C) 기구   (D) 자료

어휘 equipment 장비 amenity 편의 시설 instrument 기구 materials 자료, 자재

102

AtoZ 산업은 여러분의 필요에 딱 맞는 다수의 임대 사무가구와 사무용품을 제공합니다.

(A) 임대료, 임대하다   (B) 임대의
(C) 임차인   (D) 임대하다

어휘 plenty of 많은 rental 임대의

103

귀하의 컴퓨터에 소프트웨어 설치 시 문제가 생긴다면, 저희 고객서비스 센터로 전화하시거나 또는 이메일을 보내실 수 있습니다.

(A) 그리고   (B) ~도 아닌
(C) 또는   (D) ~에

어휘 install 설치하다

104

시의회는 대학원생 집단이 창작한 건축 제안을 정기적으로 받는다.

(A) 최근에   (B) 유사하게
(C) 매우   (D) 정기적으로

어휘 similarly 유사하게

105

기조연설이 막판에 취소되자, 행사의 주최사는 대체할 것을 찾아야 했다.

(A) 대체하다   (B) 대체할 수 있는
(C) 대체하는   (D) 대체(물)

어휘 keynote speech 기조연설 organizer 주최자 replacement 대체할 것

106

그 리더는 자신의 프로젝트 계획이 얼마나 현실적인지 팀 전원이 진행에 합의할 때까지 장황하게 설명했다.

(A) ~의 경우에 대비하여   (B) ~를 생각하면
(C) ~까지   (D) ~인지 아닌지

어휘 at length 상세히 practical 현실적인 proceed 진행하다 in case ~의 경우에 대비하여 given that ~를 고려하면

107

Sarah Luther는 새로운 인트라넷 시스템에 관한 의무 세미나에 참석하기 위해 서둘러 사무실로 돌아와야 했다.

(A) 많은   (B) 의무적인
(C) 다용도의   (D) 자발적인

어휘 numerous 많은 mandatory 의무적인 versatile 다용도의 voluntary 자발적인

108

난방 문제 때문에 영업팀은 극히 추운 방에서 회의를 해야 했다.

(A) 초과하다   (B) 초과했다
(C) 엄청난   (D) 극도로

어휘 exceedingly 극도로

109

전 직원은 회사의 새로운 정책에 대해 통지받았고 모든 규정에 동의함을 인정해야 한다.

(A) 그들의 것   (B) 그들을
(C) 그들 자신   (D) 그들은

어휘 be required to ~하라는 요구를 받다 acknowledge 인정하다 inform 알리다 in all respects 모든 점에서

110

Melba 로지스틱스는 전 세계로 빠르고 안전한 운송 서비스를 제공하는 허가받은 운송업체입니다.

(A) 전송하는   (B) 갖춘
(C) 제공하는   (D) 받는

어휘 licensed 허가된 carrier 운송 회사 rapid 빠른 forward 전송하다 equip 장비를 갖추다 provide 제공하다

111

50개국에서 300명이 넘는 사람들이 제15회 국제 환경과학 학술대회에 참가했다.

(A) ~ 중에   (B) ~로부터
(C) ~ 너머로   (D) ~를 통해

어휘 take part in ~에 참가하다

112

이사회의 승인으로 Henderson씨는 다음 달에 의장직을 맡게 될 것이다.

(A) 승인할 수 있는   (B) 승인하다
(C) 승인   (D) 양도인

어휘 board 위원회 assume (책임을) 맡다 post 지위 endorsement 승인

113

통신망 접속 규약과 관련해 문제가 있거나 궁금한 점이 있으시면 저희 IT부서에 연락해주세요.

(A) 선정   (B) 발전
(C) 규약   (D) 순서

어휘 selection 선정 advance 발전 protocol 통신 규약 sequence 순서

114

재정고문에 의하면, 사전에 상세한 조사를 하는 것이 주식을 사는 데 있어 매우 중요하다.

(A) 세부 사항
(B) 상세한
(C) 세부적인 것을 다루는
(D) 세부 사항들

어휘 financial advisor 재정고문 conduct research 연구하다 beforehand 사전에 crucial 중대한 stocks 주식 detailed 상세한

115

인사부장은 지원자를 면접 볼 때 예상외의 질문을 하는 것이 그들을 판단하는 데 유용할 수 있다고 생각한다.

(A) 게다가
(B) ~이 아니라면
(C) 그런데도
(D) ~할 때

어휘 personnel chief 인사부장 consider 고려하다 unexpected 뜻밖의 judge 판단하다

116

팀 매니저는 신제품을 부분적으로 수정하기보다는 전체적인 디자인을 재고해야 한다고 생각했다.

(A) 중심의
(B) 여분의
(C) 주요한
(D) 전체의

어휘 rather than ~보다는 partially 부분적으로 modify 수정하다

117

계약이 끝나가고 있기 때문에 회사는 주말까지 모든 소유물을 치우고 임차한 부동산을 비워야 할 것이다.

(A) 공석들
(B) 공허
(C) 공허한
(D) 비우다

어휘 remove 치우다 possession 소유(물) property 부동산 vacancy 공허, 빈자리 vacate 비우다

118

소비자 경향 보고서에 의하면, 사람들은 최근 휴가에 돈을 적게 쓰고 대신 저축을 했다.

(A) 더 적은
(B) 더 적은
(C) 많은
(D) 더 많은

어휘 consumer 소비자 instead 대신에

119

신형 노트북인 TGX 800은 기존 모델보다 급격히 개선되었고 사용이 훨씬 쉬워져 많은 호평을 받았다.

(A) 주로
(B) 급격히
(C) 간신히
(D) 임시로

어휘 improve 개선하다 mostly 주로 drastically 극단적으로 scarcely 간신히 temporarily 임시로

120

사장은 지난 몇 주간 회사의 주가가 꾸준히 떨어지는 것에 대해 극도로 걱정하고 있다.

(A) has dropped
(B) has been dropping
(C) is dropping
(D) will drop

어휘 extremely 극히 stock price 주가 steadily 꾸준히 drop 떨어지다

121

놀랍게도, 몇 가지 긴급 변경이 있었음에도 제품 출시는 상당히 순조롭게 진행되었다.

(A) 놀람
(B) 놀란
(C) 놀라운
(D) 놀랍게도

어휘 launch 출시 smoothly 순조롭게

122

Mason 엔지니어링은 더욱 고객 중심의 기업이 되기 위해 한 해 동안 몇 가지 큰 변화를 겪었다.

(A) 과소평가하다
(B) 겪다
(C) 약화시키다
(D) 이해하다

어휘 customer-focused 고객 중심의 underestimate 과소평가하다 undergo 겪다 undermine 약화시키다

123

행사가 Celia홀 대신 Hamilton홀에서 열린다는 것을 모든 참가자들에게 알리기 위해 이메일 한 통이 발송되었다.

(A) ~에 앞서
(B) ~ 대신
(C) 그래도
(D) 따라서

어휘 notify 알리다 participant 참석자 prior to ~에 앞서

124

연장자 무료 버스 승차 중지에 반대하는 집회에 거의 1,000명의 사람들이 참석했다.

(A) 참석한
(B) 발표
(C) 제시된
(D) 발표자

어휘 nearly 거의 protest 항의 discontinuation 중지 senior 연장자 present 참석한

125

수집된 개인정보는 법원 명령을 제외하고 사전 동의 없이는 제3자에게 공개되지 않는다.

(A) 분석
(B) 동의
(C) 논의
(D) 약속

어휘 personal information 개인정보 disclose 밝히다 third party 제3자 prior 사전의 except ~를 제외하고 analysis 분석 consent 동의 discussion 논의 engagement 약속

126

근본적인 대인관계의 마찰을 포함한 문제가 항상 타협으로 해결되는 것은 아니다.

(A) what
(B) that
(C) where
(D) whose

어휘 compromise 타협, 절충 resolve 해결하다 underlying 근본적인, 숨겨진 interpersonal 대인관계에 관련된 conflict 갈등

127

Jade 개인병원은 환자의 만족을 위해 굉장히 <u>헌신</u>하는 것으로 지역에서 훌륭한 평판을 쌓았다.

(A) 저지르다
(B) 헌신
(C) 수감
(D) 헌신적인

어휘 establish (명성을) 확고히 하다 reputation 평판 satisfaction 만족 commit 저지르다 commitment 헌신 committal 수감

128

식당이 번창하여 주인은 그 지역에서 사업을 확장하는 것을 고려 중이다.

(A) 생산적인
(B) 번창하는
(C) 전략적인
(D) 분투하는

어휘 expand 확장하다 region 지역 productive 생산적인 prosperous 번성하는 strategic 전략적인 struggling 분투하는

129

강의에서 그 유명 요리사는 청중들에게 <u>어떻게</u> 그렇게 간단한 조리법으로 맛있는 요리를 만들 수 있는지에 대해 말했다.

(A) 마치 ~인 것처럼
(B) ~에도 불구하고
(C) 어떻게
(D) 그때

어휘 lecture 강연 renowned 유명한 audience 청중 recipe 조리법 result in ~를 야기하다

130

IT 직원은 네트워크 문제를 바로잡으려고 오랜 시간을 보냈지만, <u>해결할 수</u> 없었다.

(A) down
(B) off
(C) out
(D) over

어휘 iron out 해결하다

PART 6

131-134 📧 이메일

수신: Amanda Green
발신: Exciting 여행사
제목: 코스타리카를 방문하세요.
날짜: 3월 19일

Exciting 여행사가 밝히는 당신이 코스타리카를 방문해야 하는 3가지 이유

1. 모험을 ¹³¹갈망한다면 코스타리카는 확실히 여러분을 위한 곳입니다. 급류 래프팅, 카약, 스쿠버다이빙, 암벽 다이빙, 스카이다이빙 등 셀 수 없이 많은 모험을 할 수 있습니다.
2. ¹³²1,000마일에 달하는 해안선과 더불어, 코스타리카는 세계에서 가장 아름다운 해변의 본고장입니다. 공유 해변과 사유 해변 모두

¹³³여러분과 같이 태양과 모래를 사랑하는 사람들을 기쁘게 해줄 것입니다.
3. 코스타리카가 지구상에서 가장 행복한 나라라고 불리는 데에는 타당한 이유가 있습니다. 사람들은 평온하고, 친근하며, 모든 방문객들이 자기 집이라고 느낄 수 있도록 각별한 노력을 하고 있습니다.
저희 코스타리카 여행 ¹³⁴패키지에 대한 자세한 내용은 웹사이트 www.excitingtravel.net을 방문해주세요.

어휘 crave 열망하다 definitely 확실히 white-water 급류의 please 기쁘게 하다 good reason 타당한 이유 go out of one's way to ~하기 위해 특별히 애를 쓰다

131

(A) 만약 ~한다면
(B) 아마
(C) 어디에
(D) ~인지 아닌지

132 신 유 형

(A) 코스타리카는 세계적으로 유명한 열대 우림을 보유하고 있으며 많은 환경 단체들이 투어를 한다.
(B) 아이들이 있다면, 여섯 개의 수영장을 보유한 저희 리조트의 이점을 누리고 싶을 것입니다.
(C) 저희는 코스타리카의 훌륭한 여행 상품을 판매하고 있습니다. 곧 만료되니 미루지 말고 오늘 전화하세요.
(D) 1,000마일에 달하는 해안선과 더불어, 코스타리카는 세계에서 가장 아름다운 해변의 본고장입니다.

어휘 rainforest 열대 우림 environmental 환경의 organization 조직 expire 만료되다 put off 미루다 coastline 해안선

133

(A) 우리 자신
(B) 그들을
(C) 그들 자신
(D) 당신 자신

134

(A) 대리점
(B) 보험
(C) (여행) 패키지
(D) 조언

어휘 agency 대리점 insurance 보험

135-138 📰 기사

Stamford로 이전하는 미디어 회사

STAMFORD—Westville에 ¹³⁵본사를 두고 있는 라이브 스트리밍 미디어 회사 Blasted는 몇 달 내로 Stamford의 남쪽 끝에 있는 복합상업지구로 이전할 계획이다. 이 회사는 Brookbend 센터에 9,500 평방 장기임대계약에 ¹³⁶서명한 후 올해 2분기 중에 이전할 예정이다. "Brookbend 센터는 설립 ¹³⁷이후 많은 첨단기술 회사들의 고향이 되었으며, Blasted가 Brookbend를 미래의 보금자리로 하는 것을 기쁘게 생각하고 있습니다." 부동산 관리자 Jonathan Turner는 성명서에서 이와 같이 말했습니다. Norton 강 옆에 위치한 Brookbend 센터는 40 에이커에 걸쳐 있습니다. 센터에는 200명까지 수용 가능한 회의실과 강당, 6개의 회의실이 있습니다. ¹³⁸또한 이곳에는 구내식당과 1,457대를 수용할 수 있는 주차장, 그리고 여러 개의 산책로가 있습니다.

135

(A) base
(B) based
(C) is basing
(D) was based

136

(A) 만든
(B) 잃은
(C) 제안한
(D) 서명한

137

(A) ~까지
(B) ~한 이후로
(C) ~까지
(D) 아직

138 신유형

(A) Turner씨는 사무실 공간을 원하는 다른 잠재 세입자들로부터 신청서를 받고 있습니다.
(B) 소식통들에 의하면 회사는 이사 후 국내 제조 능력을 확장할 예정이라고 합니다.
(C) 또한 이곳에는 구내식당과 1,457대를 수용할 수 있는 주차장, 그리고 여러 개의 산책로가 있습니다.
(D) Blasted의 행보가 고전하고 있는 제품의 수익을 올릴지 시간이 지나면 알 수 있을 것입니다.

139-142 메모

사내 메모

수신: 전 직원
발신: Oscar Mendelson
날짜: 5월 25일
제목: 신입직원을 환영합니다.

Joanne Remnick씨가 고객서비스부의 공석을 메우기 위해 Medifast사에 입사함을 알립니다. Joanne씨는 BioServe사의 고객서비스 분야에서 5년 이상 139일했습니다. 그녀는 그곳에서 일하는 동안 이 달의 직원상을 여러 번 받았으며 상급자들로부터 140적극 추천을 받았습니다.

Joanne씨의 직속상관은 Robert Vesper씨이니, 문의할 내용이 있으면 그녀의 근무 시작 전에 Robert씨와 141이야기하면 되겠습니다. Joanne씨가 Medifast팀에 합류하게 되어 기쁩니다.

Joanne씨의 첫 근무일은 6월 13일 화요일이 될 것입니다. 142건물 주변에서 Joanne씨를 보면 입사를 환영해주세요.

139

(A) is working
(B) will have worked
(C) worked
(D) works

140

(A) 매우
(B) 주로
(C) 대부분은
(D) 공정하게

141

(A) 공유하면
(B) 해결하면
(C) 이야기하면
(D) 생각하면

142 신유형

(A) 다음 주에는 이곳에 안전검사관들이 올 예정이니, 늦게 출근하지 마세요.
(B) 건물 주변에서 Joanne씨를 보면 입사를 환영해주세요.
(C) Joanne씨는 고객서비스부에서 최고의 직원 중 한 명이었고, 우리는 그녀를 그리워할 것입니다.
(D) 그때까지 반드시 이 달의 직원에 대한 제안사항을 제출해주세요.

143-146 이메일

수신: Atlas 부동산 관리대행사
발신: Buildmore사 Rita Hanson
날짜: 5월 13일
제목: 필요한 수리

5월 12일에 있었던 대화에 대한 후속 조치로 Bradford 건물 301호에 위치한 귀사 사무실의 수리를 143요청하는 바입니다. 그 사무실은 당사의 어떠한 잘못, 남용, 부주의로 인한 것이 아닌 저희가 이사 왔을 144때부터 수리가 필요했습니다. 수리가 필요한 항목은 다음과 같습니다. 안쪽 사무실 문 한 짝(걸쇠 파손), 사무실 남쪽의 난방장치(켜기/끄기가 제대로 되지 않음)

145당연히 저희는 이 문제를 가능하면 빨리 처리하고 싶습니다. 유감스럽게도 이런 문제 때문에 이 사무실에서 사업을 146하는 데 방해가 되고 있습니다. 언제 수리하실 예정인지 알려주세요.
Rita

143

(A) 청구서
(B) 견적
(C) 답장
(D) 요청

144

(A) 비록 ~일지라도
(B) ~ 때문에
(C) ~하는 때
(D) ~인지 아닌지

145 (신)(유)(형)—

(A) 당사는 최근에 디자인과 능률성 부문에서 여러 개의 상을 수상했습니다.
(B) 이 사무실은 공간 활용성과 자연광 같은 훌륭한 특성을 많이 갖추고 있습니다.
(C) 저희의 협업 제안에 대해 귀하의 회신을 기대합니다.
(D) 당연히 저희는 이 문제를 가능하면 빨리 처리하고 싶습니다.

어휘 efficiency 능률 attribute 특징 spaciousness 공간 활용성 natural light 자연광 proposal 제안

146

(A) conducting
(B) conducted
(C) conducts
(D) to conduct

어휘 conduct (특정한 활동을) 하다

PART 7

147-148 (제품설명서)

3중 믹서기 TopSpeed를 구매해주셔서 감사합니다. 저희는 사용이 쉽고 고품질인 자사의 주방용품과 식기를 자랑스럽게 생각하고 있습니다.
새 믹서기를 사용하려면 먼저 포장용기에서 부품들을 꺼내고 설치를 시작합니다. ¹⁴⁷믹서기의 본체가 무거우므로 포장의 바닥부터 개봉하면 제품이 떨어질 수 있음을 양지하십시오.
제품은 본체 1개, ¹⁴⁸칼날 2개, 통 1개, 서빙컵 4개로 구성되어 있습니다. 사용 전에 기계의 모든 부품을 깨끗이 청소하십시오. 사용할 칼날을 고르시고(¹⁴⁸큰 날 한 개, 작은 날 한 개, 다른 사이즈는 별도 판매), 본체에 칼날을 고정시킵니다. 고정되었다면 이제 사용할 준비가 되었습니다. 그다음으로 플러그를 꽂고, 재료를 넣고, 통이 꽉 닫혔는지 확인하십시오. 그러면 3중 믹서기 TopSpeed를 사용할 준비가 다 된 것입니다.

어휘 trine 3배의 pride on ~를 자랑스럽게 생각하다 appliance 가전제품 utensil (주방에서 사용하는) 기구 container 포장용기 setup 설치 blade 날 attachment 부가 장치 pitcher 주전자, 병 thoroughly 완전히 separately 별도로 screw 나사로 고정시키다 secured 고정된 plug in 플러그를 꽂다 ingredient 재료

147

고객이 제품을 꺼낼 때 주의해야 할 점은 무엇인가?
(A) 설치 설명서
(B) 칼날의 날카로움
(C) 상자를 여는 칼의 종류
(D) 박스 개봉 방식

어휘 installation instruction 설치 설명서 sharpness 날카로움

148

상자에는 몇 가지의 칼날이 포함되어 있는가?
(A) 1
(B) 2

(C) 3
(D) 4

149-150 (문자 메시지) (신)(유)(형)—

Steve Bedrosian [오전 9:34]	Mark, 귀찮게 해서 미안해요. 새 고객하고 약속 시간이 다 된 걸 알지만 부탁할 게 있어요.
Mark Fitz [오전 9:37]	무슨 일인데요?
Steve Bedrosian [오전 9:39]	¹⁴⁹제가 하루 종일 사무실에서 회의가 있어서 그러는데 돌아오는 길에 서쪽 사무실에 들러서 오늘 저녁 여기 회의 때 쓸 Bunker Hill 프로젝트 디자인 서류를 가져다줄 수 있어요?
Mark Fitz [오전 9:41]	알겠어요. 지금 고객 사무실로 가고 있어요. 멀지 않으니까 여기 일을 끝내고 잠깐 들러서 가져다줄게요. 프로젝트가 예정대로 진행되고 있나요?
Steve Bedrosian [오전 9:43]	고마워요. 그 디자인으로 원래 BH 프로젝트를 재구성할지, 아님 다음 봄에 있을 새로운 Wilder 프로젝트를 시작할 때 사용할지 논의할 거예요.
Mark Fitz [오전 9:48]	좋은 소식이네요! ¹⁵⁰그 디자인이 다시 뽑히길 기대하고 있었어요. 디자인이 떨어졌을 때 모습을 갖춰가는 방식이 정말 좋았거든요. 제가 서류를 찾아서 돌아갈 때 다시 문자 보낼게요.

어휘 bother 귀찮게 하다 client 고객 be stuck in ~에 갇히다 swing by ~에 들르다 grab 잡다 appreciate 감사하다 have discussion 논의하다 restructure 재구성하다

149

Bedrosian씨가 회의 서류를 갖고 오지 못하는 이유는 무엇인가?
(A) 그는 Bunker Hill에 가야 한다.
(B) 그는 회사에 계속 있어야 한다.
(C) 그의 동료가 휴가를 냈다.
(D) 서류가 아직 준비되지 않았다.

어휘 prevent 막다 colleague 동료

150 (신)(유)(형)—

오전 9시 48분에 Fitz씨가 I really liked the way it was shaping up이라고 말한 의미는 무엇인가?
(A) 그는 프로젝트의 디자인이 좋았다고 생각했다.
(B) 그는 회의가 잘 조직되었다고 생각했다.
(C) 그는 프로젝트가 불필요한 것들을 줄이고 있다고 생각했다.
(D) 그는 그 일정이 잘될 것이라고 생각했다.

어휘 organized 잘 정돈된 unnecessary 불필요한

151-152 (안내문)

Rosa's Italian Homestead가 4월 16일 토요일 52번가 지점을 다시 개장함을 알려드리며, 모든 분들이 저희의 새로운 외관과 메뉴를 보러 오시기 바랍니다. 지난 30년 동안 저희는 지역에 최고급 요리를 제공해왔지만, 식당을 현대화하여 디자인과 음식을 업데이트하고 싶었습니다.

Mariemont 지역에서 즐거운 시간을 보내시는 여러분께 감사의 표시로, 이번 달 한정 특별 요리를 몇 가지 제공할 예정입니다! 오셔서 ¹⁵²전통적인 시칠리아 파스타 알라 노르마, 마니코티, 신선한 해산물 요리 황새치 알라 교따를 즐기세요. ¹⁵¹첫째 주 동안, 세 코스 특별 요리를 라지 사이즈 피자 한 판 가격에 제공합니다. 들어오셔서 Rosa 식당의 신선한 맛을 경험해보세요!

어휘 location 지점 finest dish 최고급 요리 modernize 현대화하다 gratitude 감사 plate 요리

151
특별 할인은 언제 끝나는가?
(A) 며칠 후
(B) 주말
(C) 이번 달 말
(D) 다음 달 말

152
특별 재개장 메뉴로 Rosa 식당에서 제공하지 않는 음식은 무엇인가?
(A) 라지 사이즈 피자
(B) 마니코티 요리
(C) 해산물 요리
(D) 시칠리아 파스타

153-154 📧 이메일
수신: James McCullen
발신: Sebastian Bludd
제목: Winterholm 프로젝트
날짜: 4월 20일

McCullen씨께
Winterholm 프로젝트 개시 허가를 받았지만, 당신에게 몇 가지 도움을 받아야 할 것 같아요. ¹⁵³저는 새로운 건설공사를 이끄는 게 처음이지만 당신은 이런 상황에서 많은 경험을 해보셨으니 조언해주시면 감사하겠습니다.
우선, 기간이 14개월 밖에 남지 않았는데 ¹⁵⁴공사는 11월에 시작합니다. 그래서 겨울 날씨가 건설팀을 더욱 힘들게 할 것 같습니다. 적은 인원으로 작업을 시작하고 나중에 더 고용하는 게 나을까요? 대형 건축물이 될 것이고, 저희 인부들 모두에게 최상의 작업 공간을 만드는 데 상당한 시간이 필요할 것 같습니다. 저도 품질만큼이나 속도가 중요하다는 것을 알고 있지만, 제대로 해보고 싶습니다. 생각을 말씀해 주세요.
Sebastian Bludd

어휘 clearance 허가 construction site 공사 현장 experience 경험 input 조언 complete 완료하다 structure 건축물 workspace 작업 공간 recruit 새로운 구성원 come up with the idea 아이디어를 생각해 내다

153
Bludd씨가 McCullen씨에게 조언을 요청하는 이유는 무엇인가?
(A) 그는 프로젝트에 책임을 지고 싶지 않다.
(B) 그는 건설 경험이 전혀 없다.
(C) 그는 시작하기 위해 승인이 필요하다고 생각한다.
(D) 그는 프로젝트에 대한 McCullen씨의 의견을 신뢰한다.

어휘 opinion 의견

154
Bludd씨가 언급한 문제는 무엇인가?
(A) 사무실 배치
(B) 건물의 가격
(C) 부지의 크기
(D) 건설 기간 동안의 날씨

어휘 placement 배치

155-157 📝 메모
전 직원분들께
¹⁵⁶연례 여름 창고 세일이 6월 5일 시작됩니다! 전 직원이 세일에 참가하실 수 있으며 현재 본사 근처 창고에 있는 모든 제품이 60~80퍼센트 할인된 가격으로 제공됩니다. ¹⁵⁵즉, 텔레비전, 오븐, 라디오 등을 구매하실 수 있다는 것입니다.
¹⁵⁷회사 인트라넷에 직원 세일 분야를 업데이트했으니 카탈로그를 지금 찾아보실 수 있습니다! 판매가 시작되면 웹페이지 데이터가 정확하지 않을 수 있습니다. 매주 제품을 업데이트하는 데 시간이 걸릴 수 있기 때문입니다. 모든 품목은 선착순으로 판매되므로 관심이 있는 제품을 보셨다면 망설이지 마세요.
창고에 입장하실 때에는 반드시 회사 배지를 지참해야 합니다. ¹⁵⁶이번 세일은 2주만 진행되오니 1년에 한 번 있는 절약의 기회를 놓치지 마세요!

어휘 warehouse 창고 include 포함하다 currently 현재에 house 보관하다 incorrect 정확하지 않은 badge 배지 entry 입장 last 지속하다 savings 저금 opportunity 기회

155
세일 중에 어떤 종류의 제품을 구입할 수 있는가?
(A) 전자제품
(B) 주방기구
(C) 사무 장비
(D) 여름 의류

156
세일은 언제 끝나는가?
(A) 6월 5일
(B) 6월 19일
(C) 6월 30일
(D) 7월 1일

157
세일 전에 어떻게 세일 품목을 알 수 있는가?
(A) 웹사이트에 접속해서
(B) 목록을 요청해서
(C) 본사에 있는 누군가에게 연락해서
(D) 창고를 방문해서

어휘 access 접속하다 ask for ~를 요청하다

158-160 📢 광고
JD Turk Cleaners는 귀사의 사무실과 가게, 창고로 방문하여 직원들이 안전하고 깨끗한 업무 환경에서 일할 수 있도록 해드릴 것입니다. 저희 회사는 6년 동안 업계에 있으면서 철저함과 작업 태도로 수많은 상을 받았습니다. 어느 곳이든지 사무실을 관리하는 데 있어서 귀사가 믿고 맡길 수 있으리라 자부합니다. 저희 직원들은 귀사가 필요로 할 때 언제든지 준비되어 있습니다. ¹⁵⁹Glen Matthews 팀장이 현장에서 20년의 경력으로 귀사를 위해 일을 처리할 것입니다.

저희는 귀사의 중요한 업무 시간을 방해하고 싶지 않습니다. ¹⁵⁸저희를 필요로 하시면 언제든지 24시간 연중무휴로 이용할 수 있습니다. ¹⁶⁰JD Turk에 연락하시려면 916-555-2342로 전화하시거나, jdturk@mailme.com으로 메시지를 보내주십시오. 또 4023 Sacred Heart, San DiFrangeles, CA 94207로 양식을 보내실 수 있습니다.

어휘 recipient 수혜자 thoroughness 철저함 attitude 태도 faith 신뢰 interrupt 방해하다

158
JD Turk Cleaners에 대해 옳은 것은 무엇인가?
(A) 일을 빨리 끝낼 수 있다.
(B) 언제든지 일할 수 있다.
(C) 그 분야에서 최고인 사람만을 고용한다.
(D) 20년 전에 사업을 시작했다.

어휘 hire 고용하다 industry 산업

159
Matthews씨는 어떤 일을 하는가?
(A) 사무실에서 전화를 받는다.
(B) 회사의 신입직원을 채용한다.
(C) JD Turk의 현장 책임자이다.
(D) 즉시 모든 이메일에 답변한다.

어휘 field 현장 respond 답변하다 directly 곧장

160
고객이 JD Turk Cleaners와 연락할 수 없는 수단은 무엇인가?
(A) 우편   (B) 전화
(C) 이메일   (D) 웹사이트

어휘 via ~를 통하여

161-163 📄기사
¹⁶¹Garibaldi 시큐리티 서비스는 고객 인터넷 안전 보호로 소중한 Londo상을 받았다는 소식을 듣고 축하했습니다. GSS는 235명 이상의 고객을 책임지고 있으며, 시상 기간 동안 서버 장애가 없었습니다. 최근 몇 년간 GSS는 과거의 실수를 극복하고, 보안기술 분야의 선두주자가 되었을 뿐만 아니라, 기업과 고객 정보의 손실을 방지하기 위한 새로운 수단이 되었습니다.
GSS가 이 상을 수상한 것은 처음이며, 대변인은 "이 상은 고객들이 사생활을 믿고 맡길 수 있도록 우리 회사가 작년에 한 모든 노력을 인정하는 것입니다."라고 말했습니다. 대변인은 계속해서 ¹⁶²5년 전 회사 개편으로 새로운 해킹 기술과 외부로부터의 스파이 활동을 항시 살피는 데 더욱 전념할 수 있었다고 말했습니다. ¹⁶³GSS는 또한 수익과 인지도를 극대화하기 위한 노력으로 내년에 서비스 확대 또한 모색하고 있습니다.

어휘 prized 소중한 protection 보호 time frame 기간 measure 수단 spokesperson 대변인 recognize 인식하다 reorganization 재개편 stay on top of ~에 훤하다 espionage 스파이 활동 maximize 극대화하다 profit 수익

161
기사의 주요 내용은 무엇인가?
(A) 우수한 서비스를 인정받은 회사
(B) 신규 설립 회사의 실패
(C) IT회사의 주요 인사이동
(D) 정보기술산업의 최근 동향

어휘 outstanding 우수한 establish 설립하다

162
회사가 5년 전에 개편을 실시한 이유는 무엇인가?
(A) 해외사업을 확장하기 위해
(B) 고객 지원을 위한 더 나은 방법을 얻기 위해
(C) 업데이트된 기술을 구매하기 위해
(D) 고령 근로자를 대체하기 위해

어휘 replace 대체하다

163
이 회사가 가까운 미래에 할 예정이 <u>아닌</u> 것은 무엇인가?
(A) 브랜드 인지도 향상
(B) 수익 창출
(C) 사업 확장
(D) 정부 계약 추진

어휘 pursue 추구하다 contract 계약

164-167 📄광고
¹⁶⁴아이들의 멘토로 활동하면서 여름을 보내고 싶나요? 그렇다면 Camp Crystal에서 신나는 6주 프로그램에 참여하세요. ¹⁶⁵우리는 캠프에서 2주 동안 함께 일하고 훈련하면서 여러분의 어린 시절에 했던 모든 재미 있는 일들을 할 것입니다.
Camp Crystal에는 아이들이 배우고 재미있는 시간을 보낼 수 있는 장소가 세 곳이 있습니다. ¹⁶⁷먼저, 숙소 구역에서는 생활하고, 요리하고, 청소하며 그룹으로 재미있게 지냅니다. 임무를 공유하고 잡다한 일을 돕는 것은 팀워크의 본보기가 됩니다. 캠퍼들은 오두막집을 꾸미고, 식사를 만드는 것을 도울 것입니다.
다음으로, 캠프를 둘러싼 숲속에서는 모두가 야생 동물을 가까이에서 직접 볼 수 있습니다. Camp Crystal 주변에 많은 종류의 흥미로운 동물들이 살기 때문입니다. 과거 트레킹을 통해 우리는 곤충에서부터 여우와 곰까지 모든 것을 봤습니다! 훈련된 야외 지도자들이 모든 자연 속 산책을 주관하므로, 다치거나 길을 잃을 위험은 없을 것입니다.
끝으로, 가장 유명한 장소입니다. 커다란 호수가 있으며, 상담가들과 캠퍼들은 함께 수영과 보트타기를 하실 수 있습니다. 운이 좋다면, 100년간 호수 근처에서 살고 있는 커다란 거북이인 Old Jason을 보실 수 있습니다.
¹⁶⁶또한 추가금으로 음악, 요리, 미술 레슨을 제공합니다. 여러분이 가르칠 수 있는 수업이 있다면 알려주세요. Camp Crystal에 오셔서 모두가 무엇에 흥분하는지 확인해보세요!

어휘 mentor 멘토 duty 임무 chore 허드렛일 surround 둘러싸다 wildlife 야생 동물 trek 트레킹 supervise 감독하다 counselor 조언자

164
이 광고의 주된 목적은 무엇인가?
(A) Camp Crystal로 관광객 모으기
(B) 신규 여름 캠프 지도자 채용하기
(C) Camp Crystal의 변경 사항 통보하기
(D) 여름 야외 활동 소개하기

어휘 draw 끌어들이다 outdoor 야외의

165
캠프가 시작되기 전에 직원들은 얼마 동안 훈련을 받을 것인가?
(A) 며칠   (B) 1주
(C) 2주   (D) 한 달

166
Camp Crystal에서 제공하지 않는 추가 강습은 무엇인가?
(A) 요리   (B) 승마
(C) 음악   (D) 미술

167 신유형
다음 문장은 [1], [2], [3], [4] 중 어디에 들어가는가?
"먼저, 숙소 구역에서는 생활하고, 요리하고, 청소하며 그룹으로 재미있게 지냅니다."
(A) [1]   (B) [2]
(C) [3]   (D) [4]

어휘 lodging 임시숙소

168-171 이메일

수신: Sarah McGinly
발신: Frank Tyson
제목: 자사 제품
날짜: 4월 14일

McGinly씨께
근래 귀하께서 최근 사용한 교육제품군에 대한 이메일을 받았습니다. 제품 사용 경험에 대해 좋은 말씀 감사합니다. 저희 제품에 만족하시는 고객의 의견을 항상 환영하며, 168향후 출시할 앱과 게임, 소프트웨어의 종류를 결정하는 데 귀하께서 도움을 주실 기회를 드릴 수 있어 기쁘게 생각합니다.
귀하는 저희의 고객 베타 프로그램을 통해 현재 작업 중인 앱 또는 컴퓨터 소프트웨어 버전을 받으실 것입니다. 다운로드 후 무료로 사용이 가능하며, 169간단한 설문에 답변해주시고, 선호하시는 고객 웹사이트를 통해 피드백을 주시기만 하면 됩니다.
170관심이 있으시면, 첨부 양식을 작성해주세요. 양식에는 베타 테스트로 귀하가 가장 사용하고 싶은 앱과 소프트웨어의 선호 종류, 그리고 얼마나 자주 테스트에 참여하고 싶으신지 등의 내용을 담고 있습니다. 171또한 선호 고객 프로그램에 포함될 기밀 유지 서약에 서명하셔야 합니다. 저희가 이 양식들을 수령한 후, 귀하가 가장 관심을 갖는 제품을 찾은 후에 첫 번째 테스트 기간에 시작하실 수 있도록 연락을 드리겠습니다.
감사합니다. 좋은 하루 되세요.
Frank Tyson 제품책임자
Brain Games 엔터테인먼트

어휘 line up (회사의) 상품 educational 교육의 release 출시하다 questionnaire 설문지 preference 선호도 period 기간

168
Brain Games사가 McGinly씨에게 보내는 제품이 아닌 것은 무엇인가?
(A) 앱   (B) 책
(C) 게임   (D) 소프트웨어

169
이 프로그램의 일환으로 McGinly씨는 무엇을 해야 하는가?
(A) 사무실로 출근해서 일하기
(B) 담당자에게 보낼 보고서 작성하기
(C) 제품에 대한 질문에 응답하기
(D) 신제품에 대해 기자들에게 말하기

170
이 프로그램에 참여하기 위해 McGinly씨는 무엇을 해야 하는가?
(A) Tyson씨에게 직접 전화하기
(B) 신청서 양식 다운로드하기
(C) 첨부파일 다시 보내기
(D) Brain Games 엔터테인먼트 방문하기

어휘 send back 다시 보내다 attachment 첨부파일

171 신유형
다음 문장은 [1], [2], [3], [4] 중 어디에 들어가는가?
"또한 선호 고객 프로그램에 포함될 기밀유지서약에 서명하셔야 합니다."
(A) [1]   (B) [2]
(C) [3]   (D) [4]

어휘 secrecy agreement 기밀유지서약

172-175 온라인 토론 신유형

Steve Banner
[2:23 PM]
안녕하세요, Brand, Kate. 시간을 내줘서 고마워요. 우리 웹사이트의 방문자 수에 대해 물어볼 게 있어요. 데이터를 확인했는데 지난 며칠 간 고객의 방문이 급격하게 감소했더군요. 이게 무슨 일인지 아는 분 있나요?

Brand Thompson
[2:24 PM]
며칠 전에 특별 보도가 뉴스에 나왔는데, 172우리 제품들 중에 하나를 타다 부상을 입었대요. 그게 아마 관련이 있을 것 같은데요.

Kate Marna
[2:26 PM]
뭐라고요? 전 어떤 것도 들은 게 없어요. 무슨 일이에요?

Steve Banner
[2:27 PM]
저도 처음 듣는 이야기네요. 말해줄 수 있어요, Brand?

Brand Thompson
[2:30 PM]
한 지역 뉴스 채널이 보조 바퀴 Cubby 200으로 자전거 타기를 배우는 것에 대해 어떤 부모를 인터뷰했어요. 그 부모가 말하길, 172갑자기 바퀴가 떨어져 나가서 아이가 넘어졌고, 다리와 얼굴에 약간의 찰과상을 입었다고 했어요.

Steve Banner [2:32 PM]	저는 왜 그걸 몰랐을까요? [173]이 학부모에게 연락해 사과할 뿐만 아니라 제품 교체도 해드려야 합니다. 우리 제품과 고객에 대해 우리가 관심을 가지고 있다는 것을 보여주도록 합시다.
Kate Marna [2:34 PM]	Brand, 어디 뉴스 방송국인지 알려주세요. [174]제가 상황을 바로잡을 수 있도록 방송국에 연락할게요. [175]너무 늦기 전에 어서 이 불부터 끕시다!
Brand Thompson [2:35 PM]	알겠어요. 정보를 찾아봐야 할 테지만 오늘 안에 보내드릴게요.
Steve Banner [2:37 PM]	알겠어요. 알려줘서 고마워요. 걱정하는 부모들이 이 상황을 전해 듣고 방문자 수가 낮아진 것 같아요. 그러니 고객들이 다시 돌아올 수 있도록 두 사람이 같이 협조해서 일해주세요.

어휘 traffic 통신량 decline 감소하다 fill in ~에게 지금까지의 일을 들려주다 pop off 떨어져 나가다 scrape 찰과상을 내다 bring attention 이목을 끌다 extend apologies 사과하다 get in touch with ~와 연락하다 straighten out ~를 바로잡다 by word of mouth 사람들의 입에서 입으로

172
웹사이트의 방문자 수가 감소한 원인은 무엇인가?
(A) 제품 결함 (B) 가격 상승
(C) 새로운 회사 방침 (D) 잘못된 정보 하나

어휘 defective 결함이 있는 hike 급등

173
그들은 어떻게 문제를 해결하려고 노력할 것인가?
(A) 새로운 Cubby 200을 줌으로써
(B) 사과의 편지를 보냄으로써
(C) 매체를 사용하여 제품을 홍보함으로써
(D) 고객에게 제품을 사용하지 말라고 경고함으로써

어휘 promote 홍보하다

174
누가 특정 뉴스 매체에 연락할 것인가?
(A) Banner씨 (B) Thompson씨
(C) Marna씨 (D) 그들의 상사

175 신유형
오후 2시 34분에 Marna씨가 Let's put out this fire before it's too late라고 말한 의도는 무엇인가?
(A) 회사의 다른 직원들이 더 잘하도록 장려해야 한다.
(B) 더 많은 고객을 잃기 전에 신속하게 문제를 해결해야 한다.
(C) 회사의 충성 고객에게 더 많은 할인을 제공하기 시작해야 한다.
(D) 고객에게 계속 새로운 소식을 알려야 한다.

어휘 loyal 충성하는

176-180 정보…신청서

[176]Expanse 엔지니어링은 주택이나 가구, 가전 등을 임대, 구매, 판매 또는 거래하고자 하는 직원들을 위한 온라인 게시판을 열었습니다. 게시에는 약간의 비용이 들지만, 회신 또는 직원 라운지에서의 거래는 항상 무료입니다. 광고를 내려면 신청서에 필요한 정보를 빠짐없이 작성하고 요금을 지불하시기 바랍니다.

[177]요금
물건 소개 (50자 이하)	2달러
물건 소개 (50~99자)	3달러
[180]물건 소개 (100자 이상)	4달러
사진	사진당 10센트

직원 이름:	Mary Logan
구분:	판매/가구
날짜:	3월 23일

물품 설명:
[178]저는 이번 회계연도가 끝나면 이사할 예정으로, 가구를 팔고 싶습니다. 팔 물건이 세 가지 있는데요. 먼저 서랍이 4개 달린 커다란 나무 화장대입니다. 4년 됐지만 상태가 좋습니다. 그리고 흰색 소형 컴퓨터 책상은 작업하는 데 충분한 크기지만, 방 안에 둬도 가로거치지 않을 정도입니다. 마지막으로 소형 냉장고에는 여러 개의 용기와 캔 음료는 최대 6개를 넣을 수 있습니다. 세 물건 모두 한꺼번에 팔고 싶지만 필요하면 개별로도 판매가 가능합니다. [179]각 첨부 사진을 확인하시고 제게 연락해서 가격을 제시하세요!

[180]단어 수:	114단어
첨부 사진:	3장
게시 날짜:	30일

어휘 housing 주택 fiscal year 회계연도 dresser 화장대 get in the way 방해가 되다 container 그릇 make an offer 제안하다

176
회사 게시판은 어떤 서비스를 제공하는가?
(A) 소유물 주고받기 (B) 불필요한 물건 수집하기
(C) 가전제품 배달하기 (D) 서류 번역하기

어휘 exchange 교환하다 goods 소유물 translate 번역하다

177
서비스 요금은 어떻게 책정되는가?
(A) 분류에 따라서
(B) 상품의 개수에 따라서
(C) 단어 수에 따라서
(D) 게시 기간에 따라서

178
Logan씨는 왜 물건들을 판매하는가?
(A) 그녀는 새로운 것을 사려고 한다.
(B) 그녀는 회사를 그만둘 예정이다.
(C) 그녀는 돈이 필요하다.
(D) 그녀는 이사를 갈 것이다.

179

사람들이 물건의 상태를 어떻게 알 수 있는가?

(A) 웹 관리자에게 연락해서

(B) 온라인에서 사진을 보고

(C) Logan씨에게 이메일을 보내서

(D) Logan씨의 집을 방문해서

어휘 administrator 관리자

180

Logan씨는 광고에 얼마의 비용을 썼는가?

(A) 2.10달러   (B) 3.30달러

(C) 4.30달러   (D) 9.30달러

181-185 📋 일정표…이메일

신입직원 오리엔테이션 일정

4월 3일 ~ 7일

일정	시간
환영 조찬	오전 8:00 – 오전 10:00
규정 및 절차 소개	오전 10:15 – 오전 11:05
시스템 연수(고객서비스 담당자 한정) – Lana Carney	오전 11:15 – 오후 12:00
시스템 연수(엔지니어) – Vince Turner	오전 11:15 – 오후 12:00
점심	오후 12:15 – 오후 1:15
185시스템 연수 (내외근 영업) – Richard Bird	오후 1:15 – 오후 2:00
185시스템 연수 (관리 부분 연수자) – Lori Stevens	오후 1:15 – 오후 2:00
부장 브레이크아웃 세션 (부장 한정)	오후 1:30 – 오후 2:00
부서별 브레이크아웃 세션 – 매니저 소개	오후 2:15 – 오후 3:00
181팀 브레이크아웃 세션 – 모든 그룹	오후 3:15 – 오후 4:45
오리엔테이션 종료	오후 5:00

수신: 185Richard Bird; Lori Stevens

발신: Vince Turner

제목: 오리엔테이션 일정

날짜: 3월 31일 오후 2:43

안녕하세요, Rich, Lori.

신입직원 오리엔테이션이 다음 주로 다가왔는데, Towson의 매니저가 저에게 그들의 새 데이터베이스를 183만드는 것을 도울 수 있도록 바로 다음 주에 그들과 함께 일할 시간이 있는지 물었어요. 그들은 제가 아침에 그들의 사무실에서 작업을 시작하길 바라는 것 같습니다. 182,185가능하시면, 두 분 중 한 분과 제 훈련 시간을 바꾸고 싶습니다. 제가 보통 때라면 요청하지 않을 텐데, 184상위 10위 안에 드는 고객이라서 거절하고 싶지 않았습니다. 제가 우리 데이터베이스의 관리 책임자이기 때문에 그들은 제가 필요하고 또 자기들에게 잘 설명해달라고 말했습니다. 제 생각에는 설치 시에 고객에 대한 충성을 보여주는 것이 중요하다고 생각합니다.

월요일부터 수요일까지이지만, 그 주의 전체 일정을 변경하는 것이 관계자 모두에게 편할 것 같습니다. 제가 아침에 Towson과 일할 수

있도록, 두 분 중 한 분이 저와 시간을 바꾸실 수 있나요?

부탁드립니다.

Vince Turner

어휘 orientation 예비 교육 coming up 다가오는 build 구축하다 installation 설치 involved 관련된 entire 전체의

181

팀 세션은 시간이 얼마나 소요되는가?

(A) 30분   (B) 45분

(C) 한 시간   (D) 한 시간 반

182

이메일을 쓴 목적은 무엇인가?

(A) 오리엔테이션에서 무엇을 논의할 것인지 묻기 위해

(B) 어떤 경영진이 참석하는지 확인하기 위해

(C) 교육 프로그램 운영하는 사람을 파악하기 위해

(D) 일정 변경을 요청하기 위해

어휘 determine 알아내다 run 운영하다

183

이메일의 첫 번째 문단, 두 번째 줄의 building과 의미상 가장 가까운 단어는 무엇인가?

(A) 더하는   (B) 만드는

(C) 확대하는   (D) 건설하는

어휘 enlarge 확대하다 construct 건설하다

184

Turner씨는 왜 고객의 부탁을 거절하지 않는가?

(A) 그는 언제나 그들을 돕겠다고 약속했다.

(B) 그들은 중요한 단체이다.

(C) 그들은 그 없이 데이터베이스를 사용할 수 없다.

(D) 그들이 방문비를 지불했다.

185

Turner씨는 언제 신입 엔지니어들과 이야기하기를 원하는가?

(A) 오전 11시 15분   (B) 오후 1시 15분

(C) 오후 1시 30분   (D) 오후 5시

186-190 📋 정보…이메일…송장 신 유 형

파손된 수하물

귀하의 수하물이 파손된 채 도착한다면, 186가방 수령 후 7일 이내에 파손을 신고하셔야 합니다. 공항에 있는 지상 근무요원에게 연락하거나, 고객서비스부로 메시지를 보내셔도 됩니다. (cs@forwardair.com)

파손된 수하물에 대한 Forward Airlines의 책임은 제한적입니다. 자사의 수하물 정책에 대한 자세한 내용은 이곳에서 확인하시기 바랍니다. Forward Airlines Baggage Policy

189일반적으로, 닳거나 찢어지는 일상적인 파손에 대해 귀사는 책임을 지지 않습니다. 여기에는 다음 사항을 포함합니다.

*주의 취급에도 불구하고 발생할 수 있는 자국, 절단, 긁힘, 흠, 움푹

들어간 흔적과 자국
189*끈, 주머니, 손잡이, 옷걸이의 고리, 바퀴, 외부 잠금장치, 보안 줄 또는 지퍼를 포함한 수하물의 돌출부 손상 또는 손실
*부적합하게 포장된 수하물(예: 과적)

수신: Forward Airlines 고객서비스부 <cs@forwardair.com>
발신: Beverly Rodriguez <brodriguez@pronto.net>
제목: 파손된 수하물
날짜: 5월 22일

담당자께
최근에 저는 홍콩에서 로스앤젤레스로 돌아오면서 Forward Airlines를 이용했습니다. 제가 맡겼던 가방이 파손되어 있는 것을 보고 저는 경악했습니다. 187그날 바로 가방을 수리점에 가져가 수리를 했습니다. 이 메시지에 청구서를 첨부했습니다. 수리 대금 전액을 환불받을 수 있기를 바랍니다. 188이번이 Forward Airlines을 이용하면서 처음 겪은 좋지 않은 경험이며, 이 문제가 조속히 해결되기를 바라고 있습니다.
Beverly Rodriguez

Three Star 가방수리점

187수령일	5월 17일	청구서 번호	5V803
고객 이름	Beverly Rodriguez	점원	Yannick
가방 유형	검은색, 대형 롤링백	수리 완료일	5월 21일
190가방 제조사	Stenson사		

189수리 내용: 수납식 손잡이 장치 교환

190알림: 모든 수리는 제조업체의 부품을 사용하여 제조업체의 기준을 따릅니다.	소계	35.50달러
	세금	5달러
	총액	40.50달러

어휘 baggage 짐 ground staff 지상 근무요원 scuff 흠 dent 움푹 들어간 곳 protruding 돌출된 dismayed ~에 경악한 reimburse 변상하다 retract (일부분을) 집어넣다

186
정보에 대해 사실인 것은 무엇인가?
(A) 고객은 파손에 대해 일주일 이내에 알려야 한다.
(B) 파손된 수하물은 보험처리가 된다.
(C) 고객은 자기 수하물을 사무실로 가져와야 한다.
(D) 해진 수하물은 개별적으로 취급된다.

어휘 worn 닳은, 해진

187
Rodriguez씨는 언제 로스앤젤레스에 도착했는가?
(A) 5월 15일 (B) 5월 17일
(C) 5월 21일 (D) 5월 22일

188
Rodriguez씨가 이메일에서 암시하는 것은 무엇인가?
(A) 그녀는 전에 Forward Airlines를 탄 적이 있다.
(B) 그녀는 최근에 해외로 이사를 갔다.

(C) 그녀는 직접 가방을 수리했다.
(D) 그녀는 비행기를 타고 홍콩으로 갔다.

189
Forward Airlines가 Rodriguez씨의 배상 요구를 거절할 이유는 무엇인가?
(A) 알맞은 직원에게 보고하지 않았다.
(B) 손잡이가 파손되었다.
(C) 그녀는 가방에 짐을 너무 많이 쌌다.
(D) 그녀는 배상을 요구하지 않았다.

어휘 report 보고하다 make the claim 배상 요구를 하다

190
수리에 대해 언급된 내용은 무엇인가?
(A) 비용이 예상보다 덜 들었다.
(B) 수리가 요청한 것보다 빨리 끝났다.
(C) 제품이 제조업체로 보내졌다.
(D) 교체 부품은 Stenson사의 부품이었다.

191-195 📋 주문서···이메일···정보 신 유 형

Castle Clothing 주문 개요

고객:
Eric Pratchett
5400 Hanover Rd.   주문일: 5월 14일
Smith Village, Ca 94423   배송일: 5월 17일

물품 번호	물품 이름	색상	개수	단가	합계액
SW99	스웨터	파란색	1	50달러	50달러
CR67	남자용 바지	회색/검정색	2	80달러	160달러
192BL02	가벼운 블레이저	갈색	1	150달러	194150달러
SH14	셔츠	흰색	2	40달러	80달러
				소계	440달러
				주문 총액	440달러

*캘리포니아주 거주자는 단가에 세금이 포함됩니다.
**191300달러 초과 주문의 경우 배송료는 무료입니다.

수신: Eric Pratchett <ericpratchett@strongly.net>
발신: Castel Clothing 고객관리부 <cccc@castelclothing.com>
제목: 주문건
날짜: 5월 29일

Pratchett씨께
192죄송하지만, 귀하가 주문하신 물품 번호 BL02는 현재 품절되었습니다. 저희는 재고량에 대해 100% 정확성을 유지하기 위해 최선을 다하고 있지만, 드물게 재고 오류를 범하는 경우가 있습니다.
195첨부한 것은 현재 저희 재고 품목 중에서 귀하가 구매하신 것과 유사한 품목에 대한 설명입니다. 194이 제품은 구매하신 것보다 더 저렴하기 때문에 차액은 환불될 것입니다. 193이 제품으로 교환하고 싶으신지, 원래 주문하신 품목이 나올 때까지 기다리실 것인지 알려주시기 바랍니다.
감사합니다.

Raleigh McIntosh
Castel Clothing 고객관리부

Graveline 스포츠 재킷

이 남성용 재킷은 가벼워서 따뜻한 봄에 입거나, 쌀쌀한 날에 스웨터 위에 걸칠 수 있습니다. 통기성이 있는 ¹⁹⁵100% 면으로 만들어진 이 재킷에는 앞 단추 다섯 개, 널찍한 옆 호주머니 두 개, 안쪽 가슴 주머니 한 개가 있습니다. 바람을 막아주는 스탠드 업 옷깃은 멋지고 실용적입니다. ¹⁹⁴140달러(세금 포함)에 다양한 색상으로 구매하실 수 있습니다.

어휘 quantity(qty.) 수량 unit price 단가 shipping charge 배송료 out of stock 품절된 maintain 유지하다 accuracy 정확성 inventory 재고 rare 드문 difference 차액 refund 환불하다 underneath ~의 안에 chilly 쌀쌀한 breathable 통기성이 있는 roomy 넓은 practical 실용적

191
주문 양식에서 알 수 있는 것은 무엇인가?
(A) 구매 당일 배송되었다.
(B) 추가 세금이 부과되었다.
(C) 물품이 무료로 배송되었다.
(D) 물품이 반송될 수 있다.

192
Pratchett씨가 주문한 물품 중 즉시 구할 수 없는 물품은 무엇인가?
(A) 검정 바지   (B) 회색 바지
(C) 파란 스웨터   (D) 갈색 블레이저

193
McIntosh씨가 원하는 정보는 무엇인가?
(A) 신용카드 번호   (B) 고객의 결정
(C) 배송 주소   (D) 물품 번호

194
Pratchett씨는 새 재킷에 대해 얼마의 환불을 받을 수 있는가?
(A) 10달러   (B) 40달러
(C) 50달러   (D) 80달러

195
BL02는 어떤 소재로 제작된 것으로 보이는가?
(A) 실크   (B) 나일론
(C) 면   (D) 양모

196-200 📋 일정표…목록…이메일 신유형
싱가포르 여행일정
5월 10일 ~ 13일
¹⁹⁷5월 10일 수요일

| 오후 4:00 | 싱가포르 도착 |
| 오후 7:00 | 팀원들과의 저녁식사(장소는 여러분의 재량) |

5월 11일 목요일

| 오전 10:00 ~ 오후 4:00 | 제조시설 견학, Chang씨 진행 |
| 오후 7:00 | Chang씨아 디너 크루즈 |

¹⁹⁶5월 12일 금요일

오전 10:00	싱가포르 관광
오후 2:00	제품개발팀의 발표
오후 6:30	Waverly Point에서 저녁식사 예약

5월 13일 토요일

| 오전 10:00 | 호텔 체크아웃 |
| 정오 12:00 | 샌프란시스코 행 비행기 출발 |

Singapore에서 먹을 만한 곳

Pavilion
Western 호텔에 위치한 Pavilion은 고향을 떠나온 여행자들에게 고향의 맛을 제공합니다. 여러분의 식사에 훌륭한 와인 한 잔을 ¹⁹⁸짝지어드립니다.
연중무휴

Fortini
¹⁹⁹메뉴를 요청하지 마세요. 저희 가게에는 메뉴가 없습니다. 수상 경력이 있는 저희 셰프가 여러분을 위해 선택해드리겠습니다. 후회하지 않으실 거라 약속드립니다.
연중무휴

Aubergine
프랑스 요리사 Paul Desautel는 5년 전 편안한 파리 생활을 정리하고 Aubergine를 시작했습니다. 싱가포르에서 가장 산뜻한 식당 중 하나입니다.
¹⁹⁷수요일 휴무

Chantilly
Marina 베이의 중심부에 위치한 Chantilly는 퓨전요리에 진지하게 임하고 있습니다. 세계 각지의 최고의 음식을 혼합합니다.
월요일 휴무

수신: Jocelyn Woods
발신: Brandon Ainsley
제목: 추천
날짜: 4월 28일

Jocelyn,
싱가포르로 간다는 소식을 들었어요. 정말 멋지네요! ¹⁹⁹Fortini라는 멋진 레스토랑을 절대로 놓쳐서는 안 돼요. 이탈리아어처럼 들리는데 정말 맛있는 이탈리아 음식도 있지만, 그보다 훨씬 더 많은 요리를 제공해요. 저는 이 레스토랑에 세 번 간 적이 있지만, 갈 때마다 지금까지 먹은 요리 중 최고라고 생각하며 나오게 돼요. ²⁰⁰Megan에 대해서도 걱정할 필요는 없어요. 그 요리사는 채식주의자에게 언제나 멋진 요리를 해주거든요. 모두 매우 마음에 들 것이라고 장담해요!
안전한 여행 되세요.
Brandon Ainsley

어휘 itinerary 여행 일정(표) discretion (자유) 재량 manufacturing

facility 제조시설 sightseeing 관광 depart 출발 traveler 여행자
regret 후회하다 culinary 요리의 terrific 아주 좋은, 멋진 guarantee
보장하다

196
일정에 의하면, 팀은 언제 관광지를 방문할 것인가?
(A) 수요일 (B) 목요일
(C) 금요일 (D) 토요일

197
첫날에 이 팀이 방문할 수 없는 식당은 어디인가?
(A) Pavilion (B) Fortini
(C) Aubergine (D) Chantilly

198
목록의 네 번째 줄의 pair와 의미상 가장 가까운 단어는 무엇인가?
(A) 결합하여 (B) 두 배로 만들어
(C) 보관하여 (D) 대접하여

어휘 combine 결합하다 double 두 배로 만들다

199
Ainsley씨가 추천하는 레스토랑에 대해 언급된 것은 무엇인가?
(A) 메뉴가 없다.
(B) 야외 자리가 있다.
(C) 퓨전 음식을 제공한다.
(D) 채식주의 음식만 제공한다.

200
일행 중 한 구성원에 대해 암시하고 있는 것은?
(A) 그녀는 전에 식당에 갔었다.
(B) 그녀는 이탈리아 음식을 좋아하지 않는다.
(C) 그녀는 섭취 음식에 제한이 있다.
(D) 그녀는 여행을 가지 않을 것이다.

어휘 dietary restriction 식이요법 제한

Actual Test 2

정답

1 (D)	**2** (D)	**3** (B)	**4** (D)	**5** (D)	**6** (D)	**7** (A)	**8** (C)	**9** (B)	**10** (A)
11 (A)	**12** (C)	**13** (B)	**14** (C)	**15** (A)	**16** (B)	**17** (B)	**18** (A)	**19** (C)	**20** (B)
21 (A)	**22** (A)	**23** (C)	**24** (C)	**25** (A)	**26** (B)	**27** (A)	**28** (B)	**29** (B)	**30** (C)
31 (A)	**32** (B)	**33** (D)	**34** (C)	**35** (D)	**36** (D)	**37** (B)	**38** (A)	**39** (C)	**40** (B)
41 (A)	**42** (C)	**43** (C)	**44** (B)	**45** (B)	**46** (B)	**47** (D)	**48** (D)	**49** (D)	**50** (B)
51 (D)	**52** (C)	**53** (D)	**54** (A)	**55** (D)	**56** (C)	**57** (C)	**58** (D)	**59** (B)	**60** (D)
61 (B)	**62** (B)	**63** (A)	**64** (C)	**65** (D)	**66** (A)	**67** (A)	**68** (D)	**69** (D)	**70** (B)
71 (D)	**72** (B)	**73** (D)	**74** (B)	**75** (B)	**76** (D)	**77** (D)	**78** (D)	**79** (A)	**80** (D)
81 (D)	**82** (D)	**83** (B)	**84** (B)	**85** (C)	**86** (D)	**87** (B)	**88** (D)	**89** (B)	**90** (C)
91 (B)	**92** (B)	**93** (A)	**94** (D)	**95** (A)	**96** (D)	**97** (A)	**98** (D)	**99** (C)	**100** (D)
101 (C)	**102** (C)	**103** (C)	**104** (D)	**105** (B)	**106** (A)	**107** (D)	**108** (A)	**109** (D)	**110** (A)
111 (D)	**112** (A)	**113** (A)	**114** (A)	**115** (A)	**116** (C)	**117** (D)	**118** (B)	**119** (D)	**120** (B)
121 (C)	**122** (B)	**123** (D)	**124** (A)	**125** (A)	**126** (A)	**127** (C)	**128** (C)	**129** (B)	**130** (C)
131 (C)	**132** (A)	**133** (C)	**134** (A)	**135** (A)	**136** (A)	**137** (D)	**138** (B)	**139** (B)	**140** (C)
141 (A)	**142** (D)	**143** (C)	**144** (D)	**145** (D)	**146** (D)	**147** (B)	**148** (A)	**149** (D)	**150** (B)
151 (D)	**152** (D)	**153** (C)	**154** (C)	**155** (C)	**156** (A)	**157** (C)	**158** (A)	**159** (D)	**160** (C)
161 (B)	**162** (B)	**163** (C)	**164** (B)	**165** (D)	**166** (D)	**167** (D)	**168** (A)	**169** (C)	**170** (D)
171 (D)	**172** (D)	**173** (B)	**174** (A)	**175** (D)	**176** (B)	**177** (B)	**178** (B)	**179** (B)	**180** (A)
181 (A)	**182** (C)	**183** (B)	**184** (D)	**185** (D)	**186** (B)	**187** (A)	**188** (B)	**189** (D)	**190** (D)
191 (C)	**192** (D)	**193** (D)	**194** (C)	**195** (C)	**196** (D)	**197** (A)	**198** (A)	**199** (B)	**200** (D)

PART 1

1

◁)) 캐나다

(A) One person is taking a drink from a bottle.
(B) One person is writing on a computer.
(C) They're listening to a speaker on a stage.
(D) They're sitting around a rectangular table.

(A) 한 사람은 음료수를 병으로 마시고 있다.
(B) 한 사람은 컴퓨터로 글을 쓰고 있다.
(C) 사람들이 무대 위 연설자의 말을 듣고 있다.
(D) 사람들이 직사각형 탁자 주위에 앉아 있다.

어휘 take a drink 한 잔 마시다 rectangular 직사각형의

2

◁)) 호주

(A) They're drying off with towels.

(B) They're playing with a ball.

(C) They're running toward the sea.

(D) They're standing near a net.

(A) 사람들이 타월로 몸을 말리고 있다.

(B) 사람들이 공을 가지고 놀고 있다.

(C) 사람들이 바다를 향해 뛰어가고 있다.

(D) 사람들이 네트 근처에 서 있다.

어휘 dry off 몸을 말리다

3

◁)) 영국

(A) Coffee is being poured into cups.

(B) Plates with food sit near a glass.

(C) A spoon has been left in the cup.

(D) A table is covered with vegetables.

(A) 커피를 컵에 붓고 있다.

(B) 음식이 담긴 접시가 유리컵 근처에 놓여 있다.

(C) 숟가락이 컵에 남겨둔 채로 있다.

(D) 식탁은 야채들로 덮여 있다.

어휘 pour into ~에 붓다 be covered with ~로 덮이다

4

◁)) 미국

(A) They're adding ingredients to a dish.

(B) They're cleaning some cooking utensils.

(C) They're cooking something in large pans.

(D) They're serving food in a tent.

(A) 사람들이 요리에 재료를 추가하고 있다.

(B) 사람들이 조리 기구를 닦고 있다.

(C) 사람들이 큰 냄비에 무언가를 요리하고 있다.

(D) 사람들이 텐트 안에서 음식을 제공하고 있다.

어휘 serve (음식 등을) 내다

5

◁)) 호주

(A) All flowers are being placed in baskets.

(B) Flowers are being planted in front of a door.

(C) Some plants are growing over a window.

(D) Some plants are hanging near a wall.

(A) 모든 꽃이 바구니에 담기고 있다.

(B) 꽃이 문 앞에 심어지고 있다.

(C) 몇몇 식물이 창문 너머로 자라고 있다.

(D) 몇몇 식물이 벽 근처에 매달려 있다.

어휘 basket 바구니 plant 식물; ~를 심다 hang 매달다

6

◁)) 미국

(A) He's bending down to pick something up.

(B) He's leaning on the side of the car.

(C) He's opening the car window.

(D) He's pointing at something in front of the car.

(A) 남자는 어떤 것을 집으려고 몸을 구부리고 있다.

(B) 남자는 차 옆에서 기대고 있다.

(C) 남자는 차창을 열고 있다.

(D) 남자는 차 앞에서 무언가를 가리키고 있다.

어휘 bend down 몸을 구부리다 pick up 집어 들다 lean 기대다

PART 2

7 ◁)) 미국…캐나다

How often does the interoffice mail get delivered?

(A) Twice a day.

(B) Which ones are for me?

(C) Take a 15-minute break.

어휘 interoffice 사내의 break 휴식

사내 우편물은 얼마나 자주 배달되나요?

(A) 하루에 두 번이요.

(B) 어떤 것이 제 거죠?

(C) 15분간 휴식하세요.

---

8 ◁)) 호주…영국

Are they planning to work on Saturday?

(A) Yes, it works both ways.

(B) I don't know where they are.

(C) Yes, and Sunday.

어휘 work 일하다; 유효하게 작용하다

그 사람들은 토요일에 일할 계획인가요?

(A) 네, 두 가지 방법 모두 가능해요.

(B) 저는 그들이 어디에 있는지 몰라요.

(C) 네, 그리고 일요일에도요.

---

9 ◁)) 미국…캐나다

Where is the extra copy paper?

(A) We're out of paper cups.

(B) By the plant over there.

(C) Just $9.99 per pack.

어휘 extra 여분의 copy paper 복사 용지

여분의 복사 용지는 어디에 있나요?

(A) 종이컵이 다 떨어졌어요.

(B) 저쪽 화분 옆에 있어요.

(C) 한 팩에 단돈 9.99달러입니다.

---

10 ◁)) 영국…호주

You saw the new museum exhibit, didn't you?

(A) Yes, and it was fantastic.

(B) Only if you let me pay.

(C) No one was at the meeting place.

어휘 exhibit 전시(회)

새로운 박물관 전시회를 보았죠?

(A) 네, 아주 좋았어요.

(B) 제가 계산하게 해주실 경우에만요.

(C) 회의 장소에 아무도 없었습니다.

---

11 ◁)) 영국…미국

Didn't Sarah submit her application?

(A) Not yet. By tomorrow at noon, she said.

(B) She told me to meet her at the station.

(C) Her report was 15 pages long.

어휘 application 신청(서)

Sarah가 신청서를 제출하지 않았나요?

(A) 아직요. 내일 오후까지 제출하겠다고 했어요.

(B) 그녀가 역에서 만나자고 했어요.

(C) 그녀의 보고서는 15쪽 분량이었어요.

12 🔊 캐나다…호주

I think we should get this agreement in writing.

(A) There is writing on both sides of the paper.

(B) Nobody can agree on the remodeling.

(C) Good thinking. Please request it.

어휘 agreement 협정 in writing 서면으로 request 요청하다

제 생각에 이 협정은 서면으로 해야 할 것 같아요.

(A) 종이 양면 모두 글이 있어요.

(B) 누구도 리모델링에 동의할 수 없어요.

(C) 좋은 생각이에요. 요청하세요.

---

13 🔊 호주…미국

Why did the sales team leave early today?

(A) Because it cost too much.

(B) They went to a seminar.

(C) To get a repair estimate.

어휘 cost 비용이 들다 estimate 견적서

왜 영업팀은 오늘 일찍 퇴근했나요?

(A) 비용이 너무 많이 들었거든요.

(B) 세미나에 갔어요.

(C) 수리 견적을 받으려고요.

---

14 🔊 영국…호주

Do you know when Ms. Travers is going to Sydney?

(A) I haven't heard the price.

(B) With all of her subordinates.

(C) Sometime in August.

어휘 subordinate 하급자

Travers씨가 언제 시드니에 가는지 아세요?

(A) 가격이 얼마인지 못 들어봤어요.

(B) 그녀의 부하 직원 모두 함께요.

(C) 8월 중에요.

---

15 🔊 캐나다…미국

What is the accounting head doing in Melissa's office?

(A) Don't ask me.

(B) The accounts were reviewed twice.

(C) Let me call you right back.

어휘 accounting 회계

회계 담당자가 Melissa의 사무실에서 뭘 하고 있나요?

(A) 전 몰라요.

(B) 그 회계장부는 두 번 검토됐어요.

(C) 바로 전화드릴게요.

---

16 🔊 영국…캐나다

When do you suppose he'll make his decision?

(A) I'm supposed to be in Detroit today.

(B) It could take a while.

(C) A one-in-ten chance, I'd say.

어휘 one-in-ten 10분의 1 chance 확률

언제 그가 결정을 내릴 것이라고 생각하세요?

(A) 전 오늘 디트로이트에 가기로 되어 있어요.

(B) 시간이 좀 걸릴 수도 있어요.

(C) 제가 보기엔 10분의 1확률이에요.

17 ◁)) 호주···영국

How are you getting to the conference tomorrow?

(A) Just ten minutes from here.

(B) By train, I'd expect.

(C) Tuesday, November the 15th.

내일 회의에 어떻게 갈 거예요?

(A) 여기서 10분 거리예요.

(B) 아마 기차를 타고 갈 거예요.

(C) 11월 15일 화요일이에요.

어휘 conference 대회의

---

18 ◁)) 미국···호주

Has she spoken to Mr. Sears about her time-off request?

(A) Yes, and he approved it.

(B) No. I haven't been trained yet.

(C) Wherever she goes, she'll be successful.

그녀가 Sears씨에게 휴직 요청에 대해 얘기했나요?

(A) 네. 그가 승인해줬어요.

(B) 아뇨. 저는 아직 훈련을 받지 못했어요.

(C) 어디를 가든 그녀는 성공할 거예요.

어휘 time-off 휴직

---

19 ◁)) 미국···캐나다

When can we expect an answer about this?

(A) Every third Saturday at noon.

(B) I've stopped going to the gym.

(C) In about three days.

언제쯤 이것에 대한 답을 받을 수 있을까요?

(A) 매달 셋째 주 토요일 정오에요.

(B) 체육관에 다니는 것을 그만뒀어요.

(C) 약 3일 후에요.

어휘 gym 체육관, 헬스장

---

20 ◁)) 호주···영국

The new temp is working out, isn't he?

(A) Yes. We've had record heat.

(B) Yes, as far as I know.

(C) Just a moment. I'll get him.

새로 온 임시 직원이 일하는 건 잘돼가고 있죠?

(A) 네. 기록적인 더위예요.

(B) 네, 제가 아는 한 그렇습니다.

(C) 잠시만요. 제가 그를 바꿔드릴게요.

어휘 temp 임시 직원 record heat 기록적인 더위 as far as ~하는 한

---

21 ◁)) 미국···호주

Could you order takeout for us for lunch?

(A) Sure. What do you want?

(B) The tickets are all sold out.

(C) What time did you arrive?

점심을 포장 주문으로 해주시겠어요?

(A) 그러죠. 뭐 드실 거예요?

(B) 표는 다 팔렸습니다.

(C) 몇 시에 도착하셨나요?

어휘 sold out 매진된 arrive 도착하다

22 ◁))) 영국···캐나다

Who called for Ms. Carson this morning?

(A) He didn't leave his name.

(B) About 8:00 AM.

(C) I heard her train was delayed.

오늘 아침 전화해서 Carson씨를 찾은 게 누구죠?
(A) 그는 이름을 남기지 않았어요.
(B) 오전 8시쯤에요.
(C) 그녀의 기차가 연착되었다고 들었습니다.

어휘 leave 남기다

---

23 ◁))) 미국···호주

Do you think Paul will accept the offer?

(A) There are many factories in that area.

(B) We should congratulate him.

(C) He's leaning toward yes.

Paul이 그 제안을 받아들일 거라고 봐요?
(A) 그 지역에는 공장이 많아요.
(B) 우리는 그를 축하해줘야 해요.
(C) 그는 제안을 받아들이는 쪽으로 기우는 것 같아요.

어휘 factory 공장 lean toward ~로 마음이 기울어지다

---

24 ◁))) 영국···미국

I just realized my phone ran out of battery.

(A) These phones are too heavy.

(B) We're all out of that size.

(C) Here's my charger.

휴대폰의 배터리가 방전된 걸 이제 알았어요.
(A) 이 휴대폰들은 너무 무거워요.
(B) 그 사이즈는 다 팔렸어요.
(C) 여기 제 충전기요.

어휘 run out of ~를 다 써 버리다 charger 충전기

---

25 ◁))) 캐나다···호주

Are they planning to stay overnight?

(A) I'm not sure, but I'll ask.

(B) We were there just for the weekend.

(C) Actually, I disagree.

그들은 하룻밤 묵을 예정인가요?
(A) 잘 모르겠는데, 물어볼게요.
(B) 우린 주말 동안만 그곳에 있었습니다.
(C) 사실, 저는 동의하지 않습니다.

어휘 stay overnight 하루 묵다 disagree 동의하지 않다

---

26 ◁))) 캐나다···영국

Where did these flowers come from?

(A) They went to London last year.

(B) A thank-you gift from Mr. Allen.

(C) They haven't been authorized.

이 꽃들은 어디에서 난 것인가요?
(A) 그들은 지난해 런던에 갔습니다.
(B) Allen씨가 보낸 감사 선물이에요.
(C) 그들은 허가를 받지 않았습니다.

어휘 authorize ~를 허가하다

27 호주…미국

He isn't sure he wants to go with us.

(A) Well, it's his choice.

(B) Never give up on your dreams.

(C) Those aren't my only options.

그는 우리와 같이 가고 싶다는 확신이 없어요.

(A) 그건 그의 선택이지요.

(B) 당신의 꿈을 절대로 포기하지 마세요.

(C) 제가 선택할 수 있는 게 그것들만 있는 건 아니에요.

어휘 option 선택지

---

28 영국…캐나다

Should we make the copies now or wait until tomorrow?

(A) The coffee has gotten cold.

(B) We might have last-minute changes.

(C) Not around here.

복사를 지금 할까요, 아니면 내일까지 기다릴까요?

(A) 그 커피는 식었어요.

(B) 막판 수정이 생길지도 몰라요.

(C) 여기서는 안 돼요.

어휘 last-minute 마지막 순간의

---

29 미국…영국

It's going to be a long day.

(A) That's right. By 7:00.

(B) True. But we'll get through it somehow.

(C) All of the employees are gone.

힘든 하루가 될 거예요.

(A) 맞아요. 7시까지예요.

(B) 맞아요. 그래도 어떻게든 끝낼 수 있을 겁니다.

(C) 모든 직원이 떠났어요.

어휘 get through ~를 하다, 끝내다 somehow 어떻게든

---

30 캐나다…호주

The reports have been finalized, haven't they?

(A) Yes, they were looking for you.

(B) Not yet. The oven is still heating up.

(C) I'm just checking them for the last time.

그 보고서는 최종 마무리된 거죠?

(A) 네, 그들이 당신을 찾고 있었어요.

(B) 아직이요. 오븐이 아직 예열되는 중이에요.

(C) 마지막으로 확인하는 중이에요.

어휘 finalize 마무리 짓다 heat up 뜨거워지다

---

31 미국…캐나다

Do you mind if I switch seats with you?

(A) Not at all.

(B) Yes, I'm almost there.

(C) There's no need to switch cars.

저와 자리를 바꿔주실 수 있나요?

(A) 네, 그럼요.

(B) 네, 거의 다 왔습니다.

(C) 차를 갈아탈 필요가 없어요.

어휘 switch 바꾸다, 전환하다

PART 3

Questions 32-34 refer to the following conversation. 〔◁» 호주…영국〕

W Hi. ³²I'll be away from home on holiday for the month of October. I was wondering if I could suspend my home Internet service while I'm gone.

M Yes, you can, but ³³you'll have to pay a suspension fee, $5.00 a month.

W I guess that's all right. Can you set that up for me now?

M Of course. To start the process, ³⁴I'll need your name and home address.

여 안녕하세요. ³²제가 10월 한 달 동안 휴가로 집을 비울 예정인데요. 집을 비우는 동안 인터넷 서비스를 일시적으로 정지할 수 있는지 궁금합니다.

남 가능합니다. 하지만 ³³정지 비용을 매달 5달러씩 내셔야 합니다.

여 괜찮은 것 같아요. 지금 바로 처리해주실 수 있나요?

남 물론이죠. 절차를 진행하려면 ³⁴고객님의 성함과 주소를 알아야 합니다.

어휘 away from ~에서 떠나서 suspend 일시 정지하다 suspension fee 정지 비용

---

32 여자는 10월에 무엇을 할 것인가?
(A) 세미나에 참여한다.
(B) 휴가를 떠난다.
(C) 유학을 간다.
(D) 출장을 간다.

33 남자는 서비스 일시 정지에 대해서 뭐라고 말하는가?
(A) 일시 정지는 불가능하다.
(B) 한 달 이상이어야 한다.
(C) 절차를 온라인으로 진행해야 한다.
(D) 요금이 부과될 것이다.

34 여자는 다음에 어떤 정보를 줄 것인가?
(A) 계좌번호
(B) 이메일 주소
(C) 집 주소
(D) 전화번호

어휘 overseas business trip 해외 출장 procedure 절차 charge 부과금 account 계좌

Questions 35-37 refer to the following conversation. 〔◁» 캐나다…미국〕

W Hello. My name is Megan Roberts and ³⁵I have an appointment for a personal yoga session with Ms. Jackson tomorrow morning, but ³⁶I'm not going to be able to make it. Does she have time tomorrow afternoon?

M She is booked all day tomorrow and for the rest of the week, I'm afraid. Looks like she's totally booked the whole next week, too. ³⁷If you're fine with someone else, Ms. Dalton is available tomorrow afternoon.

W I've heard she's good, too. ³⁷Okay, I'll try her.

여 안녕하세요. 제 이름은 Megan Roberts라고 하는데, 내일 아침에 ³⁵Jackson씨의 개인 요가 수업을 예약했어요. ³⁶그런데 그 시간에 갈 수 없을 것 같습니다. 내일 오후에 시간이 될까요?

남 죄송하지만, 내일 모든 시간이 예약되어 있고 그 주의 나머지도 전부 예약이 찼습니다. 다음 주도 예약이 다 찬 것으로 보입니다. ³⁷다른 강사도 괜찮으시다면 Dalton씨가 내일 오후에 가능합니다.

여 그분도 잘한다고 들었어요. 좋아요. ³⁷그분이랑 해볼게요.

어휘 session 수업

---

35 Jackson씨는 누구인가?
(A) 접수원
(B) 학교 소유주
(C) 학생
(D) 강사

36 여자가 전화한 이유는 무엇인가?
(A) 예약하기 위해
(B) 예약을 취소하기 위해
(C) 예약을 확인하기 위해
(D) 예약 일정을 변경하기 위해

37 여자는 무엇을 하기로 결정했는가?
(A) 나중에 남자에게 다시 전화하기
(B) 다른 사람을 선택하기
(C) 다음 주에 예약 잡기
(D) Jackson씨에게 말하기

어휘 receptionist 접수원 instructor 강사 confirm 확인하다

Questions 38-40 refer to the following conversation. (캐나다…영국)

W Oh, David, I was looking for you. ³⁸Do you have a minute to look at the new logos? The design firm sent them to me this morning and well, see for yourself.

M Oh, wow, these are really different from what I expected.

W Yes, but I can't quite put my finger on what is wrong. The color? The size?

M I think ³⁹the company name is hard to read on these two. And this one is too busy. You know, too many lines and . . .

W ³⁹That's it. We need something simple and clean. ⁴⁰I'll let the designers know. Hopefully, they'll come up with better ones.

여 David, 당신을 찾고 있었어요. ³⁸새 로고 봐줄 시간 좀 있어요? 오늘 아침 디자인 회사에서 저에게 로고를 보냈어요. 한번 직접 보세요.
남 와, 제가 생각한 것과 정말 많이 달라요.
여 그렇죠. 그런데 뭐가 잘못됐는지 딱 꼬집어 말할 수가 없어요. 색깔? 크기?
남 ³⁹이 두 개는 회사 이름을 읽기가 힘든 것 같아요. 그리고 이 디자인은 너무 복잡하고요. 선이 너무 많아요.
여 ³⁹맞아요. 좀 더 간단명료한 로고가 필요해요. ⁴⁰디자이너들에게 말해줘야겠어요. 더 좋은 디자인이 나오면 좋겠네요.

어휘 put one's finger on ~를 확실히 지적하다 busy (모양이) 복잡한 come up with 찾아내다

---

38 화자들은 무엇에 대해 말하는가?
(A) 회사의 심벌
(B) 신축 건물의 디자인
(C) 그림
(D) 사진

39 여자가 That's it이라고 말한 의도는 무엇인가?
(A) 그녀는 하고 싶은 말을 했다.
(B) 그녀는 그의 의견을 재미있어 한다.
(C) 그녀는 그 남자가 좋은 지적을 했다고 생각한다.
(D) 그녀는 대화를 끝내고 싶어 한다.

40 여자는 무엇을 할 것이라고 말하는가?
(A) 다른 동료에게 도움을 청한다.
(B) 디자인 회사에게 연락한다.
(C) 다른 회사를 고용한다.
(D) 새로운 슬로건을 생각한다.

어휘 amused 즐거워하는 point 의견 co-worker 동료

Questions 41-43 refer to the following conversation. (호주…미국)

W I see the Charleston Line isn't running this morning. What happened?

M ⁴¹There was a signal malfunction near Dearing Station. They think the storm last night shut down the signals.

W How long do you think before the line is running again?

M Hard to say. They've been working on it for an hour or so and I haven't heard an update. ⁴²The latest information is on our Website. ⁴³Here's a card with the Website address.

여 Charleston 노선이 오늘 아침에 운행하지 않더라고요. 무슨 일이 있었나요?
남 ⁴¹Dearing역 근처에서 신호 고장이 있었어요. 지난밤 폭풍이 신호를 차단했다고 보고 있습니다.
여 노선이 다시 운행되려면 얼마나 걸릴까요?
남 말씀드리기 어려워요. 한 시간쯤 작업하고 있는 것 같은데, 추가로 소식을 듣지 못했어요. ⁴²최신 정보는 저희 웹사이트에 있어요. ⁴³여기 웹사이트 주소가 적힌 카드예요.

어휘 signal 신호 malfunction (기계) 고장 line (기차) 노선 run (차가) 운행하다

---

41 지연된 원인은 무엇인가?
(A) 기계 문제
(B) 직원 채용 문제
(C) 교통체증
(D) 차 사고

42 남자는 누구인가?
(A) 정비사
(B) 승객
(C) 역무원
(D) 웹사이트 디자이너

43 남자는 여자에게 무엇을 주었는가?
(A) 노선도
(B) 환불금
(C) 자기 회사의 URL
(D) 지연에 대한 최신 정보

어휘 staffing 직원 채용 traffic jam 교통체증 mechanic 정비사

Questions 44–46 refer to the following conversation. 〔◁)) 호주…영국〕 신·유·형

W Hi, there. ⁴⁴I'd like to sign up for the boat tour tomorrow. Uh, do you have any space left in the morning?

M How many people are there?

W Two adults and two children.

M In that case, you'll have to take the afternoon tour. ⁴⁵The boats are not that big, actually. They only hold eight people.

W I see. And ⁴⁴they go by the floating markets where we can buy souvenirs, right?

M That's right. The vendors sell all kinds of accessories and food. It's one of our most popular tours.

W Excellent. ⁴⁶My friend recommended we do this tour. ⁴⁴It's one of the main reasons we came here.

어휘 sign up for ~를 신청하다 in that case 그런 경우에는 floating market 수상 시장 souvenir 기념품 vendor 노점상

여 안녕하세요. ⁴⁴내일 보트 투어를 신청하고 싶은데요. 아침에 남은 자리가 있을까요?
남 몇 명 신청하세요?
여 어른 두 명과 아이 두 명이요.
남 그렇다면 오후 투어에 등록하셔야 해요. ⁴⁵보트가 크지 않거든요. 8명만 탈 수 있죠.
여 알겠어요. ⁴⁴보트가 기념품을 살 수 있는 수상 시장으로 가는 게 맞죠?
남 맞아요. 노점상들이 온갖 종류의 액세서리와 음식을 팝니다. 저희 투어 중에서 가장 인기 있어요.
여 훌륭하네요. ⁴⁶제 친구가 이 투어를 추천해줬어요. ⁴⁴우리 가족이 여기에 온 주된 이유 중 하나예요.

---

44 여자의 가족은 내일 무엇을 할 것인가?
(A) 낚시하러 가기
(B) 기념품 구매하기
(C) 집으로 돌아가기
(D) 친구 만나기

45 남자가 보트에 대해 언급한 것은 무엇인가?
(A) 빠르다.
(B) 작다.
(C) 수리가 필요하다.
(D) 하루에 한 번만 운행한다.

46 여자는 어떻게 투어에 대해 알게 되었는가?
(A) 책자에서
(B) 친구를 통해
(C) TV 프로그램에서
(D) 인터넷 광고로

어휘 memento 기념품 brochure 소책자

Questions 47–49 refer to the following conversation. 〔◁)) 미국…캐나다〕

M Amy, now that we're all moved in, we have to let our neighbors know about us. How should we advertise?

W Hmm. ⁴⁷After paying the rent and deposit on this place, we have hardly any money left for advertising.

M True, but I think if we can get some local people in here for their morning coffee, they'll tell their friends, who will tell their friends . . .

W Yeah, ⁴⁸word of mouth doesn't cost us a thing. But to start it off, why don't we use social media?

M Okay. ⁴⁹I'll post a picture of some of our drinks and pastries on my social networking sites.

어휘 rent 집세 deposit 보증금 word of mouth 입소문

남 Amy, 이제 다 이사했으니, 여기 이웃들에게 우리를 알려야 해. 우리를 어떻게 광고할까?
여 ⁴⁷이곳 임대료와 보증금을 지불하고 나면 광고로 쓸 돈이 거의 없어.
남 맞아. 우리가 여기에서 모닝커피를 마실 지역민들을 오게 하면, 그들이 친구에게, 또 그 친구가 다른 친구에게 말하지 않을까?
여 그래, ⁴⁸입소문은 돈이 들지 않지. 그렇지만 우선은 SNS를 이용하는 게 어때?
남 좋아. ⁴⁹내가 SNS에 우리 음료하고 페이스트리가 나온 사진을 올릴게.

47 여자가 재정 상태에 대해 암시하는 것은?
(A) 화자들은 은행에 빚이 있다.
(B) 화자들은 돈을 많이 벌고 있다.
(C) 화자들은 광고할 돈이 충분하다.
(D) 화자들은 여분의 돈이 없다.

48 여자가 word of mouth doesn't cost us a thing라고 말한 의도는 무엇인가?
(A) 그녀는 더 저렴한 방법이 있다고 생각한다.
(B) 그녀는 남자가 한 말이 마음에 들지 않는다.
(C) 그녀는 광고비가 얼마가 들지 잘 모른다.
(D) 그녀는 소개하는 데 돈이 들지 않는다는 것을 안다.

49 남자는 곧 무엇을 할 것이라고 말하는가?
(A) 무료로 음료를 나눠준다.
(B) 재무학 강의를 듣는다.
(C) 친구들에게 말한다.
(D) 인터넷에 사진을 올린다.

어휘 in debt 빚을 진 make money 돈 벌다 referral 소개 take a class 강의 듣다

Questions 50–52 refer to the following conversation. (영국…캐나다)

M Hi. I'm in a bit of a hurry. ⁵⁰I need to see my client in 30 minutes. Which lunch specials do you think are quickest to make?

W Well, ⁵¹all our meals are made to order, but the hamburger plate is fairly fast. It comes with a choice of salad or soup.

M Hmm, what's your soup today?

W Potato cream with bacon.

M I think I'll have a salad and the hamburger plate. ⁵²And an iced tea.

W Got it. ⁵²I'll be right out with your drink.

남 안녕하세요. 제가 좀 급해요. ⁵⁰30분 후에 고객을 만나야 하거든요. 어떤 점심 특선이 가장 빨리 나오나요?

여 ⁵¹모든 음식은 주문 후 만들어져요. 그래도 햄버거는 꽤 빨리 나와요. 샐러드나 수프 중 하나를 선택하세요.

남 오늘의 수프는 뭐죠?

여 베이컨을 곁들인 감자 크림입니다.

남 샐러드와 햄버거 먹을게요. ⁵²그리고 아이스티 한 잔도요.

여 네. ⁵²금방 음료를 가져다드리지요.

어휘 made to order 주문 제작된, ~의 주문을 받아 만드는

---

50 남자가 서두르는 이유는 무엇인가?
(A) 면접이 있어서
(B) 약속이 있어서
(C) 기차를 타야 해서
(D) 빨리 집에 가고 싶어서

51 식당의 음식에 대해 언급된 것은 무엇인가?
(A) 모두 지역의 공급업체에서 가져온다.
(B) 모두 유기농이다.
(C) 미리 준비된다.
(D) 주문 시 요리된다.

52 여자는 남자에게 무엇을 먼저 가져다줄 것인가?
(A) 햄버거
(B) 샐러드
(C) 아이스티
(D) 감자 수프

어휘 in a hurry 서두르는 supplier 공급업체 organic 유기농의 ahead of time 미리

Questions 53–55 refer to the following conversation. 🔊 호주…미국

W ⁵³Thank you for joining us on our program today, Mr. Sullivan. You've been busy in these past few months, giving talks and interviews.

M Uh, yes, it's all been a bit overwhelming. When ⁵⁴my research on oceans was published, I had no idea people would be so interested.

W ⁵³Could you tell our viewers what's next for ⁵⁴your proposal to clean the world's oceans?

M Well, that's a good question. No one has taken on the project I suggested. I'm still hopeful though, that some private company or a group of governments will contribute the necessary funds for it. It's very urgent, as you know.

W Yes, I know. ⁵⁵Now, let's show a video you and your team made to explain the project in more detail.

여 Sullivan씨, ⁵³오늘 저희 프로그램에 참여해주셔서 감사합니다. 지난 몇 달 동안 강연과 인터뷰로 바빴잖아요.

남 네, 모든 게 조금 벅찼어요. ⁵⁴해양에 관한 제 연구가 출판되었을 때, 사람들이 그렇게 관심을 가질 줄 몰랐습니다.

여 ⁵⁴세계 해양을 정화하기 위한 Sullivan씨의 제안에 관한 다음 행보를 ⁵³우리 시청자들에게 말해주시겠어요?

남 좋은 질문입니다. 아무도 제가 제안한 프로젝트를 맡지 않았습니다. 그래도 저는 사기업이나 정부단체가 프로젝트에 필요 자금을 기부할 것이라는 데에 여전히 희망을 갖고 있습니다. 아시다시피, 아주 급한 일이잖아요.

여 네, 알고 있습니다. ⁵⁵이제 당신과 팀이 프로젝트에 대해 더 자세히 설명하는 영상을 보죠.

어휘 overwhelming 압도적인 private 민간의 contribute 기부하다

---

53 화자들은 어디에 있는가?
(A) 대학교
(B) 시상식
(C) 라디오 방송국
(D) TV 스튜디오

54 남자의 연구는 무엇에 관한 것인가?
(A) 환경 문제
(B) 정치적 이슈
(C) 민간 부문의 성장
(D) 세계 경제

55 화자들은 다음에 무엇을 할 것인가?
(A) 인터뷰를 계속한다.
(B) 청중의 질문을 듣는다.
(C) 몇몇 데이터를 본다.
(D) 영상을 시청한다.

어휘 ceremony 의식 concern 문제 political 정치의

Questions 56–58 refer to the following conversation with three speakers. 🔊 호주…미국…캐나다 신유형

W1 Mr. Stuart, ⁵⁶I hope your toothache is better now. When would you like to schedule your next appointment?

M Uh . . . how about the same day and time next week, Thursday, August 4th at 10:00 AM?

W1 Dr. McCloud may be away that day. Let me check with her. Oh, there she is. Dr. McCloud, will you be here next Thursday?

W2 No, ⁵⁷I have to attend an annual dental conference.

M I see. Well, ⁵⁸I can come here next Friday, the 5th.

W2 ⁵⁸I'll be back by then, so I can see you in the afternoon.

여1 Stuart씨, ⁵⁶이젠 치통이 가라앉았으면 좋겠네요. 다음 예약은 언제로 잡고 싶으세요?

남 다음 주 같은 요일, 같은 시간대인 8월 4일 목요일 오전 10시가 어떨까요?

여1 McCloud 선생님이 그날 자리를 비울지도 몰라요. 제가 확인해 볼게요. 아, 저기 계시네요. 선생님, 다음 주 목요일에 나오실 건가요?

여2 아뇨, ⁵⁷연례 치과회의에 참석해야 해요.

남 그렇군요. ⁵⁸저는 다음 주 금요일인 5일에 여기 올 수 있어요.

여2 ⁵⁸그때는 돌아오니, 오후에 뵐 수 있겠네요.

어휘 toothache 치통 attend 참석하다 annual 연간의

---

56 남자는 누구인가?
(A) 치과의사
(B) 간호사
(C) 환자
(D) 접수원

57 McCloud 선생에 대해 언급된 것은?
(A) 이번 주 예약이 다 찼다.
(B) 곧 퇴근한다.
(C) 회의에 갈 것이다.
(D) 이제 쉴 것이다.

58 Stuart씨의 다음 예약은 언제인가?
(A) 다음 주 목요일 아침
(B) 다음 주 목요일 오후
(C) 다음 주 금요일 아침
(D) 다음 주 금요일 오후

Questions 59-61 refer to the following conversation with three speakers. (◁)) 영국…호주…미국 신유형

M1 <u>59 Tomorrow, we have to take inventory in the stockroom,</u> so I'll need you both to stay a bit later. Say, two hours.

W Fine with me. I could use the overtime.

M2 Uh, <u>60 I have a class that starts at 7:30.</u> I can't miss it since I was absent twice already. The third absence and you have to drop the class.

M1 Okay, John, you can leave in time for your class. If we aren't done yet, Sarah and I will finish up. Is that all right with you, Sarah?

W Sure. <u>61 I don't have any plans tomorrow.</u>

남1 59우리가 내일은 창고 재고 조사를 해야 하니 두 분 다 좀 더 늦게까지 남아주세요. 두 시간 정도요.

여 저는 괜찮아요. 초과 근무가 필요해요.

남2 60저는 7시 30분에 시작하는 수업이 있어요. 벌써 두 번이나 결석했기 때문에 빠질 수 없어요. 세 번 결석하면 그 수업은 끝이에요.

남1 그래요, John. 수업 시간에 맞춰 나가도록 해요. 그래도 끝나지 않는다면 Sarah와 제가 마무리 지을게요. 괜찮아요, Sarah?

여1 그럼요. 61저는 내일 아무 계획도 없어요.

59 화자들은 내일 상점에서 무엇을 할 것인가?
(A) 판매 준비하기
(B) 재고 목록 작성하기
(C) 박스로 물건 포장하기
(D) 신상품 전시하기

60 John이 내일 늦게까지 있을 수 없는 이유는 무엇인가?
(A) 진료 예약이 있어서
(B) 다른 직장이 있어서
(C) 도시를 벗어날 예정이라서
(D) 학교에 다녀서

61 여자에 대해 옳은 것은 무엇인가?
(A) 초과 근무를 싫어한다.
(B) 내일 시간이 있다.
(C) 일정에 대해 확신하지 못한다.
(D) 승진을 원한다.

Questions 62-64 refer to the following conversation and advertisement. (◁)) 영국…호주

M Jennifer, <u>62 I need to get a new jacket</u> and you said you wanted a new shirt, right? What do you say we go to the sale at Lacy's? Looking at this advertisement, we can save money if we go there this weekend.

W Not only do I need a new shirt, but I also need a pair of shoes. The problem is <u>63 I'm going to be out of town to go to my cousin's wedding ceremony this weekend.</u> I'll be back Sunday night.

M Don't worry. <u>64 We can go after work on Monday.</u>

남 Jennifer, 62나는 새 재킷이 필요한데, 당신은 새 셔츠를 사고 싶다고 했잖아요? Lacy에서 세일하는데 가보는 게 어때요? 광고를 보니까 이번 주말에 가면 돈을 절약할 수 있겠어요.

여 새 셔츠도 필요하지만, 신발 한 켤레도 필요해요. 문제는 63이번 주말에 사촌 결혼식에 가려면 시외로 나가야한다는 거예요. 일요일 밤에 돌아올 예정이고요.

남 걱정 마세요. 64월요일에 퇴근하고 가면 돼요.

Lacy 10월 세일	
7일 ~ 13일	
빠를수록 할인율이 커집니다!	
25% 할인!	금요일부터 일요일
64 20% 할인!	월요일과 화요일
15% 할인!	수요일
10% 할인!	목요일

62 남자는 무엇을 사길 원하는가?
  (A) 가방
  (B) 재킷
  (C) 신발
  (D) 셔츠

63 여자는 이번 주말에 무엇을 할 것인가?
  (A) 행사에 참석하기
  (B) 옷 몇 벌 구매하기
  (C) 집에서 쉬기
  (D) 출장 가기

64 광고에 의하면, 화자들은 얼마나 할인받을 것인가?
  (A) 10퍼센트
  (B) 15퍼센트
  (C) 20퍼센트
  (D) 25퍼센트

어휘 relax 휴식을 취하다

Questions 65-67 refer to the following conversation and schedule.

W Thanks for making the agenda for the board meeting, William. I'm afraid there's going to have to be a change though.

M Oh, really? What's that?

W ⁶⁵My boss, Ms. Sinclair has an urgent matter to handle with a client tomorrow morning. She won't get back here until 11:00.

M I see. I'm sure we can switch some things around.

W Actually, ⁶⁶it's all taken care of. I've already asked the sales team to present their report earlier.

M Oh, great. Then ⁶⁷I'll remake the agenda and send it out to everyone before I leave tonight.

W Sorry for the extra work.

M Don't mention it.

여 임원회의 일정표를 만들어줘서 감사해요, William. 그런데 변경이 좀 있을 거예요.

남 정말이요? 뭐가 바뀌죠?

여 ⁶⁵제 상사인 Sinclair씨가 내일 아침에 고객과 긴급하게 처리해야 할 일이 생겼어요. 11시까지 돌아오시지 못할 거예요.

남 그렇군요. 다른 일정과 바꿀 수 있을 거예요.

여 사실은 ⁶⁶다 처리됐어요. 영업팀에 보고서를 좀 더 일찍 발표해달라고 이미 요청했어요.

남 잘됐네요. 그러면 ⁶⁷제가 일정표를 다시 작성해서 오늘 밤 퇴근 전에 모두에게 보낼게요.

여 더 일하게 해서 미안해요.

남 별말씀을요.

임원회의 일정
11월 1일
⁶⁶10:00   Erin Sinclair
10:30   Leo Anderson
11:30   영업팀
12:00   Matt Moore 사장님

어휘 agenda 예정표 present 발표하다

---

65 여자의 상사는 내일 11시 전까지 무엇을 할 것인가?
  (A) 임원회에 참석한다.
  (B) 지원자를 면접 본다.
  (C) 발표 준비를 한다.
  (D) 고객을 만난다.

66 일정표에 의하면, 영업팀은 몇 시에 보고서를 발표할 것인가?
  (A) 10시
  (B) 10시 반
  (C) 11시 반
  (D) 12시

67 남자는 무엇을 하겠다고 말하는가?
  (A) 일정 수정
  (B) 보고서 완료
  (C) 초대장 발송
  (D) 영업팀과의 대화

어휘 edit 수정하다

Questions 68-70 refer to the following conversation and list. 🔊 미국···캐나다 신유형

M Hello, I heard about your sale on watches. Can I see them?

W Yes, but only certain brands are discounted. These over here. This Charter 400 is a best seller.

M Okay, I'll try it. Ah, no. ⁶⁸I don't like the feel of the band. It's too itchy. Can I try a different one?

W Of course. Maybe you would like a leather band better. Here's a stylish one in brown.

M ⁶⁹Ah, that feels better, but do you have a black one?

W Not in the store currently. But ⁷⁰I can order it for you and have it sent to your house, free of charge.

M Sounds good. Thank you.

남 안녕하세요? 이곳에서 시계를 할인하고 있다고요. 좀 볼 수 있을까요?

여 네, 특정 브랜드만 할인됩니다. 이쪽에 있는 것들이요. Charter 400이 가장 잘 팔리는 모델입니다.

남 좋아요, 한번 차볼게요. 이런, ⁶⁸시곗줄의 느낌이 좋지 않네요. 너무 간지러워요. 다른 걸 차봐도 될까요?

여 물론이죠. 가죽 줄을 더 좋아하실 수도 있겠네요. 여기 스타일리시한 갈색 줄이요.

남 ⁶⁹훨씬 느낌이 낫네요. 그런데 검은색이 있나요?

여 지금 매장에는 없어요. 하지만 ⁷⁰주문해서 무료로 댁까지 보내드릴 수 있어요.

남 좋네요. 감사합니다.

제품명	시곗줄 재질	시곗줄 색상
Chater 400	금속	은색
Elling 2Z	금속	금색
Millseed CR	가죽	갈색
⁶⁹Vextron 7T	가죽	검정색

어휘 itchy 가려운, 가렵게 하는 leather 가죽

68 남자가 처음으로 착용해본 시계는 무엇이 문제인가?
(A) 알맞은 색상이 아니었다.
(B) 너무 비쌌다.
(C) 너무 무거웠다.
(D) 불편했다.

69 신유형 목록에 의하면, 남자는 어떤 시계를 주문할 것인가?
(A) Charter 400
(B) Elling 2Z
(C) Millseed CR
(D) Vextron 7T

70 여자가 남자에게 무료로 제공하는 것은?
(A) 여분 시곗줄
(B) 배송 서비스
(C) 선물 포장
(D) 주차

어휘 uncomfortable 불편한 wrapping 포장

PART 4

Questions 71-73 refer to the following telephone message. 🔊 호주

Hello, my name is Samantha and ⁷¹I own a print shop in your neighborhood. I noticed your company has just moved here and I wanted to let you know what we do. In addition to the usual printing and copying, we offer Website and logo design services. For new customers such as yourself, we are priced very competitively, say . . . on business cards, if you need some with your new address. ⁷²We offer the quickest turnaround of all shops in this area, even same-day service on certain jobs. ⁷³I'll be dropping a flyer by your office later this week. Hopefully, we can speak then about your printing needs. Thank you.

안녕하세요? 제 이름은 Samantha이고 ⁷¹귀사의 근처에서 인쇄소를 운영하고 있습니다. 막 이곳으로 이사 오신 것을 알게 되어, 저희가 하는 일을 알려드리고 싶어요. 저희는 일반적인 인쇄나 복사 외에도 웹사이트와 로고 디자인 서비스도 제공합니다. 귀사와 같은 신규 고객에게는, 예를 들어 새 주소가 박힌 명함과 같은 상품을 경쟁력 있는 가격으로 제공합니다. ⁷²저희는 이 지역의 모든 가게들 중에서 가장 빠른 작업시간을 보장하며, 심지어 일부 작업은 당일 완성도 가능합니다. ⁷³이번 주에 전단지를 선생님 사무실에 갖다 놓겠습니다. 필요로 하시는 인쇄 작업에 대해 의논할 수 있기를 바랍니다. 감사합니다.

어휘 neighborhood 근처 notice 알아차리다 competitively 경쟁적으로 turnaround 작업시간 flyer 전단지

71 화자의 직업은 무엇인가?
(A) IT 직원
(B) 경찰관
(C) 우체국 직원
(D) 상점 주인

72 화자에 의하면, 그녀의 사업의 특징은 무엇인가?
(A) 가장 싸다.
(B) 가장 빠르다.
(C) 가장 크다.
(D) 가장 오래되었다.

73 화자는 곧 무엇을 할 것이라고 말하는가?
(A) 다른 지역으로 이사한다.
(B) 새 지점을 연다.
(C) 광고를 게시한다.
(D) 청자의 회사를 방문한다.

어휘 postal 우편의 post 게시하다

Questions 74-76 refer to the following broadcast. 🔊 미국

Good news for local hockey fans. ⁷⁴It looks like we'll be getting our first professional hockey team here in Stanleyville. The owner of the Pirates, a team that has played for over a decade in Greenborough, released a written statement earlier today saying he's moving his team here. ⁷⁵Among the many attractions to this area were the energetic fans and world-class ice arena, the statement said. We sent a reporter to City Hall and, ⁷⁶as you'll see after the commercial break, Stanleyville Mayor Evans had a very enthusiastic reaction to the historic announcement. Don't go away.

지역 하키 팬들을 위한 좋은 소식입니다. ⁷⁴지역의 첫 프로 하키 팀을 여기 Stanleyville에서 창단하게 될 것 같습니다. Greenborough에서 10년 넘게 경기한 Pirates의 구단주는 오늘 아침에 이곳으로 팀의 연고지를 옮길 것이라는 성명서를 발표했습니다. 성명서에서 ⁷⁵우리 지역의 매력으로 역동적인 팬과 세계적인 빙상 경기장을 꼽았습니다. 시청으로 기자를 보냈습니다. ⁷⁶광고 후에 Stanleyville의 Evans 시장이 이 역사적인 발표에 대해 아주 열렬히 반응하는 모습을 보실 것입니다. 채널 고정하세요.

어휘 release 발표하다 written 서면으로 된 attraction 매력 commercial break 광고 시간 enthusiastic 열광적인

74 방송은 주로 무엇에 관한 것인가?
(A) 새로운 스포츠 시설
(B) 새로운 스포츠 팀
(C) 은퇴하는 선수
(D) 스포츠 시합

75 Stanleyville에 대해 언급된 것은 무엇인가?
(A) 새 시장이 선출되었다.
(B) 훌륭한 아이스 링크가 있다.
(C) 전에 스포츠 행사를 개최한 적이 있다.
(D) 1개 이상의 프로 팀을 가지고 있다.

76 청자들은 다음으로 무엇을 들을 것인가?
(A) 시장의 연설
(B) 기자의 말
(C) 기상 예보
(D) 광고

어휘 host 개최하다 speech 연설

Question 77-79 refer to the following announcement. 🔊 캐나다

⁷⁷Attention Tally Ho Wine shoppers. ⁷⁸It is now 7:45 and our store will close in 15 minutes. Please bring your selections to the front for checkout. We are open from 10:00 AM to 9:00 PM Monday through Friday and ⁷⁸10:00 AM to 8:00 PM on Saturday and Sunday. For your convenience, ⁷⁹we also have a Website where you can purchase all of the items you see in our store, plus some bottles of wine that are available online only. To access the shopping feature, just use your loyalty card number and create a password. The address is www. tallyhowines.com.

⁷⁷Tally Ho Wine 쇼핑객 여러분. ⁷⁸현재 시각은 7시 45분이고 15분 후에 영업이 종료될 예정입니다. 선택하신 제품을 매장 앞 계산대로 가져오시기 바랍니다. 저희는 평일 오전 10시부터 저녁 9시까지, 그리고 ⁷⁸토요일과 일요일에는 오전 10시부터 저녁 8시까지 운영합니다. 고객님의 편의를 위해 ⁷⁹가게에서 보시는 모든 제품들을 저희 웹사이트에서 구매하실 수 있으며, 일부 와인은 오직 인터넷으로만 구매하실 수 있습니다. 저희 특매품을 구매하시려면 고객 카드 번호를 사용하시고 비밀번호를 설정하시면 됩니다. 주소는 www.tallyhowines.com입니다.

어휘 selection 선택된 것 checkout 계산대 shopping feature 쇼핑 특매품

77 어떤 종류의 가게에 대한 안내인가?
(A) 델리
(B) 백화점
(C) 식료품점
(D) 와인숍

78 안내는 언제 방송되고 있는가?
(A) 월요일
(B) 수요일
(C) 금요일
(D) 일요일

79 온라인 선택에 대해 언급된 것은 무엇인가?
(A) 매장보다 선택의 폭이 넓다.
(B) 최근에 다시 만들어졌다.
(C) 매장보다 저렴하다.
(D) 안전하다.

어휘 secure 안전한

Question 80-82 refer to following news report. (◀)) 영국

And now we turn to regional news. **80**The government has released the economic numbers for last quarter and for the first time in three years, there has been an upturn in production and job growth. The report cites two industries in particular that are responsible for the good news, biotechnology and manufacturing. We've been covering the biotech boom a lot recently, so we thought we'd get a different perspective today. **81,82**Our reporter Kevin Chang sat down with the president of KRL Manufacturing to ask about his company's recent growth.

이제 지역 뉴스로 넘어가겠습니다. **80**정부는 지난 분기의 경제 수치를 발표했고 3년 만에 처음으로, 생산과 고용 성장에서 상승이 있었다고 발표했습니다. 보고서에서는 특히 생명공학 분야와 제조업 분야, 두 업계가 이 좋은 소식에 한몫했다고 합니다. 생명공학의 호황에 대해서는 최근에 이미 여러 차례 취재를 했기 때문에 오늘은 다른 시각을 듣기로 했습니다. **81,82**저희 방송국 기자 Kevin Chang이 KRL 제조회사 사장과 함께 앉아 회사의 최근 성장에 대해 질문하겠습니다.

어휘 regional news 지역 뉴스 quarter 분기 upturn 상승 cite (이유·예를) 들다 in particular 특히 biotechnology 생명공학 manufacturing 제조업 cover 취재하다 perspective 관점

---

80 화자는 무엇에 대해 논의하는가?
(A) 새로운 정부 정책
(B) 새로운 지역 시설
(C) 업무상 인사이동
(D) 최근 경제 뉴스

81 Kevin Chang은 누구인가?
(A) 생명공학 전문가
(B) 회사 소유주
(C) 정부 대변인
(D) 뉴스 관계자

82 청자들은 다음으로 무엇을 들을 것인가?
(A) 광고
(B) 생명공학 보고서
(C) 언론 브리핑
(D) 인터뷰

어휘 personnel 직원의 expert 전문가 economics 경제학

Questions 83-85 refer to the following telephone message. (◀)) 호주

Hi, Carlos. **83**I just wanted to tell you how wonderful our awards ceremony was, thanks to your great recommendation of the Four Leaf banquet hall. The staff there was so helpful and the food was wonderful. I understand why you go back there every year for your firm's party. I actually asked them about having our end-of-year party there also. They were booked on the night we had chosen, but my co-workers and I loved it so much, **84**we're thinking about changing nights. **85**They are filling up quickly, so you should probably confirm your party date with them soon. Anyway, take care, Carlos!

안녕하세요, Carlos. **83**당신이 Four Leaf 연회장을 추천해준 덕분에 저희 시상식이 정말 훌륭했다고 말하고 싶었어요. 그곳 직원들은 아주 친절했고 음식도 훌륭했어요. 당신이 회사 모임을 매년 그곳에서 하는 이유를 알겠어요. 제가 그쪽에 저희 회사 연말 파티를 여는 것에 대해 물어보았어요. 우리가 선택한 날 밤에는 예약이 있었는데 동료들과 저는 그곳에 너무 만족해서 **84**파티 날짜를 바꾸는 걸 고려하고 있어요. **85**그곳은 예약이 금방 차니까 당신도 빨리 파티 날짜를 그쪽에 확정해줘야 할 거예요. 어쨌든, 잘 지내요, Carlos!

어휘 co-worker 동료 fill up 차다 confirm 확정하다

83 여자가 전화한 이유는 무엇인가?
- (A) 약속을 변경하기 위해
- (B) 감사를 표현하기 위해
- (C) 예약하기 위해
- (D) 식당을 추천하기 위해

84 여자는 파티에 대해 무엇을 결정해야 한다고 하는가?
- (A) 어떤 음식을 내놓을지
- (B) 언제 파티를 열지
- (C) 어디서 파티를 열지
- (D) 누구를 초대할지

85 🔵신🔵유🔵형 They are filling up quickly라는 말이 암시하는 것은 무엇인가?
- (A) 고객들이 충분히 먹었다.
- (B) 고객들이 집에 일찍 가고 싶어 한다.
- (C) 예약할 수 있는 날짜가 며칠 없다.
- (D) 직원들이 곧 일을 마칠 것이다.

어휘 appreciation 감사

Questions 86-88 refer to the following talk. 🔊 캐나다

Welcome to today's seminar on starting your own business. [87]We'll be covering all the basics of running a small business, from advertising to financing to location. [88]You'll be hearing from real business owners on each of the topics this morning. Then, after lunch, we'll have the speakers lead small group discussions so you can ask specific questions on your situation. [86]We ask that you hold your questions until the afternoon sessions. Also, we'd like you to fill out a survey at the end of the seminar. You'll find it in the information packets on each chair. Just drop them in the box at the door as you leave. Well, let's get started.

오늘 자영업 창업 세미나에 오신 것을 환영합니다. [87]저희는 광고, 자금 조달, 위치 등 소규모 사업을 운영하는 데 필요한 모든 기본을 다룰 예정입니다. [88]오전에는 실제 사업주들로부터 각 주제에 대한 이야기를 들으실 겁니다. 그러고 나서, 점심식사 후에는 자신의 상황에 대해 구체적으로 질문할 수 있도록 연사들이 소그룹 토론을 이끌 것입니다. [86]질문은 오후 세션까지 보류해주시기 바랍니다. 또한 세미나가 끝나면 설문지를 작성하시기 바랍니다. 의자마다 놓여 있는 자료집에서 설문지를 찾으실 수 있습니다. 나가실 때 문 쪽에 있는 상자에 넣어주세요. 자, 시작하겠습니다.

어휘 financing 자금 조달 information packet 자료 묶음

---

86 언제 청중들이 질문을 할 수 있는가?
- (A) 그들이 나갈 때
- (B) 언제든지
- (C) 점심시간 동안
- (D) 오후 세션에

87 🔵신🔵유🔵형 We'll be covering all the basics of running a small business라는 말이 의미하는 것은 무엇인가?
- (A) 그들은 소기업용 보험을 신청할 것이다.
- (B) 그들은 참가자들에게 창업의 다양한 측면에 대해 가르칠 것이다.
- (C) 그들은 소규모 사업장 일자리를 찾는 참가자들을 면접 볼 것이다.
- (D) 그들은 이전 세미나에서 배운 모든 기술을 복습할 것이다.

88 청중들은 다음에 무엇을 할 것인가?
- (A) 양식을 작성한다.
- (B) 소그룹으로 나뉜다.
- (C) 점심을 먹는다.
- (D) 강연을 듣는다.

어휘 instruct 가르치다 aspect 면 review 복습하다

Since we have less than a week before the move, I wanted to go over our assignments again. ⁸⁹Robert, your team will of course be in charge of the computer equipment. I mean, the movers we've hired will box it all up, but I'd like you to supervise and make sure everything is set up correctly at the new office. ⁹⁰Jocelyn, you're in charge of supplies. Again, you just have to make sure to label the boxes the movers pack and then put everything away in an organized way. Finally, Luis, can you update the Website to show our new location? Well, ⁹¹on second thought, Luis, wait until the actual move-in day, December 12. Thanks everyone.

이사까지 일주일도 채 남지 않았기 때문에 우리에게 할당된 업무를 다시 점검하고 싶습니다. ⁸⁹Robert, 당신 팀은 당연히 컴퓨터 장비를 책임질 거예요. 우리가 고용한 이삿짐 운송업자들이 전부 포장하지만, 당신이 새 사무실에서 감독하면서 모든 것이 제대로 설치되는지 확인해주세요. ⁹⁰Jocelyn, 당신은 사무용품을 담당해주세요. 이삿짐 업체에서 포장한 상자에 당신이 라벨을 붙이고 모든 것을 잘 정돈되게 치워야 합니다. 마지막으로, Luis, 우리 새 주소가 보이도록 웹사이트를 갱신해주겠어요? 음, Luis, ⁹¹다시 생각해보니 그건 실제 이사하는 날인 12월 12일까지 기다려주세요. 모두 감사합니다.

어휘 assignment 임무 in charge of ~를 담당하여 supplies 사무 용품 organized way 정리된 방식 on the second thought 다시 생각해보니 move-in day 이사하는 날

89 Robert가 일하는 부서는 어디인가?
(A) 회계
(B) IT
(C) 사무 관리
(D) 영업

90 Jocelyn은 일주일도 안 남기고 무엇을 할 것인가?
(A) 이삿짐 업체를 고용한다.
(B) 새 사무실을 청소한다.
(C) 사무용품을 정리한다.
(D) 박스를 포장한다.

91 화자가 on second thought라고 말한 이유는 무엇인가?
(신/유/형)
(A) 그녀는 청자들이 뭔가를 다시 생각해보길 원한다.
(B) 그녀는 처음에 말했던 것과 다른 것을 하고 싶어 한다.
(C) 그녀는 이사에 시간이 부족하다고 생각한다.
(D) 그녀는 이사가 더 빨리 이뤄져야 한다고 생각한다.

어휘 administration 관리, 행정 organize 정리하다 run out 다 떨어지다

⁹²We are indeed lucky to have an award-winning history professor addressing our book club tonight. Actually, Dr. Fleming recently retired from teaching and is touring around the country promoting his new book on Egyptian treasure. There's even talk of a movie version of his fascinating tale. ⁹³First he's going to read an excerpt of his book *Jewels in the Sand*. Then he'll take questions from the audience. We have a wireless microphone so everyone can hear you. ⁹⁴If you'd like to ask a question, just stand and someone will bring the microphone to you. Okay, without further ado, please welcome Dr. Fleming.

⁹²오늘 밤, 수상 경력이 있는 역사학 교수님을 저희 북클럽에서 소개하게 되어 큰 행운입니다. Fleming 박사님은 최근에 교직에서 은퇴하고 이집트 보물에 대한 신간을 홍보하며 전국을 순회하고 있습니다. 이분의 매력적인 이야기를 영화화하는 것에 대한 논의도 있습니다. ⁹³우선 교수님이 Jewels in the Sand에서 발췌한 내용을 읽어드릴 겁니다. 그러고 나서 청중들로부터 질문을 받을 것입니다. 모두가 들을 수 있도록 무선 마이크가 준비되어 있습니다. ⁹⁴질문하고 싶으신 분은, 그냥 일어서 계시면 마이크를 가져다드립니다. 거두절미하고, Fleming 박사님을 환영해주세요.

어휘 award-winning 수상 경력이 있는 address 다루다 fascinating 매력적인 excerpt 발췌 wireless 무선의 without further ado 거두절미하고

92 청중들은 누구인가?
(A) 서점 직원들
(B) 클럽 회원들
(C) 교수들
(D) 학생들

93 청중들은 다음에 무엇을 들을 것인가?
(A) 책의 발췌문
(B) 영화 개요
(C) 대학 강의
(D) 질의응답

94 화자가 청중들에게 요청하는 것은 무엇인가?
(A) 무대 위로 올라가기
(B) 소그룹으로 나누기
(C) 마이크 앞에 줄서기
(D) 질문이 있으면 일어서기

어휘 / summary 개요 make a line 줄서다

Questions 95–97 refer to the following telephone message and schedule. (◀)) 호주

Hello, Mr. Black? 95 This is Regina Worthy from Capel Studios returning your call about reserving a recording studio on November 14th. I'm afraid we won't be open November 14th, 15th, or 16th. We're renovating our studios on those days. 96 We'll re-open on Thursday the 17th, so if you can call me back, I'll book a session for you. I'm sorry for the inconvenience this may cause you, Mr. Black. The good news is that 97 we'll be offering a grand re-opening special—you'll get 10 percent off your total price within five days of our re-opening. We look forward to hearing from you soon. Thank you.

안녕하세요, Black씨. 95Capel 스튜디오의 Regina Worthy예요. 11월 14일 녹음실 예약 건으로 회신드렸습니다. 죄송하지만 11월 14, 15, 16일에는 저희 스튜디오가 열지 않아요. 그 기간 동안 스튜디오 내부공사를 진행할 예정이에요. 9617일 목요일에 열 예정이니 나중에 다시 전화를 주시면 제가 시간을 예약해드리겠습니다. 불편을 끼쳐 죄송합니다, Black씨. 좋은 소식이라면 저희가 재오픈 특별 세일을 한다는 것입니다. 97재오픈 후 5일 동안은 총 금액의 10%를 할인받으실 수 있어요. 조만간 연락 주세요. 감사합니다.

Black씨의 일정

	10시	1시	3시
14일 월요일	녹음		
15일 화요일	영업 상담		면접
16일 수요일	중역 회의	원격 회의	고객 야유회
17일 목요일	출장 ·············	··············	·············→
9618일 금요일	세미나	발표	

어휘 / recording studio 녹음실 renovate 개조[보수]하다

---

95 화자는 어떤 사업을 하고 있는가?
(A) 오디오 녹음
(B) 전자제품 판매
(C) 요식업
(D) 악기 판매

96 🔵신🟡유🟢형 일정표에 의하면, Black씨는 언제 화자의 사업장에 방문할 수 있는가?
(A) 월요일 오전 10시
(B) 화요일 오후 1시
(C) 목요일 오후 1시
(D) 금요일 오후 3시

97 화자가 Black씨에게 제공하는 것은 무엇인가?
(A) 할인
(B) 사은품
(C) 무료 주차
(D) 무료 업그레이드

Questions 98-100 refer to the following excerpt from a meeting and map. ◁)) 미국

I'll try to keep this last agenda item brief. We've been informed by the building manager that ⁹⁸the cost for our parking spaces in this building will be doubled next year uh, starting in January. We really can't afford that, so we need to find a new parking lot. Here's a map of the surrounding area. It looks like we have four choices but numbers 1 and 2 are pretty far away, so they're out. ⁹⁹Number 4 is not the cheapest, but it's more secure than number 3 since they have a guard on duty 24 hours. ^{99,100}I think security should be our top priority. What do you all think?

마지막 안건은 짧게 끝내도록 해보겠습니다. 건물 관리자가 ⁹⁸이 건물의 주차장비가 2배 오른다고 알려왔습니다. 내년 음, 1월부터요. 우리는 비용을 감당할 수 없어서 다른 주차장을 찾아봐야 합니다. 이것이 인근 지역의 지도입니다. 우리에겐 네 가지 선택권이 있는 것처럼 보이지만, 1번과 2번은 꽤 멀리 있어서 선택지에서 제외하겠습니다. ⁹⁹4번은 가장 싸지는 않지만 3번보다는 안전합니다. 24시간 보안요원이 있거든요. ^{99,100}제 생각에는 안전이 우리의 최우선입니다. 여러분의 생각은 어떠세요?

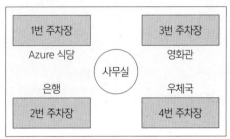

어휘 surrounding 주변 지역의 brief 짧은 afford ~할 형편이 되다 priority 우선순위

---

98 현재의 주차장에 대해 언급된 것은?
(A) 허물 것이다.
(B) 수리를 위해 폐쇄할 것이다.
(C) 직원들이 보안에 대해 우려하고 있다.
(D) 가격을 올릴 것이다.

99 지도에 의하면, 화자는 새 주차장으로 어느 곳을 선호하는가?
신유형
(A) Azure Restaurant 근처
(B) 은행 근처
(C) 우체국 근처
(D) 영화관 근처

100 주차장을 고를 때 화자가 가장 중요하게 생각하는 것은?
(A) 시간
(B) 위치
(C) 가격
(D) 안전

어휘 tear down 허물다 raise 올리다

PART 5

101

사건 보고서를 읽은 후, 공장장은 직원들이 안전 문제에 관해 서로 다른 견해를 가졌다는 것을 알게 되었다.

(A) 모양새   (B) 관광명소
(C) 견해   (D) 주의

어휘 incident 사건 sight 시각; 명소

102

금융업계에서 Mark Hudson은 수년 동안 뛰어난 비즈니스 리더로 알려졌다.

(A) 성취하다   (B) 성취할 수 있는
(C) 뛰어난   (D) 업적

어휘 financial 금융의 accomplished 뛰어난

103

보안 소프트웨어 대기업인 VESCO는 내년 봄 즈음에 전 세계에 신상품을 출시할 것이다.

(A) has been launching   (B) has launched
(C) is launching   (D) will be launched

어휘 giant 거대 기업 launch 출시하다

104

Catfox 브라우저의 최신 버전은 이용할 수 있을 때 자동으로 다운로드될 것이다.

(A) 초대된   (B) 편집된
(C) 관심 있어 하는   (D) 최신의

어휘 automatically 자동으로 edit 편집하다

105

그 직원은 관리자로 승진하기 전에 IT부서에서 겨우 1년 일했다.

(A) 승진하다   (B) 승진
(C) 승진의   (D) 촉진된

어휘 get a promotion 승진하다

106

호텔의 청구서 오류 때문에, Smiths씨 가족의 이틀 숙박 요금이 과도하게 청구되었다.

(A) ~ 때문에   (B) ~를 제외하고
(C) ~할 경우에   (D) ~하도록

어휘 excessively 지나치게 overcharge (금액을) 많이 청구하다

107

데이터 전송 속도는 보통 초당 100에서 150킬로바이트 사이이며, 사용자의 장치 유형에 따라 달라진다.

(A) 드러내다   (B) 전환시키다
(C) 기록하다   (D) 달라지다

어휘 device 장치 emerge 모습을 드러내다 convert 전환시키다

vary (상황에 따라) 달라지다

108

Kyle Boyd는 영업 경험은 없었지만, 천성적으로 명랑한 성격이 제품 판매에 매우 도움이 되었다.

(A) 천성적으로   (B) 자연스러움
(C) 본성   (D) 자연의

어휘 inexperienced 경험이 부족한 benefit 이익 naturally 천성적으로

109

패션잡지는 젊은 여성을 위한 새로운 제품군을 창작한 데서 Amy Kitano를 올해의 디자이너로 꼽았다.

(A) create   (B) created
(C) creates   (D) creating

110

질문에 거의 답하지 못했기 때문에 Jim Barrow가 발표를 완벽히 준비하지 않았음이 명백했다.

(A) 완벽히   (B) 관대하게
(C) 단단히   (D) 광범위하게

어휘 obvious 분명한 barely 거의 ~ 아니게 fully 완벽하게 generously 관대하게 securely 단단히 widely 광범위하게

111

편리한 위치에도 불구하고, 그 새 레스토랑은 심지어 주말에도 전혀 바쁘지 않았다.

(A) around   (B) for
(C) in   (D) on

112

시장은 새로운 시청 건물에 두 건축회사가 협업하여 만든 특별한 천장이 생길 것이라고 발표했다.

(A) 협업하다   (B) 협업
(C) 협업하는   (D) 합작으로

어휘 collaborate 협업하다

113

지난번 회의가 잘되지 않았기에, 그 지도자는 이번에 다가오는 프로젝트에서 합의에 이르기를 바라고 있다.

(A) 의견 일치   (B) 정의
(C) 경기   (D) 만족

어휘 reach a consensus on ~에 합의를 보다 definition 정의

114

Patterson씨는 잘나가는 비즈니스 컨설턴트로서, 그의 직업적 목표는 고객이 자신의 목표를 성취하도록 돕는 것이다.

(A) 그들의 것   (B) 그들을
(C) 그들 스스로   (D) 그들

115

막판에 장소가 바뀌는 바람에 주최측은 이 행사에 등록한 모든 참가자들에게 연락해야 했다.

(A) that
(B) what
(C) which
(D) whom

어휘 venue 장소 register 등록하다

116

행동 분석에 관한 다음 조사의 목적은 충격적인 소식에 대한 전형적인 반응을 연구하는 것이다.

(A) 유능한
(B) 형식적인
(C) 전형적인
(D) 말기의

어휘 reaction to ~에 대한 반응 capable 유능한 formal 형식적인 typical 전형적인 terminal 말기의

117

Lisa Foster는 집에 방해 요소가 많기 때문에 집에서 효율적으로 일한다는 것이 생각했던 것보다 어렵다는 것을 알게 되었다.

(A) 효율성들
(B) 효율성
(C) 효율적인
(D) 효율적으로

어휘 distraction 집중을 방해하는 것 efficiently 효율적으로

118

대부분의 응답자들이 신제품이 '유용하다' 또는 '매우 유용하다'고 생각했기 때문에 마케팅 책임자는 설문 결과에 만족했다.

(A) 거의
(B) 대부분의
(C) 대개
(D) 가장

119

개발팀은 휴대폰으로 원격 조종할 수 있는 가정용 로봇의 완성을 축하하기 위해 작은 파티를 열었다.

(A) 거의 ~ 않은
(B) 공동으로
(C) 수동으로
(D) 원격으로

어휘 completion 완성 jointly 공동으로 manually 수동으로 remotely 원격으로

120

Gene 전자의 새로운 100인치 평면 TV는 내년 봄에 5가지 색상으로 출시될 예정이다.

(A) ~로부터
(B) ~으로
(C) ~의
(D) ~와 함께

121

광산회사는 그 방대한 지역을 거대한 천연자원의 보고로 믿었고, 그것이 현명한 투자였다고 보았다.

(A) 투자하다
(B) 투자된
(C) 투자
(D) 투자자

어휘 vast 방대한 immense 어마어마한 storehouse 창고 investment 투자

122

회사의 실적이 개선되기를 기대하며, 그 자동차 회사의 사장은 회사의 경영구조를 점검하기로 결정했다.

(A) 과대평가하다
(B) 점검하다
(C) 간과하다
(D) 추월하다

어휘 performance 성과 overestimate 과대평가하다 overhaul 점검하다 overlook 간과하다 overtake 추월하다

123

철저한 진상규명 요구가 늘어난 것은 제기된 그 회사의 비밀 자금에 대해 사람들이 얼마나 분개하고 있는지를 보여주었다.

(A) call
(B) called
(C) calling
(D) calls

어휘 thorough 철저한 investigation 조사 alleged 주장된

124

신입직원의 프로젝트 계획이 너무나 정교해서 매니저를 포함한 부서의 모든 사람들이 상당히 감명받았다.

(A) 정교한
(B) 자세히 말하는
(C) 공들여서
(D) 정교함

어휘 elaborate 정교한; 자세히 설명하다

125

그 연구는 초등학교와 중학교 시절이 제2외국어를 습득하는 데 최고의 시기라는 점을 시사하고 있다.

(A) 습득
(B) 인수
(C) 소유
(D) 경영권 인수

어휘 acquisition 습득 buyout 인수 takeover 경영권 인수

126

새로 문을 연 호텔은 시내와 가깝고 호화로운 편의시설을 갖추고 있으며, 게다가 가격도 적당하다.

(A) 게다가
(B) 대신에
(C) 반면에
(D) 그렇지 않다면

어휘 reasonably 타당하게

127

관리자가 인트라넷에 업로드한 데이터는 손실되었으며, 기술자에 의하면 이런 일은 별로 흔하지 않다고 한다.

(A) 행사
(B) 가끔의
(C) 가끔
(D) 행사들

어휘 occasion (특정한) 때; 행사 occasionally 가끔

128

방문객들이 안내실에서 사무실 전체를 볼 수 있기 때문에 부장은 모두에게 책상을 정돈하고 있으라 말했다.

(A) 가까이
(B) 공정하게
(C) 정돈된
(D) 적절하게

어휘 orderly 정돈된

129

인터뷰에서 그 회사의 사장은 자신이 항상 수익<u>보다</u> 진실성을 중시하기 때문에 성공할 수 있었다고 말했다.

(A) 건너서   (B) ~보다
(C) (시간, 거리) ~보다   (D) ~ 위에

> **어휘** value 소중하게 여기다 integrity 진실성 profit 이윤

130

결과가 어떻든지 간에, Sarah Daly가 새 지점의 매니저로 고려된 것은 큰 영광이었다.

(A) 정말로   (B) 그럼에도 불구하고
(C) 어떤 ~일지라도   (D) ~하는 동안

> **어휘** outcome 결과

PART 6

131-134 (안내문)

모든 Marshburg시 거주자들에게 알림

Marshburg 시청은 10월 10일부터 21일까지 ¹³¹수리 보수를 할 예정입니다. 모든 사무업무는 2주간 시립 도서관에서 운영될 예정이지만, 10월 24일부터 28일까지는 시청으로 복귀해야 ¹³²하므로 운영하지 않을 예정입니다. 공사기간 중 전화번호와 팩스번호는 동일합니다. ¹³³하지만 업무시간은 변경될 것입니다.

> 새 업무시간:
> 월~금 오전 10시 ~ 오후 4시
> 토, 일 휴무

¹³⁴추가로, 10월 24일과 28일 사이에 사무실 이전을 돕고자 하는 주민들은 도서관에서 등록해주시기 바랍니다. 지원자 누구에게나 점심과 음료가 제공될 것입니다.

> **어휘** under renovation 수리 중인 operate 가동되다 remain 여전히 ~이다 duration 기간 local resident 지역 주민 volunteer 자진하다; 자원봉사자

131

(A) 수리하다   (B) 수리된
(C) 수리   (D) 수리공

132

(A) ~ 때문에   (B) 만일 ~한다면
(C) ~이긴 하지만   (D) ~인지 아닌지

133 (신유형)

(A) 우편주소는 아래와 같습니다.
(B) 새로운 전화번호는 웹사이트에 있습니다.
(C) 하지만 업무시간은 변경될 것입니다.
(D) 업무시간은 동일할 것입니다.

> **어휘** below 아래에

134

(A) 추가로   (B) 두 번째로
(C) 그러므로   (D) 그래도

135-138 (이메일)

수신: Samantha Patel
발신: Perry Fonda
제목: 11월 8일 지원 요청
날짜: 11월 2일

안녕하세요, Samantha.
¹³⁵부탁할 게 있어요. 제가 다음 주 화요일인 11월 8일 4시에 Tolliver Fund 직원들을 만날 예정인데, 지원이 정말 필요해요. 이번이 저에게는 중요한 고객을 확보할 수 있는 첫 번째 큰 기회라서, ¹³⁶실패하고 싶지 않아요. 저는 진짜 신입이잖아요. 당신 같은 고참 파트너가 같은 자리에 ¹³⁷없으면 그들이 저를 진지하게 생각하지 않을 것 같아요. 잠깐 들러서 자기소개라도 할 시간이 있나요? 큰 도움이 될 거예요. ¹³⁸그 시간에 바쁘시면, 제게 몇 가지 조언을 해주시는 것도 좋아요. 이곳에서 일을 시작했을 때의 팁들을 조금만 알려주세요.
감사합니다.
Perry

> **어휘** land 획득하다 take ~ seriously (사람·사물을) 진지하게 생각하다 stop in ~에 들르다 in advance 미리

135

(A) 부탁   (B) 업무
(C) 요청   (D) 바람

> **어휘** favor 부탁

136

(A) 실패하다   (B) 오해하다
(C) 중지하다   (D) 속상하게 하다

> **어휘** upset 속상하게 하다

137

(A) ~ 사이에   (B) ~ 전에
(C) ~ 외에   (D) ~ 없이

138 (신유형)

(A) 그 파일을 검토한 후에, 어떻게 생각하는지 알려주세요.
(B) 그 시간에 바쁘시면, 제게 몇 가지 조언을 해주시는 것도 좋아요.
(C) 당신이 안 된다면 이해해요. 저는 최선을 다할 거예요.
(D) 당신의 일정을 알려주면 맞춰보도록 할게요.

> **어휘** look over 검토하다 pointer 조언 match 맞추다

139-142 (기사)

Junko 화장품은 수요일에 건조한 겨울 날씨에 맞춰 신규 보습제 라인을 ¹³⁹출시할 것이라고 발표했다. ¹⁴⁰Skin Drink라고 하는 이 제품 라인은 각 피부별 4가지 타입의 로션으로 구성되어 있다. Junko의 CEO는 "Skin Drink는 ¹⁴¹부드럽고 쾌적한 피부를 갖기 원하는 모든 연령대의 사람들을 겨냥했습니다. 그리고 무향 수분크림과 자외선

차단 효과를 지닌 제품을 제공할 것입니다."라고 말했다. 이 로션은 Junko 제품을 판매하는 약국이나 화장품 판매대에서 5파운드에서 6파운드 50펜스 사이의 142가격으로 책정될 것이다.

어휘 cosmetics 화장품 moisturizer 보습제 aim ~를 겨냥하다 fragrance-free 향기가 없는

139
(A) 고려하다　　　　　(B) 출시하다
(C) 개장하다　　　　　(D) 시험하다

140 신유형—
(A) 다른 Skin Drink 제품들과 같이, 이 보습제에는 천연 성분들이 함유되어 있다.
(B) 회사는 제품을 출시하기 직전까지 제품명을 비밀에 부치고 있다.
(C) Skin Drink라고 하는 이 제품 라인은 각 피부별 4가지 타입의 로션으로 구성되어 있다.
(D) 판매 전망이 비관적이어서, 회사의 미래가 불확실하다.

어휘 ingredient 성분 keep under wraps 비밀에 부치다 release 출시 forecast 전망 gloomy 우울한 uncertain 불확실한

141
(A) 부드러운　　　　　(B) 부드럽게 하다
(C) 부드럽게　　　　　(D) 부드러움

어휘 smooth 부드러운

142
(A) could price　　　　(B) have been priced
(C) priced　　　　　　(D) will be priced

143-146 정보
취업박람회
11월 13일 일요일 오후 1시 ~ 5시, Canary 가족공원

독특하고 흥미로운 취업박람회가 이번 달 Canary 가족공원에서 열립니다. 이 박람회는 전적으로 Canary 가족공원의 143접대업 분야에 초점을 맞추고 있습니다! 모든 연령대가 가장 많이 찾는 이곳 유원지에서 일하기를 희망하신다면, 11월 13일 일요일에 방문해주세요. 144150개의 임시직 어느 자리에든 지원할 수 있는 기회가 될 것입니다. 몇몇 직무는 연말을 지나서도 계약이 연장될 것입니다! 145단 한 번의 신청으로 Canary 가족공원에 있는 식당과 호텔, 관광지의 모든 자리에 지원이 됩니다.
꿈에 그리던 직업을 가질 수 있는 이번 기회를 146놓치지 마세요!

어휘 entirely 완전히 attraction 관광지

143
(A) 광고　　　　　　　(B) 공학
(C) 접객　　　　　　　(D) 연구

어휘 engineering 공학 hospitality 접대, 접객

144 신유형—
(A) 지원서에 반드시 추천서 세 개를 포함시켜 11월 13일까지 보내주십시오.
(B) 이번 주말에 있을 개장 행사에 친구들과 가족들이 참여하도록 독려해주십시오.
(C) 저희는 마케팅 및 광고 분야에서 경험이 풍부한 관리자를 찾고 있습니다.
(D) 150개의 임시직 어느 자리에든 지원할 수 있는 기회가 될 것입니다.

어휘 reference 추천서 encourage 독려하다 experienced 숙련된 temporary 임시의

145
(A) 또 다른　　　　　　(B) 각각
(C) 어느 하나의　　　　(D) 단지

146
(A) 얻다　　　　　　　(B) 붙잡다
(C) 부수다　　　　　　(D) 놓치다

어휘 grab 붙잡다

PART 7

147-148 쿠폰
지금 TOMAS BROWN에서 30% 할인!
100달러 이상 온라인 구매 시
본 행사는 11월 1일 종료됩니다.
쇼핑을 즐기세요.
100달러 이상 구매마다 1달러를 Blue Triangle에 기부합니다.
조건
147*온라인 의류 구매에만 유효합니다.
*미국 내에서만 유효합니다.
*고객당 한 번에 한합니다.
148*다른 할인과 중복하여 사용할 수 없습니다.

어휘 donate 기부하다 term 조건, 규정 valid 유효한 in conjunction with ~와 함께

147
이 쿠폰은 무엇에 사용할 수 있는가?
(A) 가방　　　　　　　(B) 셔츠
(C) 시계　　　　　　　(D) 신발

148
쿠폰에는 어떤 제한이 있는가?
(A) 단독으로만 사용할 수 있다.
(B) 특정 브랜드에만 유효하다.
(C) 11월 30일에만 유효하다.
(D) 1달러를 쓴 후에 유효하다.

어휘 place a limit 한계를 두다 by oneself 단독으로

149-150 (📋 안내문)

회원님들께 알립니다

11월 9일에 체육관 및 시설에 대한 연례 정기점검을 실시할 예정이니 숙지해주시기 바랍니다. 이 점검은 모든 장비와 스튜디오, 수영장, 탈의실 및 기타 회원들이 머무는 모든 곳의 안전을 확인하기 위한 것입니다.

유지보수는 오전 6시부터 시작해서 11월 9일 전일 계속합니다. ¹⁴⁹체육관은 11월 10일 오전 6시에 회원들께 재개됩니다. 이 폐장으로 인해 11월 8일 개장이 오후 11시까지 연장됩니다. ¹⁵⁰체육관만 해당된다는 데에 주의하세요. 스튜디오나 수영장은 포함되지 않습니다. 문의사항은 관리자에게 연락하십시오.

불편을 끼쳐 사과드리며, 지속적인 후원에 감사드립니다.

어휘 maintenance 유지 gymnasium 체육관 facility 시설 ensure 확실하게 하다 entirety 전체 extend 연장하다 continued 지속적인 patronage 후원

149

유지 보수는 언제 완료될 것인가?
(A) 11월 9일 정오까지
(B) 11월 10일 개시까지
(C) 11월 10일 점심시간까지
(D) 11월 11일 개시까지

150

회원이 11월 8일에 평상시보다 더 늦게 사용할 수 있는 시설은 무엇인가?
(A) 댄스 스튜디오   (B) 체육관
(C) 수영장   (D) 스포츠 용품점

151-152 (📱 문자 메시지) 신유형—

Jane Dodson [오전 9:39]	제가 탄 기차가 Picau에서 멈췄어요. 약 20분 정도 지연될 거 같아요. 저는 회의에 늦을 것 같아요. 죄송해요.
Nick Wise [오전 9:42]	Madex에서 불이 났다고 들었어요. 괜찮아요. ¹⁵¹어쩔 수 없는 상황인데요. 가능할 때 오세요.
Jane Dodson [오전 9:45]	이해해주셔서 감사합니다! 이제 기차가 움직이네요. 곧 뵐 수 있을 거예요.
Nick Wise [오전 9:48]	알겠어요. 그러면 10시 15분에 카페 la Olay에서 만나는 게 어때요?
Jane Dodson [오전 9:50]	좋아요.
¹⁵²Jane Dodson [오전 10:07]	지금 막 Madex역에 도착했어요. 5분 후 카페에 도착할 거예요.
Nick Wise [오전 10:09]	저는 야외 테이블에 앉아 있어요.

어휘 be held up 꼼짝 못하다 out of one's hands 어쩔 수 없는

151 신유형—

오전 9시 42분에 Wise씨가 쓴 it's out of your hands가 의미하는 것은 무엇인가?
(A) 다른 동료가 Dodson씨의 프로젝트를 맡을 것이다.
(B) Dodson씨는 그 분야의 전문가가 아니다.
(C) Madex에서 지연이 시작되었다.
(D) 그 지연은 Dodson씨가 통제할 수 없다.

어휘 take over 넘겨받다 specialist 전문가 field 분야

152

Dodson씨는 10시에 어디에 있었는가?
(A) 카페 la Olay   (B) 자기 사무실
(C) Madex역   (D) 기차 안

153-154 (📋 광고)

MONIQUE BLANC 프랑스어

여러분은	저는
-말하고	– 편안하게 수업하고
-재미있게 즐기고	– 창조적인 스타일이며
-배웁니다	– 시험 대비도 합니다

¹⁵³원어민과 프랑스어를 배워요!
모든 연령과 실력에 관계없이 환영합니다.

전화: 080-5555-3245   이메일: Monique.blanc@bisco.com

후기:
"Monique의 수업은 정말 재미있었습니다! 저는 프랑스어 초보자였지만, 지금은 프랑스로 여행을 가서 제가 배운 것을 사용할 수 있을 만큼 자신감이 생겼습니다. 감사합니다!" — Mary Newman
"저는 항상 프랑스어를 배우는 게 어려웠지만 ¹⁵⁴기말고사 준비를 해야 했습니다. Blanc씨는 제가 받을 수 있는 최고의 점수를 받을 수 있도록 도와주었고, 그 점이 정말 감사합니다." — Gary Bush

어휘 preparation 대비 ability 능력 testimonial 추천의 글 confident 자신 있는 achieve 성취하다 grateful 감사하는

153

Blanc씨에 대해 언급된 것은 무엇인가?
(A) 그녀의 학업 성적
(B) 그녀의 위치
(C) 그녀의 모국어
(D) 그녀의 경력

어휘 academic 학업의 achievement 성취

154

Bush씨는 왜 Blanc씨에게 감사를 표하는가?
(A) 프랑스에서 여행할 곳을 그에게 조언해주었다.
(B) 그녀가 개인 교습을 해주었다.
(C) 그녀가 학업성취에 도움을 주었다.
(D) 그녀가 좋은 점수를 주었다.

155-157 📋 설문조사

SILVER FERN 호텔 그룹
고객만족도 조사

저희 호텔에서 투숙한 경험을 토대로 다음 설문조사를 작성해주세요.
아래 등급에 따라 해당 칸에 0에서 4까지의 숫자를 기입해주세요.

매우 불만족	불만족	보통	만족	매우 만족
0	1	2	3	4

고객서비스(안내, 대기/바 직원, 객실청소 담당자)	4
룸서비스(알맞은 시간, 편안함, 선택)	4
식당(분위기, 음식, 식기류)	4
¹⁵⁷바(분위기, 음료 선택)	1
청결 상태(모든 구역)	4
소음 정도(외부 및 내부)	3
위치(관심 있는 장소로부터의 거리)	3
가격(전반)	3
서비스 용품(선택, 기능성, 연령)	2

기타 의견사항

¹⁵⁵전반적으로 Silver Fern 투숙은 매우 만족스러웠습니다. ¹⁵⁶직원들이 뛰어났는데, 특히 Smyth씨는 제가 편안히 지낼 수 있도록 특별히 신경 써주셨습니다. ¹⁵⁷그렇지만 바에 다양한 음료가 구비되었음에도 제가 가장 좋아하는 칵테일을 찾을 수 없었고, 바 직원도 그 칵테일에 대해 알지 못했습니다. 내년에 다시 투숙할 때 메뉴에 있으면 좋겠네요! 시내로 가는 무료 셔틀 서비스가 보너스로 제공되기는 했지만, 편의시설을 이용할 시간이 없었습니다. 다시 한 번 감사드립니다. 다음에도 기대할게요!

어휘 corresponding 상응하는 in accordance to ~에 따라서 extremely 매우 timeliness 시기적절함 tableware 식기류 ambience 분위기 external 외부의 internal 내부의 distance 거리 overall 전반적으로 exceptional 특출한 go the extra mile 한층 더 노력하다

155
고객은 호텔을 어떻게 평가하는가?
(A) 보통이다.
(B) 탁월하다.
(C) 대부분 만족스럽다.
(D) 형편없다.

어휘 average 평균의

156
Smyth씨의 직업은 무엇인가?
(A) 호텔 직원
(B) 호텔 투숙객
(C) 호텔 매니저
(D) 택시 운전사

157
고객이 만족하지 못한 것은 무엇인가?
(A) 편의시설의 선택
(B) 시내에서 떨어진 거리
(C) 음료의 다양성
(D) 직원의 친절함

어휘 diversity 다양성 friendliness 친절함

158-160 📰 기사

휴대폰은 이제 도서관이나 학교보다 두 배나 많은 정보를 제공한다고 합니다. ¹⁵⁸이것은 우리가 기존의 방식으로 아이들을 계속 가르쳐야 하는가라는 의문을 불러일으킵니다. 교육부 장관과 교사들은 이 문제에 있어 기존의 방식을 고수하지만, 첨단기술 기업과 대부분의 젊은 이들은 새로운 학습 방법을 요구하고 있습니다.

¹⁵⁹Poko와 Djiib 같은 회사들은 홈스쿨링 또는 '어디에서나 가능한 학교 교육'을 더 가능하게 만들고, 미래를 위한 기술을 개척하고 있습니다. Poko의 CEO인 Jim Frank는 "아이가 이러한 기술을 통해 얻을 수 있는 지식의 깊이와 넓이는 교실에서 교사가 제공할 수 있는 것보다 훨씬 광범위합니다."라고 하며, "사회와 우리의 삶이 발전하는 만큼, 교육 방법을 바꾸지 않으면서 자녀의 앞길을 가로막고 있습니다."라고 말했습니다.

정부 관계자들은 이 새로운 아이디어를 완전히 이해하고 얼마나 실현 가능한 것인지 파악하기 위한 시도로 간담회를 열었습니다. 관계자들은 10월 3일에 공개회의를 열어 부모들과 다른 이해 당사자들로부터 이야기를 듣고자 합니다. Paul Simonson 교육부 장관은 "모두를 위해서 ¹⁶⁰저는 이번 시 회의에 시민들이 참석하기를 촉구합니다. 이 중요한 사안에 대해 모든 이의 의견이 필요합니다."라고 말했습니다.

어휘 raise a question 의문을 불러일으키다 traditional 전통 firmly 확고히 approach 접근법 pioneering 선구적인 depth 깊이 breadth 넓이 vast 광범위한 fully 완전히 comprehend 이해하다 establish 규명하다 viable 실현 가능한 urge 촉구하다

158
기사는 주로 무엇에 관한 것인가?
(A) 다른 방식의 학교 교육
(B) 새로운 사립학교
(C) 10월 3일의 특별 기념식
(D) 휴대폰의 미래

어휘 schooling 학교 교육 commemoration 기념식

159
Jim Frank는 어떤 분야에서 일하는가?
(A) 금융
(B) 정부
(C) 출판
(D) 기술

어휘 finance 금융 publishing 출판

160
정부 관계자는 사람들에게 무엇을 하도록 권장하는가?
(A) 자녀에게 홈스쿨링을 시작하기
(B) 기술 회사에 투자하기
(C) 회의에서 의견을 표명하기
(D) 지역 교사들과 대화하기

어휘 invest 투자하다 voice (의견을) 말로 표현하다

161-163 📧 이메일

수신: rich.jack@hmail.com
발신: hostelworld@promotions.com
제목: 금주의 호텔
날짜: [163]10월 3일 월요일

HOTELWORLD
세상을 만끽하세요.

금주의 호텔
Golden Arms 여관: 영국의 Bleat

[161]영국 시골 지역의 멋지고 무성한 청록의 땅에 위치한 이 여관은 런던 시민 또는 북부 잉글랜드를 여행하고자 하는 분들에게 완벽한 주말 휴가지입니다. 집 주변에는 광대한 잔디밭이 있어서 저녁 산책과 볼링 또는 크로켓을 즐길 수 있습니다. 여관 자체가 19세기 고딕 양식을 연상시키는 놀라운 건축 양식을 보여줍니다. 아치 밑의 현관에 앉아 무료 아침식사를 즐기세요.

[162]모든 객실은 투숙객에게 과거의 매력을 담은 섬세한 복원을 통해 여관의 역사에 대한 식견을 줍니다. 각 객실에는 특별실 시설(별도 욕조 포함)과 퀸 사이즈 침대 및 24시간 룸서비스도 있습니다. 기타 편의시설로는 큰 식당가와 무도회장, 도서관, 18홀 골프장, 마구간 등이 있으며, 이 모든 것이 관내에 있습니다.

[163]이번 달 말 전에 예약하면, 둘째 날의 숙박료를 50% 할인해드립니다. 실망하지 마시고 지금 예약하세요!

어휘 situate 위치시키다 lush 무성한 getaway 휴가지 stroll 산책 display 보여주다 remarkable 놀라운 reminiscent 연상시키는 porch 현관 insight into ~에 대한 식견 restoration 복원 preserve 보존하다 stable 마구간 ground 구역

161
여관에 대해 옳은 것은 무엇인가?
(A) 현대식 건축을 보여준다.
(B) 시골 지역에 위치한다.
(C) 주로 사업가들을 위한 곳이다.
(D) 무료 점심을 제공한다.

어휘 rural 시골의

162
객실은 어떻게 묘사되는가?
(A) 안락하다.　　　　　　(B) 역사적이다.
(C) 호화롭다.　　　　　　(D) 넓다.

어휘 cozy 안락한 luxurious 호화스러운 spacious (공간이) 넓은

163
할인 기간은 얼마나 되는가?
(A) 일주일　　　　　　　(B) 2주일
(C) 거의 한 달　　　　　(D) 한 달 반

164-167 📋 안내문

Breztel사 부주의 운전 정책
새로운 부주의 운전 정책을 읽고 서명한 후, 상사에게 제출하십시오.

Breztel사는 [164]직원들의 안전을 향상시키고 운전 중 불필요한 위험을 제거하기 위해 9월 1일부터 부주의 운전 정책을 제정했습니다. 우리는 부주의한 운전이 확산되는 것을 막기 위한 노력으로 이와 같은 규칙을 만들었고, 이는 회사 차량을 운행하는 모든 직원, 또는 개인 차량을 운행하는 동안 회사에서 발급한 휴대폰을 사용하는 직원에게 적용됩니다.

*차량 운행 중에 (차량이 움직일 때든 신호등에서 멈추었을 때든) 휴대폰을 사용할 수 없습니다. 이는 다음을 포함하나, 이에 국한되지 않습니다. 전화 응답 또는 전화 걸기, 전화 통화에의 참여 및/또는 이메일, 인스턴트 메시지 및/또는 문자 메시지 확인과 회신

*휴대폰을 사용해야 하는 경우, 갓길 또는 안전한 장소에 안전하게 차를 세워야 합니다.

*또한 직원은 다음을 수행해야 합니다.
(A) 자동차의 시동을 걸기 전에 휴대폰을 끄거나 무음 또는 진동 모드로 두십시오.
(B) [165]운전하는 동안 전화를 받거나 메시지를 보낼 수 없다는 것을 알리기 위해 음성 메시지 인사를 바꾸는 것을 고려하십시오.
(C) 고객, 동료 및 사업 파트너에게 이 정책을 설명하고 전화를 바로 받지 못하는 이유를 설명하십시오.

위의 규정을 준수하지 않는 것이 적발된 Breztel사 직원은 먼저 서면 경고를 받게 될 것입니다. [167]이 경고는 직원의 영구 인사 파일에 추가됩니다. [166]두 번째 위반 시 의무적으로 1주일 무급 휴가를 받을 것입니다. 세 번째 위반 시 Breztel사에서 해고될 것입니다.

어휘 distracted 부주의한 eliminate 제거하다 risk 위험 enact 제정하다 commit to ~에 헌신하다 epidemic 급속한 확산 operate 운영하다 handheld 손에 들고 쓰는 engage in ~에 참여하다 pull over 차를 대다 vibrate mode 진동 모드 compliance (법) 준수 infraction 위반 terminate 해고하다

164
새로운 정책의 목적은 무엇인가?
(A) 지역 법규를 준수하기 위해
(B) 사고를 예방하기 위해
(C) 좋은 운전 기술을 가르치기 위해
(D) 운전자가 깨어 있도록 상기시키기 위해

어휘 purpose 목적 prevent 예방하다

165
음성 메일과 관련하여 무엇을 제안하는가?
(A) 정기적으로 확인해야 한다.
(B) 꺼야 한다.
(C) 언제 회신이 가능한지 설명해야 한다.
(D) 전화에 응답하지 않는 이유를 설명해야 한다.

166
회사 정책을 두 번 위반한 직원은 무엇을 받게 되는가?
(A) 직책 변경　　　　　　(B) 경고장
(C) 회사로부터 해고 통지　(D) 무급 휴직

어휘 violate 위반하다 termination 해고 통지 suspension 휴직

167 신유형

다음 문장은 [1], [2], [3], [4] 중 어디에 들어가는가?

"이 경고는 직원의 영구 인사 파일에 추가됩니다."

(A) [1]　　　　　　　　　　(B) [2]

(C) [3]　　　　　　　　　　(D) [4]

어휘 permanent 영구적인

168-171 📄 편지

3월 18일

Vaughn씨께

시간을 들여 저희 회사와의 불만족스러운 경험에 대해 써주셔서 감사드리며, ¹⁶⁸이 문제에 대해 진심으로 사과드립니다. 저희는 고객의 기대를 충족시키고, 그러지 못한 경우 해결책을 제공하는 것이 가장 중요한 일이라고 여기고 있습니다.

따라서 ¹⁶⁹저희는 귀하의 요청을 받아들여 같은 제품 번호와 같은 색상의 소파를 무료로 교체해드릴 것이며 내일 아침에 귀하께 배송될 것입니다. 귀하께서 받은 배송 서비스가 좋지 않았다는 점에 대하여, 저희는 모든 운전자를 대상으로 새로운 교육을 실시했으며, 내일은 변화를 느끼시기를 바랍니다.

또한 이 기회를 빌려, 저희의 더 나은 고객서비스를 위해 귀하께 개인적인 서비스를 제공하고자 합니다. 50달러 상품권과 제 서명이 있는 명함을 동봉하였습니다. ¹⁷⁰매장 방문 시 직원에게 이 카드를 보여주시면 매장이 있는 동안 개별적인 도움을 받으실 수 있습니다.

저희 회사 내의 불일치해 보이는 운영에 유의하도록 알려주셔서 다시 한 번 감사드립니다. ¹⁷¹저희 회사의 성장과 미래의 성공을 보장한다는 면에서 매우 감사한 일입니다. 저희를 다시 신뢰해주시고 앞으로도 만족하는 고객이 되어 주시길 바랍니다.

감사합니다.

Arun Devdas

고객서비스 관리자

어휘 sincere 진심 어린 utmost 가장 중요한 meet 충족시키다 expectation 기대 instance 사례 resolution 해결 dispatch 배송하다 in light of ~를 고려하여 enclosed 동봉된 voucher 상품권 discrepancy 불일치

168

Devdas씨가 Vaughn씨에게 편지를 보낸 이유는 무엇인가?

(A) 유감을 전하기 위해

(B) 만족감을 표현하기 위해

(C) 회사 제품에 대해 알리기 위해

(D) 새 연락처 정보를 요청하기 위해

어휘 convey 전달하다 regret 후회

169

Devdas씨는 Vaughn씨에게 무엇을 약속했는가?

(A) 곧 교육을 실시하는 것

(B) 다음 주문 시 무료배송을 제공하는 것

(C) 추가금 없이 새 소파를 제공하는 것

(D) Vaughn씨의 결정을 존중하는 것

어휘 respect 존중하다

170

Vaughn씨가 동봉된 카드를 사용하면 무엇을 제공받을 수 있는가?

(A) 무료 선물　　　　　　　(B) 추가 할인

(C) 업데이트된 카탈로그　　　(D) 특별한 도움

어휘 assistance 도움

171 신유형

다음 문장은 [1], [2], [3], [4] 중 어디에 들어가는가?

"저희 회사의 성장과 미래의 성공을 보장한다는 면에서 매우 감사한 일입니다."

(A) [1]　　　　　　　　　　(B) [2]

(C) [3]　　　　　　　　　　(D) [4]

어휘 appreciate 평가하다

172-175 💬 온라인 토론 신유형

Ken Brown [13:02]	두 분 모두 안녕하세요! 주문건은 아직 안 끝났어요?
Jack Taylor [13:12]	안녕하세요, Ken. 아직 안 끝났어요. 예상치 못한 소방 훈련 때문에 예상보다 시간이 더 걸렸어요.
Ken Brown [13:14]	흔한 일은 아니죠. 얼마나 했어요?
Jack Taylor [13:15]	우리가 금일 주문건의 절반쯤 했을 때 시스템이 꺼졌어요. Levi는 창고로 돌아가서 절반 남은 주문에 쓸 박스를 준비하고 있어요.
Ken Brown [13:15]	좋아요. 그런데 블랙리스트에 있는 주문들 기억해요?
Jack Taylor [13:16]	¹⁷³완전히 까먹고 있었네요! Levi를 불러서 사무실로 오는 길에 가져오라고 할게요.
Ken Brown [13:17]	¹⁷⁴괜찮아요. 지금 작업장에서 사무실로 돌아가고 있어요. 제가 가지고 갈게요.
Levi O'Conner [13:25]	안녕하세요, Ken. 그냥 확인 차 왔어요. 창고가 아주 엉망이에요. 수습하는 데 꽤 걸릴 거 같아요.
Ken Brown [13:27]	걱정 마요, Levi. 할 수 있는 만큼만 하고 가능한 빨리 사무실로 돌아가요. 오늘 3시까지 주문건을 마쳐야 해요.
Levi O'Conner [13:28]	고마워요, Ken! 시간이 되는 사람 있으면 여기 일 좀 부탁하게 보내줘요.
Jack Taylor [13:30]	¹⁷⁵방금 Bruce한테 작업장에서 나오라고 얘기했어요. 당신을 도와주러 갈 거예요.
Levi O'Conner [13:31]	반가운 소식이네요. 고마워요.

어휘 anticipate 예상하다 fire drill 소방 훈련 shut down 멈추다 stockroom 창고 blank 아무 생각이 안 나다 shop floor 작업 현장

172

주로 논의되는 것은 무엇인가?

(A) 소방 훈련　　　　　　　(B) 상품 리콜

(C) 신규 고객　　　　　　　(D) 주문 처리

어휘 processing 처리

173 신유형

Taylor씨가 13시 16분에 I totally blanked on those!라고 쓴 것은 무엇을 의미하는가?

(A) 제대로 볼 수 없다.
(B) 무엇인가를 까맣게 잊고 있었다.
(C) 자유 시간이 많다.
(D) 다시 일할 준비가 되지 않았다.

174

블랙리스트는 누가 들고 올 것인가?

(A) Brown씨   (B) O'Conner씨
(C) Taylor씨   (D) Taylor씨의 조수

175

Bruce씨는 어디로 갈 것인가?

(A) 입구   (B) 사무실
(C) 가게   (D) 창고

어휘 entrance 입구

176-180 리뷰…이메일

E-Street 모델 X

Matcha 모터스에서 생산한 새로운 전기자동차에 대한 기밀 유출이 너무 많았기에 저는 이번 주말 첫 공개에서 놀랄 게 없을 것으로 예상했습니다. 하지만 제가 완전히 틀렸더군요! 일단 제가 새 모델의 내부를 살짝 들여다봤을 때, 저는 이 차가 판도를 뒤바꿀 것이라는 걸 깨달았습니다. 모델 B와 마찬가지로 176운전자나 탑승자 앞에 계기판이 없습니다. 대신, 가운데 탑재된 컴퓨터 모니터로 차를 제어합니다. 이것은 좌측 주행 국가 또는 우측 주행 국가에 수출할 때 드는 상당한 비용을 절약시키기에 Matcha 모터스에게는 합리적인 선택입니다. 기술 또한 대단합니다. 배터리 충전 게이지부터 엔터테인먼트 및 실내온도 조절장치에 이르기까지 모델 X의 모니터는 단순하고 직관적입니다.

그럼에도, 이 모델에 대해 가장 믿을 수 없는 것은 바로 가격입니다. 4만 달러가 조금 안 되는 가격부터 시작하는 이 차는 180대중을 위한 전기자동차입니다. 물론, 178듀얼 모터를 사용하려면 약 1만 달러를 더 지불해야 하지만, 한 번 충전으로 속도와 장거리 운전을 즐기는 분들은 구매할 만한 가치가 있습니다.

충전에 관해 말하자면, Matcha 모터스의 CEO는 모델 X가 나오기 전에 전국 300개 이상의 충전소를 약속하고 있습니다. 모델 X는 2년 반을 기다려야 하지만, 사전 주문이 회사의 웹사이트 www.matchamotors.com에서 진행되고 있습니다. 차를 예약하기 위해, 원하는 추가 옵션에 따라 최소 4천 달러는 각오해야 합니다. 177이 후기를 쓴 사람으로서 저는 꽂혔습니다. 배달 날짜를 세고 있어요…. — Shaun Hansen

---

수신: Shaun Hansen <shaunh@wheels.com>
발신: Olga Malayov <omalayov@matchamotors.com>
제목: 모델 X 후기

Hansen씨께

자사의 최신 모델에 대한 귀하의 열정적인 후기에 감사드립니다. 귀

하께서 새로운 E-Street 운전대에 앉았을 때 실망하지 않으실 것이라고 확신합니다. 귀하께서 독자들에게 알리고 싶어 하실까 하여, 차에 관한 정보를 몇 가지 더 드립니다.

첫째로, 참석하신 행사에서 나눠드린 홍보자료에 실수가 있었음을 말씀드립니다. 178두 번째 모터의 가격은 후기에서 언급하신 것보다 2천 달러 정도 저렴합니다. 그러므로 모델 X가 소비자들에게 더욱 매력적으로 다가올 것입니다.

179두 번째로, 저희는 생산 목표치를 올렸으며, 이제는 전에 발표한 것보다 6개월 빨리 모델 X를 받아 볼 수 있을 것으로 기대합니다. 내년 말까지 Matcha 모터스는 우리나라의 3대 자동차 제조사를 합친 것보다 더 많은 차를 생산하게 될 것입니다.

마지막으로, 선주문이 높은 기대치를 초과했기 때문에 저희는 모델 X의 대기자 명단을 시작해야 했습니다. 그러나 생산 목표치 상승으로, 향후 3년 이내에 모델 X를 원하는 모든 소비자에게 서비스를 제공할 수 있기를 바랍니다.

Olga Malayov

어휘 leak 누출 unveiling 첫 공개 peek 살짝 엿보다 game-changer 상황 전개를 완전히 바꿔놓는 중요한 것 instrument panel 계기판 mounted 설치된 intuitive 직관적인 commit (돈·시간을) 쓰다 hooked 중독된 glowing 열정적인 pass along to ~에게 알리다 press packet 홍보용 자료 exceed 초과하다

176

후기에 의하면, Matcha 모터스는 어떤 기능에 비용을 절약하는가?

(A) 배터리   (B) 제어판
(C) 모터   (D) 좌석

177

Hansen씨는 누구인가?

(A) Matcha 모터스의 대변인   (B) 언론인
(C) 기술 전문가   (D) 광고 전문가

어휘 journalist 언론인

178

모델 X의 추가 모터 비용은 얼마인가?

(A) 2천 달러   (B) 8천 달러
(C) 1만 달러   (D) 4만 달러

179

Malayov씨가 생산에 관해 언급한 것은 무엇인가?

(A) 생산이 지연되었다.
(B) 생산 속도가 빨라졌다.
(C) 해외에서 생산되고 있다.
(D) 구조조정 중이다.

어휘 speed up 속도를 더 내다 restructure 구조조정을 하다

180

후기의 두 번째 단락, 두 번째 행의 masses와 의미상 가장 가까운 단어는 무엇인가?

(A) 대중   (B) 수량

(C) 다양성 (D) 부

어휘 variety 다양성

181-185 📧 이메일…정보

수신: info@yoganation.com
발신: Evel Hun <e-hun@foro.com>
제목: 패키지 상품
날짜: 6월 30일 일요일

선생님,

제가 우연히 지역 체육관에서 선생님의 패키지 상품을 설명하는 팸플릿을 보았는데, 몇 가지 궁금한 게 있습니다.

제가 요가 수업을 듣고 싶은데, **185가능한 한 자주** 선생님의 수업에 참여하고 싶습니다. BAI 패키지는 수업이 있을 때마다 참여할 수 있다는 것을 보았습니다. **181성인 대학생은 할인이 되는지요?**

이 전단지를 오늘 보았는데, 주말이어서 7월 1일 월요일 전까지는 제 이메일을 못 보실 것 같네요. **181그래도 제가 할인된 비용으로 등록할 수 있을까요?**

182친구와 저는 시범 수업으로 어떤 요일이 더 좋을지 모르겠습니다. 추천 좀 해주실 수 있으세요?

빠른 답변 기다리고 있겠습니다.

Evel Hun

YogaNation

YogaNation의 종신회원에 관심이 있으시면 아래 월간 상품을 참고해주세요.

패키지	세부 사항	요금(추가 수업)
185BAI	원하는 만큼 모든 수업 수강 가능	월 400달러
PUR	한 달에 12개 수업 수강 가능	월 360달러(**183수업당 30달러**)
GAR	한 달에 6개 수업 수강 가능	월 210달러(수업당 35달러)
CHA	선불 방식	**184수업당 40달러**

첫 패키지 구매 시 일회성으로 **185연회비 200달러**가 부과됩니다. 이 팸플릿으로 회원권 20%를 할인받으세요.
6월 30일까지 유효합니다.

어휘 come across 우연히 보다 describe 설명하다 mature student 성인 대학생 be entitled to 권리가 있다 reduction 할인 charge 부과하다 initially 처음에

181

이메일의 주된 목적은 무엇인가?
(A) 가격 인하가 되는지 확인하기 위해
(B) 강사에게 정규수업 참석을 알리기 위해
(C) 강사가 그녀의 관심사를 알도록 하기 위해
(D) 성인 대학생반 개시를 제안하기 위해

어휘 price cut 가격 인하

182

YogaNation이 Hun씨에게 해줄 일은 무엇인가?

(A) 상품에 대해 보다 자세히 설명하기
(B) 좋은 체육관 추천하기
(C) 날짜에 대한 정보에 답하기
(D) 그녀와 친구를 시범 수업에 등록시키기

183

더 저렴한 추가 수업을 제공하는 패키지는 무엇인가?
(A) BAI (B) PUR
(C) GAR (D) CHA

184

누가 한 번의 수업을 듣기 위해 40달러를 지불할 것인가?
(A) BAI 회원 (B) PUR 회원
(C) GAR 회원 (D) CHA 회원

185

회원이 되려면 Hun씨는 최대 얼마를 내야 하는가?
(A) 200달러 (B) 400달러
(C) 560달러 (D) 600달러

186-190 📧 안내문…양식…이메일 신유형

Redlands 주민센터에서 성인들을 위한 동계 신규 강좌를 엽니다

*친구, 이웃과 함께 재미있는 수업을 들으세요.
*새로운 기술을 배우거나 오래된 관심을 되살려보세요.
***188모든 수업은 지역에서 그 분야의 전문가들이 가르칩니다.**
*다음 강좌 중에서 선택하세요.

· 사계절 야외 사진 촬영   · 프랑스 요리
· 나만의 허브 키우기   · 스케치 및 소묘
· 필라테스 입문   · 창의적 글쓰기
· 컴퓨터 기초   · 입문자를 위한 투자법

이 강좌들을 비롯해 다른 강좌들의 목록이 저희 웹사이트(www.redlandscommctr.com)에 올라가 있습니다. **186웹사이트에서 온라인 등록 양식을 작성하시고 신용카드로 지불하실 수 있습니다.** 질문이 있으시면 Jolene에게 이메일 주소 joleneb@redlandscommctr.com으로 문의하세요. 수업시간에 뵐게요!

등록 양식

Redlands 주민센터 성인 학습

이름: Whitney Burke   나이: 43
주소: 46 Wilderest Lane, Redlands
전에 Redlands 주민센터의 강좌를 수강하신 적이 있습니까? 아니요.
이 강좌를 어떻게 알게 되었습니까? **187친구가 수업을 듣고 말해주었습니다.**

강좌 ID	강좌명	선생님
RAD 105	**188나만의 허브 키우기**	Ralph Munez
RAD 148	입문자를 위한 투자법	Jennifer Cho
RAD 197	컴퓨터 기초	Neil Jackson
189RAD 239	사진 고급반	Suzanne Olsen

수신: wburke@firemail.com
발신: frankdodds@redlandscommctr.com
날짜: 10월 28일
제목: 귀하의 Redlands 강좌 신청

Burke씨께
Redlands 주민센터의 강좌를 등록해주셔서 감사합니다. 한 개의 강좌를 제외하고 귀하가 선택하신 모든 강좌를 제공해드릴 수 있습니다. 아쉽게도, ¹⁸⁹Suzanne Olsen 선생님은 이번 겨울에 강좌를 진행할 수 없게 되었습니다. ¹⁹⁰남편의 직장 때문에 갑작스럽게 이사를 해야 하기 때문입니다. 불편을 끼쳐 죄송합니다. 이 강좌는 봄에 새로운 강사를 초빙하여 진행할 것입니다.
또한, 귀하께서 신청서에 저희 센터에서 수업을 들은 친구가 있다는 언급을 하셨기에, 소개 할인에 대해 알려드립니다. 만약 누군가를 소개할 경우, 두 분 다 해당 학기 모든 수업료의 5%를 할인받으실 수 있습니다. 친구의 이름을 알려주시면 할인 조치하겠습니다.
등록해주셔서 감사합니다. 수업에서 뵙겠습니다.
Frank Dodds

어휘 revive 소생시키다 relocate 이사하다 inconvenience 불편함
referral discount 소개 할인

186
주민들은 어떻게 수업에 등록할 수 있는가?
(A) 센터를 방문하여
(B) 양식을 작성하여
(C) 미리 돈을 납입하여
(D) 직원에게 연락하여

187
Burke씨는 수업을 어떻게 알게 되었는가?
(A) 소개를 통해
(B) TV 광고를 통해
(C) 인터넷을 통해
(D) 공지를 통해

188
Munez씨에 관해 알 수 있는 것은 무엇인가?
(A) 그는 수년 동안 같은 수업을 가르쳤다.
(B) 그는 지역의 허브 전문가이다.
(C) 그는 Burke씨와 같은 수업을 듣고 있다.
(D) 그는 그 지역을 떠날 것이다.

189
겨울에 어떤 수업에 문제가 있는가?
(A) RAD 105   (B) RAD 148
(C) RAD 197   (D) RAD 239

190
왜 한 강좌는 들을 수 없는가?
(A) 그 강좌는 봄에만 제공된다.
(B) 실수로 수업 목록에 추가되었다.
(C) 강사가 아프다.

(D) 강사가 이사를 간다.

어휘 mistakenly 실수로 add to ~에 추가하다 ill 아픈

191-195 📧 이메일…이메일…쿠폰 신 유 형 —

수신: 고객서비스부 <cs@steelworks.com>
발신: Brian W <brianw@pershing.com>
제목: 나의 믿음직한 다리미
날짜: 11월 29일

관계자분께
저는 약 6년 동안 Press-on 400이라는 모델의 다리미를 썼고, 이 믿음직스러운 제품에 만족하고 있습니다. ¹⁹¹그런데 최근 다리미의 온도가 올라가지 않는 문제가 생겼습니다. 코드를 확인했는데 거기에는 문제가 없는 것 같았습니다. 표면도 깨끗하게 닦았지만 달라지지 않았습니다. 저는 이 훌륭한 다리미를 버리기는 싫은데 수리하는 게 가능한지 궁금합니다. ¹⁹⁴Glendale Valley 근처에 수리점이 있다면 알려주세요. 아니면, 어디로 보내야 할지 알려주시면 인근 지역 밖으로 우편물로 보낼 의향이 있습니다.
미리 감사드립니다.
Brian Wilcox

수신: Brian W <brianw@pershing.com>
발신: Customer Service <cs@steelworks.com>
제목: 회신: 나의 믿음직한 다리미
날짜: ¹⁹⁵11월 30일

Wilcox씨께
¹⁹²죄송하지만 Press-on 400은 약 2년 전에 단종되었습니다. 저희는 해당 모델에 대한 수리 서비스를 제공할 수 없지만, 귀하의 고객 충성도를 소중히 생각하며, 귀하를 저희 고객으로 계속 모시고 싶습니다. 이를 위해 귀하의 다리미가 가진 모든 기능에 더 많은 기능을 갖춘 자사의 최신 모델인 PressMagic 500을 구매할 경우 사용하실 수 있는 30달러짜리 쿠폰을 동봉해드립니다. 자사의 향상된 스팀 기능으로 까다로운 주름도 펴줄 것입니다. 또한 ¹⁹³PressMagic은 이전 모델보다 무거운 원단도 다룰 수 있습니다. 증서에 열거된 모든 판매점에서 혜택을 보시기 바랍니다.
감사합니다.
Jane Carver
Steel Works 고객서비스부

STEEL WORKS
다음 판매점에서 이 증서를 보여주시고 Steel Works의 제품을 30달러 할인받으세요.

B's Home Store	Appliances and More	¹⁹⁴Home Super Store	Johnson Goods
25081 Highway 53 Rosedale, UT	85 South Mall Drive Carsonville, NY	5903 E. Styx Way Glendale Valley, UT	898 Beverly St. Tatterville, NV

*본 쿠폰은 다른 프로모션 상품과 연계하여 사용할 수 없습니다.
*본 쿠폰은 현금으로 교환할 수 없습니다.
¹⁹⁵*본 쿠폰은 12월 31일까지 유효합니다.

어휘 reliable 믿을 만한 surface 표면 be willing to 흔쾌히 ~하다 immediate 아주 가까이에 있는 discontinue 중단하다 retain 유지하다 to that end 그 목적을 달성하기 위하여 enclose 동봉하다 certificate 증명서 in combination with ~와 결합하여 redeem (상품권을) 현금으로 바꾸다

191

Wilcox씨의 제품에 무슨 문제가 있는가?

(A) 제어 버튼이 고장 났다.

(B) 코드가 찢어졌다.

(C) 발열체가 파손되었다.

(D) 증기 기능이 작동하지 않는다.

어휘 split 찢다 heating element 발열체

192

Carver씨가 Wilcox씨의 요청을 받아들일 수 없는 이유는 무엇인가?

(A) 그는 보증기간이 연장되지 않았다.

(B) 그는 가게의 서비스 지역 밖에 거주한다.

(C) 그의 제품이 리콜되었다.

(D) 그의 제품이 더 이상 생산되지 않고 있다.

어휘 grant 승인하다 warranty 보증 recall (하자가 있는 제품을) 회수하다

193

PressMagic 500에 대해 언급된 것은 무엇인가?

(A) 디자인이 더 좋다.

(B) 발열 범위가 더 높다.

(C) 더 신뢰할 수 있다.

(D) 두꺼운 옷에도 작동된다.

어휘 thick 두꺼운

194

Wilcox씨는 어디에서 쿠폰을 사용할 것으로 보이는가?

(A) Appliances and More

(B) B's Home Store

(C) Home Super Store

(D) Johnson Goods

195

Wilcox씨가 쿠폰을 사용할 수 있는 기간은 얼마나 되는가?

(A) 약 일주일   (B) 약 2주일

(C) 약 한 달   (D) 약 일 년

196-200 📋 광고…주문서…이메일 신유형

Three Brothers Catering

주문의 양에 구애받지 않습니다. 고객의 기쁨이 저희의 목표입니다!

[196]Three Brothers Catering은 10년 이상 업계에 종사하면서 수년간 수백 명의 배고픈 고객들을 만족시켜드리고 있습니다. 저희는 기업 행사, 지역 단체나 개인 모임의 점심 또는 저녁식사를 제공합니다. 얼마나 기대하시든지 저희는 모두를 만족시킬 자신이 있습니다. [200]월

말까지 첫 고객이 되면 사무실 점심식사를 무료 배송으로 받으실 수 있습니다. www.3broscatering.com에서 저희의 메뉴를 (풀 컬러입니다) 살펴보십시오. 마음에 드는 음식을 보셨다면 555-8139로 전화해주세요.

Three Brother Catering

Three Brothers Catering

8391 Castle View Drive
Los Animas, NM

고객명: Leslie Jones   날짜: 11월 7일   장소: Jones and Co.

주문	수량	단가	총액
모둠 샌드위치	12	3.95	47.40
[199]싱싱한 샐러드	5	3.50	17.50
다양한 병음료	12	1.00	12.00
전체 요리	1	12.00	12.00

수신: rep@3broscatering.com
발신: ljones@jonesnco.com
제목: 주문상 변동
날짜: 11월 5일

안녕하세요, Joseph씨.

모레로 요청한 제 주문을 변경하는 게 너무 늦지 않았으면 해요. [197,198]Youngston 지점에서 세 명의 직원이 우리 모임에 함께 한다고 들었어요. 그들은 우리와 점심을 함께 하지는 않지만, 그들을 위해 음료라도 준비해야 할 것 같아요. 그래서 모임은 15명이 되었어요. [199]그리고 샐러드에도 변경이 있어요. 한 사람이 샐러드를 원하지 않는대요. 다른 건 괜찮아요. 촉박하게 전하는 것이지만 저도 어쩔 수 없었어요. [200]첫 주문인 만큼 여전히 특별 가격의 혜택을 받을 수 있길 바랍니다.

감사합니다.

Leslie Jones

어휘 catering 음식 공급업(체) aim to ~를 목표로 하다 decade 10년 corporate 기업의 the day after tomorrow 모레 beverage 음료 short notice 촉박한 통보 eligible 자격이 있는

196

Three Brothers Catering에 관하여 언급된 것은 무엇인가?

(A) 요리 수업도 제공한다.

(B) 몇 개의 상을 수상했다.

(C) 새로운 서비스이다.

(D) 10년도 더 전에 문을 열었다.

197

Jones씨는 어떤 행사를 여는가?

(A) 사업상의 오찬   (B) 개업식

(C) 은퇴 기념 파티   (D) 오픈 하우스

어휘 grand opening 개업

198

Jones씨는 왜 음료 주문을 변경해야 하는가?

(A) 더 많은 사람들이 온다.

(B) 더 많은 사람들이 커피를 원한다.

(C) 몇몇 사람들이 다이어트 음료를 요구했다.

(D) 몇몇 사람들이 오지 않을 것이다.

199

Jones씨는 몇 개의 샐러드가 필요한가?

(A) 3   (B) 4

(C) 5   (D) 12

200

Jones씨는 무엇을 받길 기대하는가?

(A) 15% 할인   (B) 무료 선물

(C) 회원 우대 프로그램   (D) 무료 배송

Actual Test 3

정답

1 (A)	**2** (A)	**3** (B)	**4** (C)	**5** (B)	**6** (D)	**7** (A)	**8** (C)	**9** (C)	**10** (B)
11 (B)	**12** (A)	**13** (B)	**14** (C)	**15** (B)	**16** (A)	**17** (A)	**18** (B)	**19** (C)	**20** (C)
21 (A)	**22** (B)	**23** (A)	**24** (C)	**25** (B)	**26** (A)	**27** (B)	**28** (B)	**29** (C)	**30** (A)
31 (C)	**32** (C)	**33** (C)	**34** (B)	**35** (D)	**36** (B)	**37** (B)	**38** (C)	**39** (A)	**40** (B)
41 (A)	**42** (D)	**43** (B)	**44** (D)	**45** (B)	**46** (C)	**47** (D)	**48** (D)	**49** (D)	**50** (A)
51 (A)	**52** (A)	**53** (A)	**54** (A)	**55** (C)	**56** (D)	**57** (D)	**58** (A)	**59** (B)	**60** (D)
61 (A)	**62** (D)	**63** (B)	**64** (A)	**65** (A)	**66** (D)	**67** (B)	**68** (D)	**69** (D)	**70** (B)
71 (D)	**72** (C)	**73** (D)	**74** (A)	**75** (C)	**76** (C)	**77** (B)	**78** (A)	**79** (A)	**80** (A)
81 (D)	**82** (A)	**83** (D)	**84** (B)	**85** (D)	**86** (D)	**87** (D)	**88** (A)	**89** (A)	**90** (A)
91 (A)	**92** (C)	**93** (B)	**94** (A)	**95** (B)	**96** (C)	**97** (D)	**98** (A)	**99** (A)	**100** (B)
101 (C)	**102** (D)	**103** (A)	**104** (C)	**105** (C)	**106** (D)	**107** (C)	**108** (D)	**109** (D)	**110** (A)
111 (B)	**112** (D)	**113** (D)	**114** (A)	**115** (C)	**116** (B)	**117** (B)	**118** (C)	**119** (D)	**120** (D)
121 (A)	**122** (C)	**123** (C)	**124** (C)	**125** (C)	**126** (D)	**127** (C)	**128** (A)	**129** (A)	**130** (C)
131 (B)	**132** (B)	**133** (A)	**134** (C)	**135** (D)	**136** (A)	**137** (B)	**138** (B)	**139** (A)	**140** (A)
141 (A)	**142** (C)	**143** (A)	**144** (B)	**145** (B)	**146** (A)	**147** (B)	**148** (A)	**149** (B)	**150** (B)
151 (B)	**152** (B)	**153** (A)	**154** (D)	**155** (C)	**156** (C)	**157** (A)	**158** (B)	**159** (C)	**160** (D)
161 (C)	**162** (A)	**163** (C)	**164** (B)	**165** (D)	**166** (D)	**167** (B)	**168** (C)	**169** (B)	**170** (A)
171 (B)	**172** (D)	**173** (C)	**174** (D)	**175** (A)	**176** (A)	**177** (B)	**178** (B)	**179** (A)	**180** (C)
181 (D)	**182** (D)	**183** (A)	**184** (A)	**185** (A)	**186** (D)	**187** (B)	**188** (A)	**189** (B)	**190** (D)
191 (D)	**192** (C)	**193** (C)	**194** (B)	**195** (A)	**196** (D)	**197** (A)	**198** (D)	**199** (A)	**200** (D)

PART 1

1

◁)) 캐나다

(A) The men are looking at a screen.
(B) The men are sitting in chairs.
(C) The woman is cleaning a window.
(D) The woman is drinking something.

(A) 남자들은 화면을 보고 있다.
(B) 남자들은 의자에 앉아 있다.
(C) 여자는 창문을 닦고 있는 중이다.
(D) 여자는 무언가를 마시고 있는 중이다.

어휘 screen 화면

2

(◁)) 미국

(A) People are standing near tables.

(B) People are eating at tables.

(C) Tables are piled with papers.

(D) People are moving files off the tables.

(A) 사람들이 탁자 가까이에 서 있다.

(B) 사람들이 탁자에서 식사를 하고 있다.

(C) 탁자에 종이가 쌓여 있다.

(D) 사람들이 탁자에서 파일을 치우고 있다.

어휘 be piled with ~로 쌓여 있다

3

(◁)) 호주

(A) They are running along a bank of a lake.

(B) A man is fishing in a lake.

(C) They are getting in a boat.

(D) A man is putting his fishing pole together.

(A) 사람들이 강둑을 따라 뛰고 있다.

(B) 남자가 호수에서 낚시를 하고 있다.

(C) 사람들이 배에 타고 있다.

(D) 남자는 자신의 낚싯대를 조립하고 있다.

어휘 run along ~를 따라 뛰다 put together 조립하다 fishing pole 낚싯대

4

(◁)) 영국

(A) Cars are going into a tunnel.

(B) Cars are parking in a garage.

(C) Cars are traveling along a road.

(D) Cars are yielding to a motorcycle.

(A) 자동차들이 터널로 진입하고 있다.

(B) 자동차들이 차고에 주차되고 있다.

(C) 자동차들이 길을 따라 이동하고 있다.

(D) 자동차들이 오토바이에 양보하고 있다.

어휘 garage 차고 yield 양보하다

5

(◁)) 호주

(A) They are dancing in a hall.

(B) Some people are holding hands in a circle.

(C) They are watching a live performance.

(D) Some people are walking out of a building.

(A) 사람들이 홀에서 춤을 추고 있다.

(B) 몇몇의 사람들은 손을 잡고 원을 그리고 있다.

(C) 사람들이 라이브 공연을 보고 있다.

(D) 몇몇 사람들은 건물 밖으로 나가고 있다.

어휘 hold hands 손을 잡다

6

(◁)) 미국

(A) A man is paying for some items.

(B) A woman is giving an item to a man.

(C) A man is taking pictures at a fair.

(D) A woman is carrying a bag in her hand.

(A) 남자는 물건 값을 지불하고 있다.

(B) 여자가 남자에게 물건을 주고 있다.

(C) 남자가 박람회에서 사진을 찍고 있다.

(D) 여자는 손에 봉투를 들고 있다.

어휘 fair 박람회

PART 2

7 （（◀）） 호주…미국

Where do you want to meet?

(A) In front of the station.

(B) She can't find the files.

(C) Tomorrow at 1:00.

어디서 만날까요?

(A) 역 앞에서요.

(B) 그녀는 파일을 찾지 못해요.

(C) 내일 1시에요.

---

8 （（◀）） 영국…미국

Could you let us know as soon as possible?

(A) Not as far as I know.

(B) That route is always delayed.

(C) Yes, of course. I'll call you.

가능한 한 빨리 알려줄 수 있습니까?

(A) 제가 알기로는 아니에요.

(B) 그 경로는 항상 지연돼요.

(C) 네, 당연하죠. 전화드리겠습니다.

어휘 route 경로

---

9 （（◀）） 캐나다…호주

When are you leaving for your vacation?

(A) It was less than $1,500.

(B) I've never seen such crowds.

(C) Not until Wednesday.

휴가 언제 가세요?

(A) 1,500달러보다 낮았어요.

(B) 그렇게 많은 사람들을 본 적은 없어요.

(C) 수요일 전에는 안 떠나요.

어휘 crowd 군중

---

10 （（◀）） 영국…캐나다

Should we update the price on the Website?

(A) I haven't heard of that brand before.

(B) No. Let's wait till the end of the day.

(C) It has doubled in five years.

웹사이트의 가격을 갱신해야 할까요?

(A) 그 브랜드에 대해서 들어본 적이 없어요.

(B) 아뇨. 오늘까지 기다려 봅시다.

(C) 5년 만에 두 배로 뛰었습니다.

---

11 （（◀）） 호주…캐나다

How long has Ms. Mason been in that meeting?

(A) I wish the line would move more quickly.

(B) Since 11:00 this morning.

(C) The small conference room.

Mason씨가 얼마 동안 회의를 하고 있나요?

(A) 줄이 좀 더 빨리 줄었으면 좋겠어요.

(B) 오늘 오전 11시부터요.

(C) 작은 회의실이에요.

어휘 conference room 회의실

12 (미국…영국)

The user reviews have been mostly positive, haven't they?

(A) Yes, over 80 percent gave three stars or more.

(B) No, I haven't reviewed the plans yet.

(C) The movie was just so-so, in my opinion.

어휘 ✓ review 비평; 검토하다

사용자 후기가 대부분 긍정적이죠?

(A) 네. 80퍼센트 이상이 별을 세 개 이상 주었어요.

(B) 아니요. 아직 계획을 검토하지 않았어요.

(C) 제 생각에 그 영화는 그저 그런 것 같아요.

---

13 (캐나다…호주)

Why hasn't the mail been delivered yet?

(A) I'll call to make a reservation.

(B) Maybe because of the bad weather.

(C) There's a post office around the corner.

왜 아직 우편물 배달이 안 되었을까요?

(A) 예약을 위해 전화를 하겠습니다.

(B) 아마도 날씨가 나빠서겠지요.

(C) 모퉁이를 돌면 우체국이 있어요.

---

14 (미국…영국)

It's the end of the month already.

(A) I left my phone in the taxi.

(B) It seems we're all booked.

(C) We've been so busy. The time has flown by.

어휘 ✓ Time flies by. 시간이 빠르게 지나간다.

벌써 월말이네요.

(A) 택시에 제 휴대폰을 두고 내렸어요.

(B) 저희가 예약이 꽉 찬 것 같습니다.

(C) 너무 바빴죠. 시간이 참 빨리 갔네요.

---

15 (미국…호주)

What do you want me to do with the old monitors?

(A) I'd like everyone's attention, please.

(B) Let's try to sell them online.

(C) No one is monitoring their progress.

어휘 ✓ monitor (컴퓨터) 모니터; 감시하다

오래된 모니터는 어떻게 했으면 좋겠어요?

(A) 모두 주목해주세요.

(B) 인터넷에서 팔아보죠.

(C) 아무도 그들의 진행과정을 감시하고 있지 않아요.

---

16 (영국…캐나다)

Who knows when the president is going to make a decision on the project?

(A) I guess we should just work on other things.

(B) She knows everyone in the room.

(C) These reports are the most current.

어휘 ✓ work on ~에 착수하다

사장님이 그 프로젝트에 대한 결정을 언제 내릴지 누가 알겠어요?

(A) 우리는 그저 다른 일에 착수해야 할 것 같아요.

(B) 그녀는 이 방의 모든 사람들을 알아요.

(C) 이 보고서들이 가장 최신이에요.

17

How do you spell your last name?

(A) F-U-L-L-E-R.

(B) Originally from Germany.

(C) Using black ink, always.

어휘 spell 철자를 말하다[쓰다]

귀하의 성의 철자가 어떻게 되나요?

(A) F, U, L, L, E, R입니다.

(B) 원래 독일에서 왔습니다.

(C) 항상 검정색 잉크를 사용하죠.

---

18 (◁)) 호주···미국

Is it possible to change the staff meeting next week?

(A) Our best wishes to you in the future.

(B) Possible, but difficult. Why?

(C) We are open until 7:00.

다음 주 직원회의를 변경하는 것이 가능한가요?

(A) 앞으로 잘되시길 바랍니다.

(B) 가능하지만 어렵죠. 왜요?

(C) 저희는 7시까지 영업합니다.

---

19 (◁)) 영국···캐나다

When does the customer want the service to begin?

(A) Through the end of the year.

(B) It's just $59 per month.

(C) On May 1.

어휘 per month 매달

그 고객이 언제 서비스를 시작하길 원하나요?

(A) 연말까지 계속이요.

(B) 매달 단돈 59달러입니다.

(C) 5월 1일이요.

---

20 (◁)) 호주···미국

Has she gone home for the day or is she coming back to the office?

(A) She lives in Springville.

(B) She doesn't need a call back.

(C) She said she'll return by 5:00.

그녀가 퇴근을 했나요, 아니면 사무실로 복귀하나요?

(A) 그녀는 Springville에 살아요.

(B) 그녀에게 다시 전화할 필요가 없어요.

(C) 그녀가 5시까지는 돌아오겠다고 했어요.

---

21 (◁)) 영국···호주

Where are the completed applications?

(A) In this folder.

(B) It'll be hard to find a qualified applicant.

(C) Talking with Ms. Simpson.

어휘 qualified 자격이 있는

완료된 지원서는 어디에 있나요?

(A) 이 폴더 안에 있어요.

(B) 조건에 맞는 지원자를 찾기가 어려울 거예요.

(C) Simpson씨와 이야기하는 것이요.

22 (⏸️ 캐나다…영국)

Conference Room B is free now, isn't it?

(A) It holds 15 people.

(B) Check the schedule.

(C) It's free for groups of five or more.

B회의실이 지금 공실이죠?

(A) 15명을 수용할 수 있습니다.

(B) 일정표를 확인하세요.

(C) 5명 이상의 단체는 무료입니다.

어휘 free 비어 있는, 무료의 hold (사람을) 수용하다

---

23 (⏸️ 미국…캐나다)

Are there any spaces left for the seminar?

(A) Only two, I'm afraid.

(B) The seminar's about marketing.

(C) When should I pay for it?

세미나에 자리가 남아 있나요?

(A) 두 자리밖에 안 남았습니다.

(B) 마케팅에 관한 세미나입니다.

(C) 제가 언제 결제하면 되나요?

어휘 pay for ~에 대해 지불하다

---

24 (⏸️ 호주…영국)

Has Mr. Powell read the contract yet?

(A) His contact information has been updated.

(B) Instead of your assistant.

(C) I left it on his desk this morning.

Powell씨가 계약서를 읽었나요?

(A) 그의 계약 정보가 갱신되었어요.

(B) 당신의 조수 대신이에요.

(C) 오늘 아침에 그분 책상 위에 올려놓았어요.

어휘 contract 계약서 update 갱신하다

---

25 (⏸️ 미국…호주)

The sales team went to the conference, didn't they?

(A) Yes, we have a double room.

(B) No, it was canceled at the last minute.

(C) I'm not sure where the reports are.

영업팀은 회의에 참석했지요?

(A) 네. 더블룸이 있습니다.

(B) 아뇨. 막판에 취소되었습니다.

(C) 보고서들이 어디에 있는지 잘 모르겠습니다.

어휘 at the last minute 막판에

---

26 (⏸️ 캐나다…영국)

None of the new recruits are coming to the after-work party.

(A) I guess they're busy.

(B) There are ten of them in all.

(C) It was held at the restaurant on the corner.

신입직원들 아무도 쫑파티에 오지 않네요.

(A) 그들은 바쁜 것 같아요.

(B) 그들은 총 열 명이에요.

(C) 모퉁이에 있는 식당에서 열렸습니다.

27 ◁)) 미국…호주

Who should we get to redecorate the lobby?

(A) They might deliver. Let me check.

(B) I'll ask around for a recommendation.

(C) Ms. Clark has a degree in finance.

어휘 recommendation 추천(장) degree 학위

복도를 누구에게 다시 장식하게 하죠?

(A) 그들이 아마 배달해줄 거예요. 제가 확인해 볼게요.

(B) 돌아다니면서 추천할 사람을 물어볼게요.

(C) Clark씨는 재무학 학위가 있습니다.

---

28 ◁)) 캐나다…미국

Do you want to announce the plans tomorrow?

(A) Yes, let's go out of town for the weekend.

(B) No. We should do it today.

(C) I just want some peace and quiet.

어휘 peace and quiet 평온

그 계획을 내일 발표하시겠습니까?

(A) 네. 주말에 교외로 놀러 갑시다.

(B) 아뇨. 오늘 해야 합니다.

(C) 그냥 조용히 좀 쉬고 싶어요.

---

29 ◁)) 영국…캐나다

All of the surveys have been returned.

(A) Some of them went to lunch down the street.

(B) I didn't know she'd returned already.

(C) We should go through them as soon as possible.

어휘 return 돌려주다, 돌아오다

모든 설문지를 돌려받았어요.

(A) 몇몇은 길을 따라 점심을 먹으러 갔어요.

(B) 그녀가 벌써 돌아왔는지 몰랐어요.

(C) 되도록 빨리 검토해야 해요.

---

30 ◁)) 캐나다…미국

Do you mind closing the window?

(A) Not at all.

(B) Yes, they're all sold out.

(C) There isn't room for everyone.

창문 좀 닫아도 될까요?

(A) 상관없어요.

(B) 네. 모두 판매되었습니다.

(C) 모두를 수용할 공간이 없어요.

---

31 ◁)) 영국…호주

I don't remember the last time I enjoyed a movie so much.

(A) It's only playing for another three days.

(B) You remember my brother, David.

(C) You're right. It was really good.

마지막으로 이렇게 영화를 재미있게 보았던 게 언제였는지 기억이 안 나요.

(A) 딱 3일 더 상영합니다.

(B) 제 동생 David를 기억하죠?

(C) 맞아요. 정말 좋았어요.

PART 3

Questions 32-34 refer to the following conversation. (◁)) 호주…영국)

W Hello, I'm with the Mystery Shopper Network. ³²We conduct research about shoppers' experiences in various stores. I see you have a bag from Nelson Marks department store. Would you mind if I asked you some questions?

M Um, actually, ³³I'm meeting someone in a few minutes.

W I understand. It won't take long. Were you shopping for yourself today or for someone else?

M ³⁴I bought a birthday present for my son, a shirt and tie. I really have to go now. Sorry.

여 안녕하세요. 저는 Mystery Shopper Network 소속입니다. ³²저희는 여러 매장에서 쇼핑객들의 경험에 대해 설문조사를 하고 있어요. Nelson Marks 백화점 쇼핑백을 가지고 계시군요. 몇 가지 좀 물어봐도 될까요?

남 사실 ³³저는 몇 분 있다가 만날 사람이 있어서….

여 알겠습니다. 오래 걸리지 않을 겁니다. 오늘 쇼핑은 본인을 위한 것인가요, 아니면 다른 사람을 위한 것인가요?

남 ³⁴아들 생일 선물로 셔츠와 넥타이를 샀습니다. 지금 정말 가봐야 해요. 죄송합니다.

어휘 conduct research 조사하다

32 여자의 직업은 무엇인가?
(A) 의류 디자이너
(B) 백화점 점원
(C) 조사원
(D) 남자의 직장 동료

33 남자는 왜 서두르고 있는가?
(A) 회사에 늦었기 때문에
(B) 몸이 좋지 않아서
(C) 누군가를 보러 가는 길이라서
(D) 방금 급한 전화를 받아서

34 남자는 구매 물품에 대해 뭐라고 말하는가?
(A) 새로 나온 제품이다.
(B) 자신을 위한 것이 아니다.
(C) 찾기 쉬웠다.
(D) 세일 중이었다.

Questions 35-37 refer to the following conversation. (◁)) 캐나다…미국)

W I'm so nervous about my presentation, Jared. ³⁵I'm worried I'll just forget what to say.

M You'll be fine. You've practiced many times and you have your notes in order, right?

W Yes, I do. ³⁶Maybe I can just go through it one more time, very quickly.

M No. It's almost 3:00. ³⁷We have to go to the conference room. If you can't remember what to say, just look at your notes. You can do it!

여 Jared, 발표 때문에 저 너무 긴장돼요. ³⁵무슨 말을 할지 잊어버릴까봐 걱정이 돼요.

남 괜찮을 거예요. 연습도 많이 했고 노트는 순서대로 가지고 있잖아요?

여 네, 아주 빨리 ³⁶한 번 더 훑어볼 수 있을 것 같아요.

남 아뇨. ³⁷이제 거의 3시예요. 회의실로 가야 해요. 만약 무슨 말을 할지 기억이 안 나면 그냥 노트를 봐요. 할 수 있어요!

어휘 in order 순서대로 된 go through ~를 훑어보다

35 여자는 왜 걱정하는가?
(A) 여러 사람 앞에서 말해야 해서
(B) 변경내용을 잊을까봐
(C) 제시간에 갈 수 없어서
(D) 실수를 할까봐

36 여자가 지금 하고 싶어 하는 것은 무엇인가?
(A) 집으로 가기
(B) 좀 더 연습하기
(C) 의사를 방문하기
(D) 쪽지 몇 장 작성하기

37 이후 두 사람은 어디로 갈 것인가?
(A) 구내식당
(B) 회의실
(C) 휴게실
(D) 사장실

Questions 38-40 refer to the following conversation. 〔◁》 영국…캐나다〕

M Excuse me. I'm looking for the manager.

W I'm the general manager. How can I help you?

M <u>38,39</u>I just wanted to ask why the menu has changed. I come here a lot with my family and we have enjoyed the variety in the past, but now there are hardly any main dishes. They all seem like appetizers.

W We decided to make the change to attract more people here after work. You know, to serve food that goes well with alcohol.

M That's too bad. <u>40</u>I'm afraid you've just lost some loyal customers. I wish you could've kept at least some of our favorite dishes.

남 실례합니다. 매니저를 찾고 있는데요.

여 제가 총책임자입니다. 무엇을 도와드릴까요?

남 38,39메뉴가 왜 바뀌었는지 궁금해서요. 저는 가족들과 이곳에 자주 오는데, 예전에는 다양한 음식들을 먹었는데 지금은 메인 요리가 거의 없어요. 전부 전채 요리만 있는 것 같아요.

여 퇴근 후 사람들을 더 끌어모으기 위해서 변화를 주기로 했어요. 주류와 잘 어울리는 음식을 제공하기 위해서요.

남 안 좋은 소식군요. 40유감스럽지만, 지금 막 단골 몇 사람을 잃으셨네요. 저희가 좋아하는 요리를 최소 몇 개라도 남겨 놓았으면 좋았을 텐데요.

어휘 appetizer 전채 go well with ~와 잘 어울리다

---

38 대화가 일어나는 장소로 알맞은 곳은 어디인가?
(A) 은행
(B) 주방용품 가게
(C) 식당
(D) 슈퍼마켓

39 남자는 무엇에 대해 불평하는가?
(A) 좁아진 선택권
(B) 시끄러운 환경
(C) 품질 불량
(D) 무례한 사람들

40 〔신유형〕 남자가 I'm afraid you've just lost some loyal customers라고 말한 이유는 무엇인가?
(A) 그는 가격 인상이 불만이다.
(B) 그는 더 이상 그곳을 방문하지 않을 것이다.
(C) 서비스가 좋지 않아 몇몇 사람들이 자리를 떴다.
(D) 어떤 사람들은 지배인이 무능하다고 생각한다.

어휘 kitchenware 주방용품 atmosphere 분위기 rude 무례한 incompetent 무능한

Questions 41-43 refer to the following conversation. 〔◁》 호주…미국〕

W Hello, I ordered some books on your Website a few days ago and I just received the package today. There are two copies of three of the books, but I only ordered one each. The order number is CW-AM-395.

M <u>41</u>I can help you with that. Oh, I think I see what happened. <u>42</u>You already had some of the titles in your shopping basket and then you added them into your basket again a few days ago. That's how you ended up with multiple copies.

W Well, I don't want more than one copy of each book.

M I understand. Just send back the books you don't want. <u>43</u>You should get your money back within two weeks.

여 안녕하세요? 며칠 전에 귀사의 웹사이트에서 몇 권의 책을 주문해서 오늘 막 소포를 받았습니다. 책 세 권이 두 부씩 있는데, 저는 한 부씩 주문했거든요. 주문번호는 CW-AM-395입니다.

남 41도와드리겠습니다. 아, 어떻게 된 일인지 알겠네요. 42고객님의 장바구니에 이미 몇 권의 책이 들어가 있었고, 그러고 나서 며칠 전에 다시 그 책들을 장바구니에 추가했어요. 그래서 여러 권이 배송되었습니다.

여 저는 책마다 한 부 이상은 원하지 않아요.

남 알겠습니다. 원하지 않는 책들은 반송해주세요. 432주 안에 환불받으실 수 있을 거예요.

어휘 copy (책) 한 부 title 서적 end up with 결국 ~하게 되다 get money back 환불받다

41 남자의 직업은 무엇인가?
(A) 고객서비스 담당자
(B) 사서
(C) 우체국 직원
(D) 배달원

42 여자가 가진 문제의 원인은 무엇인가?
(A) 컴퓨터의 오류
(B) 배송상의 실수
(C) 재고 부족
(D) 사용자의 실수

43 여자는 2주 안에 무엇을 받게 될 것인가?
(A) 쿠폰
(B) 환불
(C) 추가 품목
(D) 판촉물

어휘 stock shortage 재고 부족 oversight 실수

Questions 44–46 refer to the following conversation. 캐나다…미국

W William, **44** I just heard the Red Line has a problem. It has completely stopped running.

M Oh, no. Many of our employees use the Red Line to get home. We'd better make an announcement since it's almost the end of the day.

W Can we wait just a minute? **45** I'd like to find out what alternate services the train company is offering. I'll look on their Website.

M Good idea. **46** I have to meet with the personnel manager, Ms. Selleck, for a few minutes. Come to her office when you have the information.

여 William, **44**방금 빨간 노선에 문제가 있다고 들었어요. 운행이 완전히 중단되었어요.

남 이런, 많은 직원들이 빨간 노선을 타고 귀가해요. 이제 퇴근 시간이 다 되어 가니 알리는 게 낫겠어요.

여 잠깐 기다려줄래요? **45**열차 회사에서 대안으로 제공하는 서비스가 뭐가 있는지 찾아보고 싶어요. 회사 웹사이트에서 찾아볼게요.

남 좋은 생각이네요. **46**저는 인사부장 Selleck씨를 잠시 만나 봐야겠습니다. 알려줄 게 있으면 그녀의 사무실로 와주세요.

어휘 alternate 대안이 되는

44 대화의 주된 내용은 무엇인가?
(A) 매니저의 제안
(B) 새 입사 지원자
(C) 공공 서비스 웹사이트
(D) 교통수단의 지연

45 여자는 다음에 무엇을 할 것인가?
(A) 시 안내센터에 전화하기
(B) 인터넷에서 무언가를 확인하기
(C) 부장의 사무실로 가기
(D) 새로운 고객 만나기

46 남자는 여자에게 어디로 오라고 요청하는가?
(A) 고객과 회의하는 곳
(B) 커피숍
(C) 부장의 사무실
(D) 기차역

어휘 job candidate 입사 지원자

Questions 47–49 refer to the following conversation. 영국…호주 신 유 형

M Oh, hi Molly. I heard you got back yesterday. **47** How was your trip?

W It was great, Peter. **47** Very relaxing. Watching the sunset on the beach was fantastic. So . . . what's been going on here?

M Well, you missed a lot last week. There was a big shake-up in the sales department and two people left.

W You're kidding! What happened?

M **48** The new sales manager has been making changes that people don't like. I guess those two salespeople couldn't take it anymore.

W **49** It sounds like the president should have a long talk with the sales manager. Just to tell him to go slow with the changes.

남 Molly, 안녕하세요? 어제 돌아왔다고 들었어요. **47**여행은 어땠어요?

여 좋았어요, Peter. **47**아주 느긋하게 보냈어요. 해변에서 보는 일몰은 환상적이었고요. 그런데… 무슨 일이 있었던 거예요?

남 지난주에 당신이 휴가 간 동안 많은 일이 있었어요. 영업부에 대대적인 조직 개편이 있었는데, 두 사람이 퇴사했어요.

여 말도 안 돼요! 무슨 일이래요?

남 **48**새 영업 부장이 사람들이 싫어하는 변화를 주고 있어요. 그 두 영업자는 더 이상 버틸 수 없었나봐요.

여 **49**사장님이 영업 부장과 긴 이야기를 해야 할 것 같네요. 그냥 천천히 변화를 주라고 말이죠.

어휘 sunset 일몰 shake-up 대대적인 개편

---

47 여자는 지난주에 무엇을 했는가?
(A) 세미나에 참석했다.
(B) 면접을 보았다.
(C) 출장을 떠났다.
(D) 휴가를 갔다.

48 남자는 영업 부서에 대해 뭐라고 하는가?
(A) 새 층으로 이사를 간다.
(B) 세미나가 성공적이지 못했다.
(C) 최근 그 부서에 신입직원들이 들어왔다.
(D) 새로운 리더는 평판이 좋지 않다.

49 여자는 사장이 무엇을 해야 한다고 생각하는가?
(A) 회사 정책을 바꿔야 한다.
(B) 빠른 시일 내에 모든 직원과 이야기해야 한다.
(C) 영업 부장을 새로 고용해야 한다.
(D) 부장에게 일을 서두르지 말라고 지시한다.

어휘 unpopular 인기 없는 instruct 지시하다 go easy 서두르지 않고 하다

Questions 50–52 refer to the following conversation. 🔊 영국…캐나다 신 유 형

M Hi, ⁵⁰I visited your gym for a free trial today and I'm afraid I left my bicycle helmet there. It's black with a red stripe.

W Yes, I see it here in the lost and found box.

M Oh, good. Can I come get it now?

W Well, we're closing in about five minutes. We open at 6:00 tomorrow morning.

M Okay, I do need it since ⁵¹I ride my bike to work. But I live fairly close by, so I can pick it up on the way to work.

W Great. Uh, what did you decide about joining our gym?

M ⁵²I'm still considering it. It's a bit more expensive than my old gym.

남 안녕하세요? ⁵⁰제가 오늘 무료 체험으로 그쪽 체육관을 갔었는데, 그곳에 자전거 헬멧을 두고 왔어요. 검은색 바탕에 빨간색 줄무늬예요.

여 네, 여기 분실물 상자에 있습니다.

남 다행이네요. 지금 가지러 갈 수 있나요?

여 저희가 5분 후에 영업을 종료해요. 내일은 오전 6시에 문을 열고요.

남 알겠어요. ⁵¹제가 자전거로 출근해서 꼭 필요해요. 제가 아주 가까이에 사니까 출근길에 찾으러 갈 수 있어요.

여 잘됐네요. 저희 체육관에 등록하는 건 마음을 정하셨나요?

남 ⁵²아직 고민 중이에요. 제가 예전에 다니던 체육관보다 약간 더 비싸서요.

어휘 free trial 무료 체험 lost and found 분실물 보관소 fairly 상당히 close by 가까이에

---

50 남자는 왜 체육관에 전화했는가?
(A) 그곳에 무엇인가를 놓고 왔기 때문에
(B) 몇 가지 정보를 알고 싶어서
(C) 신청서를 가져오는 것을 잊었기 때문에
(D) 체육관이 열었는지 확인하고 싶어서

51 남자는 어떻게 출근하는가?
(A) 자전거로
(B) 버스로
(C) 승용차로
(D) 지하철로

52 남자는 왜 체육관에 등록하지 않을 것으로 보이는가?
(A) 비용이 너무 비싸서
(B) 집에서 멀어서
(C) 좋아하는 장비가 구비되어 있지 않아서
(D) 필요한 시간에 운영하지 않아서

Questions 53-55 refer to the following conversation. （◁)) 호주…미국

W I heard ⁵³the boss is finally going to announce a new marketing manager this week. Who do you think would do a better job, Steve or Iris?

M Oh, ⁵⁴I'm the wrong person to ask. You know Iris was the one who trained me. She's kind of been like a mentor to me since I started here.

W That's right, I remember. You have a good reason to prefer Iris. ⁵⁵As far as experience, though, Steve has more since he's been here for ten years.

M That's true. But, I'll still root for Iris.

어휘 as far as ~에 관한 한 root for ~를 응원하다

여 ⁵³사장님이 드디어 이번 주에 새 마케팅 부장을 발표한대요. Steve와 Iris 중에 누가 더 일을 잘 할 것 같아요?

남 ⁵⁴저는 그 질문을 받을 사람은 아니네요. 당신도 알겠지만 Iris는 저를 훈련시킨 분이에요. 제가 여기서 일을 시작한 이후로 일종의 멘토가 돼주었죠.

여 맞아요. 기억나요. Iris를 더 선호할 만한 충분한 이유네요. ⁵⁵경력으로 보면 Steve는 10년 동안 근무를 했기 때문에 경력이 더 많죠.

남 그렇죠. 하지만 전 Iris를 응원할 거예요.

---

53 대화의 주된 내용은 무엇인가?
(A) 동료의 승진
(B) 남자의 이력
(C) 여자의 업무
(D) 사장의 은퇴

54 남자가 I'm the wrong person to ask 라고 말한 의도는 무엇인가?
신유형
(A) 그는 객관적인 판단을 할 수 없다.
(B) 그는 그 일에 관해서는 선호하는 것이 없다.
(C) 그는 마케팅에 대해 잘 모른다.
(D) 그는 답변에 대해 생각할 시간이 필요하다.

55 여자는 Steve에 대해 뭐라고 하는가?
(A) 신상품에 대한 아이디어가 있다.
(B) 회사에서 가장 오래 근무했다.
(C) Iris보다 경험이 많다.
(D) 곧 성명을 발표해야 한다.

어휘 objective 객관적인 matter 문제

Questions 56-58 refer to the following conversation with three speakers. （◁)) 캐나다…미국…호주 신유형—

W1 ⁵⁶Here is the final contract, ready for your signature, Mr. Allen.

M ⁵⁷I appreciate your hard work on selling my house. I didn't expect it to happen so quickly. I guess it's a good market for sellers right now.

W1 Yes, you're right. We are very busy in this office at the moment. Uh, now, on this page we'll need a witness to sign, so I've asked my assistant to join us. Carol, can you come over here and sign your name here under Mr. Allen's?

W2 Yes, Okay. There you go.

M Well, is that all? Any more paperwork to do?

W1 Not at this time. We'll take this to the buyers and start the payment process. You should receive the money within about six weeks.

W2 ⁵⁸I'll send you an e-mail when everything has been finalized.

M Thank you both so much.

어휘 signature 서명 witness 증인 payment 지불

여1 ⁵⁶여기 최종 계약서에 사인만 하시면 됩니다, Allen씨.

남 ⁵⁷저희 집 매매에 힘써 주신 것에 대해 감사드려요. 이렇게 빨리 거래가 이루어질 줄은 생각도 못했어요. 지금 시장이 판매자에게는 좋은 것 같네요.

여1 네, 맞아요. 지금 저희 사무실이 아주 바빠요. 자, 이 페이지에 서명할 증인이 필요하니 제 조수에게 합류해달라고 부탁했어요. Carol, 이쪽으로 와서 Allen씨의 서명 아래에다 서명해주겠어요?

여2 네, 물론이죠. 됐습니다.

남 다 끝났나요? 서류 작업이 더 필요한가요?

여1 지금은 다 끝났어요. 저희가 계약서를 구매자들에게 갖다주고 대금 처리를 시작하겠습니다. Allen씨는 약 6주 안에 돈을 받으실 거예요.

여2 ⁵⁸모두 마무리되면 제가 이메일을 보내드릴게요.

남 두 분 모두 감사합니다.

56 남자가 요청받은 것은 무엇인가?
(A) 설문조사 작성하기
(B) 계약 협상하기
(C) 금액 지불하기
(D) 서명하기

57 여자들은 어디에서 일하는가?
(A) 은행
(B) 건축 회사
(C) 법률 회사
(D) 부동산 사무실

58 Carol은 무엇을 약속하는가?
(A) 나중에 남자에게 연락하기
(B) 더 많은 서류 작업 준비하기
(C) 은행 직원에게 말하기
(D) 남자의 회사를 방문하기

어휘 / negotiate 협상하다 real estate 부동산

Questions 59–61 refer to the following conversation. (캐나다…영국) 신 유 형

W Hi. Could you help me? ⁵⁹I'm looking for a going-away present for my colleague who is moving to a different state next week. Do you have any suggestions?

M How about this nice travel umbrella? It has a convenient strap.

W That looks great. I think he'll like this brown one. Could I get it gift-wrapped?

M Of course. If you'll just wait a few minutes.

W Actually, I need to do one more errand and then get back to my office for a meeting. ⁶⁰Could I have it delivered later today?

M We can get it to you tomorrow morning. Will that be soon enough?

W Yes, I guess so. ⁶¹We're having a party for my co-worker at lunchtime, so I definitely need to have it before then.

M I will make sure it's there in the morning.

여 안녕하세요. 저 좀 도와주시겠어요? 다음 주에 다른 주로 이사를 가는 ⁵⁹제 직장 동료에게 줄 작별 선물을 찾고 있어요. 추천해주실 물건이 있나요?

남 이 멋진 여행용 우산은 어떤가요? 편리한 끈이 달려 있습니다.

여 좋네요. 제 생각에 그는 갈색을 좋아할 거 같아요. 선물을 포장해주실 수 있나요?

남 물론이죠. 잠시만 기다려주세요.

여 실은 제가 한 가지 일을 더 처리하고 회의가 있어서 사무실로 돌아가야 하는데요. ⁶⁰오늘 있다가 배달해줄 수 있나요?

남 배달은 내일 아침에 가능할 것 같아요. 늦지 않으시겠지요?

여 네, 그럴 것 같아요. ⁶¹점심시간에 그 동료를 위한 파티가 있으니까, 그전에는 꼭 필요해요.

남 아침에 확실히 배달해드릴게요.

어휘 / going-away present 작별 선물 strap 줄 errand 심부름

---

59 여자는 무엇을 사려고 하는가?
(A) 생일 선물
(B) 작별 선물
(C) 은퇴 선물
(D) 결혼 선물

60 여자는 남자에게 무엇을 부탁하는가?
(A) 창고 확인하기
(B) 할인해주기
(C) 다른 물품 추천하기
(D) 그녀에게 물품 보내기

61 여자는 내일 정오에 무엇을 할 예정인가?
(A) 모임에 참석한다.
(B) 배송료를 지불한다.
(C) 파티에 내놓을 음식을 만든다.
(D) 동료를 공항에 데려다준다.

Questions 62–64 refer to the following conversation and timetable. (영국…호주)

M Hello. One ticket for *All Star Players* at 5:30, please.

W Oh, I'm sorry. That time slot is sold out. Would you like to wait for the later showing?

M Uh, I can't. ⁶²I'm having dinner with a friend at 8:00. I guess ⁶³I'll see *Brave And Braver* then. I heard it was good.

W Yes, ⁶⁴I saw it yesterday myself. It was very funny.

남 안녕하세요? 5시 30분 All Star Players 표 한 장이요.

여 죄송하지만, 그 시간은 매진되었습니다. 그다음 상영 시간까지 기다리시겠어요?

남 안 되는데요. ⁶²8시에 친구와 저녁을 먹기로 했거든요. ⁶³그러면 저는 Brave And Braver를 봐야겠네요. 이것도 좋다고 들었어요.

여 네. ⁶⁴어제 저도 봤는데, 정말 웃겼어요.

```
                    T-REX 극장

                    1번 상영관
    All Star Players      ▶ 5:30 – 7:40
                         ▶ 8:00 – 10:10

                    2번 상영관
    63Brave And Braver   ▶ 5:40 – 7:30
                         ▶ 7:50 – 9:40
```

62 남자는 이후에 무엇을 한다고 말하는가?
(A) 자기 생각을 공유한다.
(B) 저녁을 만든다.
(C) 사무실로 돌아간다.
(D) 친구를 만난다.

63 【신유형】 상영표에 의하면, 남자는 몇 시 영화를 볼 것인가?
(A) 5:30
(B) 5:40
(C) 7:50
(D) 8:00

64 Brave And Braver는 어떤 종류의 영화인가?
(A) 코미디
(B) 다큐멘터리
(C) 드라마
(D) 공상 과학

Questions 65–67 refer to the following conversation and survey. 〔◁) 미국…캐나다〕 【신유형】

M Rachel, we've gotten the results of our customer satisfaction survey back and I'm not too pleased about some of the comments.

W Oh, really, Mr. Danvers? Which ones are concerning to you?

M Well, for example, 65"poor quality of cleaning" from Anderson& Associates.

W Right. 66I spoke with Mr. Anderson and explained we had a new person in training at that time and it wouldn't happen again.

M 67What about this one, "schedule problems"? We can surely do something about that.

W Of course. 67I will call the customer right away and work out a better timetable for them.

남 Rachel, 자사 고객 만족도 조사결과를 받았어요. 몇몇 의견에 대해서는 그다지 만족스럽지 않네요.

여 정말요, Danvers씨? 어떤 것들이 맘에 걸리시나요?

남 예를 들면, 65Anderson&Associates에서는 '형편없는 청소상태'라고 했어요.

여 맞아요. 66제가 Anderson씨와 이야기하면서 당시 교육 중인 신규 직원이 있었다고 설명했고, 다시는 이런 일이 없을 거라고 얘기했어요.

남 67'일정 문제'라는 건 뭔가요? 이건 꼭 처리해야 할 것 같은데요.

여 물론이죠. 67지금 바로 고객에게 전화해서 더 나은 일정을 잡도록 할게요.

고객 만족도 조사	
업체	의견
Anderson&Associates	형편없는 청소 상태
67Blackmoor, Inc.	일정 문제
Parker&Sons	너무 비쌈
Vesper Group	항시 만족

어휘 satisfaction survey 만족도 조사 comment 의견 work out ~를 생각해내다

---

65 화자들은 어떤 업종에서 일하는가?
(A) 청소 업체
(B) 법률 회사
(C) 대여 업체
(D) 훈련소

66 형편없다는 평에 대해 여자가 설명하는 것은 무엇인가?
(A) 게으른 직원들
(B) 질이 낮은 용품
(C) 신규 경영
(D) 미숙한 직원

67 【신유형】 조사표에 의하면, 여자는 곧 누구에게 전화할 것인가?
(A) Anderson&Associates
(B) Blackmoor, Inc.
(C) Parker&Sons
(D) Vesper Group

어휘 rental agency 대여 업체

Questions 68-70 refer to the following conversation and coupon. (<)) 호주…미국) 신 유 형

W　Hello, <u>68,69 I'd like to reserve two spots for your full package spa treatment tomorrow.</u>

M　Tomorrow, let me see—we only have time in the afternoon. Would that be okay?

W　Yes. Actually, the later the better since I have to work until 4:30.

M　Fine, then <u>69 I'll put you down for 5:00.</u> Do you have any coupons?

W　Oh, yes, I almost forgot about that. <u>68 I have the coupon on my phone.</u>

M　Great. Just show it when you pay.

W　Thanks. <u>70 My co-worker and I are really looking forward to getting your full package.</u>

여　여보세요? 68,69내일 풀 패키지 스파 트리트먼트 두 자리를 예약하고 싶은데요.

남　내일이요? 잠시만요…. 오후에만 예약이 가능한데, 괜찮으신가요?

여　네, 늦을수록 좋아요. 제가 4시 30분까지 일을 하거든요.

남　좋아요. 그러면 695시로 예약을 잡아드릴게요. 할인권이 있으신가요?

여　아, 그러네요. 깜빡할 뻔했네요. 68제 휴대폰에 쿠폰이 있어요.

남　좋아요. 계산할 때 보여주시면 됩니다.

여　감사합니다. 70제 동료와 저는 풀 패키지를 정말 기대하고 있어요.

```
        Serenity 스파 서비스 선택
  ◦마사지 …………… 50달러
  ◦얼굴 관리 ………… 35달러
  ◦손 관리 …………… 25달러
  ◦발 관리 …………… 20달러

68이 온라인 쿠폰을 보여주시고 풀 패키지
를 100달러에 이용하세요.
```

어휘 treatment (청결·보호를 위한) 처리

68 쿠폰에 의하면, 여자는 얼마를 지불할 것
신 유 형 인가?
(A) 25달러
(B) 35달러
(C) 50달러
(D) 100달러

69 여자는 언제 트리트먼트를 받는가?
(A) 오늘 4시 30분
(B) 오늘 5시
(C) 내일 4시 30분
(D) 내일 5시

70 여자는 누구를 데리고 갈 것인가?
(A) 남편
(B) 직장 동료
(C) 딸
(D) 엄마

PART 4

Questions 71-73 refer to the following talk. (◁)) 호주)

Thank you all for your help today. Digitizing all of the library's resources is a big job. Obviously, **72we need more volunteers to help, so if you know of anyone, let me know.** **71I'll be holding an information session for new volunteers next week here at City Library.** It should only take two hours or so to show people how to use the scanner and software. Of course, there's no pay, but we have plenty of free parking and **73some local restaurants have offered to deliver lunches to our volunteers.**

오늘 여러분의 도움에 감사드립니다. 71도서관의 모든 자료를 디지털화하는 것은 큰일입니다. 분명한 것은, 72우리는 더 많은 자원봉사자들의 도움이 필요하니 자원봉사할 누군가를 알고 계시다면 저에게 알려주세요. 71다음 주에 이곳 시립 도서관에서 신입자원봉사자들을 위한 설명회가 열립니다. 스캐너와 소프트웨어를 사용하는 방법을 보여주는 데 두 시간 정도 걸릴 것입니다. 보수는 지급되지 않지만, 무료 주차장이 많고 73지역 식당 몇 군데에서 자원봉사자들에게 점심 배달을 지원해주고 있습니다.

어휘 digitize (정보를) 디지털화하다 resource 자원 information session 설명회

71 화자는 어디에 있는가?
(A) 주민센터
(B) 시청
(C) 컴퓨터 수리점
(D) 도서관

72 화자는 청자들에게 무엇을 요청하는가?
(A) 소프트웨어에 대해 배우기
(B) 점심 배달하기
(C) 더 많은 자원봉사자들 모집하기
(D) 기기 다루기

73 지역 업체에서 제공하는 것은 무엇인가?
(A) 컴퓨터 수업
(B) 할인 쿠폰
(C) 무료 소프트웨어
(D) 식사

Questions 74-76 refer to the following recorded message. (◁)) 미국)

74Thank you for calling the Chelsea Fun Park information line. The Chelsea Fun Park is open seven days a week from 10:00 AM to 7:00 PM. **75We are closed on some national holidays except in the summer months, June through August. We also close once a month for maintenance.** A list of closing days is listed on our Website at www.chelseafunpark.com. If you wish to hear a listing of special events, please press "1". For information about accessibility and facilities for families, please press "2". **76For prices and group discounts, please press "3".**

74Chelsea 유원지 안내센터에 전화해주셔서 감사합니다. Chelsea 유원지는 일주일 내내 오전 10시부터 오후 7시까지 운영합니다. 75저희는 여름 기간인 6월부터 8월은 제외하고 일부 국경일에 문을 열지 않습니다. 또한 유지 관리를 위해 한 달에 한 번씩 문을 닫습니다. 문을 닫는 날은 저희 웹사이트 www.chelseafunpark.com에 게시되어 있습니다. 특별 행사에 대해 듣고 싶으시면 1번을 눌러주세요. 접근성과 가족 시설에 대한 정보는 2번을 눌러주세요. 76가격 및 단체 할인은 3번을 눌러주세요.

어휘 seven days a week 일주일 내내 national holiday 국경일 maintenance 유지보수 accessibility 접근(성)

74 메시지는 어떤 업종을 위한 것인가?
(A) 놀이동산
(B) 주민센터
(C) 어린이 극장
(D) 학교

75 여름철에는 며칠 동안 문을 닫는가?
(A) 하루
(B) 이틀
(C) 사흘
(D) 닫지 않는다.

76 입장권 가격에 대한 정보를 들으려면 어떻게 해야 하는가?
(A) 1번을 누른다.
(B) 2번을 누른다.
(C) 3번을 누른다.
(D) 웹사이트를 방문한다.

Questions 77-79 refer to the following advertisement. (🔊 캐나다)

Thinking of taking a trip? Forget the hassle of the airport and the crowds at train stations. ⁷⁷Travel with us on Blue Star Bus Lines. When you use Blue Star, just show up at any of our conveniently located terminals, many of which feature free park-and-ride services, and leave the driving to us. ⁷⁸Blue Star also offers flexible ticketing. If you want to return early or stop over at a different city, you can change your ticket with no penalty up to 24 hours in advance. ⁷⁹For more information, including testimonials from satisfied customers, please visit our Website, www.bluestarbuses.com.

여행을 고려하고 계신가요? 혼잡한 공항과 붐비는 기차역은 잊으세요. ⁷⁷Blue Star 버스와 함께 여행하세요. Blue Star 버스를 이용하실 때에는, 편리한 곳에 위치한 저희 터미널로 오기만 하세요. 터미널에서는 무료 주차 환승 서비스를 이용하시고 운전은 저희에게 맡겨주세요. ⁷⁸Blue Star는 또한 유연한 발권 서비스를 제공합니다. 일찍 돌아오거나 다른 도시에 들르고 싶다면, 24시간 전에는 어떠한 위약금 없이 승차권을 변경하실 수 있습니다. ⁷⁹만족하신 고객들의 추천글을 포함하여 더 많은 정보를 원하시면 저희 웹사이트 www.bluestarbuses.com을 방문하세요.

> **어휘** hassle 번거로운 일 park-and-ride service 주차 환승 서비스 penalty 위약금

77 무엇을 광고하는가?
(A) 비행기 여행
(B) 버스 회사
(C) 열차 여행
(D) 여행사

78 회사는 고객에게 무엇을 제공하는가?
(A) 변경 가능한 승차권
(B) 빠른 서비스
(C) 낮은 가격
(D) 많은 운행노선

79 광고에 의하면, 웹사이트에서 볼 수 있는 것은 무엇인가?
(A) 고객 후기
(B) 일정 정보
(C) 승차권 가격
(D) 관광 안내

> **어휘** changeable 바뀔 수 있는

Questions 80-82 refer to the following report. (🔊 영국)

⁸⁰I've been asked to report on the progress of the product redesign. ⁸¹Since we received feedback from customers that our travel iron was too heavy to use, the product design team has worked hard to come up with a way to fix the problem. They found a different material to make the iron, so the finished product should be about half a kilogram lighter. We hope to have the new product ready to ship to stores by the end of next month. ⁸²We are planning to send out coupons to all the customers on our mailing list at that time.

⁸⁰저는 제품 재설계 진행 상황을 보고해달라는 요청을 받았습니다. ⁸¹자사의 여행용 다리미가 사용하기에는 너무 무겁다는 고객의 피드백을 받았기 때문에 제품 디자인팀은 문제를 해결할 방법을 찾기 위해 열심히 일했습니다. 디자인팀에서 다리미를 만들 수 있는 새로운 물질을 발견하여, 완성품의 경우 약 500그램 더 가벼워졌습니다. 새 제품이 다음 달 말까지 상점에 출하될 준비가 끝나길 바랍니다. ⁸²그때에는 우리 우편물 수신자 명단에 있는 모든 고객에게 쿠폰을 보낼 계획입니다.

> **어휘** iron 다리미 come up with (해답·돈을) 찾아내다 finished product 완제품 mailing list 우편물 수신자 명단

80 무엇에 대해 보고하고 있는가?
(A) 제품 설계
(B) 제품 진열
(C) 제품 회수
(D) 제품 판매

81 화자가 언급하는 문제는 무엇인가?
(A) 색상
(B) 기능
(C) 가격
(D) 중량

82 고객은 다음 달 말에 무엇을 받을 수 있는가?
(A) 할인
(B) 피드백 양식
(C) 경품
(D) 특별 초대권

> **어휘** weight 무게

Thank you all for coming today. I will cover three main points in my lecture about making our town more eco-friendly. And then I'll be taking questions from all of you, concerned citizens. ⁸³If you don't mind holding your questions to the end, that will help me. To be honest, ⁸⁴I'm a bit nervous. It's the first time I've given this speech in front of such a large group. But I'm committed to making a difference in our community, so ⁸⁴I'm just going to bite the bullet and do this. ⁸⁵My first point is about increasing our recycling efforts.

오늘 참석해주셔서 감사합니다. 강의에서 저는 우리 마을을 좀 더 환경친화적으로 만드는 것에 대한 세 가지 주요 사항을 다룰 것입니다. 그러고 나서 관심을 가져주시는 시민 여러분의 질문을 받겠습니다. ⁸³괜찮으시다면 끝날 때까지 질문은 기다려 주시면 감사하겠습니다. 솔직히 ⁸⁴조금 긴장되네요. 이렇게 많은 사람들 앞에서 강연하는 것은 처음입니다. 하지만 저는 우리 지역에 변화를 주기 위해 최선을 다하려고 합니다. ⁸⁴그래서 저는 용기를 내서 강연할 예정입니다. ⁸⁵저의 첫 번째 요점은 재활용에 더 노력하는 것입니다.

어휘 cover (문제를) 다루다 take questions 질문을 받다 be committed to ~에 전념하다 bite the bullet 이를 악물고 하다 recycling 재활용

83 청자들에게 요청하는 것은 무엇인가?
(A) 화자에 대해 인내심을 갖기
(B) 끝나면 화자에게 박수를 보내기
(C) 사진 촬영을 자제하기
(D) 질문은 기다렸다가 하기

84 화자는 왜 I'm just going to bite the bullet and do this라고 말하는가?
(A) 그녀는 곧 점심을 먹을 것이다.
(B) 그녀는 긴장되지만 강연하려고 한다.
(C) 그녀는 청중들이 어떻게 생각하는지 듣고 싶다.
(D) 그녀는 도시 내 폭력을 멈추고 싶다.

85 다음으로 화자는 무엇에 대해 이야기할 것인가?
(A) 사람들을 투표에 참여시키는 방법
(B) 도시의 문제 해결 방법
(C) 지역 학교의 개선 방안
(D) 불필요한 물품의 재활용 방법

어휘 clap 손뼉을 치다 refrain from ~를 삼가다 violence 폭력 unwanted 원치 않는

Hi, this message is for Wendell Jasper. This is Frederick Booker from Booker Manufacturing. I'm pleased to hear you liked the design and quality of the luggage handles you ordered from us a few months ago. But, well, ⁸⁶this current order for lock components has me a bit concerned. As you know, ⁸⁷we're a relatively small operation—only 20 full-time staff and technicians working the equipment. Uh, so your order of 6,000 units by the end of the summer is going to be a challenge. ⁸⁸After all, that's only six weeks away. Give me a call back at your earliest convenience to discuss this. Thanks.

안녕하세요, Wendell Jasper씨에게 메시지를 남깁니다. 저는 Booker 제조회사의 Frederick Booker입니다. 몇 달 전에 저희에게 주문하신 가방 손잡이의 디자인과 품질이 마음에 드셨다니 기쁩니다. 하지만 ⁸⁶이번 잠금장치 부품 주문건은 제가 좀 걱정스럽습니다. 고객님도 아시다시피 저희는 장비를 운용하는 정규 직원과 기술자가 총 20명에 불과한 ⁸⁷비교적 작은 사업장입니다. 그래서 이번 여름 안에 고객님의 주문 6천 개를 처리하는 것은 쉽지 않을 것 같습니다. ⁸⁸겨우 6주밖에 남지 않았습니다. 이 문제를 논의하기 위해 가능한 빨리 저에게 전화를 주세요. 감사합니다.

어휘 component 부품 relatively 비교적 operation 사업(체) full-time staff 상근 직원 after all 결국에는 at your earliest convenience 가급적 빨리

86 청자는 화자에게 무엇을 부탁했는가?
(A) 장비 설계
(B) 가방 설계
(C) 일부 손잡이 제작
(D) 일부 잠금장치 제작

87 화자의 사업에 대해 언급된 것은 무엇인가?
(A) 디자인상을 받았다.
(B) 사업을 해외로 확장하고 있다.
(C) 자금난을 겪고 있다.
(D) 큰 회사가 아니다.

88 화자의 말 After all, that's only six weeks away가 암시하는 것은 무엇인가?
(A) 마감일이 촉박하다.
(B) 주문이 곧 완료된다.
(C) 일정이 완벽하다.
(D) 여름이 너무 빨리 지나간다.

Questions 89–91 refer to the following excerpt from a meeting. (◁) 캐나다)

Okay, let's move on to the next item. ⁸⁹What I'm about to say shouldn't be a surprise to anyone. We've been trying to save on our office costs, as you know, by reducing our electricity and paper usage. I noticed recently that we spend a lot of unnecessary money on color copies. ⁹⁰I'd like to ask that for in-house documents, you only use black ink. Of course, for presentations, if you absolutely need to have a graphic or picture in color, go ahead. But otherwise, ⁹¹please change your print function settings to "black and white only" the next time you print.

좋아요. 다음 안건으로 넘어가죠. ⁸⁹제가 지금 하려는 말은 누구도 놀랄 일이 아닐 겁니다. 아시다시피 우리는 전기와 종이 사용량을 줄임으로써 사무실 비용을 절감하려고 노력했습니다. 최근에 저는 우리가 컬러 복사에 불필요하게 많은 돈을 쓰고 있다는 것을 알게 되었습니다. ⁹⁰사내 문서는 검은색 잉크만 사용하시면 됩니다. 물론 프레젠테이션을 위해 도표나 컬러 사진이 꼭 필요한 경우에는 사용하십시오. 하지만 그렇지 않으면 다음에 인쇄할 때에는 ⁹¹프린터 인쇄 기능 설정을 '흑백'으로 변경해주세요.

89 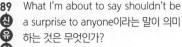 What I'm about to say shouldn't be a surprise to anyone이라는 말이 의미하는 것은 무엇인가?
(A) 회사가 돈을 절약하려고 하는 것은 이번이 처음이 아니다.
(B) 화자가 그 이야기를 다시 언급을 하는 것은 예상치 못한 일이다.
(C) 청자들은 방금 전까지도 그 정책에 대해 잘 알지 못했다.
(D) 청자들은 화자가 한 말을 잊었을 수도 있다.

90 화자는 어떤 불필요한 비용을 줄이려 하는가?
(A) 컬러 토너
(B) 전기
(C) 종이
(D) 컴퓨터 서버

91 화자는 청자들에게 컴퓨터로 무엇을 하라고 요청하는가?
(A) 설정 변경하기
(B) 비밀번호 재설정하기
(C) 백업 서버에 파일 저장하기
(D) 새 프린터 사용하기

Questions 92–94 refer to the following introduction. (◁) 영국)

Thank you all for coming to ⁹²this seminar today about increasing your company's Website traffic. Even if you've had a Web presence for a while, I'll be teaching you some new tricks to get some more clicks. ⁹³Over the last 15 years. I've helped hundreds of businesses with their Websites, so I'm sure you'll learn a lot today. In the first hour, I'll give a presentation about getting new people to your site. Then, in the next hour, I'll talk about keeping customers once they've visited your site. Of course, ⁹⁴if you have any questions, go ahead and interrupt me. Well, let's get started.

⁹²여러분 회사의 웹사이트 방문자 수를 증가시키기 위한 오늘 세미나에 참석해주신 모든 분께 감사드립니다. 한동안 웹사이트를 유지해오셨겠지만, 더 많은 클릭을 유도하는 몇 가지 새로운 비법을 알려드리겠습니다. ⁹³지난 15년 동안, 저는 수 백여 기업들의 웹사이트와 관련해 도움을 줬습니다. 그래서 저는 오늘 여러분이 많은 것을 배워갈 것이라고 확신합니다. 처음 한 시간은 웹사이트에 신규 방문자가 오도록 하는 것에 대해 설명하겠습니다. 그다음 한 시간은 고객이 여러분의 웹사이트 방문 후에도 계속 이용할 수 있도록 하는 법에 대해서 말씀드리겠습니다. ⁹⁴질문이 있으시다면 언제든지 질문하세요. 그럼 시작하겠습니다.

92 무엇에 관한 세미나인가?
(A) 신규 웹사이트 구축
(B) 현지 업체 지원
(C) 웹사이트 방문자 수 증가
(D) 웹사이트 업데이트

93 화자가 자신의 경험에 대해 언급한 것은 무엇인가?
(A) 15년 전에 자신의 첫 번째 웹사이트를 만들었다.
(B) 오랫동안 업체들을 도왔다.
(C) 웹디자인으로 상을 받았다.
(D) 세미나에 참석하여 새로운 기술을 배웠다.

94 발표 도중에 청자들이 무엇을 하도록 권장되는가?
(A) 질문하기
(B) 제안하기
(C) 필기하기
(D) 녹음장치 사용하기

Questions 95–97 refer to the following telephone message and chart. (◁)) 호주

Hi, I have a question about a pair of shoes I ordered from your online store. I received them yesterday but unfortunately, they don't fit. ⁹⁶I'm a size 7 here in the US and I ordered the correct size, according to the size conversion chart on your Website. But it seems I need one size up. ⁹⁵I'm wondering, how soon can I get a larger pair sent to me if I return these today? ⁹⁷I'm leaving on a business trip next week and I'd really like to have these comfortable shoes since I'll be doing a lot of walking. Please call me back at 555-2839.

안녕하세요? 제가 그쪽 온라인 상점에서 주문한 신발에 대해 문의할 게 있습니다. 어제 상품을 받았는데, 신발 치수가 맞지 않아요. ⁹⁶웹사이트에 나와 있는 치수 변환표에 의하면 저는 미국 치수로 7이고, 저는 정확한 사이즈를 주문했습니다. 하지만 저한테는 한 치수 위의 신발이 필요한 것 같네요. ⁹⁵궁금한 것은, 이 상품을 오늘 반품하면 언제쯤 교환 상품이 도착할까요? ⁹⁷제가 다음 주에 출장을 가는데 그곳에서 많이 걸을 예정이어서 편안한 이 신발이 꼭 필요합니다. 555-2839로 연락주세요.

신발 사이즈 일람표	
미국	유럽
6	36
7	38
⁹⁶8	40
9	42

어휘 conversion 변환

95 화자가 전화를 한 이유는 무엇인가?
(A) 환불을 요청하려고
(B) 반품 정보를 받으려고
(C) 치수표를 요청하려고
(D) 여행 일정을 변경하려고

96 일람표에 의하면, 화자는 어떤 신발 사이즈가 필요한가?
(A) 36
(B) 38
(C) 40
(D) 42

97 화자는 곧 어디에 갈 예정인가?
(A) 캠핑 여행
(B) 유람선 여행
(C) 도보 여행
(D) 출장

Questions 98–100 refer to the following telephone message and information. 🔊 미국

Hello. This message is for Penelope Morris. ⁹⁸My name is Stanley Evans, head administrator at City Hospital. I received your e-mail about wanting a tour of the hospital for your group of city officials. ⁹⁹I would be happy to lead that for you. Of the dates you gave, next Wednesday at 3:00 is the best for me. Please confirm by phone or e-mail with the group number. To answer your other question, yes, we have free monthly seminars for the public. ¹⁰⁰It sounds like you'd be interested in the one called Healthy Diets for a Long Life. Look on our Website for more details. Looking forward to meeting you soon, Penelope.

안녕하세요? Penelope Morris에게 메시지를 남깁니다. ⁹⁸저는 시립 병원의 수석 관리자인 Stanley Evans입니다. 시청 관계자로 구성된 단체가 병원 견학을 하고 싶다는 귀하의 이메일을 받았습니다. ⁹⁹기꺼이 안내해드리겠습니다. 귀하께서 제시한 날짜 중에서 다음 주 수요일 3시가 가장 좋을 것 같습니다. 전화나 이메일로 참석 인원을 확인해주세요. 귀하의 다른 질문에 답변을 드리자면, 그렇습니다. 저희는 일반인을 위한 월간 무료 세미나를 열고 있습니다. ¹⁰⁰귀하는 '장수를 위한 건강식' 세미나에 관심이 있으실 것 같네요. 자세한 내용은 저희 웹사이트를 참조하세요. 귀하를 뵙기를 기대하고 있습니다.

일반인을 위한 무료 세미나

시립 병원 후원

5. 22.	모두를 위한 운동
¹⁰⁰6. 19.	장수를 위한 건강식
7. 24.	휴가 중에도 건강한 식사하기
8. 21.	행복 유지하기

어휘 head administrator 수석 관리자 public 일반인 sponsor 후원하다

---

98 화자는 누구인가?
(A) 관리자
(B) 의사
(C) 시 공무원
(D) 여행사 직원

99 다음 주에 화자는 청자를 위해 무엇을 할 예정인가?
(A) 투어 안내하기
(B) 파티 주최하기
(C) 수술하기
(D) 세미나에서 강연하기

100 일정에 의하면, Morris씨는 언제 세미나에 참석할 것으로 보이는가?
(A) 5월 22일
(B) 6월 19일
(C) 7월 24일
(D) 8월 21일

어휘 operation 수술

PART 5

101

호텔 Lila의 온라인 후기에는 요금이 너무 비싸다는 불만이 있었지만 Smith씨 부부는 요금이 적당하다고 생각했다.

(A) 과도한 　　　　　　　(B) 고급의
(C) 적당한 　　　　　　　(D) 귀중한

어휘 rate 요금 excessive 과도한 reasonable 적당한 valuable 귀중한

102

TSG 출판사에서 새 아동 도서 시리즈에 그림을 그릴 수 있는 경험 많은 삽화가를 찾고 있습니다.

(A) 삽화를 넣다 　　　　　(B) 삽화를 넣은
(C) 삽화 　　　　　　　　(D) 삽화가

어휘 illustrator 삽화가

103

Sophie Anderson은 고등학교를 졸업한 직후 자신의 사업인 Real Wear사를 시작했다.

(A) 그녀의 　　　　　　　(B) 그녀의 것
(C) 그녀 자신 　　　　　　(D) 그녀는

104

야간 근무자 자리에 지원하시려면 온라인 지원서를 작성해주십시오.

(A) 고용 　　　　　　　　(B) 의무
(C) 자리 　　　　　　　　(D) 책임

어휘 apply for ~에 지원하다 employment 고용 responsibility 책임

105

조사 결과, 참가자의 95퍼센트 이상이 자신과 관련 없는 정보나 홍보를 받았다고 했다.

(A) 연관성 　　　　　　　(B) 적합성
(C) 관련 있는 　　　　　　(D) 관련되어

어휘 relevant 관련 있는, 적절한

106

건물의 증축이 거의 끝나가므로 우리는 개관식을 계획해야 할 것입니다.

(A) ~하는 한 　　　　　　(B) 비록 ~일지라도
(C) ~이면 좋을 텐데 　　　(D) ~이므로

107

Suri 테크의 제품은 품질이 뛰어날 뿐만 아니라, 대부분의 이름 있는 브랜드의 제품보다 훨씬 더 경제적이다.

(A) 모든 　　　　　　　　(B) 매우
(C) 훨씬 　　　　　　　　(D) 매우

어휘 economical 실속 있는 brand-name 상표가 붙은

108

셔틀버스는 아침 9시부터 저녁 8시까지 쇼핑몰과 중앙역 사이를 계속해서 운행한다.

(A) 지속 　　　　　　　　(B) 계속되는
(C) 지속적인 　　　　　　(D) 계속해서

어휘 continuously 계속해서

109

총무과에서 회사 야유회를 취소할지 연기할지 결정하는 데 어려움을 겪고 있다.

(A) 전에 　　　　　　　　(B) 심지어 ~조차
(C) ~한 것 　　　　　　　(D) ~인지 아닌지

어휘 administrative affairs 행정사무

110

영업담당자는 중요 고객과의 오찬에 사장과 동행하라는 말을 듣고 기뻤지만 긴장했다.

(A) 동행하다 　　　　　　(B) 완수하다
(C) 포함하다 　　　　　　(D) 포함하다

어휘 luncheon 오찬 accompany 동행하다 involve 포함하다

111

Matt Bender는 경리과로 부서 이동을 한 후, 전산 소프트웨어를 익히는 데 시간이 좀 필요했다.

(A) acquaint 　　　　　　(B) acquainted
(C) acquainting 　　　　 (D) acquaints

어휘 payroll 급료 지불 명부 get acquainted with ~를 익히다

112

John Harris는 조직에 기여한 공으로 회사 3년차에 부장으로 승진했다.

(A) 기여하다 　　　　　　(B) 기부된
(C) 기여하는 　　　　　　(D) 기여

어휘 promote 승진시키다 contribution 기여, 이바지

113

성과급은 개인의 실적에 따라 매년 6월과 12월 두 번 지급될 예정이다.

(A) 배경 　　　　　　　　(B) 재정
(C) 점검 　　　　　　　　(D) 실적

어휘 finance 재정 performance 실적

114

디자인 대회의 우승자가 발표되는 날짜는 아직 정확하게 정해지지 않았다.

(A) when 　　　　　　　　(B) where
(C) which 　　　　　　　(D) whose

어휘 exact 정확한

115

인터넷상의 수천 개의 자료들을 <u>검색할</u> 때에는 원하는 결과를 얻기 위해 종종 몇 가지 기술이 필요하다.

(A) beneath
(B) over
(C) through
(D) under

어휘 beneath 아래에 search through ~를 검색하다

116

후보자는 그 직책에 <u>충분한</u> 경험이 있지만, 인사 부장은 그가 긍정적인 태도가 부족하다고 생각했다.

(A) 거대한
(B) 충분한
(C) 전문적인
(D) 추가의

어휘 lack ~이 없다 enormous 거대한

117

<u>기술적으로</u> 말해서, 이 나라의 바이오 연료 산업은 지난 수십 년 동안 크게 발전해왔다.

(A) 기술적인
(B) 기술적으로
(C) 기술들
(D) 기술

어휘 biofuel 바이오 연료

118

마케팅 부장은 기술자가 나타나기를 기다리기<u>보다는</u> 스스로 자기 컴퓨터의 문제를 해결하려고 했다.

(A) 더 좋은
(B) 나중에
(C) ~라기 보다
(D) 다른

119

전무이사는 현지 직원들로부터 <u>후한</u> 대우를 받았기 때문에 지방 지점으로의 출장을 매우 즐겼다.

(A) 효과적으로
(B) 특히
(C) 일반적으로
(D) 관대하게

어휘 treat 대하다 effectively 효과적으로 generously 후하게

120

Elton사가 그 땅을 적정 가격에 구매한다면 그들은 연말까지 새로운 장소로 <u>이전할</u> 것이다.

(A) have been moved
(B) moved
(C) are moved
(D) will move

121

임금 인상 협상이 합의에 이르지 못하자, 노조는 선택지의 여지 없이 파업에 <u>들어갈</u> 수밖에 없었다.

(A) 시작하다
(B) 착수
(C) 처음의
(D) 처음에

어휘 wage-hike 임금 인상 union 조합 strike 파업 initiate ~에 착수하다

122

수년간의 침체 끝에 물류업계에 약간의 회복 <u>기미</u>가 보인다.

(A) 암시
(B) 인상
(C) 조짐
(D) 중재

어휘 struggle 몸부림 recovery 회복 logistics 물류 implication 암시 indication 조짐 intervention 중재

123

Acro Hill 호텔에서 투숙객들은 옥상 테라스의 장관을 즐기며 편안히 <u>지내실</u> 수 있습니다.

(A) enjoy
(B) enjoyed
(C) enjoying
(D) enjoys

어휘 magnificent 멋진, 장대한

124

두 팀은 회의에서 탁자 <u>맞은편</u>에 앉아 각자의 계획을 관철시키기 위해 노력하고 있었다.

(A) 서로 대립되는
(B) 반대하다
(C) 맞은편의
(D) 반대

어휘 push through (강행하여) 통과시키다 oppose 반대하다 opposite 맞은편의

125

그 전국 슈퍼마켓 체인점은 자사의 90개 매장 중 50개 매장을 경쟁업체에 판매함으로써 부채를 <u>상쇄하려고</u> 했다.

(A) 청구하다
(B) 입력하다
(C) 상쇄하다
(D) 풀어주다

어휘 seek to ~ 하려고 (시도)하다 debt 부채 charge 청구하다 input 입력하다 offset 상쇄하다

126

업계의 최신 기술에 <u>뒤지지 않기</u> 위해 그 자동차 회사의 사장은 여러 권의 전문 잡지를 정기적으로 읽는다.

(A) along
(B) for
(C) to
(D) with

어휘 keep up with (뉴스·유행을) 알다

127

제약 회사의 보고서에 의하면, <u>대략</u> 세 명 중 한 명꼴로 식품 알레르기가 있는 것으로 추정된다.

(A) 거친
(B) 대충 만드는 사람
(C) 대략
(D) 거칠

어휘 estimate 추산하다 rough 거친 roughly 대략

128

노련한 판매원은 6개월 동안 신입직원을 <u>열정적으로</u> 지도했고, 그를 놀랄 만한 성과로 이끌었다.

(A) 열정적으로
(B) 정기적으로
(C) 비교적
(D) 잠재적으로

어휘 mentor 지도하다 enthusiastically 열정적으로 periodically 정기적으로 potentially 잠재적으로

129
Mildred 병원은 환자 치료 결과와 최첨단 시설 분야에서 국내 최고의 수준이다.

(A) ~ 중에   (B) 높이
(C) ~하는 경우에   (D) ~라는 것

어휘 state-of-the-art 최신의 rank among ~ 사이에 자리 잡다

130
그 자신이 숙련된 조종사인 Jeff Long은 비행 학교의 교관이자 항공 잡지의 칼럼니스트이기도 하다.

(A) 그는   (B) 그를
(C) 그 자신   (D) 그의

어휘 skilled 숙련된 aviation 항공

PART 6

131-134 (안내문)

Eat Healthy, Be Active 커뮤니티 워크숍 시리즈

Eat Healthy, Be Active 커뮤니티 워크숍 시리즈는 정부의 <건강과 체력에 대한 식생활 지침>을 바탕으로 영양사들과 운동 131전문가들에 의해 개발되었습니다. 이 시리즈의 6개 워크숍에는 132각각 학습계획, 학습목표, 실습, 비디오 및 인쇄물이 포함됩니다. 이 워크숍은 다양한 지역사회에서 지역 교육자, 건강증진 전문가, 영양사, 기타 성인을 대상으로 교육하는 사람들을 위해 설계되었습니다. 이 워크숍은 6월간 River시 주민센터에서 주말마다 무료로 제공됩니다. 133모든 참가자는 시리즈 완료 후에 평생교육 수료증을 받습니다. 센터나 온라인 www.rivercitycommcenter.org134에서 등록하세요.

어휘 develop 개발하다 learning objective 학습 목표 hands-on 직접 해보는 nutritionist 영양사 a wide variety of 매우 다양한 enroll 등록하다

131
(A) 특별한   (B) 전문가들
(C) 전공하다   (D) 전공하는 것

어휘 specialize 전공하다

132
(A) (수가) 적은   (B) 각각
(C) 모든   (D) 총

133 신유형
(A) 모든 참가자는 시리즈 완료 후에 평생교육 수료증을 받습니다.
(B) 주민센터의 수업의 질을 높이기 위한 의견이나 제안은 언제든지 환영합니다.
(C) 보수공사가 예상보다 오래 걸릴 것 같아서 일부 수업을 취소해야 했습니다.
(D) 저희 센터에서는 현재 현금뿐만 아니라 모든 주요 신용카드를 받습니다.

어휘 continuing education 평생교육

134
(A) ~를 위해   (B) ~의 곁에서
(C) ~에서   (D) ~ 쪽으로

135-138 (이메일)

수신: Gina Caruso
발신: Yuki Madison
날짜: 7월 5일
제목: 공연 요청

Caruso씨께
저는 지난밤 Bluebird 카페의 관객이었고 당신의 어쿠스틱 기타와 피아노 곡에 135매우 감명받았습니다. 저는 Starling시에서 열리는 연례 음악 축제에 음악가들을 섭외하는 일을 하는데, 방금 연주자 중 한 명이 참석을 136취소했습니다. 긴급한 요청이라는 것을 알지만 137만약 그녀를 대신해서 귀하가 참가해주신다면 정말 감사하겠습니다. 138출연료 제안 및 기타 세부 사항들에 관한 서류를 첨부했습니다. 검토하신 후 가능한 빨리 저에게 연락주실 수 있겠습니까?
Yuki Madison
Starling 시 음악축제 조직위원

어휘 performance 공연 step in for ~를 대신해서 하다 eternally 영원히

135
(A) 거의 ~아닌   (B) 거의
(C) 고르게   (D) 매우

어휘 evenly 고르게 deeply 깊이, 매우

136
(A) 취소하다   (B) 지속하다
(C) 연주하다   (D) 참석하다

137
(A) ~하는 바로 그 순간에   (B) 만약 ~라면
(C) ~ 때문에   (D) 게다가

138 신유형
(A) 저는 금요일까지 사무실에 없지만 메시지는 확인하겠습니다.
(B) 출연료 제안 및 기타 세부 사항들에 관한 서류를 첨부했습니다.
(C) 이 축제는 7월 30일과 31일 사이에 Starling 시립 공원에서 열립니다.
(D) 콘서트에 대해 고려 중인 다른 가수가 세 명 더 있습니다.

어휘 fee 보수, 사례

139-142 (안내문)

Valley Ridge 터널 주말 지연

Valley Ridge 시 토목과에서 진행 중인 Valley Ridge 터널 복구 및 보수 공사로 인하여, 여름이 끝날 때까지 32번, 89번, 171번, 482번 고속버스의 주말 운행은 양방향 운행에 상당한 지연이 139예상됩니다.

터널 ¹⁴⁰수리로 인해 한 개의 통로가 일시적으로 폐쇄되며, 남은 통로로 양방향 통행이 이루어집니다. ¹⁴¹결과적으로, 한 차선만이 각 방향에서 개방될 것입니다. 금요일 밤 시를 빠져나가는 교통이 특히 혼잡할 것으로 예상되니, 자차 운전자이든 대중교통 이용객이든 ¹⁴²추가 이동 시간을 고려해주세요.

어휘 significant 커다란 accommodate 충당하다

139
(A) expect (B) expected
(C) expecting (D) expects

140
(A) 수리 (B) 서비스
(C) 폐쇄 (D) 교통

어휘 shutdown 폐쇄

141 신유형
(A) 결과적으로, 한 차선만이 각 방향에서 개방될 것입니다.
(B) 시내버스는 이제 지정된 장소에 유모차를 태울 수 있습니다.
(C) 사실은, 최근 시 토목기사들이 Valley Ridge의 모든 도로를 조사하였습니다.
(D) 기사들은 보수 작업이 내년까지 계속될 수 있다고 말했습니다.

어휘 designated 지정된

142
(A) 추가하다 (B) 추가
(C) 추가의 (D) 추가적으로

143-146 메모
직원 여러분,
저는 최근에 4층 회의실의 상태에 대한 ¹⁴³항의를 많이 받았습니다. 분명 여러분 중 몇몇은 회의실에서 점심을 먹고 나갈 때 쓰레기를 ¹⁴⁴가져가지 않았을 것입니다. 오후에 그곳에서 회의하는 사람들을 매우 불쾌하게 만들고 있지요. 회의실 휴지통에 냄새나는 음식 쓰레기를 버리지 말아 주세요. ¹⁴⁵이런 종류의 쓰레기는 휴게실에 있는 쓰레기통을 사용하세요. 문제가 계속된다면 저는 점심시간 ¹⁴⁶동안 회의실을 잠그는 수밖에 없습니다.
감사합니다.
Timothy Reynolds 사무장

어휘 state 상태 unpleasant 불쾌한 wastebasket 휴지통

143
(A) 항의 (B) 칭찬
(C) 갈등 (D) 논란

어휘 compliment 칭찬 controversy 논란

144
(A) take (B) taken
(C) taking (D) to take

145 신유형
(A) 우리 모두가 제때 시간표를 제출하는 걸 더 잘할 수 있어요.
(B) 이런 종류의 쓰레기는 휴게실에 있는 쓰레기통을 사용하세요.
(C) 사장님이 재활용 정책의 중요성에 대해 말씀하실 거예요.
(D) 회의 음식을 맞춤 주문할 테니 빨리 주문하세요.

어휘 address 연설하다

146
(A) ~ 동안 (B) ~에
(C) ~하는 때 (D) ~하는 동안

PART 7

147-148 안내문

Robinson 공원 지역민들에게 알림

¹⁴⁷어린이용 공간의 리모델링과 무료 공연을 위한 원형극장 공사로 Olonda 공원을 일시적으로 폐장함을 알려드립니다. 전체 작업 완료까지 4~6개월 정도가 예상되며 내년 봄에 재개방 축제를 크게 열 것으로 기대하고 있습니다. 이것은 Meyer Springs 설립 100주년 기념에 맞춰 완성될 것이고, 저희는 행사를 위해서 공원에서 파티를 열 것입니다. Olonda 공원의 폐장 기간 동안 방문객들은 지역 내 학교와 가깝고 편리한 위치에 있는 Lindley 공원과 Jinat 공원을 확인하여 이용하시기를 바랍니다. ¹⁴⁸문의사항은 시장 사무실(mayorsoffice@meyersprings.gov)로 문의하시거나, 7월 5일에 있을 다음 시의회 회의에 참석해주시기를 바랍니다.

어휘 district 지역 notification 통지 amphitheater 원형극장

147
공원을 폐장하는 이유는 무엇인가?
(A) 다음 주말에 있을 큰 행사를 대비하기 위해서
(B) 개보수 및 건물을 추가하기 위해서
(C) 공원의 도로 및 보도를 보수하기 위해서
(D) 노후 시설물을 철거하기 위해서

어휘 tear down ~를 파괴하다

148
주민들은 7월 5일에 무엇을 하도록 권고받는가?
(A) 공원 내 공사에 대해 문의하기
(B) 시의 계획에 반대 의사 표명하기
(C) 신설 시립 공원에 관한 안내 책자 얻기
(D) 도시 개발의 세부 내용 듣기

어휘 opposition 항의 urban 도시의

149-150 (문자 메시지) 신유형

Mark Seagal [오후 2:43]
Tom? 거기 있어요?

Tom Hill [오후 2:45]
네. 마침 연락 주셨네요. Mark씨 고객들 중 한 명이 3시 회의에 늦는다고 전화했어요.

Mark Seagal [오후 2:46]
그래서 제가 문자를 하는 거예요. 저는 지금 75번 고속도로예요. 그런데 앞에 무슨 문제가 있는 게 분명해요. 149차가 몇 마일이나 꽉 막혀 있어요.

Tom Hill [오후 2:48]
149그럼 그분들도 같은 도로에 있나 보네요. 저한테 전화로 말했던 대로예요. 회의에 제시간에 도착하실 수 있으세요?

Mark Seagal [오후 2:49]
150못할 것 같아요. 우리 모두 회의에 늦을 것 같네요. 그분들에게 상황을 알려주세요.

Tom Hill [오후 2:50]
알았어요. 전화해서 오늘 회의를 그대로 할지, 일정을 조정할지 알아보고 알려줄게요.

Mark Seagal [오후 2:51]
좋아요. 고마워요.

> **어휘** be backed up (차가) 꽉 막히다

149
회의는 무엇 때문에 연기되었는가?
(A) 자동차 고장 때문에
(B) 교통체증 때문에
(C) 열차 지연 때문에
(D) 도로 공사 때문에

> **어휘** defer 연기하다 breakdown (차) 고장

150 신유형
오후 2시 49분에 Seagal씨가 I don't think so라고 말한 의미는 무엇인가?
(A) 그는 데이터가 부정확했다고 믿는다.
(B) 그는 회의에 제시간에 참석하지 못한다.
(C) 그는 Hill씨의 생각에 동의하지 않는다.
(D) 그는 열차가 제시간에 도착할지 의심하고 있다.

> **어휘** incorrect 부정확한 doubt 의심하다

151-152 (광고)
Waypoint가 올 가을에 새로운 미디어 플레이어 Armada 시리즈를 출시할 예정입니다. 이 최신 장비는 (저장) 공간과 선택의 폭이 넓습니다. 151직장이나 학교에서 최신 흐름을 잘 알기 위해서는 이동 중에도 가장 인기 있는 영상들을 보고 공유할 수 있는 것이 중요합니다. 그래서 모든 Armada는 HD 영상이 표준입니다. 요즘은 좋아하는 음악을 가지고 다니는 것이 중요하여, Waypoint는 음질을 잃지 않고도 저장 공간을 늘리는 방법을 찾았습니다. 가장 높은 수준의 음질로 152Armada 1은 3천 곡을 저장할 수 있습니다. 한 단계씩 올라갈 때마다 3천 곡씩 더 저장할 수 있습니다. 여러분이 최대로 음악을 저장하고 싶으시다면, Armada 5는 최고의 음질로 1만 5천 곡을 저장할 수 있습니다. 지금 사전 예약 주문을 받고 있습니다. 그러니 이 놀라운 기기를 구입할 기회를 놓치지 마세요.

> **어휘** staple 주 요소 fidelity 충실도 generate 만들어내다 pre-order 사전 예약 주문 slip through one's fingers 손가락 사이로 빠져나가다

151
Armada 시리즈에 대해 옳은 것은 무엇인가?
(A) 다양한 색상으로 구매할 수 있다.
(B) 영화를 담을 수 있다.
(C) 음악을 녹음할 수 있다.
(D) 다른 기기보다 무게가 덜 나간다.

> **어휘** weigh 무게가 ~이다

152
Armada 2에는 얼마나 많은 곡을 담을 수 있는가?
(A) 3,000곡
(B) 6,000곡
(C) 9,000곡
(D) 15,000곡

153-154 (이메일)
수신: Melissa Scroggins
발신: Harold Lloyd
날짜: 8월 4일
제목: 수업 진행

Melissa씨께
귀하의 대학에서 강의해달라는 요청 감사합니다. 고려해 볼 만한 일이긴 하지만, 지금은 귀하의 요청을 받아들일 수가 없습니다. 153현재 제 팀이 진행 중인 프로젝트를 위해 현장에 있어야 하거든요. 운이 좋으면 연초에 끝날 것입니다. 물론 장담할 수는 없습니다. 귀하의 제안이 유효하다면, 저는 내년에 가능한 날짜에 대해서 논의하고 싶습니다. 물리학에 열정적인 젊은이들을 보고, 이야기하고, 발전시켜 나가는 것은 항상 저에게 큰 즐거움을 줍니다. 연말쯤에 154제가 어떤 부분이나 주제에 대해 말하기를 원하시는지에 대한 세부 사항을 보내주시면, 저는 학생들을 위해 해야 할 것을 준비하겠습니다. 수개월의 이메일 끝에 귀하를 뵐 수 있기를 기대합니다.
Harold Lloyd 박사
Andromeda 산업 수석 천체 물리학자

> **어휘** site 현장 wrap it up 일을 끝내다 There are no guarantees. 장담할 수 없다. stand (제안이 아직도) 유효하다 passionate 열렬한 put a face to a name (이름만 알다가) 실제로 만나다

153
Lloyd 박사의 연구는 언제 완료될 예정인가?
(A) 1월
(B) 3월
(C) 8월
(D) 12월

154
Lloyd씨는 Scroggins씨에게 무엇을 요청하는가?
(A) 직접 만나서 세부 사항을 논의하기
(B) 대학에서 강의 준비하기
(C) 프로젝트 제안서에 대한 이메일을 그에게 보내기
(D) 강의에 대한 세부 사항을 그에게 보내기

155-157 (정보)
157가전제품 및 DIY에 대한 여러분의 모든 필요를 충족시키는 Cooper City의 최신 센터인 Schmidt에 오신 것을 환영합니다. 155가

게에 개점 기념 쿠폰 책자를 가져오셔서 가장 적합한 쿠폰을 골라보세요. 집에 새 가전제품을 들이시려는 경우에는 ¹⁵⁶첫 번째 쿠폰을 제시하시면 제품 가격의 15%를 절약할 수 있을 뿐만 아니라 배송도 무료입니다. 또 염두에 두신 TV가 있다면, ¹⁵⁶그다음 쿠폰을 사용하시면 무료 설치와 함께 3개월간 위성 TV 서비스가 제공됩니다! 마지막으로, 집 안에 이런저런 잔손질을 직접 하려고 하신다면 ¹⁵⁶여기 세 번째 쿠폰으로 무료 공구 세트를 받으실 수 있습니다. 필요한 것을 알려주시면 기꺼이 도와드리겠습니다. 7월 1일에 시작하는 Schmidt 개점 축하 행사에서 뵙기를 바랍니다.

어휘 booklet 소책자 suit ~에 적합하다 satellite 위성 handy 솜씨 좋은 entitle ~할 자격을 부여하다 complimentary 무료의

155
Schmidt은 왜 고객에게 쿠폰을 제공하는가?
(A) 명절 세일 주간을 시작하려고
(B) 가게의 창립 기념일을 축하하려고
(C) 가게의 영업 첫날을 기념하려고
(D) 고객에게 감사를 표시하려고

156
몇 개의 서비스가 쿠폰으로 제공되는가?
(A) 1   (B) 2
(C) 3   (D) 4

157
Schmidt에서 고객이 찾을 수 없는 품목은 무엇인가?
(A) 자동차 용품   (B) 가정용 오락기기
(C) 주방기기   (D) 페인트 붓

158-160 📧 이메일
수신: Rohm Ellington <rellington@vastmail.com>
발신: Pathway Tours <csr@pathwaytours.com>
제목: 캐나다 여행
날짜: 6월 1일

Ellington씨께
Pathway Tours를 선택해주셔서 감사합니다. ¹⁵⁸이 이메일은 귀하의 캐나다 여행에 대한 확인 이메일입니다. 귀하의 여행에 관해 문의 사항이 있으시면 언제든지 답변해드리겠습니다. 어떤 식으로든지 귀하를 도울 수 있다면 말씀해주세요. 여행 인원은 총 38명일 것으로 예상되며, 모두가 2인으로 방을 사용하시게 됩니다. 한 명 이상의 동행이 있으신 분은 가족실로 예약해드립니다. 저희는 식당과 시장 등 많은 곳을 방문할 예정이니 알레르기나 음식에 제한이 있으시다면 저에게 알려주시길 바랍니다.
여행 항공편은 오전 9시 32분에 출발하기로 예정되어 있으니, 모두 17일 오전 7시 30분까지 공항에 모이기를 요청드립니다. ¹⁵⁹문제가 생긴다면 여행 가이드 중 한 명에게 가능한 한 빨리 말씀해주시기 바랍니다. 비행기는 기다릴 수 없지만, 필요하다면 그들 중 한 명은 비행기가 도착한 후에 캐나다에서 귀하를 만날 것입니다. 도착 후 두 명의 가이드 Gina Lyons씨와 John Hogan씨가 이 여행을 이끌 예정입니다. ¹⁶⁰두 분 다 캐나다 태생이며, 대부분을 그곳에서 살았습니다. 두 가이드가 가장 인기 있는 장소뿐만 아니라 오직 지역민들만 알

고 있는 숨겨진 보물들도 보여줄 것입니다.
Pamela Strathmore
Pathway Tours 고객상담원

어휘 confirmation 확인 restriction 제약 spot 장소 hidden 숨겨진 treasure 보물 local 현지인 CSR 고객상담원

158
이메일의 주된 목적은 무엇인가?
(A) 여행 가이드에 관련한 도움을 요청하기 위해서
(B) 고객과의 여행을 확인하기 위해서
(C) 고객에게 여행을 제안하기 위해서
(D) 고객에게 항공편에 늦지 말라고 알리기 위해서

159
고객이 비행기를 놓친다면, 누가 공항에서 대기할 것인가?
(A) 현지 여행사 직원   (B) 택시 운전사
(C) 여행 가이드   (D) Strathmore씨

160
Strathmore씨는 왜 두 가이드가 이 여행에 적합하다고 생각하는가?
(A) 둘 다 이 지역의 역사 전문가이다.
(B) 매우 인내심이 많고 다른 사람들을 기다릴 줄 안다.
(C) 지방 사투리를 쓰고 번역할 수 있다.
(D) 둘 다 이 지역에서 나고 자랐다.

어휘 local dialect 지방 사투리

161-163 📋 설문지
Fair Trade 잡지는 독자분들께 잡지에 대한 의견을 요청드립니다. 저희는 매달 기사에 대해 독자분들이 무엇이 좋고 싫은지 알고 싶습니다. 의견을 받는 기한이 끝날 때에는 무작위로 선정된 참가자들 중 세 명에게 상품을 드립니다. 작성된 양식을 보내주시는 모든 분들이 상품 추첨에 참여하실 수 있습니다.

Q. 잡지에서 가장 좋아하는 섹션은 무엇입니까?
A. 저희 회사는 여러 나라에 지사를 두고 있기 때문에 ¹⁶¹저는 세계 곳곳에서 열리는 회의에 참석해야 합니다. 따라서 비즈니스 에티켓 섹션은 반드시 읽어야 합니다. 제가 좋아하는 또 다른 섹션은 가장 큰 섹션인 월간 보고입니다. 그 섹션은 산업 리더의 관점에서 보는 사업 마인드에 대해 매우 가치 있는 통찰력을 줍니다.

Q. 좋아하지 않는 섹션이 있습니까?
A. ¹⁶²쓸모없는 섹션은 커버스토리라고 생각합니다. 보통은 자신들이 어떻게 성공했는지에 대해서 잘 말해주지 않는 거물급 인사나 기업의 사장에 대한 허튼 글입니다. 보통 그 섹션은 그 인사가 휴가 중에 무엇을 하는지만 자세히 설명합니다. CEO나 고위경영진이 아닌 사람들은 그 부분을 읽고 싶지 않습니다. 이 섹션을 매일 열심히 일하는 보통 사람들의 기사로 대체하는 것은 어떨까요? 이 잡지가 가능하게 만드는 저희 같은 사람들을 대변해주시길 바랍니다.

Q. 저희 잡지를 개선할 수 있는 다른 방법이 있습니까?
A. 웹사이트가 잡지와 함께 운영되므로 ¹⁶³잡지 구독자를 위한 보너스 혜택은 어떤가요? 웹사이트의 회원 섹션에 접속할 수 있도록 하거나, 주간 뉴스 업데이트나 판매 전략에 대한 뉴스를 제공하는 특별 기

사에 접속할 수 있도록 말입니다.

161
독자가 에티켓 페이지에서 즐겨 읽는 것은 무엇인가?
(A) 타국가의 직원들이 일하는 법
(B) 다른 업체들이 일하는 법
(C) 익숙하지 않은 상황에서 행동하는 법
(D) 신규 고객을 환영하는 법

162
독자는 왜 주요 기사가 유용하지 않다고 생각하는가?
(A) 충분한 정보를 제공하지 않는다.
(B) 유명 인사들을 소개하지 않는다.
(C) 일반 독자에게는 너무 전문적이다.
(D) 쉬운 주제만을 다룬다.

163
독자는 잡지를 위해 무엇을 제안하는가?
(A) 독자들이 유명한 리더들에게 질문할 수 있도록 하기
(B) 독자들과 뉴스 제작자 간에 간담회 열기
(C) 일부 독자들을 위한 웹사이트 특별 섹션 만들기
(D) 잡지 구독자에게 추가로 할인해주기

164-167 📄 기사

Ellison Waters의 신간 At Odds with Business는 약간의 도움만 있다면 가장 어려운 업무상의 결정을 어떻게 하면 누구나 쉽게 극복할 수 있는지를 보여주는 훌륭한 기술서입니다.

Waters씨는 이 책은 "22년간의 힘든 일과 경험의 정점이며, 젊은 시절에 겪었던 모든 일을 기록한 것이다."라고 말했습니다. 165Waters씨의 책은 그의 어린 시절로 시작해서 대학 시절까지 이어지는, 전기문이자 지침서입니다. 167그러고 나서, 그가 오늘날 비즈니스계의 전설이 되기까지 영향을 준 사람들에 대한 소개로 이야기가 넘어갑니다. 예를 들면, 166Sam Nash 같은 미래의 경쟁자들은 Waters씨에게 사업으로의 문을 열어주었습니다. 그는 또한 사업 인생 초반에 했던 선택들을 포함시켜서, 실패에서 얻은 교훈과 뭔가를 하지 않는 방법에 대해 보여줍니다. 이러한 실패는 다른 사람들이 똑같은 실수를 하지 않도록 하여 가치가 큽니다.

Waters씨가 책에서 열거한 기술을 이해한다고 해서 여러분이 차세대 산업계의 거인이 되지는 못하겠지만, 그의 정신이 어떻게 작용하는지, 새로운 아이디어를 창출하기 위해 그의 회사를 어떻게 활용하는지에 대해 이 책은 약간의 통찰력을 줍니다. 164사업에 뛰어들거나 회사의 제품 수요를 창출하기 위한 새로운 방법을 알고자 하는 모든 사업가에게 이 책을 추천합니다.

164
평론가는 책에 대해 어떻게 생각하는가?
(A) 사업 관련 팁을 충분히 주지 않는다.
(B) 사업을 배우기에 좋은 방법이다.
(C) 필자의 배경을 이해하기 힘들다.
(D) 실패에 대해 너무 많이 할애한다.

165
책의 앞부분에는 무엇이 명시되어 있는가?
(A) 읽어야 하는 경영 도서
(B) 경영 기법
(C) 사업가로서 Waters씨
(D) 학창 시절의 Waters씨

166
Sam Nash는 누구 인가?
(A) Waters씨의 고문　　　　(B) Waters씨의 파트너
(C) Waters씨의 친척　　　　(D) Waters씨의 적수

167 신 유 형
다음 문장은 [1], [2], [3], [4] 중 어디에 들어가는가?
"그러고 나서, 그가 오늘날 비즈니스계의 전설이 되기까지 영향을 준 사람들에 대한 소개로 이야기가 넘어갑니다."
(A) [1]　　　　　　　　　　(B) [2]
(C) [3]　　　　　　　　　　(D) [4]

168-171 📄 기사

전 세계의 많은 기업가들이 올해의 가장 큰 무역 박람회를 위해 다음 주에 로스앤젤레스에 옵니다. 168전자제품과 컴퓨터, 게임 업계의 선두주자들이 소비자와 경쟁 업체 모두에게 출시 예정 제품군을 보여주기 위해 최선을 다할 것입니다.

일주일간의 박람회가 시작되면 텔레비전과 카메라, 신규 게임기나 모바일 기기 등 많은 제품들이 전시될 것으로 기대됩니다. 171박람회 첫 3일 동안 놀라운 일들이 대부분 일어나기 때문에, 훨씬 더 빨리 알게 될 것입니다. 169박람회 중 3일간 열리는 모든 공개 행사에 참가하는 많은 소비자들을 포함하여, 기간 중 하루에만 최소 25,000명 이상의 사람들이 행사에 올 것으로 예측됩니다.

이 행사에서 업계에 종사하지 않는 개인들이 중요한 이유는, 제품과 많은 시간을 보내는 사람들이 그들이며, 사용 후기를 남김은 물론, 집에 가져가서 자랑할 무료 상품도 받기 때문입니다. 설문조사에 응한 소비자들 중 40퍼센트 이상이 신제품을 보면 사탕 가게의 아이처럼 느껴진다고 말했습니다. 170놀랍게도, 올해 참가 확정자들의 74퍼센트는 제품의 기술적인 디자인을 보러 온다고 했습니다.

168

행사의 목적은 무엇인가?

(A) 새 전자제품의 매매를 위하여
(B) 마케팅 조사를 하기 위하여
(C) 앞으로 나올 제품을 소개하기 위하여
(D) 기술 진보를 공유하기 위하여

어휘 advance 진보

169

일반인들에게 공개된 행사는 며칠간 진행되는가?

(A) 1일   (B) 3일
(C) 5일   (D) 7일

170

기사에 의하면, 사람들이 행사에 참석하는 이유는 무엇인가?

(A) 제품의 디자인을 보기 위해서
(B) 최신 장치를 구매하기 위해서
(C) 해당 분야의 전문가와 대화하기 위해서
(D) 출시 전에 새 전자제품을 사용해보기 위해서

어휘 gadget 장치

171 신유형 ─

다음 문장은 [1], [2], [3], [4] 중 어디에 들어가는가?

"박람회 첫 3일 동안 놀라운 일들이 대부분 일어나기 때문에, 훨씬 더 빨리 알게 될 것입니다."

(A) [1]   (B) [2]
(C) [3]   (D) [4]

172-175 📱 온라인 토론 신유형 ─

Drew Manson [오후 12:34]	안녕하세요. 함께 해주셔서 감사합니다. 조별 프로젝트를 발표하기까지 겨우 3주 남았는데, 우리가 어디까지 했는지 확인하고, 필요하다면 도움을 요청하는 게 좋겠다는 생각이 들었습니다.
Michael Ino [오후 12:35]	저희 팀은 확실히 지원을 받아야 한다고 생각해요. 저희는 창조적 한계에 부딪혔어요.
Elaine Gregg [오후 12:35]	제가 도와드리면 좋겠는데요. 뭘 하면 될까요?
Michael Ino [오후 12:37]	172제품이 실제 작동하는 방식을 경영진에게 어떻게 하면 잘 보여줄 수 있을까요? 175발표 형식에 맞추어 표현이 잘 안 되네요.
Drew Manson [오후 12:38]	경영진에게 제품이 어떻게 작동되는지 짧게 시연해줄 수도 있을 것 같은데요. 어떻게 생각하세요?
Michael Ino [오후 12:40]	좋은 생각이긴 한데, 어떻게 3주 안에 견본을 만들 수 있을까요? 급하게 서두르다가 전혀 안 될까 봐 걱정이에요. 그러면 재앙이겠죠.
Elaine Gregg [오후 12:42]	173이번 주에 저희 팀이 견본에 주력해 볼 수 있을 것 같아요. 그러고 나서 당신 팀에 넘겨줄게요. 시연을 할 때 두 팀이 제대로 사용하는 방법을 알고 있다면 큰 도움이 될 거예요. 그렇죠?

Michael Ino [오후 12:43]	좋은 생각이에요. 저희 팀에게는 여러분 모두와 함께 협력해서 일할 거라고 알릴게요.
Drew Manson [오후 12:44]	174좋아요. 다음 주에 진행 상황을 들어보죠.

어휘 backup 지원 translate (다른 형태로) 옮기다 demonstration 시연 demo 견본 disaster 재난 in tandem with ~와 협력하여

172

Ino씨가 프로젝트에서 자기가 맡은 부분에 도움이 필요한 이유는 무엇인가?

(A) 경영진으로부터 어려운 부탁을 받았기 때문에
(B) 자료 수정에 애를 먹었기 때문에
(C) 더 저렴한 재료를 찾아야 하기 때문에
(D) 제품을 잘 선보이길 원하기 때문에

어휘 correct 바로잡다

173

누가 먼저 견본에 착수할 것인가?

(A) Ino씨의 팀   (B) Manson씨의 팀
(C) Gregg씨의 팀   (D) 모든 IT 부서원

174

일주일 후에는 어떤 일이 있을 것인가?

(A) 그들은 매니저들과 회의를 할 것이다.
(B) 그들은 그들의 고객에게 시험용을 보여줄 것이다.
(C) 그들은 새로운 프로젝트를 시작할 것이다.
(D) 그들은 Manson씨에게 프로젝트에 대한 소식을 알릴 것이다.

어휘 trial 시험(용)

175 신유형 ─

오후 12시 37분에 Ino씨가 It doesn't translate well라고 말한 의도는 무엇인가?

(A) 제품에 대해 효과적으로 설명하기 어렵다.
(B) 다른 나라에서는 시연하기 어려울 것이다.
(C) 사진으로는 다른 사람들에게 안 된다.
(D) 많은 사람들이 이해하기 힘든 말이다.

176-180 📱 광고…이메일

Jericho사는 179올 여름에 새로 합류할 팀원을 찾고 있습니다. 고객서비스 및 영업 경험이 있으신 분과 이 직책에 대해 이야기하고 싶습니다. 177자사의 재능 있는 영업 직원들은 신문, 잡지, 검색 엔진, 광고와 같은 과거와 현대의 기법을 사용하도록 교육을 받습니다. 하여 개인과 기업에게 그들의 제품과 관련해 국내와 해외의 마케팅 및 광고에 대해 상담합니다. 1771983년에 비전을 가진 두 남자가 이 업계에서 크게 성공해보자는 생각으로 회사를 설립했습니다. 176Jericho사는 첫 8년간의 운영 이후 오늘날 광고업계 상위 5개의 회사 중 하나로 평가받습니다. 177저희는 광고, 판매, 마케팅, 협상에 관해 결단력 있는 사람들을 찾고 있습니다. 2억 명 이상이 우리의 캠페인을 보았고, 저희는 올해 비전을 두 배로 늘리기를 원합니다. 우리는 언제나 원대한 아이디어를 환영

하며, 우리의 사업을 세계적인 리더로 변모시킬 수 있는 방법을 듣고 싶습니다. ¹⁷⁹대학 졸업 신입도 지원이 가능합니다.

관심이 있으시다면 Irvine 사무실의 Lance Everson씨에게 864-555-7093으로 전화를 주시거나, jobsjericho@walls.com으로 이메일을 보내주십시오.

수신: Lance Everson <jobsjericho@walls.com>
발신: Robert Gibson <robertgib11@smokeymt.edu>
날짜: 5월 20일
제목: 일자리

Everson씨께

¹⁷⁸저는 Jericho사의 일자리에 매우 관심이 있으며 가능한 빠른 시일 내에 취업 기회에 관해 이야기를 나누고 싶습니다. ¹⁷⁹저는 Smokey Mountain 대학 4학년이며 올해 말 경영경제학 학위를 받을 예정입니다. 저는 반에서 상위이고, 마을에 있는 지역의 광고 사무실인 Hunter&Michaels에서 아르바이트를 하고 있습니다. 저는 광고에 대한 열정을 ¹⁸⁰가지고 있으며 더 큰 직책으로 지역 광고 및 마케팅 분야에서 저의 경험을 사용하고 싶습니다. 저는 항상 전국의 시장에 제품을 소개하는 새로운 방법에 대해 생각하고 있으며, 인터넷 마케팅과 분석에 기술을 도입하여 우리 브랜드가 더 많은 소비자에게 노출될 수 있도록 할 것입니다. 이러한 이유로, 제가 Jericho사에 적합하다고 생각합니다. 감사합니다.

Robert Gibson

어휘 domestically 국내에서 take ~ by storm ~에서 대성공을 거두다 determined 단호한 negotiation 협상 transform 변형시키다 senior 졸업반 학생 analytics 분석 (정보)

176
Jericho사는 어떤 회사인가?
(A) 광고 회사
(B) IT 회사
(C) 출판사
(D) 소매업체

어휘 publisher 출판사 retailer 소매업(체)

177
광고에 언급되지 않은 것은 무엇인가?
(A) 직원 훈련
(B) 매출액
(C) 직무 자격
(D) 회사 연혁

어휘 sales figures 매출액 qualification 자격

178
이메일의 주된 목적은 무엇인가?
(A) 입사 제안을 수락하려고
(B) 일자리에 지원하려고
(C) 직책에 대한 자세한 정보를 물어보려고
(D) 면접을 끝까지 하려고

어휘 follow up on ~를 끝까지 하다

179
Gibson씨는 무엇 때문에 직책을 얻지 못하겠는가?
(A) 현재 학업 상태
(B) 그의 학교 성적

(C) 대학 전공
(D) 추천자 미달

어휘 status 상태

180
이메일의 네 번째 줄의 share와 의미상 가장 가까운 단어는 무엇인가?
(A) 나누다
(B) 주다
(C) 가지고 있다
(D) 어울리다

181-185 일정표···메모

7월 17일 회의 안건	시간
¹⁸⁵Amory Brothers 대표단 도착	오전 9:00
소개 및 첫 번째 안건	오전 9:30
멀티미디어 쇼케이스 ¹⁸²*반드시 오디오 파일을 사용하세요.	오전 10:00
우리 회사가 성장을 이룰 수 있는 방법 논의 *질의응답 시간을 가질 수 있습니다.	오전 11:00
Amory Brothers 사장과의 오찬	오후 12:00
두 회사 경영진과의 그룹 토론	오후 1:00
최종 협상 *이 부분에 좀 더 빨리 다다르기를 바라지만, 이때에는 압박을 할 것입니다.	오후 2:00
¹⁸¹임시 계약서 작성	오후 2:30
당일 회의 종료	오후 4:00

메모

수신: Mark Reynolds, Amy Abbott
발신: Jennifer Tyson
날짜: 7월 15일
제목: 7월 17일 회의 안건

안녕하세요, Mark와 Amy.
7월 17일 Amory Brothers와의 회의에 관한 정보를 보내드립니다. 우리에게 큰 회의인 만큼 그날에 있을 모든 일에 대해 확실하게 알려드리고 싶습니다.
¹⁸¹이 계약은 우리 회사가 오디오 산업에서 입지를 되찾는 데 도움이 될 수 있고, 그렇게 되도록 두 분이 도와줄 것이라 봅니다. ¹⁸⁵Amory의 대표단이 도착하면 D회의실로 안내해주세요. 여러분을 위해 그곳에서 모든 것을 준비해놓겠습니다.
¹⁸⁴Amory Brothers는 오디오 업계에서 우량 기업이며 최고의 가수부터 세계 최고의 영화사까지 이르는 모든 사람들과 일합니다. ¹⁸³그들의 전문 분야는 가능한 한 작은 오디오 청취 기기를 써야 하는 우주 프로그램과 정부를 돕는 소형 장치를 만드는 것입니다. 그들은 자신들의 관심사에 빠르게 생각하고 반응하는 프로젝트 리더를 기대하고 있으며, 두 분이 향후 오디오 분야에서 우리 회사가 어떻게 최고가 될 수 있는지 보여주리라 믿습니다. Amory Brothers의 향후 계획에 우리가 최고의 선택이라는 것을 그들이 알게 될 것이라고 확신합니다!
Jennifer Tyson
Hitbox Sound 사장

어휘 management 경영진 preliminary 예비의 draw up 작성하다 regain 되찾다 foothold 발판 count on ~를 믿다 specialty 전문 concerns 관심사

181
회의의 목적은 무엇인가?
(A) 새 오디오 장치에 대해 설명하기 위해
(B) 새 프로그램을 대표단에게 보여주기 위해
(C) 합병을 독려하기 위해
(D) 회사의 계약을 성사시키기 위해

182
Tyson씨는 Mark와 Amy에게 쇼케이스에서 무엇을 하라고 상기시키는가?
(A) 고객의 질문에 답변하기
(B) 가능하면 빨리 끝내기
(C) 가급적 많은 세부내용 설명하기
(D) 준비된 파일 사용하기

183
고객사가 선두 기술을 가지고 있는 분야는 무엇인가?
(A) 오디오 장비　　　　　(B) 컴퓨터
(C) 자동차　　　　　　　(D) 비디오 장비

184
Amory Brothers에 대한 Tyson씨의 생각으로 옳지 않은 것은 무엇인가?
(A) 그들은 작은 회사이다.
(B) 그들은 최고의 회사 중 하나이다.
(C) 그들은 함께 일할 수 있는 대응 능력이 있는 회사가 필요하다.
(D) 그들은 계약을 이익이라고 생각할 것이다.

어휘 responsive 즉각 반응하는 beneficial 이로운

185
Mark와 Amy는 언제 방문객들을 만날 것인가?
(A) 오전 9:00　　　　　(B) 오전 9:30
(C) 오전 10:00　　　　　(D) 오후 12:00

186-190 📄 요약…일정표…이메일 신유형
화가 Peter Solvang의 작품 개요

· 초기: Solvang은 생애 후반에 유명해진 폭넓은 필법을 사용하여 다양한 색(아크릴)으로 작업했다.
· 중기: [187]이 시기에 Solvang은 현대 초상화 몇 점을 그리기 시작했는데, Carson과 Eustace의 영향을 연상시킨다.
· 말기: [186]죽기 전 10년 동안 Solvang은 오직 검은색만으로 감정을 표현했다. 그는 대담하고 어두운 획이 색 자체의 빛을 반영한 것이라고 말했다.

Public Access Channel 7월 프로그래밍 일정표

[188]7월 17일 월요일　은퇴 자금 마련 시작하기　17:00~17:15
투자 전문가 Ravita Singh은 은퇴를 위한 투자 시작은 결코 이르지 않다고 말합니다. 가장 좋으면서도 가장 안전한 투자에 대한 조언과 유의 사항을 시청하세요.

7월 18일 화요일　화요일의 타코와 기타 대접 음식　15:30~16:00
멕시코 요리사 Juanita Valdez가 또 멋진 요리법을 공유합니다. 슈퍼마켓에서 쉽게 찾을 수 있는 재료를 사용하여 오늘 밤 배고픈 사람들을 기쁘게 할 수 있습니다.

[189]7월 19일 수요일　Peter Solvang 회고 방송　20:00~21:30
Solvang은 프랑스의 가장 위대한 현대 화가로 불립니다. 시리즈의 두 번째로, [187]오늘 밤은 그의 70년 경력에서 중기의 작품에 대해 알아봅니다.

7월 20일 목요일　아름다운 고택　20:30~21:30
오래된 집의 주인들은 할 일이 많습니다. 주간 방송을 통해 가정 수리 및 유지보수의 기초를 보다 쉽게 가르치고 있습니다. 돈을 절약하고 스스로 만들어보세요!

수신: Public Access Channel Information <pacinfo@pacabroadcasting.gov>
발신: Riley Springer <rspringer@vastmail.com>
날짜: 7월 20일
제목: 프로그램에 대한 질문

안녕하세요?
[189]지난밤 방송된 화가에 대한 프로그램을 재방송하는지 알고 싶습니다. 프로그램의 마지막 10분만 시청해서 그 프로그램의 이름은 모릅니다. [190]저는 지역 대학에서 미술사를 가르치고 있으며 프로그램의 일부를 수업 중에 사용하고 싶습니다. 가능하면 다시 보는 방법이나 녹화물을 구매하는 방법을 알려주시겠습니까?
Riley Springer

어휘 brush stroke 필법 branch out (새 분야를) 시작하다 portrait 초상화 bring to mind 연상시키다 influence 영향(력) guru 전문가 tune in 시청하다 retrospective 회고전 DIY (소비자가) 직접 수리하다 re-broadcast 재방송하다

186
Peter Solvang은 언제 검은색만 사용했는가?
(A) 초창기에
(B) Eustace를 만나기 전에
(C) 경력 중반부에
(D) 인생 후반부에

187
예술 TV 프로그램은 무엇에 집중하는가?
(A) 필법 지도
(B) 작가의 초상화 시기
(C) 자연의 밝은 색상
(D) 그림에서 아크릴의 사용

어휘 tutorial 개별 지도

188
돈에 대한 프로그램은 언제 방송되는가?
(A) 월요일　　　　　　　(B) 화요일
(C) 수요일　　　　　　　(D) 목요일

어휘 air 방송하다

189
Springer씨는 어떤 프로그램에 대해 질문하는가?
(A) 은퇴 자금 마련 시작하기
(B) Peter Solvang 회고 방송
(C) 화요일의 타코와 기타 대접 음식
(D) 아름다운 고택

190
Springer씨에 대해 언급된 것은 무엇인가?
(A) 그녀는 예술가이다.
(B) 그녀는 투자 전문 은행원이다.
(C) 그녀는 오래된 집을 소유하고 있다.
(D) 그녀는 교육 분야에서 일한다.

191-195 📑 광고…송장…이메일 신 유 형

Auburn Motors의 임대 특가

어떠한 이유로든 차를 살 마음의 준비가 되어 있지 않으시다면, 저희 임대 옵션은 완벽하며, 장기적으로 사는 것보다 비용이 적게 들 수도 있습니다!

¹⁹¹새로 나온 어떤 *모델이든 36개월간 매달 200달러에 임대하고 계약 시 2,500달러만 지불하시면 됩니다. 이 가격은 다른 어느 경쟁사보다 더 저렴한 금액입니다.

임대 보증금은 없습니다. 임대 계약 기간 동안 언제든지 철회할 수 있습니다. 36개월간 (차 구매보다 싼) 가격에 합당한 차를 구매하는 선택권을 행사하세요. 이는 자격이 되는 신청자에게 제공됩니다. 철저한 신용조사가 Verify사에 의해 이루어집니다.

¹⁹²*Wellspring 5000 세단, Fox Trot XR 스포츠카, Jasmine 33 하이브리드, Emerald Bay 미니밴

자동차 임대 최종 청구서

이름: Timothy Loins

¹⁹²제조사/모델: 하이브리드
¹⁹³총 임대 기간: 12개월

반환 시 누적 주행거리: 12,389
유지보수: 새 브레이크 패드

¹⁹⁴주행거리 비용	389 x 0.15	58.35
지방세		49.50
유지비		245.25
마지막 달 요금		200.00
총액		553.10

¹⁹⁴*차량 임대는 연간 12,000마일 무료입니다. 초과하면 마일당 0.15달러가 부과됩니다.

발신: Timothy Lions <timothylions@bizplus.net>
수신: Auburn Motors <info@auburnmotors.com>
날짜: 7월 3일
제목: 자동차 임대료

방금 Auburn Motors에서 자동차 임대료 최종 청구서를 받았는데 착오가 있는 것 같습니다. 아마 직원의 실수인 것 같아요. ¹⁹⁴차를 반납할 때 기록이 10,389마일이었습니다. ¹⁹⁵주행 기록계 사진을 찍었으니 이메일에 첨부합니다. 추가 운행 요금은 환불해주세요.
감사합니다.

Timothy Lions

어휘 costly 돈이 많이 드는 brand-new 신품의 security deposit 임대 보증금 clerical 사무직의 odometer 주행 기록계

191
Lions씨는 계약금으로 얼마를 지불했는가?
(A) 200달러　　　　(B) 553.10달러
(C) 1,200달러　　　(D) 2,500달러

192
Lions씨가 임대한 차량은 어떤 종류인가?
(A) Emerald Bay　　(B) Fox Trot XR
(C) Jasmine 33　　　(D) Wellspring 5000

193
Lions씨는 언제 차량을 반납했는가?
(A) 계약하고 일주일 뒤에
(B) 계약하고 몇 개월이 지난 뒤에
(C) 계약하고 1년 뒤에
(D) 계약하고 3년 뒤에

194
Lions씨가 환불을 요청하는 금액은 얼마인가?
(A) 49.50달러　　　(B) 58.35달러
(C) 200달러　　　　(D) 245.25달러

195
Lions씨가 이메일과 함께 보낸 것은 무엇인가?
(A) 차량 제어반 사진　　(B) 차 외부 사진
(C) 그의 계약서 원본　　(D) 임대 광고

어휘 control panel 제어반 exterior 외부

196-200 📑 정보…이메일…목록 신 유 형

San Marcos 제25회 연례 가정 장식용품 전시
¹⁹⁷7월 21~24일 오전 9:30 – 오후 5:30

캘리포니아 샌마르코스의 Javier 센터

7월 21일 프로그램

· 개회사　　　　오전 10:00 – 오전 10:30　　　주 무대
전시회 주최자인 Westbrook 디자인의 Felicia Knowles가 환영사를 합니다.

· 가정 패션 동향　　오전 11:30 – 오후 12:30　　동관
현지 업체인 Bridget Homes의 직원이 현재의 동향을 설명합니다.

· ¹⁹⁶내년 유행 예측　　오후 1:30 – 오후 2:00　　서쪽 별관
디자인계의 아이콘 Robert Waxman이 내년에 유행할 디자인에 대한 그의 통찰력을 공유합니다.

· 새 출품자 갤러리　전일　　　　중앙 구역
새 업체들이 선보이는 제품들을 놓치지 마세요.

발신: Marc Ephraim <mephraim@ephraimdes.com>
수신: Janessa Blackwell <jblackwell@ephraimdes.com>

날짜: 7월 17일
제목: 가정 장식용품 전시

안녕하세요, Janessa.
Javier 센터에서 있을 행사에서 당신이 저를 도와줬으면 해요. 제 팀과 제가 부스는 ¹⁹⁸다룰 수 있지만, ¹⁹⁷첫날은 하루 종일 갤러리에 몇 사람을 교대로 보내야 합니다. 1시부터 5시까지 시간이 가능한가요? 그리고 두 사람이 더 필요로 할 수 있으니 추천할 만한 직원이 있다면 알려주세요. 한 가지 더요. ¹⁹⁹첨부된 제품 목록을 보고 CSH-45의 가격을 확인해주겠어요? 특수 직물 때문에 그 제품이 더 비싸다는 것은 알고 있는데, 우리가 최종 가격을 얼마로 책정했는지 모르겠네요.

Marc Ephraim
Ephraim 디자인

Ephraim 디자인 전시회 제품 목록

	제품 번호	치수	가격
덮개 천			
직조	UF-WV21	다양함(조각)	개별 표시
현대식	UF-MO11	"	"
전통식	UF-TR95	"	"
작은 찬장			
얼룩덜룩한 녹색	CPB-MG3	²⁰⁰높이85/ 너비76/깊이40	125달러
프랑스풍 회색	CPB-FG5	"	125달러
프로방스풍 파란색	CPB-PB7	"	135달러
지중해풍 파란색	CPB-MB9	"	130달러
¹⁹⁹쿠션 덮개			
꽃 무늬	CSH-55	40x40	45달러
동물 무늬	CSH-32	40x40	45달러
¹⁹⁹디자이너 도안	CSH-45	55x55	50달러
전통 무늬	CSH-64	55x55	50달러

어휘 exhibition 전시회 give a welcome speech 환영사를 하다 pavilion 부속 건물 rotate 교대시키다 dimension 치수 upholstery (소파의) 덮개 remnant 조각, 자투리 mottled 얼룩덜룩한

196
참가자들은 앞으로의 동향을 어디에서 들을 수 있는가?
(A) 중앙 구역
(B) 동관
(C) 주 무대
(D) 서쪽 별관

197
Ephraim씨가 Blackwell씨의 도움을 필요로 하는 때는 언제인가?
(A) 7월 21일
(B) 7월 22일
(C) 7월 23일
(D) 7월 24일

198
이메일의 첫 번째 줄 cover와 의미상 가장 가까운 단어는 무엇인가?
(A) 장식하다
(B) 숨기다
(C) 포장하다
(D) 포함하다

어휘 hide 숨기다

199
Ephraim씨는 Blackwell씨에게 어떤 제품에 대해 물었는가?

(A) 디자이너 도안의 쿠션 덮개
(B) 꽃 무늬 쿠션
(C) 현대식 덮개 천
(D) 직조 식탁보

200
찬장 목록에서 공통된 것은 무엇인가?
(A) 색상
(B) 재료
(C) 가격
(D) 크기

어휘 material 재료

Actual Test 3 ··· 103

Actual Test 4

정답   🔊 LC MP3 Actual Test **4**

1 (A)	**2** (C)	**3** (C)	**4** (C)	**5** (B)	**6** (D)	**7** (A)	**8** (C)	**9** (B)	**10** (B)
11 (B)	**12** (C)	**13** (A)	**14** (B)	**15** (C)	**16** (A)	**17** (B)	**18** (A)	**19** (B)	**20** (A)
21 (C)	**22** (A)	**23** (B)	**24** (A)	**25** (B)	**26** (C)	**27** (C)	**28** (A)	**29** (C)	**30** (B)
31 (C)	**32** (C)	**33** (C)	**34** (B)	**35** (B)	**36** (B)	**37** (B)	**38** (B)	**39** (D)	**40** (D)
41 (A)	**42** (C)	**43** (B)	**44** (C)	**45** (A)	**46** (C)	**47** (B)	**48** (D)	**49** (C)	**50** (A)
51 (B)	**52** (D)	**53** (D)	**54** (C)	**55** (A)	**56** (A)	**57** (A)	**58** (A)	**59** (A)	**60** (D)
61 (C)	**62** (D)	**63** (A)	**64** (C)	**65** (C)	**66** (C)	**67** (D)	**68** (B)	**69** (B)	**70** (A)
71 (B)	**72** (A)	**73** (B)	**74** (D)	**75** (B)	**76** (D)	**77** (D)	**78** (B)	**79** (D)	**80** (C)
81 (C)	**82** (B)	**83** (B)	**84** (C)	**85** (D)	**86** (D)	**87** (C)	**88** (C)	**89** (A)	**90** (B)
91 (B)	**92** (A)	**93** (A)	**94** (B)	**95** (C)	**96** (C)	**97** (C)	**98** (C)	**99** (D)	**100** (C)
101 (D)	**102** (C)	**103** (D)	**104** (C)	**105** (B)	**106** (D)	**107** (C)	**108** (B)	**109** (C)	**110** (A)
111 (B)	**112** (C)	**113** (B)	**114** (B)	**115** (B)	**116** (D)	**117** (C)	**118** (D)	**119** (D)	**120** (A)
121 (C)	**122** (C)	**123** (A)	**124** (C)	**125** (C)	**126** (C)	**127** (B)	**128** (C)	**129** (C)	**130** (D)
131 (C)	**132** (D)	**133** (B)	**134** (D)	**135** (A)	**136** (D)	**137** (B)	**138** (B)	**139** (D)	**140** (B)
141 (A)	**142** (B)	**143** (A)	**144** (B)	**145** (C)	**146** (A)	**147** (C)	**148** (D)	**149** (B)	**150** (A)
151 (B)	**152** (A)	**153** (B)	**154** (D)	**155** (C)	**156** (A)	**157** (D)	**158** (C)	**159** (B)	**160** (A)
161 (C)	**162** (A)	**163** (C)	**164** (A)	**165** (D)	**166** (B)	**167** (D)	**168** (A)	**169** (A)	**170** (B)
171 (A)	**172** (B)	**173** (D)	**174** (D)	**175** (D)	**176** (D)	**177** (D)	**178** (D)	**179** (B)	**180** (B)
181 (C)	**182** (B)	**183** (B)	**184** (C)	**185** (A)	**186** (C)	**187** (D)	**188** (B)	**189** (A)	**190** (A)
191 (C)	**192** (D)	**193** (A)	**194** (C)	**195** (D)	**196** (B)	**197** (A)	**198** (B)	**199** (D)	**200** (B)

PART 1

1

🔊 캐나다

(A) She's touching a piece of equipment.

(B) She's talking with someone near a copier.

(C) She's looking at a video monitor.

(D) She's playing an instrument.

(A) 여자는 장비를 만지고 있다.

(B) 여자는 복사기 근처에서 누군가와 이야기하고 있다.

(C) 여자는 비디오 모니터를 보고 있다.

(D) 여자는 악기를 연주하고 있다.

어휘 copier 복사기 instrument 악기

2

◁)) 미국

(A) He's cutting some grass.

(B) He's cleaning a window.

(C) He's operating a construction vehicle.

(D) He's painting something on a road.

(A) 남자가 잔디를 깎고 있다.

(B) 남자가 창문을 닦고 있다.

(C) 남자가 공사 차량을 운전하고 있다.

(D) 남자가 길에 뭔가를 그리고 있다.

어휘 construction vehicle 공사 차량

3

◁)) 호주

(A) A dog is being petted.

(B) A man is riding a bicycle.

(C) Some people are looking down at a dog.

(D) A dog is sitting on a bench.

(A) 개가 쓰다듬어지고 있다.

(B) 남자는 자전거를 타고 있다.

(C) 몇몇 사람들이 개를 내려다보고 있다.

(D) 개가 벤치 위에 앉아 있다.

어휘 pet 쓰다듬다 look down 내려다보다

4

◁)) 미국

(A) Lights are hanging from the ceiling.

(B) Pictures are arranged by the door.

(C) Tables have been set for a meal.

(D) Windows are open near the door.

(A) 천장에 전등이 걸려 있다.

(B) 문 옆에 그림이 배치되어 있다.

(C) 식사를 위해 식탁이 준비되어 있다.

(D) 문 근처에 창문이 열려 있다.

어휘 arrange 정렬하다 set for a meal 식사 준비를 하다

5

◁)) 호주

(A) They're driving through traffic.

(B) Some people are getting in a car.

(C) They're stopping at a signal.

(D) Some people are leaving a building.

(A) 사람들이 교통체증을 뚫고 운전하고 있다.

(B) 몇몇 사람들이 차에 타고 있다.

(C) 사람들이 신호등에서 멈춰 서 있다.

(D) 몇몇 사람들이 건물을 나가고 있다.

어휘 get in (탈것)에 타다 traffic 교통(량)

6

◁)) 영국

(A) Motorcycles are being fixed.

(B) Motorcycles are parked end to end.

(C) Motorcycles are being washed.

(D) Motorcycles are parked next to each other.

(A) 오토바이들이 수리되고 있다.

(B) 오토바이들이 한쪽 끝과 다른 한쪽 끝이 닿게 주차되어 있다.

(C) 오토바이들이 세차되고 있다.

(D) 오토바이들이 서로 나란히 주차되어 있다.

어휘 next to each other 나란히 end to end 끝과 끝을 붙여서

PART 2

7 🔊 미국···캐나다

Would you be able to help me later?

(A) Sure. How about 3:00?

(B) I'm afraid I didn't catch his name.

(C) No. They're out at the moment.

이따가 저를 도와주실 수 있나요?
(A) 물론이죠. 3시 어때요?
(B) 그 사람 이름을 못 들은 것 같아요.
(C) 아니요. 그들은 지금 외출 중입니다.

어휘 catch one's name 이름을 못 알아듣다

---

8 🔊 호주···영국

Why do we need new security badges?

(A) No one can stay past 8:00 PM.

(B) Because she got a new one.

(C) The building has a new system.

왜 새로운 보안 배지가 필요한가요?
(A) 저녁 8시가 지나면 아무도 있을 수 없어요.
(B) 그녀가 새것을 얻었기 때문이에요.
(C) 건물에 새로운 시스템이 설치됐거든요.

어휘 security 보안 past (시간상) 지나서

---

9 🔊 미국···캐나다

Who is supposed to sign my time sheet?

(A) She already filled it out online.

(B) Ask Mr. Peters.

(C) I have no more questions.

누가 내 시간표에 서명하기로 되어 있죠?
(A) 그녀는 이미 온라인으로 그것을 작성했어요.
(B) Peters씨에게 물어보세요.
(C) 저는 더 이상 질문이 없어요.

어휘 be supposed to ~하기로 되어 있다

---

10 🔊 영국···호주

The supplies are being delivered tomorrow, aren't they?

(A) You picked him yourself, didn't you?

(B) Yes, as far as I know.

(C) Just $4.99 for shipping.

비품이 내일 배달되는 거죠?
(A) 직접 그를 뽑으셨지 않나요?
(B) 네, 제가 아는 한 그래요.
(C) 배송료는 단돈 4.99달러예요.

어휘 supplies 비품 shipping 배송

---

11 🔊 영국···미국

I was told this is the newest version of the software.

(A) There's a mistake on my bill.

(B) That's right. It's version 4.0.

(C) Can you make a copy of this contract?

이것이 소프트웨어의 최신 버전이라고 들었어요.
(A) 제 계산서에 실수가 있어요.
(B) 맞아요. 4.0 버전입니다.
(C) 이 계약서를 복사해주겠어요?

어휘 version 판, 버전

12 (🔊) 캐나다…영국

What do you want me to do with these reports?

(A) The report said Highway 50 is closed today.

(B) I want all staff informed immediately.

(C) Could you file them away for me?

이 보고서를 제가 어떻게 하길 원하시나요?

(A) 오늘 50번 고속도로가 폐쇄되었다고 보도됐어요.

(B) 즉시 모든 직원들이 알길 바랍니다.

(C) 저한테 서류를 정리해서 주겠어요?

어휘 file away (서류를) 정리하다

---

13 (🔊) 캐나다…미국

Where are the new clients going?

(A) On a tour with the manager.

(B) I'm always thinking ahead.

(C) Wherever they will fit securely.

새 고객들이 어디로 가고 있나요?

(A) 매니저와 함께 둘러보는 중이에요.

(B) 저는 언제나 미리 생각하고 있지요.

(C) 어디든 단단히 고정될 수 있는 곳이에요.

어휘 on a tour 관광[견학] 중인 think ahead 미리 생각하다

---

14 (🔊) 영국…호주

How much rice should we order?

(A) Until nearly 6:00.

(B) Same as last time—10 kilos.

(C) From the outlet over there.

쌀을 얼마나 주문할까요?

(A) 거의 6시까지요.

(B) 지난번과 똑같이 10kg이요.

(C) 저쪽 할인점에서요.

어휘 outlet 할인점

---

15 (🔊) 캐나다…미국

When does the next bus leave for the airport?

(A) Tickets are $25 per person.

(B) Do you prefer a window or an aisle seat?

(C) Not for another 35 minutes.

다음 버스는 언제 공항으로 출발하나요?

(A) 표는 1인당 25달러입니다.

(B) 창문 쪽과 통로 쪽 중 어느 쪽 좌석이 좋으세요?

(C) 앞으로 35분 동안은 없어요.

어휘 aisle seat 복도 좌석

---

16 (🔊) 호주…캐나다

Should we invite Elise to join us?

(A) She's tied up with her project.

(B) To the Tidewater Café.

(C) No. The food was just so-so.

Elise를 초대해서 함께 할까요?

(A) 그녀는 프로젝트에 발이 묶였어요.

(B) Tidewater 카페요.

(C) 아니요. 음식은 그저 그래요.

어휘 so-so 그저 그런 be tied up with ~에 발이 묶이다

17 ◁)) 호주…영국

How much will the new system cost?

(A) We're not sure of the release date.

(B) Between 4 and 5,000 dollars.

(C) It's straight from the manufacturer.

어휘 release date 출시일 straight 곧장 manufacturer 제조업체

새 시스템은 비용이 얼마나 들까요?
(A) 우리는 출시일에 대해 확실히 몰라요.
(B) 4천에서 5천 달러 사이가 될 거예요.
(C) 제조업체에서 곧장요.

---

18 ◁)) 캐나다…미국

Where should I put this box of pictures?

(A) In the storage cabinet, thanks.

(B) My camera's in the shop.

(C) The frames are expensive.

어휘 storage 창고

이 사진 상자를 어디에 놓을까요?
(A) 보관 캐비닛이에요. 감사합니다.
(B) 제 카메라는 수리점에 있어요.
(C) 액자가 비싸요.

---

19 ◁)) 미국…캐나다

Do you want to meet at my office?

(A) No. I haven't met her yet.

(B) Sounds good. Give me your address.

(C) In case I'm late, start without me.

어휘 in case ~할 경우에

제 사무실에서 만나겠어요?
(A) 아뇨. 아직 그녀를 못 만났어요.
(B) 좋아요. 당신의 주소를 알려주세요.
(C) 제가 늦을 경우에는 저 없이 시작하세요.

---

20 ◁)) 호주…영국

Who decided to buy the new curtains?

(A) The office manager.

(B) Let's ask Mr. Carson for the money.

(C) The decorator will visit our office tomorrow.

어휘 decorator 실내 장식가

누가 새 커튼을 사기로 결정했죠?
(A) 사무실 매니저요.
(B) Carson씨에게 돈을 요청합시다.
(C) 장식하는 분이 내일 우리 사무실을 방문할 거예요.

---

21 ◁)) 미국…호주

Should I invite Bob to the party?

(A) Yes. The party's been canceled.

(B) You should go to bed early.

(C) Sure. It looks like he could use a break.

파티에 Bob을 초대할까?
(A) 네. 파티가 취소됐어요.
(B) 당신은 일찍 자야죠.
(C) 물론이지. 그는 휴식이 필요한 것 같아.

22 （1）） 영국…캐나다

Where is your showroom located?

(A) Next to the bank on Maple Street.

(B) Our airport hotel is convenient.

(C) From 10:00 to 5:00.

어휘 showroom 전시실

전시장은 어디에 있습니까?

(A) Maple가의 은행 옆이에요.

(B) 저희 공항 호텔이 편해요.

(C) 10시부터 5시까지예요.

---

23 （1）） 미국…호주

There isn't any more tea, is there?

(A) There are more participants than expected.

(B) Sorry. We ran out.

(C) I wish you could come.

어휘 run out 다 떨어지다

차가 더는 없지요?

(A) 예상보다 참가자가 많아요.

(B) 죄송해요. 다 떨어졌어요.

(C) 당신이 와줬으면 해요.

---

24 （1）） 영국…미국

Why don't we ask for volunteers first?

(A) I doubt anyone will volunteer.

(B) There are no more slots left.

(C) They'll be ready at 10:00.

어휘 slot (조직에서의) 자리

먼저 자원봉사자를 찾는 게 어때요?

(A) 아무도 지원하지 않을 것 같아요.

(B) 자리가 더 이상 남아 있지 않아요.

(C) 그들은 10시에 준비가 될 거예요.

---

25 （1）） 캐나다…호주

Are you going to the seminar next week?

(A) Yes. It was a useful one.

(B) No. I'm too busy.

(C) I have an appointment today.

다음 주에 세미나에 갈 거예요?

(A) 네. 유용했습니다.

(B) 아니요. 너무 바빠요.

(C) 오늘 약속이 있어요.

---

26 （1）） 호주…영국

We don't often get storms like this here.

(A) Let's check with him later.

(B) They're often delayed by weather.

(C) Yes. This one is scary.

어휘 scary 무서운

이곳에서 이런 폭풍은 자주 일어나지 않아요.

(A) 나중에 그와 확인해봅시다.

(B) 날씨 때문에 지연되는 경우가 잦아요.

(C) 네. 이번 것은 무섭네요.

27 (◁)) 호주…미국

How about switching shifts with Susan tomorrow?

(A) That's one way to think about it.

(B) She prefers this blue shirt.

(C) Her shift is too late for me.

어휘 switch 바꾸다 shift 교대 근무

내일 Susan과 교대해서 근무하는 게 어때요?

(A) 그것에 대해 생각해볼 수 있는 한 가지 방법이네요.

(B) 그녀는 이 파란 셔츠를 좋아해요.

(C) 그녀의 근무 시간이 저한테는 너무 늦어요.

---

28 (◁)) 영국…캐나다

Are these 100 brochures going to be enough or should we order more?

(A) Let's start with these.

(B) I can't work this new copier.

(C) No. They can't come tomorrow.

이 100개의 책자로 충분할까요, 아니면 더 주문할까요?

(A) 이것들로 시작합시다.

(B) 저는 이 새 복사기를 작동 못 하겠어요.

(C) 아니요. 그들은 내일 올 수 없어요.

---

29 (◁)) 미국…영국

I hope the manager talks to Priscilla soon.

(A) Whenever she wants.

(B) All of the managers are out.

(C) Why? Is there a problem?

매니저가 Priscilla에게 빨리 얘기하면 좋겠어요.

(A) 그녀가 원하는 때면 언제든지요.

(B) 모든 매니저가 나가 있습니다.

(C) 왜요? 무슨 문제가 있어요?

---

30 (◁)) 캐나다…호주

Are they taking the train back?

(A) Yes. We are on the express.

(B) I think they're driving.

(C) No. I haven't heard back from him.

어휘 express 급행

그들이 기차를 타고 돌아오나요?

(A) 네. 저희는 급행을 타고 있어요.

(B) 운전해서 오는 것 같아요.

(C) 아니요. 그에게서 들은 게 없어요.

---

31 (◁)) 미국…캐나다

What made them change their minds?

(A) I don't have any change, sorry.

(B) Our vacation was pleasant.

(C) The new contract terms were attractive.

어휘 change 바꾸다; 잔돈 contract terms 계약 조건

무엇 때문에 그들이 마음을 바꾸었나요?

(A) 죄송하지만, 잔돈이 없어요.

(B) 우리의 휴가는 즐거웠어요.

(C) 새로운 계약 조건이 매력적이었거든요.

PART 3

Questions 32–34 refer to the following conversation. 🔊 캐나다…미국

W ³²When we go to our client, the Bradley firm, should we take a company car or the train? They moved recently and now they are out near the airport. No trains go there directly, as far as I know.

M In that case, ³³it makes more sense to drive. I'll put in a request for a car. We're going this Friday, right?

W ³²Uh, actually, it's next Friday. This Friday is a national holiday.

M Oh, that's right. How could I forget? ³⁴I'm going camping with my family.

여 ³²우리 고객사인 Bradley 회사에 갈 때 회사 차를 타고 가야 할까요, 아니면 기차를 타야 할까요? 그 회사는 최근 이전해서 지금은 공항 근처에 있어요. 제가 알기로는 그곳까지 직행으로 가는 기차는 없어요.

남 그렇다면 ³³운전해서 가는 게 맞겠네요. 제가 차를 요청을 할게요. 이번 주 금요일에 가는 것 맞죠?

여 ³²아뇨. 다음 주 금요일이에요. 이번 주 금요일은 국경일이에요.

남 맞네요. 어떻게 그걸 잊어버리지? ³⁴제가 가족과 캠핑을 가거든요.

어휘 firm 회사 make sense 타당하다 put in a request 신청하다

32 다음 주에 화자들은 어디로 가는가?
(A) 출장
(B) 캠핑 여행
(C) 고객의 사무실
(D) 휴양지

33 화자들은 무엇을 타고 목적지에 도착할 것인가?
(A) 비행기
(B) 버스
(C) 자동차
(D) 열차

34 이번 주 금요일에 대해 언급된 것은?
(A) 이용 가능한 회사 차량이 없다.
(B) 남자는 가족과 함께 시간을 보낼 것이다.
(C) 여자는 새로운 곳으로 이사할 것이다.
(D) 회사 야유회가 있다.

Questions 35–37 refer to the following conversation. 🔊 영국…호주

M Ah, Emily, I was just about to call you about the exhibit tomorrow. We're still going, right?

W Of course. I've been looking forward to it. ³⁵Pop art is my favorite type of art. So, should we meet at the gallery or have dinner first?

M ³⁶Let's have dinner first. I've been wanting to try the new Greek place, Olympian. It's only a few streets over from the gallery.

W Great. So ³⁶let's meet in front of Olympian at 6:00. That should give us enough time to eat and ³⁷make the artist's introduction at 7:30.

남 Emily, 내일 전시회 때문에 전화하려던 참이었어요. 우리 가는 거죠?

여 물론이죠. 기대하고 있었어요. ³⁵팝아트는 제가 가장 좋아하는 예술이에요. 우리 전시장에서 만날까요, 아니면 저녁을 먼저 먹을까요? ─

남 ³⁶저녁을 먼저 먹어요. 새로 생긴 그리스 식당인 올림피언에 가보고 싶었어요. 갤러리에서 얼마 안 떨어져 있어요.

여 좋아요. 그럼 ³⁶6시에 올림피언 앞에서 만나요. 그러면 식사할 시간은 충분하고, ³⁷7시 30분에 예술가의 소개도 들을 수 있을 거예요.

35 여자는 무엇을 좋아한다고 하는가?
(A) 그리스 음식
(B) 현대 미술
(C) 새 카페
(D) 팝 음악

36 화자들은 어디에서 만날 예정인가?
(A) 갤러리
(B) 식당
(C) 미술용품 가게
(D) 여자의 아파트

37 화자들은 내일 7시 30분에 무엇을 할 것인가?
(A) 저녁을 만든다.
(B) 예술가의 이야기를 듣는다.
(C) 미술 수업에 참여한다.
(D) 새로운 식당에 가본다.

Questions 38-40 refer to the following conversation. (🔊 영국…캐나다)

M Hi, I'm calling about a new account that a friend of mine told me about. It's free and uh . . . What's it called?

W ³⁸I think you're talking about our first-time-customer promotion account. ³⁹We've had a lot of calls about that today. I can help you with that over the phone.

M Well, it's actually for my son. He's in college and I want him to have a local bank account. But he's not here right now.

W That's okay. ⁴⁰Please tell him to call us later. The offer is only good until Friday though, so don't delay.

M Thank you. I'll tell him to call today.

어휘 account 계좌 promotion 홍보 good 유효한

남 안녕하세요? 신규 계좌 때문에 전화했어요. 제 친구가 말해줬거든요. 무료인데, 그걸 뭐라고 했더라?

여 ³⁸저희의 신규 고객 프로모션 계좌에 대해 말씀하시는 것 같군요. ³⁹오늘 그 건으로 전화를 많이 받았어요. 전화상으로 도와드릴 수 있어요.

남 사실 제 아들을 위한 거예요. 대학에 다니고 있는데 그 애한테 지역 은행 계좌가 있었으면 해서요. 하지만 지금 그 애는 여기 없어요.

여 괜찮습니다. ⁴⁰나중에 전화하라고 해주세요. 이 행사는 금요일까지 유효하니 미루지 마세요.

남 감사합니다. 오늘 전화하라고 할게요.

---

38 남자는 여자에게 무엇에 대해서 묻고 있는가?
(A) 대학 지원서
(B) 홍보 캠페인
(C) 그의 예금계좌
(D) 아들의 장학금

39 🔵신🔵유🔵형 여자는 왜 We've had a lot of calls about that today라고 말하는가?
(A) 많은 사람들이 통화 중이라고 불평했다.
(B) 같은 고객과 여러 차례 대화를 했다.
(C) 그녀는 모든 전화에 지쳤다.
(D) 새로운 행사가 인기가 있다.

40 여자는 남자에게 무엇을 추천하는가?
(A) 친구에게 조언을 구할 것
(B) 그녀를 다시 만나러 올 것
(C) 나중에 다시 전화할 것
(D) 서두를 것

어휘 checking account 예금계좌 scholarship 장학금 busy 통화 중인 repeatedly 되풀이하여

Questions 41-43 refer to the following conversation. (🔊 호주…미국)

W Excuse me. ⁴¹Everyone else has already got their bag, but I don't see mine.

M I'm sorry about that. ⁴¹It may have gotten put on a different flight. Can I have your last name and where you're coming from?

W It's Denison and I just arrived from Atlanta.

M Okay, Ms. Denison, ⁴²I see your luggage number and it didn't make it on the flight from Atlanta, but will be coming on the next flight arriving in about an hour. You can wait here or we can deliver it to your hotel or home.

W ⁴³Please send it to my hotel. I'm really tired and want to lie down.

어휘 flight 항공편

여 실례합니다. ⁴¹다른 사람들은 벌써 가방을 찾아 갔는데, 제 가방은 보이지 않네요.

남 죄송합니다. ⁴¹다른 비행기에 실렸을 수도 있어요. 성함과 출발지를 말해주시겠어요?

여 이름은 Denision이고, 애틀랜타에서 막 도착했어요.

남 네, Denison씨, ⁴²손님의 수하물 번호가 보이는데요, 애틀랜타에서 출발한 비행기에는 수화물이 실리지 않았지만, 다음 비행기로 한 시간 후에 도착할 거예요. 여기서 기다리시거나, 아니면 저희가 호텔이나 집으로 배달해드릴 수 있습니다.

여 ⁴³제 호텔로 보내주세요. 저는 지금 너무나도 피곤해서 당장 눕고 싶어요.

41 화자들이 있는 곳은 어디인가?
(A) 공항
(B) 여행가방 가게
(C) 기차역
(D) 여행사

42 무엇이 문제인가?
(A) 남자가 예약하는 것을 잊었다.
(B) 남자가 여자에게 요금을 더 부과하였다.
(C) 여자의 물건이 함께 도착하지 않았다.
(D) 여자의 이름 철자가 틀렸다.

43 여자는 다음에 어디로 갈 것인가?
(A) 병원
(B) 호텔
(C) 애틀랜타
(D) 자신의 집

Questions 44-46 refer to the following conversation. (1) 미국···캐나다

M Angela, ⁴⁴have you seen the test version of our new Website? We need to get everyone's feedback on it by tomorrow when I meet with the designers.

W Oh, yes, I'm just looking at it now. I really like the clean divisions on the side. It makes our product information much easier to see. ⁴⁵One thing I would change, though, is the size of the words in the middle. It's much too big.

M I agree. I will ask the designers to change that. Plus, the logo needs to stand out more.

W ⁴⁶Do you want me to come to the meeting with you?

M ⁴⁶I think I can handle it. I've been working with them for a couple of weeks on this.

남 Angela, ⁴⁴우리 새 웹사이트의 시험 버전 봤어요? 제가 내일 디자이너들을 만날 때까지 모두에게서 웹사이트에 대한 피드백을 받아야 해요.

여 네, 이제 막 보고 있는 중이에요. 저는 측면의 명확한 구분이 정말 좋아요. 그것 때문에 우리 제품 정보를 보기가 훨씬 더 쉬워요. 하지만 ⁴⁵한 가지 제가 바꾼다면, 중간에 있는 글자 크기예요. 너무 커요.

남 같은 생각이에요. 디자이너들에게 바꾸라고 요청할게요. 거기에다 로고는 더 눈에 띄었으면 하고요.

여 ⁴⁶제가 회의에 같이 가면 좋겠어요?

남 ⁴⁶제가 할 수 있을 것 같아요. 이 일에 관해서 디자이너들과 몇 주 동안 같이 일했거든요.

어휘 division 경계, 구분 stand out 눈에 띄다 handle 처리하다

---

44 화자들이 주로 의논하는 것은 무엇인가?
(A) 고객 주문
(B) 피드백 양식
(C) 새 웹사이트
(D) 시험 제품

45 여자는 어떤 변화를 제안하는가?
(A) 글꼴 크기 줄이기
(B) 로고 강조하기
(C) 글자를 더 진하게 만들기
(D) 전체 디자인 수정하기

46 🔵신 🔵유 🔵형 남자가 I think I can handle it라고 말한 의도는 무엇인가?
(A) 남자는 혼자서 시스템을 설정할 수 있다.
(B) 남자는 여자의 피드백이 필요 없다.
(C) 여자가 디자이너들을 만날 필요가 없다.
(D) 여자가 남자를 태워줄 필요가 없다.

어휘 trial 시험적인 decrease 줄이다 emphasize 강조하다

Questions 47–49 refer to the following conversation. 〔📢 영국…호주〕 신 유 형 —

M ⁴⁷Storage Solutions customer care line. How can I help you?

W Yes, ⁴⁸I was trying to order some containers on your Website, but I keep getting an error message. It says my credit card is invalid, but I've ordered from you before.

M I can help you with that. Can I have your name, please?

W Yes, it's Theresa Gregson.

M Okay, I see you in our system. It says your credit card is expired.

W Oh, I must be using my old card. Can I update the information now?

M ⁴⁹I'm afraid you'll have to do that online. I'll tell you the process if you'd like.

어휘 invalid 효력 없는 expired 만료된

남 ⁴⁷스토리지 솔루션 고객관리부입니다. 무엇을 도와드릴까요?

여 네, ⁴⁸웹사이트에서 그릇을 주문하려고 했는데 계속 오류 메시지가 떠요. 신용카드가 유효하지 않다고 하는데, 전에 주문한 적이 있거든요.

남 제가 도와드리겠습니다. 성함이 어떻게 되시죠?

여 Theresa Gregson입니다.

남 알겠습니다. 저희 시스템에 고객님이 보이네요. 신용카드가 기한이 지났다고 되어 있습니다.

여 제 옛날 카드를 쓰고 있었나 보네요. 지금 정보를 업데이트할 수 있나요?

남 ⁴⁹죄송하지만, 그건 고객님께서 온라인으로 해주셔야 합니다. 원하시면 과정을 말씀드릴게요.

47 남자는 누구인가?
(A) 카드사의 대리인
(B) 고객서비스 담당자
(C) 신규 고객
(D) 점원

48 여자의 문제는 무엇인가?
(A) 컴퓨터가 작동하지 않는다.
(B) 주문한 것이 아직 도착하지 않았다.
(C) 주문이 잘못되어 있다.
(D) 지불 방법이 받아들여지지 않는다.

49 남자는 다음에 무엇을 할 것인가?
(A) 카드 회사에 전화한다.
(B) 여자의 구매 기록을 확인한다.
(C) 절차를 설명한다.
(D) 여자의 전화를 넘겨준다.

어휘 transfer 넘겨주다

Questions 50–52 refer to the following conversation. 〔📢 호주…미국〕

W Hi, ⁵⁰I'm calling about your grocery delivery service. My neighbor told me about it and I think it would really help me since I just started working full time.

M It is very convenient for working people. Can I first ask where you live? We have different delivery days for different areas.

W I'm in the Rosewood neighborhood. ⁵¹If I could get the delivery on Monday, it would help me a lot.

M I'm afraid we're only delivering on Tuesdays to Rosewood at the moment. ⁵¹But if we get more customers there, we could add another delivery day.

W ⁵¹,⁵²I'll ask my friends around here if they want to join.

어휘 grocery 식료품 delivery 배달 neighborhood 동네 at the moment 지금

여 안녕하세요? ⁵⁰식료품 배달 서비스와 관련해 전화드렸습니다. 제 이웃이 그 서비스에 대해 말해줬는데, 제가 막 전일제로 일하기 시작해서 저에게는 정말 도움이 될 것 같아요.

남 일하는 분들에게는 그 서비스가 아주 편리합니다. 어디에 사시는지 여쭤도 될까요? 지역에 따라 배송 날짜가 다르거든요.

여 저는 Rosewood 동네에 살고 있어요. ⁵¹월요일에 배달받으면 큰 도움이 될 것 같아요.

남 죄송하지만, 지금은 화요일에만 Rosewood로 배달하고 있어요. ⁵¹하지만 그쪽에 더 많은 고객이 생기면 배송일을 더 추가할 수 있어요.

여 ⁵²근처에 사는 친구들에게 함께 할지 물어볼게요.

50 화자들이 주로 의논하는 것은 무엇인가?
(A) 식품 배달 서비스
(B) 동네 행사
(C) 남자의 일정
(D) 여자의 새 직업

51 여자는 어떤 변화를 보고 싶은가?
(A) 다양한 서비스
(B) 다른 일정
(C) 더 친절한 직원
(D) 더 낮은 가격

52 여자는 무엇을 하겠다고 말하는가?
(A) 다른 지역으로 이사한다.
(B) 직업을 바꾼다.
(C) 서비스를 신청한다.
(D) 이웃에게 얘기한다.

Questions 53-55 refer to the following conversation. 🔊 영국…캐나다

M ⁵³Mr. Stanley, our manufacturer, just called and he said he can't get the part for our new fans for another six weeks.

W Six weeks? ⁵⁴The summer will nearly be over by then!

M Don't worry. I talked to Mr. Stanley and explained that our fans are sold out in almost every store and we need to restock them immediately. ⁵⁵He's going to check with a different supplier and get back to me by the end of the day.

W Let me know what he says. If it's more bad news, we'll have to start looking for another manufacturer.

남 ⁵³우리 제조업체에서 Stanley씨가 방금 전화했는데, ⁵³,⁵⁴6주간 우리 새 선풍기의 부품을 댈 수 없대요.

여 6주요? ⁵⁴그때쯤이면 여름이 거의 끝날 거예요!

남 걱정 마세요. Stanley씨와 이야기했어요. 우리 선풍기가 거의 모든 매장에서 다 팔려서, 금방 다시 재고를 채워야 한다고요. ⁵⁵Stanley씨가 다른 납품업체와 확인하고 오늘 안으로 저에게 말해줄 거예요.

여 Stanley씨가 뭐라고 하는지 제게 알려줘요. 더 나쁜 소식이라면, 다른 제조업체를 찾아봐야 할 거예요.

어휘 part 부품 restock 다시 채우다

---

53 화자들이 의논하는 문제는 무엇인가?
(A) 고객 불만
(B) 재무 문제
(C) 제품 회수
(D) 공급 문제

54 🔵유형 The summer will nearly be over by then이라는 여자의 말이 암시하는 것은 무엇인가?
(A) 그때는 더위가 덜할 것이기 때문에 행복하다.
(B) 회사는 여름이 지나면 문을 닫을 것이다.
(C) 그때는 제품이 필요하지 않게 될 것이다.
(D) 그때는 근로자들이 더 바빠질 것이다.

55 저녁에 무슨 일이 있을 것인가?
(A) 제조사에서 회신이 올 것이다.
(B) 재고 정리 세일이 시작될 것이다.
(C) 화자들은 재고조사를 할 것이다.
(D) 상품이 시장에 출시될 것이다.

어휘 clearance sale 재고 정리 세일 do an inventory 재고조사를 하다 put ⊠ on the market ~를 팔려고 내놓다

Questions 56-58 refer to the following conversation with three speakers. 🔊 미국…캐나다…영국 🔵유형

M1 ⁵⁶We've experienced a lot of growth at our company in the last six months and we may need to move offices. I'd like you two to look at properties nearby and report back to me by the end of the month.

W Sure, Mr. Martin. ⁵⁷I have a realtor friend who could show us some places. I'll set up an appointment with her right away.

M2 Is there a specific price range we should be looking at?

M1 Well, we pay $3,500 per month for this office. I hope not to pay more than $4,000.

M2 That might be difficult. ⁵⁸The rents in this area have really increased since the new station went in.

W Yes, my friend said the same thing. But we will try to find the best deal.

남1 ⁵⁶지난 6개월간 회사가 많은 성장을 해서 사무실을 이전해야 할 수도 있습니다. 두 분은 가까운 부동산을 보시고 이번 달 말까지 저에게 보고해주세요.

여 알겠습니다, Martin씨. ⁵⁷장소를 몇 개 보여줄 부동산 중개업자 친구가 있어요. 당장 그녀와 약속을 잡을게요.

남2 우리가 봐야 할 가격대가 있나요?

남 이 사무실은 매월 3,500달러씩 내요. 저는 4,000달러 이상은 내지 않았으면 좋겠어요.

남2 그건 힘들 거예요. ⁵⁸새 역이 들어 온 후로 이 지역의 임대료가 정말 많이 올랐어요.

여 제 친구도 같은 말을 했어요. 하지만 가장 좋은 거래를 찾아보자고요.

어휘 realtor 부동산 중개업자 set up an appointment 약속을 잡다 price range 가격대 rent 임차료

56 화자들의 회사에 대해 언급된 것은?
    (A) 사업이 잘되고 있다.
    (B) 신입직원을 채용하고 있다.
    (C) 해외 지역으로 이전한다.
    (D) 수입보다 더 많이 지출하고 있다.

57 여자는 무엇을 하겠다고 말하는가?
    (A) 친구에게 연락하기
    (B) 계약서들 살펴보기
    (C) 예약하기
    (D) 새 지점 방문하기

58 그 지역의 임대료가 인상된 이유는 무엇인가?
    (A) 교통편 향상
    (B) 경제 성장
    (C) 안전 개선
    (D) 신축 사무실 공사

어휘 improved 개선된

Questions 59-61 refer to the following conversation with three speakers. (◁)) 영국…호주…캐나다) 신 유 형

M Hi, Ellen. I haven't seen you since you moved to your new place. How are you liking it?

W1 It's great. ⁵⁹The only thing is I have to take the train to work now. I don't really understand the complicated train system and it's always so crowded.

M Nina, you take the train to work, right? Which direction are you coming from?

W2 Northeast. ⁶⁰I take the Yellow Line and transfer at Seven Oaks Station to the Blue Line.

W1 Oh, I come from the east and I take the Yellow Line, too. I didn't think about changing lines at Seven Oaks.

W2 Oh, yes. It's much easier than going all the way to City Center. The train gets very crowded if you do that.

W1 Thanks for the tip, Nina.

W2 And ⁶¹they just made an app for the trains. You can look up all the times and see if there are delays. Here, ⁶¹Ellen, I'll show you on my phone.

어휘 crowded 붐비는 direction 방향 transfer 환승하다

남 안녕하세요? Ellen. 당신이 새 집으로 이사한 후로 못 봤네요. 집은 마음에 들어요?
여1 훌륭해요. ⁵⁹문제가 있다면 이젠 기차로 출근해야 한다는 거예요. 복잡한 기차 시스템을 잘 이해하지 못하겠고, 항상 너무 붐벼요.
남 Nina, 당신이 기차로 출근하잖아요? 어느 쪽에서 와요?
여2 북동 방향이요. ⁶⁰저는 노란색 노선을 타고 Seven Oaks에서 파란색 노선으로 갈아타요.
여1 저는 동쪽에서 오는데 저도 노란색 노선을 타요. Seven Oaks에서 갈아탈 생각을 하지 못했네요.
여2 네, 도심까지 쭉 가는 것보다 훨씬 쉬워요. 그렇게 가면 기차가 너무 붐벼요.
여1 조언 고마워요, Nina.
여2 그리고 ⁶¹기차용 앱이 있어요. 기차 시간표를 찾아보고 지연되는 것도 확인할 수 있어요. ⁶¹Ellen, 여기 내 전화기에서 보여줄게요.

---

59 Ellen은 새로 이사한 곳의 어떤 점을 싫어하는가?
    (A) 회사로의 접근성
    (B) 붐비는 역
    (C) 주택의 색
    (D) 방의 크기

60 Seven Oaks역에 대해서 뭐라고 말할 수 있는가?
    (A) 새로 생긴 역이다.
    (B) 도시의 서쪽에 있다.
    (C) 여자들은 그 역에 대해 몰랐다.
    (D) 두 노선이 그곳을 통과한다.

61 Nina는 이후 무엇을 할 것인가?
    (A) 새 집 찾기
    (B) 출발 시간 확인하기
    (C) Ellen에게 앱 보여주기
    (D) 기차 타기

Questions 62–64 refer to the following conversation. 🔊 영국…호주 신 유 형

M Hi, Mary Brock? ⁶²This is Alan Hall from City Life Magazine. I'm calling to let you know that your catering company has won "The Best in the City" award from our readers.

W Really? I'm so flattered. ⁶³We came in second place last year but, oh, I don't know what to say!

M Well, congratulations. It seems you've become more popular since last year.

W I guess so.

M ⁶²,⁶⁴I'd like to schedule a time to do an interview with you and possibly take some pictures in your office.

W Uh, okay. I'm pretty busy this week. ⁶⁴Is next Monday too late?

M No, that would be fine. Does 3:00 PM work for you?

W Sounds great. Thank you, Mr. Hall.

남 Mary Brock씨인가요? ⁶²City Life 매거진의 Alan Hall입니다. 귀하의 출장음식업체가 저희 독자가 뽑은 '도시 최고' 상을 수상했습니다.

여 정말요? 으쓱해지네요. ⁶³저희가 작년에는 2위를 했는데요. 뭐라고 해야 할지 모르겠네요!

남 축하드립니다. 작년 이후로 인기가 더 높아진 것 같아요.

여 그런 것 같아요.

남 ⁶²,⁶⁴인터뷰할 시간을 정하고 싶어요. 그리고 사무실에서 사진도 몇 장 찍을 것 같아요.

여 이번 주에는 꽤 바빠요. ⁶⁴다음 주 월요일은 너무 늦나요?

남 아뇨, 괜찮아요. 오후 3시 어떠세요?

여 좋습니다. 감사합니다, Hall씨.

어휘 catering 음식 공급 be flattered 으쓱해지다 come in second place 2위를 하다

---

62 남자는 누구인가?
(A) 출장음식업자
(B) 시 공무원
(C) 식료품점 관리자
(D) 기자

63 여자의 사업에 대해 언급된 것은?
(A) 작년에 그 상을 탈 뻔했다.
(B) 작년에 이전했다.
(C) 올해 사무실을 개조했다.
(D) 올해 창업했다.

64 다음 주 월요일에 무슨 일이 있을 것인가?
(A) 대회 결과가 발표될 것이다.
(B) 잡지가 발행될 것이다.
(C) 여자의 사무실에서 화자들이 만날 것이다.
(D) 여자는 면접을 볼 것이다.

어휘 relocate 이전하다

Questions 65–67 refer to the following conversation and bill. 🔊 호주…미국

W Hi, I'm ready to check out but I think ⁶⁵there's a mistake on my bill. I didn't take anything out of the mini bar.

M Oh, let me check that. Room 343, right? I think I see what happened. ⁶⁶Your name is similar to another guest's name. That's why the charges got switched. Does everything else look correct?

W Um, yeh . . . Wait, what's this service charge?

M That's something we add for all our guests on the weekend.

W Oh, I see. Then everything's fine. ⁶⁷Here's my credit card.

여 안녕하세요? 체크아웃하려고 하는데 ⁶⁵계산이 잘못된 것 같아요. 전 미니바에서 아무것도 꺼내지 않았거든요.

남 확인해보겠습니다. 343호실 맞죠? 무슨 일이 있었는지 알 것 같아요. ⁶⁶손님의 성함이 다른 손님의 성함과 비슷하네요. 그래서 요금이 바뀐 거예요. 다른 건 다 맞나요?

여 잠깐만요. 이 서비스 요금은 뭐죠?

남 그것은 주말이면 모든 손님에게 추가되는 것입니다.

여 그렇군요. 그러면 모든 게 괜찮습니다. ⁶⁷여기 제 신용카드요.

Sinclair 호텔	
1. 숙박 요금	80달러
2. [65]미니바	17달러
3. 룸서비스	12달러
4. 봉사료	8달러
총액	117달러

어휘 bill 계산서 mini bar (호텔 객실의) 소형 냉장고

---

65 계산서에 의하면, 얼마가 제외될 것인가?
(A) 8달러
(B) 12달러
(C) 17달러
(D) 80달러

66 남자는 무엇 때문에 문제가 일어났다고 하는가?
(A) 청소부의 실수
(B) 컴퓨터 오류
(C) 이름 혼동
(D) 예약 변경

67 남자는 다음에 무엇을 할 것 같은가?
(A) 상사에게 전화한다.
(B) 컴퓨터에서 뭔가를 확인한다.
(C) 여자에게 열쇠를 준다.
(D) 결제를 처리한다.

어휘 process 처리하다

Questions 68–70 refer to the following conversation and coupon. 📢 미국…캐나다

M [68]This sofa is so comfortable. And it will look great in my new apartment. I'm worried about the price though. [69]Can I use this coupon I found online?

W [69]Sure. And you're in luck! Today only, everything from our Inverness line is an extra 5 percent off!

M Oh, [69]so you mean this sofa has an additional discount today? Wow, that is lucky. I'll take it.

W Great. [70]Just come to the counter and we'll get started on your delivery and payment details.

남 [68]이 소파는 정말 편해요. 제 새 아파트에 두면 멋져 보일 거예요. 그런데 가격이 걱정되네요. [69]온라인에서 찾은 이 쿠폰을 사용할 수 있나요?

여 [69]그럼요. 운이 좋으시네요! 오늘 단 하루만, 저희 Inverness 라인의 모든 것이 5%의 추가 할인이 돼요!

남 [69]그럼 오늘 이 소파에 추가 할인이 있다는 말인가요? 와, 운이 좋네요. 이걸로 할게요.

여 좋습니다. [70]계산대로 오세요. 배송과 결제 세부 사항에 대해 얘기해보죠.

ABC 가구	
할인 쿠폰	
[65]소파류	10% 할인!
식탁	20% 할인!
침대	20% 할인!

9791196597504

(7월 31일까지 유효)

어휘 be in luck 운이 좋다

---

68 남자가 상품에 대해 언급한 것은?
(A) 가장 좋아하는 색이다.
(B) 그의 집에 적합하다.
(C) 그의 집에 비해 크다.
(D) 그의 예산 범위 내에 있다.

69 쿠폰에 의하면, 구매 시 남자는 얼마나 할인받을 것인가?
(A) 10%
(B) 15%
(C) 20%
(D) 25%

70 남자는 다음에 무엇을 할 것인가?
(A) 배송 일정 세우기
(B) 온라인으로 가격 확인하기
(C) 다른 품목 찾기
(D) 품목 재기

PART 4

Questions 71–73 refer to the following recorded message. 🔊 호주

Thank you for your continued patience. Our customer service representatives are busy helping other customers at this time. Please stay on the line and your call will be answered in the order in which it was received. **71,72 Please make sure you have your frequent flyer number and flight schedule with destinations ready to give to the next available representative.** **73 Less heavy call volumes are expected between 8:00 and 9:00 AM and between 5:00 and 6:00 PM.** Or, you can visit our Website at www.skyquik.com to make your reservation online.

계속 기다려 주셔서 감사합니다. 현재 저희 고객서비스 담당자는 다른 고객을 돕고 있습니다. 전화를 끊지 않으시면 전화 온 순서대로 응대해드리겠습니다. 71,72고객님의 상용 고객 번호와 도착지를 포함한 비행 일정을 준비해주시고, 다음에 연결되는 담당자에게 알려주시기 바랍니다. 73오전 8시부터 9시, 오후 5시부터 6시 사이에는 통화량이 적을 것으로 예상됩니다. 또는 저희 웹사이트 www.skyquik.com에 접속하여 온라인으로 예약하실 수 있습니다.

71 어떤 업종의 메시지인가?
(A) 호텔
(B) 항공사
(C) 전자제품 가게
(D) 온라인 의류 매장

72 발신자에게 준비하라고 요청하는 것은 무엇인가?
(A) 회원 번호
(B) 휴대폰 번호
(C) 주문 번호
(D) 여권 번호

73 발신자에게 대기가 짧은 시간에 다시 전화하라고 안내한 시간은 언제인가?
(A) 오전 10시
(B) 오후 5시 30분
(C) 오후 7시
(D) 오후 8시 30분

Questions 74–76 refer to the following excerpt from a meeting. 🔊 미국

74 Thank you for inviting me here today to talk about our exciting line of copying equipment. I think you will be impressed with all the functions of these new copiers. I notice that you're using our competitor's machine and that's fine. You might want to think about upgrading to our PaperQ 2000, **75 which copies at twice the speed of the one you have and costs just the same.** **76 I'd like to show you a video now.** It will give you a very visual idea of what our machine can actually do.

74오늘 저희 회사의 흥미로운 복사기 제품군에 대해 이야기하기 위해 이곳에 초대해주셔서 감사합니다. 이 두 대의 새 복사기가 가진 모든 기능에 깊은 인상을 받으실 것입니다. 여러분이 저희 경쟁사의 제품을 사용하는 것을 알지만, 괜찮습니다. 비용은 같으면서 75복사 속도는 지금 제품보다 두 배인 저희 PaperQ 2000으로 업그레이드하는 것에 대해 생각해보실만 합니다. 76지금 영상을 보여드리겠습니다. 저희 제품이 실제로 할 수 있는 것을 시각적으로 보여줄 것입니다.

74 화자가 청자들과 만나고 있는 이유는 무엇인가?
(A) 소프트웨어가 어떻게 작동하는지 설명하기 위해
(B) 새로운 시스템에서 그들이 필요한 것을 알아내기 위해
(C) 신입직원에게 회사의 정책을 알려주기 위해
(D) 장비를 소개하기 위해

75 화자에 의하면 그의 제품이 경쟁사의 제품보다 이점인 것은 무엇인가?
(A) 더 싸다.
(B) 더 빠르다.
(C) 품질이 더 높다.
(D) 더 가볍다.

76 청자들은 다음에 무엇을 할 것인가?
(A) 발표 듣기
(B) 새로운 시스템에 로그인하기
(C) 사무용 장치 사용하기
(D) 영상 시청하기

Questions 77–79 refer to the following advertisement. ◁)) 캐나다

Whether you're new to running or an experienced runner, Air Space K running shoes are made with you in mind. ⁷⁷Thanks to a revolutionary new fabric, they are sturdy enough to last for years, yet they are the lightest on the market today. You'll feel like you're walking on air. Air Space K shoes are available at Thom's Shoes. Come in soon to get fitted by our shoe specialists. ⁷⁸We use the latest technology to find out your shoe size and foot shape. Plenty of free parking and ⁷⁹mention this ad for a free pair of socks.

달리기에 처음 입문한 분이든, 노련한 러너이든, Air Space K 러닝화는 여러분을 고려하여 만들어졌습니다. ⁷⁷혁신적인 새로운 원단 덕분에 수년을 견딜 수 있을 만큼 견고하면서도 현재 시중 제품 중 가장 가볍습니다. 마치 공중을 걷는 듯한 느낌을 받으실 것입니다. Air Space K 신발은 Thom's Shoes에서 구매 가능합니다. 어서 오셔서 저희 신발 전문가들이 맞춰드리는 서비스를 받아보세요. ⁷⁸저희는 최신 기술을 사용하여 여러분의 신발 치수와 발 모양을 찾습니다. 넓은 무료 주차 공간이 있으며 ⁷⁹이 광고를 언급하시면 양말 한 켤레를 무료로 드립니다.

> **어휘** revolutionary 혁신적인 fabric 직물 sturdy 튼튼한 mention 언급하다

77 Air Space K 신발에 대해 언급된 내용은 무엇인가?
(A) 달리기를 시작한 사람들만을 위해 만들어졌다.
(B) 온라인으로만 구매할 수 있다.
(C) 시장에 나온 제품 중 가장 싸다.
(D) 새로운 원단이 사용되었다.

78 매장의 기술은 어떤 역할을 하는가?
(A) 맞춤 신발 만들기
(B) 발 크기 측정하기
(C) 고객에게 달리는 방법 가르치기
(D) 고객에게 달리는 곳 보여주기

79 사은품을 받으려면 고객은 어떻게 해야 하는가?
(A) 쿠폰 지참하기
(B) 신발 두 켤레 구매하기
(C) 설문지 작성하기
(D) 광고를 들었다고 말하기

Questions 80–82 refer to the following announcement. ◁)) 영국

Attention ladies and gentleman. ⁸⁰Those of you waiting for the 8:30 showing of *For Once And For All*, you may now enter the theater. Please have your tickets out to give to our staff. Then proceed to Theater 3. ⁸¹For those waiting for the 8:45 showing of *Star Games*, please do not get in line yet. We will call you in about five minutes. ⁸²As part of our public transportation promotional campaign this month, just show your public transportation receipt or card for 10 percent off all of our snacks and drinks. And please feel free to pick up a copy of *Movie News* on your way out.

신사 숙녀 여러분 주목해주세요. ⁸⁰8시 30분에 상영하는 For Once And For All을 기다리시는 분들은 이제 상영관에 입장하실 수 있습니다. 입장권을 꺼내어 저희 직원에게 주시고, 3번 상영관으로 입장하세요. ⁸¹8시 45분에 상영하는 Star Games를 기다리시는 분들은 아직 줄을 서지 말아주세요. 약 5분 후에 안내해드리겠습니다. ⁸²이번 달 대중교통 홍보 캠페인의 일환으로 대중교통 영수증이나 카드를 보여주시면, 모든 스낵과 음료를 10% 할인해드립니다. 나가시는 길에는 자유롭게 Movie News 한 부씩 가져가세요.

> **어휘** proceed ~로 향하다

80 청자들은 어디에 있는가?
(A) 콘서트 장소
(B) 식료품점
(C) 영화 극장
(D) 스포츠 장소

81 5분 후에 일어날 일은 무엇인가?
(A) 경기가 시작될 것이다.
(B) 출연자가 나타날 것이다.
(C) 또 다른 안내방송이 있을 것이다.
(D) 간식을 먹을 수 있을 것이다.

82 지하철 카드를 보여주는 청자는 무엇을 받게 될 것인가?
(A) 잡지 한 권
(B) 음식 할인
(C) 사은품
(D) 특별 좌석

Questions 83–85 refer to the following talk. 🔊 호주

Hello, folks. Welcome to Tony's Café. My name is Brenda and I'll be your server today. In addition to what's on our menu, we have some morning specials on the board over there. I recommend the blueberry pancakes—we're famous for them. Just to let you know, though, **83we will stop taking breakfast orders in about ten minutes.** **84If everyone is drinking coffee, I can bring you a carafe that's enough for four. It'll be cheaper than ordering coffee individually.** Let me give you a few minutes to look at our menu and **85I'll be right back with your water.**

안녕하세요, 여러분. Tony 카페에 오신 걸 환영합니다. 저는 Brenda이고, 오늘 여러분의 서빙을 맡을 것입니다. 메뉴에 있는 것 외에도, 저쪽에 있는 보드에 아침 스페셜 메뉴가 적혀 있습니다. 저는 블루베리 팬케이크를 추천드립니다. 저희 가게에서 유명합니다. 알려드리자면, 83약 10분 후에 아침식사 주문을 마감할 예정입니다. 84일행 모두가 커피를 마신다면, 네 명은 충분히 마실 수 있는 유리병에 가져다드릴 수 있습니다. 개별적으로 커피를 주문하는 것보다 저렴할 것입니다. 메뉴를 살펴보실 동안 85저는 물을 가져다드리겠습니다.

어휘 in addition to ~에 더하여 carafe 유리병 individually 개별적으로

83 화자가 we will stop taking breakfast orders in about ten minutes라고 말한 의도는 무엇인가?
(A) 청자들은 서둘러 나가야 한다.
(B) 청자들은 무엇을 먹을지 빨리 정해야 한다.
(C) 화자는 교대 근무가 거의 끝나간다.
(D) 화자는 아침식사가 떨어질 것이다.

84 화자는 청중들에게 무엇을 제안하는가?
(A) 음료를 따로따로 주문하기
(B) 식사비를 개별적으로 지불하기
(C) 공통의 음료를 나눠 마시기
(D) 전채 음식 먹어보기

85 화자는 청자들에게 곧 무엇을 가져다줄 것인가?
(A) 커피
(B) 메뉴판
(C) 은 식기류
(D) 물

어휘 separately 따로따로

Questions 86–88 refer to the following report. 🔊 미국

86I've been asked to report on the progress of our Website update. **87We've had to rebuild whole sections, which got hacked,** as I mentioned last month. Those are almost complete and the new products section is nearly updated with our new product line. By the middle of next week, we should be able to test a few purchases. **88My department wants to assure everyone that by Friday of next week we will be up and running again.** In addition to re-creating the Website, we have installed a stronger firewall so this problem won't occur again. Does anyone have any questions?

86웹사이트 업데이트 진행 상황을 보고해달라는 요청을 받았습니다. 지난달에 말씀드린 바와 같이 87해킹당한 부분을 전부 원상 복구시켰습니다. 그 부분들은 거의 완료되었으며, 신상품 섹션은 우리의 신상품 라인과 함께 거의 업데이트되었습니다. 다음 주 중반까지 몇 가지 구매 테스트를 할 수 있을 것입니다. 88제 부서는 다음 주 금요일까지 일을 마무리하고 재가동할 수 있을 거라 확신합니다. 웹사이트를 다시 만드는 것 외에도 더 강력한 방화벽을 설치했으므로 이 문제가 다시는 발생하지 않을 것입니다. 질문 있으신 분 계십니까?

어휘 rebuild 재건하다 whole 전체의 assure 확인하다 install 설치하다 firewall 방화벽

86 보고하는 사람은 누구인가?
(A) 소방 공무원
(B) 제품 디자이너
(C) 웹디자이너
(D) IT 직원

87 무엇이 문제였는가?
(A) 사무실 화재로 장비가 손상되었다.
(B) 제품에 결함이 있는 것으로 나타났다.
(C) 웹사이트가 해킹을 당했다.
(D) 어떤 직원이 안전하지 않은 웹사이트를 사용했다.

88 언제 문제가 완벽하게 해결되는가?
(A) 내일
(B) 다음 주 중반
(C) 다음 주말
(D) 다음 달

Questions 89-91 refer to the following broadcast. (캐나다)

Good afternoon, everyone. This is Marsha Newell reporting live from the new Tech Heaven store downtown. ⁸⁹It's very crowded since the latest device from Nova Electronics, the smart watch, was released today. Representatives of the company say they are producing the watch as fast as they can, but ⁹⁰there are a limited number of watches available at this time. I'm not sure how many are left because, well, ⁹⁰the store opened at 9:00 and it's almost 2:00 now. If you don't make it down here in time, you can order one online, though ⁹¹I heard there is a waiting list of six weeks.

여러분, 좋은 오후입니다. 도심에 새로 연 Tech Heaven 매장에서 생방송을 진행하는 Marsha Newell입니다. ⁸⁹오늘 출시된 Nova Electronics의 최신 제품인 스마트 시계 때문에 이곳은 매우 혼잡합니다. 회사의 대변인은 가급적 빨리 시계를 생산하고 있지만, ⁹⁰현재로서는 제한된 개수만 구매할 수 있다고 합니다. 가게는 9시에 열었고 지금 거의 2시가 다 되어가기 때문에 남은 수량이 얼마나 될지 모르겠습니다. 제때 매장에서 구매하실 수 없다면 온라인에서도 주문할 수 있지만 ⁹¹약 6주치의 대기 명단이 있다고 합니다.

어휘 latest device 최신 제품

---

89 화자는 어떤 종류의 제품에 대해 보도하고 있는가?
(A) 소형기기
(B) 노트북 컴퓨터
(C) 음악 재생 장치
(D) 비디오카메라

90 🛈🔔🔄 the store opened at 9:00 and it's almost 2:00 now라는 화자의 말이 암시하는 것은 무엇인가?
(A) 계산대의 줄이 점점 짧아지고 있다.
(B) 인기 품목이 지금쯤이면 매진됐을 수도 있다.
(C) 점원들은 이미 피곤하다.
(D) 가게가 곧 문을 닫는다.

91 온라인으로 주문한 고객은 언제 물품을 받을 수 있는가?
(A) 3주 후
(B) 6주 후
(C) 약 2달 후
(D) 6개월 후

어휘 gadget (간단한) 기계 장치

Questions 92-94 refer to the following telephone message and report. (영국)

Hello, Catherine. ⁹²This is Stuart in the accounting department. I'm calling about the expense report for the trade show. Your report was fine, but I can't find the receipts for one or more of your meals. ⁹³When I add up the receipts you gave me for your meals, the total comes to only $250. ⁹⁴If you have any more receipts, please drop them by my office. I'm trying to get all the reports processed by 5:00 today, so I'd appreciate having the receipts as soon as possible. Thank you.

안녕하세요, Catherine. ⁹²회계부의 Stuart예요. 무역 박람회 경비 보고서 때문에 전화드렸어요. 보고서는 괜찮은데 식사 영수증 한두 개를 찾을 수 없네요. ⁹³저에게 주신 식사 영수증을 합산하면, 총액은 250달러밖에 되지 않아요. ⁹⁴영수증을 더 갖고 계시면 제 사무실로 가져다주세요. 오늘 5시까지 모든 보고서를 처리하려 하니, 가급적 빨리 영수증을 가져다주시면 고맙겠습니다. 감사합니다.

지출 품의

출장 목적: 무역 박람회   부서: 영업
이름: Catherine Snow   부장: Isabelle Perkins

날짜	상세	교통비	호텔비	식비	기타
8/20, 23	로스앤젤레스 왕복 비행	350달러			
8/20~22	3박		800달러		
8/20~22	식사			⁹³300달러	
8/20~22	렌터카	200달러			

어휘 accounting department 회계부 trade show 무역 박람회 add up 합산하다

92 화자는 어떤 부서에서 일하는가?
(A) 회계
(B) 행정
(C) 인사
(D) 영업

93 품의서에 의하면, Catherine은 얼마의 영수증을 제출해야 하는가?
(신)(유)(형)
(A) 50달러
(B) 200달러
(C) 250달러
(D) 350달러

94 Catherine이 요청받은 것은 무엇인가?
(A) 항공권 예약하기
(B) 화자에게 영수증 가져다주기
(C) 예약 변경하기
(D) 양식 작성하기

Questions 95–97 refer to the following talk and graph. 🔊 호주

In the meeting today, ⁹⁵we're going to go over our recent mobile phone sales numbers and talk a bit about what we want to do in the upcoming months. As you can see on the graph, ⁹⁶we had a spike in phone sales corresponding with the blowout sale at all our branches. While the sale was very successful, it was disappointing to see numbers drop so drastically the next month. But, ⁹⁷we have a couple of ideas to get more customers into our stores next month to buy, buy, buy. I'll now let Rachel explain what we have in mind.

오늘 회의에서 ⁹⁵우리는 최근의 휴대폰 판매 수치를 검토하고 다가오는 몇 달 동안 하고 싶은 바에 대해 이야기해보겠습니다. 그래프에서 알 수 있듯이, ⁹⁶모든 지사에서 했던 파격 세일에 해당하는 기간에 판매가 급증했습니다. 판매는 매우 성공적이었던 반면, 다음 달에는 판매 수치가 급격하게 떨어지는 것이 실망스러웠습니다. 하지만 ⁹⁷다음 달에 고객들을 우리의 매장으로 오게 해서 구매하고 또 구매하게 할 수 있는 아이디어가 두어 가지가 있습니다. Rachel이 우리의 아이디어를 설명할 것입니다.

※월별 매출 그래프는 문제지를 참조하세요.

어휘 go over 검토하다 spike 급등 corresponding 상응하는 blowout sale 파격 세일 drastically 급격하게

---

95 화자는 어디에서 일하는가?
(A) 케이블 서비스 회사
(B) 가정용 가구 업체
(C) 이동통신 회사
(D) 여행사

96 그래프에 의하면 언제 세일을 했는가?
(신)(유)(형)
(A) 6월
(B) 7월
(C) 8월
(D) 9월

97 Rachel은 무엇에 대해 이야기할 것인가?
(A) 지점 개장
(B) 새로 온 판매 직원
(C) 몇 가지 새로운 영업 전략
(D) 실망스러운 판매 수치

Questions 98–100 refer to the following the following excerpt from a meeting and flyer. 🔊 미국

Thanks, everyone, for coming to this last-minute meeting. It won't take long ⁹⁸because I know you're busy with the quarterly report. As you know, our charity run for medical research is coming up in two weeks. Thanks to Lee's great design work, we have a really colorful and unique flyer this year. I have a question, though, before we take it to the printer. It's about the placement of our Website address. Right now it's in the top left corner, but ⁹⁹I'm wondering if it would be better near our phone number. ¹⁰⁰What do you all think?

이렇게 갑작스럽게 잡은 회의에 참석해주셔서 감사합니다. ⁹⁸여러분이 분기별 보고서 작성으로 바쁜 것을 알기 때문에 오래 걸리지는 않을 겁니다. 아시다시피, 자사의 의학 연구를 위한 자선 달리기가 2주 후에 시작됩니다. Lee의 훌륭한 디자인 작업 덕분에, 올해 우리는 정말 화려하고 특별한 전단지를 갖게 되었습니다. 인쇄 전에 여러분에게 질문이 있습니다. 웹사이트 주소의 배치에 관한 질문이에요. 지금은 상단 왼쪽 구석에 있는데, ⁹⁹저는 우리 회사의 전화번호 근처에 있는 게 더 나을 것 같아서요. ¹⁰⁰여러분의 생각은 어떠세요?

www.walshassoc.com

B

의학 연구
달리기 대회

A

C

7월 22일 토요일
가족 모두가 참여해요.
Walsh&Assoc. 협찬

D

⁹⁹전화: 555-6332

어휘 last-minute meeting 갑작스럽게 잡은 회의 quarterly 분기별의 placement 배치

---

98 화자가 일하는 곳은 어디인가?
(A) 인쇄소
(B) 체육관
(C) 사무실
(D) 쇼핑몰

99 전단지에 의하면, 화자는 웹 주소를 어디
신 에 넣고 싶어 하는가?
유
형 (A) A
(B) B
(C) C
(D) D

100 청자들은 다음에 무엇을 할 것인가?
(A) 행사에 참여하기
(B) 전단지 인쇄하기
(C) 의견을 제시하기
(D) 화자를 도와 전단지를 나눠주기

PART 5

101

부서장이 출근할 때 탄 급행열차는 기계적 문제로 1시간 지연되었다.

(A) 해로움   (B) 실수
(C) 개정   (D) 문제

어휘 division head 부서장 revision 개정

102

경영 위험 관리 프로세스를 보다 예측 가능하고 일관성 있게 개선하기 위해 장기적인 테스트가 필요했다.

(A) 예측하다   (B) 예측 가능성
(C) 예측 가능한   (D) 예측

어휘 refine 개선하다 predictable 예측 가능한

103

두 개의 포스터 견본이 제출되었지만 둘 다 팀장에게 감명을 주지 않았고, 팀은 다른 것을 생각해야 했다.

(A) 둘 다   (B) 각각
(C) 둘 중 어느 한쪽의   (D) 둘 중 어느 것도 아닌

어휘 present 제출하다 strike 감명을 주다

104

비영리 단체는 운이 좋게도 지역 은행에서 3만 달러의 금전적 원조를 받았다.

(A) 교육의   (B) 유익한
(C) 금전적인   (D) 직원의

어휘 nonprofit 비영리적인 fortunate 운이 좋은 informative 유익한
monetary 금전적인

105

Sunshine 시큐리티는 가정용이나 사업장용으로 의무적인 구매 없이 무료 현장 견적을 내드립니다.

(A) 의무를 지우다   (B) 의무
(C) 의무적으로 ~하게 하다   (D) 의무를 진

어휘 on-sit 현장의 obligation 의무

106

예정된 직원회의에 앞서, 조수는 참석자 전원을 위해 인쇄물을 모두 출력해야 했다.

(A) ~까지   (B) ~를 제외하고
(C) 얼추   (D) ~에 앞서

어휘 print out 출력하다 handout 인쇄물

107

Ian Lee는 지난주에 해외지점의 자리를 제안받았지만, 기회를 잡아야 할지 여전히 고민하고 있다.

(A) 거의   (B) 오직
(C) 여전히   (D) 아직

108

평년보다 시원한 여름이 주된 원인이 되어, 전국적으로 에어컨의 판매가 뚝 떨어졌다.

(A) 큰   (B) 크게
(C) 큼   (D) 더 큰

어휘 owing to ~ 때문에

109

상품권이 이메일에 pdf형식으로 첨부되어 있으니 체크인할 때 호텔 직원에게 보여주세요.

(A) attached   (B) attaching
(C) is attached   (D) is attaching

110

그 잡지 기사는 농촌의 농업 문제로 대중의 관심을 향하게 하는 데 성공했다.

(A) 향하게 하다   (B) 강제로 ~하다
(C) 촉진하다   (D) 도달하다

어휘 agricultural 농업의 direct ~의 방향으로 향하게 하다 force
강제로 ~하다 promote 촉진하다 reach 도달하다

111

Naomi Boomer는 Fairmont 호텔로 급히 달려갔는데, 그곳에서 그녀는 고객을 만나기로 했다.

(A) when   (B) where
(C) which   (D) who

어휘 rush 급히 움직이다

112

관리부장은 중앙공원이 회사의 야외 행사에 매우 적합할 것이라고 생각했다.

(A) 적합하다   (B) 적합
(C) 적합한   (D) 적합하게

113

새로운 스마트폰 시리즈 Xtreme의 가장 주목할 특징은 사용자를 인증하는 지문 센서입니다.

(A) 매력   (B) 특징
(C) 상표   (D) 보물

어휘 noticeable 현저한 fingerprint 지문 authenticate 진짜임을
증명하다 fascination 매혹 feature 특징 trademark 상표

114

관광버스는 최소 20분 동안 도시의 전경을 즐길 수 있는 장소에서 멈출 것입니다.

(A) ~까지   (B) ~ 동안
(C) ~까지   (D) ~와 함께

어휘 panoramic view 전경

115

최고경영자는 회사가 지난 분기에 <u>가장 높은</u> 매출을 기록했다는 소식을 듣고 기뻐했다.

(A) 더 높은
(B) 가장 높은
(C) 더 낮은
(D) 가장 낮은

어휘 delighted 기뻐하는

116

마케팅 책임자는 설문 결과에 대한 신입직원의 <u>빈틈없는</u> 분석에 깊은 인상을 받았다.

(A) 배려하는
(B) 필사적인
(C) 경의를 표하는
(D) 빈틈없는

어휘 considerate 배려하는 desperate 필사적인 respectful 경의를 표하는 thorough 빈틈없는

117

Catty사는 신제품의 성공 덕분에 작년 <u>누적 손실액</u> 850만 달러를 줄일 수 있었다.

(A) 잃다
(B) 손해 보는
(C) 손실액
(D) 잃어버린

어휘 accumulated 누적된 loss 손실(액)

118

우리 시의 청소 프로젝트에 관심이 있는 사람이라면 누구나 이 웹사이트를 통해 그 진행 과정을 <u>지켜볼</u> 수 있습니다.

(A) follow
(B) followed
(C) following
(D) to follow

어휘 follow (진행 상황을 계속) 지켜보다

119

자신의 다채로운 경력에 대해 <u>열정적으로</u> 이야기하는 바람에 강연자는 주어진 시간을 이미 넘겼다는 것을 깨닫지 못했다.

(A) 은밀하게
(B) 협력하여
(C) 엄청나게
(D) 열정적으로

어휘 confidentially 은밀하게 cooperatively 협력하여 enormously 엄청나게 passionately 열렬히

120

나날이 빠르게 발전하는 기술로, 전문가와 구직자는 자신의 분야에서 최신 정보를 얻는 것이 중요하다.

(A) it
(B) one
(C) that
(D) there

어휘 advance 증진하다

121

고객의 비전을 완벽하게 <u>실현시키기</u> 위해 고객과 긴밀한 관계를 맺는 데 최선을 다하고 있습니다.

(A) 실현 가능한
(B) 깨달음
(C) 실현하다
(D) 실현된

어휘 make every effort 온갖 노력을 다하다 establish a relationship 관계를 맺다 realize (목표를) 실현하다

122

Tim Davidson은 20년 이상 자선단체에서 일하며 모금활동에서 <u>전문지식</u>을 쌓았다.

(A) 헌신
(B) 이해력
(C) 전문지식
(D) 접근

어휘 charity organization 자선단체 fund-raising 자금 조달, 모금 comprehension 이해력 expertise 전문지식

123

긴 토론에 모두들 지쳐 보였다. <u>그리하여</u> 관리자는 빨리 회의를 끝냈다.

(A) 그런 이유로
(B) 마찬가지로
(C) 그동안에
(D) 그럼에도 불구하고

어휘 exhausted 기진맥진한 accordingly 그런 이유로 likewise 마찬가지로 meanwhile 그동안에

124

그 지역 제과점은 진열창에 다채로운 빵과 패스트리들을 <u>맛있어 보이</u>게 진열하는 것으로 유명하다.

(A) 식욕
(B) 전채
(C) 맛있어 보이는
(D) 식욕을 돋워

어휘 assorted 다채로운 appetizing 맛있어 보이는

125

이번 달 말까지 송장에 표시된 <u>지불</u> 금액을 저희에게 보내주시기 바랍니다.

(A) 계산된
(B) 균형 잡힌
(C) 빚진
(D) 환불된

어휘 amount 액수 indicate 표시하다 balance 수입과 지출이 맞아떨어지다

126

식물학자는 River 시립 정원이 지역의 온화한 기후로 인해 <u>많은 득을</u> 보고 있다고 말합니다.

(A) 부유한
(B) 더욱 풍부한
(C) 풍부하게
(D) 풍부함

어휘 botanist 식물학자 benefit 득을 보다 richly 풍부하게

127

해안가 개발 프로젝트는 일주일 전에 <u>끝났어야</u> 하지만, 아직 완성의 근처도 못 갔다.

(A) had been
(B) should have been
(C) was
(D) would be

어휘 nowhere 아무데도 (없다)

128

부장은 Molly Shannon의 보고서를 매우 기대했지만, 그녀는 아직 완전히 마무리 짓지 못했다.

(A) 간신히 (B) 훨씬
(C) 완전히 (D) 매우

129

Emerson 그룹은 자금이 부족하거나 다른 특별한 도움이 필요한 사람들을 돕는 데 전념하고 있습니다.

(A) help (B) helped
(C) helping (D) helps

어휘 be dedicated to ~에 전념하다

130

보안을 강화하기 위해, Madison사는 3개의 출입구마다 경비원을 배치하기로 결정했다.

(A) 배치 (B) 이동하는
(C) 부지 (D) 배치하다

어휘 enforce 강화하다 premises (건물에 딸린) 부지 station 배치하다

PART 6

131-134 📄 안내문

Harvey Collins 특별 상영회

7월 15일 토요일

West End Lovers부터 All the Beautiful Tomorrows까지, Harvey Collins의 연기 경력은 50년 넘게 ¹³¹계속되었습니다. 이제 Crestone Picture House 아카이브에서 최초로 Collins씨의 수상작 중 하이라이트를 ¹³²모았습니다. 이 중 일부 영상은 세계 곳곳에서 촬영하는 동안에 찍은 것으로 최초 공개되는 삭제 장면과 촬영장의 뒷모습을 보여줍니다. 상영작들은 Crestone 아카이브의 사무관 Kathryn Villa가 소개합니다. ¹³³또한 그녀는 영화가 끝날 때마다 청중의 질문을 받을 것입니다.

이 무료 행사는 좌석이 한정되어 있으니 빨리 예매하시길 바랍니다. 아래의 링크 주소 https://www.eventbook/harveycollins/crestonearchives.com에서 ¹³⁴예약하세요.

어휘 clip 영상 중 일부만 따로 떼어서 보여주는 부분 outtake 삭제된 부분 footage 장면

131

(A) had spanned (B) is spanned
(C) spanned (D) spans

어휘 span (얼마의 기간에) 걸치다

132

(A) 가다 (B) 얻다
(C) 이사하다 (D) 놓다

어휘 put together 모아놓다

133 신유형

(A) 그녀는 일에 관한 모든 공개 질의를 담당하고 있습니다.
(B) 또한 그녀는 영화가 끝날 때마다 청중의 질문을 받을 것입니다.
(C) Crestone 영화관은 현재 수리 중입니다.
(D) 성인은 1인당 5달러이고, 아이들은 무료입니다.

어휘 inquiry 질문

134

(A) 할인 (B) 목록
(C) 구매 (D) 예약

135-138 📧 이메일

수신: cs@bbluggage.com
발신: matildaikeda@greenmail.com
제목: PakTek40
날짜: 8월 10일

담당자님께

저는 약 3주 전에 PakTek40 배낭을 구매했습니다. 다양한 주머니와 작은 공간들이 있다는 점이 정말 마음에 듭니다. 제가 자전거로 출근해서 짐을 넣어 둘 ¹³⁵칸이 많이 필요하기 때문이죠. ¹³⁶그런데, 가방의 메인 지퍼가 걸렸는데 제가 고칠 수 없네요. 기름을 조금 발라봤지만 전혀 움직이지 않습니다. 제가 이것을 ¹³⁷기사로 보내야 할지, 구매처에 가져가야 할지 모르겠습니다. 이 문제를 해결하기 위해 제가 ¹³⁸무엇을 해야 하는지 알려주세요. 감사합니다.

어휘 carry 가지고 다니다 apply (크림을) 바르다

135

(A) 칸 (B) 노력
(C) 부분 (D) 대안

어휘 compartment 칸 alternative 대안

136 신유형

(A) 어제 앞면에 있는 작은 주머니의 바닥이 찢어진 것을 발견했습니다.
(B) 가게에서 집에 돌아오자마자, 그 위에 페인트를 쏟았습니다.
(C) 끈이 너무 짧아서 자전거에 쓸 수 없습니다.
(D) 그런데, 가방의 메인 지퍼가 걸렸는데 제가 고칠 수 없네요.

어휘 tear 찢어진 곳 spill 흘리다 strap 줄, 끈 stuck 꼼짝 못하는

137

(A) ~와 같이 (B) ~인지 아닌지
(C) ~일지라도 (D) 어디로

138

(A) 어떻게 (B) 무엇을
(C) 언제 (D) 누구를

139-142 📄 기사

시 전역에 페리 운항이 곧 시작됩니다

Rockridge 139노선은 오는 10월을 시작으로, 최초의 도시 전역을 가르는 페리가 될 것입니다. 예정된 다른 두 개의 노선은 내년 초에 시작합니다. 140Rockridge는 시에서 통근 시간이 가장 길기 때문에 첫 번째 서비스 지역이 됩니다. 이 노선은 Rockridge에서 Brantley 7번 부두 141종점까지 가며, 중간에 시 중앙 터미널 정류장도 들립니다. 요금은 3달러입니다. 그러나 시의 나머지 다른 교통 요금과 통합되지는 않으며, 따라서 배에서 지하철로 142무료 환승할 수 없습니다.

어휘 citywide 도시 전역으로 route 노선 integrate 통합하다

139
(A) 다리 (B) 방향
(C) 지도 (D) 노선

140 신 유 형
(A) 시 관계자는 역에서 무료 버스를 제공함으로써 관광객을 새 공원으로 끌어들이기를 바라고 있습니다.
(B) Rockridge는 시에서 통근 시간이 가장 길기 때문에 첫 번째 서비스 지역이 됩니다.
(C) 시의회는 다음 월례회의에서 새로운 서비스의 비용과 정차 항구에 대해 투표할 예정입니다.
(D) 안전감독관에 의하면, 사고가 발생했을 때 페리는 보통 속도로 이동하고 있었습니다.

어휘 commute time 통근 시간 inspector 감독관

141
(A) 최종의 (B) 완결했다
(C) 완결하다 (D) 마침내

어휘 finalize 완결하다

142
(A) 빠른 (B) 무료의
(C) 완전한 (D) 안전한

어휘 complete 완전한

143-146 📄 안내문

7월 3일 토요일 오전 11시부터 Doe Reservoir 해변에서 열리는 연례 회사 야유회에 모든 직원과 직원 가족들을 143초대합니다. 올해에도 배구, 소프트볼, 수영, 수상 스키(최소 3척의 보트를 띄웁니다!)를 144특별히 포함할 계획입니다! 145물론, 디저트 경연이 그날 가장 인기 있는 행사가 될 것입니다. 회사는 기본 바비큐 음식(채식주의자 주요리 포함)과 스포츠용품을 제공하며, 나머지는 개별적으로 준비하시길 146바랍니다. 여러분의 디저트를 잊지 마세요! 6월 21일까지 Luke Harris에게 얼마나 많은 사람을 데려올지 알려주시기 바랍니다. 멋진 시간이 되길 기대합니다!

143
(A) are invited (B) invited
(C) inviting (D) will be inviting

144
(A) 촉진하다 (B) 특별히 포함하다
(C) 작동되다 (D) 지속시키다

어휘 feature 특별히 포함하다 sustain 지속시키다

145 신 유 형
(A) 전 직원이 지난주에 입사한 새로운 멤버 Josh를 기쁘게 맞이했습니다.
(B) 기념식에 대한 의견이 있다면 다음 주 토요일 전에 Marie에게 알려주세요.
(C) 물론, 디저트 경연이 그날 가장 인기 있는 행사가 될 것입니다.
(D) 사용하던 제품을 자선 단체에 기증할 분들은 7월까지 가져오시면 됩니다.

146
(A) 격려되는 (B) 격려
(C) 격려하는 사람 (D) 격려하다

PART 7

147-148 📄 메모

147Parker&Sons에서 지난 40여 년간 근무했던 Howard Trumbo는 이번 달 말에 은퇴할 예정입니다. Trumbo씨의 유머와 근면함은 업계에 잘 알려져 있으며, 그는 경험하지 못한 세계 곳곳을 여행하고 보기 위해 자신의 황금기를 사용하고 싶다고 말했습니다. 그가 하는 모든 일이 잘되길 바랍니다.

그의 자리에 오기로 한 148Janet Newsome는 지난 5년간 그룹의 리더로 있었으며, 앞으로 회사를 성공적인 미래로 이끌 것으로 기대됩니다. 새로운 팀원이 새로운 책무에 익숙해지는 동안, 몇 주 변화가 있을 것입니다.

어휘 transition 변화, 이동 task 일

147
공지의 목적은 무엇인가?
(A) 상을 받은 사람을 축하하기 위해
(B) 합병 전환에 대한 정보를 주기 위해
(C) 퇴사하는 사람에 대해 직원에게 알리기 위해
(D) 회사의 신규 팀원을 환영하기 위해

148
Newsome씨에 관한 내용으로 옳은 것은 무엇인가?
(A) 그녀는 몇 주 전에 은퇴했다.
(B) 그녀는 해외로 출장을 갈 것이다.
(C) 그녀는 다른 사무실로 전근을 할 것이다.
(D) 그녀는 몇 년간 팀을 이끌어왔다.

어휘 transfer 옮기다

149-150 📱 문자 메시지 신유형

BRIAN GRUNSWALD [9:20]	곧 역에 도착할 예정입니다. 제가 만날 분은 어디에서 기다리고 있나요?
ANITH HEENAN [9:21]	149서쪽 출구의 커피숍 옆이요. 당신이 제안한 장소예요.
BRIAN GRUNSWALD [9:23]	저도 그렇게 생각했는데, 여기에 그가 없네요. 그가 전화했나요?
ANITH HEENAN [9:24]	제가 알기로는 아니요. 어느 커피숍에 있어요?
BRIAN GRUNSWALD [9:26]	Mario에요. 출구로 나오면 첫 번째 커피 가게예요.
ANITH HEENAN [9:27]	150그가 문자를 보냈는데 승강장에서 돌아오고 있대요. 그는 지금 가는 중이에요.
BRIAN GRUNSWALD [9:28]	네. 여기서 기다리면서 찾아보죠.
ANITH HEENAN [9:28]	금방 거기에 도착할 거예요.

어휘 exit gate 출구 message 메시지를 보내다 turn around 방향을 바꾸다 look out for ~를 찾다

149
Grunswald씨는 만나기로 한 사람을 어디에서 볼 것인가?
(A) 출구 옆에서
(B) 카페 옆에서
(C) 역 근처에서
(D) 승강장에서

150 신유형
9시 27분에 Heenan씨가 he got turned around on the platform이라고 말한 의미는 무엇인가?
(A) 그는 가야 할 방향에 대해 혼란스러워 했다.
(B) 그는 물건들을 살피기 위해 승강장을 돌아다니기 시작했다.
(C) 그는 다른 장소에서 만나길 원했다.
(D) 그는 사람들이 많은 곳에서 걷고 있었다.

151-152 📝 메모
Conway 회계사무소는 전 직원 휴가 프로그램을 발표합니다! 151한 해 동안 열심히 일하신 것에 대한 감사를 표하며, 사무실 파티가 언제나 최선은 아니기에, 9월 첫 번째 주를 시작으로 3개 주 지역 여러 곳을 번갈아가며 무료로 당일치기 여행을 보내드릴 것입니다.
이 당일 여행은 힘들었던 한 달 동안의 초과 근무 후 모두에게 휴식과 긴장을 풀 기회가 될 것입니다. 모두가 여행을 즐길 수 있기를 바라는 마음에서, 각 여행은 사무실에서 3시간 이내 거리에서 이루어질 것이며, 152선택 사항으로 전일 스파, 별장에서의 일급 서비스, VirtuaPlex에서의 가상세계가 포함됩니다. 선택의 수가 20개가 넘습니다!
누구나 이 프로그램을 사용할 수 있지만 날짜는 선착순입니다. 그러니 너무 오래 고민하지는 마세요. 회사 인트라넷을 통해 등록하고 '직원의 날'이라고 표시된 링크를 찾아 휴가일을 정하세요.

어휘 getaway 휴가 complimentary 무료의 rotate 번갈아 하다 day trip 당일 여행 unwind 긴장을 풀다 lodge 별장 virtual 가상의

151
왜 회사는 직원들에게 당일 여행을 제공하는가?
(A) 프로젝트 완료에 대한 보상
(B) 직원들의 노력에 대한 감사의 표시
(C) 수상에 대한 감사의 표시
(D) 직원들의 연말 상여금

어휘 reward 보상

152
프로그램에 대한 설명으로 옳지 <u>않은</u> 것은?
(A) 주로 야외 활동이다.
(B) 무료로 제공된다.
(C) 가는 데 오래 걸리지 않을 것이다.
(D) 9월 초에 시작될 것이다.

153-154 📰 기사
두 회사의 경쟁사에게는 잠재적으로 나쁜 소식입니다만, 153TES 시스템과 Holiday 테크놀로지가 경쟁이 치열한 기술 시장에서 시장 점유율을 높이고자 새로운 비즈니스 파트너 관계를 맺고 함께 협력할 것이라고 보도되고 있습니다. 두 회사가 결합하면 세계에서 가장 큰 컴퓨터 소프트웨어 회사가 될 것입니다.
승인된다면, TES 시스템은 비용 효율이 높은 기술을 사용하여 판매 수익을 높이기 위한 노력으로 Holiday를 위한 부품을 만들기 시작할 것입니다. 154TES 시스템은 재정비된 자재를 사용하여 제조사의 비용을 크게 절감할 수 있다고 합니다. 153비록 두 회사 모두 '합병'이라는 단어의 사용을 주저했지만, 이런 상황에서는 합병으로 보입니다. TES 대변인 Greg Harrison은 "이 파트너십으로 두 회사는 수익을 증대시키는 한편, 생산 비용을 낮춤으로써 각 회사에 이익이 될 것입니다."라고 말했습니다.

어휘 margin 판매 수익 cost-effective 비용 효율이 높은 refurbish (헌것을) 새롭게 하다 be reluctant to ~를 주저하다 spokesman 대변인

153
기사의 주된 내용은 무엇인가?
(A) 회사의 재정 상태
(B) 잠재적 합병
(C) 새로운 기술 개발
(D) 재활용 의식 제고

어휘 fiscal 재정의 awareness 의식

154
TES 시스템은 어떻게 비용을 절감하는가?
(A) 효율적인 제조 공정을 갖고 있다.
(B) 해외로 제조를 위탁한다.
(C) 비용을 절반으로 줄일 것이다.
(D) 부품에 더 저렴한 재료를 사용한다.

어휘 outsource (생산을) 외부에 위탁하다

155-157 📄 메모

Dream Net 전 직원들께

몇 달간의 협의 끝에 155새로운 장비를 몇 대를 우리 사무실에 들여오기로 결정했습니다. 전 직원들이 기계에 대해 알고, 사용법도 배우는 기회를 가지길 바랍니다. 장비 설치를 위한 준비로 인해 월요일부터 2층 일부 구역의 출입을 막을 것입니다. 이 새 장비가 무엇이냐? 여러분은 이제 이곳에서 최고 수준의 의료 3D 프링팅을 배울 수 있어 아주 기쁘실 겁니다.

우리의 많은 고객들이 말했듯이, 이 새로운 기술에 대해 고객들이 재활치료소 네트워크에 들어오는 데 관심을 보이며, 자사는 이 서비스의 선두 공급업체가 될 수 있다고 믿습니다. 많은 고객들이 본인이 돕고자 하는 사람들과 이 기술을 이용하고 싶다고 밝혔으며, Wish 재단과 함께 우리는 이러한 꿈이 실현되도록 도울 수 있습니다. 1563D 프린터로 제작한 손이든 발이든, 도움이 필요한 모든 이를 돕는 팀의 일부로서 우리는 최선을 다 할 수 있습니다.

157일단 장비가 설치되면 며칠간 기본 훈련이 있을 것이고, 그다음에는 이 기계를 직접 다루는 팀원들을 위한 집중 프로그램이 있을 것입니다. 질문이나 그 밖의 다른 의견들은 Jackie Stevens에게 내선 49번 또는 이메일 jstevens@dreamnet.com로 보내주시기 바랍니다.

어휘 get a chance 기회를 얻다 block off 막다 state 말하다 rehabilitation clinic 재활치료소 assist 돕다 intensive 집중적인

155
새로운 장비는 어디에 도입되는가?
(A) 진료소
(B) 신규 고객의 사무실
(C) Dream Net 사무실
(D) Wish 재단 사무소

156
회사는 어떤 종류의 일을 하는 것으로 보이는가?
(A) 장애인에게 도움을 준다.
(B) 첨단 스캐너로 이미지를 만든다.
(C) 사무기기를 판매한다.
(D) 기술을 사용하여 서버를 생성한다.

어휘 disability 장애

157
다음 주에 있을 일은 무엇인가?
(A) 회사는 Wish 재단과의 파트너십을 발표할 것이다.
(B) 회사는 신제품 디자인에 대해 논의할 것이다.
(C) 회사는 의료 네트워크에 가입할 것이다.
(D) 회사는 훈련 프로그램을 제공할 것이다.

158-160 📄 견적서

Ken Brockton 자동차 수리점

1928 Ball Road
Culver City, CA 90232
1598월 7일

손상 부분	- 차량 앞 왼쪽 펜더 부분 손상 - 왼쪽 전조등 및 케이싱 - 범퍼의 균열 및 페인트 긁힘
158수리 부분	- 차량 앞 왼쪽 펜더의 수리 및 표면 처리 - 전조등 교체 - 범퍼 균열 수리 - 범퍼 광택 및 왁스 처리
159예상 수리 시간	4일*
견적 비용	850달러*
160보험 사항	- 자동차 보험(60% 지불) - 보험 증서 번호 0323-268-9890
차체 기사	Clark Flynn
정비사	Aaron Bernard
고객	Nicholas Tunney 65 Arrow Lane Los Angeles, CA 90096 424-555-7404

유의 사항: 시간과 비용은 변경될 수 있습니다. 당사의 정책상 수리 전에 고객에게 이러한 변경을 알립니다.

어휘 fender (자동차의) 펜더 crack (갈라져서 생긴) 금 scrape 긁힌 흔적 smooth 매끈하게 하다 polish 광택을 내다 policy 보험 증서 subject to ~될 수 있는

158
몇 개의 자동차 부품이 수리되는가?
(A) 1개   (B) 2개
(C) 3개   (D) 4개

159
수리를 가장 빨리 끝낼 수 있는 날은 언제인가?
(A) 8월 9일   (B) 8월 11일
(C) 8월 13일   (D) 8월 15일

160
비용에 대해서 알 수 있는 것은 무엇인가?
(A) 보험사에서 일정 부분의 금액을 보상할 것이다.
(B) 8월 30일에 지불해야 한다.
(C) 최종 금액이다.
(D) Tunney씨는 850달러를 지불해야 한다.

어휘 cover (돈을) 대다 due 지불해야 하는

161-163 📄 이메일

수신: Marcus Thorn <thorninyourside@nsm.com>
발신: Anthony Weldon Mtonyweldon@cwm.com>
날짜: 1619월 23일
제목: Cinema Write 잡지 구독

Marcus씨께
지난 10년 동안 저희 잡지를 구독해주셔서 감사합니다. 귀하와 같은 구독자분들 덕분에 저희는 전 세계에 있는 시나리오 작가들을 위한 일등 잡지를 꾸준히 제공할 수 있습니다.
161다음 달 말에 귀하께서 구독이 만료되어, 재구독할 생각이 있으신

지 확인해야 한다고 생각했습니다. ¹⁶²귀하는 최고 등급의 구독자이시기 때문에 '본인만 해당하는' 특별 혜택을 제공해드릴 수 있습니다. 이 특별 혜택을 통해, 2년간 구독료의 60%를 할인받으실 수 있으며, 50년간의 최우수 수상 영화에 쓰인 각본 원본을 담은 기념 도서 2권도 받으실 것입니다.

¹⁶³오늘 재구독하시고 또 다른 혜택도 확인하세요. 요즘 업계에서 가장 인기 있는 각본가와 만나서 소통할 수 있는 기회를 가질 수 있습니다! 참석하고자 하는 모든 분께 플래티넘 레벨 온라인 과정을 제공할 예정입니다. 이곳에서 전문가의 강연을 듣고, 질문하며, 지금의 시장에서 각본을 가장 잘 팔 수 있는 방법에 대한 조언도 얻으실 수 있습니다.

Marcus씨, 어떠신가요? 잡지 구독을 연장하고 매달 최고의 잡지를 집에서 받아보실 준비가 되셨나요?

Anthony Weldon

어휘 supporter 지지자 screenwriter 시나리오 작가 renew 갱신하다 be authorized to ~의 권한이 있다. commemorative 기념하는 interact 소통하다 tier 계층

161

Thorn씨의 구독은 언제 만료되는가?

(A) 9월 말   (B) 10월 초
(C) 10월 말   (D) 11월 초

162

Thorn씨가 특별 프로그램을 제안받는 이유는 무엇인가?

(A) 최고 등급의 회원이기 때문에
(B) 많은 돈을 기부했기 때문에
(C) 10년 넘게 잡지사에서 일했기 때문에
(D) 잡지를 친구에게 소개했기 때문에

163 신유형

다음 문장은 [1], [2], [3], [4] 중 어디에 들어가는가?

"오늘 재구독하시고 또 다른 혜택도 확인하세요."

(A) [1]   (B) [2]
(C) [3]   (D) [4]

164-167 기사

West 시장과 시의회는 오늘 우리 시의 강둑 지역을 부활시킬 계획을 발표했습니다. Banks of Riverdale이라 명명된 이 계획은 ¹⁶⁴수많은 오래된 창고와 건물을 철거하고 좀 더 가족친화적인 명소로 전환시켜, 방문객들이 Riverdale 도심을 더 경험할 수 있도록 할 것입니다. 또한 강 옆에는 놀이터와 그네 등 모두가 즐길 수 있는 시설을 갖춘 공원 최소 2곳이 새롭게 조성될 것입니다.

여론조사에 응한 시민들 중 절반 이상이 ¹⁶⁵도심 지역은 이미 이 지역에서 가장 좋은 도시 중 하나로 여겨지지만 이를 더 향상시켜 아름답게 할 필요가 있다고 말했습니다. ¹⁶⁶프로젝트를 이끄는 담당자들은 완전한 개보수 작업이 수년 전에 고려되었지만, 시의 스포츠팀들이 관련한 성공적인 프로젝트와 그들이 낸 수익 덕분에 이제야 자금을 조달할 수 있게 되었다고 했습니다.

West 시장에 의하면, 프로젝트의 초반은 올 봄에 시작될 것이며, 경기장에서 가장 가까운 지역을 우선 보수하거나 철거할 것입니다. 거

기부터 ¹⁶⁴담당자들은 새로운 식당과 쇼핑 구역이 그 지역에 처음 온 사람들과 와봤던 사람들 모두에게 인기를 얻길 바라고 있습니다. ¹⁶⁷향후 몇 주간 계획이 확정되면 이 프로젝트에 대해 더 많은 소식을 들으실 수 있습니다.

어휘 resurrect 부활시키다 visitor experience 관광객 체험 enhance 향상시키다 revenue 수익 generate 발생시키다 catch on with ~의 인기를 얻다

164

시는 강둑 지역을 어떻게 개선할 것인가?

(A) 식당 및 관광지를 조성함으로써
(B) 아이들을 위한 놀이동산을 만듦으로써
(C) 강의 수질을 깨끗하고 안전하게 만듦으로써
(D) 창고들을 시의 다른 지역으로 이전시킴으로써

165

Riverdale에 대해 언급된 것은 무엇인가?

(A) 호수 근처에 있다.
(B) 프로 스포츠팀을 찾고 있다.
(C) 곧 새 경기장을 개장할 계획이다.
(D) 지역에서 최고의 도시 중 하나로 여겨진다.

166

왜 시 정부는 보수 계획을 진행하기로 결정했는가?

(A) 다수의 토론 끝에 지역민들이 동의했다.
(B) 마침내 계획을 가능하게 할 자금이 생겼다.
(C) 대형 스포츠 경기 전에 도시를 개선하고 싶었다.
(D) 언론으로부터 비판을 받아 도시의 모습을 새롭게 하고 싶었다.

어휘 criticism 비판

167 신유형

다음 문장은 [1], [2], [3], [4] 중 어디에 들어가는가?

"향후 몇 주간 계획이 확정되면 이 프로젝트에 대해 더 많은 소식을 들으실 수 있습니다."

(A) [1]   (B) [2]
(C) [3]   (D) [4]

168-171 안내문

저희 Streamline이 다음 달에 더 큰 사무실로 이전함을 모든 고객과 거래처에 알립니다. ¹⁶⁸지난 몇 년 동안 여러분 덕분에 믿을 수 없는 성장을 이뤘습니다. 여러분의 친절한 리뷰와 홍보에 감사의 말씀을 드립니다. 지금의 Streamline은 고객 여러분에 의한 것이라고 믿고 있으며, 저희는 최선을 다하여 여러분께 서비스하고 있음을 말씀드리고 싶습니다.

9월 1일부터 저희는 Geraldine 지역에 있는 새 사무실로 이전을 시작할 것입니다. 사무실은 97번가와 Taft가 모퉁이에 위치하며, Houseman 빌딩의 1층부터 5층까지 사용합니다. ¹⁶⁹Houseman 사무실의 주차장은 건물 뒤편에 있으며 약 100대를 주차할 수 있습니다. 1층에서는 일상적인 업무가 이루어질 것이고 ¹⁷⁰2층은 회의와 면접이 이루어질 예정이며, 3층부터 5층까지는 제작 스튜디오로서, 이곳에 마련할 무대와 세트에서 고객의 사업을 위한 완벽한 아이디어를

창조하겠습니다.
¹⁷¹문의에 대비하여, 새 본사로 이전을 시작하면서 예전 사무실과 새 사무실 두 곳에 고객 응대 인원을 둘 것입니다. 저희 웹사이트 www.streamline.com을 방문하시거나, 555-2389로 전화 주십시오.

어휘 unbelievable 믿기 어려울 정도인 spread the word 말을 퍼트리다 day-to-day operation 일상 업무

168
Streamline이 사무실을 이전하기로 결정한 이유는 무엇인가?
(A) 최근에 사업이 큰 성공을 거두었다.
(B) 고객들이 시내와 가까워지도록 요청했다.
(C) 새로운 제품들을 위한 공간이 필요했다.
(D) 사업 운영을 간소화했다.

어휘 streamline 간소화하다

169
새 사무실을 방문하면 어디에 주차해야 하는가?
(A) 건물 뒤   (B) 건물 앞
(C) 건물 옆   (D) 건물 지하

170
프레젠테이션을 하는 고객은 몇 층으로 갈 것인가?
(A) 1층   (B) 2층
(C) 3층   (D) 4층

171
일부 직원이 예전 사무실에 남아 있는 이유는 무엇인가?
(A) 고객의 문의에 대답하기 위해
(B) 오래된 장비를 청소하기 위해
(C) 진행 중인 프로젝트 완료를 위해
(D) 중요한 고객을 만나기 위해

172-175 온라인 토론 신 유 형

GREG HUNT	모두 안녕하세요. ¹⁷²다음 달 전시회에 대한 소식이 있나요?	[11:30]
TONY PLAYER	어제 전시회에 대한 이메일을 받았어요. 아직 못 받았어요?	[11:31]
JIM JONSON	전 받았어요. 우리 모두 같은 방을 써야 한다고 했어요. 맞죠?	[11:33]
GREG HUNT	네? 어떻게 네 명이 한 방을 쓰죠? 정어리마냥 꽉 찰 거예요!	[11:34]
TONY PLAYER	그들은 어떻게 그게 가능할거라고 생각한 거죠? ¹⁷³그 방에는 침대가 두 개뿐인데요.	[11:36]
JIM JONSON	문제네요. 전 일주일 동안 바닥에서 자고 싶지 않아요.	[11:37]
RON BURKE	저 이제 왔어요. ¹⁷³방에 대해 운영진에게 물어봤더니 알아보겠대요.	[11:39]
GREG HUNT	좋아요. 그럼 올해에는 제품을 어떻게 선보일지 생각해 봐요.	[11:39]

TONY PLAYER	일종의 상호작용을 하는 전시를 생각해봤어요.	[11:40]
JIM JONSON	의견 좋네요. 그러면 우리가 설명할 때 사람들은 해볼 수 있잖아요.	[11:42]
RON BURKE	좋은 계획이에요. ¹⁷⁴Tony와 Jim이 첫 발표를 맡는 게 어때요?	[11:42]
TONY PLAYER	알았어요. 오늘 오후에 연습할게요.	[11:44]
JIM JONSON	시연 길이 전략은 뭐죠? ¹⁷⁵길게 끌고 싶지 않은데요.	[11:47]
GREG HUNT	10분에서 15분 이내로요. 가급적 많은 사람들이 봤으면 해요.	[11:48]
TONY PLAYER	그리고 행사장에서 사람들이 사진을 찍지 못하게 막는 것도 해야죠.	[11:49]
RON BURKE	물론이죠. 경쟁사가 우리의 아이디어를 '빌려' 가는 건 원치 않아요.	[11:50]
GREG HUNT	좋아요. 일하러 갑시다. 그리고 어떻게 진행할지 생각해서 금요일에 만나요.	[11:51]

어휘 stuffed 속을 채운 interactive 상호작용을 하는 game plan 전략 length 길이

172
팀은 무엇을 준비하고 있는가?
(A) 고객을 위한 프레젠테이션
(B) 업계 행사
(C) 시합
(D) 영업 회의

173
Burke씨는 왜 운영진과 연락했는가?
(A) 프로젝트에 대해 묻기 위해
(B) 비용을 낮추기 위해
(C) 새 장비를 요청하기 위해
(D) 방 크기에 대해 말하기 위해

174
첫 발표는 누가 할 것인가?
(A) Burke씨와 Player씨
(B) Hunt씨와 Burke씨
(C) Jonson씨와 Hunt씨
(D) Jonson씨와 Player씨

175 신 유 형
11시 47분에 Jonson씨가 We don't want to go long이라고 말한 의도는 무엇인가?
(A) 그는 사진 촬영 시간을 좋아하지 않는다.
(B) 그는 행사가 일찍 끝날 것으로 예상한다.
(C) 그는 멀리 이동하는 것을 꺼린다.
(D) 그는 시연이 짧은 것을 선호한다.

176-180 📧 이메일…이메일

수신: Brian Sinclair
발신: John Sheridan
제목: 새로운 회사 정책
날짜: 7월 17일

안녕하세요, Brian.

회사의 신규 여름 운동 프로그램의 초안을 보내드립니다. 피드백 주시면 감사하겠습니다.

이제 여름이 왔으니 Lang&Huston의 직원들이 하루를 시작하는 흥미롭고 새로운 방법을 도입하고자 합니다. [176]오전 8시부터 누구나 참여하는 30분 준비운동을 시작할 것입니다. 올해 모두가 건강하고 활동적이도록 전 직원을 장려하고 있습니다. 첫째 주 아침 세션을 시작할 특별한 손님을 모실 겁니다만, 깜짝 놀랄 소식을 밝혀서 일을 [177]망치고 싶지 않습니다.

이 프로그램은 우리의 몸과 마음 모두를 스트레칭 하기에 좋은 방법이 될 것입니다. 그 후에는 회의를 열고 일상 업무를 향상시키기 위해 우리가 할 수 있는 일에 대해 토론할 것입니다. 모두가 참석하기를 바라며, [178]3일 월요일부터 시작하니 오전 8시까지 A 회의실로 꼭 와주시기 바랍니다.

John Sheridan 인사부 부사장
Lang&Huston사

수신: John Sheridan
발신: Brian Sinclair
제목: 회신: 새로운 회사 정책
날짜: 7월 17일

안녕하세요, John.

오전 운동 프로그램에 대한 보내주신 이메일을 읽었습니다. 하지만 몇 가지를 변경해야 할 것 같습니다. 제가 읽기로는 의무적 참여로 느껴지는데, 직장에서 어느 누구에게도 운동 수업 참여를 강제할 수는 없습니다. 참여를 원하는 직원에게 무료로 수업을 제공하는 것은 어떤지요? 그리고 [179]누구든지 이 기회에서 제외될 수 없기 때문에 다른 시간대들도 제공해야 할 것입니다. [178]또한 특별 손님을 비밀로 하는 일도 없어야 합니다. 전 직원을 즐겁게 참여시키기 위해 특별 손님을 섭외한다면, 참여를 독려하기 위해서 그 점을 이용해야죠. [180]그리고 한 주의 시작과 끝에 팀 빌딩을 할 수 있도록, 한 주를 시작하는 날과 마지막 날에 그 일정을 잡는 건 어떨까요?

Brian Sinclair 영업 부장
Lang&Huston사

어휘 draft 초안 warm-up exercise 준비 운동 kick off 시작하다 spoil 망치다 mandatory 의무적인 exclude 제외하다 remove 제거하다

176

Sheridan씨는 직원들이 무엇을 하길 원하는가?
(A) 건강 서비스 업계의 리더가 되기
(B) 서로 더 경쟁하기
(C) 작년보다 더 나은 판매율 기록하기
(D) 동료들과 함께 운동하기

어휘 competitive 경쟁을 하는

177

첫 번째 이메일에서 두 번째 단락, 네 번째 줄의 spoil과 의미상 가장 가까운 단어는 무엇인가?
(A) 도와주다 (B) 창조하다
(C) 수리하다 (D) 망치다

어휘 ruin 망치다

178

Sinclair씨는 언제 특별 손님에 대해 공개할 것을 제안하는가?
(A) 가능한 한 늦게 (B) 첫 번째 수업에서
(C) 돌아오는 월요일에 (D) 8월 3일 전에

어휘 reveal 드러내다

179

Sinclair씨는 무엇을 할 것을 제안하는가?
(A) 신입직원에게 강의 제공하기
(B) 다양한 시간대 열어두기
(C) 미리 등록하기
(D) 개인 선호도 확인하기

어휘 personal preference 개인적 선호

180

Sinclair씨는 수업이 어느 날에 가장 적합하다고 생각하는가?
(A) 월요일과 화요일 (B) 월요일과 금요일
(C) 목요일과 금요일 (D) 토요일과 일요일

181-185 📧 주문서…이메일

사무용품 도매 주문서

이름: Wolffe Marketing	배송지: 2002 Republic
주소: 66 Order Ave	Boulevard
Springfield, IL	Nashville, [183]TN
62702	37201
날짜: [182]6월 24일	

송장 번호: C2032

물품	수량	단가	총액
복사용지(박스)	[181]10	40달러	400달러
사무용 책상 30x48x23	10	100달러	1,000달러
사무용 의자(검은색)	10	60달러	600달러
합계			2,000달러
회원 할인*: 10%			1,800달러 (#OSW23789)
[183]세금**: 10%			180달러
최종 가격			1,980달러

*회원 할인은 회원 번호가 필요합니다.

**[183]켄터키, 테네시, 미시시피, 앨라배마로 발송되는 주문에 대해서는 판매세가 붙지 않습니다.

수신: 고객서비스부 <csr@osw.com>
발신: Leila Saldana <leilasaldana@packmail.com>
제목: 주문 번호 OSW23789

날짜: [182]7월 1일

고객서비스부 앞

저희 사무실에서는 귀사의 인터넷몰에서 신입직원용 새 가구(주문번호 2032)를 주문했습니다. 주문은 지난달에 하였습니다. [182]오늘 모든 것이 수령지로 잘 도착했지만, 알아두셔야 할 두 가지 오류가 있습니다. [185]저희가 주문한 사무용 의자는 검은색이었는데, 수령한 의자 열 개가 모두 빨간색이었습니다. 그 의자들이 아주 좋은 의자이긴 하지만 저희 사무실 디자인에 좀 더 적합한 것이 좋겠습니다. [183]다른 문제는 제가 구매한 물품에 대한 판매세에 관한 것입니다. 이에 대해 가격 조정을 받을 수 있나요?

신입직원들이 12일에 출근을 시작하기 때문에 [184]최대한 빨리 의자를 교환하고 싶습니다. 의자 교환 허가증과 함께 귀사의 창고로 의자를 반송하는 데 드는 운송비에 대한 변제를 요청드립니다.

읽어주셔서 감사합니다.

Leila Saldana

Wolffe 마케팅 현장 매니저

어휘 sales tax 판매세 Attn (글에서) ~ 앞, 귀하 price adjustment 가격 조정 authorization 허가(증) reimbursement 변제

181
송장에서 알 수 있는 것은 무엇인가?
(A) 청구 주소와 배송 주소가 같다.
(B) 배송료가 추가되었다.
(C) 각 물품의 수량이 같다.
(D) 사무가구들만 주문되었다.

182
Wolffe 마케팅은 비품을 얼마나 기다렸는가?
(A) 며칠   (B) 약 일주일
(C) 몇 주   (D) 약 한 달

183
Saldana씨는 얼마를 돌려받을 것인가?
(A) 150달러   (B) 180달러
(C) 200달러   (D) 380달러

184
Saldana씨는 공급업체에게 무엇을 요청하는가?
(A) 다음 구매 시 할인
(B) 주문 반품 승인
(C) 교환 허가서
(D) 전체 주문에 대한 상환

185
주문에 어떤 문제가 있었는가?
(A) 물품의 색상이 잘못되었다.
(B) 물품이 잘못된 주소로 배송되었다.
(C) 물품의 개수가 잘못되었다.
(D) 의자의 가격이 잘못되었다.

186-190 📋 광고…신청서…온라인 후기 신 유 형

이제 이사 오셔서 케이블 TV와 인터넷 설치가 필요하신가요? 케이블 방송 서비스에 문제가 있으신가요? Jim the Cable Guy에 오늘 전화 주세요.

· 저렴한 가격
· 편리한 서비스 시간
· [186]현지 소유 및 운영

아래의 상품은 지역 내 대부분의 고객이 사용하실 수 있습니다.

TV+인터넷 50달러/월	인터넷만 25달러/월
-200개 채널과 HD 화질 무료	-표준 속도 인터넷
-표준 속도 인터넷	-무료 설치(인터넷 주문 시에만)
TV만 40달러/월	**[189]디럭스 75달러/월**
-200개 채널 포함	-250개 채널 및 HD 화질
-HD 화질은 추가 요금 발생	-고속 인터넷 및 무료 설치

Jim the Cable Guy
서비스 신청서

이름: Candace Bauman
원하는 방문 시간*: [188]월요일, 수요일, 목요일에는 12시~1시, 주말에는 정오 전에
주소: 3801 San Carlos Drive Esposito, California
연락처: 555-2839
거주지 유형: 아파트
*위 시간에 방문한다고 장담할 수 없지만, 귀하의 일정에 맞추려 [187]노력하고 있습니다.

★★☆☆☆ 저는 새로 이사 온 집으로 Jim의 케이블 서비스를 신청했고, 남자분(Jim이 아님)이 오늘 설치를 위해 방문했습니다. 그분이 30분 늦게 와서 저는 실망했습니다. [188]제가 점심시간에 나와 있었던 것이어서 결국 회사에 늦게 복귀하게 되었습니다. [190]그분은 또한 소음을 많이 냈고, TV 위에 걸려 있던 제 사진 중 하나를 깨뜨렸습니다. [189]저는 귀사의 서비스 중 가장 비싼 요금을 지불했기에 훨씬 더 전문적인 설치기사를 기대했습니다. — Candace

어휘 residence 거주지 strive to ~하려 노력하다 frustrated 불만스러워하는 end up 결국 (어떤 처지에) 처하다

186
Jim the Cable Guy의 소유주에 대해 언급된 것은 무엇인가?
(A) 공학 학위를 가지고 있다.
(B) 수십 년간 그 사업을 갖고 있다.
(C) 그 지역에 산다.
(D) 최근에 새로운 곳으로 이사했다.

187
신청서의 여덟 번째 줄의 strive와 의미상 가장 가까운 단어는 무엇인가?
(A) 영향을 미치다   (B) 경쟁하다
(C) 반대하다   (D) 애를 쓰다

188

Jim the Cable Guy의 직원은 언제 Bauman씨의 집에 방문했는가?

(A) 월요일 오전   (B) 수요일 정오

(C) 금요일 정오   (D) 토요일 아침

189

Bauman씨는 어떤 상품을 선택했는가?

(A) 디럭스   (B) 인터넷만

(C) TV와 인터넷   (D) TV만

190

Bauman씨는 무엇에 대해 불평했는가?

(A) 설치기사의 행실   (B) 케이블 서비스 가격

(C) TV 화면의 품질   (D) 인터넷 속도

어휘 behavior 행실

191-195 📧 이메일···이메일···목록 신유형

수신: Theodore Slate <tslate@jumbo.com>

발신: Cassandra Holly <cholly@jumbo.com>

날짜: 9월 26일 월요일

제목: 팝업 스토어

안녕하세요, Theo.

조사를 좀 해줄래요? ¹⁹³제가 10월 6일부터 일주일간의 휴가 동안 우리 회사의 최고 판매 상품 몇 가지를 시내에 있는 팝업 스토어에서 판매하고 싶어요. ¹⁹¹온라인에서 제품을 판매했는데 판매가 잘됐어요. 우리 제품에 대해 주민들이 알고 있는지 잘 모르겠어요. 우리가 가게를 차릴 수 있는 가게 앞 공간이나 야외 공간이 있는지 한번 둘러봐주겠어요? 고마워요.

Cassie

수신: Cassandra Holly <cholly@jumbo.com>

발신: Theodore Slate <tslate@jumbo.com>

날짜: 월요일 10월 3일

제목: 회신: 팝업 스토어

안녕하세요, Cassandra.

Oaktown에서 가시적인 방법으로 ¹⁹²우리 수제 가방을 선보이고 싶다는 아이디어가 정말 좋네요. 팝업 스토어에 관심이 있을 만한 장소를 몇 군데 찾았습니다. 이 메시지에 목록을 첨부했어요. 저는 첫 번째와 두 번째가 가장 좋을 것 같아요. 제일 크고 당장 이용 가능하기 때문이지요. 하지만 교통의 관점에서만 보면, 마지막 장소가 시내의 붐비는 길에 위치해 있기 때문에 완벽할 수도 있을 것 같습니다. 의견을 말해주세요. ¹⁹⁴보고 싶은 곳이 있다면 그곳의 주인과 약속을 잡을 수 있습니다.

Theo

건물 유형	위치	면적	세부 사항
가게 앞 공간	391 Main가	45m²	바로 사용 가능
쇼핑몰 공간	Oaktown – 동쪽 동	42m²	비쌈
역 주변 매점	Greenbay 역 출구	31m²	¹⁹⁵보안 문제

가게 앞 공간	208 Redmond 대로	40m²	¹⁹³10월 중순부터 사용 가능

어휘 week-long 일주일간의   storefront 거리에 면한 점포   outdoor venue 야외 공간   attach 첨부하다   standpoint 관점   wing 부속 건물   boulevard(Blvd.) 도로, 대로

191

Holly씨는 왜 팝업 스토어를 원하는가?

(A) 판매할 여분의 상품이 있기 때문에

(B) 이제 막 사업을 시작했기 때문에

(C) 더 많은 현지 고객을 유치하고 싶어서

(D) 새로운 제품군을 소개하고 싶어서

192

Slate씨의 회사는 어떤 종류의 상품을 생산하는가?

(A) 의류   (B) 화장품

(C) 보석   (D) 지갑

193

Redmond 대로에 있는 장소는 왜 선택되지 않을 것인가?

(A) 적시에 이용할 수 없어서

(B) 너무 비싸서

(C) 너무 멀어서

(D) 너무 비좁아서

194

Slate씨는 무엇을 한다고 제안하는가?

(A) 더 조사하기

(B) 건물 목록 작성하기

(C) 약속 잡기

(D) Holly씨에게 몇 가지 신제품 보여주기

195

매점에 대해 언급된 것은 무엇인가?

(A) 쇼핑몰과 가깝다.

(B) 시내에 있다.

(C) 가장 큰 장소이다.

(D) 안전하지 않을 수 있다.

196-200 📢 광고···일정표···이메일 신유형

BROWN 호텔

Center Grove의 중심부에 있습니다.

¹⁹⁶Brown 호텔은 Center Grove에서 가장 유명한 명소 중 하나로, 컨벤션 센터 근처의 King 스퀘어에서 가깝습니다. 호텔에는 커피숍과 풀서비스 식당이 있습니다. 9월 한 달 동안의 특별한 혜택을 알려드립니다.

– ¹⁹⁸평일 2박을 1박 가격으로 제공합니다.*

– 3개 이상의 더블룸을 예약하는 단체는 20% 할인을 받으실 수 있습니다.**

*월요일이 국경일인 경우 적용되지 않습니다.

**다른 혜택과 중복하여 쓸 수 없습니다.

Center Grove에서 열리는 박람회 일정표

9월 23-25일

9월 23일 **198토요일	
오전 10:00	Center Grove 도착
오전 11:00	전시 부스 설치
오후 1:00 ~ 5:00	Welch 컨벤션 센터에서의 전시
**9월 24일 **198일요일	
오전 10:00	전시회 개장
오전 10:00 ~ 오후 4:00	전시
오후 7:00	팀원과 함께 저녁식사
**9월 25일 월요일(국경일)	
오전 09:00	199Center Grove 총책임자와 조찬
오전 11:00	197Center Grove 팀과 캠페인 계획(작업하면서 점심식사)
오후 3:30	Winchester로 비행기 타고 복귀

수신: Kate Johnson <kjohnson@mytex.com>
발신: Bradley Dexter <bdexter@mytex.com>
날짜: 9월 11일 월요일
제목: 다가오는 출창에 대해

안녕하세요, Kate.
Center Gorve에서 열리는 전시회에 간다고 들었어요. 제가 작년에 전시회에 갔을 때 정말 재미있었어요. 우리 지점 직원들이 아주 친절해서 즐거운 시간을 보내게 해줄 거예요. 199훌륭한 아침식사를 먹으려면 총책임자에게 Stanley라는 강 바로 옆에 있는 식당에 데려다달라고 하세요. 그곳의 오믈렛은 환상적이에요.
어쨌든, Brown 호텔에 대한 광고를 찾았어요. 우리가 작년에 머물렀던 곳이에요. 박람회장까지 가는 데 정말 편리하고 200만을 바라보는 전경이 아주 좋으니, 만이 보이는 방으로 요청하세요.
호텔에서 이번 달에 제공하는 두 가지 할인 중 하나를 받을 수 있기를 바랄게요.
좋은 여행 되세요.
Bradley Dexter

어휘 landmark 명소 weeknight 평일 저녁 exhibition venue 박람회장

196
Brown 호텔에 대해 언급된 것은 무엇인가?
(A) 보수된 지 얼마 안 되었다.
(B) 유명한 곳이다.
(C) 24시간 룸서비스를 제공한다.
(D) 사업가들이 주된 고객이다.

197
Johnson씨와 그녀의 팀은 월요일 정오경에 무엇을 할 것인가?
(A) 사업 전략 논의 　　(B) 외식
(C) 부스 철거 　　(D) 전시회에서 작업

어휘 take down (구조물을) 치우다

198
이 팀이 호텔의 반값 할인을 받을 수 없는 이유는 무엇인가?
(A) 충분히 오래 투숙하지 않는다.
(B) 주말에 투숙할 것이다.
(C) 호텔 회원 카드가 없다.
(D) 충분한 방을 예약하지 않을 것이다.

199
Johnson씨는 언제 동료들과 Stanley에 갈 수 있는가?
(A) 토요일 점심시간 　　(B) 일요일 오전
(C) 일요일 저녁 　　(D) 월요일 아침

200
Dexter씨는 호텔에서 무엇을 하는 것을 추천하는가?
(A) 추가 베개 요청하기
(B) 특정 방향으로 방 얻기
(C) 음악회장 가기
(D) 기념품점 방문하기

Actual Test 5

정답   ◁)) LC MP3 Actual Test 5

1 (C)	2 (D)	3 (D)	4 (B)	5 (A)	6 (D)	7 (A)	8 (C)	9 (A)	10 (C)
11 (B)	12 (B)	13 (B)	14 (C)	15 (A)	16 (A)	17 (B)	18 (C)	19 (A)	20 (B)
21 (B)	22 (A)	23 (C)	24 (B)	25 (A)	26 (B)	27 (C)	28 (B)	29 (A)	30 (C)
31 (B)	32 (A)	33 (D)	34 (D)	35 (B)	36 (C)	37 (C)	38 (D)	39 (A)	40 (B)
41 (D)	42 (D)	43 (D)	44 (C)	45 (D)	46 (C)	47 (B)	48 (B)	49 (A)	50 (A)
51 (B)	52 (B)	53 (A)	54 (C)	55 (C)	56 (D)	57 (B)	58 (D)	59 (B)	60 (D)
61 (C)	62 (B)	63 (A)	64 (B)	65 (C)	66 (B)	67 (C)	68 (C)	69 (B)	70 (C)
71 (D)	72 (B)	73 (C)	74 (D)	75 (A)	76 (B)	77 (A)	78 (D)	79 (B)	80 (A)
81 (C)	82 (A)	83 (C)	84 (B)	85 (B)	86 (A)	87 (C)	88 (D)	89 (A)	90 (B)
91 (A)	92 (A)	93 (C)	94 (A)	95 (C)	96 (C)	97 (A)	98 (D)	99 (D)	100 (D)
101 (D)	102 (C)	103 (A)	104 (B)	105 (A)	106 (A)	107 (C)	108 (C)	109 (B)	110 (D)
111 (A)	112 (B)	113 (D)	114 (D)	115 (A)	116 (C)	117 (C)	118 (C)	119 (C)	120 (C)
121 (D)	122 (C)	123 (D)	124 (D)	125 (D)	126 (B)	127 (D)	128 (C)	129 (B)	130 (B)
131 (C)	132 (C)	133 (B)	134 (A)	135 (C)	136 (A)	137 (A)	138 (A)	139 (C)	140 (C)
141 (D)	142 (B)	143 (C)	144 (C)	145 (C)	146 (A)	147 (B)	148 (C)	149 (B)	150 (B)
151 (C)	152 (A)	153 (C)	154 (B)	155 (B)	156 (D)	157 (C)	158 (D)	159 (D)	160 (D)
161 (A)	162 (C)	163 (C)	164 (D)	165 (D)	166 (D)	167 (C)	168 (B)	169 (C)	170 (B)
171 (A)	172 (B)	173 (C)	174 (B)	175 (D)	176 (D)	177 (C)	178 (B)	179 (A)	180 (B)
181 (B)	182 (D)	183 (B)	184 (C)	185 (D)	186 (C)	187 (D)	188 (C)	189 (D)	190 (D)
191 (A)	192 (D)	193 (B)	194 (B)	195 (B)	196 (B)	197 (A)	198 (A)	199 (B)	200 (A)

PART 1

1

(◁)) 호주)

(A) He's standing on a bench.
(B) He's fishing in a lake.
(C) He's sitting on a bench.
(D) He's walking with a friend.

(A) 남자는 벤치 위에 서 있다.
(B) 남자는 호수에서 낚시를 하고 있다.
(C) 남자는 벤치에 앉아 있다.
(D) 남자는 친구와 함께 걷고 있다.

2

미국

(A) They're helping customers with purchases.
(B) They're pouring wine in glasses.
(C) They're putting bottles on shelves.
(D) They're standing behind a cash register.

(A) 사람들이 고객의 구매를 돕고 있다.
(B) 사람들이 와인을 잔에 따르고 있다.
(C) 사람들이 선반 위에 병을 놓고 있다.
(D) 사람들이 금전등록기 뒤에 서 있다.

어휘 pour (음료를) 따르다 cash register 금전등록기

3

호주

(A) Chairs are stacked up by a door.
(B) A man is placing dishes on a table.
(C) People are having meals in a dining room.
(D) Umbrellas are shading café tables.

(A) 의자들은 문 옆에 쌓여 있다.
(B) 남자는 접시를 식탁 위에 놓고 있다.
(C) 사람들이 식당 안에서 식사를 하고 있다.
(D) 파라솔들이 카페 식탁에 그늘을 만들고 있다.

어휘 stack up 계속 쌓이다 place 놓다 umbrella 파라솔 shade 그늘지게 하다

4

미국

(A) A vehicle is running on the bridge.
(B) A vehicle is stopped outside.
(C) Someone is checking under the hood of a vehicle.
(D) Someone is taking a bag out of the vehicle.

(A) 차량이 다리 위를 달리고 있는 중이다.
(B) 차량이 밖에 정지해 있다.
(C) 누군가가 차량의 후드 아래를 확인하고 있다.
(D) 누군가가 차량에서 가방을 꺼내고 있다.

어휘 vehicle 차량 take ⊠ out ~를 빼다

5

캐나다

(A) Clothing is hung on a rod.
(B) Chairs are folded by a table.
(C) Purses are lying on the ground.
(D) Women are talking near a building.

(A) 옷이 긴 막대에 걸려 있다.
(B) 의자들이 테이블 옆에 접혀 있다.
(C) 지갑들이 땅에 널려 있다.
(D) 여자들이 건물 근처에서 이야기하고 있다.

어휘 fold 접다 lie 놓여 있다

6

영국

(A) The gear shift is attached to the steering wheel.
(B) The glove box is open.
(C) There is no side mirror.
(D) The steering wheel is on the left side.

(A) 변속 기어가 핸들에 부착되어 있다.
(B) 사물함이 열려 있다.
(C) 사이드 미러가 없다.
(D) 핸들이 좌측에 있다.

어휘 gear shift 변속 기어 glove box 사물함 steering wheel 자동차 핸들

PART 2

7 (◀)) 캐나다…영국)

Who should I talk to about updating my address?

(A) Landon in Personnel, I think.

(B) The calendars are over there.

(C) I don't have any updates yet.

제 주소를 갱신하는 건 누구에게 말해야 하나요?

(A) 제 생각에는 인사부의 Landon이요.

(B) 달력은 저쪽에 있어요.

(C) 저는 아직 갱신할 게 없어요.

어휘 update 최신의 것으로 만들다

---

8 (◀)) 미국…호주)

Could I have a moment of your time?

(A) It's only 4:00.

(B) If only I had known sooner.

(C) Of course. How can I help?

잠시 시간을 좀 내주실 수 있나요?

(A) 4시밖에 안되었어요.

(B) 좀 더 일찍 알았더라면 좋았을 텐데요.

(C) 물론이죠. 무엇을 도와드릴까요?

---

9 (◀)) 캐나다…미국)

Where are the markers I bought yesterday?

(A) I think I put them in the supply cabinet.

(B) They were on sale.

(C) At the office equipment store.

제가 어제 산 매직펜은 어디에 있나요?

(A) 제가 비품 캐비닛에 넣어둔 것 같아요.

(B) 그것들은 세일 중이었어요.

(C) 사무용품 가게에요.

어휘 marker 매직펜

---

10 (◀)) 호주…영국)

He followed up on your questions, didn't he?

(A) He won't be able to pass, I'm afraid.

(B) The doctor isn't in now.

(C) Yes. He answered all my questions.

그가 당신 질문에 답변해줬지요?

(A) 유감스럽지만, 그는 통과할 수 없습니다.

(B) 의사 선생님은 부재중입니다.

(C) 네. 그가 제 질문에 모두 답해줬습니다.

---

11 (◀)) 미국…캐나다)

How many folders come in a package?

(A) Less than $5.00.

(B) Ten, I guess.

(C) We shouldn't buy them.

한 묶음에 폴더가 몇 개 들어 있나요?

(A) 5달러보다 적어요.

(B) 10개인 것 같아요.

(C) 우리는 그것들을 사면 안 돼요.

12 〔◁〕 호주…영국

I don't know which phone number is hers.

(A) She's looking for her phone.

(B) I think it's the top one.

(C) Nobody knows where she is.

그녀의 전화번호가 어떤 것인지 모르겠어요.

(A) 그녀는 자기 휴대폰을 찾고 있어요.

(B) 제일 위에 있는 번호 같아요.

(C) 그녀가 어디에 있는지 아무도 몰라요.

---

13 〔◁〕 미국…호주

Why are the chairs stacked up in the conference room?

(A) Room A at 3:30.

(B) They're cleaning the carpets tonight.

(C) Because he's too busy right now.

왜 회의실에 의자들이 쌓여 있나요?

(A) 3시 30분에 A실이에요.

(B) 오늘 밤 카펫을 청소할 거예요.

(C) 그는 지금 너무 바쁘니까요.

---

14 〔◁〕 캐나다…영국

Has she gotten back to you about the project yet?

(A) I haven't heard the weather report.

(B) No. They're not coming over.

(C) Yes, and it's going ahead.

그녀가 프로젝트에 대해 아직 당신한테 연락 안 했어요?

(A) 저는 일기예보를 못 들었어요.

(B) 아뇨. 그들은 오지 않을 거예요.

(C) 했죠. 진행될 거예요.

어휘 go ahead 진행되다

---

15 〔◁〕 호주…캐나다

Which vehicle is big enough for five people?

(A) I recommend the SUV since you have luggage, too.

(B) Only three days to go.

(C) We charge extra for mileage.

5명이 충분히 탈 수 있는 큰 차는 어떤 건가요?

(A) 짐도 많으시니, 저는 SUV를 추천합니다.

(B) 3일밖에 안 남았어요.

(C) 마일당 추가 요금이 부과됩니다.

어휘 mileage 마일 계산

---

16 〔◁〕 미국…영국

There are no parking spaces left.

(A) Let's try at that other lot.

(B) There's one more space left in the workshop.

(C) We'll have to postpone, I guess.

남은 주차 공간이 없어요.

(A) 다른 주차장으로 가봐요.

(B) 작업장에 남은 공간이 하나 더 있어요.

(C) 제 생각엔 연기해야 할 것 같아요.

어휘 lot (토지의) 한 구획

---

17 〔◁〕 영국…호주

Can I get two large coffees to go, please?

(A) All of the seats are taken.

(B) Sure. That'll be $5.50.

(C) These are the last batch.

커피 큰 걸로 2잔 테이크아웃이요.

(A) 모든 좌석이 꽉 찼습니다.

(B) 네. 5.50달러입니다.

(C) 이게 마지막 묶음입니다.

어휘 batch 한 묶음

---

18 🔊 캐나다…미국

When will the president make the announcement?

(A) He's announced our new policy.

(B) The profits were through the roof.

(C) At 3:00, I heard.

사장님이 언제 발표하실까요?
(A) 그가 우리의 새 정책을 발표했어요.
(B) 이윤이 급등했어요.
(C) 제가 들은 바로는 3시예요.

어휘 be through the roof 급등하다

---

19 🔊 미국…호주

The theater has a cloakroom, doesn't it?

(A) As far as I know, yes.

(B) It's being torn down.

(C) The new play is fantastic.

극장에 물품 보관소가 있죠?
(A) 제가 알기로는 있어요.
(B) 허물어지고 있어요.
(C) 새 연극이 환상적이에요.

어휘 cloakroom 휴대품 보관소

---

20 🔊 영국…캐나다

Who is the woman next to Mr. Elmore?

(A) He's not coming back today.

(B) I've never seen her before.

(C) She can't make it to the party today.

Elmore씨 옆에 있는 여자는 누구인가요?
(A) 그는 오늘 돌아오지 않아요.
(B) 저는 처음 보는데요.
(C) 그녀는 오늘 파티에 갈 수 없어요.

---

21 🔊 호주…캐나다

Would you like me to do anything else before I leave?

(A) I'd like to thank you all for being here.

(B) No. That's everything. Thanks.

(C) Whenever you can come is fine.

제가 가기 전에 다른 할 일이 있나요?
(A) 참석해주신 여러분께 감사드립니다.
(B) 아뇨. 그게 전부예요. 고마워요.
(C) 올 수 있으면 언제든지 와도 좋아요.

---

22 🔊 호주…영국

The company is opening an office in Singapore.

(A) Oh, that's news to me.

(B) By next fall.

(C) Round trip or one way?

회사가 싱가포르에 지점을 열어요.
(A) 저는 처음 듣는 소식이에요.
(B) 내년 가을까지요.
(C) 왕복인가요, 편도인가요?

어휘 round trip 왕복 여행 one way 편도

---

23 캐나다…미국

Do you think the offer will be accepted?

(A) We don't accept credit cards.

(B) When you have enough time.

(C) No one knows for sure.

제안이 받아들여질 거라고 봐요?

(A) 저희는 신용카드를 받지 않습니다.

(B) 시간이 많으실 때에요.

(C) 아무도 확신할 수 없죠.

---

24 호주…캐나다

Why isn't this printer working?

(A) We bought a new printer this morning.

(B) It must be out of ink.

(C) Because we sold it.

왜 이 프린터는 작동하지 않나요?

(A) 오늘 아침에 새 프린터를 샀어요.

(B) 잉크가 다 떨어져서 그럴 거예요.

(C) 우리가 팔았으니까요.

---

25 영국…미국

Did you buy a laptop computer or tablet?

(A) Neither. I'm still shopping around.

(B) None of the tech people are available.

(C) My work computer is pretty old.

노트북 샀어요, 태블릿 샀어요?

(A) 둘 다 안 샀어요. 아직 보는 중이에요.

(B) 상담 가능한 기술자가 아무도 없어요.

(C) 제 업무용 컴퓨터는 꽤 오래되었어요.

---

26 미국…호주

Where do you suggest we stay?

(A) Until at least 5:00 PM.

(B) The hotel near the airport is convenient.

(C) We're all booked, I'm afraid.

우리가 어디에서 머물면 좋을까요?

(A) 늦어도 오후 5시까지요.

(B) 공항 근처 호텔이 편리해요.

(C) 죄송하지만, 예약이 꽉 찼습니다.

---

27 캐나다…영국

Feel free to call me with any questions.

(A) Are there any questions?

(B) My number is 555-3892.

(C) Thanks. I'll do that.

문의사항이 있으면 언제든지 전화주세요.

(A) 질문이 있나요?

(B) 제 전화번호는 555-3892입니다.

(C) 고마워요. 그렇게 할게요.

---

28 호주…미국

Why don't you join us for dinner tonight?

(A) I'll make a reservation if you like.

(B) Sorry, I already have plans.

(C) We're going to Emma's Café at lunchtime.

오늘 밤 같이 저녁을 먹는 게 어때요?

(A) 괜찮으시면 제가 예약할게요.

(B) 미안하지만, 선약이 있습니다.

(C) 우리는 점심시간에 Emma 카페에 갈 거예요.

29 ◁)) 영국···미국

Was there an invoice from the supplier?

(A) It should be inside the box.

(B) We need to switch them.

(C) Yes. We paid extra for it.

납품업체한테서 받은 송장이 있었나요?

(A) 박스 안에 있을 거예요.

(B) 그것들을 교체해야 해요.

(C) 네. 추가로 비용을 지불했어요.

---

30 ◁)) 미국···캐나다

What do you want to do this weekend?

(A) They're open on Sunday afternoons.

(B) There's not enough time for that.

(C) Whatever you want.

이번 주말에 뭐 하고 싶어요?

(A) 가게는 일요일 오후에 문을 열어요.

(B) 그걸 하기에는 시간이 충분하지 않아요.

(C) 당신이 하고 싶은 거요.

---

31 ◁)) 영국···호주

Do you want me to show you the cafeteria?

(A) Aren't you in sales department?

(B) I was given the full tour yesterday, thanks.

(C) Okay. Here's a map.

구내식당을 구경시켜드릴까요?

(A) 영업부 소속이 아니신가요?

(B) 고맙지만, 어제 전부 구경했어요.

(C) 좋아요. 여기 지도요.

PART 3

Questions 32-34 refer to the following conversation. ◁)) 호주···영국

W Hi, Jim. I was wondering if I could get your advice on something.

M Sure, Sarah, come on in. How can I help you?

W Well, ³²I'm putting together the budget for this year's awards ceremony, but I'm not really sure how much money we will need.

M Hmm. ³³When I did it last year, I ended up having some money left over. The expenses are a lot lower than you think.

W Oh, that's good because ³⁴the president asked me to keep the cost down.

여 안녕하세요, Jim. 제가 조언을 좀 얻을 수 있을까요?

남 그럼요, Sarah. 들어와요. 무엇을 도와줄까요?

여 그게, ³²올해 시상식 예산을 편성하려고 하는데, 돈이 얼마나 필요할지 정말로 모르겠어요.

남 ³³제가 작년에 그 일을 했을 때 결국에는 돈이 조금 남았어요. 비용은 당신이 생각하는 것보다 훨씬 저렴해요.

여 좋네요. ³⁴사장님이 비용을 낮추라고 하셨거든요.

어휘 put together 짜 맞추다 awards ceremony 시상식 expenses 비용

---

32 화자들은 무엇에 대해 논의하고 있는가?

(A) 회사 축하 행사

(B) 연봉

(C) 리더십의 변화

(D) 신제품 판매

33 남자는 지난해에 무엇을 했는가?

(A) 승진을 했다.

(B) 부서를 이동했다.

(C) 프로젝트에 비용을 과다 지출했다.

(D) 행사를 계획했다.

34 회사의 사장은 여자에게 무엇을 하도록 지시했는가?

(A) 넓은 장소 예약하기

(B) 지불하기

(C) 빨리 판매고 올리기

(D) 돈을 적게 쓰기

어휘 overspend 너무 많이 쓰다

Questions 35–37 refer to the following conversation. 🔊 캐나다…미국

W Good morning, this is Dr. Allen's office.

M Hello, ³⁵**I'm calling to cancel, well . . . uh, hopefully reschedule my appointment.** It's for this morning and I'm just too busy at work. I can't make it.

W No problem. I can find a time later this afternoon.

M I'm afraid that's no good, either. I've got meetings until 6:00. If you had a slot tomorrow around 3:00, that would be great. My name is Eric Cameron, by the way.

W Okay, Mr. Cameron, ³⁶**I have you down at 3:00 tomorrow.** ³⁷**Please don't forget to bring your latest insurance card.**

여 안녕하세요. Allen 의원입니다.

남 안녕하세요. ³⁵제가 예약을 취소하려고, 음… 할 수 있으면 제 예약 일정을 변경했으면 해요. 오늘 아침 예약이었는데, 제가 일이 너무 바빠서요. 도저히 못 가네요.

여 괜찮습니다. 오늘 오후로 시간 변경이 가능해요.

남 그것도 안 될 것 같아요. 오늘 6시까지 회의가 있어서요. 내일 3시경에 자리가 있다면 그게 좋을 것 같습니다. 그나저나 제 이름은 Eric Cameron입니다.

여 네, Cameron씨. ³⁶내일 3시로 변경했습니다. ³⁷최근 발급받은 보험증을 꼭 가져오세요.

어휘 slot 시간, 틈 down (더 낮은 장소나 위치에로) 아래로 insurance card 보험증

35 전화의 목적은 무엇인가?
(A) 예약 취소
(B) 예약 변경
(C) 예약 확인
(D) 예약 잡기

36 남자는 언제 여자의 진료소에 갈 것인가?
(A) 오늘 아침
(B) 오늘 오후
(C) 내일 3시
(D) 내일 6시

37 여자는 남자에게 무엇을 상기시키고 있는가?
(A) 남자의 연례 건강검진
(B) 남자의 다음 주 약속
(C) 남자의 보험 정보
(D) 남자의 지난달 납입

어휘 checkup 건강검진

Questions 38–40 refer to the following conversation. 🔊 호주…미국

W Oh, Martin, I heard you are moving to a new apartment closer to the office.

M Yes, Jessica. I found a really great one-bedroom apartment only a couple of stops away on the train from here. One problem, though. ³⁸**I have to sell my couch. It takes up too much space in my new place.**

W That brown leather one? ³⁹**I loved sitting on it at your party a few months ago.** It was so comfortable. I might be interested in it if the price is right.

M Ah, actually, ⁴⁰**I'm showing it to somebody afternoon. He said he was fine with my price.**

여 Martin, 사무실에서 가까운 새 아파트로 이사 간다고 들었어요.

남 네, Jessica. 정말 좋은 침실 한 개짜리 아파트를 찾았어요. 여기서 기차로 두 정거장 밖에 안 돼요. 하지만 한 가지 문제가 있어요. ³⁸제 소파를 팔아야 한다는 거요. 소파가 새 집에 비해 너무 크거든요.

여 갈색 가죽 소파요? ³⁹몇 달 전에 당신이 파티했을 때 앉아봤는데 좋더라고요. 너무 편했어요. 가격이 맞는다면 제가 살 생각이 있어요.

남 사실, ⁴⁰오후에 소파를 보여주기로 한 사람이 있어요. 그 사람이 제 가격이 괜찮대요.

어휘 stop 정거장 take up (공간을) 차지하다

38 왜 남자는 소파를 판매하는가?
(A) 새것을 구매했다.
(B) 해외로 이사한다.
(C) 소파가 오래된 편이다.
(D) 새 아파트에는 너무 크다.

39 여자에 관해 뭐라고 말할 수 있는가?
(A) 전에 남자의 아파트에 가본 적이 있다.
(B) 아파트의 주인이다.
(C) 곧 파티를 열 것이다.
(D) 방금 새로운 도시로 이사했다.

40 (신유형) I'm showing it to somebody this afternoon이라는 남자의 말이 암시하는 것은 무엇인가?
(A) 그는 여자가 자기 아파트를 사는 것을 원하지 않는다.
(B) 그는 소파를 살 사람을 찾았을 수도 있다.
(C) 누군가가 자기 아파트에 관심이 있다고 생각한다.
(D) 그는 소파를 얼른 팔고 싶다.

Questions 41–43 refer to the following conversation. 🔊 캐나다…영국

W Aron, I'm having a hard time deciding who to promote to the assistant manager position. Since Trevor quit suddenly, we've been without an assistant on the evening shift.

M Well, who are your top choices? ⁴²We need someone reliable to keep our grocery store running smoothly during the busy hours.

W ⁴¹Either Susan or Mike. They have both been working here for more than three years and they both have good relations with the other employees.

M Hmm, that is tough. ⁴³Why don't you ask them each to write a statement about why they would be a good manager?

여 Aron, 부매니저로 누구를 승진시킬지 결정하느라 애를 먹고 있어요. Trevor가 갑자기 그만둬서 야간 근무조에 부매니저가 없었잖아요.
남 당신이 생각하고 있는 사람은 누구예요? 바쁜 시간에도 ⁴²가게를 원활하게 운영하는 데 믿을 만한 사람이 필요해요.
여 ⁴¹Susan이나 Mike요. 두 사람 다 여기서 3년 넘게 일했고, 다른 직원들과의 관계도 좋아요.
남 어렵네요. ⁴³각자에게 자신이 훌륭한 관리자가 될 이유에 대해 써보도록 하는 건 어때요?

> 어휘 assistant manager 부관리자 shift 교대조 have good relations with ~와 좋은 관계를 맺다 tough 어려운 statement 진술(서)

---

41 결정을 내리는 데 있어서 여자가 가진 난관은 무엇인가?
(A) 적당한 후보자가 없다.
(B) 상사로부터 압박감을 느낀다.
(C) 시간적 압박을 느낀다.
(D) 두 명의 좋은 후보자가 있다.

42 화자들은 어디에서 일하는가?
(A) 공장
(B) 옷 가게
(C) 패스트푸드점
(D) 슈퍼마켓

43 남자는 무엇을 제안하는가?
(A) 온라인에 구직광고를 올리기
(B) 다른 상점을 방문하여 정보 얻기
(C) 합동 면접 보기
(D) 지원자들에게 글을 받아 읽어보기

> 어휘 pressure 압박

Questions 44–46 refer to the following conversation. 🔊 캐나다…미국

W Well, ⁴⁴it doesn't look good for our company marathon on Thursday.

M Oh, no. What is the forecast?

W ⁴⁴Rain starting at noon and lasting throughout the day.

M How about Friday? ⁴⁶Maybe we can postpone the marathon to Friday.

W Let me check the app here on my phone. Uh, it says cloudy in the morning and clear in the afternoon.

M That sounds perfect. Not too hot. ⁴⁵I'll post a message on the company intranet to tell everyone that ⁴⁶we're delaying it by a day.

어휘 forecast 예보 throughout ~ 동안 쭉 intranet 내부 전산망

여 ⁴⁴목요일 회사 마라톤 때 날씨가 좋지 않을 것 같아요.

남 안 돼요. 예보가 어떤데요?

여 ⁴⁴정오부터 비가 내리기 시작해서 하루 종일 이어지네요.

남 금요일은요? ⁴⁶마라톤을 금요일로 미룰 수 있을지도 몰라요.

여 제 휴대폰 앱으로 확인해볼게요. 오전에는 구름이 끼지만 오후에는 맑음이에요.

남 완전 좋아요. 너무 덥지도 않고요. ⁴⁵회사 인트라넷에 메시지를 올려서 모두에게 ⁴⁶마라톤이 하루 늦춰진다고 할게요.

---

44 행사의 문제는 무엇인가?
(A) 예산을 크게 초과했다.
(B) 화자들이 장소를 찾을 수 없다.
(C) 날씨가 나쁠지도 모른다.
(D) 참가자가 충분하지 않다.

45 남자는 무엇을 할 것이라고 말하는가?
(A) 직원회의 소집하기
(B) 행사를 언론에 알리기
(C) 직원 게시판에 공지 게시하기
(D) 내부 네트워크에 정보 올리기

46 행사는 언제 개최될 것인가?
(A) 오늘
(B) 목요일
(C) 금요일
(D) 다음 주 월요일

어휘 largely 크게

Questions 47–49 refer to the following conversation. 🔊 호주…영국

W Hi, I'd like to make a reservation for Friday, November 24.

M Yes, ma'am. ⁴⁷I can help you with that. What type of room do you need?

W Just a single, the cheapest you have. I'm actually arriving late and ⁴⁸leaving early for a conference on Saturday.

M I see. Okay, we have a single for $89. Would that be okay?

W That's great. And I'll also need a shuttle from the airport.

M I can arrange that for you. ⁴⁹Let me get your name and phone number first.

어휘 arrange 마련하다

여 안녕하세요. 11월 24일 금요일에 예약하고 싶습니다.

남 네, 손님. ⁴⁷도와드리겠습니다. 어떤 방이 필요하신가요?

여 가장 싼 1인실이요. 늦게 도착해서 ⁴⁸토요일에는 회의 때문에 일찍 나가거든요.

남 알겠습니다. 89달러짜리 1인실 방이 하나 있습니다. 괜찮으신가요?

여 좋아요. 그리고 공항 셔틀버스도 필요해요.

남 준비해드릴 수 있습니다. ⁴⁹먼저 성함과 전화번호를 알려주세요.

---

47 남자가 일하는 곳은 어디인가?
(A) 컨퍼런스 센터
(B) 호텔
(C) 여행사
(D) 항공사

48 여자의 여행의 목적은 무엇인가?
(A) 결혼식
(B) 업무
(C) 휴가
(D) 가족 모임

49 여자는 남자에게 무엇을 줄 것인가?
(A) 자신의 연락처 정보
(B) 자신의 신용카드 번호
(C) 자신의 비행 정보
(D) 자신의 예약 번호

어휘 vacation 휴가 contact 연락

Questions 50-52 refer to the following conversation. 🔊 호주…미국

W   Tom, you're going to talk to the president about your idea today, right?

M   Uh, you mean, about having a weekly meeting in a different room? Yes, if I get up the courage. He might think that because ⁵⁰I just started to work here, I should keep my mouth shut.

W   Well, ⁵¹you have my vote. I was thinking the same thing. The old place is just too small.

M   Thanks, Tess. Because of you, ⁵²I'm going to his office right now to talk with him.

어휘 get up the courage 용기를 내다

여   Tom, 오늘 당신의 생각에 대해 사장님과 이야기하죠?

남   다른 회의실에서 주간 회의를 하자는 것 말이죠? 네. 용기가 생기면요. ⁵⁰저는 이제 여기서 일을 시작했기 때문에 사장님은 제가 조용히 있어야 된다고 생각할 수도 있어요.

여   ⁵¹제 표는 이미 획득했어요. 저도 같은 생각을 하고 있었거든요. 오래된 그곳은 너무 작아요.

남   고마워요, Tess. 당신 덕분에 ⁵²지금 당장 말씀 드리러 사장님실로 가겠어요.

---

50 남자에 대해 언급된 것은 무엇인가?
(A) 그는 사무실의 신입이다.
(B) 그는 사장이 되길 원한다.
(C) 그는 새 프로젝트에 배정되었다.
(D) 그는 여자를 돕고 싶다.

51 여자가 you have my vote라고 말한 의미는 무엇인가?
(A) 여자는 남자가 선거에 나가기를 바란다.
(B) 여자는 남자의 생각을 지지한다.
(C) 여자는 관리직 자리에 남자를 뽑으려 한다.
(D) 여자는 남자에게 좋은 평을 해줄 것이다.

52 이후 남자는 어디로 갈 가능성이 높은가?
(A) 시청
(B) 사장의 사무실
(C) 투표 장소
(D) 여자의 사무실

어휘 assign 배정하다 run (선거에) 출마하다 election 선거 managerial 관리의

Questions 53-55 refer to the following conversation. 🔊 영국…캐나다 신유형

M   Mary, ⁵³have you looked at the new Internet that was installed over the weekend?

W   No, not yet, but ⁵⁴I have to log in quickly before my meeting at 9:30. I need a new password, right?

M   Yeah, the IT department sent you a new one by e-mail last week.

W   Honestly, I've been busy since last week and haven't checked my e-mails carefully. I have a big presentation this afternoon and I haven't finished it yet.

M   ⁵⁵If you need any help or someone to practice with, let me know. I'm free all morning.

W   Thanks, Dave. I appreciate it. Let me check my password first, then I'll let you know.

남   Mary, ⁵³주말에 설치된 새 인터넷을 살펴봤어요?

여   아뇨, 아직이요. 하지만 ⁵⁴9시 30분 회의 전에 빨리 로그인해야 해요. 새 비밀번호가 필요하지요?

남   네, 지난주에 IT부서에서 이메일로 새 비밀번호를 보내줬어요.

여   사실은, 지난주부터 바빠서 이메일을 꼼꼼히 확인하지 않았어요. 오늘 오후에 중요한 발표를 해야 하는데 아직 마무리하지 못했어요.

남   ⁵⁵도움이나 같이 연습할 사람이 필요하면 알려주세요. 전 아침 내내 한가해요.

여   고마워요, Dave. 고맙게 생각하고 있어요. 먼저 비밀번호를 확인한 다음에 알려줄게요.

---

53 주말 동안에 무엇이 바뀌었는가?
(A) 컴퓨터 네트워크
(B) 부서 공간
(C) 직원들의 책상
(D) 사무실의 위치

54 여자는 무엇을 해야 한다고 하는가?
(A) 보고서 끝내기
(B) 발표 노트 찾기
(C) 컴퓨터에 접속하기
(D) 남자에게 업무 주기

55 남자는 여자에게 무엇을 제안하는가?
(A) IT부서에 전화해주기
(B) 그녀의 비밀번호를 바꿔주기
(C) 그녀의 발표를 들어주기
(D) 사무실을 구경시켜주기

Questions 56-58 refer to the following conversation with three speakers. ◁)) 캐나다…미국…영국 신유형

W Robert, ⁵⁶I don't know how we're going to get through all these applications! I never expected so many.

M1 Well, we did advertise in two more places than we usually do. Those Websites are really popular among recent college graduates.

W You're right. But now, we have too many to sort through with just the two of us.

M1 ⁵⁷Why don't I ask my assistant Tony to help? Oh, there he is. Tony, are you busy now?

M2 Not really. I just finished entering all the data you asked me to.

M1 Good. ⁵⁸Could you do the initial screening of the applicants? I'll tell you what we're looking for.

M2 Sure, ⁵⁸I'll start on that right away.

여 Robert, ⁵⁶이 모든 지원서들을 어떻게 다 봐야 할지 모르겠어요! 이렇게 많을 거라고는 상상도 못했어요.

남1 우리가 평소보다 두 군데 더 광고했어요. 그 웹사이트들은 최근 대학 졸업자들 사이에서 인기가 많아요.

여 맞아요. 하지만 우리 둘이서 살펴보기에는 너무 많아요.

남1 ⁵⁷제 조수인 Tony에게 도와달라고 요청하는 게 어때요? 아, 저기 있네요. Tony, 지금 바빠요?

남2 아뇨. 요청하셨던 데이터 입력을 지금 막 끝냈어요.

남1 좋아요. ⁵⁸지원자들을 1차로 심사할 수 있겠어요? 우리가 찾는 사람을 알려줄게요.

남2 좋아요. ⁵⁸지금 바로 시작할게요.

어휘 get through ~를 끝내다 college graduate 대학 졸업자 sort through 자세히 살펴보다 enter 입력하다 initial screening 첫 심사 applicant 지원자

56 여자는 왜 놀라는가?
(A) 그녀의 상사가 회사를 떠나서
(B) Robert가 회의에 늦어서
(C) 지원자들이 자격이 없어서
(D) 구직 후보자들이 많아서

57 Robert가 제안하는 것은 무엇인가?
(A) 더 많은 웹사이트에 광고하기
(B) 누군가에게 도움을 요청하기
(C) 몇몇 대학에 연락하기
(D) 빨리 면접 약속 잡기

58 이후 Tony는 무엇을 할 것인가?
(A) 지원서 작성하기
(B) 컴퓨터에 자료 입력하기
(C) 지원자들 면접하기
(D) 일부 지원자들 검토하기

어휘 look through 검토하다

Questions 59-61 refer to the following conversation. ◁)) 캐나다…영국 신유형

W Hi, ⁵⁹I'm calling several caterers trying to get an estimate for a dinner at my company. About 35 people. Could you tell me approximately how much the meal would cost?

M It depends what type of food you'd like. For example, chicken is cheaper than beef. If it's casual, we make small finger food that's even cheaper.

W Oh, ⁶⁰we're going to have a sit down dinner because it's a board meeting. I'm thinking maybe a buffet line.

M Hmm, 35 people, buffet style. Will you be needing beverages, too?

W No, we have wine and other drinks at the office.

M ⁶¹I can put some numbers together and send you an e-mail. Remember, though, that these aren't final costs. I can't give you a real quote until after you pick specific dishes.

여 안녕하세요? ⁵⁹저는 회사에서 하는 저녁식사 견적을 받으려고 여러 출장음식업체에 전화하고 있습니다. 인원은 약 35명이에요. 대략적으로 비용이 얼마인지 알려주실 수 있으세요?

남 가격은 고객이 원하는 음식의 종류에 따라 다릅니다. 예를 들면, 닭고기는 소고기보다 저렴하지요. 격식을 차리지 않는 자리라면 소량의 핑거 푸드가 있고, 그건 더 쌉니다.

여 ⁶⁰이사회 회의라서, 앉아서 하는 저녁식사예요. 저는 뷔페를 생각했습니다.

남 35명이고, 뷔페 스타일이군요. 음료도 필요하십니까?

여 아뇨, 사무실에 와인과 다른 음료가 있습니다.

남 ⁶¹계산해서 이메일로 보내드릴게요. 그렇지만 그게 최종 금액은 아닙니다. 명확하게 요리를 고르기 전에는 최종 견적을 드릴 수 없습니다.

어휘 approximately 대략 finger food (손으로 쉽게 집어 먹을 수 있는) 핑거 푸드 sit down dinner 앉아서 하는 식사 specific 명확한

---

59 남자의 직업은 무엇인가?
(A) 이사진
(B) 출장음식업자
(C) 사무 보조원
(D) 행사 조직원

60 여자는 어떤 행사 때문에 전화했는가?
(A) 생일 파티
(B) 퇴직 파티
(C) 시상식 연회
(D) 경영진 모임

61 남자는 여자에게 무엇을 보낼 것인가?
(A) 브로슈어
(B) 메뉴
(C) 가격 견적
(D) 와인 리스트

어휘 organizer 조직자 executive 경영진

Questions 62–64 refer to the following conversation and price list. 🔊 미국…호주

M Hi, ⁶²I'd like a ticket to the special exhibit on dinosaurs, please.

W Of course. Would you be interested in watching our special movie about the exhibit? ⁶³It's not that long and it gives a bit of detail about the exhibit.

M I see. I think I have time to watch it since it's not very long. Yes, ⁶²I'd like a ticket with the movie.

W Here's your ticket. And this is a brochure about our upcoming exhibits and information about becoming a museum member. Members get 10 percent off all tickets.

M Thank you. ⁶⁴I'll think about joining.

남 ⁶²공룡 특별 전시 입장권 한 장이요.

여 알겠습니다. 전시회에 관한 특별 영상을 보는 데 관심이 있으신가요? ⁶³그렇게 길지 않고, 전시에 대한 세부 사항을 알려주거든요.

남 그렇군요. 상영 시간이 길지 않다니 볼 수 있겠네요. 네, ⁶²영상이 포함된 입장권을 구매할게요.

여 입장권 여기 있습니다. 그리고 이건 앞으로 있을 전시와 박물관 회원이 되는 것에 관한 정보가 담긴 안내 책자입니다. 회원은 모든 입장권 구매 시 10% 할인이 됩니다.

남 감사합니다. ⁶⁴가입은 생각해볼게요.

Rockford 자연사 박물관 입장권 가격표	
·일반 전시	18달러
‑오디오 가이드 포함	22달러
·공룡 전시	10달러
⁶²‑영상 시청 포함	14달러

어휘 upcoming 다가오는

62 가격표에 의하면, 남자는 입장료로 얼마를 지불했는가? 신 유 형
(A) 10달러
(B) 14달러
(C) 18달러
(D) 22달러

63 여자는 영상에 대해 뭐라고 말하는가?
(A) 특별 전시에 대해 설명해준다.
(B) 몇 가지 특수 효과가 있다.
(C) 상영 시간이 길다.
(D) 시간마다 상영된다.

64 남자는 무엇을 할 것이라고 말하는가?
(A) 나중에 박물관에 다시 오기
(B) 여자의 제안 고려하기
(C) 박물관에 가입하기
(D) 다른 날에 영상 시청하기

Questions 65-67 refer to the following conversation and book shelf. 🔊 영국…호주

M Excuse me. I'm looking for a book I heard about on the radio. Something with *Hotel* in the title. It's set in 19th century Europe.

W You must be talking about *Hotel Metropole*. **⁶⁵It's gotten great reviews! We can hardly keep it on the shelves.**

M Yes, that's it! Oh, I hope you still have a copy. **⁶⁶If I like it, I'm going to recommend it to my book club.**

W I'm sure we do because I stocked them this morning. **⁶⁷They're over there next to the science fiction. You see? Below the biographies?**

M Ah, yes. Thank you so much.

남 실례합니다. 라디오에서 들은 책을 찾고 있는데요. 제목이 Hotel 뭐뭐예요. 19세기 유럽을 배경으로 하고 있습니다.

여 Hotel Metropole을 이야기하시는 것 같네요. ⁶⁵평이 아주 좋은 책이지요. 책장에 꽂아놓기만 하면 바로 나가요.

남 네, 그거예요! 책이 아직 남아 있으면 좋겠네요. ⁶⁶마음에 들면, 제 북클럽에 추천할 거예요.

여 제가 오늘 아침에 채워놨기 때문에 분명 남아 있을 거예요. ⁶⁷공상과학소설 옆에 있습니다. 보이세요? 전기 아래예요.

남 그렇군요. 정말 고맙습니다.

미스터리	전기
공상과학	⁶⁷공포
역사	판타지

어휘 be set in ~를 배경으로 하다 stock 채우다 biography 전기 문학

65 여자는 책에 대해서 뭐라고 말하는가?
(A) 후기가 엇갈린다.
(B) 읽기 어렵다.
(C) 인기가 있다.
(D) 유럽을 배경으로 한다.

66 남자는 왜 그 책을 읽고 싶어 하는가?
(A) 과제로 읽어야 하기 때문에
(B) 추천할 만한지 보고 싶기 때문에
(C) 그 책을 극찬하는 후기를 읽었기 때문에
(D) 여자가 강력히 추천했기 때문에

67 🔵신 🔵유 🔵형 책장에 의하면, 남자는 어떤 종류의 책을 찾고 있는가?
(A) 판타지
(B) 역사
(C) 공포
(D) 미스터리

Questions 68-70 refer to the following conversation and list. 🔊 캐나다…미국

W Hi, I was hoping to get some fabric for a piece of art I'm working on. It's pretty big, so I'd need a lot of it.

M **⁶⁸What kind of fabric were you looking for?** Wool or cotton or cotton or . . . ?

W I need something very light and almost see-through. I was thinking of chiffon or gauze.

M I'm looking at the stock information on my computer, and I'm afraid we only have a small amount of chiffon. We could order it from our other stores and that would take, uh, probably about a week.

W Hmm, **⁶⁹I'd like to finish my piece on the weekend.** I think **⁷⁰I'll go with the gauze.**

여 안녕하세요. 제가 작업하고 있는 예술품에 쓸 원단을 찾고 있는데요. 그게 꽤 커서 많은 양이 필요해요.

남 ⁶⁸어떤 종류의 원단을 찾고 있습니까? 울? 면? 그것도 아니면?

여 저는 아주 가볍고 속이 비치는 원단을 찾고 있어요. 시폰이나 거즈요.

남 컴퓨터로 재고 정보를 보고 있는데, 죄송하지만 시폰이 조금밖에 없네요. 다른 곳에 있는 저희 가게에 주문해서 받아볼 수 있는데, 한 일주일 정도 걸릴 것 같습니다.

여 ⁶⁹주말에는 제 작품을 끝내고 싶어요. ⁷⁰거즈로 해야겠네요.

재고 목록

물품 번호	원단	재고량
C92	면	18미터
Ch19	시폰	1미터
⁷⁰G05	거즈	10미터
W83	울	7미터

어휘 see-through (옷감이) 속이 다 비치는 chiffon 시폰 inventory 재고(품)

68 대화가 이루어지고 있는 장소는 어디인가?
(A) 식당
(B) 옷 가게
(C) 원단 가게
(D) 예술품 가게

69 여자는 주말에 무엇을 할 것이라고 말하는가?
(A) 갤러리에 가기
(B) 예술 작품 완성하기
(C) 재고 확인하기
(D) 회사에서 일하기

70 신유형 목록에 의하면, 여자는 어떤 원단을 살 것인가?
(A) C92
(B) Ch19
(C) G05
(D) W83

PART 4

Questions 71–73 refer to the following telephone message. (호주)

Hello. My name is Melanie Nevins and **71**I'm planning on attending your winery's grand opening next week. **72**When I sent in my reservation card, I marked one person, but I'd like to update that to two people. **73**A friend of mine from California will be in town and I thought he might enjoy seeing our local wine being produced. You can reach me at 555-1871 if you have any questions. Thanks for restoring the old winery and opening it up to the public. I'm looking forward to the event next week.

안녕하세요. 저는 Melanie Nevins입니다. **71**다음 주에 당신의 와이너리 개점에 참석할 계획입니다. **72**제가 예약 신청서를 보냈을 때 한 명만 표시했는데, 두 사람으로 변경하고자 합니다. **73**캘리포니아에서 친구가 올 건데, 그 친구가 이 지역에서 생산되는 와인을 보고 좋아할 것 같습니다. 궁금한 게 있으시면 555-1871로 연락해주세요. 오래된 와이너리를 복원하고 대중에게 공개해주셔서 감사합니다. 다음 주 행사에서 뵙겠습니다.

어휘 winery 와인 양조장 produce 생산하다 restore 복원하다

71 화자는 다음 주에 어떤 행사에 참여하는가?
(A) 준공식
(B) 지역 축제
(C) 식당 개업
(D) 와이너리 투어

72 화자는 왜 청자에게 연락을 달라고 요청하는가?
(A) 행사에 관한 질문에 답하기 위해
(B) 추가 손님을 확인하기 위해
(C) 참가를 취소하기 위해
(D) 행사장에 가는 길을 알려주기 위해

73 화자는 누가 방문할 것이라고 말하는가?
(A) 업무 관계자
(B) 사업주
(C) 친구
(D) 친척

어휘 building dedication 준공식

Questions 74–76 refer to the following introduction. (미국)

We are so honored tonight to have renowned French Chef Pascal **74**here at our community cooking club to **75**show us how to make French food at home. It really isn't as hard as it looks. **76**Chef Pascal has been cooking since he was eight years old, and, as he says in his new book, his mother taught him more about cooking than he ever learned in cooking school. Tonight, he will be making bouillabaisse and ratatouille. These two dishes combined are a simple and satisfying meal the whole family can enjoy. Let's give a warm welcome to Chef Pascal.

오늘 밤 영광스럽게도 유명 프랑스 요리사 Pascal씨가 **74**이곳 우리 지역 요리 클럽에서 **75**집에서 프랑스 요리를 만드는 법을 보여주십니다. 보이는 것만큼 어렵지 않습니다. **76**Pascal씨는 8살 때부터 요리를 시작했으며, 그의 새 책을 보면, 요리 학교에서 배운 것보다 어머니가 더 많이 가르쳐주셨다고 합니다. 오늘 밤, 그는 부야베스와 라타투이를 만들 것입니다. 이 두 가지 요리면 온 가족이 즐길 수 있는 간단하고 만족스러운 식사가 됩니다. 요리사 Pascal씨를 따뜻하게 맞이해주시기 바랍니다.

어휘 renowned 유명한 satisfying 만족스러운

74 청자들은 누구인가?
(A) 독서 클럽 회원
(B) 서점 직원
(C) 지역의 지도자
(D) 요리 클럽 회원들

75 화자에 의하면, Pascal씨는 곧 무엇을 할 것인가?
(A) 기술 시연하기
(B) 그의 책 낭독하기
(C) 그의 책에 서명하기
(D) 청자들로부터 질문 받기

76 Pascal씨는 자신이 선택한 분야에 대해 언제 관심을 갖기 시작했는가?
(A) 첫 책을 쓴 이후
(B) 어린 시절에
(C) 프랑스를 처음 떠났을 때
(D) 요리 학교에 다니는 동안

어휘 demonstrate 보여주다

Questions 77-79 refer to the following announcement. (캐나다)

Attention passengers. **77 We are about to pull into dock at Marina 7.** **78 Please line up at the door near the snack bar on the upper deck to exit. Only this exit on the front of the boat will be open.** When you disembark, please make sure to bring all your belongings with you. There is a tourist information center as you step off the ramp, just in front of the fountain. **79 The staff at the center speak Chinese, Japanese, Korean, and English.** We are happy you chose Sea Star Lines for your journey today. Please come sail with us again.

승객 여러분께 알립니다. 77우리는 7번 선착장에 정박합니다. 78하선하시려면 상갑판 스낵바 근처 문 쪽에 줄을 서주시기 바랍니다. 배의 앞에 있는 이 출구만 개방될 것입니다. 하선하실 때는 반드시 소지품을 모두 챙기시기 바랍니다. 경사로를 내려가시면 분수 바로 앞에 관광안내소가 있습니다. 79센터의 직원들은 중국어, 일본어, 한국어, 영어를 구사할 수 있습니다. 오늘 여행에 저희 Sea Star Lines를 선택해주셔서 기쁩니다. 다음에도 저희와 함께 하시길 바랍니다.

어휘 pull into ~에 도착하다 disembark (배에서) 내리다 ramp 경사로 fountain 분수 sail 항해하다

77 안내는 어디에서 이루어지고 있는가?
(A) 배
(B) 관광버스
(C) 기차
(D) 비행기

78 스낵바 근처에 있는 것은 무엇인가?
(A) 관광안내 데스크
(B) 출구로 가는 계단
(C) 화장실
(D) 유일한 출구

79 누가 여러 언어를 사용하는가?
(A) 식당 종업원
(B) 서비스 센터의 직원
(C) 스낵바 직원
(D) 배의 승무원

Questions 80-82 refer to the following advertisement. (영국)

If you have been disappointed with language learning systems in the past, you'll be pleasantly surprised by the newest release from EduLang. **80 Say Hello! is a Web-based language learning program** that helps you become fluent in a foreign language within six weeks. **81 It uses repetition and cool graphics to help you make progress and to keep you coming back.** For one low monthly fee, you can use Say Hello! on your mobile phone or PC at home or office. Started by educators in several fields nearly a decade ago, **82 EduLang is the award winning company** that has released some of the most popular educational software in the country.

과거의 언어 학습 시스템에 실망하셨다면, EduLang이 최근 출시한 프로그램이 매우 기쁘실 겁니다. 80Say Hello!는 웹 기반의 언어학습 프로그램으로서 6주 이내에 외국어를 유창하게 할 수 있도록 도와줍니다. 81반복 학습과 멋진 그래픽을 사용하여 여러분의 학습 진행을 돕고, 계속해서 공부할 수 있도록 해줍니다. 저렴한 월 사용료로 휴대폰 또는 집이나 사무실의 PC로 Say Hello!를 사용할 수 있습니다. 약 10년 전 여러 분야의 교육자들에 의해 시작된 82EduLang은 수상 경험이 있는 회사로, 우리나라에서 가장 인기 있는 교육 소프트웨어를 출시한 적이 있습니다.

어휘 foreign language 외국어 repetition 반복 make progress 진전을 이루다

80 어떤 제품이 광고되고 있는가?
- (A) 학습 앱
- (B) 시리즈 도서
- (C) 언어 캠프 프로그램
- (D) 언어 개인 레슨

81 광고에 의하면, Say Hello!는 어떻게 사용자들의 학습동기를 유지시키는가?
- (A) 정기적인 할인을 제공함으로써
- (B) 승급 포상을 제공함으로써
- (C) 흥미로운 이미지를 사용함으로써
- (D) 인기 있는 음악을 사용함으로써

82 EduLang에 관해 언급된 것은 무엇인가?
- (A) 수상 경력이 있다.
- (B) 소프트웨어 산업에서 신생 기업이다.
- (C) 업계에서 가장 인기 있는 회사이다.
- (D) 과학기술 전문가에 의해 시작되었다.

어휘 incentive 장려책 honor 명예 start-up 신규 업체

Questions 83-85 refer to the following telephone message. (◁)) 호주)

Hi, Dominic, **83** this is Claudia from personnel. I got all the paperwork on **85** your new marketing department employee, George Barnes, this morning. Thank you. Um, I noticed that one of the forms is not complete. I'm not sure why that is, but maybe he didn't see that it had a back side. Anyway, **84** I was hoping to finalize everything later today. Since payroll needs to add him to the records soon, **85** could you let him stop by my office to finish up the paperwork? Thanks, Dominic.

안녕하세요, Domonic. **83** 인사부의 Claudia입니다. 오늘 아침에 **85** 당신의 새 마케팅 부서 직원 George Barnes에 대한 서류를 모두 받았어요. 고마워요. 그런데, 제가 보니까 양식 중 하나가 작성이 다 안 됐더라고요. 왜 그런지 모르겠지만, 아마도 서류에 뒷면이 있는 것을 보지 못한 것 같아요. 어쨌든, **84** 오늘 중으로 모든 것을 마무리 짓고 싶어요. 경리과에서 그를 명단에 곧 추가해야 하니 **85** 그에게 제 사무실에 들러서 서류 작업을 끝내게 해주시겠어요? 고마워요, Dominic.

어휘 back side 뒷면 payroll 급여 지급

---

83 화자가 일하는 부서는 어디인가?
- (A) 마케팅
- (B) 경리
- (C) 인사
- (D) 영업

84 🛑 화자가 I was hoping to finalize everything later today라고 말한 의미는 무엇인가?
- (A) 그녀는 Dominic이 곧 그녀에게 전화를 주기를 바란다.
- (B) 그녀는 Dominic이 서둘러주길 바란다.
- (C) 그녀는 최종 보고서 관련하여 도움을 원한다.
- (D) 그녀는 일찍 떠나기를 원한다.

85 누가 오늘 화자의 사무실에 방문해야 하는가?
- (A) Dominic
- (B) George
- (C) 마케팅 사장
- (D) 경리부 이사

Questions 86-88 refer to the following radio broadcast. (◁)) 미국)

Good morning and thank you for listening to KWAL. **86** Before we get back to the classical music, I'd like to let everyone know about a fantastic event coming up at the downtown amphitheater. **87** Our local chamber orchestra, The Walden Strings, led by conductor Marshall Young, will be giving free concerts both Saturday afternoon and Sunday evening. These concerts are sponsored by Walden Bank and the local business association. **88** Seating is limited and tickets will be available starting Wednesday morning. **86** Let's return now to a piece by Bach.

좋은 아침입니다. KWAL을 들어주셔서 감사합니다. **86** 클래식 음악으로 돌아가기 전에, 모든 분들에게 시내 원형극장에서 열리는 환상적인 행사에 대해 알리고 싶습니다. **87** Marshall Young이 지휘하는 우리 지역의 실내악단 The Walden Strings가 토요일 오후와 일요일 저녁에 무료로 콘서트를 열 예정입니다. 이 콘서트는 Walden 은행과 지역 비즈니스 협회가 후원합니다. **88** 좌석은 한정되어 있으며, 입장권은 수요일 오전부터 발권이 가능합니다. **86** 이제 바흐의 작품으로 돌아가죠.

어휘 chamber orchestra 실내악단 conductor 지휘자

---

86 화자는 어떤 종류의 라디오 프로그램을 진행하는가?
(A) 클래식 음악
(B) 지역 뉴스
(C) 로큰롤
(D) 토크쇼

87 화자에 의하면, Marshall Young은 누구인가?
(A) 은행 직원
(B) 지역 사업체 리더
(C) 오케스트라 지휘자
(D) 라디오 방송국 직원

88 Seating is limited라는 화자의 말이 암시하는 것은 무엇인가?
(A) 청취자들은 특별 좌석을 예약할 수 있다.
(B) 청취자들은 앞좌석만 예약할 수 있다.
(C) 청취자들은 수요일에만 표를 예약할 수 있다.
(D) 청취자들은 빨리 표를 구해야 한다.

Questions 89-91 refer to the following telephone message. 〔◀)) 캐나다〕

Hi, Marilyn. ⁸⁹I'm calling to say a big congratulations on getting Employee of the Year. When I heard the news, I was not surprised in the least. ⁹⁰No one deserves this more than you. ⁹¹You've been working so hard on the opening of our new branches in two states, plus training your team leaders. I'd like to treat you to a drink some time this week. Please let me know when you are free. You can ask your husband to join us if you like. See you soon, Marilyn.

안녕하세요, Marilyn. ⁸⁹올해의 직원에 선정된 것을 정말로 축하한다고 말하고 싶어서 전화했어요. 그 소식을 들었을 때 저는 조금도 놀라지 않았어요. ⁹⁰당신 말고는 그 상을 받을 만한 사람은 없거든요. ⁹¹당신은 두 개 주에서 새 지점들을 여느라 정말 열심히 일했어요. 거기에 당신의 팀 리더들을 교육하는 것도요. 이번 주에 언제 술 한잔 대접하고 싶어요. 당신이 편할 때를 알려주세요. 괜찮다면 당신 남편도 함께 해요. 곧 봐요, Marilyn.

어휘 in the least 조금도 ~ 않다

---

89 전화를 한 주된 목적은 무엇인가?
(A) 동료를 축하하기 위해서
(B) 동료에게 수상에 대해 알리려고
(C) 동료를 저녁식사에 초대하기 위해
(D) 동료에게 도움을 요청하기 위해

90 화자가 No one deserves this more than you라고 말한 의미는 무엇인가?
(A) 모두가 청자가 상을 타기를 바랐다.
(B) 다른 직원들은 수상하지 못할 것이다.
(C) 화자의 팀에는 아무도 없다.
(D) 우리 모두 더 나은 결과를 얻을 만했다.

91 올해 화자의 회사에 대해 언급된 것은 무엇인가?
(A) 다른 장소들로 확장했다.
(B) 많은 사람들을 고용했다.
(C) 다른 장소로 이전했다.
(D) 상을 받았다.

Questions 92-94 refer to the following talk. 〔◀)) 영국〕

Welcome everyone to tonight's year-end celebration! After a difficult two years, ⁹³we've had an amazing turnaround at Stronghold, Inc. this year and it's all thanks to you. Word has spread within the industry about ⁹²how we handle data security and protect our customers, both consumer and corporate, and ⁹³we're now considered the industry leader. So, how are we going to thank you for all making this a great year? Well, in addition to raises, ⁹⁴we are giving you the opportunity to help grow our company overseas. We are looking for leaders, and that person could be you. If you are interested in heading a new branch, please talk to Ms. Smith in personnel.

오늘 밤 연말 행사에 오신 여러분을 환영합니다! 어려웠던 지난 2년이 지나고, ⁹³올해 Stronghold사는 놀랄만한 반등을 했으며, 이 모든 것은 여러분 덕분입니다. ⁹²우리가 어떻게 데이터 보안을 다루고, 소비자 및 기업 두 고객 모두를 보호하는지에 대해서는 업계에 잘 알려졌으며 ⁹³이제 우리는 업계의 리더로 간주되고 있습니다. 그러면, 이 멋진 한 해를 만들어준 여러분에게 어떻게 보답할까요? 임금 인상 외에도 ⁹⁴여러분에게 해외에서 회사의 성장을 도울 수 있는 기회를 드리려고 합니다. 우리는 리더를 찾고 있고, 리더는 여러분이 될 수 있습니다. 여러분 중에 새 지점을 이끄는 데 관심이 있으시면, 인사부의 Smith씨에게 말해주세요.

어휘 turnaround 호전, 반등 raise 임금 인상 head ~를 이끌다

---

92 Stronghold사는 어떤 종류의 사업을 하는가?
- (A) 정보 보안
- (B) 투자
- (C) 법률 사무소
- (D) 부동산

93 올해 회사에 좋았던 일은 무엇인가?
- (A) 회사가 해외로 진출했다.
- (B) 회사가 경험이 많은 직원들을 고용했다.
- (C) 회사의 명성이 높아졌다.
- (D) 판매가 사상 최고를 기록했다.

94 화자는 청자들에게 무엇을 제안하는가?
- (A) 관리 직책
- (B) 추가 보안
- (C) 더 큰 사무실
- (D) 연말 보너스

어휘 law firm 법률 사무소 hit a record high 최고치를 기록하다

Questions 95–97 refer to the following excerpt from a meeting and chart. (◁)) 호주

Okay, everyone, we have a lot to talk about, so let's get started. **95**The new store building will be ready soon and we want to have a smooth transition with the least disruption to customers and, of course, sales. As I was trying to decide when to move, I looked at a sales chart from this time last year. **96**You can see that one week we weren't as busy. Of course, we don't know that it will be the same this year. But **97**typically sales follow a pattern year to year.

좋아요, 여러분. 할 얘기가 많으니 시작합시다. **95**새 매장 건물은 곧 완공될 예정이며, 우리는 고객의 혼란을 최소화하고, 또한 당연히, 판매까지 부드럽게 전환되기를 원합니다. 이사할 시기를 결정하고자 작년 이맘때의 매출표를 보았습니다. **96**한 주에는 우리가 그렇게 바쁘지 않았다는 것을 알 수 있습니다. 물론, 올해도 지난번과 똑같을지는 알 수 없습니다. 하지만 **97**일반적으로 매출은 매년 어떤 패턴을 따라가지요.

※주별 매장 매출(11월) 그래프는 문제지를 참조하세요.

어휘 disruption 혼란 transition 전환 typically 일반적으로 year to year 매년

---

95 화자는 어떤 유형의 사업에 종사하는가?
- (A) 숙박업
- (B) 제조업
- (C) 소매업
- (D) 건설업

96 신유형 매출표에 의하면, 가게는 언제 이전할 것으로 보이는가?
- (A) 11월 첫째 주
- (B) 11월 둘째 주
- (C) 11월 셋째 주
- (D) 11월 넷째 주

97 화자는 매출에 대해서 뭐라고 말하는가?
- (A) 매출이 매년 비슷하다.
- (B) 계절성 캠페인 기간 중에 매출이 오른다.
- (C) 올해는 평소보다 매출이 더 낮다.
- (D) 달 안에서도 매출이 매우 다르다.

어휘 about the same 거의 같은 vary 달라지다

Questions 98–100 refer to the following announcement and store directory. (◁)) 미국

98Thank you for shopping at Diamond Department Store during our annual sale. We have terrific savings on all floors this week, and today only, we have some extra special savings for women. **99**All women's outerwear, including jackets and coats, are an extra 20 percent off our already low price. You can also find great deals on children's clothing, Men's accessories and shoes for everyone in your family. **100**Don't forget to show your loyalty card when you make your purchases for a chance to win a trip for two to Hawaii in our lottery drawing.

98Diamond 백화점의 연례 세일 기간에 쇼핑해주셔서 감사합니다. 이번 주 백화점 전 층에서 비용을 엄청나게 절약하실 수 있으며, 오늘 단 하루, 여성분들을 위한 특별 추가 할인이 있습니다. **99**재킷과 코트를 포함해서 모든 여성용 겉옷이 이미 할인된 가격에서 20퍼센트가 더 추가 할인됩니다. 또한 좋은 가격에 아동 의류와 남성용 액세서리, 가족 모두를 위한 신발을 구매하실 수 있습니다. **100**제비 뽑기에서 2인 하와이 여행권을 얻을 수 있는 기회를 잡으시려면, 구매 시 잊지 말고 고객 카드를 보여주세요.

Diamond 백화점 층별 안내	
⁹⁹4층	여성복
3층	신발
2층	남성복
1층	화장품

어휘 terrific 엄청난 savings 절약 outerwear 겉옷 lottery drawing 제비 뽑기

---

98 매장은 얼마나 자주 세일을 하는가?
(A) 분기마다
(B) 반년마다
(C) 한 달에 한 번
(D) 일 년에 한 번

99 신 유 형 안내판에 의하면, 오늘 어디에서 추가 할인을 받을 수 있는가?
(A) 1층
(B) 2층
(C) 3층
(D) 4층

100 고객이 경품을 받을 기회를 얻으려면 어떻게 해야 하는가?
(A) 설문지 작성
(B) 물품 최저액 구매
(C) 쿠폰 제시
(D) 고객 카드 사용

PART 5

101

Cosmos House는 200명이 넘는 재능 있는 건축가와 디자이너가 있는 업계의 선도기업이다.

(A) 선진의
(B) 계산된
(C) 흥미 있어 하는
(D) 재능 있는

어휘 calculated 계산된 talented 재능 있는

102

이민자 규정은 외국인이 적합한 자격 없이 그 나라에서 일하는 것을 금하고 있다.

(A) 규제하다
(B) 규제
(C) 규정
(D) 규제력을 지닌

어휘 immigration 이민 permit 허용하다 appropriate 적절한 status 신분, 자격 regulation 규정

103

Gibson씨의 팀에 있는 모두가 신제품 신발의 성공에 기여했다.

(A) 모두
(B) 누구든 ~하는 사람
(C) 서로
(D) 서로

104

저희는 계속해서 일급 서비스를 제공해드리는 데 도움이 되는 여러분의 의견을 환영합니다.

(A) 동기 부여
(B) 의견
(C) 초대
(D) 운영

어휘 continually 계속해서 motivation 동기 부여 operation 운영

105

오직 이번 주에만 easybuy.com에서 엄선된 품목에 특별 할인을 해드립니다.

(A) 선발된
(B) 선택하는
(C) 선택
(D) 선택들

어휘 select 선발하다

106

비록 그 소프트웨어 회사는 비교적 알려지지 않았지만, 그들의 신제품이 회사를 유명하게 할지도 모른다.

(A) 비록 ~일지라도
(B) ~에도 불구하고
(C) 게다가
(D) ~까지

어휘 unknown 알려지지 않은

107

배송료가 300달러여야 했지만, 청구서에서 공급업체는 소매업자에게 100달러를 더 청구했다.

(A) ~보다 위에
(B) 높이
(C) 더 많이
(D) 위로

108

저희 고객센터는 모든 문의에 대해 빠짐없이 답변하고자 일주일 내내 가동됩니다.

(A) 납득시키다
(B) 결정하다
(C) 확실하게 하다
(D) 특징으로 하다

어휘 convince 납득시키다

109

마케팅팀에게는 다행스럽게도, 광고가 이례적으로 잘되었고 전면 보도되었다.

(A) 다행한
(B) 다행스럽게
(C) 행운
(D) 재산

어휘 exceptionally 예외적으로 coverage (매체의) 보도

110

Wayfair사는 최신 소프트웨어를 알맞은 가격에 공급하는 데 헌신합니다.

(A) provide
(B) provided
(C) provision
(D) providing

어휘 affordable 알맞은 provision 공급

111

전문가에 의하면, 풍력 발전은 일반적으로 도시의 옥상에 설치되는 것보다 개방된 시골 지역에서 훨씬 더 잘 작동된다고 한다.

(A) 훨씬
(B) 더 멀리
(C) 더 적은
(D) 더 많은

어휘 mount 설치하다

112

Movie Times 디지털 버전의 구독자이시라면 저희의 온라인 아카이브에 접근하실 수 있습니다.

(A) 구독하다
(B) 구독자
(C) 구독자들
(D) 구독

어휘 archive 기록보관소

113

부서장은 자기 새 사무실 벽지를 흰색으로 할지, 아니면 연한 회색으로 할지 고르는 데 애를 먹고 있었다.

(A) 그리고
(B) 그러나
(C) ~도 아니다
(D) 또는

114

그 최고경영자는 항상 빈틈없는 연구와 분석을 시행하여 실패의 위험을 최소화할 수 있다고 말한다.

(A) 복잡한
(B) 장황한
(C) 시험적인
(D) 빈틈없는

어휘 redundant 장황한 tentative 시험적인

115

Mark Tyler는 Zane 산업의 초창기에 재직했는데, 그때에는 직원 수가 적었다.

(A) when
(B) where
(C) which
(D) whose

116

합병에 대한 직장 동료들의 열광에도, Lisa Olsen은 그 소식에 흥미가 없었다.

(A) at
(B) in
(C) of
(D) with

어휘 enthusiasm 열광

117

일자리 제안이 거절하기에는 너무나 매력적이었지만, Lee Boule은 다른 주로 통근하는 것을 주저했다.

(A) 마음을 끄는
(B) 매력
(C) 매력적인
(D) 보기 좋게

어휘 pass up 거절하다 reluctant 주저하는

118

회계부서에서는 양식에 영수증이 첨부된 비용에 대해서만 상환해준다는 점을 유의해주세요.

(A) 재평가
(B) 참고
(C) 상환
(D) 복제품

어휘 reassessment 재평가 reference 참고 reimbursement 상환 replica 복제품

119

Amy Lynn은 지난주부터 매일 발표를 연습했기 때문에 동료들은 그녀가 준비되었다고 믿는다.

(A) could have practiced
(B) had practiced
(C) has practiced
(D) practices

어휘 deliver (연설을) 하다

120

저희 협회 가입에 대한 귀하의 문의에 대해, 기쁜 마음으로 회원 세부사항에 대해 의논하겠습니다.

(A) ~ 때문에
(B) 똑같이
(C) ~에 대해
(D) ~와 함께

어휘 association 협회

121

Milan 부동산은 Colton 테크의 과거 부지를 인수했는데, 총 1백만 평방피트 가까이 된다.

(A) 수익을 올리다
(B) 순수익을 올리다
(C) 총계를 내다
(D) 총 ~이 되다

어휘 site 부지 gross ~의 총수익을 올리다 net 순이익을 올리다 sum 총계를 내다 total 총 ~이 되다

122

관리부장이 거리에서 자기 고객인 Ford씨를 알아봤다면, 인사했을 겁니다.

(A) recognition
(B) recognize
(C) recognized
(D) recognizing

어휘 recognize 알아보다

123

영수증 없이 제품을 환불할 경우, 다음 구매에 쓸 수 있는 매장 적립금으로 받게 됩니다.

(A) above
(B) over
(C) through
(D) toward

어휘 apply toward ~에 쓰다

124

Sue Ellis는 3년 전에 팀장이 되었고, 그 뒤 다음 해에 영업부장으로 승진했다.

(A) 연대순으로
(B) 줄곧
(C) 진심으로
(D) 그 뒤에

어휘 chronologically 연대순으로 subsequently 그 뒤에

125

ZDE 철강의 기업 역사의 마지막 장에는 1980년대 회사의 확장에 관한 내용이 있다.

(A) 확장시키다
(B) 확장할 수 있는
(C) 확대시키는 사람
(D) 확장

어휘 expansion 확장

126

회사의 규정에 의하면, 공장 검사는 두 달에 한 번씩 수행해야 한다.

(A) ~ 동안
(B) 한 번
(C) 그때
(D) 이내에

127

가장 내구성 있는 탑승 수하물로, 여행자들은 여행하는 동안 불편을 겪지 않으실 것입니다.

(A) 엄격한
(B) 비교할 만한
(C) 활기찬
(D) 내구성이 있는

어휘 carry-on luggage 탑승 수하물 rigorous 엄격한 comparable 비교할 만한 vigorous 활기찬 durable 내구성이 있는

128

그 자동차 회사는 제조 과정에서 에어백에 결함이 있었기 때문에 1백만 대 이상의 자동차 리콜을 발표했다.

(A) 결함
(B) 결함이 있는
(C) 결함이 있게
(D) 결함들

어휘 recall 회수 manufacture 제조하다 defectively 불완전하게

129

몇몇 심리 치료는 다른 치료법들보다도 더 지속적인 영향을 미칠 수 있다.

(A) 마지막의   (B) 지속적인
(C) 계속되었다   (D) 마지막으로

어휘   psychological 심리의   treatment 치료   last 마지막의; 지속되다   lasting 지속적인

130

공식 매입계약을 맺기 위해서 감독자는 잠재 매각업체 최소 두 곳의 견적서를 제출해야 한다.

(A) 신청서   (B) 견적서
(C) 자격요건   (D) 포함하다

어휘   purchase agreement 매입 계약   vendor 매각자   comprise 포함하다

PART 6

131-134 (📄 안내문)

Oak Grove 도서관이 사업 오찬회를 진행합니다

11월 7일 화요일 오전 11:30부터 오후 12:30까지 Oak Grove 도서관에서 무료 사업 오찬회를 131주최합니다. 기업가와 중소기업가분들은 132각자의 점심을 지참하시고, Oak Grove 도서관에서 사업 성장에 도움이 되는 디지털 기술을 배우시면 됩니다. Digital Age의 소유주인 James Olson이 여러분의 온라인 가시성을 향상시킬 수 있는 열 가지 방법을 무료로 공유할 것입니다. 이 행사는 Monroe Country 상공회의소와 133협력하여 진행됩니다. 134더 자세한 정보를 원하시면 555-2591로 전화하셔서 James를 찾아주세요.

어휘   entrepreneur 사업가   boost 신장시키다   visibility 가시성

131

(A) 출장음식을 제공하다   (B) 설립하다
(C) 주최하다   (D) 계획하다

어휘   host 주최하다

132

(A) 그들의 것   (B) 그들을
(C) 그들의   (D) 그들 자신

133

(A) 협력하다   (B) 협력
(C) 협력의   (D) 협력적으로

어휘   in collaboration with ~와 협력하여

134 (신유형)

(A) 더 자세한 정보를 원하시면 555-2591로 전화하셔서 James를 찾아주세요.
(B) 참가자들은 입구에서 소정의 금액을 내야 합니다.

(C) 우천 시 행사가 취소됩니다.
(D) 도서관은 11월 6일 월요일에 휴관합니다.

어휘   call off 취소하다   in case of rain 만일 비가 오면

135-138 (📄 기사)

San Marcos가 Harriston에 새 매장을 엽니다

HARRISTON— San Marcos가 Harriston에 첫 번째로 입점합니다. 이 커피숍 체인은 화요일에 Harriston 지점에 대한 135계획을 발표했습니다. San Marcos에 의하면, 이 지점은 내년 2월에 개장할 예정이며, 3년 전 전국적으로 더 많은 농촌 지역에 투자를 136시작했던 회사 계획의 일환이라고 합니다. 137회사 관계자들은 그들의 목표가 지역 청년들에게 취업의 기회를 주는 것이라고 말했습니다. 또한 San Marcos는 현지 기업들과 협력하여 지점에 제품을 공급할 계획입니다. Harriston시 관계자들은 지점이 시내 지역으로 더 많은 유동 인구를 138불러오는 데 도움이 될 것이라며 들뜬 모습이었습니다.

어휘   initiative 계획, 결정   rural community 농촌   across the nation 전국적으로   foot traffic 유동 인구

135

(A) 개발   (B) 운영
(C) 계획   (D) 약속

136

(A) began   (B) had begun
(C) have begun   (D) will have begun

137 (신유형)

(A) 회사 관계자들은 그들의 목표가 지역 청년들에게 취업의 기회를 주는 것이라고 말했습니다.
(B) San Marcos는 라틴 아메리카와 아프리카의 몇 개 국가에서 회사 소유의 커피콩을 재배합니다.
(C) 이 투자는 은퇴한 부부와 젊은이들 모두에게 안전할 것으로 예상됩니다.
(D) 일반적으로 농촌은 경기 호전의 혜택을 가장 덜 받습니다.

어휘   retired 은퇴한   upturn 호전

138

(A) 가져오다   (B) 유지하다
(C) 제공하다   (D) 발생하다

139-142 (📄 이메일)

발신: Henri Saveaux <hsaveaus@visitparis.fr>
수신: Amalia Francis <amaliaf@bloggers.net>
날짜: 12월 12일
제목: 재게재 허가

Francis씨께
저는 파리에 있는 작은 출판사에서 일합니다. 저희는 분기마다 프랑스에 관한 관광 영어 잡지를 출간합니다. toursaroundtheworld.com에서 귀하의 블로그 게시물을 보았습니다. 글이 매우 139재미있었고, 그림과 지도가 좋았습니다. 140저희 독자들이 좋아할 것 같은데,

글을 2월 호에 실을 수 있을지 궁금합니다. 물론, 저희 잡지에 기고해주신 것에 대해 ¹⁴¹통상적인 원고료를 지불할 것입니다. 귀하의 글이 정말 매력적인데, 혹시 정기적으로 기고하고 싶으신지요? 두 제안 중 ¹⁴²어느 하나에든, 둘 다에든 동의 여부를 알려주십시오.

Henri Saveaux

> **어휘** publishing company 출판사 put out 출간하다 contribution 기고문 captivating 매혹적인

139
(A) 즐겁게 해주다   (B) 재미있는
(C) 재미있게   (D) 오락

> **어휘** entertainingly 재미있게

140 신유형
(A) 각 호는 세계의 곳곳의 도시에 초점을 맞추고 있으며, 다음 도시는 베를린이 될 것입니다.
(B) 당신의 삽화가 정말 아름다워서 파리에 있는 저희 화랑에 걸어두고 싶습니다.
(C) 저희 독자들이 좋아할 것 같은데, 글을 2월 호에 실을 수 있을지 궁금합니다.
(D) 파리로 돌아갈 때, 센강 근처에 있는 저희 새 사무실을 방문해주세요.

> **어휘** issue (잡지의) 호

141
(A) 유리한   (B) 적은
(C) 감소한   (D) 통상적인

> **어휘** reduced 감소한

142
(A) 모든   (B) 둘 중 어느 하나
(C) 수많은   (D) 둘 중 어느 하나도 아닌

143-146 정보
박물관 할인 입장권

패션 박물관, 로마 박물관, Torrance 미술관의 박물관 할인 입장권을 구입하셔서 입장료를 크게 절약하세요! ¹⁴³내년에는 Torrance에 더 많은 박물관이 개관할 예정입니다. 온라인이나 안내데스크 또는 관광 안내소에서 입장권을 ¹⁴⁴구매하실 수 있습니다.

· 성인: 21.50파운드
· 노인(65세 이상) / 학생: 18.50파운드
· 어린이(6~16세): 11.75파운드
· 20명 이상의 단체: 1인당 13파운드

정기권

패션 박물관, 로마 박물관, Torrance 미술관에 1년 내내 입장할 수 있는 ¹⁴⁵최고의 가치를 지닌 이 정기권 또한 상기 언급된 것과 같은 방식으로 구매하실 수 있습니다. 여러분이 이 지역에 사시는 경우, 또는 Torrance에 정기적으로 방문하시는 경우에라도, 이 정기권이 ¹⁴⁶완벽합니다.

· 성인: 30파운드
· 노인(65세 이상) / 학생: 25파운드
· 어린이(6~16세): 14파운드

> **어휘** adult 성인 senior 노인 season ticket 정기권 describe 서술하다 even if ~라 하더라도

143 신유형
(A) 안타깝게도, 지금은 모든 건물들이 보수를 위해 문을 닫았습니다.
(B) 걸어서 서로 10분 이내에 위치한 이 세 곳의 입장권 세 장을 구매하실 수 있습니다.
(C) 내년에는 Torrance에 더 많은 박물관이 개관할 예정입니다.
(D) 기차로 Torrance를 방문하시려면, Torrance 서부역에서 하차하세요.

144
(A) 신청하다   (B) 확인하다
(C) 구매하다   (D) 예약하다

145
(A) 입장 가능한   (B) 이용할 수 있는
(C) 최고의   (D) 분명한

> **어휘** accessible 입장 가능한

146
(A) 완벽한   (B) 완벽
(C) 완벽하게   (D) 완벽함

PART 7

147-148 정보

새 Haven 스웨터의 수명 연장을 위해 여러분이 좋아하는 새로 산 상의를 관리하는 방법에 대한 조언과 팁을 드립니다. 우선, 이 원단은 매우 섬세하기 때문에 일반 세탁기 및 건조기 사용은 추천하지 않습니다. ¹⁴⁷이리저리 뒹굴리면 천이 늘어지고, 몇 번 세탁하면 찢어질 수 있습니다. 스웨터는 드라이업자 같은 세탁 전문가에게 맡겨 적절하게 세탁하세요.

또한 선명한 색깔과 깔끔한 원단을 유지할 수 있도록 ¹⁴⁸스웨터를 입지 않을 때에는 건조하고 어두운 상자에 보관하실 것을 추천합니다. 옷을 꺼내 입으시려면 부드러운 모직 빗을 사용해 스웨터의 보풀이나 머리카락을 제거하셔야 합니다. 다른 것을 사용하신다면, 거친 플라스틱이나 금속 브러시는 효과적일 수는 있지만 옷에 손상을 줄 수 있습니다.

> **어휘** delicate 섬세한 conventional 평범한 toss and tumble 대굴대굴 뒹굴다 stretch 늘어지다 tear 찢어지다 lint 보푸라기 coarse 거친 bristle (솔의) 털

147

제품을 숙련된 세탁업자에게 보내지 않는다면 어떻게 될 것인가?

(A) 주름이 생길 수 있다.
(B) 찢어질 수 있다.
(C) 줄어들지도 모른다.
(D) 변색될지도 모른다.

어휘 wrinkled 주름이 있는 rip 찢어지다 shrink 줄어들다

148

정보에 의하면, 사용자는 제품을 어디에 보관해야 하는가?

(A) 밝은 방
(B) 옷장
(C) 덮개로 닫는 건조한 용기
(D) 통풍이 잘 되는 공간

어휘 ventilate 통풍시키다

149-150 (안내문)

¹⁴⁹10월 1일부로 시행될 새로운 휴가 정책과 관련해 Yongwater사의 전 직원에게 공지합니다. ¹⁵⁰전 직원은 목표 휴가일 최소 2주 전에 경영진에게 알려야 합니다. 갑작스러운 휴가 요청은 해당 시점에 필요성을 검토하겠습니다. 일부 직원이 정규시간에 근무할 수 없더라도 회사가 중단 없이 업무를 계속할 수 있도록 정책이 갱신됩니다. 이를 통해 회사는 필요할 경우 임시직도 충원할 수 있습니다. 휴가를 쓰는 날짜와 사유를 적어주시면 경영진이 검토하겠습니다. 협조해주셔서 감사합니다.

어휘 in regard to ~에 관해 time-off 휴식 unexpectedly 갑자기 interruption 중단

149

10월에 무슨 일이 일어나는가?

(A) 새로운 컴퓨터 시스템이 도입될 것이다.
(B) 휴가 시기에 관한 새 규정이 적용될 것이다.
(C) 회사에서 임시 직원을 고용할 것이다.
(D) 경영진이 바뀔 것이다.

150

직원들은 언제 서류를 제출해야 하는가?

(A) 매월 초   (B) 휴가 가기 보름 전쯤
(C) 2주 후   (D) 다음 날

151-152 (정보)

Martinez Goods는 여러분이 이것 없이는 살 수 없겠다는 제품을 만들기 위해 열심히 일하고 있습니다. 그래서 저희는 전자레인지 Jericho 5000 제품을 자랑스럽게 발표합니다. 저희 설계자들은 이 가정용 기기가 여러분이 필요로 하는 모든 기능을 갖추고 있는지 확인하기 위해 안전성 검사 등의 시험에 많은 시간을 할애했습니다. ¹⁵¹과거에 Jericho 모델을 구입하신 바, 귀하께서 저희 최신 모델에 대한 중요 결정에 도움을 주셨으면 합니다. 저희는 단골 고객들을 위해 최고의 제품을 만들고자 하며, 여러분의 도움으로 그렇게 할 수 있다고 생각합니다. 아래 설문조사를 완료하는 데에는 약 5~7분밖에

걸리지 않으며, ¹⁵²감사의 표시로 저희 웹사이트에서 다음 구매 시 사용 가능한 10% 할인 쿠폰을 드리겠습니다.

어휘 royal customer 단골

151

Martinez Goods에서는 누구에게 설문 참여를 요청하는가?

(A) 웹사이트 방문자는 누구나
(B) 어린아이의 부모들
(C) 이전 고객들
(D) 자사 디자이너들

152

설문을 작성하면 응답자에게는 무엇이 제공되는가?

(A) 할인권   (B) 사은품
(C) 특별 할인 링크   (D) 감사 이메일

어휘 responder 응답자

153-154 (문자 메시지) 신 유 형

Brad Young [오후 1:32]	¹⁵³Ray가 아침에 보낸 새로운 인사 관련 제안에 대해 어떻게 생각해요? 내년 회사의 비전과 잘 맞을 거 같아요.
Jessica Imono [오후 1:36]	아직 시간이 없어서 충분히 살펴보진 않았는데, 제가 본 바로는 좋아 보였어요.
Brad Young [오후 1:37]	당신의 의견을 듣고 싶었어요. 이메일에 '보너스'라고 표시된 추가 부분을 읽어봤나요?
Jessica Imono [오후 1:40]	아뇨, 어디에 있었어요? 이메일에서 첨부파일은 보지 못했어요. 다시 확인해볼게요.
Brad Young [오후 1:42]	이메일에 첨부되어 있거나, 이메일 하단에 링크로 있을 수도 있어요. 제가 지금 보내줄 수 있는데요.
Jessica Imono [오후 1:43]	그게 좋겠네요. ¹⁵⁴확실히 여기엔 없어요.
Brad Young [오후 1:44]	좋아요. 몇 분 있다 다시 확인해보고 이야기 나누도록 해요.

어휘 human resources 인적 자원 forward 전달하다

153

대화의 주제는 무엇인가?

(A) 회사 직원   (B) 회사 문제
(C) 인사 계획   (D) 분실물

154 신 유 형

오후 1시 43분에 Imono씨가 It's definitely not here라고 말한 의미는 무엇인가?

(A) 그녀는 웹페이지에 접근할 수 없다.
(B) 그녀는 그 정보를 찾을 수 없다.
(C) 이메일이 분실된 것이 틀림없다.
(D) 그 정보는 다른 곳에 게시돼야 한다.

155-157 📧 이메일

수신: Emerson Palmer <emersonp@nextmail.com>
발신: Reginald Teller <representative@dasexpress.com>
날짜: 9월 28일
제목: 주문 번호 820-00812

Palmer씨께

주문하신 저희 디지털 안테나와 스피커와 관련해 이메일을 드립니다. ¹⁵⁵유감스럽게도, 이번 주에 저희 창고 근처에서 매우 강한 폭풍우가 있었고, 이로 인해 건물에 심각한 피해를 입었습니다. 그래서 구매하신 제품을 즉시 배송해드릴 수 없습니다. 건물을 수리하는 데 1~2주가 소요되며, 주문 재개를 위한 준비로 며칠이 더 소요될 것입니다. 귀하께서는 주문건에 대해 몇 가지 선택권이 있습니다. ¹⁵⁶우선은, 지연에 동의하시면 귀하의 주문은 계속 유효하며, 저희는 가급적 빨리 배송해드리겠습니다. 그다음은, 유사 제품으로 대체하여 국내의 다른 창고에서 발송해드리는 것입니다. 마지막으로, 원하신다면 주문을 취소하실 수 있습니다. ¹⁵⁷48시간 이내에 가장 적합한 선택을 하셔서 알려주십시오. 저희가 응답을 받지 못하면 주문은 유효한 상태로 진행될 것입니다. 이로 인해 불편을 끼쳐드려 죄송합니다.

감사합니다. 좋은 하루 되세요.

Reginald Teller 고객서비스 담당자

> **어휘** resume 재개하다 active 유효한 substitute 대체하다

155

배송은 왜 지연되는가?
(A) 배송 문제 때문에
(B) 악천후 때문에
(C) 잘못된 라벨 부착 때문에
(D) 재고 부족 때문에

> **어휘** inclement 궂은 mislabel ~에 라벨을 잘못 붙이다 shortage 부족

156

고객에게 제공되는 선택권이 <u>아닌</u> 것은 무엇인가?
(A) 물품 교체
(B) 주문 취소
(C) 차후 물품 발송
(D) 운송비 환불

> **어휘** alternate 교체의 cancellation 취소 shipping cost 운송비

157

Palmer씨가 응답하지 않는다면 이틀 후에 무슨 일이 일어나는가?
(A) 주문이 취소된다.
(B) 주문이 청구된다.
(C) 주문이 처리된다.
(D) 주문이 배송된다.

158-160 📢 광고

가을이 다가오는 지금, 내년을 위해 몸매를 가꾸기에 가장 좋은 시기입니다! ¹⁵⁸Gregg 체육관은 에어로빅, 심장 강화 운동, 요가, 무술, 근육 기르기, 체중 감량 프로그램 관련 최신 기술을 제공합니다. 휴가 전에 살을 빼고 싶거나, 단순히 운동을 하고 싶다면, 저희는 여러분을 위한 계획이 있습니다.

¹⁵⁹저희 체육관의 비수기 Body Saver 시리즈는 모두를 위한 작은 혜택을 제공합니다. 한 개 수업을 풀타임 시즌으로 수강하거나, 두 개의 수업을 한 개의 가격으로 수강하거나, 또는 방문 시 원하는 수업을 섞어 듣는 시스템을 선택할 수 있습니다. ¹⁶⁰잠시 방문하셔서 저희 전문 강사와 체험하고, 어떻게 삶을 더 개선할 수 있는지 보고, 운동하면서 재미를 느껴보세요.

¹⁵⁸체육관은 일주일 내내, 매일 오전 6시부터 새벽 12시까지 영업하므로 언제든지 원하시는 일정에 맞추실 수 있습니다. ¹⁵⁸저희는 17번가와 Winslow가가 교차하는 도시 중심부에 위치하고 있으며, 지하철에서 걸어서 두 블록밖에 안 됩니다.

> **어휘** get in shape 몸매를 가꾸다 cardio 심장 강화 운동 martial art 무술 shed 없애다 off-season 비수기 test drive 시험 운전 conveniently 편리하게도

158

광고에서 언급되지 <u>않은</u> 것은 무엇인가?
(A) 운동의 유형
(B) 근무 시간
(C) 위치
(D) 자격 요건

159

광고에 의하면, Gregg 체육관의 특징은 무엇인가?
(A) 많은 직원
(B) 역 바로 옆
(C) 24시간 운영
(D) 특별 할인

160

서비스를 어떻게 시험해 볼 수 있는가?
(A) 친구를 동반해서
(B) 온라인 신청으로
(C) 현장에서 회원이 되어서
(D) 직접 방문해서

161-163 📧 이메일

수신: Amelia Hunters <ahunters@sloanefoundation.com>
발신: Rachel Benson <rbenson@nextmail.com>
날짜: 10월 10일
제목: Sloane 역사 전시

안녕하세요, Amelia.

¹⁶¹이번 주말에 우리와 함께 Sloane 역사 전시에 갈지 궁금해서 연락했어요. 이 전시회는 가을에 하는 가장 멋진 전시회 중 하나랍니다. 미술감독은 우리 지역의 역사와 관련된 박물관의 소장품 모두를 우리에게 보여줄 수 있도록 승인을 받았고, 또 ¹⁶²우리 재단에서 제공하는 많은 것들이 포함될 거예요. 항상 금고에 보관되어 대중이 볼 수 없던, 그리고 제가 보고 싶었던 물품들이 많이 있어요. ¹⁶³심지어 도시의 원래 디자인도 전시될 것이라고 들었어요. 당신은 역사에 관심이 많아 이 기회를 놓치고 싶지 않겠지요.

내일 저녁 8시 전까지 연락을 주면, 그 시간에 가고 싶어 하는 모든 사람을 위해 입장권을 준비해 놓을게요. 6명 정도의 일행이 있을 거고, ¹⁶²출발 전에 사무실에서 모일 거예요.

Rachel

> **어휘** permission 승인 foundation 재단 vault 금고

161

이메일의 목적은 무엇인가?

(A) Hunters씨에게 행사 참여를 물어보기 위해
(B) 직장에서 조퇴 허락을 맡기 위해
(C) Hunters씨를 점심에 초대하기 위해
(D) 이메일에 답장하기 위해

162

이번 주말에 Benson씨는 Hunters씨를 어디에서 만나길 원하는가?

(A) 매표소 　　　　　　(B) 시청
(C) 재단 사무실 　　　　(D) 박물관

163 신유형

다음 문장은 [1], [2], [3], [4] 중 어디에 들어가는가?

"심지어 도시의 원래 디자인도 전시될 것이라고 들었어요."

(A) [1] 　　　　　　　(B) [2]
(C) [3] 　　　　　　　(D) [4]

164-167 📧 이메일

수신: Amy Loughton <amyloughton01@parspace.com>
발신: Kevin Redd <kevinredd@beldingnperk.com>
날짜: 8월 25일
제목: Belding&Perk사의 영업 팀장 직책

안녕하세요, Amy.

지난주에 사무실에 오셔서 영업 팀장 직책에 관련해 말씀해주셔서 감사합니다. ¹⁶⁴당신이 팀에 가져올 수 있는 것에 대한 생각과 내년 판매를 촉진시킬 몇 가지 당신이 언급한 기술까지, 대화가 아주 유익했습니다. 저는 당신에게 그 직책을 제안하고 싶고, 다음 달 1일부터 우리와 함께 일하기를 바랍니다.

당신이 힘차게 시작하기를 바라며, 당연히, ¹⁶⁵소개하는 자리와 더불어 팀원들과의 정식 회의도 필요합니다. 영업 팀장으로서 모든 팀의 목표 및 마감을 정하고, 경영진과는 격주로 상황 보고 회의를 하고, 대규모 영업 회의도 도와야 합니다. ¹⁶⁷처음에는 일이 꽤 많은 것처럼 들리겠지만, 당신이 따라갈 수 있다고 믿어요. 함께 하는 처음 몇 주간 당신이 일에 파묻히는 것을 원치 않으니, ¹⁶⁶첫 달은 제가 당신과 더 긴밀하게 일하겠습니다.

업무일 전후로 문의할 내용이 있다면 언제는 알려주세요.

Kevin Redd
Belding&Perk 영업 부장

어휘 technique 기법 start off (어떤 일을) 시작하다 introductory 소개하는 biweekly 격주로

164

Redd씨는 Loughton씨와의 면접에서 어떤 점을 좋아했는가?

(A) 그녀의 명랑한 성격
(B) 그녀의 영업 경험
(C) 그녀의 관리 능력
(D) 그녀의 판매 아이디어

165

Loughton씨는 회사에서의 첫 주를 어떻게 준비할 것인가?

(A) 다른 직원들과 교육을 받는다.
(B) 주어진 업무를 완수할 것이다.
(C) 부하 직원들에게 할 연설문을 작성할 것이다.
(D) 여러 차례 회의를 할 것이다.

166

누가 9월에 Loughton씨를 도울 것인가?

(A) Redd씨의 조수
(B) 영업팀 직원들
(C) 전임 영업 팀장
(D) 영업 부장

167 신유형

다음 문장은 [1], [2], [3], [4] 중 어디에 들어가는가?

"처음에는 일이 꽤 많은 것처럼 들리겠지만, 당신이 따라갈 수 있다고 믿어요."

(A) [1] 　　　　　　　(B) [2]
(C) [3] 　　　　　　　(D) [4]

어휘 keep up (진도·속도를) 따라가다

168-171 📧 이메일

수신: Jackson Waters <jwaters@noratech.com>
발신: Emily Brewer <eb001@goerslove.com>
날짜: 11월 1일 수요일
제목: 자사 제품 관련 회의

안녕하세요, Waters씨.

잘 지내고 계신지요. ¹⁶⁸내일 회의 일정을 다음 주로 조정해도 되는지 알고 싶습니다. 저희는 가능하면 최신의 제품 정보를 모두 알려드리고 싶지만, 오늘 저녁에나 보고서를 받을 것 같습니다. 당신에게 프레젠테이션을 하기 전에 저희가 보고서를 읽고 철저히 검토했으면 합니다. ¹⁶⁹전반적으로 제품 정보를 읽고 확인하는 데 2~3일이 걸립니다. 제품 보고서를 더 일찍 받으면, 당연히 알려드리겠습니다. ¹⁷⁰주말에는 이 정보를 처리하고 작업할 시간이 조금 더 있으니, 회의에서 보여드릴 제품 시연을 준비하도록 하겠습니다. ¹⁷¹저희로서는 다음 주 초가 괜찮을 것 같습니다. 괜찮으신지요?

답변을 기다리며, 양사 모두에게 중요한 프로젝트에 함께 해주셔서 감사합니다.

Emily Brewer

어휘 thoroughly 철저히

168

이메일의 목적은 무엇인가?

(A) 제품 설명을 요청하기 위해
(B) 회의 시간 연기를 요청하기 위해
(C) 회의 시간을 연장하기 위해
(D) 회의에 대한 최신 정보를 주기 위해

169

팀이 정보를 검토하는 데 얼마의 시간이 소모될 것인가?

(A) 몇 시간 　　　　　(B) 하루

(C) 며칠   (D) 한 주

어휘 go through ~를 살펴보다

170

Brewer씨가 Waters씨에게 제안하는 것은 무엇인가?
(A) 완성된 부품   (B) 시연
(C) 인쇄된 보고서   (D) 지원 서류

171

Brewer씨가 Waters씨를 만날 가능성이 가장 높은 날은 언제인가?
(A) 월요일   (B) 목요일
(C) 금요일   (D) 토요일

172-175 📱 온라인 토론 신 유 형

Randal Bunch [오전 11:34] 오늘 Francis를 본 사람 있어요? 나랑 이야기하기로 했는데.

Ingrid Colane [오전 11:35] ¹⁷²오늘 아침에 전화를 받고서는 나가야 한다고 했습니다. 고객 사무실에 가는 것 같았어요.

Randal Bunch [오전 11:35] 알았어요. Kilnesmith에 대해 새로운 소식이 있나요?

Brian Lagerwood [오전 11:40] 그건 제가 말씀드릴 수 있을 것 같아요. 그 고객은 제가 Francis와 함께 일하고 있어요.

― Ingrid Colane이 대화방을 나갔습니다. ―

Randal Bunch [오전 11:41] 좋아요, Brian. Francis가 그들과 꽤 오랫동안 일한 것으로 알아요. 그들이 우리의 제안을 받아들일 거라 봐요?

Brian Lagerwood [오전 11:41] ¹⁷⁴저와 Francis가 지난 몇 달 동안 그들을 여러 번 만났어요. 우리 회사 아니면 다른 회사로 결정될 거예요. 10월 13일까지는 결정할 겁니다.

Randal Bunch [오전 11:44] 좋아요. 저는 적어도 9월까지 결과를 알기를 바랐어요. 그들이 우리의 제안을 받아들이도록, 우리가 할 수 있는 일이 있는지 알고 싶어요. ¹⁷³만약 그들이 제안을 받아들이지 않는다면 우리 다음 회계연도의 재무 상태에 상당한 차질이 있을 거예요.

Brian Lagerwood [오전 11:45] 제가 듣기로 Bromley에서 Klinesmith에 돈을 더 준다고 했지만 단기 거래였습니다. 저희 거래가 두 배 더 길 겁니다. ¹⁷⁵우리가 더 구미가 당기도록 해야 할까요?

Randal Bunch [오전 11:46] 아마도요. 하지만 우리가 그들과 함께 이 건을 할 수 있다는 걸 확실히 합시다. ¹⁷⁴우리는 단기 간에 다른 공급자를 찾을 여력이 없어요.

Brian Lagerwood [오전 11:47] 소식이 업데이트되는 대로 알려드릴게요.

어휘 account 고객 come down to 결국 ~이 되다
sweeten the pot 제안을 매력적인 것으로 만들다

172

Colane씨는 Francis씨가 무엇을 하고 있다고 말하는가?

(A) 출장 가는 중이다.
(B) 고객과 만나고 있다.
(C) 더 좋은 거래를 따기 위해 노력하고 있다.
(D) 가족을 방문하는 중이다.

173

Bunch씨는 Kilnesmith와의 거래를 어떻게 설명하는가?
(A) 복합적이다.   (B) 힘들다.
(C) 아주 중요하다.   (D) 오래 간다.

어휘 complex 복잡한 demanding 힘든 essential 극히 중요한

174

Lagerwood씨가 최근에 관련된 일은 무엇인가?
(A) 새로운 창고 장소 찾기
(B) 잠재 공급업체와 회의하기
(C) 출장 준비하기
(D) 내년도 재무 세부 내용 작업하기

어휘 potential 잠재적인

175 신 유 형

오전 11시 45분에 Lagerwood씨가 Should we sweeten the pot? 이라고 말한 의도는 무엇인가?
(A) 그들의 계약이 더 나은 이유를 설명해야 하는지 알고 싶다.
(B) 그들이 결정할 시간을 연장해줘야 하는지 알고 싶다.
(C) 그들을 회의에 초대해야 하는지 알고 싶다.
(D) 더 나은 제안을 해야 하는지 궁금해 한다.

176-180 📄 프로그램···리뷰

Shade: The Mark on Banker Hill

Steven Bird 각본

Lindy Allen 감독

Richard Shade는 말이 거칠고 냉철한 탐정으로 이 도시를 자기 손바닥 보듯이 훤히 알고 있다. ¹⁷⁷그는 첫 사건을 맡았던 때부터 동료 탐정들에게 존경을 받아왔다. 도시는 어둡고 음산하다. 그는 오늘이 그의 인생에서 행운의 날, 아니면 최악의 날일 거라고 느낀다. 영화 속 범죄 탐정의 아이콘 중 하나인 Shade가 경찰 수사망 밖에서 일하면서 ¹⁷⁶그가 믿는 유일한 경찰인 Maxwell Young과 여러 가지 논쟁을 한다. Steven Bird는 원작 영화를 가져와 오늘날의 관객들을 위해 각색했고, 현재의 기술을 사용하여 이야기를 둘러싼 현대적인 분위기를 만들어냈다.

또한 우리는 누군가가 남편의 유산을 훔치려 한다며 Shade의 사무실에 나타나 도움을 청하는 의문의 여자 Gloria Grey를 만난다. 그녀는 Shade가 사무실에서 낮잠을 잘 때 들어가서, 돈을 손에 넣기 위해서는 무엇이든 할 수 있는 여자라는 것을 증명한다. Banker Hill의 거리는 위험하지만, Richard Shade와 같은 사람에게는 살인도 일어날 수 있는 곳이다.

상영시간: 117분

Shade: The Mark on Banker Hill은 ¹⁷⁸고전 영화의 리메이크작으로, 휴식을 찾고 있는 운이 다한 탐정의 이야기이다. 원래 이 영화는

1950년대에 개봉된 Shade 시리즈 중 하나였고, 이제 이 장르에 있어 고전으로 여겨진다.

¹⁷⁹이 버전에서 Shade의 캐릭터는 좀 더 부드러워졌고, 사설탐정은 이제 더 빠른 사고를 하는 조커이다. ¹⁸⁰Richard Shade의 역으로 분한 Johnny Baxter는 그간 좀 더 유머러스한 뮤지컬 배우로서 배역을 맡았었다. ¹⁷⁹그런데 Baxter는 원작의 배우가 자랑스러워할 만큼의 성공적인 퍼포먼스를 선보인다. 원작과는 확실히 다르지만, Baxter는 그 역을 위해 태어난 것처럼 그 장면들을 처리한다. Marianne Lewis는 여주인공으로서 환상적이고, 확실히 전도유망한 스타로 보일 것이다. ¹⁷⁸이 두 명을 중심으로 이야기가 전개되기 때문에 영화에서 그들이 서로 얼마나 잘 풀어나가는지 주목해야 하지만, 나머지 작은 배역들도 기억할 만한 장면들이 있다.

Shade는 Grand 스튜디오의 새로운 영화 시리즈의 첫 번째 작품으로 제작되었으며, ¹⁷⁸이 영화가 범죄 영화를 보는 방식을 바꾸지는 않을 것이지만, 현시대에 캐릭터를 설정할 수 있는 좋은 방법이다.

어휘 tough-talking 독설의 hard-boiled 냉철한 like the back of one's hand ~에 훤하다 case 사건 dispute 논쟁 inheritance 유산 let oneself in ~로 들어가다 down-on-one's-luck 운이 다한 private eye 사설탐정 cast 배역을 맡기다; 출연자 come through with ~를 내놓다 revolve around (이야기가) ~를 중심으로 전개되다

176
Richard Shade가 믿는 사람은 누구인가?
(A) Gloria Grey
(B) Johnny Baxter
(C) Lindy Allen
(D) Maxwell Young

어휘 have faith in ~를 믿다

177
프로그램의 첫 번째 단락, 두 번째 줄의 fresh와 의미상 가장 가까운 단어는 무엇인가?
(A) 추가적인
(B) 활동적인
(C) 새로운
(D) 날것의

어휘 raw 날것의

178
영화에 관해 사실이 아닌 것은?
(A) 다시 제작되었다.
(B) 감독이 원작 영화를 바꾸지 않았다.
(C) 영화에는 2명의 주인공이 있다.
(D) 영화는 오늘날의 경향을 반영했다.

어휘 reproduce 다시 만들어내다 reflect 반영하다

179
리뷰는 새로운 버전의 영화가 가진 어떠한 변화에 초점을 맞추는가?
(A) 주인공
(B) 음악
(C) 전반적인 분위기
(D) 시나리오

180
Baxter씨는 보통 어떤 종류의 작업을 하는가?
(A) 액션
(B) 코미디

(C) 드라마
(D) 공포

181-185 이메일…이메일

수신: Elijah Graham <elijah2019@inoutbox.com>
발신: Tower 호텔 <frontdesk@towerhotelten.com>
날짜: 9월 5일
제목: 예약 확인

Graham씨께

¹⁸¹10월 3일부터 12일까지 귀하의 예약 요청을 받았으며 711호실이 준비됨을 확인해드립니다. 또한, ¹⁸³10월 4~6일 3일간 오전 5시 30분에 모닝콜 서비스도 확인했습니다.

¹⁸¹귀하의 투숙 기간 동안 Richmond Harvest 축제가 열림에 따라 호텔과 주변 지역은 매우 혼잡할 것입니다. 시에서는 일주일간의 축제 중 적어도 하루는 약 10만 명의 사람들이 방문할 것으로 보고 있습니다. 거래에 감사드리며, 더욱 편안한 숙박이 되도록 저희가 할 수 있는 일이 있다면 주저하지 말고 문의해주시길 바랍니다.

포함 서비스	모닝콜
	¹⁸²무료 아침식사 방 청소
711호실 1박에 92달러 (¹⁸⁴10월 3~12일, 9박)	총액: 828달러

Tower 호텔을 선택해주셔서 감사합니다.
Jason Richards 호텔 매니저
테네시주 리치먼드 Tower 호텔

수신: Tower 호텔 <frontdesk@towerhotelten.com>
발신: Elijah Graham <elijah2019@inoutbox.com>
날짜: 9월 6일
제목: 예약 및 수정

Richards씨께

예약을 빨리 확인해주셔서 감사합니다만, 오류가 있습니다. ¹⁸⁴저는 11일에 떠날 예정으로, 12일에는 방이 필요 없습니다. 새 날짜로 다시 예약하고 확인해주실 수 있나요?

그리고 저는 Richmond Harvest 축제에 대해 몰랐습니다. 그래서 그것이 문제가 될지도 모르겠습니다. ¹⁸³고객과 함께 시내에서 업무를 볼 거라 지각하지 않기 위해 모닝콜을 요청했습니다. 이제는 그 주에 교통이 불편할 것 같아 걱정이네요. ¹⁸⁵투숙객들을 위한 셔틀버스나 호텔 버스를 제공해주시나요? 택시를 기다리다가 회의에 늦고 싶지 않아요.

Elijah Graham

어휘 wake-up call 모닝콜 correction 수정 unaware 모르는

181
축제는 언제 열리는가?
(A) 9월 말
(B) 10월 초
(C) 10월 중순
(D) 10월 말

182
호텔은 Graham씨에게 어떤 서비스를 제공할 것인가?

(A) 다과   (B) 세탁
(C) 룸서비스   (D) 무료 식사

어휘 refreshments 다과

183
Graham씨는 언제 회의를 하기로 예정되어 있는가?
(A) 10월 3일~5일   (B) 10월 4일~6일
(C) 10월 3일~11일   (D) 10월 11일~12일

184
Graham씨는 호텔에 며칠을 머물 계획인가?
(A) 6   (B) 7
(C) 8   (D) 9

185
Graham씨는 호텔에 무엇에 대해 묻는가?
(A) 주차 공간   (B) 축제 일정
(C) 객실 크기   (D) 교통수단

186-190 📧 이메일…이메일…상품권 신유형

수신: Levey Vacuums <leveyvacuums@service.net>
발신: Felix Muncey <fmuencey@indinet.com>
날짜: 11월 18일
제목: PowerRave 3000

관계자분께
저는 거의 10년 동안 Levey PowerRave 3000 진공청소기를 사용했습니다. 그런데 지난달에 청소기가 갑자기 작동을 멈췄습니다. 저는 청소기를 다시 작동시키기 위해 제가 생각할 수 있는 모든 것을 시도해보았지만, 아무 효과가 없었습니다. 사용설명서의 문제 해결 부분을 읽어보기도 했습니다만 결과는 같았습니다. [189]저는 인디애나폴리스에 있는 현지 수리점에도 가져갔지만 주인 말로는 고칠 수 없다고 했습니다. [186]마지막으로, 수리를 위해 공장에 보낼 수 있는지 알아보려고 연락드렸습니다. 지금껏 청소기를 아주 잘 써왔는데 교체하고 싶지 않습니다.
감사합니다.
Felix Muncey

수신: Felix Muncey <fmuencey@indinet.com>
발신: Levey Vacuums <leveyvacuums@service.net>
날짜: 11월 19일
제목: 회신: PowerRave 3000

Muncey씨께
문의 감사합니다. 귀하의 PowerRave 30000이 더 이상 작동하지 않는다니, 유감입니다. 죄송하지만 이 모델은 단종되었습니다. 하지만 귀하께서 PowerRave가 마음에 드신다니, 당사의 새 모델인 [188]Clean Machine XT(소매가 250달러)도 마음에 드실 것으로 확신합니다.
Clean Machine XT는 자사의 최신 청소기 모델로서, 여러 가지 매력적인 기능을 갖추고 있습니다. [187]이 모델의 '특별 소재'로 인해, 시중의 다른 어떤 유사한 청소기보다 훨씬 가벼우며, 출력의 손실도 없습

니다. 또한, Clean Machine의 혁신적인 디자인 덕분에 작은 모서리와 가구 밑도 접근이 가능합니다.
Levey 청소기 브랜드에 대한 귀하의 충성에 감사의 뜻으로 Clean Machine XT 구입 시 할인 혜택을 드리고자 합니다. 이 메시지에 쿠폰을 첨부했으니, 인쇄하셔서 근처의 공식 판매점 중 한 곳에 보여주십시오. 앞으로도 계속 고객님을 모시기를 바랍니다.
Marcia Lopez
고객관리부

---

[190]발행일: 11월 19일
(모바일 기기 또는 종이 형태로) 이 쿠폰을 판매자에게 보여주고 [188]Clean Machine XT를 20% 할인받으세요.

Al's Vacuums Gary, IN	**Morristown Appliance** Morristown, IN
Flat Irons Appliance Evansville, IN	[189]**S&B Vacuums** Indianapolis, IN

*다른 제품이나 모델에는 적용되지 않습니다.
*다른 할인과 중복하여 적용할 수 없습니다.
[190]*발행일로부터 6개월 뒤 쿠폰이 만료됩니다.

어휘 trouble shooting 고장 해결 as a last resort 최후의 수단으로 one-of-a-kind 특별한 sacrifice 희생시키다 outlet 판매 대리점 retain 보유하다 make 제품

186
첫 번째 이메일의 목적은 무엇인가?
(A) 근처에 있는 수리점에 대해 묻기 위해
(B) 제품에 대한 불만을 얘기하기 위해
(C) 공장 수리에 대해 문의하기 위해
(D) 환불을 요구하기 위해

187
어떤 점이 Clean Machine XT를 특별하게 만드는가?
(A) 힘   (B) 가격
(C) 크기   (D) 무게

188
쿠폰을 사용하면 청소기는 얼마가 되는가?
(A) 100달러   (B) 150달러
(C) 200달러   (D) 250달러

189
Muncey씨와 같은 도시에 위치한 소매점은 어디인가?
(A) Al's Vacuums   (B) Morristown Appliance
(C) Flat Irons Appliance   (D) S&B Vacuums

190
쿠폰은 언제 만료되는가?
(A) 11월 30일   (B) 12월 31일
(C) 1월 19일   (D) 5월 19일

191-195 (기사…일정표…이메일) 신유형

수상 작가인 Roland Evans는 독자들이 4년을 기다리게 했지만, 마침내 그의 베스트셀러 Surprise, Surprise!의 후속작을 냈습니다. 11월 25일은 No Surprise Is a Good Surprise의 하드커버 판이 공개되는 날로 달력에 표시해야 합니다. 홍보담당자에 의하면 ¹⁹¹Evans씨는 책을 완성하기 위해 작년에 거의 6개월 동안 자기 산장에 틀어 박혀 살았다고 합니다. 그리고 운 좋게 미리 견본을 읽은 모든 비평가들은 기다릴 가치가 있었다고 말합니다.

분명히, No Surprise Is a Good Surprise는 Surprise, Surprise!에서 독자들이 사랑했던 멋진 등장인물들과 흥미진진한 액션들을 모두 조합하고 있습니다. 이제 우리의 궁금증은, 이 위대한 책들을 커다란 스크린으로 불러올 영화가 제작 중에 있느냐는 것입니다. 이것에 대해서 Evans씨는 의심스러울 정도로 함구하고 있습니다. 그저 어떤 놀라운 일이 우리를 기다리고 있을지 지켜보아야 할 것입니다.

Franklin 서점 12월 행사 일정

날짜	¹⁹³12월 4일 오후 8시	12월 7일 오후 3시	¹⁹⁴12월 11일 오후 7시	12월 14일 오후 1시	12월 20일 오후 8시
작가	Lucia Tanak	Elise Pauley	Roland Evans	Emil Vargus	Erin Gutierrez
도서 종류	판타지	어린이	¹⁹²청소년	역사	공상과학

수신: Johan Klein <jkdemon@fastline.com>
발신: Franklin 서점 <customer@franklinbooks.com>
날짜: 12월 21일
제목: 행사 일정표

Klein씨께

연락 감사합니다. ¹⁹⁴Evans씨의 행사에서 불만스러운 경험을 하셨다니 죄송합니다. 저희 웹사이트에서는 공간이 한정되어 있어 좌석이 선착순으로 제공된다고 나와 있습니다. 조금 늦게 도착하셨다면, 귀하께서 말씀하신 대로 좌석을 구하지 못하는 것은 어쩔 수 없는 일입니다. 사인 대기 줄이 길었던 것도, 초청 작가의 인기를 저희가 어떻게 할 수 없습니다.

¹⁹⁵작가마다 1회 이상의 행사를 개최해달라는 의견은 전달하겠습니다. 제 상사는 고객의 의견을 중요하게 받아들입니다. 귀하께서 좋아하는 다른 작가가 온다면 또 저희 서점과 함께하시길 바랍니다.

Frannie Poleman
Franklin 서점

어휘 follow-up 후속편 smash 대성공 hardback 하드커버 be holed up (어떤 장소에) 숨다 mountain cabin 산장 publicist 홍보담당자 reviewer 비평가 advance copy 신간 견본 blend 섞다 suspiciously 수상쩍게

191

Evans씨에 대해 언급된 것은 무엇인가?
(A) 산속에 거처가 있다.
(B) 영화를 만들고 있다.
(C) 긴 휴가를 보내고 있다.
(D) 집필을 그만두고 싶어 한다.

어휘 shelter 주거지 quit 그만두다

192

No Surprise Is a Good Surprise는 어떤 종류의 책인가?
(A) 어린이   (B) 판타지
(C) 공상과학   (D) 청소년

193

Franklin 서점에 대해 알 수 있는 것은 무엇인가?
(A) 오후 8시에 문을 닫는다.
(B) 12월에는 아침에 행사를 하지 않았다.
(C) 넓은 행사 공간이 있다.
(D) 일주일에 한 번씩 행사를 개최한다.

194

Klein씨는 언제 Franklin 서점의 행사에 참여했는가?
(A) 12월 4일   (B) 12월 11일
(C) 12월 14일   (D) 12월 20일

195

Poleman씨는 Klein씨를 위해 무엇을 하겠다고 약속하는가?
(A) 다음번에 작가가 올 때 전화하기
(B) 상사에게 그의 제안을 전달하기
(C) 행사에서 그의 자리를 보장해주기
(D) 그에게 할인 쿠폰 보내기

196-200 (이메일…제품정보…이메일) 신유형

발신: Jarvis Sloan <jsloan@allproav.net>
수신: Stephanie Ross <sross@ultrawave.com>
날짜: 11월 7일
제목: 프레젠테이션 장비

Ross씨께

¹⁹⁶저희 프레젠테이션 장비 종류에 관해 이메일을 보내주셔서 감사합니다. 이메일에 사양을 첨부했습니다. 첨부파일에서 특징 요약 및 가격 범위를 확인하실 수 있습니다. ²⁰⁰각 제품의 컬러 사진과 도움이 되는 영상 등 자세한 내용은 저희 웹사이트 www.allproav.net을 방문해주십시오. 또한 계정을 만들어서 저희 웹사이트를 통해 직거래로 물품을 구매하실 수 있습니다.

시청각 장비와 관련하여 귀사의 필요를 충족시키기 위해 제가 도움이 된다면, 주저하지 말고 연락 주십시오.

Jarvis Sloan
All-Pro Audio-Visual사
555-2839

All-Pro Audio-Visual사

프로젝터 – 휴대용, 사내용

· 2.5GB 또는 4GB 내장 메모리 선택
· Wi-Fi 연결
· USB 기능
· 휴대용 모델은 가볍기 때문에 휴대가 용이합니다.

· LED 램프는 교체가 필요 없습니다.
· 메모리 용량에 따라, 가격대는 299~495달러입니다.

스크린

· 휴대용 – 손쉬운 설치 및 분해(이동 케이스 포함)
· 장착용(영구) – 전기 또는 수동 풀다운
· [198]92~120인치
· 크기에 따라, 가격대는 99~159달러입니다.

스마트보드

· 회의실에 두는 거대한 태블릿 형태
· [197]상호작용하는 스크린으로 여러 사람의 입력이 가능합니다.
· 멀티터치 스크린
· 그리기와 쓰기를 위한 드라이 이레이즈 표면
· 가격대는 559~999달러입니다.

프레젠테이션 분야 최신 기술인 스마트보드는 정말 최첨단입니다! 약간 비싸지만, 스마트보드로 할 수 있는 협업 기능은 제값을 합니다.

수신: Jarvis Sloan <jsloan@allproav.net>
발신: Stephanie Ross <sross@ultrawave.com>
날짜: 11월 9일
제목: 회신: 프레젠테이션 장비

Sloan씨께
빠른 답장에 감사드리며, [199]저는 스마트보드를 구매하는 것에 관심이 있지만, 스타트업 사업의 예산상 당장 이 유형의 제품을 구매하기가 쉽지 않습니다. 추후에 새 제품들을 소개하실 때 낮춘 가격이라도 계속 알려주세요.
현재 [198]저는 가장 싼 프로젝터와 추가로 92인치 스크린에 관심이 있습니다. [200]제가 이 제품들을 구매할 수 있는 방법을 알려주세요. 사양서에는 그 정보가 없네요.
감사합니다.
Stephanie Ross
Ultra Wave

어휘 spec sheet 사양서 brief 개요 audio-visual 시청각의 hesitate 주저하다 portable 휴대용의 in-house (조직) 내부의 connectivity 연결 capability 능력 cutting-edge 최첨단의 pricey 값비싼 inspire ~에 영감을 주다 reduction 축소

196
Sloan씨는 왜 Ross씨에게 이메일을 보냈는가?
(A) 그녀의 불만에 답하기 위해
(B) 그녀의 문의에 답하기 위해
(C) 그녀와 회의 시간을 잡기 위해
(D) 그녀의 업무에 감사하기 위해

197
정보에 의하면, 스마트보드의 장점은 무엇인가?
(A) 스마트보드에서는 그룹으로 더 쉽게 함께 일할 수 있다.
(B) 영상 화면으로 사용할 수 있다.
(C) 상자에 넣어 쉽게 운반할 수 있다.
(D) 프로젝터보다 저렴하다.

198
Ross씨가 스크린을 사기 위해 지불할 금액은 얼마인가?
(A) 99달러
(B) 159달러
(C) 299달러
(D) 495달러

199
Ross씨가 스마트보드에 대해 언급한 것은 무엇인가?
(A) 상사가 그 기능을 이해하지 못한다.
(B) 회사가 구매할 만한 돈이 없다.
(C) 회사에서 스마트보드는 필요 없다.
(D) 동료들이 한 번도 스마트보드를 사용해 본 적이 없다.

어휘 afford (경제적) 여유가 있다

200
Ross씨에 대해 암시하는 것은 무엇인가?
(A) 그녀는 웹사이트를 보지 않았다.
(B) 그녀는 설립 회사의 대표이다.
(C) 그녀는 Sloan씨의 회사의 신입직원이다.
(D) 그녀는 Sloan씨에게 프레젠테이션을 할 것이다.